Strategic Management

IN ACTION

SECOND EDITION

Strategic Management
IN ACTION

SECOND EDITION

MARY COULTER

SOUTHWEST MISSOURI STATE UNIVERSITY

Prentice
Hall

Upper Saddle River, New Jersey 07458

Library of Congress Cataloging-in-Publication Data

Coulter, Mary K.

  Strategic management in action / Mary K. Coulter.—2nd ed.

    p.   cm.

  Includes index.

  ISBN 0–13–040006–8

  1. Strategic planning.   I. Title.

HD30.28.C696   2002

658.4'012—dc21   00–059840

Executive Editor: David Shafer
Managing Editor (Editorial): Jennifer Glennon
Assistant Editor: Michele Foresta
Editorial Assistant: Kim Marsden
Media Project Manager: Michele Faranda
Executive Marketing Manager: Michael Campbell
Marketing Assistant: Katie Mulligan
Managing Editor (Production): Judy Leale
Production Editor: Emma Moore
Production Assistant: Keri Jean
Permissions Coordinator: Suzanne Grappi
Associate Director, Manufacturing: Vincent Scelta
Production Manager: Arnold Vila
Manufacturing Buyer: Diane Peirano
Design Manager: Patricia Smythe
Senior Designer: Steve Frim
Interior Design: SettingPace
Cover Design: Steve Frim
Cover Illustration/Photo: Stock Illustration Source, Inc.
Associate Director, Multimedia Production: Karen Goldsmith
Manager, Print Production: Christina Mahon
Composition: Rainbow Graphics
Full Service Project Management: Bennie Sauls/Rainbow Graphics
Printer/Binder: Courier

Credits and acknowledgments borrowed from other sources and reproduced, with permission,
in this textbook appear on appropriate page within text.

10 9 8 7 6 5 4

ISBN 0–13–040006–8

To Ron, Sarah, and Katie

Brief Contents

Contents

CHAPTER 2: THE CONTEXT OF MANAGING STRATEGICALLY   32

Pedagogical Material

CHAPTER 3: ASSESSING OPPORTUNITIES AND THREATS: DOING AN EXTERNAL ANALYSIS   74

Pedagogical Material

CHAPTER 4: ASSESSING STRENGTHS AND WEAKNESSES: DOING AN INTERNAL ANALYSIS   120

Pedagogical Material

CHAPTER 5: FUNCTIONAL STRATEGIES   158

Pedagogical Material

CHAPTER 6: COMPETITIVE STRATEGIES   208

Pedagogical Material

CHAPTER 7: CORPORATE STRATEGIES 248

Pedagogical Material

CHAPTER 8: STRATEGIC MANAGEMENT IN OTHER ORGANIZATION TYPES   300

Small Businesses and Entrepreneurial Ventures   302

What Is a Small Business and What Is an Entrepreneurial Venture?   302

Why Are These Types of Organizations Important?   303

The Strategic Management Process in Small Businesses and Entrepreneurial Ventures   305

Specific Strategic Issues Facing Small Businesses and Entrepreneurial Ventures   311

Not-for-Profit and Public Sector Organizations   313

What Are Not-for-Profit Organizations and What Are Public Sector Organizations?   313

The Strategic Management Process in Not-for-Profit and Public Sector Organizations   316

Specific Strategic Issues Facing Not-for-Profit and Public Sector Organizations   321

The Bottom Line   326

Building Your Skills   328

Strategic Management in Action Cases   330

Pedagogical Material

APPENDIX: COMPREHENSIVE CASES FOR ANALYSIS   336

Preface

Welcome to the second edition of *Strategic Management in Action!* This book reflects my strong belief that strategic management can (and should) be interesting and exciting, and yet also can be based on sound, current academic theory. For a long time, I've felt there was a distinct need for a strategy book that effectively integrated strategy theory and strategy action—I wanted to show strategic management "in action." And *Strategic Management in Action* is a result of those beliefs!

How is this book different from the other strategic management textbooks on the market? I want to share with you what I feel are its competitive advantages—a term you will be quite familiar with after reading this text! As it did in the first edition, the book effectively integrates strategy theory and strategy action. It shows in an exciting and engaging way strategic management in action. How? Through the several new features in this edition and features retained from the first edition.

A new feature of this book is the inclusion of several chapter elements that illustrate and explore strategic management in action. One of these elements is a box theme called Strategic Management in Action. These boxes describe companies and the unique strategies they're using. Some of the companies portrayed include California Pizza Kitchen, FedEx, VISA USA, Krispy Kreme doughnuts, and E*Trade. Then, there are the FYI (For Your Information) boxes in every chapter that provide a concise overview of current strategic management issues. For example, some of the topics discussed include Corporate Reputations, Are Profits an Outdated Idea?, Why Good Companies Go Bad, The DNA of Corporate Innovation, and so forth. In order to emphasize the global importance of strategic management, there's also a chapter box feature called Strategic Management—the Global

Perspective. Some of the companies described include Giant Manufacturing Company, Ltd. (Taiwan), Nestlé SA (Switzerland), and Canadian Imperial Bank of Commerce. Finally, because strategic decision makers are often faced with ethical dilemmas, there's an ethics dilemma presented in every chapter under the heading of The Grey Zone. These were written to encourage you to think about the ethical implications inherent in strategic decisions. To make all of these chapter boxed features more relevant, most include suggestions for further research, review, or discussion. Be prepared—your professor might make assignments from any of these boxed items!

Another important change in this textbook is the addition of seven comprehensive cases. These cases include the following: Amazon.com, Eatertainment Industry, Greeting-Card Industry, Kellogg Company, Levi-Strauss, Southwest Airlines, and Starbucks. These cases were written so you can perform a thorough strategic analysis, identify strategic issues, and develop appropriate strategic choices. Additional cases I have written will be available online starting in the spring semester 2001 and may be assigned by your professor.

There's no doubt that the realities of the e-business world are having a major impact on organizational strategies. To introduce you to this topic, another new and significant feature in this book reflects the critical importance of understanding e-business and its implications for strategy. To explore e-business concepts, a boxed feature in every chapter called Strategic Management in an E-Business World addresses various aspects of e-business and how strategic decision makers are dealing with the dynamic changes taking place. Some of the topics discussed include choiceboards, Internet taxes, the appropriateness of internal analysis for e-businesses, stock options, and the competitive challenges with selling pet supplies on the Web. In addition, e-business strategies used by different companies are described and discussed.

Continued from the last edition of the book are several pedagogical tools to help you better learn and understand the concepts and theories of strategic management. For instance, the end-of-chapter Building Your Skills exercises give you the chance to "practice" the skills that successful strategic managers are going to need in tomorrow's organizations. In addition, short end-of-chapter cases (I like to call them case-ettes) provide an opportunity for you to further explore the topic in the chapter. These mini-cases provide a narrowly focused situation to examine and discuss. One change in this edition is that the chapter-opening Strategic Management in Action case can now be studied in addition to the other end-of-chapter cases. Each chapter also has several Consider This boxes that provide a number of review and discussion questions for a topic section that you've just read. Introduced in the first edition of the book, these boxes offer an excellent way for you to check your comprehension of the material you've just read and are also a great way to review chapter material. Finally, the chapter summaries are presented in a form called The Bottom Line, a term chosen very carefully. When a company focuses on the bottom line, it's focusing on the things that are the most important. Therefore, this section summarizes the important information, including key terms and definitions, in each chapter.

This edition continues to introduce the most current strategic management theories and practices. Some of these include world-class organizations, the guerrilla view of competitive advantage, online communities, data mining, real options theory, and several others. Of course, the traditional concepts of strategic management such as competitive advantage, SWOT, corporate growth, and strategy implementation are covered as well.

Another distinguishing feature of *Strategic Management in Action* retained from the first edition is that the discussion of the various strategy levels (functional, competitive, and corporate) cov-

ers formulation, implementation, and evaluation in the respective chapters. Other strategy texts cover strategy formulation in one chapter, implementation in another, and then evaluation in another. I felt that this approach made it hard for readers to see and understand the integrative nature of strategy. So, I decided it made more sense (both from the student's perspective in learning the material and from the professor's perspective in presenting the material) to discuss formulation, implementation, and evaluation as each strategy level was being discussed. So, for instance, when discussing functional strategy, you'll find information on how it's formulated, implemented, and evaluated; and likewise for the competitive and corporate levels, as well.

Finally, I want to say that I think this book is unique in the market because of its conversational and highly readable writing style. Although an author's writing style is difficult to describe (particularly your own!), I did write this text in a way to try to make strategy and strategic management clear and understandable—yet enjoyable. My teaching philosophy (and I've been teaching for almost 25 years now, have won teaching awards at my university, and am consistently ranked in the top two or three in my department based on student evaluations) has been that education *can* be fun! So, I write like I teach. But only you, the reader, can ultimately judge how well I've written the material.

I need to thank a number of people for their contributions to this book. Without them, *Strategic Management in Action, 2nd edition* wouldn't be a reality. First of all are my students—current and past. Through my experiences (most of them enjoyable!) teaching our Strategic Management course, I've developed my own personal philosophy of what's worked and what hasn't. I learn things every semester from my students, and I hope they're learning from me. Then, I'd like to say "Thanks" to my department head, Barry Wisdom, and my college dean, Ron Bottin. Thank you for your support and encouragement. And then, of course, are my departmental secretaries, Carol Hale and Anita Looney. Thank you for all you do to make my life easier.

I would also like to recognize the individuals who provided me with intelligent and thorough reviews of the first edition of *Strategic Management in Action*. I appreciate your willingness to provide thorough and thought-provoking reviews. I know the second edition is better because of the suggestions you have provided. These individuals are Dr. William P. Anthony, Florida State University; Dr. Jeryl L. Nelson, Wayne State College; Jerry Thomas, Arapahoe Community College; Patrick L. Schultz, Texas Tech. University; Frederick J. Richards, Sacred Heart University; Dr. A. D. Amar, Seton Hall University; Dr. Augustus Abbey, Morgan State University; and Dr. Richard D. Babcock, University of San Francisco.

Supplements

Instructor's Manual
Each chapter includes learning objectives, a detailed lecture outline, teaching notes to selected chapter exercises, and answers to all end-of-chapter material. Tips on where to incorporate PowerPoint slides are also included.

Test Item File
Each chapter contains multiple choice, true/false, chapter essay, and case essay questions. Together, the questions cover the content of each chapter in a variety of ways providing flexibility in testing the student's knowledge of the text.

Windows/Prentice Hall Test Manager, version 4.0
Containing all of the questions in the printed Test Item File, Test Manager is a comprehensive suite of tools for testing and assessment. Test Manager allows educators to easily create and distribute tests for their courses, either by printing and distributing through traditional methods, or by online delivery via a Local Area Network (LAN) server.

Instructor's Resource CD-ROM
Contains the electronic Instructor's Manual, Test Manager, and PowerPoint Electronic Transparencies. The PowerPoint Transparencies, a comprehensive package of text outlines and figures corresponding to the text, are designed to aid the educator and supplement in-class lectures.

Companion Web Site
The Prentice Hall Companion Web Site features an interactive and exciting online Student Study Guide. Students can access multiple choice, true/false, and Internet-based essay questions that accompany each chapter in the text. Objective questions are scored online, and incorrect answers are keyed to the text for student review. Faculty resources are also posted on this site and are password-protected. For more information, contact your local sales representative.

Acknowledgments

I'd also like to thank the wonderful people at Prentice Hall, my publisher. As usual, all of you have been just super to work with! A big THANK YOU to David Shafer, Executive Editor, Management. David, thanks for all your help and encouragement. A special thank you to Natalie Anderson for her unwavering support and for being a friend. The other people on the Management team have been just great to work with as well. These include Jennifer Glennon, Michele Foresta, and Kim Marsden. Thank you for all your hard work to make this book successful! My marketing manager, Michael Campbell, is a dream come true for an author. He is so knowledgeable about the market and the product. Michael, thank you for all your hard work. I'd also like to thank the hardworking people on the production side. Emma Moore, Suzanne Grappi, Steve Frim, and Nancy Marcello, have been truly super professionals who helped make *Strategic Management in Action, 2nd edition* look as great as it does! Thanks!

Next, I'd like to say a special thank you to a good friend and outstanding mentor—Steve Robbins, a textbook publishing icon! Steve, your friendship and advice continue to mean a lot to me! As I've said before, thanks for "taking a chance" on me and for "showing me the ropes" of textbook publishing. Although I can never fill your shoes (particularly the ones that make you a world-class and exceptionally successful sprinter), I know I'm a better writer because of you! Thanks!

Finally, I'd like to say THANKS to my family—my wonderful and truly supportive husband,

Ron, and our bright, beautiful, and remarkably well-adjusted daughters, Sarah and Katie. Words cannot express how much you guys mean to me! Thank you for being patient with me when I was focused on writing and for not complaining about the many carryout meals we've consumed! You provide that much-needed balance to my life. And what I've been able to do, is because of all three of you. Thanks!

Mary Coulter
Southwest Missouri State University

Strategic Management
IN ACTION
SECOND EDITION

1
INTRODUCING THE CONCEPTS

LEARNING OBJECTIVES

After studying this chapter, you should be able to:

1. Discuss why strategic management is important.
2. Define strategy and strategic management.
3. Describe the strategic management process.
4. Describe the three levels of organizational strategies.
5. Explain the historical evolution of strategic management.
6. Rebut misconceptions about strategy and strategic management.
7. Explain who's involved with strategic management and their role in managing strategically.

STRATEGIC MANAGEMENT IN ACTION CASE #1

Pizza Wars

"The main thing is to keep the main thing the main thing." This pretty much sums up the strategic philosophy of Papa John's Pizza (**www.papajohns.com**).[1] It's a quote that John H. Schnatter (yes, there is a "real" Papa John), founder and CEO of Papa John's International, uses to keep his troops focused on what they're doing—that is, pizza. Not salads, pasta, chicken wings, or sub sandwiches. But pizza, and only pizza. And the company feels that being focused is particularly important in the intensely competitive and cutthroat pizza industry.

Papa John's currently is number three in the industry (the other industry leaders are Pizza Hut number one, Domino's number two, and Little Caesars number four). But, Papa John's is very aggressive in its strategic assaults on the other competitors. It's the fastest-growing pizza company in America and has over 2,600 restaurants (at least at this time) throughout the United States and seven global markets. The company considers itself the quality leader among the national pizza companies and is committed to its heritage of making a superior-quality, traditional pizza. The company's slogan, "Better Ingredients. Better Pizza," can be found on its storefronts and its pizza boxes. It has a simple formula for success: Focus on one thing and try to do it better than anyone else. How? By emphasizing people, product, and service as "mission-critical" priorities.

That is, Papa John's has determined that the people, the product, and the service are critical to its successful pursuit of its strategic mission and goals. Table 1-1 summarizes the company's core values that support these priorities.

However, in early January of 2000, Papa John's found its strategies being strongly challenged. Its simple slogan, "Better Ingredients. Better Pizza," had long been a thorn in the side of Pizza Hut. Those four words were fighting words. And, Pizza Hut fought—and won. On January 3, 2000, a federal court judge in Dallas ruled that Papa John's could no longer use its trademarked four-word slogan. The judge, in an unprecedented advertising ruling, ordered that the company's broadcast and print advertising could not include the slogan after January 24, 2000. In addition, the company would have until March 3, 2000, to phase out its printed supply of other items containing the slogan, and until April 3, 2000, to remove the slogan from its restaurant signage. Although Pizza Hut had asked for $12.5 million in damages and asked that any award be tripled under the Lanham Act (a U.S. federal law aimed at controlling anti-competitive actions), the judge

ruled that Papa John's had to pay only $467,619.75 in damages. The judge also permanently prohibited Pizza Hut from broadcasting or disseminating any television, radio, or print advertising that compares any component of Pizza Hut's pizza to a like component of Papa John's pizza. And, the ruling continued that Pizza Hut may not explicitly or implicitly state or suggest that a Pizza Hut component is superior to a like Papa John's component unless the superiority claim is supported by either scientifically demonstrated attributes or superiority or taste test surveys that

demonstrate a statistically significant preference for the Pizza Hut component. These are pretty serious legal statements and directives, aren't they? Yet, the continued inroads of Papa John's into Pizza Hut's markets had triggered the legal actions on the part of Pizza Hut. The resulting judicial decision wasn't going to stop Papa John's, however. The case is on appeal, and the company's strategic managers vowed that the ruling wasn't going to change its commitment to quality or slow its momentum in the marketplace. Pizza Hut may have won this battle, but the pizza wars go on!

TABLE 1-1   Papa John's Core Values

- **Focus**
  We must keep The Main Thing, The Main Thing. We will consistently deliver a traditional Papa John's superior-quality pizza.
- **Accountability**
  We do what we say we are going to do when we say we are going to do it. We earn the right to hold others to a higher level of accountability by being accountable to ourselves, our customers, and our business partners.
- **Superiority**
  Our customer satisfaction must be consistent, quantifiable, and demonstrable. At Papa John's we expect excellence—the "best in its class" in everything we do.
- **PAPA**
  People Are Priority #1 Always. Our team members treat one another with dignity and respect.
- **Attitude**
  If you think you can or you think you can't—you're right! The difference between winners and losers is a positive mental attitude. Our attitude is a reflection of what we value: successful team members must be upbeat, proactive, and passionate about everything they do.
- **Constant Improvement**
  We never stop trying to surpass our previous best. We constantly "Raise the Bar." No matter how good we are, we will always get better.

Source: Company's Web site (**www.papajohns.com**), February 2, 2000. Used with permission.

This chapter-opening case illustrates many of the complexities and challenges that today's managers face in attempting to *manage strategically.* Papa John's strategic initiatives have implications for managers and employees throughout the entire organization. Even managers at Pizza Hut, Domino's, and Little Caesars had to decide if and how to respond to Papa John's strategic moves. And, as the case describes, Pizza Hut's managers did decide to take action. These types of strategic decisions are common in today's competitive environment for all types and sizes of organizations. Understanding how and why managers formulate strategic responses—that is, manage strategically—is what this book is about. By studying strategic management in action, you can begin to understand how different managers cope with various strategic issues and challenges. Then, whether you're a local pizza outlet manager in Omaha, a regional sales manager in San Diego, or a customer service representative at Papa John's headquarters in Louisville, Kentucky, you'll be able to assess the implications of strategic decisions. How might these decisions affect your own work, and how might they affect what your work group does? What kinds of strategic changes might be necessary?

In this introductory chapter, you'll get a flavor of what strategic management is all about. It's divided into three major sections: why is strategic management important, what is strategic management, and who's involved with it. The one thing you might notice isn't included is the *how* aspect. But don't worry! That's what the rest of the text covers—how you actually *do* strategic management. First, though, we think it's important to look at why strategic management is important and why it's important that you know something about strategic management.

WHY IS STRATEGIC MANAGEMENT IMPORTANT?

One thing you may be asking yourself about now is "Why is this stuff important to organizations and, even more directly, why is it important to me? I'm majoring in accounting, and my career goal is to make partner in one of the big five accounting firms. What do I care about strategic management?" Or you may be a computer information systems major who plans to work on e-business applications for an online retailer. You may feel that strategic management and managing strategically have little to do with you. However, one of the assumptions we make in this book is that *every*one in an organization plays a role in managing strategically. Because life after school for most of you means finding a job in order to have an income, this means you'll be working for some organization. (Even if you choose to start your own business, managing strategically is important, as we'll discuss in Chapter 8.) The very fact that you'll be working in some organization of some size and type means you'll need to manage strategically. Thus, understanding what this means and how you can be a more effective and efficient strategic decision maker is important for you personally so that your work performance will be valued and rewarded accordingly. But, in addition, the practice of strategic management is important for other reasons that pertain more directly to the organization.

One of the most significant reasons it's important to understand strategic management is that whether an organization's employees manage strategically does appear to make a difference in how well the organization performs. The most fundamental questions in strategy are why do firms succeed or fail, and why do firms have varying levels of performance? These questions have influenced what strategic management researchers have studied over the years. What have researchers found in attempting to answer these questions? Do strategic management and managing strategically make a difference? Well, the overall conclusion of numerous studies is that a small but positive relationship between strategic planning and performance does exist.[2] In other words, it appears that organizations that use strategic management concepts and techniques do have higher levels of performance. If it impacts the organization's performance (one measure of performance is the proverbial "bottom line" or profits), that would appear to be a pretty important reason to know something about strategic management and managing strategically.

Another reason for studying strategic management is that organizations of all types and sizes continually face changing situations. These changes may be minor or significant, but there's still change to cope with. Being able to cope effectively with these uncertainties in the external and internal environments *and* achieve expected levels of performance is a real challenge. However, this is where strategic management comes in. By systematically following the strategic management process, strategic decision makers examine all the important aspects in order to determine the most appropriate decisions and actions. The deliberate structure of the strategic management process "forces" organizational employees to examine relevant variables in deciding what to do and how to do it. In fact, some recent

Corporate Reputations

A nationwide survey of 10,830 people conducted by Harris Interactive Inc. and the Reputation Institute for the *Wall Street Journal* provided a listing of the top 30 companies based on their score on a Reputation Quotient (RQ). The RQ measured corporate attributes in the following categories: Emotional Appeal (how much the company is liked, admired, and respected), Social Responsibility (perceptions of the company as a good citizen in its dealings with communities, employees, and the environment), Products and Services (perceptions of the quality, innovation, value, and reliability of its products and services), Workplace Environment (perception of how well the company is managed, how it is to work for, and the quality of its employees), Vision and Leadership (how much the company demonstrates a clear vision and strong leadership), and Financial Performance (perceptions of its prof-itability, prospects, and risk). Who had the best corporate reputations? The top 10 were Johnson & Johnson, Coca-Cola, Hewlett-Packard, Intel, Ben & Jerry's, Wal-Mart, Xerox, Home Depot, Gateway, and Disney. The next 10 were Dell, General Electric, Lucent, Anheuser-Busch, Microsoft, Amazon.com, IBM, Sony, Yahoo!, and AT&T. The remaining companies included as part of the listing of 30 best corporate reputations were FedEx, Procter & Gamble, Nike, McDonald's, Southwest Airlines, AOL, DaimlerChrysler, Toyota, Sears, and Boeing. What got these companies the distinction of having a "best" corporate reputation? What will keep these companies on such a list? Although there's many things these companies do well, strategic management has to be one of the things they do exceptionally well!

Source: R. Alsop, "The Best Corporate Reputations in America," *Wall Street Journal,* September 23, 1999, p. D1.

studies of the strategy decision process suggest that the *way* strategy is developed can make a difference in performance, also. For instance, one study of strategic decision makers found that those who collected information and used analytical techniques made more effective strategic decisions than those who did not.[3] And, that's what strategic management is all about—analyzing the situation and proceeding from there to develop and implement appropriate strategies. Another study found that organizations that used several approaches to developing strategy outperformed those that used a single approach.[4] These studies further verify that the strategic management process can affect organizational performance. What this means then is that some structured, systematic approach to coping with the uncertain environments organizations face is needed, and that's what the strategic management process provides.

Consider This ◀◀|

✓   How can the strategic management process benefit you as an individual?

✓   What have studies shown about the relationship between the use of the strategic management process and an organization's performance? What are the implications?

✓   How does managing strategically help an organization cope with changes in its external and internal environments?

✓   What coordinating role does the strategic management process play?

✓   Suppose you had to explain to a friend why you're studying strategic management. What would you tell that person?

Finally, understanding strategic management is important because an organization is composed of diverse divisions, functions, and work activities that need to be coordinated and focused on achieving the organization's goals. The strategic management process fills this purpose. As they manage strategically, organizational employees representing all of the organization's diverse perspectives—from manufacturing to marketing to accounting *and* at all organizational levels—are developing and implementing strategies that will help the organization perform at desired levels. And, they're using strategic management to coordinate their actions.

Although the strategic management process itself and using it to manage strategically are important, keep in mind that it isn't a panacea and won't solve all an organization's problems or challenges. But given the fact that it's becoming increasingly difficult for organizations of all sizes and types to achieve high levels of performance, the structure and order imposed by the strategic management process, at the very least, forces employees to think about the relevant variables.

WHAT IS STRATEGIC MANAGEMENT?

The study of strategic management *is* one of the most exciting in all of the traditional business areas! That's because every decision made by an organization's managers has strategic implications. Whether it's the National Basketball Association looking to expand its market reach globally, Apple Computer's attempts to reposition itself in the PC market, your local library's decision to go online, or Papa John's Pizza's all-out pursuit of the pizza market, some aspect of strategic management is involved. One of this book's explicit assumptions is that strategic management isn't simply the responsibility of an organization's top managers. People at *all* organizational levels play a role in developing, implementing, and changing strategy. But, just what *is* strategic management? Let's take a closer look.

The Basics of Strategy and Strategic Management

To begin to understand the basics of strategy and strategic management, you need look no further than at what's happened in the discount retail industry. The industry's two largest competitors—Wal-Mart and Kmart—have battled for market dominance since 1962, the year both companies were founded. The two chains have other striking similarities as well: store atmosphere, names, markets served, and organizational purpose. Yet, Wal-Mart's performance (financial and otherwise) has entirely surpassed that of Kmart. Why? Well, that, again, is the most fundamental question in strategy: why firms succeed or fail or why firms have varying levels of performance. Organizations vary in how well they perform because of differences in their strategic positions and differences in competitive abilities.[5] But, this doesn't tell us much about what strategy or strategic management is.

Definition of Strategy. The term *strategy* has been defined in a variety of ways. Early descriptions ranged from strategies as integrated decisions, actions, or plans designed to set and achieve organizational goals to strategy as simply the outcome of the strategy formulation process.[6] Our definition of **strategy** is a series of goal-directed decisions and actions that match an organization's skills and resources with the opportunities and threats in its environment. Let's look at some key parts of this definition. First of all, strategy involves an organization's goals. The chosen strategy (or strategies) should help an organization achieve its goals. But formulating and deciding a goal-directed strategy isn't enough. Strategy also involves goal-directed actions—the activities to implement the strategy. In other words, an organization's strategy involves not only *what* it wants to do, but *how* it's going to do it. Also, a single, simple action is not a strategy; strategy is a series of related decisions and actions throughout the various levels and departments or divisions of the organization. What coordinates these organizational

---

Strategic Management in Action

Hewlett-Packard, under the direction of CEO Carly Fiorina, is moving to become an e-commerce revolutionary. Rajiv Gupta, a computer designer for Hewlett-Packard, is leading the company's strategic effort to establish an edge in e-commerce technology with a set of programming protocols called E-Speak. This E-Speak strategy is one of the most crucial components in a sweeping transformation of Hewlett-Packard from an old-fashioned maker of computers, printers, and test equipment to a twenty-first-century Internet services company. How is E-Speak a strategy? It entails a number of goal-directed decisions and actions that have matched the company's technical skills and resources with the e-commerce opportunities in the environment.

Source: J. Markoff, "Hewlett-Packard Sees Its Future as an E-Commerce Revolutionary," *New York Times,* August 2, 1999, p. C1.

decisions and actions? The organization's goals do. They serve as the framework within which strategic decisions are made. Finally, the organization's strategies should be designed so they take into account its key internal strengths (resources and capabilities) and external opportunities and threats. This "matching" idea is important to the concept of strategy and strategic management, and you'll see it frequently referred to throughout the book.

Definition of Strategic Management. **Strategic management** involves those decisions and actions in which organizational members analyze the current situation; develop appropriate strategies; put those strategies into action; and evaluate, modify, or change those strategies as needed. It entails all of the basic managerial functions: planning, organizing, implementing, and controlling. The organization's strategies must be planned (formulated), organized and put into effect (implemented), and controlled (evaluated). In other words, we can describe the basic activities of strategic management as strategy formulation, strategy implementation, and strategy evaluation. (See Figure 1-1.)

How is strategic management different from other types of management? Four aspects of strategic management set it apart. First of all, strategic management is, by nature, *interdisciplinary.*[7] It's not like other types of management that focus on specific areas such as human resources or operations. Next, strategic management is characterized by its emphasis on the interactions of the organization with its external environment—that is, strategic management has an *external focus.* As organizational employees manage strategically, one of the important things they do is look at the external environment to see how factors such as the economic situation, competitors, or the changing characteristics of the target market might impact strategic decisions and actions. Another distinguishing characteristic of strategic management is that it emphasizes the important interactions and coordination of the organization's various functional areas—that is, it has an

Figure 1-1

Basic Activities of Strategic Management

Strategy Formulation

Strategy Implementation

Strategy Evaluation

internal focus. An organization's various strategies aren't formulated and implemented in isolation. The different organizational functions (the typical ones include marketing, manufacturing, research and development, and so on) and even the different organizational levels must be coordinated as appropriate strategies are developed. Strategic management provides that coordination. Finally, what distinguishes strategic management is that it concerns the choice of *future direction* of the organization (future focus). Whether that "future" means contending with week-to-week operational issues, one-year financial planning cycles, or a significant long-term shift in markets the organization targets, organizational employees use strategic management. As organizational members determine what they're going to do and how they're going to do it, they do so in light of relevant external factors and internal capabilities. Now, think back to our chapter-opening case on Papa John's. How is strategic management illustrated? According to our description, as managers at any of the companies in this scenario evaluated the situation (using both external and internal information) and decided what future actions to take, they were using strategic management. Let's examine the specific process by which organizational employees do this.

The Strategic Management Process

A process simply means that there's a series of interrelated and continuous steps that lead to some concluding aspect. In the strategic management process, the series of steps lead to the development, modification, or change in the organization's strategies. Figure 1-2 shows the steps in the strategic management process in action. As organizational members manage strategically (i.e., as they "do" strategic management), these are the activities they're engaged in. What's involved in each of these steps?

Situation Analysis. Before deciding on an appropriate strategic direction or response, organizational employees need to analyze the current situation. This **situation analysis** entails scanning and evaluating the organizational context, the

---

Strategic Management in Action

The Fuller Brush Company may be one of the last names that come to mind when you think of the Internet. However, the company's Web site (**www.fullerbrush.com**) has attracted a lot of eyeballs. The Web site showcases many of the company's products. And, it also is being used to help distributors recruit new salespeople. Here's a company firmly grounded in the past (it began in 1906), yet one that's definitely looking to the future. Log on to the company's Web site, go to the "About Fuller Brush" section, and read the information there. Then, make a bulleted list of what types of things the company is doing. These are its "strategies."

Source: Company's Web site (**www.fullerbrush.com**), February 7, 2000.

Figure 1-2

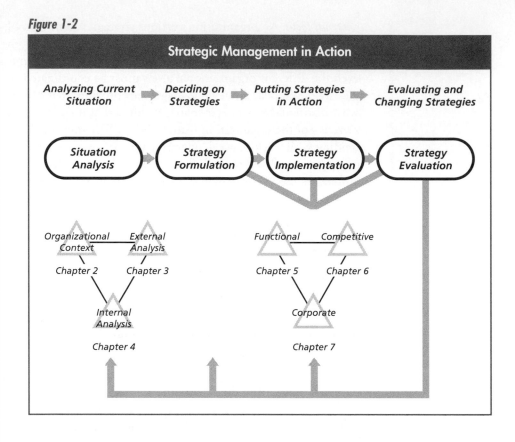

external environment, and the organizational environment. In Chapter 2, we'll be exploring relevant components of the organizational context including, for example, the new economy, the role of stakeholders, the dynamics of change, and the role of organizational culture and mission. In Chapter 3, we'll look closely at what an external analysis is and how it is done. Finally, in Chapter 4, we'll study the steps involved in doing an internal analysis and look carefully at an organization's resources, distinctive capabilities, and core competencies. Each of these parts of the strategic management process provides important clues to understanding and evaluating the organization's current situation.

Strategy Formulation. **Strategy formulation** involves the design and choice of appropriate organizational strategies. In this stage of the strategic management process, the organization's strategies are designed and developed. The typical approach to describing an organization's strategies is to look at them from three different organizational levels (see Figure 1-3).

Functional strategies (also called **operational strategies**) are the short-term (less than a year) goal-directed decisions and actions of the organization's various functional departments. What are the organization's functional departments? Typical ones include production–operations (manufacturing), marketing, research and development, human resources, financial–accounting, and perhaps information systems–information technology. But keep in mind that each organization will have its own unique functional departments. For instance, your university's functional departments might include the various academic departments and student services departments. In a retail store, the functional departments might

Figure 1-3

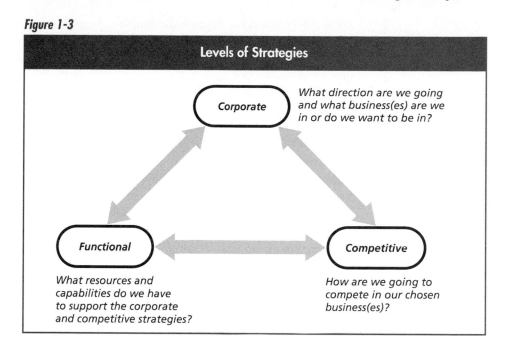

Levels of Strategies

Corporate
What direction are we going and what business(es) are we in or do we want to be in?

Functional
What resources and capabilities do we have to support the corporate and competitive strategies?

Competitive
How are we going to compete in our chosen business(es)?

include purchasing, merchandising display, selling, and accounting. We chose to start our discussion of the levels of organizational strategy with the functional–operational strategies because that's where you'll find the unique resources, capabilities, competencies, and work activities that are the source of the organization's

Strategic Management in Action

The retailing industry is an extremely competitive one, indeed. And, no one knows that better than JCPenney Company, Inc. (**www.jcpenney.com**). The 1980s and 1990s were tough years for traditional retailers as prices were slashed, new hip retailers such as Target and Old Navy stole customers away from the traditional department stores, and e-commerce retailing exploded. Talk about the need for some effective competitive strategies. Log on to the company's Web site, go to the section on Company Information, and browse through the Mission Statement, Positioning Statement, and Business Objectives and Strategies (including the sections under that link). What types of things is JCPenney doing to compete in the retail industry? Make a bulleted list of its strategies. What do you think of its strategies?

Sources: Company's Web site (**www.jcpenney.net/company**), February 7, 2000; and L. Kaufman, "Can J.C. Penney Evolve?" *New York Times*, June 26, 1999, p. B1.

competitive strategies. Because the functional–operational strategies support the organization's competitive strategies, it makes sense to discuss their formulation, implementation, and evaluation first. The various functional–operational strategies are discussed in Chapter 5.

An organization's **competitive strategies** are concerned with how it's going to compete in a specific business or industry. At this level, individual organizations compete with other individual organizations. For example, Compaq Computer competes with Dell, Gateway, and other personal computer companies. From our chapter-opening case, Papa John's competed with Pizza Hut, Dominos, and other pizza companies. The competitive strategies address what competitive advantages an organization currently has or wants to develop. All the aspects of competitive strategies and competitive moves and actions are explored in Chapter 6.

At the upper levels of the organization, **corporate strategies** are concerned with the broad and more long-term questions of "what business(es) are we in or do we want to be in, and what do we want to do with these businesses?" For instance, AOL's decision to merge with Time-Warner is a corporate strategy. Another example of corporate strategy would be PepsiCo's decisions about its soft drink division (Pepsi Cola) and its snack food division (Frito Lay). Any changes PepsiCo might choose to make in the mix of industries it competed in—as it did when it decided to spin off its fast-food restaurants (Taco Bell, Pizza Hut, and KFC) as a separate business in the late 1990s—involve changing its corporate strategy. But, what about organizations that don't compete in numerous industries? What does their corporate strategy entail? Corporate strategy in these types of single-business companies is not so much concerned with the optimal mix of corporate business(es) as it is decisions about the future direction of the organization. The various aspects of corporate direction and strategy will be discussed in Chapter 7.

Strategy Implementation. It's not enough for an organization's employees to develop or formulate great strategies. In the next stage of the strategic management process, these strategies have to be implemented. **Strategy implementation** is the process of putting the organization's various strategies into action. The approaches to implementing the various strategies should be considered as the strategies are formulated, so we'll be looking at the various aspects of strategy implementation as we discuss the strategies. In other words, in our discussion of functional or operational strategies, we'll look at how they're formulated *and* implemented and so on for each level.

Strategy Evaluation. **Strategy evaluation** is the process of evaluating how the strategy has been implemented as well as the outcomes of the strategy. An organization's employees should monitor both the actual implementation of the strategy and the performance results of implemented strategies. If these don't measure up to expectations or strategic goals, then the strategy itself or the implementation process may have to be modified or totally changed. Again, because this process is inherently part of the whole strategy package, we'll also discuss strategy evaluation as we discuss each level of strategy.

Continuing Process of Strategic Management in Action. It's important to recognize that, even though we discuss the strategic management process by isolating each step individually in order to study it, in reality it's an ongoing and continuous cycle of strategy formulation, implementation, and evaluation. As performance

Are Profits an Outdated Idea?

Do profits really matter? Is making money still an appropriate measure of organizational performance? The digital economy and the enormous dollar amounts being supplied by venture capitalists and the market values being placed on dot.com companies would tend to make you think otherwise. For example, although Amazon.com's revenues continued to skyrocket (1999 fourth-quarter sales of $650 million whereas its 1998 *total* sales were $610 million), as of 1999 it had yet to make a profit. However, according to strategic management consultants, there seems to be some rational basis for this extraordinary thinking. Companies such as Amazon.com and AOL, Inc. have little in the way of traditional capital spending that can be depreciated over several years. Instead, their capital-intensive cash outlays are funding immediate, up-front marketing costs to capture customers. These costs can range from $20 to $100 or more per customer, and are accounted for immediately on the profit-and-loss statements as expenses, thereby reducing the company's profit. So even though they're unprofitable, these companies can do all the things that profitable ones can—they can sell stock to the public, issue debt, make acquisitions, dominate a market niche, enrich management and shareholders, and achieve large market capitalizations. However, investment analysts point out that there will come a time when profits *do* matter. The investments being made by companies such as Amazon.com and AOL will eventually have to lead to profits.

Sources: "Amazon Has a Plan, but Isn't Telling," *Springfield News-Leader*, January 30, 2000, p. 6B; B. Wysocki Jr., "Rethinking a Quaint Idea: Profits," *Wall Street Journal*, May 19, 1999, p. B1; and A. J. Slywotzky and D. J. Morrison, *The Profit Zone: How Strategic Business Design Will Lead You to Tomorrow's Profits* (New York: Random House, 1997).

---

results or outcomes are achieved—at *any* level of the organization—organizational members assess the implications and make any necessary adjustments to strategies. Typically, when an organization goes in a new strategic direction or develops a totally new strategy, the strategic management process is followed in sequential order starting with situation analysis. Otherwise, strategic management in action involves minor and major adjustments to organizational strategies (functional–operational, competitive, corporate) currently in effect. This may mean starting with strategy evaluation, then doing a situation assessment before proceeding to strategy formulation and implementation. The point is that the way organizations actually function doesn't always happen neatly and logically according to a prescribed sequence, but that doesn't discount the importance of the specific steps in the process.

Looking at Strategic Management's Past

Why look at the history of strategic management? By looking at the evolution of the concepts and practices of strategic management, we can better understand how and why today's managers practice strategic management in action and why organiza-

Consider This ◀◀|

✓ What is strategy? Why isn't it just a plan?

✓ What is the concept of "matching" and why is it important?

✓ What is strategic management? How is it different from other types of management?

✓ Describe the strategic management process. Why is it a process?

✓ What does a situation analysis include?

✓ Describe the levels of strategy.

✓ What connections are there between strategy implementation and strategy evaluation?

tional performance levels vary. Strategic management's past is quite fascinating, ranging from great historical military battles to current attempts to understand why firms succeed or fail.

Strategy's Military Roots. Although strategic management is a relatively young academic discipline, the concept of strategy has a long and colorful background arising from the decisions and actions used by military organizations. Historical accounts tell us that a country's military decision makers often would design battlefield strategies to gain an edge on the enemy. They would try to exploit the enemy's weak spots and attack them where they were most vulnerable, thus giving the aggressor the best chance of succeeding. Even today, military historians like to analyze great battles in terms of the strategies that each side used and try to interpret why some were successful whereas others failed. In addition, many popular children's games (such as Battleship, tic-tac-toe, and even checkers) are based on military concepts and designed around the idea of a "strategy." Most involve figuring out what your opponent is doing and taking actions based on that information. The process of analyzing the situation and crafting, implementing, and evaluating an appropriate response is quite common, although we may not think of it specifically in strategy terms.

Academic Origins of Strategic Management.[8] The fields of economics and organization theory provided the earliest academic bases for strategic management. What did economics contribute? Although mainstream economic theory, with its emphasis on rationality, predictability, and similarity, doesn't quite jive

Principles of War

The nation's leading military academies teach the Nine Principles of War. These principles have stood the test of time, and only one, the ninth, has been added since 1921. Because the marketplace is often viewed as a "battleground," these principles might be useful in developing an organization's competitive strategy. What are these nine principles?

- *The objective:* Must be clear, conclusive, and obtainable.
- *The offense:* Victory requires offensive action; defensive actions only prevent defeat.
- *Unity of command:* Forces must be under one commander with full authority and responsibility.
- *Mass:* Victory goes to the army with superior forces at the point of contact.

- *Economy of force:* Allocate only the essential minimum of forces to areas of secondary importance.
- *Maneuver:* Deploy forces so they can come together at the right place at the right time.
- *Surprise:* If you can strike at the enemy at an unexpected time or place, you can often win your objective before the enemy reacts.
- *Security:* Surprise cannot exist without security—safeguard intentions and plans.
- *Simplicity:* Objectives, strategies, plans, and orders should be clear, concise, and simple.

Now relate these nine "war" principles to what an organization does as it competes for customers. Do they make sense? Explain.

Source: W. C. Finnie, "A Four Cycle Approach to Strategy Development and Implementation," *Strategy & Leadership,* January–February 1997, p. 28.

with the realities of strategic management, it does provide an avenue for beginning to explore the role of management decisions and the possibility of strategic choices. In addition, early organizational studies by Frederick Taylor (scientific management), Max Weber (bureaucratic organizations), and Chester Barnard (administrative functions and the organization as an open system) provided important knowledge about efficient and effective organizations and the role that managers played.

Strategic Planning and Strategic Management Emerge.[9] The 1960s were a time of questioning and challenges to tradition in many different areas of society's customs and practices. This was true also in the way management was being practiced. The universalistic principles and rules of management being advocated (which proposed that there's only one correct way to manage in all situations) were being replaced by contingency ideas, which proposed that each organizational situation was different and the best way of managing depended on the situation. Organization theorists were searching for explanations of organizational differences in functioning and performance. Although strategic management hadn't yet appeared as a separate area of study, the groundwork was there for the continued exploration of organizational strategies.

During the 1960s, the publication of three important books proved instrumental in the establishment of many of the basic concepts of strategic management and distinguishing strategic management as a separate academic field. These books were Alfred Chandler's *Strategy and Structure* (1962); Igor Ansoff's *Corporate Strategy* (1965); and the Harvard textbook *Business Policy: Text and Cases* by E. P. Learned, C. R. Christensen, K. R. Andrews, and W. D. Guth (1965). Chandler's book explored how large businesses grew over time and how their organizational structures adapted to accommodate the growth. Based on his studies, he declared that structure followed strategy; that is, when an organization changed its strategy, it had to change its structure to carry out that strategy. Chandler's analysis and interpretation of the process by which large organizations such as Sears, General Motors, and DuPont grew provided a sizable boost to the importance of understanding corporate strategy. On the other hand, Ansoff's book (he was general manager of the New Jersey–based Lockheed Electronics Company) focused on strategy as providing a "common thread" for five major organizational decisions: product–market scope, growth alternatives, competitive advantage, synergy made possible by a combination of capabilities or competencies, and the make-or-buy decision. Many of Ansoff's ideas are still addressed today in the formulation of organizational strategies. Finally, the business policy textbook by Learned and his co-authors was the first to address the concept of an organization's internal strengths and weaknesses and external opportunities and threats (SWOT analysis) and how organizations should use the results of this analysis to develop appropriate strategies.

During the 1970s and 1980s strategic management became more of a distinct academic field as researchers empirically studied organizations, managers, and strategies. A dichotomy developed between those trying to understand how strategies were formed and implemented (focusing on the *process* of strategic management) and those seeking to understand the relationship between strategic choice and performance (focusing on the *content* of strategic management).[10] Process researchers studied "how" strategy is formed. Content researchers studied the

Strategic Management—The Global Perspective

The name of Giant Manufacturing Company Ltd. befits its strategic performance. Located in Taichung, Taiwan, Giant manufactures bicycles that are exported around the world. In fact, 93 percent of its bicycles are exported. In building its global brand, Giant not only distributed overseas but also built manufacturing facilities abroad. It selected the Netherlands as its manufacturing base, which people thought was crazy. After all, wages were 50 percent higher in the Netherlands than in Taichung. But, CEO Antony Lo said that shipping finished bicycles from Taiwan to Europe could take up to two months, so locating in the Netherlands made strategic sense because it allowed the company to react more quickly to customer demands such as color and size changes. Also, by manufacturing there, Giant could avoid strict European Union antidumping duties. What do you think of Lo's strategy? It does seem to be a smart one, doesn't it?

Source: W. Royal, "Made in Taiwan," *Industry Week,* February 15, 1999, pp. 56–70.

"what" of a strategic decision. Despite their differences in perspective, both process and content researchers have attempted to establish a relationship between strategic decisions and organizational performance. In addition, strategy researchers have begun looking at the important relationships between strategy content, strategy process, organizational context, and performance. Because explaining and predicting organizational performance is a primary research objective in the field of strategic management, these types of studies continue to provide important clues to how organizational employees can be effective in managing strategically.

Even with all the research that's been done on strategy (and the research that continues to be done), there still are some misunderstandings about strategy and strategic management.

Misconceptions About Strategy and Strategic Management

In explaining what strategy *is*, it may help to clarify the concept by explaining what it *isn't*. Although management researchers have studied strategic management for a number of years, there still are misconceptions about it. What are some of these misconceptions?

1. *Strategy and strategic planning are dead.* This assertion by Henry Mintzberg and other management critics focused on how strategic planning processes can become overly rigid and fixated on analysis and quantification.[11] In so doing, these critics said, the planning process and the resulting strategy can be inflexible and incapable of predicting crucial market shifts. Why is this a misconception? Well, even these critics agreed that every organization needs the focus and direction provided by its strategies and the strategic management process.[12] Although strategic planning often may be misapplied and misdirected in organizations, it certainly isn't dead.

2. *Strategy is strictly for top management.* Early studies of strategic management processes in organizations asserted that strategy and strategic management were for top managers only. Although top management does play a crucial role in establishing the direction and dealing with the "big" organizational

issues, *everyone* in the organization has a part to play. Even the welder on an automobile assembly line or a nurse's aide in a hospice care organization contributes to the strategic management process. (We'll explore the role of all organizational employees in strategic management when we get to the section on "who" does strategic management.)

3. *Strategy is about planning.* You're probably already well aware why this statement is a misconception about strategy. Our whole description of strategy and the strategic management process emphasizes that strategy isn't just about planning; it's also about doing. The perfect plan is useless unless it's implemented, evaluated, and modified as needed. Strategy and strategic management is about more than just planning. In fact, remember our definition of strategy presented earlier: a series of goal-directed decisions and *actions.* Strategy means deciding *and* acting.

4. *Strategy is stable and constant.* In a world where change is infrequent and predictable, an organization's strategy very well could be stable and constant. However, as we'll discuss more fully in the next chapter, the context that organizational employees must deal with is usually anything but predictable and calm. What's the implication? An organization's strategy can't be stable and constant. It's dynamic and flexible, changing as needed to respond to environmental opportunities and threats and organizational strengths and weaknesses.

5. *Strategic management outlines the ultimate destination and route.* This misconception is related to the previous one in that the "ultimate" strategy *could* be developed if all the variables were predictable and stable. However, we know

Why Good Companies Go Bad

Success doesn't always lead to success. In fact, one of the perplexing questions in strategic management is why good companies go bad. Why do successful companies facing major changes in their environment often fail to respond effectively? One author says it's a problem of *active inertia.* Although you may think inertia is associated with inactivity, *active* inertia is an organization's tendency to follow established patterns of behavior. Because these established patterns of behavior have been successful in the past, organizational decision makers who are victims of active inertia tend to do the same things that have worked before. After all, they rationalize, these activities have brought us high levels of success. Companies such as Firestone Tire & Rubber (for more than 70 years, the leader in the U.S. tire industry), Laura Ashley (once a powerful retail brand in fashion), and Xerox (a company once blinded to what was happening in both the copier and personal computer markets) are all examples of what can happen when good companies go bad. However, active inertia can be avoided. Instead of asking "what should we do?" effective strategic managers who want to continue and build on their companies' successes should focus on understanding the obstacles to doing what they need to do. This doesn't mean that the heritages of the past need to be destroyed, but it does mean that there should be a willingness to look at new strategic processes, relationships, and values that can better help the company meet the new challenges.

Source: D. N. Sull, "Why Good Companies Go Bad," *Harvard Business Review,* July–August, 1999, pp. 42–52.

Consider This ◀◀|

✓ What role did the military play in the development of strategy and strategic management?

✓ How did economic theory and studies of organizations contribute to strategic management?

✓ Describe the contributions of the three 1960s strategy books.

✓ How would strategy process researchers study the chapter-opening case? How about strategy content researchers?

✓ What have you learned from the history of the development of strategy and strategic management?

✓ What are the misconceptions about strategy and strategic management, and how would you refute them?

that this is an unrealistic expectation. Even in industries that aren't experiencing significant upheaval, the likelihood of designing the "perfect" strategy would be remote. In addition, it's hard to pin down exactly what the ultimate strategy would look like. What the strategic management process can do, however, is establish a systematic approach to analyzing relevant information and using this information to design, implement, and evaluate appropriate strategies.

By now, you should have a fairly good feel for what strategic management is. Knowing what strategic management *is* is important, but who specifically in organizations plays a role in managing strategically and what role do they play? That's the next topic we'll be looking at.

WHO'S INVOLVED WITH STRATEGIC MANAGEMENT?

As stated earlier, one of the major assumptions of this text is that *all* an organization's employees play an important role in the formulation, implementation, and evaluation of its strategies. Strategic management is just as important for the bank teller at a drive-through facility as it is for the bank's executive vice president in charge of commercial loans. Think back to our definition of strategic management—those decisions and actions in which organizational members analyze the current situation; decide on strategies; put those strategies into action; and evaluate, modify, or change strategies—and you can begin to see how each and every employee is involved. The only aspect that differs is the scope or range of the individual's strategic decision making and action. For example, a bank teller is concerned only with his or her direct work activities in formulating, implementing, and evaluating specific functional strategies (goal-directed decisions and actions) and making sure that his or her actions are coordinated with others, whereas the bank's executive vice president does the same either on the competitive or corporate level (or both) with several work areas. Given the importance of each and every employee in strategic management, we need to look at the groups who play key roles in the strategic management process. These groups include the board of directors, top management teams, and other strategic managers and organizational employees.

The Role of the Board of Directors in Strategic Management

What is a board of directors? For publicly owned business organizations (those whose stocks or shares are sold to the public), the **board of directors** serves as the elected representatives of the company's stockholders. They play a significant role in corporate governance—that is, in governing the decisions and actions of the organization. Table 1-2 lists some typical board responsibilities. The board's legal obligation is to represent the shareholders (stockholders) and protect their interests. Even not-for-profit organizations often have a board of advisers. In fact,

TABLE 1-2   Typical Board Responsibilities
• Review and approve strategic goals and plans
• Review and approve organization's financial standards and policies
• Ensure integrity of organization's financial controls and reporting system
• Approve an organizational philosophy
• Monitor organizational performance and regularly review performance results
• Select, evaluate, and compensate top-level managers
• Develop management succession plans
• Review and approve capital allocations and expenditures
• Monitor relations with shareholders and other key stakeholders
Other responsibilities may be assigned depending on the unique culture and needs of the organization.

Source: Based on K. McG. Sullivan and H. J. Gregory, "Board Self-Assessment," *The Corporate Board,* November–December 1995, p. 7.

your college may have a board of regents (or board of governors or whatever name it has) that evaluates top management decisions and perhaps even makes recommendations as far as future strategic decisions and actions.

Just how much a board is involved in formulating and implementing strategy has always been a sensitive issue.[13] Although in most situations, top management keeps the board of directors informed of the evolving strategy, it's also been standard, and accepted, procedure for top management to keep "ownership" of the strategy and manage it with limited board input regarding specific operational approaches (implementation issues). In fact, an organization's management and board often have unique and different perspectives on strategy. Managers are responsible for turning strategic vision and goals into operational reality. The board's responsibility, on the other hand, is to represent the interests of investors and question whether the strategies are appropriate for stockholders' interests. However, investor activism and significant changes in corporate strategy such as downsizing, global expansion, or mergers have created an increased interest in exactly what role boards should play in the strategic management process.

One approach is to view the role of the board in the firm's strategy processes from two opposing perspectives, as shown in Figure 1-4. These two board roles represent the outer boundaries in terms of the level of involvement in the strategic management process. In the initiating role, the board of directors has the highest level of involvement and acts as the initiator and creator of strategic direction. In this instance, the role of the organization's managers would be simply to operationalize the various strategies. At the other end of the continuum is the approving role in which the board has the

The Grey Zone   Suppose you're in a management position and you're asked by your company's top managers to lie about information you have that's going to be presented to the board. Is lying always wrong, or might it be acceptable under certain circumstances? What, if any, might those circumstances be? What about simply distorting information that's being presented to the board? Is that always wrong, or might it be acceptable under certain circumstances? What circumstances?

Figure 1-4

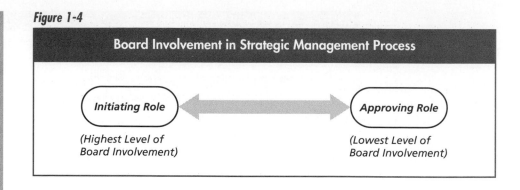

lowest level of involvement in the strategic management process. Here, the board would simply approve management's recommendations of strategic directions and actions. Of course, a wide range of board involvement exists between the two extremes. The role an organization's board of directors chooses to play in the strategic management process would depend on its desired level of involvement in organizational strategy direction and actions.

The Role of Top Management

There's absolutely no doubt that an organization's top managers play a significant role in the strategic management process. The top organizational manager typically is called the CEO (chief executive officer) and usually has a top management team composed of other executive or senior managers, such as a COO (chief operating officer), CFO (chief financial officer), CIO (chief information officer), and other individuals who may have various titles. Traditional descriptions of the CEO's role in strategic management include being the "chief" strategist, structural architect, and developer of the organization's information and control systems.[14] Other descriptions of the strategic role of the "chief executive" include key decision maker, visionary leader, political actor, monitor and interpreter of environment changes, and strategy designer.[15]

No matter how we characterize top management's job, you can be certain that from managers' perspective at the upper levels of an organization, it's like no other job in the organization. By definition, they are ultimately responsible for every decision and action of every organizational employee. One important aspect of top management's role in strategy concerns top managers as strategic leaders. As you're probably well aware, leadership is a continually popular management topic. Libraries and bookstores have numerous books on the subject. Organizational researchers continue to study it in relation to strategic management because it's important for an organization's top managers to provide effective strategic leadership. What is **strategic leadership**? It's an individual's ability to anticipate, envision, maintain flexibility, think strategically, and work with others in the organization to initiate changes that will create a viable and valuable future for the organization.[16] How can top managers provide effective strategic leadership? Six key dimensions of strategic leadership have been identified.[17] (See Figure 1-5.) These include determining the organization's purpose or vision, exploiting and maintaining the organization's core competencies, developing the organization's human capital, creating and sustaining a strong organizational culture, emphasizing ethical organizational decisions and practices, and establishing

STRATEGIC MANAGEMENT IN AN E-BUSINESS WORLD

e·biz

eBay is an interesting success story in the e-business world. Unlike some other well-known e-businesses, eBay is profitable. What's its story? The company is the world's largest personal online trading community. eBay created an entirely new market—efficient one-to-one trading in an auction format on the Web. Individuals use eBay to buy and sell items in more than 4,500 categories. Some of the more popular ones include Beanie Babies, dolls, jewelry, and sports memorabilia. Its mission is to help people trade practically anything on earth. Pierre Omidyar founded the company in 1995 because his wife, who's an avid Pez collector, said it would be really neat if she could interact and trade with other Pez collectors online. He now serves as eBay's chairman. His responsibilities include overseeing the strategic direction and growth of the company, model and site development, and community advocacy. Meg Whitman is eBay's president and CEO. After job stints at consulting and in corporate America (she worked for Procter & Gamble, Disney's Consumer Products division, Stride Rite Corporation, and Hasbro Inc.), Whitman was called by a headhunter who urged her to give up her comfortable position as general manager of Hasbro's Preschool Division for a CEO position at a no-name Silicon Valley start-up. At first, she said "no," but after visiting the California offices of eBay, she was hooked. She said, "I thought something was very right here. They had touched a consumer nerve."

Log on to eBay's Web site (**www.ebay.com**). Find the link that will take you to information about the company. Then, link to information about eBay's management team. Make a list of who's on the management team, what their responsibilities are, and what you feel they bring to the top management team. Explain whether the CEO fits the six dimensions of effective strategic leadership. Make note of other interesting information you find about the company.

Sources: Company's Web site (**www.ebay.com**), February 7, 2000; and L. M. Holson, "Defining the On-Line Chief," *New York Times,* May 10, 1999, p. C1.

appropriately balanced organizational controls. Each of these strategic leadership dimensions is an important part of the strategic management process, which we'll be discussing in detail in Chapters 2 through 7.

Other Strategic Managers and Organizational Employees

Although an organization's top managers have several important strategic leadership responsibilities in the strategic management process, managers and employees at other levels throughout the organization are also important to managing strategically. What are some of their strategic responsibilities?[18] One of their primary tasks in managing strategically is implementation. They're the people putting the strategies into action. They might be supervising the work of others (in the case of a supervisor or manager) or they may even be personally performing some of the work as well. For example, think back to the chapter-opening case. Someone had to create the advertising slogan and a marketing plan. Someone had to develop the information system for tracking quality. And, someone had to plan and implement all those new store openings. As Papa John's adjusts to its changing environment, new strategies may have to be put into action. That's the role other strategic managers and organizational employees will play.

Figure 1-5

Effective Strategic Leadership Involves

- Determining Organization's Purpose or Vision
- Establishing Appropriately Balanced Controls
- Exploiting and Maintaining Core Competencies
- Effective Strategic Leadership
- Emphasizing Ethical Decisions and Practices
- Developing Human Capital
- Creating and Sustaining Strong Organizational Culture

Source: Based on R. D. Ireland and M. A. Hitt, "Achieving and Maintaining Strategic Competitiveness in the 21st Century: The Role of Strategic Leadership," *Academy of Management Executive,* February 1999, pp. 43–57.

Consider This ◀◀|

✓ How are boards of directors involved in the strategic management process?

✓ Describe the two specific levels of board involvement in the strategic management process.

✓ What role do top managers play in strategic management?

✓ What is strategic leadership?

✓ List the six key dimensions of strategic leadership.

✓ What are the different roles that other strategic managers and organizational employees play in strategic management?

✓ Describe open book management and how it relates to the strategic management process.

Organizational employees and managers are also likely to be responsible for evaluating whether the strategies are working. If the strategies aren't achieving the desired levels of performance, then they need to be changed or modified. Although top management may establish the guidelines and policies for evaluating performance, the other strategic managers and organizational employees actually do the evaluation and take any necessary actions. In fact, many organizations—particularly, smaller ones—are involving their employees even more in strategy evaluation by opening up the financial statements (the "books"). They share this information so employees can make better decisions about their work and will understand the implications of what they do, how they do it, and the ultimate impact on the bottom line. This approach is called **open book management**.[19]

No matter what organizational level you're on or functional area you're in, you'll find yourself involved in some way with strategic management.

Whether your career goal is to be part of that top management team or whether you plan to apply your technical training in some functional area of the organization, you'll be affected by and have an effect on the organization's strategic management process. This chapter is just the beginning of your exciting journey to understand strategic management!

THE BOTTOM LINE

➤ Strategic management is important to you individually because you'll be working in some organization and will be evaluated and rewarded on how effectively and efficiently you manage strategically.

➤ Strategic management is important to organizations because it does appear to make a difference in how well the organization performs; it helps employees decide what to do and how to respond to continually changing situations; and it helps coordinate the diverse divisions, functions, and work activities. However, although strategic management is important, it won't solve all an organization's problems or challenges.

➤ A **strategy** is a series of goal-directed decisions and actions that match an organization's skills and resources with the environmental opportunities and threats.

➤ **Strategic management** involves those decisions and actions in which organizational members analyze the current situation; develop appropriate strategies; put those strategies into action; and evaluate, modify, or change those strategies as needed.

➤ The basic activities of strategic management are strategy formulation, strategy implementation, and strategy evaluation.

➤ Strategic management is different from other types of management because it is interdisciplinary, has an external focus, has an internal focus, and has a future focus.

➤ The strategic management process consists of **situation analysis** (scanning and evaluating the organizational context, the external environment, and the organizational environment), **strategy formulation** (the design and choice of appropriate organizational strategies), **strategy implementation** (putting the organization's various strategies into action), and **strategy evaluation** (evaluating how the strategy has been implemented as well as the outcomes of the strategy).

➤ In reality, the strategic management process may not always follow the prescribed sequence, but the activities are still completed.

➤ An organization will have three different types of strategies. **Functional strategies** (also called **operational strategies**) are the short-term goal-directed decisions and actions of the organization's various functional departments. **Competitive strategies** dictate how an organization is going to compete in a specific business or industry. **Corporate strategies** are broad and more long term and address issues of what businesses the organization is in or wants to be in and what it hopes to do with these businesses.

⫸ Strategic management has its roots in military strategies because military units would try to gain the edge on an enemy, much like an organization does as it tries to gain the edge on competitors.

⫸ Strategic management also has evolved out of the academic fields of economics and organization theory.

⫸ Strategic management as an academic discipline was influenced by work in the 1960s in which researchers looked for explanations of organizational differences in performance and functioning.

⫸ Also, in the 1960s, three important strategic management books were published that established some of the core ideas in strategy.

⫸ During the 1970s and 1980s, researchers looked at how strategies were formed and implemented (*process* research) and at the relationship between strategic choices and performance (*content* research).

⫸ Several misconceptions exist about strategic management including *strategy and strategic planning are dead, strategy is strictly for top management, strategy is about planning, strategy is stable and constant,* and *strategic management outlines the ultimate destination and route.* Each of these misconceptions can be rebutted.

⫸ People at *all* organizational levels play a role in developing, implementing, and evaluating strategy.

⫸ Three main groups play key roles in the strategic management process.

⫸ One of these groups is the **board of directors**, the elected representatives of the company's stockholders. Their involvement can range from an initiating role (highest level of involvement) to an approving role (lowest level of involvement).

⫸ Top management is another of these groups. The top management team (CEO and other executive or senior managers) is ultimately responsible for every decision and action of employees.

⫸ One important characteristic of top managers is their **strategic leadership**, an individual's ability to anticipate, envision, maintain flexibility, think strategically, and work with others in the organization to initiate changes that will create a viable and valuable future for the organization.

⫸ Six key dimensions of strategic leadership include determining the organization's purpose or vision, exploiting and maintaining the organization's core competencies, developing the organization's human capital, creating and sustaining a strong organizational culture, emphasizing ethical organizational decisions and practices, and establishing appropriately balanced organizational controls.

⫸ The third important group involved in strategic management is other strategic managers and organizational employees at middle and lower organizational levels. One of their primary tasks is implementation. And, they're also likely to be responsible for strategy evaluation.

⫸ Many organizations are involving employees more in strategy evaluation through **open book management**—where the organization's "books" or financial statements are shared with employees so they can see the implications of their decisions and work.

BUILDING YOUR SKILLS

1. A recent description of the role of an organizational leader identified the following: creating a clear understanding of the current reality and a healthy dissatisfaction with the current situation; helping develop a shared vision of a more desirable future situation; creating the belief that there is a viable path from the former to the latter; and creating an environment in which people are motivated to embark on the journey to that future. Do some research on the strategic leader(s) of Coca-Cola, Amazon.com, and Ford Motor Company. Use paper-based sources (business periodicals, books, etc.) or Web-based information. In a brief paper, describe how each of these strategic leaders fulfills these four roles. In addition, address the following questions: How do these descriptions of the role of a strategic leader fit with the six dimensions of strategic leadership identified in this chapter? Are they similar or dissimilar? Explain.

    (*Source:* J. Mariotti, "The Role of a Leader," *Industry Week,* February 1, 1999, p. 75.)

2. Your manager is preparing to make a presentation to your company's top management team on open book management and has asked you to gather some information on the topic. After researching the topic, write up a bulleted list of important points to give her.

3. BHAG (BEE-hag). Big Hairy Audacious Goals. This corporate buzzword describing goals that might seem impossible and that really "raise the bar" for organizations. Some examples: Goodyear Tire and Rubber aims to add $10 billion in sales in five years. Procter & Gamble intends to double in size in 10 years. Campbell Soup aspires to be seen as a peer of global brand leaders Coca-Cola and Gillette. These goals will require incredible strategic efforts on the parts of these organizations. What impact might BHAGs have on the strategic management process? How might the different groups in strategic management be affected by BHAGs? How might these groups be involved in BHAGs? What would be the advantages of having BHAGs? What might be the drawbacks?

    (*Source:* A. Bryant, "When Management Shoots for the Moon," *New York Times,* September 27, 1998, p. BU4.)

4. The CEO of one of the Baby Bells (the phone companies spun off from AT&T when it was deregulated) stated in a speech that "Strategy's the easy part. Implementing it is the hardest thing an executive will ever have to do." What's your interpretation of this remark? Do you agree? Why or why not? What are the implications for the way an organization's employees engage in strategic management?

5. "Making strategy, once an event, is now a continuous process." Explain what you think this statement means.

6. The performance of an organization's board of directors is being scrutinized more closely than ever. Complete the following assignments having to do with boards of directors.

    a. *Fortune* (**www.fortune.com**) has an annual listing of the worst boards of directors. Get the most recent listing (the list usually comes out in one of the April issues). Look up financial information on the companies on this list. Report what you find. Draw some conclusions about why these boards are cited as being among the worst.

b. *Forbes* (**www.forbes.com**) has an annual listing of Global Companies. In the 1999 listing (May 17, 1999), information is provided about shareholder participation in executive pay decisions and what executive compensation information is disclosed in 20 countries. Get this list information (check for the most recent listing) and report what you find. Which countries seem to provide the most shareholder participation? Which countries seem to provide the most information about executive compensation? What implications might these have for an organization's strategic management processes?

c. *Business Week* published a special article (January 24, 2000, pp. 142–50) on the best and worst corporate boards of directors. Read this article. What performance measures were used to determine the rankings? What do you think these performance measures describe? What does the article report are the attributes of a good board? What factors contribute to a company's ranking on the worst board list? Compare *Business Week's* list of worst boards with *Fortune's* list. Are any of the companies the same? Now take one company from the "best" list and one company from the "worst" list. Do some comparative research on each. How do the two compare? What can you learn about strategic management from these examples?

d. *Fortune* also publishes an annual ranking of the most admired companies (usually in a February issue). Get the most recent listing of the top 10. Look up financial information on the companies on this list. Look up information on the boards of directors of these companies. Report what you find. What conclusions might you draw about the role of the board in the strategic management of these most admired companies?

7. Few companies can afford to ignore the strategic challenges of the e-business era. Here are some comments made by researchers and analysts regarding the CEO's role in strategically leading an organization into this challenging territory. Explain what you think each statement means and what you think the strategic implications are. Now, do you agree with the statement? Explain your stance.

- "The Internet does change what the CEO should be doing."
- "It is critical for the top six or eight people in a company to have some hands-on experience with the Internet."
- "The CEO needs to take the lead in both understanding the technology and finding ways to put it to use in the business."
- "I view my role as making sure I have access to people who are computer and Internet experts and to make sure we don't fall behind the curve."
- "The CEO doesn't need to be a regular Web surfer in order to understand the technology well enough to be an effective champion of its use in the corporation."
- "The historical pattern in which the CEO and other business leaders set strategy and then the business units set their own strategy, and then finally the information technology department sets its strategy, just doesn't work with e-commerce."

- "The idea that a strategic plan is viewed as being operative for a year doesn't make sense in the world of the Internet. Your e-commerce strategy should be reviewed every quarter or even more frequently."

(*Source:* D. Bartholomew, "Piloting Companies in the Brave 'Net World," *Industry Week,* May 17, 1999, pp. 67–76.)

STRATEGIC MANAGEMENT IN ACTION CASES

CASE #1: Pizza Wars

Strategic Management in Action case #1 can be found at the beginning of Chapter 1.

Discussion Questions

1. What do you think Papa John's Pizza strategic philosophy ("The main thing is to keep the main thing the main thing") is talking about? Do the company's core values contribute to this strategic philosophy? Explain.

2. What are the implications of this strategic philosophy for the way strategic management is done at all levels in this organization?

3. Do you think the legal ruling will have an impact on Papa John's strategies? Explain.

4. Update the information on Papa John's. Include the following: number of stores, revenues, profits, and strategies.

CASE #2: Fighting Grime

Look in your pantry, your laundry room, your bathroom, or under your kitchen sink. Chances are your household contains at least one of Clorox Company's many cleaning products. The Clorox Company (**www.clorox.com**) manufactures and markets household cleaning and grocery products around the globe. Some of those product names you might recognize include Clorox Bleach, Glad bags, Soft Scrub bathroom cleaner, Tilex shower cleaner, Combat Plus pest control, STP automotive products, Kingsford charcoal, S.O.S. cleaning pads, Hidden Valley salad dressings, and many others.

Although most people probably know Clorox from its best-selling bleach products (it has a 60 percent share of the bleach market),

Clorox bleach is not even the company's biggest brand. That distinction belongs to the Glad line of food storage and disposal products. The Glad line was part of the acquisition of First Brands Corporation, a $2 billion acquisition that the Clorox Company completed in January of 1999. In addition to the Glad products, the acquisition brought the STP line of automotive additives and the Scoop Away and Jonny Cat litter brands under the Clorox Company's fold. It was a bold strategic move on the part of the Clorox Company.

The Clorox Company's strategic position today is much better than it was in the late 1990s. Much of that success can be traced to

G. Craig Sullivan, Clorox's CEO, who was brought on board in the early 1990s. In the early 1990s, Clorox was viewed by its competitors as knowing how to sell bleach, but not much else. There was a complacent and content management team who did an adequate job of strategically managing a tired product line. When Sullivan was hired, his first action was to let go those managers he judged to be unable to adapt to the new strategic direction he had in mind for Clorox. Half the management team left. His next step was to sell off money-losing operations such as bottled water and restaurant equipment and to acquire grime-fighting brands such as S.O.S. scrubbing pads and Lestoil cleaner that were more in line with Clorox's core products. Then, Sullivan stepped up marketing efforts for the company's existing brands such as Pine Sol and Formula 409 cleansers. But the biggest strategic change of all was the acquisition of First Brands Corporation, an acquisition that increased the Clorox Company's size by almost 50 percent overnight. In the period of one year (the time it took to complete the transaction), Clorox went from a $2.7 billion company with 6,600 employees to a $4 billion company with almost 11,000 employees.

First Brands was a lot like the "old" Clorox Company. It had a stable of solid brands that had stalled or faded from consumers' minds and thus from their purchases. However, Sullivan felt that he could make First Brands a better organization. How? A key element of his overall growth strategy was to "dust off" brands that had languished. His strategic formula: Execute. Freshen old brands, extend product lines, improve advertising, and lower costs. Revitalizing product lines is a key to the success of this strategy. Sullivan also recognizes that, in addition to successfully integrating the new businesses, it's important to continue to support and grow the company's base business. To illustrate this commitment, Clorox introduced 85 new products from its base brands in 1999, compared with only 41 in 1998.

However, not everything the Clorox Company has done has been a success. A line of Hidden Valley salad dressings aimed at children with flavors like pizza and nacho sauce got the thumbs down by kids. And, sales of the company's pest control products have slipped. But, according to one investment analyst, the company seems to be "willing to cut things off when they're not working." Another enormous strategic challenge will be maintaining the rapid growth gains of the last few years. That growth may have to come from international markets in which Clorox's presence is small, whereas that of one of its major competitors, Colgate-Palmolive, is already enormous. Yet, the management team at the Clorox Company welcomes these strategic challenges. After all, if its products can effectively fight the grime and dirt found in some customers' homes, the war in the marketplace might not seem so bad after all!

Discussion Questions

1. Do you think strategic management has contributed to the Clorox Company's success? Why or why not?
2. Given this information about the Clorox Company, at what step in the strategic management process do you think it excels? Explain your choice.
3. Using Figure 1-5, evaluate G. Craig Sullivan's strategic leadership.
4. What evidence do you see here of functional strategy? Competitive strategy? Corporate strategy?

5. Update the information on the Clorox Company by logging on to the company's Web site (**www.clorox.com**). How big is Clorox now in terms of sales? In terms of number of employ-ees? What new strategies is it pursuing, if any?

(*Sources:* Company's Web site (**www.clorox.com**), February 7, 2000; and D. Canedy, "Resurgence of a Grime Fighter," *New York Times*, March 14, 1999, p. BU1.)

CASE #3: About Face to Save Face

Thermo Electron Corporation (**www.thermoelectron.com**) is a $4 billion multi-industry company and the world's leading manufacturer of measurement instruments that monitor, collect, and analyze information for a broad range of industries. The company also has a leading position in markets for biomedical products and for paper recycling equipment and papermaking accessories. But, Thermo Electron was known as a pioneer in another way as well.

The company had long been known for its unusual, radical, and complex organization structure. Each time a new product was invented or a new market for a new technology was found, Thermo would create a whole new autonomous company to pursue the opportunity. These various subsidiary companies sold minority blocks of stock to the public in order to raise capital. This "spinout strategy" fostered innovation and allowed the company's many engineers and scientists to, in fact, become entrepreneurs. It was seen as a way to increase funding opportunities for emerging businesses that might otherwise get lost in a large company and was also intended as a way to reward executives with stock options. Here's how the strategy was supposed to work: (1) Invent or identify a promising technology or service. (2) Develop a business around the idea and put in capital from the parent company. (3) When the business started to grow, set it up as its own separate entity. (4) Sell a minority stake in the company to the public and use that capital raised in the stock market for other new ventures. (5) The corporation becomes a growing family of spun-off subsidiaries. Although this strategy was a primary contributor to the company's growth during the 1980s and 1990s, it created a level of complexity that made Thermo Electron difficult to manage. CEO Richard F. Syron said the structure resulted in operational inefficiencies, reduced stock market liquidity, and reduced the coverage of the company by stock researchers and analysts who make buy or sell recommendations. Now, the company is doing an about face.

In a move to streamline its dizzyingly complex structure, Thermo Electron announced a massive reorganization plan that included the selling off of approximately $1 billion in assets and a "spin-in" of some of its subsidiaries—that is, Thermo will be buying back the minority stakes in these businesses. Businesses to be sold off have failed to meet certain financial goals or no longer fit strategic objectives. The reorganization plan also structured Thermo into three major independent entities. According to CEO Syron, "This is a bold plan to deliver shareholder value by creating focused companies that have strong prospects for growth." And, he concluded, "Thermo Electron was founded on the principle of identifying and nurturing new technologies and bringing them to the marketplace.

With this new structure, we believe each company will be able to continue the Thermo Electron tradition of product innovation and excellence, while creating even greater opportunities for commercial success."

Discussion Questions

1. Explain how Thermo Electron Corporation's strategic management and the strategic management process is illustrated.

2. Evaluate CEO Syron's comments on the company's proposed reorganization. How might the company's board of directors be affected by the reorganization? How about the top management team? How about other organizational employees?

3. Describe Thermo Electron's spin-out strategy. What were the supposed advantages from the strategy? What were the drawbacks? Why do you think the strategy worked well for a number of years and then became ineffective?

4. What changes in functional strategy might have to occur because of this corporate change? How about changes in competitive strategy? What are the implications for understanding how strategic management works in organizations?

(*Sources:* Company's Web site (**www.thermoelectron.com**), February 9, 2000; L. Johannes, "Thermo Electron Plans a Divestiture of $1 Billion in Major Streamlining," *Wall Street Journal*, February 1, 2000, p. A4; C. H. Deutsch, "A Corporate Parent with Too Big a Family," *New York Times*, June 6, 1999, p. BU6; and W. M. Bulkeley, "Thermo Electron to Take Pretax Charge of $450 Million, 'Spin in' Subsidiaries," *Wall Street Journal*, May 25, 1999, p. A3.)

ENDNOTES

1. Information from Papa John's International Web site (**www.papa johns.com**), February 2, 2000; information from *Washington Post* Web site (**www.washingtonpost.com**), February 2, 2000; A. M. Pascual and M. Hequet, "Slice, Dice, and Devour," *Time*, October 26, 1998, pp. 64–66; and D. Roth, "This Ain't No Pizza Party," *Fortune*, November 9, 1998, pp. 158–64.

2. P. J. Brews and M. R. Hunt, "Learning to Plan and Planning to Learn: Resolving the Planning School–Learning School Debate," *Strategic Management Journal*, 20 (1999), pp. 889–913; D. J. Ketchen Jr., J. B. Thomas, and R. R. McDaniel Jr., "Process, Content and Context: Synergistic Effects on Performance," *Journal of Management*, 22, no. 2 (1996), pp. 231–57; C. C. Miller and L. B. Cardinal, "Strategic Planning and Firm Performance: A Synthesis of More Than Two Decades of Research," *Academy of Management Journal*, December 1994, pp. 1649–65; and N. Capon, J. U. Farley, and J. M. Hulbert, "Strategic Planning and Financial Performance: More Evidence," *Journal of Management Studies*, January 1994, pp. 105–10.

3. J. W. Dean Jr. and M. P. Sharfman, "Does Decision Process Matter? A Study of Strategic Decision-Making Effectiveness," *Academy of Management Journal*, April 1996, pp. 368–96.

4. S. Hart and C. Banbury, "How Strategy-Making Processes Can Make a Difference," *Strategic Management Journal*, May 1994, pp. 251–69.

5. W. P. Barnett, H. R. Greve, and D. Y. Park, "An Evolutionary Model of Organizational Performance," *Strategic Management Journal*, winter 1994, pp. 11–28.

6. A. D. Chandler Jr., *Strategy and Structure: Chapters in the History of the Industrial Enterprise* (Cambridge, MA: MIT Press, 1962); and C. W. Hofer and D. Schendel, *Strategy Formulation: Analytical Concepts* (St. Paul, MN: West Publishing, 1978).

7. O. E. Williamson, "Strategy Research: Governance and Competence Perspectives," *Strategic Management Journal*, 20 (1999), pp. 1087–108.

8. R. P. Rumelt, D. E. Schendel, and D. J. Teece, "Fundamental Issues in Strategy," in R. P. Rumelt, D. E. Schendel, and D. J. Teece, *Fundamental Issues in Strategy: A Research Agenda* (Boston: Harvard Business School Press, 1994), pp. 9–47.

9. R. E. Hoskisson, M. A. Hitt, W. P. Wan, and D. Yiu, "Theory and Research in Strategic Management: Swings of a Pendulum," *Journal of Management*, 25, no. 3 (1999), pp. 417–56; and Rumelt, Schendel, and Teece, *Fundamental Issues in Strategy.*

10. Ketchen, Thomas, and McDaniel, "Process, Content and Context."

11. H. Mintzberg, *The Rise and Fall of Strategic Planning* (Boston: Free Press, 1994); and G. Hamel and C. K. Prahalad, *Competing for the Future* (Boston: Harvard Business School Press, 1994).

12. N. Capon, book review of H. Mintzberg's *The Rise and Fall of Strategic Planning, Academy of Management Review*, January 1996, pp. 298–301; and S. J. Wall and S. R. Wall, "The Evolution (Not the Death) of Strategy," *Organizational Dynamics*, autumn 1995, pp. 7–19.

13. N. Donaldson, "A New Tool for Boards: The Strategic Audit," *Harvard Business Review*, July–August 1995, pp. 99–107.

14. S. Ghoshal and C. A. Bartlett, "Changing the Role of Top Management: Beyond Structure to Process," *Harvard Business Review*, January–February 1995, pp. 86–96.

15. R. Calori, G. Johnson, and P. Sarnin, "CEO's Cognitive Maps and the Scope of the Organization," *Strategic Management Journal*, July 1994, pp. 437–57.

16. R. D. Ireland and M. A. Hitt, "Achieving and Maintaining Strategic Competitiveness in the 21st Century: The Role of Strategic Leadership," *Academy of Management Executive*, February 1999, pp. 43–57.

17. Ibid.

18. S. W. Floyd and P. J. Lane, "Strategizing Throughout the Organization: Managing Role Conflict in Strategic Renewal," *Academy of Management Review*, January 2000, pp. 154–77.

19. J. Case, "The Open-Book Revolution," *Inc.*, June 1995, pp. 26–50.

THE CONTEXT OF MANAGING STRATEGICALLY

LEARNING OBJECTIVES

After studying this chapter, you should be able to:

1. Define competitive advantage.
2. Describe the different perspectives on ways to achieve competitive advantage.
3. Explain what makes organizational resources unique.
4. Discuss the concept of transitory (temporary) competitive advantage.
5. Describe the driving forces of the "new" business environment.
6. Explain the implications of the "new" business environment.
7. Discuss the critical success factors for the "new" business environment.
8. Differentiate between organizational vision and mission.
9. Describe the concept of a world-class organization.
10. Discuss how corporate social responsibility and ethics affect strategic management.
11. Define organizational learning.
12. Describe the characteristics of a learning organization.

STRATEGIC MANAGEMENT IN ACTION CASE #1

The Queen of Lifestyle

Martha Stewart.[1] Most people have an opinion about America's most famous homemaker—they either love her or hate her. But no matter what you think about the public person you see cooking, decorating, or gardening, you have to admire the fact that she's building an impressive company, Martha Stewart Living Omni-media, Inc. (**www.martha stewart.com**). Using her knowledge and skills in homemaking, a task probably as old as civilization itself, Martha has effectively positioned her company to exploit the future.

From the publication of her first book on entertaining back in 1982 to today's multimedia empire, Stewart has capitalized on what she does best—helping people create a type of quality lifestyle where the ultimate in cooking, decorating, entertaining, and other homemaking arts are emphasized and celebrated. And Martha's fans are loyal. Her various media properties reach over 88 million people a month. That number represents a lot of potential purchasing power!

What exactly does Martha Stewart Living Omnimedia Inc. do? The company has two primary strategic goals: to provide original "how-to" content and information to as many consumers as possible and to turn customers into "doers" by offering them the information and products they need for do-it-yourself ingenuity the "Martha Stewart" way. The business is built around core subject areas including cooking, entertaining, weddings, crafts, gardening, home, holidays, baby and children, and keeping and preserving (clothes, mementos, decorative artifacts, etc.). From these different subject areas, content is developed for different media including magazines, books, network television, cable television, newspapers and radio, and the new Web site (**www.martha stewart.com**). In addition, the core subject areas have evolved into merchandise lines at Kmart and Zellers (Martha Stewart Everyday, which includes sheets, towels, table linens, garden equipment, plants and seeds, and baby bedding), an online catalog (Martha by Mail and MarthasFlowers.com), Sears and Canadian Tire (paints), and specialty retailers (fine paints, fabrics, and crafts). Revenues from 1999 exceeded $225 million and were expected to hit the $400 million level by 2003. Books and magazines accounted for 65 percent of the company's revenues whereas television and radio accounted for 12 percent. However, merchandising revenues were up to 10 percent of the total from being a minuscule percentage. And, Stewart's fledgling Web business is poised to be a major contributor to company revenues. In 1999, Internet and direct sales accounted for approximately 13 percent of revenues. However, the Web site is still a money loser because of heavy investments in staff and Web site development. But, the Web site is popular with advertisers and consumers and is expected to become profitable soon. In October of 1999, Martha Stewart Omnimedia (listed as MSO) went public and sold shares on the New York Stock Exchange. Shares offered at the initial public offering (IPO) opened at $18, quickly doubled to $36, and settled back to around $27. Since that time, the share price has hovered around the $21 to $29 mark. The IPO raised $149 million for the company and made Stewart a billionaire on paper.

Although the company's team of strategic decision makers is well aware of the realities of the organizational context and has positioned the company quite well to exploit the changing dynamics, one major strategic challenge faces them. And that's Martha herself. Although Stewart remains the walking, talking personification of the Martha Stewart brand, Martha and her management team need to ensure that Martha Stewart the brand can outlive Martha Stewart the person. However, Stewart is approaching it like she would making one of her impressive terra-cotta-tinged roses or freshly squeezed orange juice—by taking care of the details. And if there's one thing that the queen of lifestyle is proficient at, it's the details!

The story of Martha Stewart Living Omnimedia offers an interesting illustration of the importance of interpreting, understanding, and considering the context in which an organization's employees manage strategically. The company's strategic decision makers have a fairly good idea of their competitive advantage and the dynamic and changing context they're operating in. From the development of a sustainable competitive advantage that exploits the realities of today's business environment to the creation of an organization considered the best at what it does, an organization's strategic decision makers have to understand the context within which they're managing strategically. Why is it important to look at the context of managing strategically? Because an organization's context determines the "rules" of the game it's playing and what actions are likely to work best. Just as the coach of a baseball team analyzes its specific context (such factors as the condition of the playing field, the cohesiveness of the team's players, player injuries, or maybe even the team's current rankings in its division) in deciding what game strategies might work best, so, too, must organizational decision makers be aware of the context within which strategic decisions are made and implemented. You can see how the context of managing strategically fits into the overall strategic management process in Figure 2-1.

MANAGING STRATEGICALLY AND COMPETITIVE ADVANTAGE

Managing strategically means making decisions and implementing strategies that allow an organization to develop and maintain competitive advantage.

Figure 2-1

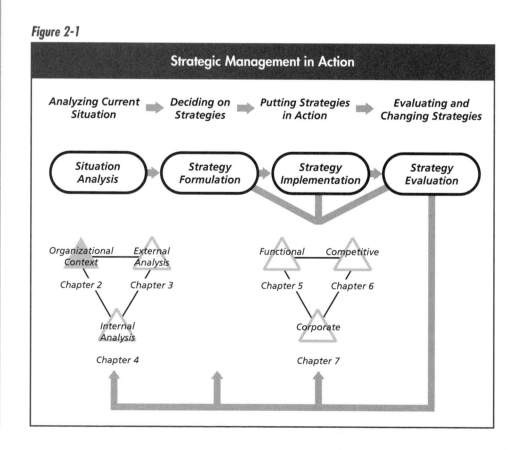

Competitive advantage is a key concept in strategic management. What is **competitive advantage**? It's what sets an organization apart—in other words, its competitive edge. When an organization has a competitive advantage, it has something that other competitors don't, does something better than other organizations do, or does something that others can't. Competitive advantage is a necessary ingredient for an organization's long-term success and survival. Even not-for-profit organizations (such as governmental agencies, community arts organizations, or social service groups) must have something that sets them apart—something unique that they offer in order to stay in business. Getting and keeping competitive advantage is what managing strategically is all about. It's tough to do, and getting tougher. The pursuit of competitive advantage leads to organizational success or failure. Although success is obviously the preferable choice, organizations don't choose to fail. Instead, poor performance can typically be traced to the failure to recognize the impact of important and dynamic external factors or the failure to capitalize on organizational resources and capabilities. These realities represent different perspectives on what it takes to capture competitive advantage—that is, to manage strategically. The first view suggests organizations look at the impact of important external factors and is called the industrial organization (I/O) view.[2] The second perspective that emphasizes exploiting organizational resources in order to develop and maintain competitive advantage is called the resource-based view.[3] In addition to these two traditional perspectives, another contemporary line of thought is the guerilla view of competitive advantage because it proposes that an organization's competitive advantage is only temporary and can be gained only by peppering the competitive marketplace with rapid radical surprises.[4] Because strategic management researchers and organizational strategists seriously desire to know where an organization's competitive advantage comes from, we need to look closer at these three perspectives. Table 2-1 summarizes the main points of each of these views.

Table 2-1   Comparison of I/O, Resource-Based, and Guerrilla Views of Competitive Advantage

	I/O View	Resource-Based View	Guerrilla View
Competitive Advantage	Positioning in industry	Possessing unique organizational assets or capabilities	Temporary
Determinants of Profitability	Characteristics of industry; firm's position within industry	Type, amount, and nature of firm's resources	Ability to change and radically surprise competitors with strategic actions
Focus of Analysis	External	Internal	External and internal
Major Concern	Competition	Resources — competencies	Continual, radical, and chaotic conditions
Strategic Choices	Choosing attractive industry; appropriate position	Developing unique resources and capabilities	Rapidly and repeatedly disrupting current situation and surprising competitors

The Industrial Organization (I/O) View

The **industrial organization (I/O) view** focuses on the structural forces within an industry, the competitive environment of firms, and how these influence competitive advantage. The best-known proponent of the I/O approach to competitive advantage is Michael Porter of Harvard University. His popular books *Competitive Strategy: Techniques for Analyzing Industries and Competitors* (Free Press, 1980) and *Competitive Advantage: Creating and Sustaining Superior Performance* (Free Press, 1985) provide a comprehensive description of how and why organizations develop competitive strategy and competitive advantage. According to Porter, five industry forces (covered in detail in Chapter 3) determine the average profitability of an industry, which in turn influence the profitability of firms within the industry. His approach emphasizes choosing the "right" industries and within those industries, the most advantageous (or competitive) positions. Porter's approach was developed from the field of industrial organization economics, which attempts to explain organizational performance by looking at the relationships of industry structure–organizational conduct–organizational performance. In other words, the structure of an industry influences what is appropriate organizational conduct (i.e., its strategic decisions and actions), which in turn influences the organization's performance. I/O researchers explore these various relationships in an attempt to explain how and why organizations differ in their performance.

Strategic Management in Action

Maybe you've never even heard of the Dictaphone Corporation (**www.dictaphone.com**), but it has been around for over 100 years as a market leader in the voice-recording industry. Dictaphone equipment used to be standard issue in offices around the United States. Executives would dictate letters, instructions, or other information, and a secretary or administrative assistant would transcribe the tape. However, as the need for voice-recording capabilities has changed, so has Dictaphone. Today, its products are no longer stand-alone voice recorders, but instead are part of enterprise-wide information systems in organizations where voice recordings are an essential part of doing business. The company views the human voice as just another form of data transmission and approaches its markets in that way. Check out the company's Web site. What does it say about the company's strategic direction? What is its vision? Its mission? How would Porter evaluate Dictaphone's strategic direction?

Sources: Company's Web site (**www.dictaphone.com**), February 23, 2000; and C. H. Deutsch, "Take a Memo: Dictaphone Is Still in Business," *New York Times*, December 27, 1999, p. C1.

Porter's idea is that getting and keeping competitive advantage means analyzing the external forces and then basing strategic decisions and actions on what is found. Not surprisingly, then, the focus of strategic analysis in the I/O view is external. Identifying and evaluating the industry and competitive forces that impact an organization entail looking at various external environmental factors. It means asking: What are the critical forces and what's happening with them? Because all firms within an industry face essentially the same external environmental forces, a major concern of the I/O view is how the firm stacks up against its competitors. Keep in mind that the I/O view proposes that competitive advantage relates to competitive positioning in the industry. Also, the I/O view suggests that both a firm's position within the industry and the underlying industry characteristics determine its potential profitability. This means that if there are a lot of negative forces in the industry or the firm has a weak position within the industry, then its profitability will be lower than average. But, if the industry is characterized by significant opportunities or the firm has a strong position within the industry, then its profitability will be above average. How do managers make sound strategic choices? According to the I/O view, it's a matter of understanding the nature of an attractive industry and then choosing an appropriate competitive position within that industry.

Although the I/O view provides important contributions to understanding how to manage strategically in order to gain competitive advantage, critics have complained that it neglects to tell the whole story. Although Porter's ideas don't ignore the characteristics of individual companies, the emphasis is clearly on understanding what is happening at the industry level. Some strategic management researchers began proposing that a complete understanding of sources of competitive advantage requires looking at the role a firm's resources played as well.

Resource-Based View

The **resource-based view (RBV)** takes the approach that a firm's resources are more important than industry structure in getting and keeping competitive advantage. It sees organizations as very different collections of assets and capabilities. No two organizations will be alike because they've not had the same set of experiences, acquired the same assets or capabilities, or built the same organizational cultures. The organization's assets and capabilities will determine how efficiently and effectively it does its work—whether that "work" involves selling hamburgers, providing health care services, or educating students. According to the RBV, certain key assets (resources) will give the firm a sustainable competitive advantage. Therefore, an organization will be positioned to succeed if it has the best and most appropriate resources for its business and strategy.

The major organizational concern according to the RBV is resources and capabilities. Although the RBV focuses on analyzing internal organizational factors, it doesn't ignore important external factors. Instead, it links an organization's internal capabilities (what it does well) with its external environment (what the market is demanding and what competitors are offering). Competitive advantage will accrue to the organization that possesses unique assets or capabilities. Organizational profitability is determined by the type, amount, and nature of a firm's resources and capabilities. Therefore, managing strategically according to the RBV involves developing and exploiting an organization's unique resources and capabilities. But, what exactly are "resources" and what makes them "unique"?

Resources can include all of the financial, physical, human, intangible, and structural–cultural assets used by an organization to develop, manufacture, and deliver products or services to its customers.[5] Financial assets encompass the actual and potential debt and equity used by the organization as well as any retained earnings or other financial holdings. Physical assets include machines, buildings, manufacturing facilities, raw materials, or any other tangible materials the organization has. Human resources include the experiences, characteristics, knowledge, judgment, wisdom, skills, abilities, and competencies of the organization's employees. Intangible assets include such things as brand names, patents, reputation, trademarks, copyrights, registered designs, and databases. Finally, structural–cultural assets include the history, culture, work systems, organizational policies, working relationships, level of trust, and the formal reporting (organizational) structure being used. All of these have some influence on the way organizational employees work.

Although every organization has resources, not all of these resources are going to be unique and capable of leading to a sustainable competitive advantage. In order to be unique, the RBV suggests that resources must be difficult to create, buy, substitute, or imitate. The issue of imitability is central to the arguments of the RBV. If competitors can copy (imitate) each other, then a sustainable competitive advantage can't be developed and above-average profits can't be earned. Figure 2-2 illustrates what it takes for organizational resources to be unique and thus a source of potential competitive advantage. Because these characteristics are important, let's look at them more closely to understand the resource-based view clearly.

Value. An organizational resource is unique if it adds value. What does it mean to "add value"? It means that the resource can be used to exploit external circumstances that are likely to bring in organizational revenues, or the resource can be used to neutralize negative external situations that are likely to keep rev-

---

Strategic Management in Action

At California Pizza Kitchen (CPK) (**www.cpk.com**), a market-leading premium pizza chain, ROCK describes the company's culture. It sets CPK apart and represents four principles that employees live by each and every day. It provides the foundation for the company's winning philosophy. What is ROCK? *R* stands for respect. *O* stands for opportunity. *C* stands for communication. And, *K* stands for kindness. Go to the company's Web site. List other resources (in the correct categories, of course!) that CPK has.

Sources: Company's Web site (**www.cpk.com**), February 23, 2000; A. Linsmayer, "Smothered by Money," *Forbes,* November 30, 1998, pp. 138–40; and K. Morris, "How to Have Your Pie and Eat It, Too," *Business Week,* November 16, 1998, pp. 100–104.

Figure 2-2

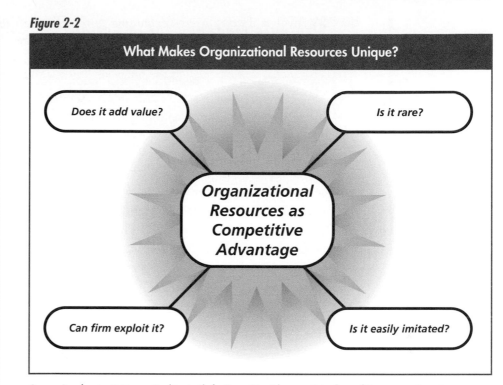

Source: Based on Jay B. Barney, "Looking Inside for Competitive Advantage," *Academy of Management Executive,* November 1995, pp. 49–61.

enue from flowing in. An organization's resources aren't valuable in a vacuum, but only when they exploit those external opportunities or neutralize the threats. As environmental factors such as customer tastes or technology change, resources can become more valuable or less valuable. So, a resource is valuable—that is, it adds value—in the context of what's happening in the external environment.

    Rare. In order for a resource to be rare, ideally no other competing firms should already possess it. If more and more competitors acquire certain resources or capabilities that have been a source of competitive advantage, then it becomes a less likely source of sustainable competitive advantage for an organization. Keep in mind, though, that even commonly held resources may be valuable if for no other reason than the firm's survival in a competitive environment. But, in order to gain a competitive advantage, a resource should be both valuable *and* rare.

    Hard to Imitate. Obviously, if a resource can't be imitated by a competitor, then any revenues it's able to generate are more likely to continue flowing in. Organizations want resources that are hard to imitate. Imitation by competitors can happen in at least two ways: duplication and substitution. Duplication is when a competitor builds the same kind of resources as the firm it's imitating. Substitution is when a firm substitutes some alternative resources for the specific resources currently being used to gain competitive advantage and achieves the same results. So, in order to keep resources unique, you want them to be hard to imitate. Some resources are much harder to reproduce than others. For example, such things as company reputation, employee trust, teamwork, and organizational culture are difficult for competitors to imitate.

Strategic Management in Action ▶

W. L. Gore & Associates (**www.gore.com**) is well known for its high-quality and revolutionary outdoor wear products. The kinds of innovative efforts exhibited by Gore's associates (not employees) are made possible by a unique organizational culture that unleashes creativity and fosters teamwork. Being an associate at Gore requires a commitment to four basic principles articulated by company founder Bill Gore: fairness to each other and everyone you come in contact with; the freedom to encourage, help, and allow other associates to grow in knowledge, skill, and scope of responsibility; the ability to make your own commitments and keep them; and consulting with other associates before undertaking actions that could impact the reputation of the company by hitting it "below the waterline." Go to the company's Web site to find out additional information about it. Do you think Gore's "resources" are unique? Explain and give examples.

Sources: Company's Web site (**www.gore.com**), February 23, 2000; D. Anfuso, "Core Values Shape W. L. Gore's Innovative Culture," *Workforce,* March 1999, pp. 48–53.

Ability to Exploit. Not only must organizational resources be valuable, rare, and hard to imitate, the organization must be able to exploit them. Does the firm have in place the formal structure, systems, policies, procedures, and processes to take full advantage of the resources it has in order to develop a sustainable competitive advantage? In other words, is it organized to exploit the full competitive potential of its resources? Without these organizational mechanisms in place, it would be difficult for an organization to create and maintain a competitive advantage.

All four of these characteristics—valuable, rare, hard to imitate, and ability to exploit—are important indicators of a resource's chances of being a source of sustainable competitive advantage. The popular business press is filled with stories of companies that have unique and valuable resources they're able to exploit. But, there are also many descriptions of organizations that have been unable to get and keep a competitive edge because they have no unique resources or they haven't been able to exploit the unique resources they do have. According to the RBV, managing strategically means continually maintaining and building organizational resources—in essence, capitalizing on what can be called the "crown jewels" of the firm. However, a question facing strategic decision makers is this: Do these crown jewels (unique resources that are sources of an organization's competitive advantage) remain the same over time? According to our next view of competitive advantage, they do not.

Guerrilla View

What do you think of when you hear the term *guerrilla?* Do you envision rapid and continual sneak attacks on an enemy position by a well-trained, competent, and skilled force? That's very much the analogy behind the guerrilla view of competitive advantage. The main premise of the **guerrilla view** is that an organization's competitive advantage is temporary. Why? Because the environment is characterized by continual, radical, and often revolutionary changes. For instance, disruptions in technological know-how, market instabilities, and other types of significant and unpredictable changes can challenge strategic managers' attempts at creating a long-term sustainable competitive advantage. Under these types of chaotic situational conditions, it's difficult to develop and maintain a permanent competitive advantage. Instead, successful organizations must be more adept at rapidly and repeatedly disrupting the current situation and radically surprising competitors with strategic actions designed to keep them off balance—in other words, acting like a guerrilla unit. And, the successful organization will repeatedly form new competitive advantages based on different rules and different asset combinations than the existing strategies being used.

All Three Views Provide Clues to Understanding Competitive Advantage

We know the important role competitive advantage plays in how an organization ultimately performs, so which of these views is most appropriate for understanding competitive advantage? Each view that we've just discussed brings a unique perspective to understanding the all-important concept. The I/O view addresses the need to look at the external environment, particularly the industry and competitors, and emphasizes the importance of understanding competitive position-

---

Strategic Management in Action

What if customers said they no longer needed packages shipped "absolutely, positively overnight"? That's the position FedEx, the world's largest express transportation company (**www.fedex.com**) and a company that prided itself for being consistently on the cutting edge of product delivery, found itself in. Overnight, its market turned upside down, and the competitive advantage FedEx had developed was no longer valuable. Customers no longer desired fast, but pricey delivery service. External changes such as instantaneous e-mail delivery of information, discount carriers that provided package tracking information online, and competitive rivals that copied FedEx's elaborate information system that once distinguished the company have all contributed to its uncertain, chaotic future. The company's strategic decision makers aren't just sitting back, however. They're looking at strategic options for succeeding in the changed world.

Sources: Company's Web site (**www.fedex.com**), February 23, 2000; and D. A. Blackmon, "Speed Limits," *Wall Street Journal,* November 4, 1999, p. A1.

ing. The RBV considers the need to look inside the organization for the unique resources and capabilities that can be exploited. This approach continues to be a popular topic for strategic management researchers attempting to clarify why organizations differ in their performance. However, the new guerrilla view forces strategic decision makers to recognize that the chaotic nature of the external environment can affect what is considered a competitive advantage and how long that competitive advantage can last.

Realistically speaking, managing strategically involves looking both externally and internally to come up with strategies that have a chance of creating a sustainable competitive advantage, even if for only a brief period of time. In this way, distinctive organizational resources and capabilities can be "matched" to changing external circumstances. Because the external environment is continually changing (i.e., new competitors come and go, customers' tastes change, technology changes, current competitors start a price war, etc.), the source of sustainable competitive advantage—the "edge" an organization has over its competitors—*is* probably found in different places at different points in time. Given these realities, how can strategic managers possibly ever hope to develop a sustainable competitive advantage—that is, manage strategically? The answer is by continually analyzing both the external and internal organizational environments. Taking advantage of any positive changes (or buffering against negative changes) with the organization's unique resources and capabilities is what it all boils down to. That's the ever-changing, yet constant, challenge for the strategic manager.

One of the most important changes strategic managers must contend with is the realities of the new business environment. That's what we'll look at next.

Consider This ◀◀|

✓ What is competitive advantage? Why is it important?

✓ Describe the important points of the industrial organization (I/O) view.

✓ Describe the important points of the resource-based view (RBV).

✓ What makes a resource unique?

✓ Describe the important points of the guerrilla view.

✓ Why are all three views important to understanding competitive advantage?

✓ How would proponents of the I/O view analyze the chapter-opening case? How about proponents of the RBV? How about proponents of the guerrilla view?

THE REALITIES OF THE NEW BUSINESS ENVIRONMENT

The business arena that organizations operate in today is a lot different than what it used to be. It's an important topic to discuss in the context of managing strategically because it establishes the "rules of the game" for doing business. Even not-for-profit organizations feel the impact of these changing realities because they, too, need resources such as labor, technology, and funding to operate. Poised here in the early years of a new century, we need to examine some important characteristics of this business environment: What forces are "driving" it? What are the implications? And, what will it take to be successful in this context? Figure 2-3 provides an overview.

Drivers of the New Business Environment

What are the driving forces of the twenty-first-century business environment? Three major ones seem to be the most critical: (1) the information revolution,

Figure 2-3

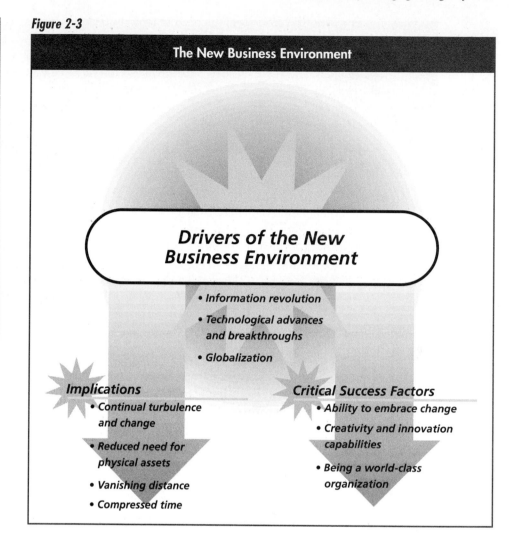

The New Business Environment

Drivers of the New Business Environment

- *Information revolution*
- *Technological advances and breakthroughs*
- *Globalization*

Implications
- *Continual turbulence and change*
- *Reduced need for physical assets*
- *Vanishing distance*
- *Compressed time*

Critical Success Factors
- *Ability to embrace change*
- *Creativity and innovation capabilities*
- *Being a world-class organization*

(2) technological advances and breakthroughs, and (3) globalization. Let's discuss each more thoroughly.[6]

The Information Revolution. If there's one driving force that has set the tone for this new business environment, it's the information revolution. *And* not only is this revolution continuing to spread, it's also accelerating. Information is now readily available to practically anyone from anywhere on the globe at any hour of the day and pretty much in any format. An investor in Los Angeles at 3 A.M. can check currency exchange rates for the yen, click on another software program, and e-mail instructions to a broker in London. A shopper in Shanghai with a fondness for maple syrup can indulge that passion by purchasing products from a small retail store in Vermont without ever physically stepping foot in the United States. How? By linking to its virtual storefront on the Web. The almost instant availability of almost any type of information has radically changed the nature of the business environment. And, in turn it affects the context of strategic management.

Although information has always been a factor in producing goods and services, previously it had been applied only to the design and use of work tools,

An EconomyTurned Upside Down?

One of the fundamental concepts you should remember from economics is the supply and demand relationship. However, that relationship is undergoing radical changes thanks to the Internet. Already we can see changes in the way people shop. This not only affects the demand for products—just a note: the number-one complaint of holiday shoppers during the 1999 holiday season was product was out of stock, a supply–demand problem—but also affects the supply side. The transactions taking place in supply chains are not only becoming more efficient, they're changing shape. The traditional "vertical" supply chain from manufacturer to wholesaler to retailer is giving way to more "horizontal" supply chains as the Internet provides buyers with better access to a wider choice of suppliers. This shift is forcing businesses to rethink every aspect of their business models—from pricing strategies to delivery choices to inventory management systems.

Sources: "Top 10 Things That Irked Holiday Shoppers," *Business Week E-Biz,* February 7, 2000, p. EB12; and M. Casey, "Internet Changes the Face of Supply and Demand," *Wall Street Journal,* October 18, 1999, p. A43K.

organizational processes, management systems, and products. A look back at history illustrates that from the early days of the industrial revolution (in the 1700s) up through what has often been described as the "productivity" revolution (in the early 1900s), information had been primarily used to achieve organizational efficiency and effectiveness. However, today we're seeing information as *the* essential resource of production, not simply as a means to an end. We're seeing a fundamental shift toward the application of knowledge to knowledge itself.[7] Whereas economists and businesspeople traditionally thought of land, labor, and capital as the main factors of production, their role in a knowledge economy is better understood as constraints. Without them, even knowledge couldn't be productive. But, in this new information business environment in which knowledge is applied to knowledge, decision makers can always use their knowledge to obtain the other necessary resources. The implication of such a profound change is that organizations can no longer simply rely on the traditional factors of production to provide a sustainable competitive advantage. They must now look to how information and knowledge can be exploited. This fundamental change highlights an important aspect of competing successfully in the new world economy. (Please note that in the last section of this chapter, we'll explore the concept of world-class organizations more thoroughly.) One of the areas in which knowledge and information have had a significant impact is in technology and innovation. That's the next driving force we'll discuss.

Technological Advances and Breakthroughs. All organizations—regardless of size, type, or location—use some form of technology to do their work. What is **technology**? It's the use of equipment, materials, knowledge, and experience to perform tasks. Some industries are, by necessity, more technology intensive (i.e., think of electronics, telecommunications, software, pharmaceuticals, etc.), but even organizations such as the American Red Cross, your neighborhood grocery store, utility companies, and steel mills use technology. Technology significantly changed the nature of competition in the last part of the twentieth century.

Approaches and tools that may have been effective in the past weren't anymore, and new ones were rapidly being developed. For example, innovations in telecommunications and computer technology had far-reaching effects for strategic managers in all types of organizations.

There's no doubt technology is changing the way we work and the type of work we do.[8] What are some of the major broad technological trends that might affect the context of managing strategically? The four we need to look at are summarized in Table 2-2.[9]

First is the increasing rate of technological change and diffusion. This means that not only are technological advances happening more frequently, they're also being more rapidly adopted by organizations. This trend is significant because it means that strategic managers must keep up with changes by speeding up the product development process. In fact, "time" has been highlighted as a critical resource by many organizations.[10]

The rapid rate of technological change has had an impact on the competitive protection offered by patents, which brings us to the second major technological trend: the increasing commercialization of innovations. **Innovation** is the process of taking a creative idea and turning it into a product or process that can be used or sold. It's more than just being creative—it's developing, making, and marketing something that can generate revenue. Some experts have cited growing evidence that the U.S. economy is in the early stages of a powerful new wave of innovation.[11] Although the use of patents traditionally provided many organizations with protection for technological discoveries that were the basis for profitable products or services, this advantage is declining in significance because technological improvements can rapidly replace the technology that's currently protected by the patent and being used to create value.

Another significant trend in technology was covered earlier—the increasing dependence on knowledge intensity. Because technology—both the creation and use of it—involves knowledge, the importance of knowledge as a resource for sustainable competitive advantage has increased significantly. The implication of this relationship is that as the use of technology increases, so does the need for knowledge. The reverse is true as well—as knowledge increases, so does the use of technology. For instance, even employees on an assembly line now must have more than manual dexterity skills and physical stamina. They need knowledge to run the sophisticated machinery found in today's manufacturing environment.

TABLE 2-2   Major Technological Trends
• Increasing rate of technological change and diffusion   • Increasing commercialization of innovations   • Increasing dependence on knowledge intensity   • Advent of increasing returns

Source: Based on Richard A. Bettis and Michael A. Hitt, "The New Competitive Landscape," *Strategic Management Journal,* summer 1995, pp. 7–19.

Strategic Management in Action

"We Bring Good Things to Life." That's the well-known corporate slogan of General Electric Company (GE). And, the company, consistently on lists of "best-managed" and "America's most admired," *does* bring good things to life. However, the company delayed taking advantage of the Internet in its business operations, almost missing the Internet revolution. But, not for long! CEO Jack Welch, calling the Internet, "the greatest change in business in his lifetime," told his executives that every GE business had better establish a Web site by the end of 1999. In addition, to make its employees more Web savvy, GE is posting its internal newsletters and other memos from Mr. Welch only online. And, e-commerce performance is being considered as part of managers' compensation. Go to GE's Web site (**www.ge.com**) and check out the e-business initiatives described there. What types of strategies is the company pursuing?

Sources: Company's Web site (**www.ge.com**), February 23, 2000; and M. Murray, "Late to the Web, GE Now Views Internet as Key to New Growth," *Wall Street Journal,* June 22, 1999, p. B1.

The last significant technological trend is the recognition that technology makes increasing returns possible. Why is this significant? Economists have long operated under the notion of diminishing returns—that is, the more you make or sell, the harder it is to keep doing so. On the other hand, increasing returns is the tendency for whatever's ahead to get further ahead. For instance, if an organization employs a technology that gives it a small lead, receives positive feedback, and locks customers into that technology, then that company has a significant competitive advantage. Probably one of the best-known examples of the potential impact of increasing returns is Microsoft Corporation. Microsoft leveraged its 60 million user customer base in DOS into Windows, then Windows 95, then Windows 98, and now into Windows 2000. The customers are "bound" to that technology and the company's "lock" on the marketplace allows it to stay ahead and get further ahead because it's the accepted standard.

The increasing pace of technological breakthroughs and the importance of continual innovation are quite evident. Within the context of managing strategically, technology and innovation are obviously going to influence an organization's sustainable competitive advantage. The challenge is capturing and exploiting the unique advantages of technology by using the organizational innovation process to create valuable products and processes. What makes these activities even more challenging is that technology advances and innovation are occurring globally, not just in the domestic arena. The challenges and opportunities of globalization are the third driving force we're going to look at next.

Globalization. The third driving force of the new business environment is **globalization**, the international linkage of economies and cultures that fosters a business and competitive situation in which organizations have no national boundaries. We've been hearing about the concept of globalization for so long now (you, undoubtedly, hear about it in every business class you take) that it almost seems a cliché. However, it *is* important and continues to be a dominant characteristic of the business environment.[12] More than ever, organizations are witnessing the globalization of the business and competitive landscape and are taking part in it. The days when all our consumer products—for instance, the shoes we wore, the cars we drove, and the food we ate—were produced in the United States are long gone. Now, it's common for the products we purchase and consume to be provided by a foreign company or by a domestic company that also does business globally. Even small businesses are impacted by the global business environment. How does the context of globalization influence managing strategically? Two specific ways are (1) in the global marketplace and (2) through global competitors.

It's not an understatement to say that the whole world is a potential marketplace. Providing products to meet consumer needs and wants has taken on a global perspective. Potential markets are found all the way from small villages in China to Johannesburg to Moscow to Mexico City, and all points in between. This global marketplace provides significant opportunities for organizations to market their goods and services. Creating sustainable competitive advantage may require looking globally, not just domestically, for customers. But, the global marketplace shouldn't be viewed as only an outlet for products; it's also a critical source of resources as well. Financial, material, human, and knowledge resources are available globally and should be acquired wherever it strategically makes sense to do so. In other words, geographic boundaries shouldn't constrain an organization's strategic decisions and actions. However, not only does this mean domestic organizations can operate anywhere in the world, it also means foreign organizations—that is, competitors—can, too.

As global markets open, global competition becomes a reality. Competitors

STRATEGIC MANAGEMENT IN AN E-BUSINESS WORLD

From idea generation to customer service, companies are using technology to boost productivity at every stage in the business process. Let's look at some examples. At the innovation stage, Royal Dutch/Shell's "GameChanger" teams are using the Internet to generate new business ideas. In the product design stage, Honeywell uses the Internet to help fashion a customized prototype of products from a fan blade to a golf club head. Ford Motor Company redesigned its purchasing function so its 30,000 suppliers can use its AutoXchange online trading bazaar. In its logistics function, cement maker Cemex uses Internet-based truck dispatch systems to speed deliveries to customers. And, to better serve its customers, GE Power Systems lets customers use the Internet to compare the performance of their turbine engines against other GE turbine engines in the market. These are just a few examples of the way that e-business is affecting the way that companies do business. Organizational strategies will continue to change as companies redesign their strategies around e-business applications.

Source: J. Reingold, M. Stepanek, and D. Brady, "Why the Productivity Revolution Will Spread," *Business Week,* February 14, 2000, p. 116.

can come from anywhere and they, too, will be looking for a sustainable competitive advantage. Although the rewards of a global market are attractive, the bar also has been pushed a little higher. Competing in a global marketplace is more challenging because now, all of a sudden, you're dealing with competitors who've had their own unique set of experiences and resources, making it much more difficult to understand their strategic approach and intent. However, global competitors don't always have to be a negative threat to each other. They might find that their most effective strategy to achieve a sustainable competitive advantage is to partner together in some type of an arrangement to make or market products. In fact, in Chapter 7 where we discuss corporate strategy, we'll look at global strategic alliances and how organizations are using these.

Globalization is more than just producing, marketing, and distributing goods and services throughout the world. "It is a new way of thinking."[13] It's solving customers' needs no matter where the customers are. It's segmenting markets on a global basis and sourcing people, capital, technologies, and ideas from anywhere in the world. Globalization has transformed and continues to transform the new business environment.

Each of these driving forces of the new business environment—the information revolution, technological advances, and globalization—is affecting the context within which strategic decision makers manage strategically. What are the implications of these forces for strategic decision makers?

Implications of These Driving Forces

Look back at Figure 2-3 (p. 43), and you'll see that there are four major implications arising out of the driving forces of the new business environment. These include continual turbulence and change, the reduced need for physical assets, vanishing distance, and compressed time. Let's examine each of these more closely.

1. *Continual turbulence and change.* Change, and for many organizations, turbulent and chaotic change, is an undeniable reality of today's business environment. *All* organizations must deal with change, if not on a daily basis,

Global Success

A survey of executives identified five issues they believe to be the most critical to becoming a high-performance global organization. These five issues and the percentage of CEOs who said these were the most critical are as follows:

- Programs and processes that reward innovation and risk taking 60%
- Leadership talent 57%
- Knowledge sharing 57%
- Translating the global vision into strategy and tactics 48%
- Communicating the global vision 41%

Take each of these issues and explain what you think it means. Do you agree that these are the most critical global issues facing strategic decision makers? Explain your answer.

Source: M. A. Verespej, "Global Quandary," *Industry Week,* November 15, 1999, pp. 9–10.

then on an increasingly frequent basis. **Change** is any alteration in external environmental factors or internal organizational arrangements. Often, changes in external conditions or even in internal ones stimulate the need for organizational change. **Organizational change** is any alteration in what an organization does and how it does it. For instance, changes in technology (an external factor) have opened up new avenues for organizations that have created Web sites where electronic greeting cards can be purchased and sent electronically. Because of this change, the large corporate greeting-card companies have been forced to rethink how they do business and to make organizational changes. Or, take, for instance, changing demographic trends (another external factor). The baby boomlet (resulting from the large group of baby boomers who have had and are having children), the increasing Hispanic population, and other demographic changes have forced organizations to alter the types of products they offer, the packaging of these products, and the promotional techniques they use to sell these products. Strategic decision makers are looking for rules to follow and yet are looking for ways to break the rules in order to prosper in this new business environment where change is the norm, not the exception. Turbulence and change are realities in the new business environment.

2. *Reduced need for physical assets.* The business environment confronting business organizations even just a few years ago was one in which having a large number of physical assets (manufacturing facilities, office buildings, equipment, inventory, etc.) was critical for financial success. The more physical assets you had, the more economically powerful you were. However, that's not the case in today's economy. Success in today's economy isn't reliant simply on physical assets. Instead, value can be found in intangible factors such as information, people, ideas, and knowledge. Companies such as General Electric (GE), eBay, American Airlines, Amazon.com, and even Toyota are finding that they can achieve a sustainable competitive advantage with non-physical assets such as customer database information, online ordering systems, continual product and process innovation, and employee knowledge sharing.

3. *Vanishing distance.* The influence of physical distance on an organization's strategic decisions and actions has all but disappeared! Whereas geography traditionally played an important role in determining customers and competitors, that's no longer the reality. An organization's potential market can be found anywhere. The limitations once imposed because of physical distance have vanished. The world is your customer, but this also means that the world is your competitor. The opportunities—and challenges—for strategic decision makers have never been greater.

4. *Compressed time.* As the limitations of physical space have disappeared, so, too, have the limitations of time. Where it used to take Pony Express riders weeks to deliver information via the mail, we now have the U.S. Postal Service delivering mail in two to three days, and even overnight. But, as you already know, the time frame is even more compressed than that now. Electronic mail and interactive Web sites give us almost instantaneous delivery of information. This instant interactivity (between customer and business, between employees, between companies and suppliers, or between

STRATEGIC MANAGEMENT IN AN E-BUSINESS WORLD

Choiceboard. You probably haven't heard this term before, but it's associated with e-business strategies. It refers to a strategy in which companies provide customers with interactive, online systems that allow customers to design their own products by choosing from a menu of attributes, components, prices, and delivery options. Instead of being a passive recipient of a product that the company has designed, the customer becomes an active designer by making choices. Many companies already use choiceboards. For example, Dell's online configurator allows customers to design their computers. Customers can create their own dolls with Mattel's My Design Barbie. Investors can assemble their own investment portfolios with Schwab's mutual fund evaluator. And, customers can even design their own golf clubs with Chipshot.com's PerfectFit system. The use of choiceboards will undoubtedly continue to spread as customers demand more input into the products they want. See if you can find other examples of choiceboards in use.

Source: A. J. Slywotzky, "The Age of the Choiceboard," *Harvard Business Review,* January–February 2000, pp. 40–41.

friends and family) has created a context within which there are, to use a sports analogy, no time-outs and no substitutions! If an organization doesn't stay on top of changes, its marketplace advantage will be temporary, at best. Although it isn't easy to stay on top of changes, it's important. For example, take Dell Computer. It's been able to hold on to its marketplace advantage by understanding the benefits and challenges of compressed time. Michael Dell, founder and CEO of Dell Computer, has built a successful organization on the basis of staying on top of changes through instantaneous interactivity. The company builds computers directly from buyers' requests. Then, using its lightning-fast inventory and purchasing cycles, Dell builds and ships out computers almost as soon as the customer's order is received. Also, Dell uses information from customers' orders to adapt to emerging trends way ahead of the curve. Dell is a good example of an organization that understands the external context and what it takes to be successful in this new business environment. What *does* it take to be successful given the realities of the new business environment?

Consider This ◀◀|

✓ Describe the three major driving forces of the new business environment.

✓ How is the information revolution affecting the context of managing strategically?

✓ What is technology?

✓ What technological trends are affecting the context of managing strategically?

✓ What is innovation?

✓ Define globalization.

✓ How do global factors impact the context of managing strategically?

✓ Describe the four major implications of the driving forces of the new business environment.

✓ Define change. Define organizational change.

Critical Success Factors

Three critical factors for succeeding in this new business environment are shown in Figure 2-3 (p. 43): ability to embrace change, creativity and innovation capabilities, and being a world-class organization. Let's look at why each of these success factors is critical.

1. *Ability to embrace change.* If there's one word that captures the essence of this new business environment, it's *change.* Do you like change? Probably not. Few people enjoy or even seek out change. Most of us think change is annoying, scary, or both. We like order and structure, not chaos. But change is a given in this new business environment. Being successful in this kind of turbulent environment means not only being tolerant of change but also seeking it out and embracing it with open arms. Change can bring not only opportunities to exploit but also challenges in dealing successfully with the changes. In any type of organizational change efforts, the caliber of organizational strategic leadership can spell the difference between success and failure.

   Strategic decision makers play an important role as change agents. Effective change doesn't happen by itself. There's got to be someone (or groups of "someones") to initiate and oversee the process. **Change agents** are individuals or groups who strategically manage the formulation, implementation, and evaluation of organizational change efforts. Whether it's major or minor changes in organizational strategy, change "drivers" are needed. Strategic decision makers can play this important role. Ideally, an organization's top-level strategic decision makers provide a sense of long-term direction and offer support and rationale for needed changes.[14] But, strategic leaders at any level of the organization play an important role in managing the change process.

Strategic Management—The Global Perspective

Heading up the world's largest food company (Nestlé SA), CEO Peter Brabeck has had to act as a change agent. Since taking over in 1997, Brabeck has nudged the giant, slow-moving Swiss company (more than 8,000 brands, over 2,000,000 employees, and revenues approaching $50 billion in U.S. dollars) toward some revolutionary changes. For example, when the company introduced Pure Life, a global water brand for developing countries, it was the biggest rollout of a global brand from scratch—a first for the company. And, the company's marketing and advertising campaigns for Nescafé instant coffee, one of its most famous megabrands, has been unified globally. The new ads target a younger market and are focused on repositioning Nescafé as a trendy coffee beverage. Another change Brabeck is spearheading involves providing more information and establishing relationships with Wall Street investors and analysts. This is a major shift from Nestle's former standoffish approach. In a company that many consider too big, Brabeck's willingness to "shake things up" is welcomed. Says Brabeck, "We are more dynamic than many recognize us to be, and we will be more dynamic and aggressive in the future. We have to be, because in today's environment, the faster ones kill the slower ones." Check out the company's Web site (**www.nestle.com**). Do you think Nestlé is succeeding at being dynamic and aggressive? Explain your answer.

Sources: E. Beck, "Switzerland's Nestlé Is Expected to Report Strong Sales and Profits," *Wall Street Journal,* February 25, 2000, p. A17; "Nestlé Agrees to Buy Maker of Nutrition Bars," *Wall Street Journal,* February 24, 2000, p. A8; Company's Web site (**www.nestle.com**), February 23, 2000; and E. Beck, "Nestlé CEO Pushes Company to Change," *Wall Street Journal,* June 24, 1999, p. A18.

Any type of change is difficult for all involved. (Think about how you react when you find a substitute professor in class one day, or if your professor changes the course assignment schedule to accommodate a change in plans. Most of us respond by being anxious, maybe even angry.) Although strong strategic leadership throughout all organizational levels and areas can't eliminate all the challenges associated with change, it can smooth the process and facilitate successful implementation of the change. Considering the numerous dynamic forces facing today's organizations, strong strategic leadership can play a significant role in providing an appropriate and supportive organizational environment in which employees are encouraged to take responsibility for problems and take action to solve them.[15]

2.   *Creativity and innovation capabilities.* Here's an abbreviated statement of just how critical this factor is: "Create and innovate or lose!" It's that simple. In this dynamic, chaotic world we've described where technological change, information revolution, and globalization are the order of the day, strategic decision makers must be prepared to create new products and services and adopt state-of-the-art technology if their organizations are to compete suc-

FYI

The DNA of Corporate Innovation

The members of the Innovation Network Inc. (**www.thinksmart.com**) put their heads together and developed the Innovation DNA Model. This model identifies the following nine dimensions that need to be in place for organizational innovation to occur:

1.   *Change, ideas, passion, and trends.* These provide the stimuli needed to move away from the status quo.

2.   *Challenge.* The bigger the challenge and the passion behind it, the more energy innovation efforts will need.

3.   *Customer focus.* All innovation should be focused on creating value for customers, external or internal, and it requires understanding their needs.

4.   *Creativity.* Everything starts from an idea and the best way to get ideas is to generate a lot of possibilities.

5.   *Communication.* Open communication of ideas, information, and feelings is the lifeblood of innovation.

6.   *Collaboration.* Innovation is a group process.

7.   *Completion.* Innovations require "doing" — that is, decision making, delegating, scheduling, monitoring, and feedback skills; and completed projects should be celebrated.

8.   *Contemplation.* Learning from completed projects builds a knowledge base that creates an upward cycle of success.

9.   *Culture.* Organizational cultural factors create the playing field for all the other concepts.

Research a company (GE, Ford Motor, Microsoft, or pick your own) and assess it on these nine dimensions. Be sure to document your sources, and be prepared to share your findings in class.

Sources: Innovation Network Inc. Web site (**www.thinksmart.com**), February 28, 2000; and S. Caudron, "The Economics of Innovation," *Business Finance,* November 1999, pp. 23–27.

cessfully and survive. **Creativity**, the ability to combine ideas in a unique way or to make unusual associations between ideas, is an important capability.[16] A creative person or organization develops novel approaches to doing work or unique solutions to problems. But, it doesn't stop there. We know from our earlier chapter discussion that innovation is the process of taking a creative idea and then turning it into a product or process that can be used to generate revenue. An innovative organization is characterized by its ability to channel creativity into useful outcomes. Both capabilities, being creative and being innovative, are critical to strategic success in this new business environment.

3. *Being a world-class organization.* Given the importance of creating a sustainable competitive advantage in light of the realities of the new business environment, you'd probably agree that ensuring an organization's long-run survival and success isn't an easy task. Even not-for-profit organizations face the challenge of managing strategically in such a context. What can strategic decision makers do to surmount this seemingly overwhelming challenge? One strategic management concept that has considerable potential for helping organizational decision makers meet the challenge is that of the world-class organization.[17] What is a **world-class organization**? It's one that continually acquires and utilizes knowledge in its strategic decisions and actions in order to be the best in the world at what it does. Recall our earlier discussion of the realities of the new business environment with respect to information and knowledge and increasing globalization, and you can begin to appreciate why being a world-class organization is an important goal. Even if an organization operates in a single geographic location, it should still strive to be the best at what it does in its own little "world" or competitive arena. What characteristics does a world-class organization have? The major ones are shown in Figure 2-4. These characteristics are important to becoming a world-class organization. However, the decision to be a world-class organization starts with developing an organizational vision and mission.

Organizational Vision and Mission. Yes, it's equally important for an organization to have both an organizational vision *and* mission. Although some people view the two as one and the same concept, we're going to look at them as different. **Organizational vision** is a broad comprehensive picture of what a leader wants an organization to become. It's a statement of what the organization stands for, what it believes in, and why it exists. The vision provides a vibrant and compelling picture of the future. It presents a view beyond what the organization "is" to what the organization "could be."[18] You may think that the concept of a vision is something off-the-wall, hard to grasp or describe, and very peculiar—something that sounds good on paper, but does nothing to improve the organization's performance. Yet, if organizational leaders can articulate a distinct vision, organizational members may be more motivated to contribute increased levels of effort.[19] For instance, at Microsoft Inc. the vision "A computer on every desk and in every home," which had guided organizational decisions and actions throughout the company's history of explosive growth, was changed to "Empower people through great software anytime, any place, and on any device." The company's strategists broadened the vision statement because of continuing changes in the business environment. Also, look again at the chapter-opening case for a descrip-

Figure 2-4

Major Characteristics of World-Class Organizations

Strong Customer Focus

Significant Technological Support

Continual Learning and Improvement

World-Class Organization

Egalitarian Climate

Flexible Organization Structure

Creative Human Resource Management

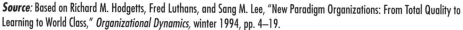

Source: Based on Richard M. Hodgetts, Fred Luthans, and Sang M. Lee, "New Paradigm Organizations: From Total Quality to Learning to World Class," *Organizational Dynamics*, winter 1994, pp. 4–19.

tion of the vision at Martha Stewart Omnimedia and how this affected strategic decisions.

What should organizational vision include? Four components have been identified as important to organizational vision.[20] First is that the vision be built on a foundation of the organization's core values and beliefs. These values and beliefs address what's fundamentally important to the organization, whether it's conducting business ethically and responsibly, satisfying the customer, emphasizing quality in all aspects, or being a leader in technology. And, the vision should stress whatever those core values might be. Just how important are values to doing business? One study found that six out of ten large U.S. corporations have developed a specific statement of values.[21] Although a statement of values doesn't guarantee success, it can provide employees with a sense of work and behavioral expectations. For example, if employees know that outstanding customer service is valued by the organization, then they can make decisions and act in ways that champion customer service.

Second, the vision should elaborate a purpose for the organization. An organization must have a purpose for even existing. Every organization—profit or not-for-profit, large or small, local or global—has a purpose, and that purpose is specified in the organization's vision. That way, all organizational stakeholders are explicitly aware of why this organization exists.

> ### Strategic Management in Action
>
> Although many old-line manufacturers dream of transforming themselves into nimble technology companies, Corning Inc. (**www.corning.com**) has actually pulled off that difficult transformation. Maybe you (or older family members or friends) still have Corning casserole dishes in your kitchen. The Corning that manufactured those dishes and other glassware still works mostly in glass, but in forms that most people would not recognize. The company has shifted its focus to products such as optical fiber and liquid crystal display screens. In fact, the company's statement of "Who We Are" is "Corning Incorporated creates leading-edge technologies for the fastest-growing markets of the world's economy." This "new" Corning is poised to profit from a high-tech world.
>
> *Sources:* Company's Web site (**www.corning.com**), February 23, 2000; and T. Aeppel, "Corning's Makeover: From Casseroles to Fiber Optics," *Wall Street Journal,* July 16, 1999, p. B4.

The third component of organizational vision is that it should include a brief summary of what the organization does. Although the vision should not provide explicit details of what the organization does (this is done in the various mission statements, discussed shortly), it should explain what it's doing to fulfill its purpose. And, this is a good time to say that while they're related, there *is* a difference between an organization's purpose and what it does. For example, several organizations may have the purpose of ecological preservation, but the way they go about carrying out that purpose (i.e., what they do) may be different.

The last component of organizational vision is that it should specify broad goals. Goals provide a target that all organizational members work toward meeting. Goals also serve to unify organizational members toward a common end. An organization's vision can and should be a guiding force in every decision.

Although organizational vision provides an overall picture of where the entire organization would like to be in the future, a **mission** is a statement of what the various organizational units do and what they hope to accomplish in alignment with the organizational vision. An organization will have only one vision and potentially several missions (divisional, departmental, project work group, or any number of others) that contribute to the pursuit of the organizational vision. A unit's mission statement provides a focus for unit employees as they make strategic decisions and implement them. Although it's not as comprehensive and broad as the organizational vision, a unit's mission statement still provides an overview of the unit's purpose, what it does, and its goals. Each unit's mission statement also aligns with the organizational vision. Ideally what you have is a broad framework within which organizational members know what they're doing and why they're doing it. This shared vision provides direction for managing strategically and determining whether progress is being made. The vision also should reflect the organization's commitment to social responsibility and ethical decision making.

The Grey Zone   Are vision and mission statements just a bunch of words? A study of several securities firms and investment banks showed that many hours had been spent crafting elegant mission statements that extolled the virtues of teamwork, integrity, and respect for the individual. Yet, the partners at those firms treated their young analysts like second-class citizens. They gave them work that wasn't commensurate with their skills, were openly impolite to them, and in many instances, were verbally abusive toward them. When these conditions were described to the top decision makers, they said that kind of behavior couldn't be happening—it went against their companies' mission statements. Yet, this type of situation doesn't occur only in securities firms. Could this situation have been prevented? If so, how? If not, why not? How can strategic decision makers make sure that vision and mission statements are more than empty words?

Corporate Social Responsibility and Ethics. How much and what type of social responsibility business organizations should pursue has been a topic of heated debate for a number of years. **Corporate social responsibility (CSR)** is the obligation of organizational decision makers to make decisions and act in ways that recognize the interrelatedness of business and society.[22] CSR recognizes the existence of various stakeholders and how organizations deal with them. But, it's in the definition of "who" organizations are responsible to that we find a diversity of opinions.

According to the traditional view, corporations existed solely to serve the interests of one stakeholder group—the stockholders.[23] Milton Friedman has been the biggest advocate of this view. He argued that corporate social programs and actions must be paid for in some way and add to the costs of doing business. Those costs have to be either passed on to customers in the form of higher prices or absorbed internally. In either case, profit margins might suffer because customers might buy less at higher prices or

The Greening of Strategic Management

FYI

A number of highly visible ecological problems and environmental disasters has brought about a new awareness and spirit of environmentalism among strategic decision makers. Increasingly, strategic decision makers have begun to confront questions about the natural environment and its impact on organizations. This recognition of the close link between an organization's decisions and actions and its impact on the natural environment is referred to as the **greening of management.** As organizations become "greener," we find more and more of them issuing detailed reports on their environmental performance. The Global Reporting Initiative (**www.globalreporting.org**), sponsored by the Coalition for Environmentally Responsible

Economies (CERES), has published structured but flexible guidelines for a green reporting process for organizations that wish to participate. Bristol-Myers Squibb (**www.bms.com/ehs**), the global health and personal care products company, and Royal Dutch/Shell (**www.shell.com**) both take environmental reporting seriously. Check out all these Web sites. What guidelines does the Global Reporting Initiative provide? What do the environmental reports of Bristol-Myers Squibb and Royal Dutch/Shell look like? Can you find other examples of green reports?

Sources: Information from Web sites (**www.globalreporting.org**), (**www.bms.com**), (**www.shell.com**), February 28, 2000; and A. Kolk, "Green Reporting," *Harvard Business Review*, January–February 2000, pp. 15–16.

organizational costs would increase. But, you do need to understand that Friedman didn't say that organizations shouldn't be socially responsible. In fact, he felt they *should* be. But, his argument was that the extent of the responsibility was to maximize shareholder returns.

However, the traditional—and purely economic—perspective of corporate social responsibility has given way to a belief that organizations have a larger societal role to play and a broader constituency to serve than just stockholders alone. Yet, balancing various stakeholder demands is a complicated process because stakeholders often have a wide range of needs and conflicting expectations.[24] What this means for managing strategically as a world-class organization is recognizing the commitment to make decisions and to implement those decisions in ways that will enhance the various stakeholder relationships. **Stakeholders** are individuals or groups who have a stake in or are significantly influenced by an organization's decisions and actions and who, in turn, can influence the organization. What types of stakeholders might an organization have to deal with? Figure 2-5 identifies some of the most common. Many organizations believe strong and socially responsible stakeholder relationships make them more competitive. For example, the New York–based Council on Economic Priorities, (**www.cepnyc.org**) annually singles out companies for being role models of social responsibility. Its 1999 Corporate

Figure 2-5

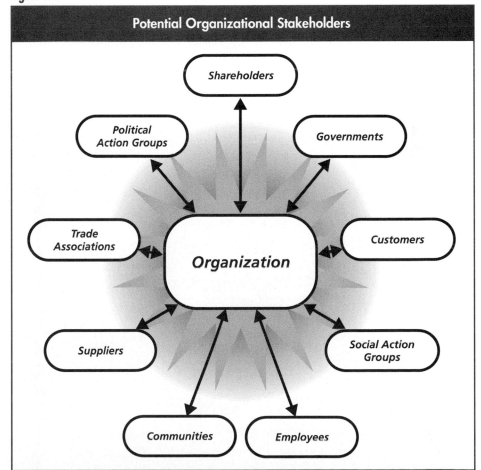

Conscience Award winners included the following: for global ethics, Pfizer Inc. and SmithKline Beecham, PLC; for environmental stewardship, Ecover Products and Lyons Falls Pulp & Paper Company; for employee empowerment, Grupo M and IBM; and for community partnership, FNMA—Fannie Mae.[25] Many other companies understand the importance of strong stakeholder relationships. Although corporate social responsibility emphasizes the broad picture of an organization's societal interactions, it's also important that these interactions take place in a context of "doing the right thing." That's where the concept of ethics comes in.

By this time in your life, you've undoubtedly faced numerous ethical dilemmas, both in academics and, if you're employed, at your job. (In fact, the Grey Zone ethical dilemmas in each chapter of this book emphasize the importance of understanding the role of ethics in strategic decision making.) For example, is it ethical to make a copy of inexpensive computer software for a friend who's short of money or to "donate" copies of completed case homework or other assignments to your sorority or fraternity? Or say that you're a telemarketing representative. Is it ethical for you to pressure customers to purchase a product just so you can win a prize? **Ethics** involves the rules and principles that define right and wrong decisions and behavior. In other words, as we live our lives—attend school, work at a job, engage in hobbies, and so forth—certain decisions and behaviors are ethically "right," and certain decisions and behaviors are ethically "wrong." Considering the varied interpretations of right and wrong, you can see what a complex topic ethics is to address. Although we will not get into an extended discussion of the origin of ethics here, be aware that ethical considerations should play a role in managing strategically. In fact, some individuals believe that ethics is both a personal and organizational issue and should be part of the strategic management process.[26]

Ethics in Real Life

An ethics code should be more than great public relations. The success or failure of corporate ethics programs has a lot less to do with such things as written ethics codes and compliance hot lines, and everything to do with why employees think the programs were established in the first place. According to a study conducted by the ethics and responsible business practices group at Arthur Andersen LLP, the tools that work best to reduce unethical conduct in companies include being consistent in policies and actions, rewarding ethical conduct, treating employees fairly, and exercising executive leadership in setting a good example. What works least well? According to this study, it was referring employees to a code of conduct and training employees in the code of conduct. The lead researcher in the study says that she hopes executives will learn three things from the study:

1. Really, genuinely, "walk the talk, practice what you preach, live out what you say."
2. Be fair. Equal treatment, equal application of policy, and equitability are the key issues.
3. Spend money where it counts, where it can affect how your organizational members are really feeling.

What do you think of these suggestions? Do you agree? Why or why not? Why are ethics codes encouraged so much when they don't seem to work? What are the implications of these ideas for managing strategically?

Source: J. S. McClenahen, "Your Employees Know Better," *Industry Week*, March 1, 1999, pp. 12–13.

Strategic Management in Action

Stakeholders *do* play a significant role in the strategies that organizations ultimately choose. For instance, when Ben & Jerry's Homemade, a company well-known for its socially responsible approach to doing business, decided to seek a buyer, a group of owners of Ben & Jerry's ice cream shops rallied to make the point that they didn't want a corporate takeover that would pose a threat to the company's image. Another example of the role that stakeholders play in organizational strategies is Procter & Gamble, which after years of protests from animal rights groups, decided to stop animal testing for a broad range of products including cosmetics, shampoos, detergents, cleansers, and paper goods. McDonald's Corporation also has faced protests from animal rights activists who want the company to demand better treatment of farm animals. And, Gerber and H. J. Heinz, two food processors, have been grilled by Greenpeace, the activist European environmental group, over the use of genetically engineered food. Although these examples illustrate some of the more radical stakeholder demands, all organizations must understand the demands of stakeholders and the impact on strategic choices.

Sources: C. L. Hays, "Shops Rally to the Ben & Jerry's Cause(s), *New York Times,* January 25, 2000, p. C2; R. Gibson, "Animal Rights Flare Up as McDonald's Is Torched, PETA Breaks Off Talks," *Wall Street Journal,* August 13, 1999, p. B8; L. Lagnado, "Strained Peace," *Wall Street Journal,* July 30, 1999, p. A1; G. Fairclough, "Procter & Gamble Makes Move Away from Animal Tests," *Wall Street Journal,* July 1, 1999, p. B10; and D. Canedy, "P&G to End Animal Tests for Most Consumer Goods," *New York Times,* July 1, 1999, p. C2.

What does this mean for managing strategically? It means recognizing the ethical implications of the outcomes of strategic decisions and actions. It means considering more than just being in compliance with the law as organizational strategies are formulated and implemented. For example, Avon Products Inc. sells its cosmetic products mainly to women. When Avon asked women what their number-one health concern was, breast cancer was the overwhelming answer. In response, Avon created its Worldwide Fund for Women's Health. This umbrella organization has spread around the globe. The company's biggest women's health program in this fund is the Breast Cancer Awareness Crusade in the United States. Through this program, the company's sales force educates women about breast cancer by distributing brochures about the disease on their sales visits. In this instance, Avon's strategic decision makers chose to develop and implement a sales strategy that addressed a significant customer concern. Was it the "right" thing to do? Well, Avon's decision makers think so. Not only were they being ethical in their dealings with customers, those customers responded by boosting company sales.[27] Although not every strategic decision and action will be this broad in scope, the ethical implications for managing strategically are clear: As you're managing strategically, ask yourself, what's the "right" thing to do in making this decision or taking this action?

Organizational Learning. The final aspect of world-class organizations is the significant role that organizational learning plays. **Organizational learning** is the intentional and ongoing actions of an organization to continuously transform itself by acquiring information and knowledge and incorporating these into organizational decisions and actions. A learning organization can either create or acquire new ideas and information and then use these to make decisions and take action. Organizational learning has been shown to be an important means for an organization to gain competitive advantage.[28] Table 2-3 lists some of the characteristics of a learning organization. As you can see from this table, a learning organization values all kinds of learning. But most importantly, managers in a learning organization incorporate learning into every aspect of the strategic management process.

How does an organization "learn"? Four basic ways were identified in a survey of organizational learning practices. (See Figure 2-6 on page 62.) Let's look at each of these a little closer. When an organization cultivated new capabilities in teams or individuals, they were described as using competence acquisition. These types of organizations continuously sought new ways to work and promoted learning as part of their fundamental organizational strategies. According to the survey, another way that organizations learned was by experimentation. These organizations continuously tried out new ideas and attempted to be the first to the marketplace with new processes or products. The most popular category in the survey for the way organizations learned was continuous improvement. This type of learning was characterized by the desire to master each step in a process before moving on to the next. The popularity of this approach shouldn't be surprising given the significant adoption by organizations of total quality management techniques and its emphasis on continual improvement. An organization that used continuous improvement wanted to become the recognized technical leader for a specific product or process. Finally, the last way that organizations were said to learn was by boundary spanning. In this approach to learning, an organization would continuously scan other companies' efforts and measure its

TABLE 2-3 Characteristics of a Learning Organization
• Learns continuously, collaboratively, and openly
• Values *how* it learns as well as what it learns
• Invests in staying on top of what's happening in its industry
• Learns faster and smarter than its competitors
• Rewards both "failure" learning (learning from what goes wrong) as well as "success" learning (learning from what goes right)
• Takes risks but doesn't jeopardize organization's basic security
• Encourages organizational members to share information
• Develops and exhibits an organizational culture that promotes learning
• Uses what it learns in developing and implementing strategies

Sources: P. M. Senge, *The Fifth Discipline* (New York: Doubleday, 1990); and Richard M. Hodgetts, Fred Luthans, and Sang M. Lee, "New Paradigm Organizations: From Total Quality to Learning to World Class," *Organizational Dynamics,* winter 1994, pp. 4–19.

Communities of Practice

A new organizational form that promises to radically change knowledge sharing, learning, and change is emerging. It's called the **community of practice**. What is a community of practice? It's a group of people bound together by shared expertise and passion for a joint interest or endeavor. The primary output from the group is knowledge. This community of practice may actually meet face-to-face, or it may be a meeting of the minds via e-mail. It may not have an explicit agenda of items to cover and may not even follow the agenda if it does have one. But, the one thing that characterizes this community of practice is the sharing of experiences and knowledge in free-flowing, creative ways. What benefits can communities of practice bring to organizations? They have the potential to add value in the following ways: They help drive strategy; they start new lines of business; they solve problems quickly; they transfer and spread best practices among organizational units; they develop professional skills that allow them to act as mentors and coaches; and they help companies recruit and retain talent. So, in many ways, the communities of practice within an organization can serve to build and exchange that all important knowledge.

Source: E. C. Wegner and W. M. Snyder, "Communities of Practice: The Organizational Frontier," *Harvard Business Review*, January–February 2000, pp. 139–45.

Consider This ◀◀

✓ Describe the three critical factors for succeeding in this new business environment.

✓ What role do change agents play in managing strategically?

✓ Differentiate between creativity and innovation.

✓ What is a world-class organization? Why is the concept of world class important?

✓ Describe organizational vision and what it should include.

✓ Describe a mission and what it should include.

✓ What is corporate social responsibility?

✓ Who are stakeholders and why are they important to managing strategically?

✓ Why is ethics important to strategic decision makers?

✓ What is organizational learning?

✓ What are some characteristics of learning organizations?

✓ Why is the concept of organizational learning important to managing strategically?

progress against them. These organizations also would diligently pursue information from outside the organizations—that is, they'd cross or "span" the boundaries in looking for information.

Even more interesting about this survey of organizational learning approaches was that these four types of learning were found to impact differently on organizational competitiveness and on an organization's ability to change.[29] On both measures, companies that learned by experimentation scored the highest. Competence acquisition was next highest, followed by continuous improvement, and boundary spanning. But, this doesn't mean that experimentation is the proper learning approach for all organizations. Instead, organizational decision makers need to identify what type of learning is most appropriate for their organizations and encourage the sharing of ideas throughout the organization. Learning and the application of learning will be critical to organizational success given the realities of the new economy and the dynamics of change.[30] What's the payoff? Employees making decisions about strategies in a world-class organization as they attempt to create a sustainable competitive advantage in light of the increasingly competitive global environment.

Figure 2-6

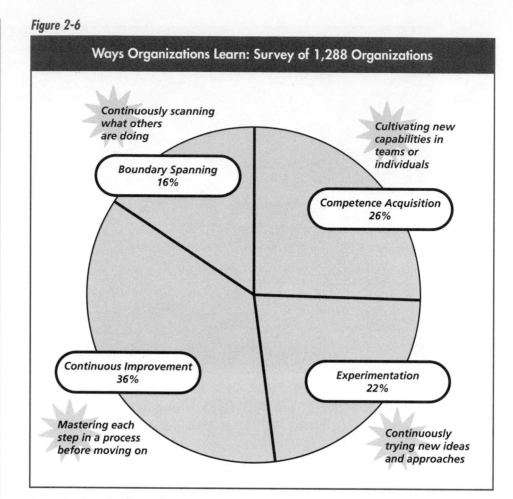

Ways Organizations Learn: Survey of 1,288 Organizations

Continuously scanning what others are doing

Boundary Spanning
16%

Cultivating new capabilities in teams or individuals

Competence Acquisition
26%

Continuous Improvement
36%

Experimentation
22%

Mastering each step in a process before moving on

Continuously trying new ideas and approaches

Source: Based on Helen Rheem, "The Learning Organization," *Harvard Business Review,* March–April 1995, p. 10.

THE BOTTOM LINE

▶ **Managing strategically** means making decisions and implementing strategies that allow an organization to develop and maintain competitive advantage.

▶ **Competitive advantage** is what sets an organization apart; its competitive edge.

▶ Competitive advantage is a necessary ingredient for an organization's long-term success and survival.

▶ There are three different views of competitive advantage.

▶ The **industrial organization (I/O) view** was developed by Michael Porter and focuses on the structural forces within an industry, the competitive environment of firms, and how these influenced competitive advantage. This view proposes that getting and keeping competitive advantage meant analyzing the external forces and then basing strategic decisions and actions on what was found.

⊪➤ The **resource-based view (RBV)** proposes that a firm's resources are more important than industry structure in getting and keeping competitive advantage, and sees organizations as very different collections of assets and capabilities.

⊪➤ **Resources** can include all of the financial, physical, human, intangible, and structural–cultural assets used by an organization to develop, manufacture, and deliver products and services to its customers.

⊪➤ Although every organization has resources, not all of these resources are going to be unique and capable of leading to a sustainable competitive advantage.

⊪➤ To be unique, resources must add value, be rare, be hard to imitate, and be able to be exploited.

⊪➤ The **guerrilla view** of competitive advantage proposes that an organization's competitive advantage is temporary because the environment is characterized by continual, radical, and often revolutionary changes.

⊪➤ All three views provide unique perspectives on understanding competitive advantage.

⊪➤ The business arena that organizations operate in today is a lot different than what it used to be.

⊪➤ The driving forces of the twenty-first-century business environment include the information revolution, technological advances and breakthroughs, and globalization.

⊪➤ In this new environment, organizations can no longer rely on the traditional factors of production to provide a competitive advantage, but must look to how information and knowledge can be exploited.

⊪➤ **Technology** is the use of equipment, materials, knowledge, and experience to perform tasks. Technology is changing the way we work and the type of work we do.

⊪➤ Four technological trends affect the context of managing strategically: the increasing rate of technological change and diffusion; the increasing commercialization of **innovation** (the process of taking a creative idea and turning it into a product or process that can be used or sold); the increasing dependence on knowledge intensity; and the possibility of increasing (not decreasing) returns.

⊪➤ **Globalization** is the international linkage of economies and cultures that fosters a business and competitive situation in which organizations have no national boundaries.

⊪➤ Two specific ways that globalization impacts the context of managing strategically are in the global marketplace and through global competitors.

⊪➤ There are four implications of these driving forces of the new business environment: continual turbulence and change, reduced need for physical assets, vanishing distance, and compressed time.

⊪➤ **Change** is any alteration in external environmental factors or internal organizational arrangements.

➠ **Organizational change** is any alteration in what an organization does and how it does it. The organization may have to change in response to changes in external or internal factors.

➠ Success in today's economy isn't reliant simply on physical assets. Instead, value can be found in intangible factors such as information, people, ideas, and knowledge.

➠ Geography no longer is a constraint on customers and competitors. An organization's potential markets and competitors can be found anywhere.

➠ The instant interactivity has created a context in which an organization needs to stay on top of changes.

➠ The critical success factors for this new business environment include the ability to embrace change, creativity and innovation capabilities, and being a world-class organization.

➠ Being successful in this turbulent environment means seeking out change and embracing it.

➠ Strategic decision makers play an important role as **change agents**—individuals or groups who strategically manage the formulation, implementation, and evaluation of organizational change efforts.

➠ "Create and innovate or lose!" **Creativity** is the ability to combine ideas in a unique way or to make unusual associations between ideas. However, creativity isn't enough. An organization also needs to be innovative—that is, be able to take that creative idea and turn it into a product or process that can be used to generate revenue.

➠ A **world-class organization** is one that continually acquires and utilizes knowledge in its strategic decisions and actions in order to be the best in the world at what it does.

➠ The characteristics of world-class organizations include strong customer focus, continual learning and improvement, flexible organization structure, creative human resource management, egalitarian climate, and significant technological support.

➠ The decision to be a world-class organization starts with developing an organizational vision and mission.

➠ **Organizational vision** is a broad comprehensive picture of what a leader wants an organization to become. It's a statement of what the organization stands for, what it believes in, and why it exists.

➠ The four components of an organizational vision are: it must be built on a foundation of the organization's core values and beliefs; it should create a purpose for the organization; it should include a brief summary of what the organization does; and it should specify broad goals.

➠ A **mission** is a statement of what the various organizational units do and what they hope to accomplish in alignment with the organizational vision.

➠ An organization will have one vision and potentially several missions that contribute to the pursuit of the organizational vision.

➠ **Corporate social responsibility (CSR)** refers to the obligation of organizational decision makers to make decisions and act in ways that recognize the interrelatedness of business and society.

➠ The traditional view of CSR was that organizations existed to serve the interests of one stakeholder group—the stockholders.

➠ The current perspective is that organizations have a larger societal role to play and a broader constituency to serve than just stockholders alone.

➠ One area of CSR that's growing in importance is called the **greening of management**, which is a recognition of the close link between an organization's decisions and actions and its impact on the natural environment.

➠ Organizations have to recognize the existence of other **stakeholders**—individuals or groups who have a stake in or are significantly influenced by an organization's decisions and actions and who, in turn, can influence the organization.

➠ **Ethics** involves the rules and principles that define right and wrong decisions and behavior.

➠ Ethics should be considered in the context of managing strategically.

➠ **Organizational learning**—the intentional and ongoing actions of an organization to continuously transform itself by acquiring information and knowledge and incorporating these into organizational decisions and actions—plays a significant role in managing strategically.

➠ A new form of organizational learning is called the **community of practice**, which is a group of people bound together by shared expertise and passion for a joint interest or endeavor.

➠ Learning organizations are characterized by their focus on learning and sharing that learning.

➠ Organizations can learn by competence acquisition, experimentation, continuous improvement, and boundary spanning.

BUILDING YOUR SKILLS

1. Organizational vision statements can take some interesting directions. For example, the vision statement of Imagine Media (**www.imaginemedia.com**) states:

   > Imagine Media is aimed at people who have a passion. A passion for games. For business. For computers. Or for the Internet. Those are passions we share. Our goal is to feed your passion with the greatest magazines, Web sites, and CD-ROMs imaginable. We love to innovate, we love to have fun, and we have a cast-iron rule always to deliver spectacular editorial value. That means doing whatever it takes to give you the information you need. With any luck, we'll even make you smile sometimes. . . .

   What do you think of this vision statement? Does it include the four components of an organizational vision? Now, go to the company's Web site and read further about its mission. How might these statements affect the strategic choices made by the company's strategic decision makers?

   Sources: Company's Web site (**www.imaginemedia.com**), February 24, 2000; and Editor's Note page, *Business 2.0,* March 2000, p. 10.

2. "Technology is fostering a free flow of information." Using a bulleted list format, write arguments supporting that statement. Then, write arguments against that statement. Be prepared to debate one or both sides in class.

3. Knowledge management is a relatively young science. Here are some suggestions for capturing knowledge and using it effectively: (a) keep it human; (b) focus on useful knowledge or "know-how"; (c) collect artifacts such as Post-it notes and other documents and make these public; (d) avoid an insular, isolated focus; and (e) keep your knowledge fresh. Explain what you think each of these suggestions is referring to. As you write your explanations, discuss the implications for strategic decision makers.

4. For each of the following quotes, explain what you think it means and the implications for understanding the context of managing strategically.

   - "To stay ahead, you must have your next idea waiting in the wings." (Rosabeth Moss Kanter, management professor, consultant, and author)

   - "Time is a river of passing events, and strong is its current; no sooner is a thing brought to sight than it is swept by and another takes its place, and this too will be swept away." (Marcus Aurelius Antoninus)

5. The summer of 1999 wasn't a good one for Coca-Cola in Europe. First, there were widely publicized product recalls. Then, the European Commission raided the company's offices in four countries following complaints from competitors, including PepsiCo, that accused Coke of unfair business practices intended to keep rival products off store shelves. A Pepsi spokesman said, "Late last year (1998), we expressed our concern about certain Coca-Cola practices that we believe are unlawful, and this year we filed a formal complaint with the commission." A Coca-Cola spokesman denied the accusations saying, "We are confident that at the conclusion of this process, the Coca-Cola Company's business practices will be found to be within all laws and regulations."

   What ethical dilemmas do you see in this situation for Coca-Cola? For PepsiCo? How is this an example of ethics affecting the context in which strategic decision makers are managing strategically?

   Source: C. L. Hays, "Pepsi Acknowledges Role in Putting Coca-Cola Under Inquiry," *New York Times,* July 23, 1999, p. C4.

6. Every year, *Fortune* publishes a list of America's most admired companies (usually in mid-to-late February). Get the most recent list and answer the following questions.

   - Define the key attributes being used to evaluate companies.
   - What companies are on the top 10 list of most admired?
   - Why do you think these companies are at the top of the list? What are they doing differently—that is, how are they managing strategically?
   - What companies are on the bottom 10 list? How are they managing strategically?
   - What could strategic decision makers learn from both groups?

7. The quality management movement encouraged organizational managers to *do it right the first time.* Make it right the first time and you eliminate waste. Finish it right the first time and you save money, time, and customer relationships. Makes sense, doesn't it? However, what if doing it right the first time stifles cre-

ativity and risk taking? Because breakthrough innovations are rarely well-planned, mistake-free processes, wouldn't an emphasis on doing it right suppress going out on a limb to try something different? Maybe doing it right isn't as important as *doing it best*. What do you think? Write a paper exploring these concepts.

8. Research the topic of best practices. Write a paper defining what best practices are, explaining their relationship to knowledge management, and describing the implications for managing strategically.

9. Go to Arthur Andersen's online productivity tool at **www.knowledgespace.com.** Pick a topic area of interest to explore. Follow the links! Using a bulleted list format, describe the important information you find.

10. One problem that organizations wanting to become knowledge-based organizations (or learning organizations) need to overcome is *knowledge hoarding,* an old habit businesspeople used to get power, to protect themselves, and to get ahead. Getting people to share information may well be the key managerial issue in the twenty-first century. How would you overcome knowledge hoarding? Make a bulleted list of ideas. Be prepared to present these in class.

11. "At the end of the day, most technologies worth their salt will provide one or two business benefits: Either they will allow a company to do something better, faster or cheaper, or they will provide a company with an opportunity to do something entirely new. Generally the first helps *save* money (productivity) whereas the second helps *make* money (profits)." Find examples of both technology benefits. Describe these examples in a paper. Be sure to explain how your examples represent each technology benefit. In addition, be sure to note your sources.

STRATEGIC MANAGEMENT IN ACTION CASES

CASE #1: The Queen of Lifestyle

Strategic Management in Action case #1 can be found at the beginning of Chapter 2.

Discussion Questions

1. What is Martha Stewart Living Omnimedia, Inc.'s competitive advantage? Explain according to the I/O view, the RBV, and the guerrilla view.

2. How is the company accomplishing its strategic objectives? (*Hint:* You will have to go to the company's Web site.)

3. Americans are increasingly outsourcing traditional homemaking functions. This trend is being driven by three factors: more women working, an older popula-

tion, and a growing affluent class. Here are some of the functions households are outsourcing:

Cooking. People used to cook at home most nights and eat out on special occasions. Now a home-cooked meal is increasingly a special occasion.

Cleaning. The number of households using an external cleaning service continues to increase.

Child care. The industry is booming and is the number-one benefit demanded by employees with young children.

Shopping. Shopping and delivery services cover areas such as dry cleaning, videos, packages, film developing, firewood, shoes needing repair, and so forth.

What impact might these trends have on MSO? Explain.

4. Update the information on MSO. Include revenues, profits, and strategic directions.

CASE #2: In the Know

Buckman Laboratories International (**www.buckman.com**), headquartered in Memphis, Tennessee, manufactures more than 1,000 specialty chemicals. The company employs over 1,200 people in 80 countries and its annual revenues exceed $320 million. Although this small, privately held company depends on its research laboratories for the products that bring in its revenues, the whole company itself is a learning laboratory.

What is it about Buckman Labs that attracts executives from AT&T, 3M, Champion International, US West, and other *Fortune* 500 companies, who trek to Memphis to see and learn? They're coming to see how the company stays so fast, global, and interactive. Bob Buckman, Buckman Lab's CEO, recognized the power of knowledge and information long before others did. Buckman and his employees began treating knowledge as the company's most important corporate asset back in 1992. They believed that being (and remaining) competitive in a knowledge-intensive global environment required three things: (1) closing the gap between the organization and the customer, (2) staying in touch with each other, and (3) bringing *all* of the company's brainpower together to serve each customer. Buckman was concerned with staying connected, sharing knowledge, and functioning anytime, anywhere, no matter what.

Buckman Labs has organized its employees and their work around its knowledge network, K'Netix®. This global electronic communications network resulted from Buckman's being confined to bed after rupturing disks in his back. Lying there, unable to stand or even to sit up, Buckman felt isolated and uninformed about what was happening in the company while he was flat on his back. He started thinking about how important information and knowledge were—not just to him, but to *all* of Buckman Labs' employees. What he needed and what his employees needed was a steady stream of information about products, markets, and customers. And this information had to be easily accessible and easily shared. As an ardent reader of business and management information, Buckman had read a comment from a well-known and well-respected CEO (Scandinavian Airlines' former CEO, Jan Carlzon) that stuck in his mind: "An individual without information cannot take responsibility; an individual who is given information cannot help but take responsibility."

Buckman realized that the way to maximize each of his individual employee's power was to connect each employee to the world. He wrote down what his ideal knowledge transfer system would do. Here's what he wrote: (1) It would be possible for people to talk to each other directly to minimize distortion. (2) It would give everyone access to the company's knowledge base. (3) It would allow each individual in the company to enter knowledge into the system. (4) It would be available

24 hours a day, 7 days a week. (5) It would be easy to use. (6) It would communicate in whatever language was best for the user. (7) It would be updated automatically, capturing questions and answers as a future knowledge base. Such a system would require a total cultural transformation—literally turning the organization upside down by getting employees to be deeply involved with collaborating and sharing knowledge. And that's what Bob Buckman set out to do. However, transforming the company from an old pyramidal, bureaucratic, command-and-control organization to an organization in which every employee would have complete access to information and in which no one would be telling employees what to do all the time wasn't easy.

Getting the physical hardware and software in place to support such a system was only half the battle. Getting employees to use the knowledge base *and* contribute to it were also important. After all, a knowledge-based company is successful only if knowledge is shared among organizational members. What was particularly difficult about this type of cultural transformation was that employees in traditional organizations had always been rewarded on their ability to hoard knowledge and thus gain power. This is how the situation at Buckman Labs was described: "There were people whose file cabinets were filled with everything they knew, and that was the source of their power." But that philosophy had to change if the knowledge system was going to work. Not long after K'Netix® went online, Buckman made his expectations clear: "Those of you who have something intelligent to say now have a forum in which to say it. Those of you who will not or cannot contribute also become obvious. If you are not willing to contribute or participate, then you should understand that the many opportunities offered to

you in the past will no longer be available." What ultimately emerged at Buckman Labs has been a mixture of visible incentives and invisible pressure to use the Buckman Knowledge Network.

Because Buckman Labs competes in a variety of businesses, often against competitors three to five times its size, its commitment to knowledge takes on a new urgency. Salespeople need the right answer for each customer and they need it fast. K'Netix® has made getting answers simple. But the company's commitment to speed, employee interactivity and knowledge sharing, and globalization would not be possible without a recognition of the context within which managing strategically takes place.

Discussion Questions

1. According to Table 2-3, is Buckman Labs a learning organization? Explain.

2. Describe Buckman Labs' strategic approaches in light of the drivers of the new business environment, the implications of these driving forces, and the critical success factors.

3. Go to Buckman's Web site. Answer the following:
   - Find the statement of mission. What is it? What other unique element(s) do you see on Buckman's statement of mission?
   - Locate the company's code of ethics. Summarize some of the company's basic principles.
   - Would you call the company a "green" company? Explain and support your answer.
   - Find the Knowledge Nurture page. What is the Buckman Room? What is the Starter Kit? What is the Library?

- Find the page that describes K'Netix®. What does it say about the Buckman Knowledge Network?

4. What could other organizations learn from Buckman Labs approach?

(*Sources:* Company's Web site (**www.buckman.com**), February 24, 2000; S. Thurm, "What Do You Know?" *Wall Street Journal,* June 21, 1999, p. R10; B. P. Sunoo, "How HR Supports Knowledge Sharing," *Workforce,* March 1999, pp. 30–32; G. Rifkin, "Buckman Labs Is Nothing but Net," *Fast Company* Web site (**www.fastcompany.com**), April 17, 1997; and A. Bruzzese, "Sharing Knowledge Breaks Hierarchy," *Springfield News Leader,* October 17, 1997, p. 7A.)

CASE #3: Banking on the Future

Diebold, Incorporated (**www.diebold.com**) is a global leader in providing integrated delivery systems and services in card-based transaction systems. Even though the company is on the cutting-edge of banking technology, it's been in business over 140 years. What does Diebold do and how has it managed this long record of success?

The company has targeted the financial services industry and four additional segments in the service sector: health care, education, retail, and government services. Diebold's primary customers include banks and financial institutions, hospitals, universities, public libraries, sports stadiums, utilities, and various retail outlets. Its service staff is one of the financial industry's largest, most comprehensively trained with over 4,500 professionals in 600 locations worldwide. The company's specific product groups include the following:

Self-Service Products. Diebold offers an integrated line of self-service banking products and ATMs. The company is a leading global supplier of ATMs and holds the market leading position in many countries around the world.

Physical Security and Facility Products. This division designs and manufactures products such as remote teller systems, vaults, safe-deposit boxes, safes, drive-up banking equipment, and so forth.

Integrated Security Solutions. This division provides global sales, service, installation, project management and monitoring of electronic security products to financial, retail, and commercial customers.

MedSelect Systems. This division develops automated, PC-based products that dispense pharmaceuticals and supplies, while simultaneously recording the information for nursing, pharmacy, and billing departments.

Campus Card Systems. This division develops and services single ID card systems that allow students to use the ID cards for a variety of activities.

Software Solutions and Services. This division provides software solutions consisting of multiple applications that process events and transactions; this division also provides professional services to assist in the implementation of software solutions.

The company does business in North America and distributes products and services directly or through wholly owned subsidiaries or majority owned joint ventures in every major country throughout Europe, the Middle East, Latin America, and in the Asia–Pacific region (excluding Japan and Korea, which use different self-service technologies).

The U.S. financial market has traditionally been Diebold's major source of revenues. Over the last few years, financial institutions within that industry have been merging and consolidating. This has left many institutions with a patchwork of information systems to integrate. What Diebold does is provide this integration, both in terms of equipment and service. In addition, the company helps these same institutions improve their competitiveness by improving and streamlining their security systems and branch facilities design. However, each of the other growth areas Diebold has targeted (education, health care, retail, and government services) stands to benefit from computerized self-service, security, and systems integration.

Discussion Questions

1. Describe Diebold's competitive advantage from each of the three perspectives on competitive advantage.

2. Does Diebold exhibit the critical success factors for the new business environment? Explain.

3. Explain the types of resources Diebold might have in each of the categories. Would any of these resources be unique? Explain.

4. What stakeholders might Diebold have to be concerned with and how might those stakeholders affect Diebold's strategic decisions and actions?

(***Sources:*** Company's Web site (**www.diebold.com**), February 23, 2000; and "Banking Trends Impact Leader in ATMs," *Better Investing,* July 1998, pp. 48–50.)

ENDNOTES

1. Information from Martha Stewart's Omnimedia Web site (**www.marthastewart.com**), February 10, 2000; and D. Brady, "Martha Inc.," *Business Week,* January 17, 2000, pp. 62–72.

2. Discussion of industrial–organization perspective based on K. R. Conner, "A Historical Comparison of Resource-Based Theory and Five Schools of Thought Within Industrial Organization Economics: Do We Have a New Theory of the Firm?" *Journal of Management,* 17, no. 1 (1991), pp. 121–54; M. Porter, *Competitive Advantage: Creating and Sustaining Superior Performance* (New York: Free Press, 1985); and M. Porter, *Competitive Strategy: Techniques for Analyzing Industries and Competitors* (New York: Free Press, 1980).

3. Discussion of resource-based view based on D. Miller and J. Shamsie, "The Resource-Based View of the Firm in Two Environments: The Hollywood Film Studios from 1936–1965," *Academy of Management Journal,* June 1996, pp. 519–43; J. M. Liedtka, "Collaborating Across Lines of Business for Competitive Advantage," *Academy of Management Executive,* May 1996, pp. 20–34; C. C. Markides and P. J. Williamson, "Corporate Diversification and Organizational Structure: A Resource-Based View," *Academy of Management Journal,* April 1995, pp. 340–67; L. W. Lam, "Does Competence Really Matter? An Empirical Investigation of the Resource-Based Explanation of Firm Performance," *SWFAD Proceedings,* March 1996, pp. 19–23; J. B. Barney, "Looking Inside for Competitive Advantage," *Academy of Management Executive,* November 1995, pp. 49–61;

J. B. Barney and E. J. Zajac, "Competitive Organizational Behavior: Toward an Organizationally-Based Theory of Competitive Advantage," *Strategic Management Journal,* winter 1995, pp. 5–9; R. Ashkenas, "Capability: Strategic Tool for a Competitive Edge," *Journal of Business Strategy,* November–December 1995, pp. 13–15; P. C. Godfrey and C.W.L. Hill, "The Problem of Unobservables in Strategic Management Research," *Strategic Management Journal,* October 1995, pp. 519–33; S. L. Hart, "A Natural Resource-Based View of the Firm," *Academy of Management Review,* October 1995, pp. 986–1014; J. B. Black and K. B. Boal, "Strategic Resources: Traits, Configurations, and Paths to Sustainable Competitive Advantage," *Strategic Management Journal,* summer 1995, pp. 131–38; P. Shrivastava, "Environmental Technologies and Competitive Advantage," *Strategic Management Journal,* summer 1995, pp. 183–200; D. J. Collis and C. A. Montgomery, "Competing on Resources: Strategy in the 1990s," *Harvard Business Review,* July–August 1995, pp. 118–28; W. B. Werther and J. L. Kerr, "The Shifting Sands of Competitive Advantage," *Business Horizons,* May–June 1995, pp. 11–17; B. Wernerfelt, "The Resource-Based View of the Firm: Ten Years After," *Strategic Management Journal,* March 1995, pp. 171–74; J. Pfeffer, "Producing Sustainable Competitive Advantage Through the Effective Management of People," *Academy of Management Executive,* February 1995, pp. 55–69; D. Schendel, "Introduction to Competitive Organizational Behavior: Toward an Organizationally Based Theory of Competitive Advantage,"

Strategic Management Journal, winter 1994, pp. 1–4; C. K. Prahalad and G. Hamel, "Strategy as a Field of Study: Why Search for a New Paradigm?" *Strategic Management Journal,* summer 1994, pp. 5–16; O. Harari, "The Secret Competitive Advantage," *Management Review,* January 1994, pp. 45–47; I. Bogaert, R. Martens, and A. Van Canwenbergh, "Strategy as a Situational Puzzle," in *Competence-Based Competition,* ed. G. Hamel and A. Heene (New York: John Wiley, 1994), p. 58; R. Hall, "A Framework for Identifying the Intangible Sources of Sustainable Competitive Advantage," in Hamel and Heene, pp. 151–54; P. J. Verdin and P. J. Williamson, "Core Competences: Competitive Advantage and Market Analysis: Forging the Links," in Hamel and Heene, p. 81; D. J. Collis, "Research Note: How Valuable are Organizational Capabilities?" *Strategic Management Journal,* winter 1994, pp. 143–52; R. Hall, "A Framework Linking Intangible Resources and Capabilities to Sustainable Competitive Advantage," *Academy of Management Journal,* November 1993, pp. 607–18; M. A. Peteraf, "The Cornerstones of Competitive Advantage: A Resource-Based View," *Strategic Management Journal,* March 1993, pp. 179–91; R. Amit and P.J.H. Schoemaker, "Strategic Assets and Organizational Rent," *Strategic Management Journal,* January 1993, pp. 33–46; R. M. Grant, "The Resource-Based Theory of Competitive Advantage: Implications for Strategy Formulation," *California Management Review,* spring 1991, pp. 114–35; J. B. Barney, "Firm Resources and Sustained Competitive Advantage," *Journal of Management,* 17, no. 1 (1991), pp. 99–120; K. R. Conner, "A Historical-Based Comparison of Resource-Based Theory and Five Schools of Thought within Industrial Organization Economics: Do We Have a New Theory of the Firm?" 1991; J. B. Barney, "Asset Stocks and Sustained Competitive Advantage: A Comment," *Management Science,* December 1989, pp. 1511–13; I. Dierickx and K. Cool, "Asset Stock Accumulation and Sustainability of Competitive Advantage," *Management Science,* December 1989, pp. 1504–11; R. P. Rumelt, "Towards a Strategic Theory of the Firm," in *Competitive Strategic Management,* ed. R. B. Lamb (Upper Saddle River, NJ: Prentice Hall, 1984), pp. 556–70; and B. Wernerfelt, "A Resource-Based View of the Firm," *Strategic Management Journal,* 14 (1984), pp. 4–12.

4. Discussion of the guerrilla view is based on C. A. Lengnick-Hall and J. A. Wolff, "Similarities and Contradictions in the Core Logic of Three Strategy Research Streams," *Strategic Management Journal,* December 1999, pp. 1109–32; V. Rindova and C. J. Fombrun, "Constructing Competitive Advantage: The Role of Firm-Constituent Interactions," *Strategic Management Journal,* August 1999, pp. 691–710; K. M. Eisenhardt and S. L. Brown, "Patching: Restitching Business Portfolios in Dynamic Markets," *Harvard Business Review,* May–June 1999, pp. 72–81; B. Chakravarthy, "A New Strategy Framework for Coping With Turbulence," *Sloan Management Review,* winter 1997, pp. 69–82; R. A. D'Aveni, *Hypercompetition: Managing the Dynamics of Strategic Maneuvering* (New York: Free Press, 1994); Collis, "Research Note"; and K. M. Eisenhardt, "Making Fast Strategic Decisions in High-Velocity Environments," *Academy of Management Journal,* December 1989, pp. 543–76.

5. J. B. Barney, "Looking Inside for Competitive Advantage," *Academy of Management Executive,* November 1995, pp. 49–61.

6. "10 Driving Principles of the New Economy," *Business 2.0,* March 2000, pp. 191–284; M. J. Mandel, "The New Economy," *Business Week,* January 31, 2000, pp. 73–77; "The Internet Age," *Business Week,* October 4, 1999, pp. 69–202; G. J. Church, "The Economy of the Future," *Time,* October 4, 1999, pp. 77–79; P. Coy and N. Gross, "21 Ideas for the 21st Century," *Business Week,* August 30, 1999, pp. 78–162; C. V. Callahan and B. R. Pasternack, "Corporate Strategy in the Digital Age," *Strategy and Business,* second quarter 1999, pp. 10–14; N. D. Schwartz, "The Tech Boom Will Keep on Rocking," *Fortune,* February 15, 1999, pp. 64–80; and D. B. Yoffie and M. A. Cusumano, "Judo Strategy: The Competitive Dynamics of Internet Time," *Harvard Business Review,* January–February 1999, pp. 71–81.

7. P. F. Drucker, *Post-Capitalist Society* (New York: Harper Business, 1993).

8. S. Kerr and D. Ulrich, "Creating the Boundaryless Organization: The Radical Reconstruction of Organizational Capabilities," *Planning Review,* September–October 1995, pp. 43–62.

9. R. A. Bettis and M. A. Hitt, "The New Competitive Landscape," *Strategic Management Journal,* summer 1995, pp. 7–19.

10. See, for example, D. D. Buss, "Embracing Speed," *Nation's Business,* June 1999, pp. 12–17; D. D. Buss, "A Wake-Up Call for Companies," *Nation's Business,* March 1998, pp. 63–67; J. W. Jones, *High-Speed Management* (San Francisco: Jossey-Bass, 1993); D. E. Vinton, "A New Look at Time, Speed, and the Manager," *Academy of Management Executive,* November 1992, pp. 7–16; J. T. Vesey, "The New Competitors: They Think in Terms of Speed-to-Market," *Academy of Management Executive,* May 1991, pp. 23–33; and G. Stalk Jr., "Time—The Next Source of Competitive Advantage," *Harvard Business Review,* July–August 1988, pp. 41–51.

11. M. J. Mandel, "You Ain't Seen Nothing Yet," *Business Week,* August 31, 1998, pp. 60–63.

12. S. A. Zahra, "The Changing Rules of Global Competitiveness in the 21st Century," *Academy of Management Executive,* February 1999, pp. 36–42; J. A. Petrick, R. F. Shcere, J. D. Brodzinski, J. F. Quinn, and M. F. Ainina, "Global Leadership Skills and Reputational Capital: Intangible Resources for Sustainable Competitive Advantage," *Academy of Management Executive,* February 1999, pp. 58–69; and H. Thomas, T. Pollock, and P. Gorman, "Global Strategic Analyses: Frameworks and Approaches," *Academy of Management Executive,* February 1999, pp. 70–82.

13. R. W. Oliver, *The Shape of Things to Come: 7 Imperatives for Winning in the New World of Business* (New York: McGraw-Hill Business Week Books, 1999), p. 23.

14. B. C. Reimann, "The New Strategic Leadership: Driving Change, Getting Results!" *Planning Review,* September–October 1994, pp. 6–8.

15. "People Power: Enlisting the Agents of Change," *Chief Executive,* May 1995, p. 516.

16. This definition is based on T. M. Amabile, "A Model of Creativity and Innovation in Organizations," in *Research in Organizational Behavior,* Vol. 10, B. M. Staw and L. L. Cummings ed. (Greenwich, CT: JAI Press, 1988), p. 126.

17. R. M. Hodgetts, F. Luthans, and S. M. Lee, "New Paradigm Organizations: From Total Quality to Learning to World Class," *Organizational Dynamics,* winter 1994, pp. 4–19.

18. S. F. Marino, "Where There Is No Visionary, Companies Falter," *Industry Week,* March 15, 1999, p. 20; D. I. Silvers, "Vision–Not Just for CEOs," *Management Quarterly,* winter 1994–1995, pp. 10–14.

19. L. Larwood, C. M. Falbe, M. P. Kriger, and P. Miesing, "Structure and Meaning of Organizational Vision," *Academy of*

Management Journal, June 1995, pp. 740–69; and S. L. Oswald, K. W. Mossholder, and S. G. Harris, "Vision Salience and Strategic Involvement: Implications for Psychological Attachment to Organization and Job," *Strategic Management Journal,* July 1994, pp. 477–89.

20. Silvers, "Vision—Not Just for CEOs."

21. G. E. Ledford Jr., J. R. Wendenhof, and J. T. Strahley, "Realizing a Corporate Philosophy," *Organizational Dynamics,* winter 1995, pp. 5–19.

22. D. J. Wood, "Corporate Social Performance Revisited," *Academy of Management Review,* October 1991, pp. 691–718.

23. M. Friedman, *Capitalism and Freedom* (Chicago: University of Chicago Press, 1962).

24. L. D. Lerner and G. E. Fryxell, "CEO Stakeholder Attitudes and Corporate Social Activity in the *Fortune* 500," *Business and Society,* April 1994, pp. 58–81.

25. Information from CEP's Web site (**www.cepnyc.org**), February 20, 2000.

26. L. T. Hosmer, "Strategic Planning as if Ethics Mattered," *Strategic Management Journal,* summer 1994, pp. 17–34; L. S. Paine, "Managing for Organizational Integrity," *Harvard Business Review,* March–April 1994, pp. 106–17; and A. E. Singer, "Strategy as Moral Philosophy," *Strategic Management Journal,* March 1994, pp. 192–213.

27. D. Kurschner, "5 Ways Ethical Business Creates Fatter Profits," *Business Ethics,* March–April 1996, pp. 20–23.

28. V. Dimovski, *Organizational Learning and Competitive Advantage: A Theoretical and Empirical Analysis,* dissertation, Cleveland State University, March 1994.

29. H. Rheem, "The Learning Organization: Building Learning Capability," *Harvard Business Review,* March–April 1995, p. 10.

30. S. L. Mintz, "A Knowing Glance," *CFO,* February 2000, pp. 52–61; N. Bontis, "Managing an Organizational Learning System by Aligning Stocks and Flows of Knowledge," *Academy of Management Proceedings,* CD-Rom, BPS, J1–J6.

3

ASSESSING OPPORTUNITIES AND THREATS: DOING AN EXTERNAL ANALYSIS

LEARNING OBJECTIVES

After studying this chapter, you should be able to:

1. Differentiate between external environmental opportunities and threats.
2. Describe how organizations are open systems.
3. Distinguish between the environment as information perspective and the environment as source of resources perspective.
4. Describe the components in an organization's specific environment.
5. Explain each of the forces in Porter's five forces model.
6. Describe the components in an organization's general environment.
7. Discuss what types of information on the external environment a strategic manager needs and where he or she might find this information.
8. Describe the types of external information different managerial levels might need.
9. Explain the benefits and challenges of doing an external analysis.

STRATEGIC MANAGEMENT IN ACTION CASE #1

Not Sold Out

The nation's theater chains are facing a critical time.[1] Although 1999 was a blockbuster year for the Hollywood studios—moviegoers spent a record $7.5 billion at the box office, up 8 percent from the year before—the theater chains that show the movies had the worst year in a number of years. How can the theater chains be doing so poorly when their main suppliers (the movie studios) are releasing so many hits? You need only look at what's happening in the theater industry's external environment and the strategic decisions that managers at the theater chains have made to begin to understand the situation.

Together, the five largest movie theater chains in the United States—Regal Cinemas (**www.regalcinemas.com**), Loews Cineplex (**www.cineplex.com**), Carmike Cinemas (**www.carmike.com**), AMC Theatres (**www.amctheatres.com**), and United Artists Theatre Circuits (**www.uatc.com**)—have close to 15,000 screens. (See Figure 3-1.) And, they're putting up more, usually in megaplexes of 20 to 30 separate theaters. But it isn't just the number of screens that's contributing to the industry's problems. Think about the movie theaters themselves: the supremely comfortable seats in stadium-style seating, the state-of-the-art sound system, the ornately decorated lobbies, and the other amenities offered at the refreshment stands including cappuccino, ice cream treats, and even full-course meals. In trying to lure customers to spend their entertainment dollars going to the movies, the theater chains have spent millions on creating an appealing and unique environment. However, as one entertainment stock analyst said, "There's no way to raise the price for tickets or Cokes fast enough to offset it." The other problem with the increasing number of movie screens is that the theater chains have limited their bargaining power with the Hollywood studios. The studios know that the chains are desperate for the first-run blockbuster films to show in their theaters and can negotiate prices accordingly. This pricing arrangement generally is that the movie studios get as much as 90 percent of ticket revenues the first week of a film's release and then drop off to about 50 percent for future weeks. However, with the large number of screens available to show new-release films, hit films have shorter runs because customers have several theaters to choose from, which hurts the theater's revenue stream.

A new twist in the pursuit of paying customers by the movie theaters is the push to offer print-at-home tickets. America Online's Moviefone unit is preparing a new program that will allow customers to print their own bar-coded movie tickets at home after purchasing them online. That way, they don't have to stand in line at the theater. The service isn't free. Customers pay a $.75 to $1.50 charge per ticket for the convenience. However, the program, which started in the summer of 2000 with United Artists Theatre and expanded to other AOL Moviefone theater-chain partners during the year, appears to be a hit with consumers.

Figure 3-1

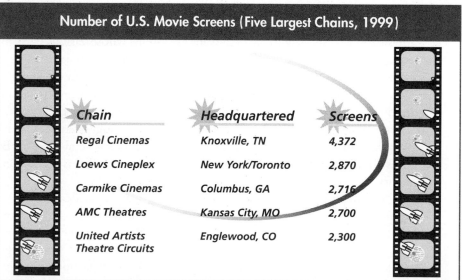

Number of U.S. Movie Screens (Five Largest Chains, 1999)

Chain	Headquartered	Screens
Regal Cinemas	Knoxville, TN	4,372
Loews Cineplex	New York/Toronto	2,870
Carmike Cinemas	Columbus, GA	2,716
AMC Theatres	Kansas City, MO	2,700
United Artists Theatre Circuits	Englewood, CO	2,300

This chapter-opening case illustrates how changes in the external environment led to changes in strategy by the strategic decision makers at the theater chains. As the case points out, external environmental factors can significantly affect companies' strategic decisions and actions. Being alert to changing trends in different external environments such as technology, customer tastes and habits, and even what your competitors are doing is an important step in formulating effective strategies. In this chapter, we'll look at the process of external analysis by first describing what an external analysis is. Then, we'll look at some details of how to do an external analysis and how to identify positive and negative aspects of the environment. Finally, we'll discuss why doing an external analysis is so important in managing strategically and why managers at all levels of the organization need to know something about understanding and analyzing what's happening outside the boundaries of their organizations.

WHAT IS AN EXTERNAL ANALYSIS?

An **external analysis** is the process of scanning and evaluating an organization's various external environmental sectors in order to determine positive and negative trends that could impact organizational performance. It's the way strategic managers determine the opportunities and threats that face their organizations. **Opportunities** are positive external environmental trends or changes that may help the organization improve its performance. **Threats,** on the other hand, are negative external environmental trends or changes that may hinder the organization's performance. In assessing your organization's current situation, it's important to know what's happening in the external environment so you can design new strategies or change your current strategies to take advantage of opportunities and to avoid threats. You can see where the external analysis fits into the strategic management in action process in Figure 3-2.

Organizations as Open Systems

The belief that an organization interacts with its environment can be traced back to the concept of organizations as open systems. The concept of systems and open systems comes from the physical sciences and their studies of living organisms. Physical scientists view living organisms as systems whose various parts (or subsystems) are interrelated, interdependent, and function as a whole. Also, as an open system these living organisms interact with their environment by taking in sustenance and other inputs and giving off outputs such as energy, waste, or other by-products. This is similar to what happens as organizations do their work. In fact, Chester Barnard, an early management theorist, first suggested back in 1938 that organizations functioned as systems.[2] However, it took several years for Barnard's ideas about organizations as systems to be accepted into mainstream management theory.

Although viewing organizations as systems—and specifically, open systems—seems entirely logical to us today, it wasn't until the late 1950s that various organizational researchers finally saw the wisdom of Barnard's concepts and suggested that organizations should also be viewed as systems.[3] In other words, organizations, too, had interrelated and interdependent parts (departments or divisions) that functioned as a whole. Any changes in any subsystems would affect the other

Figure 3-2

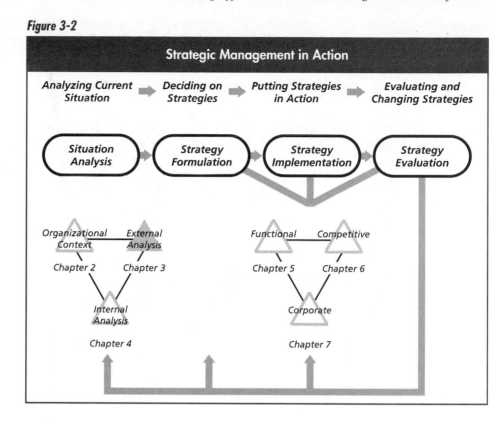

subsystems. For example, if a change is made in marketing, it influences what happens in manufacturing, accounting, human resources, or any of the organization's other functional areas. Also, organizations can be viewed as open systems in much the same way a living organism is an open system: It takes in inputs and, through some type or types of processing, produces outputs. Those inputs have to come from somewhere and the outputs must be distributed somewhere. That "somewhere" is the external environment. Thus, when we say that an organization is an **open system**, we mean that it interacts with and responds to its external environment. As an open system, an organization is affected by the environment and can also impact that environment. Figure 3-3 shows a simple example of an organization as an open system.

Perspectives on Organizational Environments

As the external environment changes, strategic decision makers may choose to respond to these new, and often vastly different, circumstances. The belief that an organization interacted with its environment has been the catalyst behind numerous attempts by organizational researchers to describe and understand organizational environments and their potential impact on an organization's performance. The various studies of organizational environments can be summarized from two different perspectives: (1) environment as a source of information and (2) environment as a source of resources. To help you better understand the impact of the environment on an organization and its ultimate performance, let's look at these perspectives more closely.

Figure 3-3

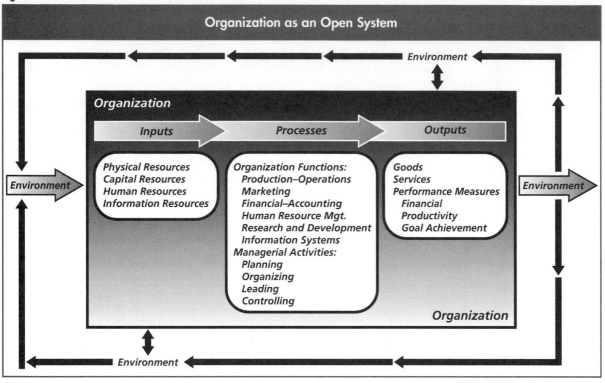

Organization as an Open System

Environment

Organization

Inputs → Processes → Outputs

Environment

Physical Resources
Capital Resources
Human Resources
Information Resources

Organization Functions:
Production–Operations
Marketing
Financial–Accounting
Human Resource Mgt.
Research and Development
Information Systems
Managerial Activities:
Planning
Organizing
Leading
Controlling

Goods
Services
Performance Measures
Financial
Productivity
Goal Achievement

Environment

Organization

Environment

Environment as Information Perspective. In this approach to organizational environments, the environment is viewed as a source of information for decision making.[4] A key aspect of this approach is the idea of **environmental uncertainty**, which is the amount of change and complexity in an organization's environment. What do we mean by these terms? The amount of change occurring in an organization's environment can be characterized as either dynamic or stable. If the organization's environment is changing rapidly, it's classified as a more dynamic one. If changes are minimal or slow in occurring, the environment is a more stable one. For instance, the environmental changes taking place in the oil refining industry are not as rapid as those, say, in the Internet service providers industry. Therefore, the Internet service providers industry would be considered more dynamic than the oil refining industry. Similarly, if decision makers must monitor a number of components in the environment, we consider that environment to be complex. If the number of environmental components is few, it's a simple environment. The more complex and dynamic the environment, the more uncertain it is, and the more information that decision makers need about the environment to be able to make appropriate decisions. So, according to this perspective, the perceived uncertainty of the environment (amount of change and complexity) dictates the amount and types of information that managers need about that environment. Where do strategic decision makers get that information? They get it from doing an analysis of the external environment—in other words, the environment serves as a source of information.

Environment as Source of Resources Perspective. In this approach, the environment is viewed as a source of scarce and necessary resources that are sought by

Strategic Management in Action

Home appliance manufacturers are tuned in to information coming from the environment about what consumers like, and they're taking note of the success of the colorful, translucent Apple iMac. When Apple introduced its iMac in August of 1998, the tangerine, blueberry, grape, and lime colors were an immediate hit with consumers. Now, manufacturers of home appliances are selling vacuums in translucent wine and yellow, steam irons in violet and aqua, and hair dryers in pink. How do you think customers will react? What other information might strategic decision makers in this industry want?

Sources: "Appliances About to Get Colorful, Translucent," *Springfield News Leader,* February 22, 2000, p. 10B; "Appliance Makers Plan Smart Devices," *New York Times,* January 17, 2000, p. C8; and A. Reinhardt, S. V. Brull, P. Burrows, and C. Yang, "The Soul of a New Refrigerator," *Business Week,* January 17, 2000, p. 42.

competing organizations.[5] As the environment becomes more "hostile" (i.e., resources become harder to obtain and control), organizations are subjected to greater uncertainty. Given these uncertain conditions, managers look for ways to acquire and control those critical resources. They do this by monitoring the environment and making appropriate decisions based on what they see happening and keeping in mind that the environment is the source of those scarce resources.

The main points of each approach to organizational environments are summarized in Table 3-1. These two different perspectives on how managers can view the organization's environment provide us with a beginning understanding of what's involved with an external analysis. Yet, how *can* managers determine what's happening in the external environment? That's where environmental scanning comes in.

Environmental Scanning and External Analysis

One impression we get from the previous discussion of both perspectives on organizational environments is that strategic decision makers need to engage in environmental scanning—to know what's happening in the external environment, whether viewing the environment as a source of information, as a source of scarce resources, or as a source of both. A strategic decision maker must be on the lookout for environmental changes. A strategic decision maker's ability to recognize and anticipate environmental changes plays a key role in shaping the organization's future because it limits or opens up strategic options. However, what does it mean to recognize and anticipate environmental changes? It means scanning the environment and evaluating what the various data and trends mean to the organization. Note that it's not enough for you just to know what's happening in your organization's environment—you also need to *assess,* to evaluate, what this information means for your organization. In other words, you need to do an external analysis and determine the opportunities and threats facing your organization. For example, look back at the chapter-opening case. Based upon their recognition

TABLE 3-1 Summary of Two Perspectives on Environment

Environment as Source of Information

- Environment viewed as source of information
- Environments differ in amount of uncertainty
- Uncertainty is determined by complexity and rate of change
- Reducing uncertainty means obtaining information
- Amount of uncertainty determines amount and types of information needed
- Information obtained by analyzing external environment

Environment as Source of Resources

- Environment viewed as source of scarce and valued resources
- Organizations depend on the environment for these resources
- Resources are sought by competing organizations
- Dependency is determined by difficulty of obtaining and controlling resources
- Reducing dependency means controlling environmental resources
- Controlling environmental resources means knowing about the environment and attempting to change or influence it

Source: Based on Richard A. Bettis and Michael A. Hitt, "The New Competitive Landscape," *Strategic Management Journal,* summer 1995, pp. 7–19.

and analysis of customer trends and technological changes, strategic decision makers at the movie theater chains chose to develop strategies that took advantage of consumers' increasing use of the Internet to purchase items, even movie tickets. These strategic decision makers recognized that customers were willing to use electronic and computer technologies as alternatives to the traditional approach of standing in line to buy movie tickets, determined that this trend provided a potential opportunity to sell more tickets, and developed strategies to take advantage of this trend.

Consider This ◀◀|

✓ What is an external analysis and what does it show managers?

✓ How is an organization an open system? How does this relate to external analysis?

✓ What does each of the perspectives on organizational environments say?

✓ What is environmental uncertainty and what role does it play in external analysis?

✓ Describe what it means for an environment to be "hostile."

✓ Why does a manager need to do more than just scan the environment?

HOW DO YOU DO AN EXTERNAL ANALYSIS?

Now that we know *what* an external analysis is, we need to look specifically at *how* you do one. What exactly do managers need to look for when they do an external analysis? Where can you find information about the external environment and how do you evaluate this information? How do managers at different organizational levels look at the external environment—that is, how do they do an external analysis? We explore these topics in this section. When you've finished reading this part of the chapter, you should know how to do an external analysis and determine an organization's opportunities and threats.

External Environmental Sectors

Obviously, it would be very difficult, if not impossible, to do an effective and comprehensive external analysis without some type of outline or format to follow. In other words, what external sectors do you need to look at to identify potential opportunities and threats?

An organization's external environment includes sectors that are directly relevant to its strategic decisions and actions and sectors that aren't directly relevant but must be considered. We're going to classify external sectors as being part of the specific environment or part of the general environment. The **specific environment** describes those external environmental sectors that directly impact the organization's decisions and actions by opening up opportunities or threats. It includes customers, competitors, suppliers, and other important industry–competitive variables. (See Figure 3-4.) The **general environment** refers to those external environmental sectors that indirectly affect the organization's strategic decisions and actions and may pose opportunities or threats. The trends and changes

Figure 3-4

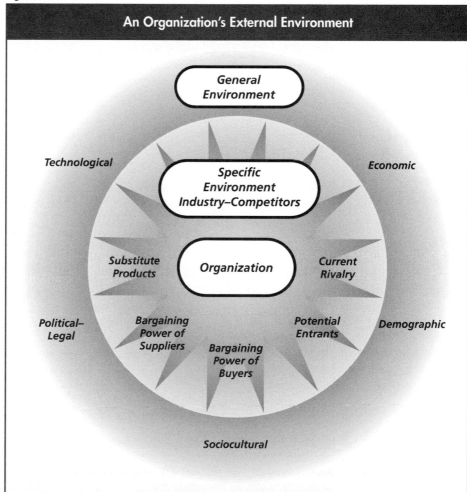

taking place in the general environment may or may not present opportunities and threats for an organization. What does the general environment include? It includes economic, demographic, sociocultural, political–legal, and technological sectors. (See Figure 3-4.) Let's look more closely at each of these environmental sectors. We'll start with the ones that are part of the specific environment.

Specific Environment

The specific environment consists of those external sectors that the organization directly interacts with. In other words, the specific environment includes industry and competitive variables. An **industry** can be defined as a group or groups of organizations producing similar or identical products. These organizations also compete for customers to purchase their products and must secure the necessary resources (or inputs) that are converted (or processed) into products (or outputs). One frequently used approach to assessing an organization's specific environment is the five forces model developed by Michael Porter.[6] (See Figure 3-5.)

Porter is an eminent strategic management scholar, and his work on industry analysis provides one framework for looking at an organization's specific environment. One assumption of his five forces model is that some industries are inherently more attractive than others; that is, the profit potential for companies in

Figure 3-5

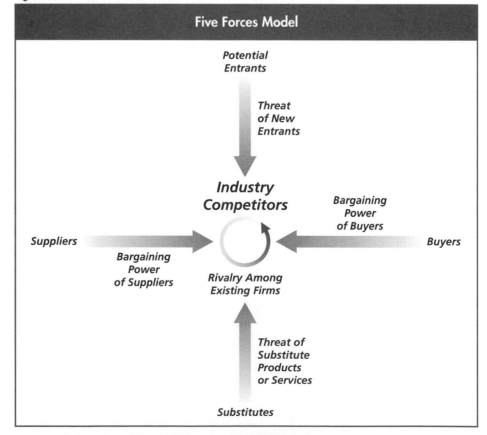

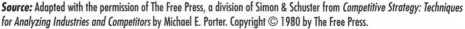

Source: Adapted with the permission of The Free Press, a division of Simon & Schuster from *Competitive Strategy: Techniques for Analyzing Industries and Competitors* by Michael E. Porter. Copyright © 1980 by The Free Press.

that industry is higher. What influences profit potential? The interaction and strength of these five competitive forces influence it. A strategic decision maker can determine the opportunities and threats in the organization's specific environment by evaluating these five forces. How do you know how to evaluate these five forces and whether they represent opportunities or threats? Let's look carefully at each so you'll know what to look for.

Current Rivalry Among Existing Firms. The existing firms in your industry are your organization's current and direct competitors. These include the organizations already in the industry that produce and market products similar to yours. For instance, in the cola soft drink industry, Coke, Pepsi, RC Cola, and Sam's Cola (to name a few) would be existing firms. In this part of the external analysis, we determine the level of rivalry among these current competitors. In other words, how intense is the rivalry? Is it intensely competitive or not? Is it "cut-throat" or "polite"? Are competitors constantly trying to take away customers from each other or do competitors seem to get along with each other? The more intense the rivalry among existing firms, the more that industry profitability, and thus your company's profitability, will suffer.

What affects the level of rivalry? Porter lists eight conditions that contribute to intense rivalry among existing competitors. First, is *numerous or equally balanced competitors.* If an industry has a number of competitors, there's a greater likelihood that some of those firms will think they can take competitive actions and no one will notice, thus keeping the industry in constant competitive turmoil. Or, if competitors are equal in terms of size or resources, they'll constantly be jockeying for position, also creating intense competitive action. The second condition is *slow industry growth.* When industry growth has slowed—in other words, consumer demand for an industry's products has leveled off—the "market share pie" is no longer increasing. For a company to keep growing means it is going to have to steal market share away from its competitors. Thus, conditions are ripe for competitors battling with each other to maintain or increase market share. The level of rivalry will be intense. For example, that's what happened in the heavy-duty truck industry as orders sharply declined for big 18-wheelers. Industry competitors such as Navistar International Corporation, Volvo GM

Strategic Management—The Global Perspective

European auto showrooms are beginning to resemble those in the United States. Consumers are wheeling and dealing to get the best deals on cars. Car manufacturers are offering more equipment on cars for the same price, and sales representatives are encouraged to bargain. Price competition is cutthroat as con- sumers shop around. This change partly reflects the adoption of the euro currency. With cars now priced in euros and in local currencies, customers can identify price differences between countries and buy cars where they're the cheapest. In addition, excess auto making in Europe is holding prices down. All in all, the level of current rivalry is as intense as it's ever been. Which of the eight conditions of current rivalry has contributed to this situation? What are the implications for both domestic and global car manufacturers? For customers?

Source: S. Miller, "Europe's Auto Market Takes On American Look," *Wall Street Journal,* September 13, 1999, p. A33.

Heavy Corporation, and Renault SA's Mack Truck responded by cutting production with the intent of trimming costs to the bone. If that strategy didn't add to profits, the next step would be to attract customers from competitors by offering them a better deal. Next, is the condition of *high fixed or storage costs*. If organizations have high fixed costs, they'll do whatever it takes to operate at capacity and thus spread out those fixed costs over a larger volume. This situation often leads to back-and-forth price-cutting by competitors in order to attract customers, which increases competitive rivalry. Also, if the industry's products are difficult or costly to store, companies will want to sell their products as quickly as possible (keeping inventory at the lowest possible levels) and often resort to price-cutting to do so. In both instances, price cuts by industry competitors keep profits low. The fourth condition that can lead to intense rivalry is *lack of differentiation or switching costs*. If the industry's product (physical good or service) is perceived to be a commodity or like a commodity (i.e., it's not unique in any way), then customers make their purchase decisions largely because of price and service. Both of these forms of competition lead to intense rivalry. For example, you might not think that the casual dining industry would face problems of differentiation. After all, industry competitors such as The Olive Garden, Red Lobster, and Chili's have spent significant dollars creating a theme and re-creating it in numerous locations. However, it's precisely that endless round of building that has created a problem of differentiation. Every format that's proven successful—American, Italian, or Mexican—has been endlessly copied until it's practically impossible to tell the theme restaurants apart. This has created intense competitive rivalry in an attempt to capture consumers' dining-out dollars. Also, if there's no cost (either actual dollars or even the amount of time you'd have to invest to learn about a new product) associated with switching from one competitor's product to another competitor's, then competitive intensity will be high because competitors will be trying to steal customers away from one another. The next condition is *capacity must be added in large increments*. In industries where capacity must be added in large increments in order to be economically feasible, then these capacity additions by competitors can create competitive disruptions. That's because the industry will suffer from continuing bouts of overcapacity, which leads to price-cutting and intense competitive rivalry. Take a look at the cruise line industry. It used to be that a 1,200-passenger boat was considered enormous. Now, new cruise ships can haul and pamper up to 4,400 passengers and new liner capacity is still being added. If passenger growth slows, there's intense competitive pressure to keep these megaliners filled. The sixth condition is *diverse competitors*. When competitors differ in their strategic approaches, philosophies, or circumstances, it's hard to judge how competitors are going to act and react as they compete. This diversity increases the level of rivalry. Next is *high strategic stakes,* which means that industry competitors have strong reasons to want to succeed (e.g., CEO's reputation, large dollar investments, etc.) and will do whatever it takes to do so, even so far as sacrificing short-run profitability. If industry competitors feel this way, then rivalry will be high. The last condition is the existence of *high exit barriers*. Porter defines **exit barriers** as "economic, strategic, and emotional factors that keep companies competing in businesses even though they may be earning low or even negative returns on investment."[7] Examples of exit barriers include highly specialized assets that can't be used in other ways or that have low liquidation value; labor agreements that must be honored; or management's unwillingness to leave a business because of pride, fear, or other psychological reasons. If there are high exit barriers, the company is, in a sense, "stuck" in that industry and thus, may use extreme tactics to compete.

One aspect of current rivalry that we need to clarify is "How do you know who your organization's current competitors are?" Obviously, if an industry includes several firms, you may find that not all of those firms are your actual direct competitors or competitors that you'd be concerned with. One solution to this definition problem is to evaluate only those competitors currently in your organization's strategic group. A **strategic group** is a set of firms competing within an industry that have similar strategies and resources. Strategy researchers have proposed that organizations within a strategic group employ similar strategies and thus compete more directly than other organizations that may also be in the industry.[8] For example, even though Mercedes-Benz and General Motors' Saturn are both in the automobile manufacturing industry, they're not considered direct competitors because they don't use similar strategies, don't have the same customer base, and don't have similar resources. In analyzing the level of current rivalry, it makes sense to look at those organizations whose strategic actions have the most potential to affect your profitability; and that means looking at those competitors in your organization's relevant strategic group.

Potential Entrants. Not only should you be concerned with the opportunities and threats presented by your current competitors, but you also need to be on the lookout for organizations moving into your industry. Why? Because these organizations bring new capacity to the industry, have the desire to gain customers (market share), and perhaps even possess substantial resources that can be used to launch competitive attacks against current competitors. The threat of potential entrants depends on the barriers to entry and the reaction by current

---

Strategic Management in Action

Sports are big business, and technology is poised to make it even bigger. It's hoped that the arrival of interactive media in the sports arena will heighten interest among fans. Whereas existing media—visual and audio—bring the action in living color to fans off the field, the new interactive technologies are even more up close and intense. Now athletes can be outfitted with transmitters embedded in helmets and other game equipment that digitize the game, recording speed, movement, and even the force of collisions. Fans get to experience the action like never before without stepping foot on the field or court. This investment in technology should differentiate the various sports franchises and contribute to continuing growth. After all, with the huge consumer interest in sports, strategic decision makers at sports franchises are looking for any strategies that can help differentiate their product.

Source: K. Tan, "Interactive Technology Boosts Sports Business," *Wall Street Journal,* January 31, 2000, p. B17A.

How Many Competitors Is Enough?

Many industries—global and domestic—are becoming more concentrated and consolidated. For example, the accounting business now has the "big five." The beverages industry has the "big three." Two names dominate the world market for commercial aviation. And, of course, there's been the Big Three in the car industry for a number of years. Why have so many industries found this arrangement of smaller number of bigger players an attractive alternative? There are practical, economic, and psychological reasons. A concentrated industry allows business leaders to retain a degree of competition without giving up too much control. In a monopoly, companies must submit to regulation or risk being broken up. In these oligopolistic situations, government regulators have done little to stop the trend of industry consolidation because of a certain paradox: A high degree of market concentration often promotes competition, whereas fragmented markets often end up costing consumers more. Market leaders need challengers to keep them on their toes. Another benefit of these oligopolistic arrangements is that it's easier to forge common standards, which is particularly helpful during times of rapid technological change. As the external environment of business organizations continues to change, we're likely to see more of these industry arrangements of a few dominant giant companies. Do you think this trend presents opportunities or threats? Explain.

Source: G. P. Zachary, "Let's Play Oligopoly!" *Wall Street Journal,* March 8, 1999, p. B1.

competitors to new entrants. **Barriers to entry** are obstacles to entering an industry. When barriers are high or current competitors can be expected to take significant actions to keep newcomers out, then the threat of entry is low. A low threat of potential entrants is positive for an industry because profitability is not divided up among numerous competitors. What are the major entry barriers? Porter described seven.

1. *Economies of scale.* Economies of scale refers to the cost savings that you get as volume increases. Increasing levels of activity in any of the organization's functions (e.g., production—producing more; marketing—selling more; research and development—innovating more; etc.) can lead to cost savings because the fixed costs are spread out over a larger volume, which drives the cost per unit down. In other words, the more we do something, the more we can bring costs down, but only to a certain level. How do economies of scale keep potential entrants out? These strategic decision makers would think twice because either they'd have to come into the industry operating at a large scale and risk retaliation by current competitors or they'd have to come in at a smaller scale and have a cost disadvantage compared to the others.

2. *Cost disadvantages from other than scale.* Established competitors may enjoy cost advantages that potential entrants can't duplicate even if they can operate at large volume. These include factors such as exclusive or protected product technology; favorable access to raw materials; favorable locations; government subsidies; or human resource advantages because of employees' cumulative level of knowledge, learning, and experience—elements reflected in the organization's learning–experience curve.

3. *Product differentiation.* Current competitors usually have worked hard and spent large sums to establish a specific product identification with customers. If it's strong enough, brand identity sets an organization apart (differentiates it) and leads to loyal customers. To overcome this brand loyalty, potential entrants have to spend heavily on customer research, advertising, packaging, and other marketing activities. This can be a significant hurdle for a new competitor that wants to enter an industry. For example, in the sporting goods industry, there's no better differentiator than Sports Authority Inc., the world's largest retail chain concentrating solely in sporting goods. Its closest rivals include Sportmart and the newest competitor, the online retailer mvp.com. Together, these three competitors have established such strong product differentiation that potential entrants are discouraged from entering the industry.

4. *Capital requirements.* If an organization has to invest significant financial resources in order to compete, this creates a barrier to entry. Potential entrants may think twice about coming into an industry in which high levels of dollars are needed even to be able to compete. That's what happened in the ski industry. As customers demanded better amenities at ski sites—good snow, groomed trails, comfortable but luxurious accommodations—the capital investment required to satisfy these customer demands rose significantly. Unless potential competitors have that kind of money, they're shut out of the industry.

5. *Switching costs.* Are you familiar with and do you consistently use one word processing package? Maybe it's Word or WordPerfect. What keeps you from using another one or ones? For most of us, it's the time and effort we'd have to invest in learning a new set of commands and keyboard shortcuts. That's an example of **switching costs**—the one-time costs facing the buyer who switches from one supplier's product to another's. These costs don't even necessarily have to be dollar costs. They can be psychological costs associated

Strategic Management in Action

The beverage giants (Coke and Pepsi) are at it again. The bottled-water business, long an industry of numerous small regional players, has become the newest battleground for the beverage companies. With the soda business maturing and bottled-water consumption increasing, it's not surprising that Coke and Pepsi want to make a splash in the market. However, they have to cope with the dilemma of getting their water on the shelves without sacrificing space for their cola products. In addition, thousands of small regional water bottlers are vulnerable to the giants' marketing tactics. It's an interesting battle that's shaping up. Analyze this situation using the seven barriers to entry from the perspective of the current competitors *and* from the perspective of the potential entrants.

Source: D. Foust, "Guess Who Wants to Make a Splash in Water," *Business Week,* March 1, 1999, p. 36.

Consider This ◀◀◀

✓ What sectors does the specific environment include? How about the general environment?

✓ What is an industry? How are the organizations in an industry similar? Different?

✓ What is the five forces model and how is it used?

✓ What eight factors determine the current level of competitive rivalry?

✓ What is a strategic group and how does it fit in with the concept of an industry? How does it fit in with the concept of current competitors?

✓ How do current industry competitors attempt to keep out potential entrants? Why would they want to do so?

with change. These switching costs serve as a barrier to entry because the industry's current customers may be reluctant to switch to a new supplier.

6. *Access to distribution channels.* You have a product to sell. You're going to need an outlet or distribution source for that product. If current competitors have already secured the logical distribution sources, a new entrant is going to have to persuade these sources to accept its product. This may mean you have to give the distributor a price break or set up cooperative advertising arrangements, both of which reduce potential profits. Therefore, closing off access to distribution channels can be a barrier to entry.

7. *Government policy.* If the government imposes laws and regulations (such as licensing requirements, controlling access to raw materials, air and water pollution standards, product safety standards, product testing time requirements, etc.), this can create a barrier to entry. Potential entrants would have to meet these requirements, which often can cost a significant amount. For example, that's what happened in the discount mail-order wine industry. Major distributors in Kentucky and Florida fought back against discount wine shops that sold by mail or by wine club subscriptions by asking state lawmakers to enforce laws that forbade wine for sale to enter a state except through officially sanctioned channels or a government liquor authority. The effect is that these laws and regulations set up a barrier to competitors wanting to come into an industry.

Bargaining Power of Buyers. Your buyers are your customers—those individuals or organizations who purchase your products. How can buyers affect industry profitability? If they have a lot of bargaining power, they can force prices down, bargain for higher quality or more services, or they might even play competitors against each other trying to see who will give them the best deal. What makes a buyer powerful? One factor is that the *buyer purchases large volumes of the seller's product.* The implication in this circumstance is that the customer is more important to the seller than the seller is to the customer. This gives that customer a lot of bargaining power. For example, the big two discount retail chains—Wal-Mart and Kmart—can account for up to 50 percent of many manufacturers' revenues. With this much buying power, these discounters can pretty much dictate selling terms. Another factor that influences a buyer's bargaining power is that the *products purchased by the customer represent a significant portion of its costs or purchases.* In this situation, customers are going to be looking for the best price and will shop around. Customers will also have significant bargaining power if *the products they purchase are standard or undifferentiated.* Here again, a customer will likely play one supplier off against another in an attempt to find the best deal. Another factor that gives the buyer greater bargaining power is if the customer *faces few switching costs.* In other words, if there are few switching costs or if switching costs are low, then the customer doesn't feel obligated to stay with the original supplier and can shop around. The buyer may also exert bargaining power if *it earns low profits*. If the customer is earning low profits, it's going to be looking for ways to reduce costs however it can, and that often means reducing its purchasing costs. In this instance, the "customer" is probably a business buying its needed resources although a customer who has limited funds (income) available is also likely to be looking for ways to bargain. Another factor that gives the customer bargaining power over the supplier is when *it has the ability and resources itself to manufacture the products it's purchasing from the industry*. If the customer can make the product it's buying, then it's in a powerful position to ask for concessions from the supplier. For example, some large businesses that purchase large quantities of electric power from local utilities have threatened to take their business elsewhere unless they get lower rates. Many of these businesses can do just that by either building their own generating plants or persuading a local government to form a municipal system to buy electric power at bulk rates. As customers, these large businesses are exerting power. Buyers also have bargaining power if *the industry's product isn't important to the quality of the buyers' products or services*. This means that if the buyer doesn't need the industry's products to get desired quality levels in its products or services, then the buyer has power to bargain with the industry over prices and services offered. On the other hand, if the industry's product *is* important to the quality of the customer's products, then the customer won't have much bargaining power. Last, buyers have bargaining power if *they have full information* about product demand, actual market prices, and supplier costs. This type of information gives the customer good ammunition to get the best possible prices from suppliers. The Internet has played a significant role in customers' access to information. Think, for example, of the car industry in which buyers can compare prices and features and bargain for the best deal.

Bargaining Power of Suppliers. If your industry's suppliers have bargaining power, they can raise prices or reduce the quality of products that your industry purchases. An industry's suppliers include any of the providers of resources or inputs: raw materials sources, equipment manufacturers, financial institutions, and even labor sources. How can you tell whether your industry's suppliers are powerful? One characteristic to look for is *domination by a few companies and more concentration than the industry*. If suppliers are few in number and are selling to a fragmented industry (i.e., the industry has a lot of small and not very powerful companies in it), then the suppliers will usually be able to exert considerable influence over prices, quality, and sales terms. Another characteristic to look for is *whether there are any substitute products*. If the supplier has to compete with possible substitutes, then it doesn't have a lot of bargaining power over

The Grey Zone

How much power do buyers really have? In the digital economy, practically any product labeled as "digital" sells. Digital marketers are labeling products digital whether they really are or not. Although the term *digital* actually means anything represented by discrete numerical values instead of approximations, it has become an all-purpose adjective for any product that wants to appear high tech. Movie theaters still using old-fashioned reel-to-reel film proclaim themselves as digital when they have an expensive sound system. Toasters that use a microprocessor to time browning are labeled digital and sell for twice the price of old-fashioned analog toasters. Is it ethical to call a product digital that really doesn't fit the scientific definition of digital just to get a premium price? Some digital experts say that it's okay because the usage just reaffirms the importance of being digital. What do you think?

the industry. But, if there aren't any good substitutes, then the supplier can exert more power over the industry. Suppliers can also exert power when *the industry is not an important customer.* If your industry is just one of many that the supplier sells to, then it could care less whether it keeps you as a customer and is more likely to exert bargaining power. On the other hand, if your industry is an important customer, the supplier will want to protect that relationship and won't try to exert bargaining power. Another characteristic to evaluate is whether *the supplier's product is an important input to the industry.* If it is, then the supplier will have more bargaining power. For example, suppliers of silicon wafers have significant power over the semiconductor industry. Even though silicon is one of the most abundant elements on earth, shortfalls in the availability of silicon wafers affects the ability of chip makers to satisfy demand for their product. This situation gives suppliers a lot of power over computer chip manufacturers. Also, it's important to know whether *the supplier's products are differentiated or if there are customer switching costs.* If the supplier's products are differentiated or if your industry would experience switching costs, then the supplier is going to be able to exert more power. For example, Department 56 is a well-known manufacturer of miniature ceramic and porcelain buildings used in Christmas decorating. Many of its pieces sell for $50 or more when first issued, but sometimes sell for thousands of dollars after they're no longer available at retail. The company keeps its differentiation strong by eliminating several pieces every year and destroying the molds. When it discovered that some of its dealers (retailers) were discounting the collectibles (a move that Department 56 felt cheapened its image), it terminated their distribution rights as a violation of policy. As a supplier, Department 56 was exerting significant power over the retailers. The final characteristic for determin-

Strategic Management in Action

Strategic decision makers at Kmart weren't too concerned when Tyco International Ltd. bought a company that makes plastic hangers it uses to display clothing. However, when Tyco bought two more hanger companies, their level of concern began to increase. Worried that Tyco was trying to corner the market on plastic hangers, Kmart began buying from one of the remaining independent suppliers. However, that hanger company was soon acquired by Tyco as well. Now, Kmart has little choice but to accept price increases for most of its supply of plastic hangers. Executives at Tyco defend their actions by saying that its strategy is to bring leadership to fragmented, inefficient industries. However, in at least a few of the industries that Tyco dominates, it profits by getting unusually large market shares, then uses its dominance to raise prices or demand concessions from customers. How does this situation illustrate the bargaining power of suppliers?

Source: M. Maremont, "Lion's Share," *Wall Street Journal,* February 15, 2000, p. A1.

ing supplier power is *the supplier's ability to provide the products that the industry is currently providing.* If the supplier can do what the industry does (i.e., produce or market the industry's products) and do it better or cheaper, then this gives the supplier more bargaining power. In other words, if the industry doesn't agree to the supplier's terms and conditions, the supplier could start doing what the industry does and attempt to put it out of business.

Substitute Products. The last of the five industry forces we need to discuss is the threat of substitute products. The best way to evaluate the threat of substitute products is to ask whether other industries can satisfy the consumer need that our industry is satisfying. For example, take a customer's need for something to drink—that is, a "thirst" need. If your company is in the cola soft drink industry, substitute products could come from other industries such as fruit drinks, alcoholic beverages, milk and milk-based products, and even mineral water. Any of these industries could fill the customer's need for something to drink. (Other companies in the cola industry would be your current competitors and would be evaluated as you look at current rivalry.) If there aren't many good substitutes for your industry's product, then this threat isn't very high. However, if there are a few good substitutes or even several not-so-good substitutes for your product, then this isn't favorable for your industry's profitability. Another good example to illustrate the threat of substitutes would be what's happened as Internet and World Wide Web usage has significantly increased. Three different industries (software companies such as Microsoft, online service providers such as AOL, and telecommunications companies such as AT&T) battled for customers' hearts and pocketbooks as the way to get online. For any of these three industries, the substitutes were good and thus posed significant threats.

By now, you should have a firm grasp of what you need to examine as you look at an organization's specific environment. Porter's five forces model provides one framework for determining the opportunities and threats of the industry and competitive environment. In Table 3-2, you'll find a quick summary of the five forces and what you need to look at as you determine whether the specific industry–competitive environment is favorable or unfavorable.

General Environment

Remember that the general environment includes those external sectors that indirectly influence an organization. These sectors include trends or changing circumstances that could have a potential positive impact on the organization (opportunity) or a potential negative impact (threat). However, not everything that happens in these sectors is going to be an opportunity or threat. Many changes take place that won't affect the organization one way or the other. We'll be looking at the five main general environment sectors: economic, demographic, sociocultural, political–legal, and technological.

Economic. The economic sector encompasses all the macroeconomic data, current statistics, trends, and changes that reflect what's happening with the economy. It doesn't include the economic statistics of an organization's industry. For

Consider This ◀◀|

✓ What makes buyers powerful?

✓ Why should an industry's competitors be concerned with how much bargaining power customers have?

✓ What makes suppliers powerful?

✓ Why should an industry's competitors be concerned with how much bargaining power suppliers have?

✓ What determines whether substitutes present a threat?

✓ Why should an industry's competitors be concerned with substitute products?

Table 3-2   Evaluating the Five Forces

Industry–Competitive Force	Threat	Opportunity
Current Rivalry		
Numerous competitors	✓	
Few competitors		✓
Equally balanced competitors	✓	
One or a few strong competitors		✓
Industry sales growth slowing	✓	
Industry sales growth strong		✓
High fixed or inventory storage costs	✓	
Low fixed or inventory storage costs		✓
No differentiation or no switching costs	✓	
Significant differentiation or significant switching costs		✓
Large capacity increments required	✓	
Minimal capacity increments required		✓
Diverse competitors	✓	
Similar competitors		✓
High strategic stakes	✓	
Low strategic stakes		✓
High exit barriers	✓	
Minimal exit barriers		✓
Potential Entrants		
Significant economies of scale		✓
No or low economies of scale	✓	
Cost disadvantages from other aspects		✓
No other potential cost disadvantages	✓	
Strong product differentiation		✓
Weak product differentiation	✓	
Huge capital requirements		✓
Minimal capital requirements	✓	
Significant switching costs		✓
Minimal switching costs	✓	
Controlled access to distribution channels		✓
Open access to distribution channels	✓	
Government policy protection		✓
No government policy protection	✓	

Table 3-2   Evaluating the Five Forces *(continued)*

Industry–Competitive Force	Threat	Opportunity
Bargaining Power of Buyers		
Buyer purchases large volumes	✓	
Buyer purchases small volumes		✓
Products purchased are significant part of buyer's costs	✓	
Products purchased aren't significant part of buyer's costs		✓
Products purchased are standard or undifferentiated	✓	
Products purchased are highly differentiated and unique		✓
Buyer faces few switching costs	✓	
Buyer faces significant switching costs		✓
Buyer's profits are low	✓	
Buyer's profits are strong		✓
Buyer has ability to manufacture products being purchased	✓	
Buyer doesn't have ability to manufacture products		✓
Industry's products aren't important to quality of buyer's products	✓	
Industry's products are important to quality of buyer's products		✓
Buyers have full information	✓	
Buyers have limited information		✓
Bargaining Power of Suppliers		
Supplying industry has few companies and is more concentrated	✓	
Supplying industry has many companies and is fragmented		✓
There are no substitute products for supplier's products	✓	
There are substitute products for supplier's products		✓
Industry being supplied is not an important customer	✓	
Industry being supplied is an important customer		✓
Supplier's product is an important input to industry	✓	
Supplier's product is not an important input to industry		✓
Supplier's products are differentiated	✓	
Supplier's products aren't differentiated		✓
There are significant switching costs in supplier's products	✓	
There are minimal switching costs in supplier's products		✓
Supplier has ability to do what buying industry does	✓	
Supplier doesn't have ability to do what buying industry does		✓
Substitute Products		
There are few good substitutes	✓	
There are several not-so-good substitutes	✓	
There are no good substitutes		✓

example, industry sales forecasts and trends aren't part of the general economic sector. However, you *would* look at those statistics in evaluating the industry and competitive environment. So, what *does* the economic sector include? The major economic information that might be important (i.e., it can be positive or negative for your organization) includes interest rates; exchange rates and the value of the dollar; budget deficit–surplus; trade deficit–surplus; inflation rates; gross national product (GNP) or gross domestic product (GDP) levels and resulting stage of the economic cycle; consumer income, spending, and debt levels; employment–unemployment levels; and workforce productivity. What you're looking at as you examine these economic statistics is the current information as well as the forecasted trends. You need to determine what impact, if any, these trends and changes will have for your organization. For example, are rising interest rates good or bad for your organization—in other words, are they opportunities or threats? If the economy is growing moderately, what does this mean for your organization? What if the dollar falls in value against the Japanese yen or against the euro? Are the implications good or bad? What if workforce productivity has leveled off and is predicted to stay stagnant? What does this mean? Take consumer debt levels. Think for a minute about what industries would be affected positively by increases in consumer debt levels. How about industries that might suffer? You need to ask these types of questions as you evaluate the economic sector for opportunities and threats. And, keep in mind, that industries (and thus the organizations in those industries) will be affected differently by these economic trends and changes. For example, declining interest rates tend to have a favorable impact on the construction industry but are less favorable for the bank card industry. Also, keep in mind that every organization in an industry faces the same economic trends and changes. That is, the inflation rate doesn't change just because your organization is McDonald's, as opposed to Wendy's. So the ultimate performance of an organization is determined by how it responds to the various economic opportunities and threats—that is, by the strategies decision makers develop. This is also true for the rest of the general environmental sectors we'll look at.

What if your organization has operations in more than one country? How would this change the type of economic analysis you have to do? Fortunately, it wouldn't change all that much. The only additional challenge you might face is finding convenient and reliable sources of statistics. However, all the industrialized and an increasing number of semi-industrialized countries collect economic data. The United Nations also collects a variety of economic information about countries. You can find information on GNP (or maybe the term *gross domestic product, GDP*, is used) that provides clues to the stage of the economic cycle and whether the country's economy is growing or contracting. You can also find information on exchange rates, trade figures, interest rates, and inflation rates. Out of these, probably the most important economic information you would want about another country would include inflation rates, interest rates, currency exchange rates, and consumer income–spending–debt levels. Because these tend to be the most volatile economic factors, upward and downward trends and changes in these figures can significantly affect strategic decisions.

Demographics. In this general environmental sector, you'll want to look at current statistical data and trends in population characteristics. The demographic sector includes the kind of information that the U.S. Census Bureau gathers: gen-

Strategic Management—The Global Perspective

The euro is the common currency for 11 of the European nations in the European Union. Although many industries will be impacted by the introduction of the euro coins and bills in January 2002, the vending machine industry is facing particularly difficult challenges. Just as in the United States, these European vending machines dispense everything from soda to cigarettes to candy. As the switchover date approaches, companies that operate vending machines will have to invest significant resources in reconfiguring their machines to accept euro coins. Then, there's the problem of what to do until the switchover is complete. Vendors don't want their machines down for too long a period of time, but they can't wait too long to make the switch. It's an interesting external dilemma requiring close attention by strategic decision makers to the economic implications.

Source: J. Tagliabue, "Vending Machines Face an Upheaval of Change," *New York Times,* February 16, 1999, p. C4.

der; age; income levels; ethnic makeup; education; family composition; geographic location; birthrates; employment status; and so forth. The data that the Census Bureau collects are used by many different types of organizations—government as well as business—in making strategic decisions. As you look at population statistics, what trends do you see in these categories that might affect your organization positively or negatively? For example, census data showed that the U.S. population of kids under age five had increased almost 20 percent since 1980, and the number of children enrolled in elementary and high school in 1999 hit a record high. What strategic implications might these types of population changes have for different organizations?

You might find it's also important to examine the interaction of these variables. For instance, which age group has the fastest-growing incomes? Or, in what geographic locations is there a greater concentration of senior citizens? Or, what is the average level of education of Asian Americans? In fact, one particular population group (another term for this is population *cohort*) that you've probably heard a lot about is the baby boomers. This group typically includes individuals who were born between the years 1946 and 1964. You hear so much about the baby boomers because there are so many of them. Through every life stage they've entered (going to elementary school, teenage years, climbing the career ladder, and now the middle-age years), they've had an enormous impact because of their sheer numbers. Although some experts believe that segmenting markets by age is inappropriate, others says it's a good clue to consumer attitudes and behavior. Some other age cohorts besides boomers that have been identified include the Depression group (born 1912–1921); the World War II group (born 1922–1927); the Postwar group (born 1928–1945); the Generation X or "zoomers" group (born 1965–1977); and Generation Y or baby-boomlet generation (born 1978–1994). This last group is predicted to be as large as, if not larger than, its boomer parents and might prove to be sources of significant demographic opportunities and threats. (One of the Strategic Management in Action cases at the end of this chapter deals with Generation Y implications.)

Demographic data can show you these types of population changes and trends. As you can probably guess, this type of information is useful for under-

> ### Strategic Management in Action ▸
>
> The nation's fast-growing Hispanic population is attracting major American corporations. Visa USA chose to go mainstream with Latin-culture commercials, specifically intended to reach people in the 18- to 34-year-old range. The advertising agency in charge of creating the ads said that ". . . Latin culture used to be for Latinos, but not anymore. Latin culture has become hip." When an advertiser the size of Visa USA follows a trend, it usually signals significant interest and acceptance among the audience it's aiming at. There's no doubt that the demographics of the Latin market are attracting the attention of consumer marketers.
>
> *Source:* P. Winters Lauro, "Visa's Latin-Tinged Mainstream Spot May Anticipate a Trend," *New York Times,* August 20, 1999, p. C4.

standing your current customer base and for targeting other potential customers. By examining the current and forecasted demographic trends, you can identify positive and negative shifts that you either try to take advantage of or stay away from (i.e., potential opportunities or threats). Some demographic trends in the United States that experts have recognized include the country's population will be growing at a decreasing rate as the large group of aging baby boomers start dying off faster than the rate babies are born; Hispanics and Asians will be the fastest-growing minority groups; the number of individuals age 50 and older will increase by 50 percent between now and 2006; and the states with the largest projected net increase in immigrants will include California, New York, Florida, New Jersey, Illinois, Texas, Massachusetts, Virginia, Maryland, and Pennsylvania.[9] Take a minute to think about the industries that might be impacted, positively and negatively, by these demographic trends.

Again, what if your organization is currently operating in other countries or is looking to expand globally? How does the need for demographic information change? Obviously, it's going to be important for your organization to have as much demographic information as possible about the global locations you're currently in or thinking about entering. The need for having information about current or potential target customers doesn't change! All industrialized and most of the larger semi-industrialized countries collect census information. Also, the United Nations collects a considerable amount of demographic-type information. However, be aware that in some of the semi-industrialized countries, the collection and statistical analysis of the information might not be as thorough or reliable as census information from the more advanced nations.

Sociocultural. There's more to understanding your current and potential customers than just their physical (demographic) characteristics. You'd also want to know what's going on culturally in your country. In other words, what's your country's culture like and is it changing? What are society's traditions, values, attitudes, beliefs, tastes, patterns of behavior, and how are these changing? The sociocultural sector encompasses these aspects. These elements aren't quite as obvious and as easy to determine as the demographic information. Anytime you're measuring and interpreting people's opinions, values, attitudes, or likes–dislikes, there's more of a challenge associated with getting the information you need. However, the fact remains that it's important for strategic decision makers to recognize both the current status and the trends in these types of information. For example, how would you interpret the results of a *Wall Street Journal* poll that showed 59 percent of the 2,001 respondents described their lives as busy and 19 percent said their lives were busy to the point of discomfort? What types of strategic implications (potential opportunities and threats) might this information have? How can you determine what's happening in the sociocultural sector? Look at the values and attitudes being expressed by people. For instance, we can identify some of the basic values that characterize the U.S. culture such as individual freedom, the work ethic, and equality of opportunity. These values influence people's behavior in the way they shop, work, raise their families, and otherwise live their lives. People's attitudes also influence their behavior. For example, male shoppers have traditionally relied on catalogs for purchasing hobby, electronic, and automotive items, but not clothing. However, catalog companies are now finding that men have tired of mall shopping and are more willing to use Internet and mail-order shopping. This change in attitude would be an opportunity for some industries and a threat for others. Some of the more noticeable attitudinal changes over the last few years (and, please note that this is by no means an exhaustive list of every relevant social change) would include the increasing fear of crime and violence; more acceptance of gambling and gaming activities; more emphasis on religion and spiritual activities, particularly by baby boomers; and increasing use of technology in schools, homes, and workplaces.

In evaluating this sector, you'd also want to look for changes or trends in people's activities, behavior, and purchases. For example, look at how The Gap responded to customers' changing attitudes about clothing purchases. Overall, people were spending fewer dollars on clothes—a potentially serious problem for

Strategic Management in Action

The sporting goods industry is going through an interesting metamorphosis. Long dominated by traditional sports companies such as Nike and Rawlings, the industry is being changed by dozens of smaller companies whose products are aimed at extreme sports enthusiasts—players who value risk taking and pushing themselves to the limits. Many of these small companies credit their recent success to the X Games, the ESPN competition that features everything from skateboarding to sky surfing to street luge. In addition, NBC network has its Gravity Games and even the venerable Olympics now allows snowboarding, thus giving more legitimacy to these extreme sports. What sociocultural trends do you see here? What are the strategic implications for different companies in this industry?

Source: "Sports Sales Get Extreme," *Springfield News Leader,* February 12, 2000, p. 7A.

a clothing retailer—and The Gap's strategic decision makers looked for strategies to reverse this trend. The strategy the managers finally settled on was to convert some of its retail stores into pared-down, no-frills outlets. After playing around with different store names, managers decided they liked the image conveyed by the name Old Navy. At Old Navy stores, consumers get low prices, quality merchandise, and a fun place to shop. The Gap managers recognized this sociocultural trend, evaluated how they could combat it, and developed this retailing format. Another example of sociocultural trends would be the increasing trend toward healthy eating and living. In fact, managers at food companies often look to what's "hot" out on the U.S. West Coast or East Coast for the latest food trends. Another sociocultural trend that many organizations have recognized and changed marketing strategies to take advantage of, is the increasingly diverse population and the different behaviors, attitudes, and values expressed by these diverse groups. In this sector, then, you're looking for those cultural and behavioral trends and changes that present potential opportunities and threats.

How does the importance of this sector change if you're in different global locations? It doesn't. You're obviously going to want this type of information for those geographic areas, also. However, getting and interpreting this information for different global locations isn't as easy as getting economic and demographic information. That's because there's no standard governmental collection of this type of information. You should keep in mind that each country has its own distinctive culture—its own generally accepted traditions, values, attitudes, beliefs, tastes, and patterns of behavior. Your challenge, then, is to understand each country's culture. In addition to knowing the current status of these elements, you'd also want to try to uncover any trends or changes—again, so you can determine potential opportunities and threats. For example, how would European consumers' increased willingness to use credit cards affect an organization's strategies? What implications might such a trend have for different industries?

Political–Legal. In this general environmental sector, you'll be looking at the various laws, regulations, judicial decisions, and political forces that are currently in effect at the federal, state, and local levels of government. It might also include regulations enacted by professional associations (such as FASB—the Financial

---

STRATEGIC MANAGEMENT IN AN E-BUSINESS WORLD

Taxes. The Internet. The two realities are worlds apart now. Yet, it's a challenging political issue that's going to have to be resolved. Proponents of taxing Internet sales include most state governments and old-fashioned bricks-and-mortar retailers. Opponents of taxing Internet sales include e-tailers and most consumers who purchase on the Internet. It's an interesting debate. Research the issue and come up with a bulleted list of arguments supporting both sides. Be prepared to take one side and debate it in class. Be sure to look at how organizational strategies might have to change if Internet sales are taxed and if they're not.

Sources: H. Gleckman, "The Great Internet Tax Debate," *Business Week,* March 27, 2000, pp. 228–36; Advisory Commission on Electronic Commerce (**www.ecommercecommission.org**), "Internet Taxes Not Likely Any Time Soon," *Springfield News Leader,* March 19, 2000, p. 12B; and D. C. Johnston, "Retailers and Governors Attack Proposal to Make the Internet a Tax-Free Zone," *New York Times,* December 16, 1999, p. C2.

Accounting Standards Board). Some of the more significant federal laws and regulations for businesses and other types of organizations are shown in Table 3-3. You'd also want to keep track of any potential legal, regulatory, and political changes, or pending judicial decisions that might take place and could impact your organization. For example, the Occupational Safety and Health Administration (OSHA) has been working to establish ergonomic (jobs and tools designed to fit the physical and psychological limits of workers) guidelines for workplaces including home offices. Although such guidelines haven't been put into effect yet, what impact might such potential guidelines have on different

---

TABLE 3-3   Examples of Significant Legislation Affecting Organizations

Occupational Safety and Health Act of 1970

Requires employers to provide a working environment free from hazards to health.

Consumer Product Safety Act of 1972

Sets standards on selected products, requires warning labels, and orders product recalls.

Equal Employment Opportunity Act of 1972

Forbids discrimination in all areas of employer–employee relations.

Worker Adjustment and Retraining Notification Act of 1988

Requires employers with 100 or more employees to provide 60 days' notice before a facility closing or mass layoff.

Americans with Disabilities Act of 1990

Prohibits employers from discriminating against individuals with physical or mental disabilities or the chronically ill; also requires organizations to reasonably accommodate these individuals.

Civil Rights Act of 1991

Reaffirms and tightens prohibition of discrimination; permits individuals to sue for punitive damages in cases of intentional discrimination.

Family and Medical Leave Act of 1993

Grants 12 weeks of unpaid leave each year to employees for the birth or adoption of a child or the care of a spouse, child, or parent with a serious health condition; covers organizations with 50 or more employees.

North American Free Trade Agreement of 1993

Creates a free trade zone between the United States, Canada, and Mexico.

General Agreement on Tariffs and Trade (GATT) of 1994

Provides for the lowering of tariffs globally by roughly 40%, extending intellectual property protection worldwide, and tightening rules on investment and trade in services.

U.S. Economic Espionage Act of 1996

Makes theft or misappropriation of trade secrets a federal crime.

industries? What industries would benefit (i.e., be an opportunity)? Which ones might suffer (i.e., be a threat)? Also, a country's political–legal climate can affect the attitudes toward business and how much regulation an industry faces. For instance, during the late 1970s and the 1980s, many U.S. industries were deregulated—airlines, trucking, phone service, and banking being the major ones. Deregulation removed a number of operating constraints and created both opportunities and threats for organizations in these specific industries and other related industries. For instance, as part of this governmental deregulation effort, the 108-year-old Interstate Commerce Commission was disbanded as of December 31, 1995. In its place now is a much smaller government agency, the Surface Transportation Board (STB), which retains some regulatory power over railroads and other transportation industries. This change obviously had different implications for railroads, trucking companies, and bus lines. Other major aspects of the political–legal sector are taxation and minimum wage laws. Obviously, the prevailing laws governing these two aspects can have a significant impact on an organization's financial performance. However, it's not only the federal laws and regulations you have to be aware of. Many states have laws and regulations that present opportunities and threats as well. For example, as people's attitudes toward gambling and gaming have softened, more and more states have created state-run lotteries and allowed riverboat casinos and other forms of gaming activities to operate. Also, all the U.S. states have income tax laws or sales tax laws or both that can be sources of opportunities and threats for organizations. Likewise, if they're applicable or could have a significant impact on your organization, you should be aware of any laws, regulations, or political–legal actions at the local governmental level.

Obviously, if your organization is operating in another country, you'd want to know the relevant laws and regulations and abide by them. In addition, you'd want to stay on top of any political changes as far as who or what political party is in power and the likelihood that new laws and regulations might be enacted. Although political stability is a given in many countries, the political situation is still volatile and unstable in some countries. You should watch these trends as well. Another significant change in the global environment is the various trade alliances among countries. These alliances—NAFTA, the European Union, and ASEAN are the three largest ones—are easing many of the political and economic restrictions on trade and creating numerous opportunities and threats. These types of global political changes are sources of global political–legal opportunities and threats.

Technological. The last general environmental sector you'll want to analyze concerns technological trends and changes. Within the technological sector, you'd look for scientific or technological improvements, advancements, and innovations that create opportunities and threats for your organization. For example, communications companies are using the latest technology to explore the untapped portions of the radio spectrum and are moving into such applications as car crash–avoidance radar or using infrared to send data over short lines of sight. Obviously, as technology advances, these types of applications will become commonplace. An even more routine application of technology can be seen in the ways that companies advertise their products. It's common now to see computerized information kiosks and Internet multimedia pages extol the virtues of products. The two organizational areas impacted most by technological innovations concern the

Strategic Management in Action

Starbucks Corporation is using advances in technology to help it design a paper coffee cup that eliminates the need for "double-cupping" or putting a corrugated sleeve around the coffee container. Research over a three-year period has resulted in a cup featuring a novel design that keeps coffee hot, meets customers' requests for less packaging, *and* protects hands from the heat. Although the new cup is believed to be more costly to produce than the standard Starbucks coffee cup, it went ahead with the technological research and development. What trends in what general external sectors do you think led Starbucks to pursue this strategy?

Source: R. Gibson, "Starbucks Plans to Test a Paper Cup That Insulates Hands from Hot Coffee," *Wall Street Journal,* March 22, 1999, p. B17.

product and process. In other words, how will technological advancements affect (positively or negatively) your organization's product(s)? Likewise, how will technological advancements affect the way you produce your products (the process)?

Probably the biggest technological advancement over the last few years that's affected the process has been the continuing computerization of an organization's activities. For example, retailers have direct computer links to suppliers who replenish inventory as needed. Manufacturers have flexible manufacturing systems that allow them to mass customize products (no, this isn't an oxymoron). Airlines have Web pages whereby customers can arrange flight times, destinations, and fares. Most organizational employees communicate by e-mail. In addition, continuing innovations in different scientific and engineering fields such as lasers, robotics, biotechnology, food additives, medicine, consumer electronics, and telecommunications provide numerous opportunities and threats for many different industries. However, keep in mind that the impact of these technological innovations is different for different industries. Some of these improvements may not offer opportunities or threats to your organization, whereas others are significant. For instance, how will technological innovations such as smart cards, 3-D computing, and satellite imaging affect different industries? Some other interesting technological trends that have been predicted to change your life include genetics-based medicines, personalized computers, multifuel automobiles, high-definition TV, home health monitors, smart maps and tracking devices, smart materials, and weight-control and anti-aging products. You'll need to uncover these types of technological changes and trends as you do your external analysis.

How would your analysis of the technological sector differ if your organization were operating globally? Obviously, the technological advancement of a country is going to affect your assessment. Some countries don't have the needed infrastructure to support or to take advantage of available technology. The phone system or telecommunications system may be unreliable or dated. Or, the power (electricity) generation system may be insufficient to support the technological requirements. The country's highway system may be in poor shape or not be conveniently located. Many variables affect whether a given technology will prove to be an opportunity or threat to your organization in another global location. For example, what would appear to be a dream market—personal computers for China's billion-plus population—has been a nightmare for computer companies. Why? Because the Chinese language would require a keyboard the size of a kitchen table. The challenge for computer companies has been to figure out strategies to deal with this technological barrier. As this example illustrates, however, it's important for you to assess the potential technological opportunities and threats that face your organization in another country.

Consider This ◀◀|

✓ What are the five components of the general environment?

✓ What are some types of economic information that you might need to consider?

✓ What does the demographics sector include?

✓ What types of information are you looking at in the sociocultural sector?

✓ Describe what the political–legal sector includes.

✓ What should you look for as you examine the technological sector?

✓ How would you analyze global general environmental sectors?

Finding Information on the External Environment and Evaluating It

Now that you know what external sectors to look at, how do you know what to look for and where to find information on these sectors? Let's first discuss what to look for. You should be looking for specific data, statistics, analyses, trends, predictions, forecasts, inferences or statements made by experts, or other types of evidence of what's happening or predicted to happen in those sectors. You will then need to evaluate whether this specific information is good or bad for your organization. Will it help your organization improve its performance currently or in the future, or will it hinder its performance? In other words, does the current external state of affairs present opportunities or threats to your organization? How about the changes or trends? These bits and pieces of information about the external environment are used by decision makers as they evaluate current strategies and design future strategies.

The approach to finding external information can range all the way from informal, unscientific observations to a formal, systematic search. For many decision makers, it's enough to talk to customers, read industry trade journals or general newsmagazines, or talk with suppliers' sales representatives. These informal, unscientific information-gathering activities often can provide sufficient clues to the changes or trends taking place in certain sectors of the external environment, and strategic decision makers can make effective strategic decisions based on this limited information. However, a thorough and comprehensive external analysis requires more of a systematic, deliberate search. In fact, having some type of formal external information system is the key to identifying specific opportunities and threats. An **external information system (EIS)** is an information system that provides managers with needed external information on a regular basis. Again, keep in mind that the whole purpose of the external analysis is to identify potential trends and changes that could positively or negatively impact your organization's performance. How often is a "regular" basis—in other words, how often do decision makers need information about external sectors? It all relates back to how complex and dynamic your organization's environment is. The more complex and dynamic the environment (i.e., the more environmental uncertainty there is), the more often you'd want information about what's occurring. For some organiza-

Spotting Trends

Spotting trends can be a good skill for strategic decision makers to have, and there's no more difficult age group to attempt to pin down as far as what they're thinking than teenagers! They may be fickle and unpredictable, but they're an enormous and attractive market for marketers because they control significant purchasing power (estimated between $140 billion and $150 billion a year and growing at a 6 percent annual rate). For companies that market products to teens, however, spotting trends is a real art *and* science. How do they do it? One thing they've discovered is that **focus groups** (a marketing research approach in which an informal group of people, with the help of a moderator, discusses a product or service and other marketing issues) don't work with teens. In group settings, teens tend to clam up, joke around, or harass the moderator. Also, ask-

ing teens direct questions about their likes and dislikes typically results in useless information. But what does work are tactics such as arming teens with disposable cameras and asking them to shoot pictures of things in their lives or asking them to complete drawings with the instructions "This is a snapshot of you. Tell us more about you—what you like, wear, listen to, read, say!" Another approach is having teens match a list of products (restaurants, clothes, etc.) with the celebrities they think are likely to be using the products. These approaches to finding information can provide strategic decision makers with significant insights into what elusive teenage minds are thinking.

Sources: "Kids' Purchasing Power," *Springfield News Leader,* March 5, 2000, p. 11B; M. J. McCarthy, "Stalking the Elusive Teenage Trendsetter," *Wall Street Journal,* November 19, 1998, p. B1; and L. Bannon, "Little Big Spenders," *Wall Street Journal,* October 13, 1998, p. A1.

tions in highly complex and very dynamic industries, this might be as often as once a month. For others, gathering and assessing external information twice a year would be enough. In some situations, once a year might be often enough to provide needed external information. No matter how uncertain the external environment is, if decision makers find that their current strategies aren't working (getting desired results), they're going to do something about them. As you know from the strategic management in action model, one of the steps in formulating appropriate strategies is determining opportunities and threats by doing an external analysis. A key concern now is where to find information on the various external sectors. Let's do some exploring!

Doing an external analysis isn't as difficult as it may sound. You may feel that you're going to have to spend hours and hours locating and interpreting information. Actually, you're going to find that the problem isn't that there's *not enough* information. The problem is that there's *too much* information. What you have to do, then, is approach it systematically. For each of the external sectors, ask yourself what specific information you think you should know, keeping in mind that industries differ in terms of the potential impact of these external trends. For example, in the economic sector, you may decide that interest rate levels will have a significant impact on your industry, so you'd want to find out current and forecasted interest rates. If your target customers are teenage girls, you'd probably want to know the population trends for this particular age group. Study each of the external sectors carefully, and identify what information you'll want in order to make intelligent strategic decisions. As a strategic decision maker, you'll come to recognize what external information is truly important to your strategic decisions, and that's what you'll want to concentrate your external analysis on. Rather than describing each and every source of information for the various external sectors (the list would constantly change and could potentially go on and on), you'll find in Table 3-4 a list of some useful information sources on each of the external sectors. Although most of these sources can be found in any library, you may want to try a high-tech alternative. Yes, you can find a lot of information online. Some of these sources are listed, as well.

Responsibilities for External Analysis at Different Managerial Levels

Obviously, the size of your organization is going to determine the number of management levels. In small and even some medium-size organizations, there may be only one or two levels. If your organization is like this, then it's important that all employees be encouraged to monitor changes in the specific (industry–competitive) environment. In fact, in many smaller organizations, front-line employees often have the most direct interactions with customers and supplier representatives. Depending on the particular situation, they may even have some contact with competitors. These employees on the "firing line" often hear comments or statements from these people outside the organization. They should know (having been educated about the importance of knowing what's happening in the organization's external environment) that this type of information can be important to strategic decision making. If any of the comments that they hear appear important or possibly indicate changing circumstances, they should share that information with managers. The managers can then determine if the situation warrants further study and possible strategy changes. In addition, if your organization is large enough to have functional area managers, they should be responsible for monitoring any trends or changes in their particular areas that could be potential opportunities or threats. Also, there should be someone in the organization (the owner–general manager or someone else) who monitors changes in the general environmental sectors. In effect, then, all of the external environmental sectors are monitored and evaluated even in smaller organizations.

In large organizations, it's not possible to do a simple, single external analysis. There are too many organizational levels and too many variables. However, this doesn't mean you just forget about doing one. Rather, it becomes even more important to involve all levels in monitoring information and making this information available for strategic decision making. For example, at Hallmark, the large greeting card company, employees noticed that customers were taking regular greeting cards and turning them into cards for their pets. To satisfy this obvious customer demand, they came up with a whole line of pet greeting cards. If these employees hadn't recognized this trend and acted on it, Hallmark might not have developed its unique and successful line of pet greeting cards and gifts. Just like smaller-size organizations, managers at lower (supervisory) levels in large organizations should encourage workers to listen to what customers are saying (compliments or complaints) or to what suppliers' sales representatives are saying. For instance, customer service employees often are an important source of information about external trends in the customer sector. This type of information about the specific environment can point out the need to change strategies, particularly at functional levels. Middle managers should coordinate any external

TABLE 3-4   Selected Sources of External Information

Industry–Competitors

Reports published by industry trade associations

Industry outlooks presented in various business periodicals *(Business Week, Fortune, Forbes, Wall Street Journal)*

Standard & Poor's Industry Surveys: Trends and Projections

Survey of Current Business

Census of Manufacturers

U.S. Industrial Outlook

Predicasts Basebook and Predicasts Forecasts

Moody's Manuals

Market Share Reporter

Encyclopedia of Business Information Sources

Various industry sourcebooks and industry-specific publications

Web Sites

Hoover's Online	**www.hoovers.com**
New York Stock Exchange	**www.nyse.com**
Industry Link	**www.industrylink.com**
Investor Home	**www.investorhome.com**
Investor Link	**www.investor-link.com**
Moody's Investor Services	**www.moodys.com**
Bloomberg	**www.bloomberg.com**
Yahoo!	**www.yahoo.com**
Dun and Bradstreet	**www.dnb.com**

Economic

Economic Report of the President

World Fact Book

Economic Indicators

Consumer Confidence Survey

Economic Outlook by U.S. Chamber of Commerce

Economic Times

Standard & Poor's Industry Surveys

International Economic Outlook by Union Bank of Switzerland

Predicasts Forecasts

U.S. Industrial Outlook

World Economic Survey by United Nations

Census of Retail Trade

Census of Manufacturing

(continues)

TABLE 3-4   Selected Sources of External Information *(continued)*

Web Sites

Bureau of Labor Statistics	**stats.bls.gov**
Board of Governors of the Federal Reserve System	**www.bog.frb.fed.us**
Business Cycle Indicators	**www.globalexposure.com**
EDGAR Database	**www.sec.gov/edgar**
Federal Reserve Bank of New York	**www.ny.frb.org**
Federal Reserve Bank of St. Louis	**www.stls.frb.org**
Export-Import Bank of the United States	**www.exim.gov**
Fedstats	**www.fedstats.gov**
STAT-USA	**www.stat-usa.gov**
Economic Statistics Briefing Room	**www.whitehouse.gov/fsbr/esbr.html**
Census Bureau	**www.census.gov**
U.S. Securities and Exchange Commission	**www.sec.gov**
Wall Street Research Net	**www.wsrn.com**

Demographic

U.S. Bureau of the Census publications
Statistical Abstract of the United States
Demographic Yearbook by United Nations
Statistical Abstract of the World
Statistical Yearbook
Productivity Measures for Selected Industries and Government Services

Web Sites

American Demographics	**www.demographics.com**
BLS	**stats.bls.gov**
Current Population Survey	**www.census.gov**
Fedstats	**www.fedstats.gov**
Statistical Abstract of the United States	**www.census.gov/statab/www/**
STAT-USA	**www.stat-usa.gov**
Census Bureau	**www.census.gov**
Department of Labor	**www.dol.gov**

Sociocultural

Publications by U.S. Department of Labor, Bureau of Labor Statistics
Statistical Abstract of the United States
Survey of Consumers by the University of Michigan's Institute of Social Research
Statistical Abstract of the World

Web Sites

Advertising Age	**www.adage.com**
Fedstats	**www.fedstats.gov**

TABLE 3-4   Selected Sources of External Information *(continued)*

Political–Legal

Congressional Reports

Reports published by industry trade associations

Web Sites

Federal Trade Commission	**www.ftc.gov**
Library of Congress	**lcweb.loc.gov**
OSHA	**www.osha.gov**
Department of State	**www.state.gov**
Environmental Protection Agency	**www.epa.gov**

Technological

Inside U.S. Business: A Concise Encyclopedia of Leading Industries

Predicasts Forecasts

Reports published by industry trade associations

Global

The Big Emerging Markets Outlook and Sourcebook

Demographic Yearbook

Statistical Abstract of the World

Statistical Yearbook

Web Sites

CIA World Factbook	**www.odci.gov/cia/publications/factbook**
Emerging Markets Companion	**www.emgmkts.com**
Export-Import Bank of the United States	**www.exim.gov**
U.S. Customs Service	**www.customs.ustreas.gov**
U.S. Department of State	**www.state.gov**
United Nations	**web.unicc.org/untpdc**

information provided from the different functional departments or divisional units and share this information with other organizational units that might benefit. The role of the middle manager in external analysis is to act more as an information gatherer and disseminator. Also, middle managers might monitor changes in general environmental sectors that are particularly important to their specific circumstances and use this information to make any needed strategic changes. That leaves top-level managers. Because of their broad perspective on situations, top-level managers see the "whole" picture. As part of establishing the organization's future direction, top-level managers should evaluate external opportunities and threats. Information about possible opportunities and threats (in either the specific or the general environmental sectors) flows up from other organizational levels. If the organization has a strategic planning department responsible for

FYI

Competitive Intelligence

One of the fastest-growing areas of environmental scanning is **competitor intelligence**—an information-gathering activity that seeks to identify who competitors are, what they're doing, and how their actions will affect your organization. Competitor intelligence experts suggest that 80 percent of what strategic decision makers need to know about competitors can be found out from their own employees, suppliers, and customers. Competitor intelligence doesn't necessarily have to involve organizational spying. Advertisements, promotional materials, press releases, reports filed with governmental agencies, annual reports, want ads, newspaper reports, and industry studies are examples of readily accessible sources of information. Trade shows and talking to your company's sales representatives can be other good sources of information on competitors. Many organizations even buy competitors' products and have their own engineers break them down (through a process called reverse engineering) to learn about new technical innovations. And the Internet is opening up new sources of competitor intelligence as many corporate Web pages include new-product information and other information such as press releases. However, the questions and concerns that arise about competitor intelligence pertain to the ways in which competitor information is gathered. Competitor intelligence becomes illegal corporate spying when it involves the theft of proprietary materials or trade secrets by any means. Often, a fine line exists between what's considered *legal and ethical* and what's considered *legal but unethical*. Check out the online "how-to" guide about competitor intelligence by going to **www.fuld.com**. What does this report have to say about competitor intelligence?

Sources: Fuld & Co. Web site (**www.fuld.com**), March 8, 2000; B. Ettore, "Managing Competitive Intelligence," *Management Review*, October 1995, pp. 15–19; K. Western, "Ethical Spying," *Business Ethics*, September–October 1995, pp. 22–23; and J. P. Herring, "The Role of Intelligence in Formulating Strategy," *Journal of Business Strategy*, September–October 1992, pp. 54–60.

doing external analysis—in other words, a more formalized strategic planning process—this information is probably monitored and compiled there.

Regardless of your managerial level, you'll be involved in some aspect of external analysis. That's further verification of one of this book's premises—that everyone in the organization is involved in managing strategically.

WHY DO AN EXTERNAL ANALYSIS?

By now, you should have a pretty good feel for what an external analysis is and how one is done, but you still may not be convinced of the necessity for knowing what's happening in your organization's external environment. In this section, we're going to look at *why* you need to do an external analysis. We also want to look at some of the challenges of doing an external analysis.

Benefits of Doing an External Analysis

We've already mentioned that the purpose of doing an external analysis is to identify potential opportunities and threats facing your organization. If you didn't examine, monitor, and evaluate the external changes and trends taking place, how could you pinpoint those opportunities and threats? It's not as if these changes would never impact your organization's performance. They would, but instead of being on top of what's taking place, you'd constantly be playing catch up and simply reacting to changes. By deliberately and systematically analyzing the external environment, you're going to be a **proactive manager**—a manager who anticipates changes and plans for those changes accordingly. In fact, a proactive manager may, at times, be able to influence various external environmental sectors to the organization's benefit (i.e., encourage changes that would affect the organization's performance positively). For example, lobbying is just one way managers can proactively manage their external environment. However, there are other reasons why an external analysis is important.

One reason is that the external analysis provides the information that strategic managers use in planning, decision making, and strategy formulation.[10] Think back to when we discussed the "environment as information" perspective. One real value in studying the external environment is the information it provides. This information is useful to the extent that strategic decision makers can determine ways to take advantage of the positive changes and ways to stay away from or adapt to the negative changes; that is, strategic decision makers can change the organization's strategies. The organization's strategies should be based on information about markets, customers, technology, and so forth.[11] Because an organization's environment is changing continually, having information about the various external sectors is important in order for decision makers to formulate strategies that "align" the organization with its environment.

The "environment as source of resources" perspective also provides another reason for doing an external analysis. Your organization's ability to acquire and control needed resources depends upon having strategies that take advantage of the environment's abundant resources and strategies that cope with the environment's limited resources.[12] Think back to how we described an organization as an open system. Because the organization depends on the environment as a source of inputs (resources) and as an outlet for outputs, it only makes sense that we'd want to design organizational strategies that allow us to get the resources we need so we can convert those resources into desired outputs. We can do that most effectively by understanding what the environment has to offer.

Another reason for doing an external analysis is the realization that today's external environment is increasingly dynamic. Turbulent market conditions, fragmented markets, less brand loyalty, more demanding customers, rapid changes in technology, and intense global competition—these are just a few of the images used to describe today's business environments. And, these types of conditions aren't the exception—they're the norm. All sizes and all types of organizations are facing increasingly dynamic environments. In order to cope effectively with these significant changes, managers need to examine the environment.[13]

The final reason we want to mention for doing an external analysis relates to whether doing so really makes a difference. In other words, what difference does doing an external analysis really make in the way an organization performs? The answer is that it *does* appear to make a difference. Various research studies generally have shown that in organizations where strategic decision makers did external analyses, performance was higher.[14] Performance was typically measured using a financial measure such as return on assets or growth in profitability. The fact that doing an external analysis appears to make a difference in performance results is a pretty good reason for wanting to know how to do one and to actually do it as part of the strategic management process.

Challenges of Doing an External Analysis

You might encounter some problems as you do an external analysis. For one thing, the environment might be changing more rapidly than you realistically can keep up with. For example, think of what happened as Internet usage absolutely exploded during the mid- and late 1990s. It seemed that technological advances, new competitors, more customers (users), and debates over possible regulations were happening faster than anyone could completely comprehend. This type of rapid change isn't just characteristic of high-tech industries—it's happening in many industries. So, even keeping track of the current situation and trends or changes can be a challenge.

Another challenge of doing external analyses is the amount of time that they can consume. We've established that systematically examining and evaluating the environment is important; yet it does take time to do it, and most strategic decision makers are busy managing and don't feel they have spare time. However, the fact remains that an external analysis *is* important to do as part of managing strategically. The key is to make the process as efficient and effective as possible. This may mean doing things such as identifying significant external sectors and monitoring those more frequently and the other sectors not as frequently; relying on specialized database searches, news clipping services, or even personalized Internet searches to monitor changes in those significant sectors; or even sharing the responsibilities for analyzing the external sectors with others in the organization. After all, many employees interact in some way with the external environment, especially through customer or supplier contacts, and can be encouraged to communicate what they hear or read about.

Finally, we need to point out the shortcomings of forecasts and trend analyses because they are a significant part of the external analysis. Forecasts aren't actual fact. They're the best predictions that experts have about what they believe is going to happen. For instance, you've probably had the experience of leaving your home without a coat and umbrella after listening to the weather forecast for a sunny, warm day only to be greeted by a cold, pouring rain. Forecasts of business, economic, or attitudinal trends aren't always accurate, either. However, the key for strategic decision makers is to be flexible, open, and alert to changing circumstances. Strategic management is an ongoing process. Strategies don't always work out the way they're intended, for whatever reason. Maybe results fall short because of some internal shortcoming or maybe because the predictions we'd made about external opportunities and threats were inaccurate. Whatever the reason, we change the strategies as needed to take advantage of new information. Therefore, even though forecasts, predictions, and trend analyses aren't always 100 percent accurate, they can provide us with a sense of the strategic direction we need to go. Even given the shortcomings, that's a pretty good reason to continue to look at them.

Consider This ◀◀▌

✓ What should you be looking for as you examine the specific and general environmental sectors?

✓ How can managers approach finding external information? How can they determine what approach they need to take?

✓ What are some information sources for each of the external sectors?

✓ How does external analysis change for different managerial levels?

✓ List some benefits of doing an external analysis.

✓ What are some challenges associated with doing an external analysis?

THE BOTTOM LINE

⟫ An **external analysis** is the process of scanning and evaluating an organization's various external environmental sectors in order to determine positive and negative trends that could impact organizational performance.

⟫ **Opportunities** are positive external environmental trends or changes that may help the organization improve its performance.

⟫ **Threats** are negative external environmental trends or changes that may hinder the organization's performance.

⟫ The belief that an organization interacts with its environment can be traced back to the concept of organizations as **open systems**, which means that the organization interacts with and responds to its external environment.

⟫ Two perspectives on organizational environments are the environment as a source of information and the environment as a source of resources.

⟫ A key aspect of the environment as information perspective is the concept of **environmental uncertainty,** which is the amount of change and complexity in an organization's environment.

⟫ The more complex and dynamic the environment, the more uncertain it is, and the more information decision makers need to be able to make appropriate decisions.

⟫ The main idea behind the perspective of the environment as a source of resources is that as the environment becomes more hostile (resources become harder to obtain and control), the more that managers need to monitor the environment and make appropriate decisions based on what they see.

⟫ It's important for strategic decision makers to engage in environmental scanning—to know what's happening in the external environment.

⟫ An organization's environment can be divided into the **specific environment** (those external environmental sectors that directly impact the organization's decisions and actions by opening up opportunities or threats) and the **general environment** (those external environmental sectors that indirectly affect the organization's strategic decisions and actions and may pose opportunities or threats).

⟫ The specific environment includes industry and competitive variables.

⟫ An **industry** is a group or groups of organizations producing similar or identical products and who compete for customers and resources.

⟫ The five forces model developed by Michael Porter is one way to assess an organization's specific environment.

⟫ The five forces assessed for relevant opportunities and threats are current rivalry among existing firms, potential entrants, bargaining power of buyers, bargaining power of suppliers, and substitute products.

⟫ Eight conditions affect the level of current rivalry: numerous or equally balanced competitors, slow industry growth, high fixed or storage costs, lack of differentiation or switching costs, capacity must be added in large increments, diverse competitors, high strategic stakes, and high **exit barriers** (factors that keep companies competing in businesses even though they may be earning low or even negative returns).

➤ One way to determine your current rivalry is by looking at your **strategic group**—a set of firms competing within an industry that have similar strategies and resources.

➤ The threat of potential entrants is determined by the **barriers to entry**—obstacles to entering an industry.

➤ The seven major entry barriers include economies of scale, cost disadvantages from other than scale, product differentiation, capital requirements, **switching costs** (the one-time financial or psychological costs facing a buyer who switches from one product to another), access to distribution channels, and government policy.

➤ Buyers' bargaining power is determined by the following factors: Buyer purchases large volumes of the seller's product, products purchased by the customer represent a significant portion of its costs or purchases, products purchased are standard or undifferentiated, few switching costs, low profits–income, have the ability and resources to manufacture the products they're purchasing, product isn't important to quality of buyers' products, and availability of full information.

➤ Suppliers' bargaining power is determined by the following factors: domination by a few companies and more concentration than the buying industry, whether there are substitute products, buying industry is not an important customer, supplier's product is an important input to buying industry, supplier's products are differentiated or there are switching costs, and the supplier's ability to provide products that buying industry is currently providing.

➤ The threat of substitute products is determined by the availability of a number of good or not-so-good substitutes.

➤ The general environment includes five main sectors: economic, demographic, sociocultural, political–legal, and technological.

➤ The economic sector encompasses all the macroeconomic data—current statistics, trends, and changes—that reflect what's happening with the economy.

➤ The demographic sector includes data and trends in population characteristics such as gender, age, ethnic makeup, education, family composition, and so forth.

➤ The sociocultural sector includes information about society's traditions, values, attitudes, beliefs, tastes, and patterns of behavior.

➤ The political–legal sector includes the various laws, regulations, judicial decisions, and political forces currently in effect at the federal, state, and local levels of government. It may also include regulations enacted by professional associations.

➤ The technological segment includes scientific or technological improvements, advancements, and innovations in both products or processes.

➤ In doing an external analysis, you should look for specific data, statistics, analyses, trends, predictions, forecasts, inferences or statements made by experts, or other types of evidence of what's happening or predicted to happen in the various external sectors. Then, you must assess whether these changes are good (opportunities) or bad (threats) for your organization.

➤ One approach to spotting trends is using **focus groups**—a marketing research approach in which an informal group of people, with the help of a moderator, discusses a product or service and other marketing issues.

⫸ The approaches to finding external information can range all the way from informal, unscientific observations to a formal, systematic search.

⫸ Some type of **external information system (EIS)** is necessary. This information system provides managers with needed external information on a regular basis.

⫸ **Competitor intelligence** is one type of environmental scanning that seeks to identify who competitors are, what they're doing, and how their actions will affect your organization.

⫸ Doing an external analysis isn't as difficult as it sounds. Just ask yourself what specific information you think you should know. Study each external sector carefully and identify what information you'll want to make good strategic decisions.

⫸ The size of your organization is going to affect who does what type of external analysis.

⫸ The benefits of doing an external analysis are as follows: It allows you to be able to pinpoint opportunities and threats; it makes you a **proactive manager**—a manager who anticipates changes and plans for those changes; it provides the information that strategic decision makers use in planning, decision making, and strategy formulation; it allows the organization to better monitor sources of needed resources; it allows strategic decision makers to be better able to cope with the increasingly dynamic environment; and finally, it does appear to make a difference in how well an organization performs.

⫸ The challenges of doing an external analysis are that the dynamic nature of the environment can be hard to keep track of; it can take a lot of time; and forecasts and trend analyses aren't always accurate.

BUILDING YOUR SKILLS

1. Inflation used to be an economic fact of life. Yet, businesses, consumers, strategic decision makers, and investors nearly everywhere in the developed world are confronting economies with low to no inflation. What are the strategic implications of a low- or no-inflation economy? What industries might find significant opportunities in such an environment? What industries might face significant threats? Explain your choices.

2. Children, aged 6 to 10, are proving to be as picky about their fashions as teenagers are. Although children have always used fashion to fit in with their peers, their desire to match the clothing that's popular among older siblings and even young adults is rising. Their tastes are no longer the cute and innocent (hearts, teddy bears, angels, and bunnies). They want the clothes, jewelry, and shoes that pop music stars and teen actors and actresses are wearing. What are the implications (opportunities and threats) for clothing manufacturers? For retailers (specialty, discount, and department stores)?

3. Experts state that the Internet is changing the nature of competition. Research this topic. *Is* it changing competition? If so, how? Write a paper summarizing your findings and explaining the implications for strategic decision makers.

4. The demographic trend of an aging baby boom generation, combined with the booming financial markets over the last decade that have allowed many people the luxury of retiring early, is creating some interesting strategic scenarios, not only in marketing opportunities and threats but also in the area of human resources. What opportunities and threats do you see in this convergence of demographic factors? How might these opportunities and threats change for different industries?

5. Understanding an industry's profit pools is an interesting twist in industry analysis. What are *profit pools*? They're the total profits earned in an industry at all points along its value chain. (The value chain consists of all the activities that add "value" to a product or service, from inputs to outputs.) Determining profit pools involves looking at your suppliers' suppliers and their suppliers as well as at your customers' customers and their customers. By examining all aspects of a product or service from its raw materials to its final destination, proponents of profit pool analysis say that you can identify where the money is actually being made and make better strategic decisions. Do some research on profit pools (another term often used is *profit zones*). Summarize your findings in a bulleted list format. What are the implications of such profit pools (or profit zones) for industry and competitor analysis?

6. The cell-phone industry in Europe is light years ahead of the United States. With their cell phones, Finns can buy a Coke from a vending machine, run a car wash, or send a digital picture to a friend. Swedes use their cell phones to pay utility bills. The French use theirs to check flight schedules, reserve hotel rooms, and scan traffic flow. Why is the United States lagging behind? Because much of this stuff requires digital networks and the Europeans have had a head start in implementing these digital networks. Going digital in the United States was more challenging because the Federal Commerce Commission chose to let competing technologies compete in the marketplace, and competitors have squabbled over whose standard would "win." Meanwhile, consumers were left with a hodgepodge of incompatible networks. Also, Americans haven't been as demanding for the newest and latest technology in their cell phones. How does this example illustrate the importance of knowing technological trends in different global locations? Sociocultural trends? Political–legal trends? Do you see any other external sectors (specific or general) at play here? Explain.

7. Two of the major competitors in the fast-food industry—Wendy's and McDonald's have positioned themselves differently. Wendy's has taken the adult approach, practically ignoring the children's market with its advertising tie-ins and toy giveaways. McDonald's has fashioned an all-out pursuit of the kids' market. Think about demographic and sociocultural trends and changes. How would each organization's interpretation of these trends and changes affect its choice of strategy? Which organization do you think is positioned better? Explain your choice.

8. Some of this decade's big social trends include the following: nutriceuticals (where drugs are delivered via your food); teen piercings; personal defibrillators; school uniforms; and home food testers (kits for testing the safety of food items). Now, you're going to do a little bit of reverse psychology. What societal and cultural values, attitudes, beliefs, tastes, patterns of behavior, and the like do you think are contributing to these trends? (You're going to have

to really stop and think about what people are feeling, what they enjoy doing, what they don't enjoy doing, and so forth. However, by recognizing the connection between sociocultural elements and product trends, you can better understand the role that sociocultural opportunities and threats play in strategy.)

9. The *Wall Street Journal* publishes a quarterly survey of politics, economics, and values (March, June, September, and December) called American Opinion. Find the latest survey and summarize what you find there. What opportunities and threats do these survey findings pinpoint?

10. A survey of purchasing habits of new products by Generation X-ers had some results that you might consider surprising: 36 percent of respondents don't buy new products at first, but buy soon thereafter; 48 percent of respondents waited at least a year before buying; 13 percent wait several years before buying; and only 3 percent buy immediately. What are the strategic implications of such findings? Would these implications change for different industries? If so, how? If not, why not?

11. A survey listed the top U.S. values including as follows (most important listed first): protecting the family, honesty, stable personal relationships, self-esteem, freedom, friendship, and respecting one's ancestors. What are the strategic implications of such findings? Would these implications change for different industries? If so, how? If not, why not?

12. Ethan Allen Interiors Inc., the traditional furniture maker and retailer, is pursuing a nontraditional path. Since September of 1999, it's been selling furniture online at its Web site (**www.ethanallen.com**). CEO and Chairman M. Farooq Kathwari, said, "The Internet is going to become a tremendously important vehicle for us. By embracing it, we can reach millions of consumers in addition to the people who visit our stores." What external trends and changes are occurring that might have led Ethan Allen's strategic decision makers to pursue this path? Compare Ethan Allen's Web site with other Web sites that sell furniture. What's your assessment of the various competitors? In addition, Ethan Allen has several store franchisees around the United States. How might an Internet strategy (designed to take advantage of opportunities in the external environment) have to be designed to deal with the special needs and concerns of the various store franchisees? What special challenges might a traditional bricks-and-mortar furniture retailer face that an Internet-only furniture retailer might not? What challenges might an Internet-only furniture retailer face? Do you think Ethan Allen's attempt to do both is wise? Explain.

STRATEGIC MANAGEMENT IN ACTION CASES

CASE #1: Not Sold Out

Strategic Management in Action case #1 can be found at the beginning of Chapter 3.

Discussion Questions

1. What external trends were strategic managers at the movie theater chains attempting to exploit?

2. If you were a strategic decision maker at one of these movie theater chains, what types of external information would you want to have?

3. Do you think the strategic decision makers have done a good job of scanning and assessing the environment? Explain.

4. What conclusion(s) about opportunities and threats can you draw from this case?

CASE #2: Tooth Wars

The battlefield is your mouth. Or more precisely, your teeth and gums. Helping people keep their teeth and gums clean and healthy is a huge market! David Giuliani, cofounder and CEO of Optiva Corporation (**www.optiva.com**) knows how important it is to stay on top of what's happening in the external environment, and is also well aware of the challenges in doing so. Today, Optiva Corporation, a privately held company, has annual revenues of over $130 million—all from selling a technologically advanced toothbrush called Sonicare. This high-tech toothbrush uses patented sonic technology, fluid dynamics, and electromechanical design to aid in removing plaque bacteria from between teeth and at the gum line.

The company's main product initially was designed by two University of Washington professors (David Engel and Roy Martin) who had developed a sonic toothbrush. A sonic toothbrush is based on the premise that a sound-wave–based device could effectively clean the plaque and tartar that are the major causes of dental disease. Engel and Martin had hoped that a large personal health care company would pick up their technology and bring it to market. However, industry giants such as Procter & Gamble, Johnson & Johnson, Sunbeam, Squibb, and others had declined, pointing to the fact that the U.S. Patent Office was filled with the sad stories of other sonic toothbrushes that had been tried and failed. What Engel and Martin felt they

had, though, was a technology that did work—that did blast teeth and gums with sound waves to keep them clean and healthy. They began looking for someone who could help bring their prototype product to fruition, and eventually connected with David Giuliani.

Giuliani's first tinkerings with the product were discouraging. The strip of metal and ceramic that held the toothbrush bristles in place kept breaking, and it required too much power to produce the needed vibrations. He was about to tell Engel and Martin that their idea was not feasible. But one day, while walking along the beach, Giuliani watched as the waves crashed over the sand, slowly eroding the beach. That process of nature was the key product design breakthrough Giuliani had been looking for! Maybe what the product needed was sound waves traveling through the mouth fluid that would then erode away plaque. After consulting with various engineers, Giuliani came up with a new design— sort of like a turning fork driven by a vibrating electromagnetic field that would provide power to the brush head. Engel and Martin spent hours in the lab observing how the vibrating brush head churned up a mixture of toothpaste and saliva on artificial teeth. They discovered that when the vibrations were tuned to 520 strokes per second (middle C on the musical scale), the churned-up fluid would start to erode plaque, even when the brush itself wasn't making contact with the teeth. This meant that the cleaning action could take place between teeth and under the gum line, the places where other toothbrushes failed to go.

Today, Optiva sells its products in the United States through warehouse clubs, mass merchandisers, department stores, and other outlets. The company also distributes its products in Canada, Japan, and the United Kingdom. Optiva likes to brag that its toothbrush has much more in common with the computer sitting on your desk than any other toothbrush in your bathroom. With its built-in microprocessor, the Sonicare toothbrush uses state-of-the-art technology to attack plaque bacteria. In addition, the company points out that 98 percent of dental professionals who have tried Sonicare recommend it to their patients. No other power toothbrush is personally used by more dental professionals. And, Sonicare is preferred by periodontists, specialists in gum care, over the other leading power toothbrushes. In the tooth wars, Optiva feels that it's well armored and well positioned.

Discussion Questions

1. What examples of environmental scanning can you see in this situation? What role do you think environmental scanning played in the company's initial operations? What role do you think environmental scanning might play now?

2. Do some research on this company and the personal care products industry. Using Porter's five forces model, assess the industry–competitive forces.

3. What types of information do you think Giuliani might want from each of the five general environmental sectors? (You don't need to look up this information. Just indicate what trends Giuliani would probably want to keep track of.)

4. What opportunities and threats do you think are facing this industry?

5. Go to the Jobs section on Optiva's Web site (**www.optiva.com**). Select four of the departments listed there. What types of external information might each of these departments need?

(*Sources:* Company's Web site (**www.optiva.com**), March 23, 2000; information from Hoover's Online (**www.hoovers.com**), March 23, 2000; C. Caggiano, "A Simple Plan in a Complex World," *Inc.*, February 1999, p. 45; and D. H. Freedman, "Sonic Boom," *Inc. 500 1997*, 1997, pp. 36–41.)

CASE #3: Going After Generation Y

"We are going to own this generation." These words reflect the not-so-subtle philosophy of dELIA*s (**www.delias.com**) cofounders, Stephen Kahn and Chris Edgar. If you've never heard of dELIA*s, you're probably not a teenager or around them.

The direct mailer–retailer runs an assortment of chains, catalogs, and Web sites targeting teenage girls and boys, and has become one of the hottest names in Generation Y retailing. Its urban fashions appeal to girls and guys everywhere. The company's database of over 4 million names gives it incredible points of contact with large numbers of kids who have significant purchasing power. Revenues are around $160 million annually and continuing to grow.

dELIA*s attracts and keeps its target customers in different ways. First, it designs and markets clothes that parents raise their eyebrows at. Also, the catalogs show these fashions with models who look like regular teenagers, not the glamorous fashion types, which heightens the appeal. And, the company's youthful image isn't just a public persona. Most of the company's employees are well under the age of 30. Its phone representatives—who are mostly high school and college students—do more than take orders. They also offer fashion tips and advice. One industry expert says, "dELIA*s speaks the language of its consumers." The company doesn't use mass-market advertising, which Generation Y consumers tend to distrust. Instead, dELIA*s gets its message out by catalog drops at schools and with hot Web sites. The company bought GURL.com, a popular fashion, chat, and game site for girls, in 1997. Now, the company is branching out into home furnishings and room decorations.

Cofounder Kahn says he defines dELIA*s business by its customers, not by product categories. He foresees a time when dELIA*s will help these customers get their first credit cards, first car loan, and first mortgage. "We'll follow them and broaden our offerings."

Discussion Questions

1. What general environmental trends, statistics, analyses, and so forth might Kahn and Edgar be particularly interested in? Where could they find this information?

2. What do you think Kahn means by his statement that dELIA*s defines its business by its customers, not by product categories? What implications does this statement have for assessing external opportunities and threats?

3. What type(s) of competitive information might dELIA*s strategic decision makers want? Would the strategic groups concept be useful for a uniquely positioned company like dELIA*s? If so, what companies might you place in their strategic group? If not, what competitors do you think dELIA*s might have? How did you choose these competitors?

4. Do some research on Generation Y. What are its demographics? How about its sociocultural characteristics? Now, check out dELIA*s Web site (**www.delias.com**). If you can, get copies of the company's catalogs. How is the company attempting to appeal to Generation Y? Would you say it's doing a good job of appealing to this generation? How might the company have to change its strategies as this generation ages?

(*Sources:* Information on dELIA*s from Hoover's Online (**www.hoovers.com**), March 22, 2000; company's Web site (**www.delias.com**), March 22, 2000; L. Clifford, "Sells Like Teen Spirit (Not)," *Fortune*, July 10, 2000, pp. 242– 43; A. Barrett, "To Reach the Unreachable Teen," *Business Week*, September 18, 2000, pp. 78–80; and E. Neuborne and K. Kerwin, "Generation Y," *Business Week*, February 15, 1999, pp. 80–88.)

ENDNOTES

1. Information from chains' Web sites (**www.amctheatres.com**, **www.carmike.com**, **www.cineplex.com**, and **www.regalcinemas.com**), March 8, 2000; "America Online to Offer 'Print-at-Home' Movie Tickets," Excite News Web site (**www.excite.coms/news/dj/**), March 8, 2000; A. Krasne, "Soon, Buy Movie Tickets Online," *PC World* (**www.pcworld.com/pcw today**), March 6, 2000; R. Grover, "Trouble in Cinema Paradiso," *Business Week*, January 17, 2000, pp. 98–100; B. Orwall, "AMC's New Chief Fine-Tunes Theater Chain's Strategy," *Wall Street Journal*, July 23, 1999, p. B6; and G. Fabrikant, "Plenty of Seats Available," *New York Times*, July 12, 1999, p. C1.

2. C. Barnard, *The Functions of the Executive* (Cambridge, MA: Harvard University Press, 1938).

3. W. R. Dill, "Environment as an Influence on Managerial Autonomy," *Administrative Science Quarterly*, 2 (1958), pp. 409–43; and J. G. March and H. A. Simon, *Organizations* (New York: John Wiley, 1958).

4. R. L. Tung, "Dimensions of Organizational Environments: An Exploratory Study of Their Impact on Organizational

Structure," *Academy of Management Journal,* 22 (1979), pp. 672–93; J. R. Galbraith, *Designing Complex Organizations* (Reading, MA: Addison-Wesley, 1973); R. B. Duncan, "Characteristics of Organizational Environments and Perceived Environment Uncertainty," *Administrative Science Quarterly,* 17 (1972), pp. 313–27; and P. R. Lawrence and J. W. Lorsch, "Differentiation and Integration in Complex Organizations," *Administrative Science Quarterly,* 12 (1967), pp. 1–47.

5. R. Bettis and C. K. Prahalad, "The Visible and the Invisible Hand: Resource Allocation in the Industrial Sector," *Strategic Management Journal,* 4 (1983), pp. 27–43; J. Freeman, "Organizational Life Cycles and Natural Selection Processes," in *Research in Organizational Behavior,* ed. B. M. Staw and L. L. Cummings (Greenwich, CT: JAI Press, 1982); H. E. Aldrich, *Organizations and Environments* (Upper Saddle River, NJ: Prentice Hall, 1979); J. Pfeffer and G. R. Salancik, *The External Control of Organizations: A Resource Dependence Perspective* (New York: Harper & Row, 1978); H. E. Aldrich and J. Pfeffer, "Environments of Organizations," *Annual Review of Sociology,* 2 (1976), pp. 79–105; S. Mindlin, *Organizational Dependence on Environment and Organizational Structure: A Reexamination of the Aston Group,* unpublished master's thesis, Cornell University, Ithaca, NY, 1974; J. Hage and M. Aiken, "Program Change and Organizational Properties," *American Journal of Sociology,* 72 (1973), pp. 503–79; and March and Simon, *Organizations.*

6. M. E. Porter, *Competitive Strategy* (New York: Free Press, 1980).

7. Ibid., p. 20.

8. J. R. Gregg, "Strategic Groups Theory: Past Nuances, Future Frontiers," *Southwest Academy of Management Proceedings,* March 1996, San Antonio, TX, pp. 29–32; J. R. Barney and R. Hoskisson, "Strategic Groups: Untested Assertions and Research Proposals," *Managerial and Decision Economics,* 11 (1990), pp. 187–98; K. Cool and D. Schendel, "Strategic Group Formation and

Performance: The Case of the U.S. Pharmaceutical Industry, 1963–1982," *Management Science,* 33 no. 9 (1987), pp. 1101–24; G. Dess and P. Davis, "Porter's [1980] Generic Strategies as Determinants of Strategic Group Membership and Organizational Performance," *Academy of Management Journal,* 27, no. 3 (1984), pp. 467–88; and M. S. Hunt, *Competition in the Major Home Appliance Industry 1960–1970,* unpublished doctoral dissertation, Harvard University, 1972.

9. F. Rice, "Making Generational Marketing Come of Age," *Fortune,* June 26, 1995, pp. 110–13.

10. B. K. Boyd and J. Fulk, "Executive Scanning and Perceived Uncertainty: A Multidimensional Model," *Journal of Management,* 22, no. 1 (1996), pp. 1–21; and R. L. Daft et al., "Chief Executive Scanning, Environmental Characteristics, and Company Performance: An Empirical Study," *Strategic Management Journal,* 9 (1988), pp. 123–39.

11. P. F. Drucker, "The Information Executives Truly Need," *Harvard Business Review,* January–February 1995, pp. 54–62.

12. C. S. Korberg and G. R. Ungson, "The Effects of Environmental Uncertainty and Dependence on Organizational Structure and Performance: A Comparative Study," *Journal of Management,* winter 1987, pp. 725–37.

13. R. S. Achrol and L. W. Stern, "Environmental Determinants of Decision-Making Uncertainty in Marketing Channels," *Journal of Marketing,* February 1988, pp. 36–50.

14. S. Kotha and A. Nair, "Strategy and Environment as Determinants of Performance: Evidence from the Japanese Machine Tool Industry," *Strategic Management Journal,* 16 (1995), pp. 497–518; R. Subramanian et al., "An Empirical Examination of the Relationship Between Strategy and Scanning," *The Mid-Atlantic Journal of Business,* December 1993, pp. 315–30; and Daft et al., "Chief Executive Scanning."

4

ASSESSING STRENGTHS AND WEAKNESSES: DOING AN INTERNAL ANALYSIS

LEARNING OBJECTIVES

After studying this chapter, you should be able to:

1. Define internal analysis.
2. Describe the relationship between organizational resources, organizational capabilities, core competencies, and distinctive organizational capabilities.
3. Explain what organizational strengths and weaknesses are.
4. Describe the primary and support activities on the value chain.
5. Explain what an internal audit is and how it can be used for an internal analysis.
6. Discuss the features of the internal environmental analysis process.
7. Describe the steps in a capabilities assessment profile.
8. Explain the criteria that could be used to assess an organization's strengths and weaknesses.
9. Discuss why an internal analysis is important.

STRATEGIC MANAGEMENT IN ACTION CASE #1

Not So Dumb

Who would have thought that a company that calls its customers "dummies" could enjoy any marketplace success? Yet, IDG Books Worldwide, Inc. (**www.idgbooks.com**) generates significant revenues (over $179 million in 1999) selling books to dummies.[1] Founded in 1990, IDG Books (IDGB), a subsidiary of the International Data Group, is a global knowledge company with a diverse portfolio of technology, consumer, and general how-to book brands; computer-based learning tools; Web sites; and Internet e-services. The company has built a reputation as a brand powerhouse.

The flagship of IDG Books is its "For Dummies" series, which includes books ranging from *Art for Dummies* to *Investing for Dummies* to *Home Improvement for Dummies*. The For Dummies series has focused on helping people learn "how-to" by making topics accessible and fun. Chairman and CEO John Kilcullen says, "IDG Books Worldwide is about turning the 'I can't' into 'I can.' " The series now has over 400 titles, has sold more than 75 million copies, and accounts for around 52 percent of the company's revenues.

Capitalizing on its high level of recognition, the For Dummies series has served as IDGB's springboard to building other successful brands, licensing nonbook products such as CDs and games, and creating exclusive customized products for strategic partners such as Epson, Lotus, Hewlett-Packard, AOL, and Siemens, among others. In 1998, IDGB acquired Cliffs Notes, the study guides that have saved many a student late at night studying for a test or writing a paper. However, not content to keep Cliffs Notes aimed only at the student market, IDGB's strategic decision makers chose to further exploit the familiar name and branched into the Cliffs Notes lifestyle series with 16 different business and technology titles. And, in 1999, IDGB acquired Macmillan General Reference, which brought into its fold a portfolio of well-recognized names including Betty Crocker's® cookbooks, Frommer's® travel guides, Howell House™ pet books, Webster's New World™ dictionaries, and Weight Watchers® diet and cookbooks.

IDGB's products are available in the United States through national retail chain booksellers, online retailers, wholesale distributors, office superstores, membership clubs, and computer–electronic superstores. In addition, the company sells its products to corporations, educational institutions, seminar and training companies, value-added resellers, catalog companies, and governmental entities. Outside the United States, IDGB's products are available in more than 90 countries. It has licensed more than 4,300 translations in 36 languages for publication by third-party publishers. As many others are doing, IDGB is now building a dynamic presence on the Internet. Its mission is to become the leading knowledge provider online as well as in print. The company's employees (around 650 total) work hard to keep it in an industry-leading position. As evidence of its success, an astounding 50 percent of the February 2000 *Publishers Weekly* computer bestsellers list was IDGB products. According to Kilcullen, IDGB's dominance in the technology content marketplace continues. He brags, "We currently maintain more than 50 percent of technology bestsellers by providing diverse, quality and timely brands that demystify technology and other complex, mission critical topics. Today, the market for expert know-how, professional productivity and lifelong learning is non-stop and we are pleased that our success in this mission has been consistently reflected in the rankings on the *Publishers Weekly* Computer Bestseller list since 1996."

What factors would you say have contributed to the success of IDG Books Worldwide? What strengths does it have? What potential weaknesses might the company have to address? In this chapter, we're going to concentrate on how to determine these important elements by discussing the internal analysis of an organization. Just as we've done in earlier chapters, we'll first look at *what* an internal analysis is, then at *how* you do one, and finally at *why* an internal analysis is an important part of managing strategically.

WHAT IS AN INTERNAL ANALYSIS?

In order to come up with the most appropriate and effective strategies, it's important to know what the organization can and cannot do particularly well, and what assets it has and doesn't have. As part of strategic management in action, an **internal analysis** is a process of identifying and evaluating an organization's specific characteristics including its resources, capabilities, and core competencies. This analysis provides important information about an organization's specific assets, skills, and actual work activities—in other words, what's good about these and what's lacking or deficient? It's the final piece in that part of the strategic management process puzzle that we've described as analyzing the current situation. (See Figure 4-1.) One important part of the internal analysis entails looking at the organization's *current* vision, mission(s), strategic objectives, and strategies. Knowing what an organization is doing currently gives strategic decision makers a beginning understanding of whether strategic changes might be necessary. Further describing *what* an internal analysis is means looking closer at the organization's resources, capabilities, and core competencies.

Figure 4-1

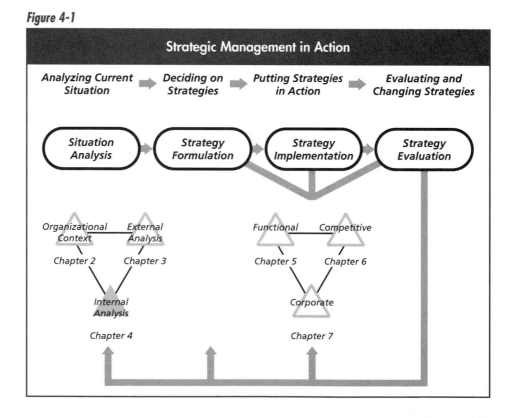

Strategic Management in Action

Analyzing Current Situation → Deciding on Strategies → Putting Strategies in Action → Evaluating and Changing Strategies

Situation Analysis → Strategy Formulation → Strategy Implementation → Strategy Evaluation

Organizational Context — External Analysis
Chapter 2 — Chapter 3
Internal Analysis
Chapter 4

Functional — Competitive
Chapter 5 — Chapter 6
Corporate
Chapter 7

A Quick Review of Organizational Resources

We've already discussed resources in relation to the resource-based view of achieving a sustainable competitive advantage (look back to Chapter 2 for a more complete description). As you will recall, resources are simply the assets an organization has for carrying out whatever work activities and processes it's in business to do (making tacos, providing at-home health care, or marketing books for dummies). These resources (or assets) can be financial, physical, human, intangible, and structural–cultural. Financial resources include debt capacity, credit lines, available equity (stock), cash reserves, and any other financial (monetary) assets. An organization's physical assets include tangible assets such as buildings, equipment and fixtures, raw materials, office supplies, manufacturing facilities, machines, and so forth. Human resources include the experiences, knowledge, judgment, skills, accumulated wisdom, and competencies of the organization's employees. At Microsoft Corporation, for example, employees' programming skills would be part of its human resources. Intangible resources are such things as brand names, patents, trademarks, databases, copyrights, or registered designs. For instance, Coca-Cola's brand name (Coke) would be one of its intangible resources; Nike's "swoosh" symbol is one of its intangible resources; the For Dummies brand name used by IDG Books Worldwide would be an intangible resource; and American Express Company's credit card customer database is one of its valuable intangible resources. Finally, structural–cultural resources include such things as organizational history, culture, work systems, policies, relationships, and the formal reporting (organizational) structure being used. For instance, 3M Corporation's organizational culture stresses risk taking and innovation by its research scientists and engineers. Because 3M's competitive advantage is based on its ability continually to develop and market innovative products, this type of culture is one of its important organizational resources.

Although an organization's tangible and intangible resources can be a source of competitive advantage, they play a more important role in determining an organization's capabilities and core competencies. Figure 4-2 illustrates this critical relationship.

From Resources to Organizational Capabilities

An organization's resources simply are the inputs needed to perform its work, whether that's making hamburgers, collecting blood plasma, or presenting a local community theater production of *My Fair Lady.* Another way to describe resources is to view them as the organization's "whats"—what it has or owns. A good example to illustrate this is someone who's considered an excellent cook. This cook will own pots and pans, spices, equipment, and other cooking materials (i.e., resources) to be used in preparing delicious meals. Likewise, an organization possesses resources that hopefully can be used to put together a sustainable competitive advantage. Although an organization's resources can be considered its "pantry of goodies," these assets are much more valuable as they're used by organizational members in their work, which is directed at helping the organization reach its goals, whatever those might be. By themselves, resources aren't productive—think of the cook who has to combine the spices and food using the appropriate equipment to put together delectable meals. Likewise, organizational resources must be processed or used in some way to get the value out of them. For example, American Express Company's customer database isn't valuable unless

Figure 4-2

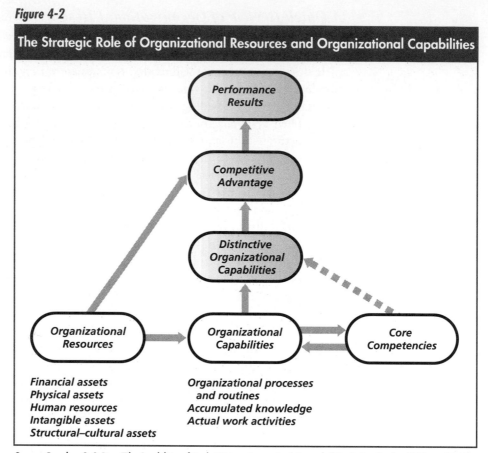

The Strategic Role of Organizational Resources and Organizational Capabilities

Source: Based on G. S. Day, "The Capabilities of Market-Driven Companies," *Journal of Marketing,* October 1994, pp. 37–52.

someone knows how to "mine" the database and use the information for making good strategic decisions. As such, the various resources are the inputs for organizational capabilities. **Organizational capabilities** are the complex and coordinated network of organizational routines and processes that determine how efficiently and effectively the organization transforms its inputs (resources) into outputs (products including physical goods and services).[2] **Organizational routines and processes** are the regular, predictable, and sequential patterns of work activity by organizational members. The organization itself is a huge network of routines and processes, encompassing such varied work activities as obtaining needed raw materials to establishing various product pricing structures to generating end-of-quarter financial and operational statistical reports. Think back to our opening case and what various capabilities—that is, organizational routines and processes—IDG Books Worldwide might need as it produces and markets its books and other learning materials.

As organizational members do their work, combining organizational resources and within the structure of organizational routines and processes, they accumulate knowledge and experience about how best to capture the value (i.e., get the most out) of the resources and turn them into possible core competencies or distinctive organizational capabilities. After all, creating organizational capabil-

Strategic Management in Action ►

How might an organization's resources and capabilities have to change when its revenues are growing by 145 percent a year? Hoover's Inc. (**www.hoovers.com**) is managing its resources and capabilities quite well under that scenario. The company sells data on 14,000 public and private businesses and institutions. Its traditional product, *Hoover's Handbook,* long available in libraries everywhere, has been surpassed by its online offerings. In fact, the company now gets more than 80 percent of its revenue from Hoover's Online. What are the implications of such a transition from a paper-based information company to an Internet-based information company on needed resources and capabilities? Explain.

Source: R. A. Oppel Jr., "A Company Short on Buzz but Long on Results," *New York Times,* July 21, 1999, p. C1.

ities isn't simply a matter of assembling resources. Instead, capabilities involve complex patterns of coordination between people, and between people and other organizational resources.[3] In fact, some organizations never get the hang of it. They're never quite able to develop efficient and effective capabilities and struggle exhaustively to survive in an increasingly dynamic and competitive marketplace. For example, look at how Wal-Mart and Kmart differ. Both have organizational resources and organizational routines and processes, yet Wal-Mart has been able to develop valuable capabilities and significant competitive advantages whereas Kmart has struggled. However, even Wal-Mart is finding that the strategic importance of organizational capabilities can change. Just because organizational capabilities were once the source of competitive advantage doesn't mean that those capabilities will continue to be a source of competitive advantage—that is, they don't always lead to a *sustainable* competitive advantage.[4]

In today's dynamic and complex environment, capabilities that are capable of leading to a competitive advantage today may not continue to do so as conditions and competitors change. To recognize and accommodate these new realities, some people have proposed that we need to think in terms of **dynamic capabilities**—an organization's ability to build, integrate, and reconfigure capabilities to address rapidly changing environments.[5] Successful competitors in the global marketplace will be firms that can demonstrate timely responsiveness, rapid and flexible product innovation, and management expertise in coordinating and redeploying organizational resources and capabilities. In fact, before any

Consider This ◄◄|

✓ What is an internal analysis?

✓ How is an internal analysis different from an external analysis?

✓ What kinds of resources might an organization possess? Give examples of each.

✓ How are resources (assets) valuable to organizations?

✓ What are capabilities?

✓ What are organizational routines and processes?

✓ How are capabilities valuable to organizations?

✓ What are dynamic capabilities?

✓ What does the dynamic capabilities approach propose?

organizational capabilities—dynamic or otherwise—can become a source of competitive advantage, they must be truly distinctive and also contribute to the development of an organization's core competencies.

From Capabilities to Distinctive Capabilities and Core Competencies

Every organization has capabilities that enable it to do what it's in business to do. Some of these capabilities will be done poorly; some will be done adequately. However, if the organization is going to develop a sustainable competitive advantage *and* be able to outperform its competition, some of these capabilities better be performed in a superior or distinct fashion. (Refer back to Figure 4-2.) Thus, **distinctive organizational capabilities** are the special and unique capabilities that distinguish the organization from its competitors. For example, Southwest Airlines has developed distinctive organizational capabilities in organizational processes and routines such as gate turnaround time, ticketing, and employee–customer interactions. Although every airline must engage in these same organizational processes and routines, Southwest has developed distinctive capabilities in these particular areas and has been able to create a competitive advantage and enjoy outstanding performance results. Other airlines have tried but have not been able to duplicate what Southwest does, making its capabilities truly distinctive. What makes capabilities distinct? Figure 4-3 outlines three characteristics that make a capability distinctive.[6] First, a distinctive capability contributes to superior customer value and offers real benefits to customers. Whatever it is that your customers value, a distinctive organizational capability enables you to provide it. Federal Express, for example, has developed a distinctive capability in providing customers with a highly efficient and effective package delivery system—

Figure 4-3

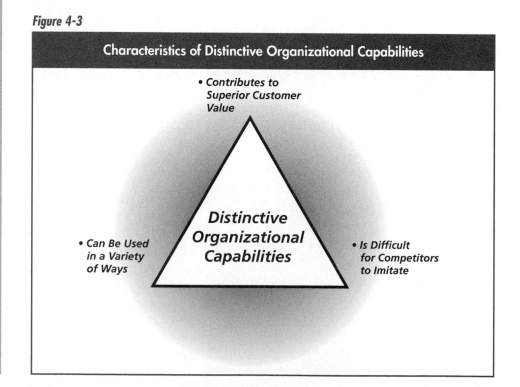

Characteristics of Distinctive Organizational Capabilities

- *Contributes to Superior Customer Value*

Distinctive Organizational Capabilities

- *Can Be Used in a Variety of Ways*

- *Is Difficult for Competitors to Imitate*

something that its customers obviously value. (On your own, try to describe some of the numerous organizational processes and routines that you think allow FedEx to do just that. Think in terms of its pickup and delivery system, tracking systems, etc.)

The second characteristic of distinctive organizational capabilities is that they should be difficult for competitors to imitate. Think back to how we described organizational capabilities as a complex and coordinated network of organizational routines and processes. Making these capabilities difficult to imitate means balancing and harmonizing a complex array of employee skills and knowledge and harnessing the considerable learning that exists in the organization. It also means recognizing how capabilities cut across functional units and how functional units can benefit from each other. If these complex interactions are strategically managed and exploited, it can be difficult for competitors to imitate even if they have similar resources and organizational processes and routines.

Finally, a distinctive organizational capability should allow the organization to use it in a variety of ways. The organizational routines and processes (what people in the organization do) shaped and honed in one area should be transferable to other areas of the organization. For example, Honda Corporation's capabilities at developing fuel-efficient, reliable, and responsive small displacement engines and drive trains has provided it with access to different markets including automobiles, motorcycles, lawn mowers, power generators, and marine outboard engines.[7]

This idea of being able to use organizational capabilities in a variety of ways is also key to understanding the role that core competencies play in this whole process. Let's take a closer look at core competencies.

Strategic Management in Action

Ever heard of H-P Labs? If not, you've undoubtedly heard of its parent, Hewlett-Packard. In fact, you probably have an H-P product (calculator, computer printer, etc.) in your backpack or at home. H-P, an icon in the computer industry, has developed significant distinctive organizational capabilities in product research and design at its corporate laboratory. H-P Labs, the company's research arm, has an illustrious track record. It's credited with developing the first pocket calculator, the first programmable calculator, and technologies used in ink-jet and laser printers. Its newest research directions are in the areas of digital photography, pervasive computing environments, and nanotechnology. Yet, the company has tended to keep quiet about its research achievements. However, the current director of the lab has been changing that approach by publicizing accomplishments. Do you think this a good move strategically? Why or why not? (Think about the characteristics of distinctive organizational capabilities.)

Sources: Company's Web site (**www.hp.com**), March 30, 2000; and D. P. Hamilton, "Venerable H-P Labs to Drop Its 'Aw, Shucks' Attitude," *New York Times*, October 21, 1999, p. B6.

The concept of core competencies was popularized by C. K. Prahalad and Gary Hamel in 1990.[8] **Core competencies** are the organization's major value-creating skills and capabilities that are *shared* across multiple product lines or multiple businesses. Let's look at an example to help explain this idea. Fingerhut Companies is the second-largest consumer catalog marketer (behind JCPenney Company) and is best known for its catalogs that promote everything from toy phones to big-screen TVs. Its target customers are low- and moderate-income customers. What is Fingerhut's core competency? It's the company's capability and skills at sorting through 500 pieces of information on each of more than 50 million active and potential customers to zero in on the best credit risks. It has used this core competency to become a leader in the catalog shopping market and has parlayed these competencies to become a major issuer of credit cards. Fingerhut (now a division of Federated Department Stores, whose other divisions include some of the biggest names in retail: Macy's, Bloomingdales, and Burdines) also has developed important competencies in the areas of e-commerce, which it is sharing with these businesses.[9] This process of sharing what an organization does best across various organizational units and developing other outlets for creating value out of these core skills and capabilities distinguishes the concept of core competencies from distinctive capabilities. However, as Figure 4-2 illustrates, core competencies cannot be a source of competitive advantage but can contribute to the development of distinctive capabilities. The major value- creating skills and capabilities (i.e., the core competencies) can become distinctive capabilities *if* they meet the test of what distinctive capabilities are. Take the example we just looked at, Fingerhut. If the company's data analysis skills (core competency) can contribute to superior customer value, can be difficult for competitors to imitate, and can be used in a variety of ways, it would then be one of Fingerhut's distinctive capabilities.

Whereas an organization's capabilities are the source of its core competencies, these core competencies also contribute to the improvement and enhancement of organizational capabilities. (Note the two-directional arrow in Figure 4-2.) Although this may seem a lot like the puzzling question of "which came first . . .

Strategic Management in Action

Ram Mukunda, CEO of Startec Global Communications, has built a company that's regarded as one of the world's leading international communications companies. Startec has succeeded by serving the needs of many ethnic communities throughout the United States and around the world. The company's core competency is communicating with customers in their native languages and then tailoring high-value programs and products to meet their changing needs. Because of its capabilities in these areas, Startec's customer base has grown nearly 4,000 percent since 1996.

Sources: Company's Web site (**www.startec.com**), January 17, 2000; and C. Ghosh, "Plugged In," *Forbes*, April 5, 1999, pp. 70–71.

the chicken or the egg," it's actually pretty simple. Organizational capabilities do come first—they're the fundamental building block for developing core competencies. Every organization has organizational processes and routines to get work done. The major value-creating skills and capabilities—that is, the organization's core competencies—are created out of its routines and processes, accumulated knowledge, and actual work activities. If these core competencies *are* established—and not every organization will be able to do so—they can, in turn, improve and enhance organizational capabilities and also contribute to the development of certain distinctive organizational capabilities. Because core competencies span the organization's various product lines or business units, they are fundamental skills and capabilities that the organization has developed and is able to exploit. Moreover, the distinction between capabilities and competencies isn't really the important thing. Instead, both represent important aspects of managing strategically.

Refer back to Figure 4-2. The remaining sections of the figure address competitive advantage and performance results. We previously discussed the concept of competitive advantage in Chapter 2. Recall that it's what sets an organization apart—its competitive edge. Whether the organization has a competitive advantage will impact its performance results, in both the long run and the short run.

Strategic Management in Action

W. W. Grainger Inc. is not a household name. However, in its industry—maintenance, repair, and operations—Grainger is a venerable competitor. As a middleman, it offers 600,000 products ranging from motors to lightbulbs, and prospers (close to $4.5 billion in annual revenues) by catering to commercial buyers and sellers. The company's catalog—it's more than 4,000 pages long—is one of the most widely distributed publications in business. With the onslaught of Internet-based business-to-business purchasing, Grainger has chosen to embrace the change by setting up its own digital storefront (**www.grainger.com**). The company estimates that 20 percent of its site traffic takes place outside normal business hours and that the average order is twice the size of those received through traditional phone and fax contacts. Grainger also developed Orderzone.com (**www.orderzone.com**), an online marketplace where customers can order from Grainger or other leading distributors in other business segments. Although Grainger is Internet-savvy and seems to have girded itself well for traditional selling and Internet-based selling, there are risks to cooperating with competitors. Check out Grainger's Web businesses. What possible strengths and weaknesses do you see?

Sources: Company's Web site (**www.grainger.com**), March 30, 2000; Orderzone Web site (**www.orderzone.com**), March 30, 2000; and B. J. Feder, "For This Supplier, the Sum of Its Parts Adds Up to Success," *New York Times,* September 22, 1999, p. 61.

Although it's possible for an organization to enjoy strong performance results in the short run without a significant competitive advantage, there are limits to how long these results can last. Without a sustainable competitive advantage, the organization's long-run success and survival are uncertain. It's important, therefore, that organizational decision makers know where the organization's strengths and weaknesses are in terms of its resources, capabilities, and competencies. Our discussion of strengths and weaknesses is the last topic in describing what an internal analysis is.

The Role of Strengths and Weaknesses

The whole reason for doing an internal analysis is to assess what the organization has or doesn't have (resources) and what it can and can't do (capabilities)—in other words, its strengths and its weaknesses. **Strengths** are resources that the organization possesses and capabilities that the organization has developed, both of which can be exploited and developed into a sustainable competitive advantage. Although not every strength has the potential to be a sustainable competitive advantage, an organization's strengths should be nurtured and reinforced as its main competitive weapons. **Weaknesses**, on the other hand, are resources and capabilities that are lacking or deficient and that prevent the organization from developing a sustainable competitive advantage. Organizational weaknesses need to be corrected if they're in important areas that are preventing the organization from developing a sustainable competitive advantage. However, because most organizations do have limited resources to correct all their problems, strategic decision makers often choose simply to minimize the impact of weaknesses as long as those weaknesses aren't in critical areas—that is, those areas that are crucial for developing a sustainable competitive advantage.

Consider This ◄◄|

- ✓ When do organizational capabilities become a source of sustainable competitive advantage?
- ✓ What are distinctive organizational capabilities and what characteristics do they have?
- ✓ What are core competencies?
- ✓ What is the relationship between organizational capabilities and core competencies?
- ✓ How do core competencies and distinctive organizational capabilities differ?
- ✓ Describe strengths and weaknesses.

Organizational members at all levels of the organization are grappling with these types of strategic decisions: What are the strengths and weaknesses in my area(s) of responsibility, and how can I strategically manage these to achieve high levels of performance? Now that you have a good understanding of *what* an internal analysis is, it's time to look at *how* you do one.

HOW TO DO AN INTERNAL ANALYSIS

How do you go about assessing the organization's resources, capabilities, and core competencies? What's involved in the process? In this section we want to look at some different techniques for analyzing an organization's internal situation. We're first going to look at an approach that views the organization's work—what it's in business to do—as a series of value-creating activities. Then we'll describe an approach that's similar to a financial audit, but, instead of just scrutinizing and evaluating financial information, it's used to examine and assess all of the internal facets of an organization. Then we'll look at an approach called an internal environmental analysis process, which combines features of the value chain analysis and the internal audit. Next, we'll cover an approach that focuses on developing a capabilities profile. Finally, we'll look at how to classify an organization's strengths and weaknesses.

Value Chain Analysis

Every organization needs customers (buyers, consumers, whatever term is used) if it's going to survive. Even a not-for-profit organization must have customers who use its services or purchase its products. The premise behind value chain analysis is that customers want (demand) some type of value from the goods and services they purchase or obtain. And just what is it that customers value? **Customer value** arises from three broad categories: The product is unique and different; the product is low priced; or the providing organization has the ability to respond to specific or distinctive customer needs quickly. In order to assess the organization's ability to provide value, strategic decision makers look at how an organization's functional activities may contribute to creating customer value. This is where value chain analysis comes in. The **value chain** is a systematic way of examining all of the organization's functional activities and how well they create customer value.

The concept of the value chain was developed by Mike Porter (the same person who created the five forces model used in analyzing an organization's industry and competitive situation) as a tool for identifying ways to create more customer value.[10] As we've discussed earlier, every organization has specific organizational routines and processes—work activities that organizational members engage in—that allow it to do whatever it's in business to do. Each of these activities creates varying levels of customer value and organizational costs. What strategic decision

---

Strategic Management in Action

Better Decisions Through Data. That's the stated mission of Fair Isaac and Company, Inc. (**www.fairisaac.com**). The company is a leading developer of data management systems and services for the financial services, direct-marketing, and personal lines insurance industries. It offers a variety of sophisticated technological tools, such as database enhancement software, predictive modeling, adaptive control, and systems automation to help its customers make better decisions through data. The value chain is one internal analysis tool that could help strategic decision makers at Fair Isaac determine how well its primary and support activities create customer value—that is, how well these activities help customers make better decisions. Log on to the company's Web site and see if you can identify primary and support activities.

Sources: Company's Web site (**www.fairisaac.com**), March 30, 2000; and "Fair Isaac and Company, Inc.," *Better Investing*, July 1998, p. 12.

makers hope is that the customer value created—as evidenced by the product(s) the organization distributes or the services it provides and what customers are willing to "pay" for that value—outweighs the costs of creating that value. In using the value chain, we're assessing the organization's ability to create customer value through its activities. In other words, what are the organization's strengths and weaknesses in these areas? How did Porter describe these activities? Figure 4-4 shows the activities Porter felt were important to assess. The nine activities included five primary activities and four support activities. Let's look first at what Porter called the primary activities. The primary activities are those that actually create customer value and include the organizational routines and processes involved with bringing resources into the business (inbound logistics), processing these resources into the organization's goods or services (operations), physically distributing them to customers (outbound logistics), marketing the goods and services to customers (marketing and sales), and servicing customers (customer service). However, we don't want to know just what these activities *are*; we want to know *how well* the organization is performing these activities. That's what we need to know in order to assess the organization's strengths and weaknesses. Table 4-1 lists some questions to ask as you assess the primary activities in the value chain.

Let's look next at the support activities in the value chain. The support activities provide support for the primary activities as well as for each other. Although it may seem that the primary activities are the most critical to the organization because they are the ones that create value, keep in mind that the "performance" of the primary activities wouldn't be possible without the support activities. For example, if IDG Books Worldwide didn't have effective human resources manage-

Figure 4-4

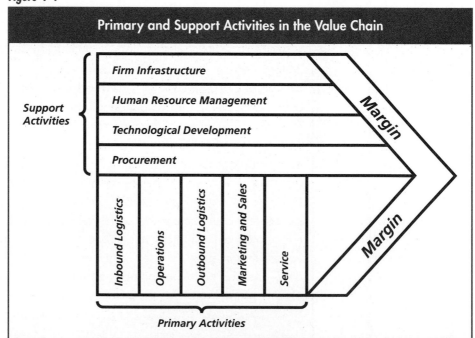

Source: Adapted with the permission of The Free Press, a Division of Simon and Schuster from *Competitive Advantage: Creating and Sustaining Superior Performance* by Michael E. Porter. Copyright © 1985 by Michael E. Porter.

TABLE 4-1   Assessing the Primary Activities in the Value Chain

Inbound Logistics

- Is there a materials control system? How well does it work?
- What type of inventory control system is there? How well does it work?
- How are raw materials handled and warehoused?
- How efficiently are raw materials handled and warehoused?

Operations

- How productive is our equipment as compared to our competitors?
- What type of plant layout is used? How efficient is it?
- Are production control systems in place to control quality and reduce costs? How efficient and effective are they in doing so?
- Are we using the appropriate level of automation in our production processes?

Outbound Logistics

- Are finished products delivered in a timely fashion to customers?
- Are finished products efficiently delivered to customers?
- Are finished products warehoused efficiently?

Marketing and Sales

- Is marketing research effectively used to identify customer segments and needs?
- Are sales promotions and advertising innovative?
- Have alternative distribution channels been evaluated?
- How competent is the sales force? Is its level of motivation as high as it can be?
- Does our organization present an image of quality to our customers? Does our organization have a favorable reputation?
- How brand loyal are our customers? Does our customer brand loyalty need improvement?
- Do we dominate the various market segments we're in?

Customer Service

- How well do we solicit customer input for product improvements?
- How promptly and effectively are customer complaints handled?
- Are our product warranty and guarantee policies appropriate?
- How effectively do we train employees in customer education and service issues?
- How well do we provide replacement parts and repair services?

Source: Based on Michael E. Porter, *Competitive Advantage: Creating and Sustaining Superior Performance* (New York: Free Press, 1985).

ment processes and routines, it wouldn't have employees to create the learning materials and to provide the exemplary level of customer service they do. If the employees can't provide this, they won't be creating value for the customer, the customer won't be willing to purchase the product, and organizational performance is going to suffer. How can you assess strengths and weaknesses in the support activities? Table 4-2 lists some questions to ask in assessing the support activities.

By assessing the organization's primary and support activities, you get a fairly good picture of its resources and capabilities (i.e., how resources are used in its work routines and processes) and of its strengths and weaknesses. To the extent

---

TABLE 4-2   Assessing the Support Activities in the Value Chain

Procurement

- Have we developed alternate sources for obtaining needed resources?
- Are resources procured in a timely fashion? At lowest possible cost? At acceptable quality levels?
- How efficient and effective are our procedures for procuring large capital expenditure resources such as plant, machinery, and buildings?
- Are criteria in place for deciding on lease-versus-purchase decisions?
- Have we established sound long-term relationships with reliable suppliers?

Technological Development

- How successful have our research and development activities been in product and process innovations?
- Is the relationship between R&D employees and other departments strong and reliable?
- Have technology development activities been able to meet critical deadlines?
- What is the quality of our organization's laboratories and other research facilities?
- How qualified and trained are our laboratory technicians and scientists?
- Does our organizational culture encourage creativity and innovation?

Human Resource Management

- How effective are our procedures for recruiting, selecting, orienting, and training employees?
- Are there appropriate employee promotion policies in place and are they used effectively?
- How appropriate are reward systems for motivating and challenging employees?
- Do we have a work environment that minimizes absenteeism and keeps turnover at reasonable levels?
- Are union—organization relations acceptable?
- Do managers and technical personnel actively participate in professional organizations?
- Are levels of employee motivation, job commitment, and job satisfaction acceptable?

Firm Infrastructure

- Is our organization able to identify potential external opportunities and threats?
- Does our strategic planning system facilitate and enhance the accomplishment of organizational goals?
- Are value chain activities coordinated and integrated throughout the organization?
- Can we obtain relatively low-cost funds for capital expenditures and working capital?
- Does our information system support strategic and operational decision making?
- Does our information system provide timely and accurate information on general environmental trends and competitive conditions?
- Do we have good relationships with our stakeholders including public policy makers and interest groups?
- Do we have a good public image of being a responsible corporate citizen?

Source: Based on Michael E. Porter, *Competitive Advantage: Creating and Sustaining Superior Performance* (New York: Free Press, 1985).

that the organization performs any of these activities more effectively or efficiently than its competitors do, it should be able to achieve a competitive advantage. The advantage of the value chain analysis technique is that it emphasizes the importance of customer value and how well an organization performs the primary and support activities in order to create customer value. However, this technique may be somewhat confusing and complex to use in assessing organizational strengths and weaknesses because organizational work activities don't always fit nicely and neatly into the primary and support activities framework. Therefore, some strategic decision makers prefer to use another approach—an internal audit.

Using an Internal Audit

Another approach to assessing organizational strengths and weaknesses is to use an internal audit of organizational functions. Just as the value chain approach starts with the premise that every organization needs customers and needs to provide value to those customers in order to achieve a competitive advantage, the internal audit approach starts with the premise that every organization has certain functions that it must perform. In pursuing a sustainable competitive advantage, these functions may be performed well or performed poorly. We base our identification of strengths and weaknesses on how well these basic organizational functions are performed. You may be familiar with the concept of a financial audit, which is simply a thorough examination of a firm's financial records and procedures. An **internal audit** is a thorough assessment of an organization's various internal functional areas. It's similar to a financial audit although it obviously focuses on much more than just the financial aspects. Strategic decision makers use the internal audit to assess the organization's resources and capabilities from the perspective of its different functions. Do the various functions have the needed resources to perform their assigned work activities and how well do they perform these assigned work activities (i.e., what are their capabilities)?

What basic organizational functions should an internal audit look at? Organizations are often characterized as having six main functional areas: production–operations, marketing, research and development, financial and accounting, management (typically includes human resource management and other general management activities), and information systems. Obviously, individual organizations are likely to have unique functions that aren't covered under these general categories, or they may not call their functions by these particular names, but these six are the most common ones. What should you examine and evaluate in each of these areas? Table 4-3 lists some key internal audit questions to use to assess the strengths and weaknesses of each of the functional areas. This assessment concentrates on the availability or lack of critical resources, and the level of performance in organizational routines and processes (i.e., the work activities being done) in each of these functional areas.

Using an internal audit approach to analyze an organization's functional activities is fairly straightforward. The analysis can be tailored to fit whatever distinctive functions an organization might have. For example, in the case of IDG Books Worldwide, an internal audit might cover its specific functional areas such as manuscript writing, manuscript design, distribution, and customer service. In addition, strategic decision makers in each of IDGB's product lines could use an internal audit to assess strengths and weaknesses in specific functions. Again, the key in assessing organization functions using an internal audit is to determine

Organizations Need Physicals, Too

Have you ever had a physical exam? If you have, you know there's an intense scrutiny of past medical history, current health issues or complaints, and lifestyle factors. And, the physical exam may point to the need for additional scrutiny with test results compared to normal ranges. Doesn't this seem to be an appropriate analogy for assessing organizations? Could the concept of a "physical exam" be applied to organizations? Here's a guide to giving your organization a physical exam.

- *Brain function:* This would be the organization's strategy and planning function. How well does your organization's "brain" function? Are the strategies and plans getting through to the rest of the organization? Is the "command center" functioning effectively and efficiently?
- *Nervous system:* You need to check your company's reflexes. Are communication and information technology systems responsive as they gather and disseminate information from the brain?

- *Eyes, ears, nose, and mouth:* These sense organs respond to the outside world. Are your marketing and sales groups "sensing" customers' needs accurately?
- *Arms, hands, legs, feet, and associated muscle groups:* These body parts convert energy into action. What kind of shape are your operations systems in? Do they acquire materials, make things, and deliver them efficiently and effectively?
- *Lungs, digestive system:* In your body, the lungs and digestive system absorb nutrients and filter waste. Are resources being absorbed efficiently? Are you getting rid of waste efficiently?
- *Heart:* You need to have a strong, highly conditioned heart to keep the rest of the body functioning properly. The organization's heart is its culture, its sense of meaning and purpose. How is the flow of your culture throughout the organization? Has it cut off circulation or is it sending out strength-giving nutrients?

Source: J. Mariotti, "Give Your Company a Physical," *Industry Week,* October 5, 1998, p. 74.

how well or poorly these functions are being performed and what resources are available to these functional areas for carrying out their work activities. The drawback of this approach is that it focuses attention on the functional areas while downplaying whether these functional areas are even important in achieving a competitive advantage. Therefore, another approach called an internal environmental analysis process attempts to address these concerns.

Using an Internal Environmental Analysis Process

We know from our discussion in Chapter 3 (on external analysis) that when strategic decision makers do an *external* analysis they go through increasingly detailed steps as they first scan and then evaluate the trends and changes taking place. What if the same type of increasingly detailed analysis were applied to the internal environment of the organization? Might it not be a more effective analytical tool for strategic decision makers? The **internal environmental analysis process** proposes assessing an organization's internal activities by first surveying strengths and weaknesses, categorizing these strengths and weaknesses in terms of

TABLE 4-3 Important Internal Audit Questions

Production–Operations

- Does the organization have reliable and reasonably priced suppliers?
- Are facilities, offices, machinery, and equipment in good working condition?
- Are facilities strategically located close to resources and markets?
- Does the organization have effective inventory control policies and procedures?
- Does the organization utilize quality control procedures? Are these procedures effective?
- How does the organization do on quality assessments?
- Does the organization have an appropriate amount of capacity?
- What is the organization's safety record?
- Does the production–operations process work smoothly and with little disruptions?
- Have production–operations goals been established, and are work activities aimed at achieving these goals?
- Do production–operations employees use appropriate operations planning and controlling tools and techniques?
- Has the organization developed any particular competencies in the areas of production–operations?

Marketing

- Does the organization segment markets effectively?
- What is the organization's market position or rank?
- Does the organization position itself well against its competitors?
- What is the organization's market share, and has it been increasing or decreasing?
- Does the organization conduct market research, and is this research effective?
- Is market research information used in making marketing decisions?
- Does the organization have an effective sales force?
- Has the organization priced its products and services appropriately?
- How is product quality, and how does it compare to that of competitors?
- Is customer service effective, and how does it compare to competitors?
- Is the advertising strategy effective?
- Are promotion and publicity strategies effective?
- Are customer complaints decreasing, increasing, or stable?
- Are customer complaints handled effectively and efficiently?
- Are present channels of distribution reliable and cost effective?
- Are marketing planning and budgeting effective?
- Do marketing employees use appropriate marketing planning and controlling tools and techniques?
- Has the organization developed any particular competencies in any of the marketing areas?

Research and Development

- Does the organization have adequate R&D facilities?
- Are the R&D employees well qualified?
- Does organizational culture encourage creativity and innovation?
- Is communication between R&D and other organizational units effective?
- Are the organization's products technologically competitive?

(continues)

TABLE 4-3   Important Internal Audit Questions *(continued)*

Research and Development *(continued)*

- If patents are appropriate, are patent applications increasing, decreasing, or stable?
- Is development time from concept to actual product appropriate?
- How many new products have been developed during the last year (or whatever time period is most appropriate)?
- Does the organization commit more, the same, or less to R&D than its competitors do?
- Do R&D employees use appropriate R&D tools and techniques?
- Has the organization developed any particular competencies in the R&D area?

Financial and Accounting

- Is the organization financially strong or weak according to the financial ratio analyses?
- What are the trends in the organization's financial ratios, and how do these compare to industry trends?
- Is the organization able to raise short-term capital?
- Is the organization able to raise long-term capital?
- What is the organization's working capital position? Is it sufficient?
- Are the organization's capital budgeting procedures effective?
- Has the organization established financial goals? Are they appropriate?
- Are dividend payout policies reasonable?
- What type of relationship does the organization have with its creditors and stockholders?
- Is there a match between the organization's sources and uses of funds?
- Do financial–accounting employees use appropriate financial–accounting tools and techniques?
- Has the organization developed any particular competencies in the financial–accounting area?

Management

- Do organization employees manage strategically?
- Are organizational goals clear and measurable? Are they communicated to organizational members?
- Is the organization's structure appropriate?
- What is the organization's culture? Does it support organizational goals and mission?
- Has the organization developed its vision? What about mission(s)?
- Does the organization attract appropriate job applicants?
- Are employee selection procedures effective?
- Does the organization provide employees with appropriate training?
- Are job descriptions and job specifications clear?
- Are jobs effectively designed?
- What is the level of employee morale?
- What is the level of employee turnover?
- Are organizational compensation and reward programs appropriate?
- Are organizational employee discipline and control mechanisms appropriate?
- How does the organization treat its employees?
- What kind of relationships does the organization have with employee groups?
- Does the organization effectively use work teams?
- Are legal guidelines followed in human resource management activities?

TABLE 4-3   Important Internal Audit Questions *(continued)*

Management *(continued)*

- Has the organization developed any competencies in its human resource management activities?
- Has the organization developed any competencies in the management area?

Information Systems–Information Technology

- How does the organization gather and disseminate information? Is it effective and efficient?
- Is the information system used by employees in making decisions?
- Is information updated regularly?
- Is information distributed effectively and efficiently?
- Do employees have access to contribute input to the information system?
- Has the organization made an investment in information technology that's greater than, equal to, or less than competitors?
- Is information technology used effectively and efficiently in all areas of the organization?
- Is the organization's information system secure?
- Is the organization's information system user friendly?
- Are training workshops or seminars provided for users of the information system?
- Are employees in the information systems–information technology area well qualified?
- Has the organization developed any competencies in the information systems–information technology area?

resources and capabilities, investigating the potential of these strengths to lead to competitive advantage, and finally evaluating the ability of these competitively relevant resources and capabilities to serve as the basis for an appropriate competitive strategy.[11] Figure 4-5 illustrates these steps.

The main aspect of this approach to internal analysis is its emphasis on linking the identification of organizational strengths and weaknesses with the devel-

Figure 4-5

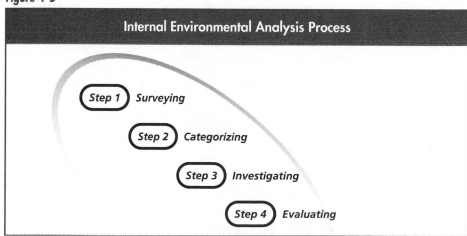

Internal Environmental Analysis Process

Step 1   *Surveying*

Step 2   *Categorizing*

Step 3   *Investigating*

Step 4   *Evaluating*

Source: Based on W. J. Duncan, P. M. Ginter, and L. E. Swayne, "Competitive Advantage and Internal Organizational Assessment," *Academy of Management Executive,* August 1998, p. 8.

Strategic Management—The Global Perspective

Have you ever heard of Sound Blaster (**www.soundblaster.com**) or experienced Sound Blaster technology? An internal environmental analysis of the company that developed Sound Blaster, Creative Technology, Ltd. (**www.creative.com**), would point to several significant resources and capabilities. Creative is the world's leading provider of multimedia products and peripherals for personal computers. The company was founded in Singapore by Sim Wong Hoo, whose vision was that multimedia would revolutionize the way people interacted with their PCs. Creative has earned global leadership status for its innovations in interactive audio, graphics, PC-DVD, video, and communications technology, and as an industry pioneer in the creation of multimedia standards. Go to the company's Web site and read about its many accomplishments. Think of the types of resources and capabilities that have enabled the company to reach the performance levels it has.

Sources: Company's Web site (**www.creative.com**), March 30, 2000; and M. Shari and P. Engardio, "The Sweet Sound of Success," *Business Week,* September 8, 1997, p. 56.

opment of an appropriate competitive advantage. Its intent is to encourage strategic decision makers to think about strengths and weaknesses in terms of their strategic relevance, rather than just auditing functional activities of the organization. Let's take a closer look at each of the steps in this approach.

The first step in this approach, surveying, involves generating extensive lists of organizational strengths and weaknesses in the organization's primary and support activities as described by the value chain. It involves looking at what the firm does well and where it needs improvement. However, just superficially identifying strengths and weaknesses isn't enough, which brings us to the second step—categorizing. In this step, strategic decision makers take a deeper look at these strengths and weaknesses in terms of the resources and capabilities represented and whether these resources and capabilities have the potential to lead to competitive advantage. Once the organizational strengths and weaknesses have been evaluated in terms of the underlying resources and capabilities, the third step involves investigating how and where these factors actually add value. The critical task in this stage is pinpointing the primary or support activity that possesses the potential for building or losing competitive advantage. Finally, in the fourth step, the competitively relevant resources and capabilities are evaluated in terms of their ability to become the basis for a sustainable competitive advantage.

Although the other two approaches to internal analysis we've discussed assume that the purpose of assessing the internal organizational primary and support activities (the value chain) or the organization's functional areas (internal audit) is to pinpoint key strengths that are likely to lead to competitive advantage and key weaknesses that must be cor-

Consider This ◀◀▏

✓ Describe what a value chain analysis shows.

✓ When will a customer find value in a product?

✓ What are the primary activities in the value chain? The support activities?

✓ What is an internal audit and what does it look at?

✓ How is an internal audit different from the value chain analysis?

✓ Describe the steps in an internal environmental analysis process.

✓ How is this approach similar to the value chain analysis? How is it different?

✓ How is this approach similar to the internal audit? How is it different?

rected, this approach to internal analysis more clearly delineates it. In that sense, it reminds us that an internal analysis is part of the bigger picture of formulating, implementing, and evaluating organizational strategies. However, the disadvantage of this approach is that by using the value chain as its basis for assessing strengths and weaknesses, it suffers from the same drawbacks we discussed earlier.

Capabilities Assessment Profile

The last approach we want to discuss for doing an internal analysis is a capabilities assessment profile. It's similar to the internal environmental analysis process because it focuses on a deeper evaluation of an organization's strengths and weaknesses, but it's different in that it focuses on only an organization's capabilities. This approach was developed because strategic decision makers had few guidelines for identifying and evaluating their organization's distinctive capabilities.[12] The analysis of capabilities is complex because capabilities develop out of the way resources are combined and coordinated in the organization's basic work processes and routines. They're not as easily identifiable as organizational functions or even the value-creating primary and support activities. However, the complex nature of capabilities also makes it hard for competitors to imitate, which makes them a good source of a sustainable competitive advantage. Therefore, we need some guidelines for identifying the organization's distinctive capabilities. That's what the capabilities assessment profile approach provides.

The capabilities assessment actually consists of two phases: (1) identifying distinctive capabilities and (2) developing and leveraging these distinctive capabilities.[13] Because our main interest at this point is analyzing the internal aspects of the organization, we're going to concentrate on phase 1, identifying distinctive capabilities. Phase 2 addresses strategy development issues that are beyond the scope of our discussion of how to do an internal analysis. Figure 4-6 illustrates the steps in phase 1—identifying these distinctive organizational capabilities.

Earlier in the chapter, we described what makes capabilities distinct. Let's review those characteristics quickly. First, distinctive capabilities should contribute to superior customer value and offer customers real benefits. Next, they should be difficult for competitors to imitate. Finally, distinctive capabilities should be usable in a variety of ways by the organization. This brief reminder about the characteristics of distinctive organizational capabilities is important because they've influenced the type of information gathered in a capabilities assessment. In fact, the first step in assessing organizational capabilities—*preparing a current product–market profile*—emphasizes organization–customer interactions. In this step, we identify what we're selling, whom we're selling to, and whether we're providing superior customer value and offering the customer desirable benefits. To do this, we need information about specific products and markets; principal competitors in each of these product–market segments; and performance measures, such as sales growth rates, market share, competitive position, contributions to division sales and earnings—for each of the product–market segments.

Once we have a current (and thorough) product–market profile, the next step in a capabilities assessment is *identifying sources of competitive advantage and disadvantage in the main product–market segments*. We want to know why customers choose our products instead of those of our competitors. This assessment would involve information on specific cost, product, and service attributes. What

Figure 4-6

Identifying Distinctive Organizational Capabilities

Step 1 *Prepare current product–market profile.*

Step 2 *Identify sources of competitive advantage and disadvantage in the main product–market segments.*

Step 3 *Describe all the organizational capabilities and competencies.*

Step 4 *Sort the core capabilities and competencies according to strategic importance.*

Step 5 *Identify and agree on the key capabilities and competencies.*

Source: Based on Kenneth E. Marino, "Developing Consensus on Firm Competencies and Capabilities," *Academy of Management Executive*, August 1996, pp. 40–51.

are these "attributes" we need to identify? When customers purchase a product (physical good or service), they're actually purchasing a bundle of attributes that they believe will satisfy their needs.[14] These attributes vary by product and market. For example, camera customers may be interested in product attributes such as picture clarity, camera speeds, camera size, or price. Airline customers might

STRATEGIC MANAGEMENT IN AN E-BUSINESS WORLD

Even with all the talk about e-business, many big companies are going slowly when it comes to an Internet strategy. A survey of 78 large companies by PricewaterhouseCoopers (PWC) and the Conference Board showed that nearly 80 percent of these businesses responded that Internet business accounted for less than 5 percent of their revenues. Only 17 percent rated themselves as e-commerce innovators. About 25 percent of the companies were able to process transactions online and less than half had tools in place to evaluate e-commerce performance. Are these results surprising? Maybe not. One of the PWC consultants stated, "The strategic process [at these large companies] can't be the traditional annual affair. They need to have a much more flexible quickly reactive way of managing ideas and opportunities." What do you think of these survey results? What are the implications for assessing capabilities and competencies? Will an e-business world change the way strategic decision makers look at internal strengths and weaknesses? Explain.

Source: B. Tedeschi, "Big Companies Go Slowly in Devising Net Strategy," *New York Times*, March 27, 2000, p. C4.

choose a particular airline based on attributes such as safety record, close adherence to arrival–departure schedules, customer service, meal availability, convenience of arrival–departure times, and price. Community arts customers might choose a live theater performance on attributes such as familiarity with the play, actors or actresses starring in the play, or ticket price. Again, in this step we're attempting to identify those attributes that our customers value in our products and what competitive advantages or disadvantages these attributes provide us.

With this information, then, we're ready to uncover what organizational capabilities lead to those sources of competitive advantage and disadvantage. Step 3 involves *describing organizational capabilities and competencies.* To identify these capabilities, you would need to closely examine the resources, skills, and abilities of the organization's various divisions. Let's look at an example to help explain this. Suppose that you're a strategic manager at one of the nation's airlines. Your analysis of sources of competitive advantage and disadvantage (step 2) showed that one of the reasons customers choose your airline over those of competitors is because scheduled flights left on time consistently. In step 3, you'd need to uncover what resources, skills, and abilities led to this competitive advantage. You might find, for example, that consistent departures were the result of a well-trained ground crew who loaded baggage efficiently and effectively; appropriate numbers of customer service representatives who processed passengers quickly; a system of paperless ticketing and boarding passes; and pilots who knew the ins and outs of getting quick control tower clearance for takeoff. This type of intense analysis of the various organizational resources and organizational routines and processes behind the capabilities is an important step. It forces strategic decision makers to understand what really happens (and what has to happen) in order to deliver superior customer value and benefits. Even strategic decision makers in not-for-profit organizations should assess what organizational resources and organizational routines and processes lead to customers' willingness to support, sponsor, and advocate their products and programs. This is probably the most difficult of all the steps in the capabilities profile. Yet, it's also the one that yields the most

---

Strategic Management in Action

A capabilities assessment profile might reveal that your once-distinctive capabilities are no longer so. Sports Authority, Inc., one of the nation's biggest sports-equipment retailers, is finding that its ability to appeal to baby boomers isn't leading to a competitive advantage. Aging baby boomers are not quite as physically active as they once were and their desire for sports gear is fading. To deal with these new realities, the company is gearing itself toward women and children. One strategic question inherent in this new direction is whether its previous competencies and capabilities can keep it competitive.

Sources: Company's Web site (**www.sportsauthority.com**), March 20, 2000; and A. I. Flores, "Sports Authority Takes Steps to Whip Itself into Shape," *Wall Street Journal,* August 3, 1999, p. B4.

important information because it gets to the heart of the matter—the most basic aspects of organizational operations and the inherent interactions as an organization's work is performed by organizational members.

What's next? Step 4 involves *sorting these core capabilities and competencies according to their strategic importance.* In other words, which of these capabilities are most important for building the future of the organization? Judging which capabilities are strategically important is a matter of evaluating each one according to three criteria: (1) Does the capability provide tangible customer benefits? (2) Is the capability difficult for competitors to imitate? and (3) Can the capability provide wide access to a number of different markets? Do these criteria sound familiar? Well, they should—we described them earlier as the characteristics of a distinctive capability. This analysis will show you that organizational capabilities differ in their level of strategic importance. Those that are most important strategically should be placed at the top of the list and on down. By sorting organizational capabilities according to level of strategic importance, strategic decision makers gain an understanding of their organization's critical strengths and weaknesses. But, there's still one more step in a capabilities assessment profile.

The final step involves *identifying and agreeing on the key competencies and capabilities.* Based upon the ranking of strategic importance, decision makers can easily identify the organization's key competencies and capabilities. But, what's difficult is agreeing that these *are* the key ones. Obviously, when we pinpoint certain organizational capabilities as more critical to competitive advantage than others, it's likely to affect future resource allocation and organizational support for various organizational units and divisions. Therefore, even though organizational members may be impacted differently, getting agreement on the organization's key capabilities is an important step in capabilities assessment. Without agreement on these critical capabilities, managing strategically for a sustainable competitive advantage will be extremely difficult.

Although the capabilities assessment approach provides a thorough analysis of the organization's important strategic capabilities, it's a complicated process. This approach appears to be most useful to upper-level strategic managers because it forces an assessment of the vast number of underlying organizational capabilities, which, because of what they are—complex interactions of organizational routines and processes—don't always fit nicely and neatly into narrowly defined specific functional areas.

Classifying an Organization's Strengths and Weaknesses

Each of the approaches to internal analysis can be used to identify the organization's resources and capabilities. Whether it's from the perspective of analyzing the customer value created by the organization's primary and support activities, from the perspective of auditing the organization's various functional areas, from the perspective of assessing the link between organizational strengths and weaknesses and competitive advantage, or from the perspective of identifying the organization's distinctive capabilities, we get a broad picture of the organization's resources and work routines and processes. However, that's only half the picture. We have to do more than just *identify* these factors. We've also got to *assess* where the organization has strengths and weaknesses in each of these areas. What are its strong points? What are its weak points? What resources and capabilities can be enhanced and exploited for a sustainable competitive advantage? What resources

Strategic Management—The Global Perspective

He's not as well-known as Bill Gates of Microsoft or Jerry Yang of Yahoo!, but Masayoshi Son has built a business that's making some noise. Softbank is Japan's number-one distributor of software and hardware and has a 70 percent interest in the high-tech media firm Ziff-Davis. In addition, Son has been aggressively investing in Internet companies and now has stakes in more than 300 of these companies including Yahoo!, Buy.com, E-Loan, E*Trade, and others. However, some experts have expressed serious doubts about Softbank's seemingly chaotic Internet empire. These concerns are ones often expressed about Internet companies—they look fabulously wealthy on paper, but they're chewing up ever-increasing amounts of cash with little cash being generated. An assessment of the strengths and weaknesses of Softbank's empire might be in order. Do some research on this company. What strategic changes have taken place? Has the company exploited its strengths and improved its weaknesses? What do you think of this company's strategic direction?

Sources: Information on Softbank from Hoover's Online (**www.hoovers.com**), March 31, 2000; and N. Weinberg, "Master of the Internet," *Forbes,* July 5, 1999, pp. 146–51.

and capabilities are lacking or not used effectively? Strategic decision makers should make these types of assessments as they analyze the information about the various internal organizational areas, whether from the value chain approach, internal audit approach, internal environmental analysis process approach, or capabilities process approach. In order to assess whether resources and capabilities are strengths or weaknesses and whether certain ones could be sources of sustainable competitive advantage, we've got to have some criteria against which to measure them. What criteria can we use to judge a strength or weakness?[15] Figure 4-7 identifies four such criteria.

One criterion that could be used to determine whether resources and capabilities are strengths or weaknesses is past performance trends. These criteria could include any organizational performance measures such as financial ratios, operations efficiency statistics, employee productivity statistics, or data on adherence to quality control standards. Any internal organizational performance area that's measurable could be assessed by looking at the trends. For instance, is market share increasing or decreasing? Are liquidity ratios going up or down? Is the number of product returns increasing or decreasing? Are employee training expenditures reducing production reject rates? For example, in our chapter-opening case, IDGB's CEO undoubtedly examines various organizational performance trends before making strategic decisions. These types of quantitative measures can be used as indicators of organizational strengths and weaknesses. Although performance trends can show important information about the organization's continuing use of resources and capabilities, it doesn't show us whether performance is up to standards.

Therefore, another criterion to use in assessing organizational strengths and weaknesses is to look at specific performance goals or targets and how actual performance measures up against these. **Organizational goals** are statements of desired outcomes. Every organization should have specific goals at all levels and in all internal functional areas that state *what* it hopes to do or accomplish within a

Figure 4-7

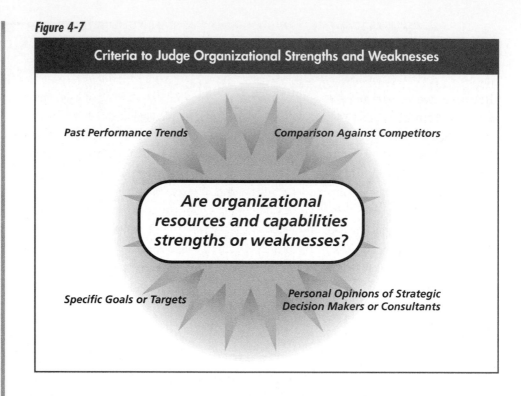

Criteria to Judge Organizational Strengths and Weaknesses

Past Performance Trends

Comparison Against Competitors

Are organizational resources and capabilities strengths or weaknesses?

Specific Goals or Targets

Personal Opinions of Strategic Decision Makers or Consultants

certain time frame. These goals provide direction by specifying what and how organizational resources and capabilities are used in carrying out the organizational vision and mission(s). By comparing actual performance in the various organizational areas against stated goals, we can assess strengths and weaknesses. This assessment provides clues to how well the various internal areas are performing. However, just looking at how internal organizational performance measures up to the goals and looking at performance trends isn't enough to help us determine whether these strengths or weaknesses can be used to influence the development of potential sustainable competitive advantage. To do this, we need some comparisons against our competitors—which is another criterion we can use to measure strengths and weaknesses.

By comparing our organization's resources and capabilities against those of our competitors, we can see how we stack up against those who are battling for the same customers' dollars. Remember from the last chapter that as part of our *external* analysis, we looked at competitors. However, as part of the internal analysis, we need to focus on not only *what* our competitors are doing but also *how* they're doing. Getting this information isn't quite as easy as getting our own internal organizational performance information. This information may include such things as surveys and rankings published in external information sources. For instance, *Fortune* publishes an annual corporate reputations survey that ranks industry competitors according to what company is most admired and on down. *Business Week* publishes annual rankings of research and development expenditures. We might also find competitor information in sources such as articles in business or general newsmagazines, other types of public documents such as annual reports or Securities and Exchange Commission filings, industry association newsletters, networking at professional meetings, customer contacts, and even the competitor's Web homepage. A key consideration for gathering informa-

FYI

There's Something About Market Share

One commonly used comparison against competitors is market share. Is it an appropriate measure? Nearly every business is mesmerized by market share—keeping it or increasing it. Conventional wisdom about the importance of market share was that the biggest market share would give a company the biggest revenues and the lowest cost per unit. That approach may have worked in the 1960s through 1980s. However, the reality of the new environment is that increasing market share may not be the route to continued competitive advantage and profitability. Having the most customers doesn't automatically translate into having the most profits. In fact, one study conducted by a consulting firm found that 70 percent of the time, the company with the largest market share didn't have the highest rate of return. What strategic decision makers need to address is how customers' needs are changing and how they can best meet those changing needs. Maybe *that's* how companies need to measure themselves against their competitors—by how well they are meeting customers' changing needs. What do you think? Do you agree with the premises of this argument regarding the decreased importance of market share? What are the implications for doing an internal analysis?

Sources: R. Brooks, "Alienating Customers Isn't Always a Bad Idea, Many Firms Discover," *Wall Street Journal*, January 7, 1999, p. A1; C. Boyd, "Management Issue: The Myth of Market Share," Management Issues Web site, December 17, 1998; R. Miniter, "The Myth of Market Share," *Wall Street Journal*, June 15, 1998, p. A28; and A. Slywotzky and D. J. Morrison, "When Baseball Is in Trouble, How GE Makes Money, and Other Insights into the True Origin of Corporate Profits," *Fortune*, May 11, 1998, pp. 183–84.

tion on your competitors is whether your competitive intelligence methods are ethical. (See The Grey Zone ethical issue.) For example, whereas there's nothing unethical about scouring published sources for competitor information, ethical

The Grey Zone

Here are some techniques that have been suggested for gathering competitor information: (1) Pretend to be a journalist writing a story. Call up competitors' offices and interview them. (2) Dig through a competitor's trash. (3) Sit outside a competitor's place of business and count how many customers go in. (4) Get copies of your competitors' in-house newsletters and read them. (5) Call the Better Business Bureau and ask if competitors have had any complaints filed against them and if so, what kind of complaints. (6) Have friends call competitors for price lists, brochures, or other marketing information. Do you think these methods are ethical or unethical? Why? What ethical guidelines might you propose for strategic decision makers when doing competitor intelligence?

issues might arise if you decide, for instance, to rummage through a competitor's trash bins for information or access its electronic databases by hacking in. Although there are no easy answers in these ethical dilemmas, be alert to the perceived "rightness" or "wrongness" of your competitive intelligence gathering methods.[16]

The last criterion we want to discuss for judging organizational strengths and weaknesses is the use of personal or subjective opinions of strategic decision makers or consultants. Sometimes, the best way to assess strong or weak areas is to get the personal opinion of those who are directly involved in the activity. Quantitative performance measures, such as trends or comparisons against standards, don't always capture what's really going on in a particular functional area. Not every resource or capability may be appropriate for quantitative measurement.

STRATEGIC MANAGEMENT IN AN E-BUSINESS WORLD

Are the tools and techniques of internal assessment appropriate for an e-business world? Although some comprehensive approach to assessing organizational strengths and weaknesses is necessary in any type or size of organization, we may need to tailor aspects of these assessments to e-business organizations. PricewaterhouseCoopers has developed its emm@ or E-Business Maturity Model, which analyzes Web sites in nine categories from strategy to performance to technology. In addition, the emm@ tool measures Web presence on a scale from "minimal to full e-business." Other e-business consultants are developing tools to help organizations assess how they stack up against the competition and how they can do better. Do you think such specialized assessments are necessary? Why or why not?

Source: J. Oleck, "Do You Rank as a Full E-Business?" *Business Week,* January 17, 2000, p. 6.

Qualitative opinions or assessments of organizational members can be useful in determining areas of strength or weakness. Also, if outside consultants are working with any of the organization's divisions or units, what's their opinion? What do they see as strengths or weaknesses? Although this particular criterion is impossible for you to use in case analysis in this class (unless you're studying a local organization), it's likely to be useful as another way to assess strengths and weaknesses when you're working in some organization and managing strategically. (Yes, you will have a professional life after school!)

By now, you should have a fairly good idea of what's involved in actually *doing* an internal analysis and identifying strengths and weaknesses. It's more than simply identifying an organization's internal resources and capabilities. It's also assessing whether those resources and capabilities are sufficient and can be sources of sustainable competitive advantage. Although we've discussed what internal analysis is and how to do one, we haven't yet addressed *why* it's an important part of managing strategically. We're going to cover that next.

Consider This ◀◀|

✓ What does a capabilities assessment profile provide?

✓ Describe the five steps in assessing organizational capabilities.

✓ How do you judge which organizational capabilities are strategically important?

✓ What criteria can be used to judge organizational resources and capabilities as either strengths or weaknesses? Describe.

✓ What are organizational goals, and how do they affect the determination of strengths or weaknesses in organizational resources and capabilities?

✓ Describe the role ethics plays in determining organizational strengths and weaknesses.

✓ Why is an internal analysis an important part of managing strategically?

WHY DO AN INTERNAL ANALYSIS?

Doing an internal analysis is important for two basic reasons: (1) It's the only way to identify an organization's strengths and weaknesses, and (2) it's needed for making good strategic decisions. Let's explain these reasons a little more completely.

As we stated at the beginning of the chapter, an internal analysis is a process of identifying and evaluating an organization's specific characteristics including its resources, capabilities, and core competencies. The outcome of the process is important information about an organization's specific assets, skills, and work routines and processes. What strengths do we have because of our specific resources and capabilities? What weaknesses are there in our specific resources and capabilities? If we didn't do this analysis, we wouldn't have this critical strategic information. But, this information in and of itself isn't useful. It's how strategic decision makers *use* this information that's important.

With the information from an internal analysis, strategic decision makers can make intelligent judgments about what competitive advantages the organization might currently have, what might potentially be developed into competitive advantages, and what might be preventing competitive advantages from being developed. This internal information, coupled with the information from the external analysis and information about the organizational context, provides the basis for deciding what strategic actions are necessary for sustainable competitive advantage.

THE BOTTOM LINE

- An **internal analysis** is a process of identifying and evaluating an organization's specific characteristics including its resources, capabilities, and core competencies.

- One important part of the internal analysis is looking at the organization's current vision, mission(s), strategic objectives, and strategies.

- An organization's resources can be financial, physical, human, intangible, and structural–cultural.

- Although an organization's tangible and intangible resources can be a source of competitive advantage, they play a more important role in determining an organization's capabilities and core competencies.

- **Organizational capabilities** are the complex and coordinated network of organizational routines and processes that determine how efficiently and effectively the organization transforms its inputs (resources) into outputs (products including goods and services).

- **Organizational routines and processes** are the regular, predictable, and sequential patterns of work activity by organizational members.

- Creating organizational capabilities isn't simply a matter of assembling resources. Capabilities involve complex patterns of coordination between people and between people and other organizational resources.

- The concept of **dynamic capabilities** suggests that organizations must have the ability to build, integrate, and reconfigure capabilities to address rapidly changing environments.

- Before organizational capabilities can become a source of competitive advantage, they must be truly distinctive.

- **Distinctive organizational capabilities** are the special and unique capabilities that distinguish the organization from its competitors.

- Three characteristics of distinctive organizational capabilities are that it must contribute to superior customer value, it should be difficult for competitors to imitate, and it should allow organizations to use it in a variety of ways.

➠ The concept of **core competencies**, developed by Prahalad and Hamel, describes the organization's major value-creating skills and capabilities that are *shared* across multiple product lines or multiple businesses.

➠ This process of sharing what an organization does best is what distinguishes the concept of core competencies from distinctive capabilities.

➠ Core competencies cannot be a source of competitive advantage but can contribute to the development of distinctive capabilities, which lead to a competitive advantage.

➠ The major value-creating skills and capabilities (the core competencies) can become distinctive capabilities if they meet the test of what distinctive capabilities are.

➠ Core competencies also contribute to the improvement and enhancement of organizational capabilities. However, capabilities do come first.

➠ **Strengths** are resources that the organization possesses and capabilities that it has developed, both of which can be exploited and developed into a sustainable competitive advantage.

➠ **Weaknesses** are resources and capabilities that are lacking or deficient and that prevent the organization from developing a sustainable competitive advantage.

➠ There are four approaches to doing an internal analysis: value chain analysis, internal audit, internal environmental analysis process, and capabilities assessment profile.

➠ The value chain focuses on **customer value**, which arises from (1) the product being unique and different, (2) the product being low priced, and (3) the organization having the ability to respond to specific or distinctive customer needs.

➠ The **value chain** was developed by Mike Porter and is a systematic way of examining all of the organization's functional activities and how well they create customer value.

➠ These organizational activities include the primary activities—those that actually create customer value and include inbound logistics, operations, outbound logistics, marketing and sales, and customer service—and the support activities—those that provide support for the primary activities and include procurement, technological development, human resource management, and firm infrastructure.

➠ The advantage of the value chain analysis is that it emphasizes the importance of customer value and how effectively the organization creates it. However, the drawback is that this approach may be confusing and complex to use because organizational work activities don't always fit into the primary and support activities framework.

➠ The **internal audit** is a thorough assessment of an organization's various internal functional areas.

➠ These internal functional areas typically include production–operations, marketing, research and development, financial and accounting, management, and information systems.

➠ The advantage of the internal audit approach is that it's fairly straightforward and can be tailored to fit whatever distinctive functions an organization might have.

➠ The drawback of the internal audit approach is that it focuses attention on the functional areas while downplaying whether these functional areas are even important in achieving a competitive advantage.

➠ The **internal environmental analysis process** proposes assessing an organization's internal activities in four steps: (1) surveying strengths and weaknesses, (2) categorizing these strengths and weaknesses in terms of resources and capabilities, (3) investigating the potential of these strengths to lead to competitive advantage, and (4) evaluating the ability of these competitively relevant resources and capabilities to serve as the basis for a competitive strategy.

➠ The advantage of this approach is that it clearly pinpoints key strengths that are likely to lead to competitive advantage.

➠ The drawback of this approach is that it uses the primary and support activities framework, which tends to be not as easy to use.

➠ The capabilities assessment profile is used to identify an organization's distinctive capabilities.

➠ The steps in a capabilities assessment profile include (1) preparing a current product–market profile, (2) identifying sources of competitive advantage and disadvantage in the main product–market segments, (3) describing organizational capabilities and competencies, (4) sorting these core capabilities and competencies according to their strategic importance, and (5) identifying and agreeing on the key competencies and capabilities.

➠ The advantage of the capabilities assessment profile approach is that it provides a thorough analysis of the organization's important strategic capabilities.

➠ The drawback is that it's a complicated process.

➠ Identifying strengths and weaknesses is only half the picture. They must be assessed against some criteria.

➠ Four criteria that can be used to assess organizational strengths and weaknesses include organizational performance measures, **organizational goals** (statements of desired outcomes), comparison against competitors, and personal or subjective opinions of strategic decision makers or consultants.

➠ Doing an internal analysis is important because it's the only way to identify an organization's strengths and weaknesses, and it's needed for making good strategic decisions.

BUILDING YOUR SKILLS

1. The conventional view that leading brands maintain their market leadership for long periods of time may be wrong says a marketing professor at New York University. A study of several top brands led to this conclusion. Companies can no longer assume that they will be able to retain their brand leadership over decades. (a) What type of resources are brands? (b) What are the implications of these findings for internal analysis? (c) Could brands ever

be the ultimate competitive weapon? Why or why not? (d) Could a brand ever be a weakness? Explain.

(*Source: Wall Street Journal,* February 10, 2000, p. A1.)

2. The *Value Line Survey* is an invaluable resource whose worth lies in the wealth of fundamental information it crams onto a single page for investors seeking information. The *Survey* is the most widely used investment service and is available free on the shelves of most public libraries. Now the company that publishes the *Value Line Survey* plans to offer for a premium price, a new select service that will provide one stock recommendation per month. However, the problem is that the recommendations will come from the *Survey* rankings that masses of people already have access to. The Value Line rankings work so well that too many people try to act on them, thus diminishing the value of the select service. What happens when a product is a prisoner of its own success? How can an organization prevent this from happening? What are the implications for internal analysis?

(*Source:* R. S. Salomon Jr., "Value Line's Self-Defeating Success," *Forbes,* June 15, 1998, p. 294.)

3. Are you a Nick fan? The Nickelodeon TV network is a $1 billion multimedia powerhouse. CEO Herb Scannell has taken the company into animated feature films, high-volume licensing and merchandising, digital cable channels, educational TV partnerships, Web sites, and global expansion. Research Nickelodeon (yes, you can watch the network as part of this assignment or log on to the Web site at **www.nick.com**), and make a bulleted list of some of the strengths and weaknesses that you see.

(*Source:* L. Mifflin, "Following a Tough Act," *New York Times,* June 17, 1999, p. C1.)

4. A study by Fuld & Company, a competitive-intelligence firm, found that companies fail to use as much as 70 percent of the online business data they buy. Why do you think strategic decision makers might not look at business data? Why are such actions a problem? What recommendations might you have for strategic decision makers regarding business data?

(*Source:* "Expensive Unused Data Are Clogging Up Budgets and Decision-Making," *Wall Street Journal,* July 1, 1999, p. A1.)

5. Volvo, the Swedish car maker, is going for a sexier image. Known as the soccer mom's car of choice, 90 percent of Volvo's buyers are married, have two kids, are in the mid to late forties, and make about $125,000 a year. Volvo *wants* customers who are just hitting 30, probably not married, childless, and making $75,000 a year. What are the implications of such a strategic change on organizational resources and capabilities?

(*Source:* F. Warner, "Volvo, Seeking Younger Buyers Tries to Create a Sexier Image," *Wall Street Journal,* August 26, 1999, p. B1.)

6. How to ask the right questions is an important skill for strategic decision makers. Here are some questions that might be useful:
   - How can we do that? (Don't ask "Why can't we do that?")
   - How else can we do that? What else could we do?
   - Will you help me? Can you explain that to me again?
   - Who, what, why, where, when, how, and how much?
   - Who will do what and by when?

Would these types of questions be useful in doing an internal analysis? Why or why not?

(*Source:* J. Mariotti, "Asking the Right Questions," *Industry Week,* November 15, 1999, p. 78.)

7. Richard Branson's Virgin Group PLC is a privately held empire that includes five main businesses: Virgin megastores, Virgin Mobile cellular company, Virgin Atlantic airline, Virgin Direct financial services, and Virgin railroads. Not content with slapping Virgin's logo on everything from planes to clothing to music stores, Branson now wants to expand his Web site into a worldwide e-commerce portal much like Amazon.com. What do you think of this move? Log on to the company's Web site (**www.virgin.com**) and research the company. What possible strengths and weaknesses can you identify from your research?

(*Source:* A. R. Sorkin, "Taking Virgin's Brand into Internet Territory," *New York Times,* February 14, 2000, p. C1.)

8. In the cosmetics industry, knowing what and how the various competitors are doing could be important strategic information in developing a sustainable competitive advantage. Suppose that you're a manager at Prescriptives. What types of competitive intelligence information would you want, and where would you find it? Create a table that lists this information. Be prepared to support your ideas in class. (You'll probably need to do some outside research—library, Internet, or otherwise—to complete this assignment.)

9. Knowledge assets have been defined as "everything that contributes to profitability and isn't a physical or financial asset." Do some research on measuring knowledge assets. Write a paper discussing the problems associated with measuring knowledge assets and how to address those problems.

(*Source:* K. Kroll, "Calculating Knowledge Assets," *Industry Week,* July 5, 1999, p. 20.)

10. Find five examples of companies' goals. List these goals on a sheet of paper. Then, do some reverse thinking here, and list what organizational resources and capabilities would be needed to accomplish those goals.

STRATEGIC MANAGEMENT IN ACTION CASES

CASE #1: Not So Dumb

Strategic Management in Action case #1 can be found at the beginning of Chapter 4.

Discussion Questions

1. What resources and capabilities does IDG Books appear to have? Are any of these capabilities distinctive? Explain.

2. What strengths and weaknesses does IDG Books appear to have? How could it prevent its strengths from becoming weaknesses?

3. What approach to internal analysis would you suggest that CEO Kilcullen use in assessing his organization's strengths and weaknesses? Why?

4. Explain IDGB's success using Figure 4-2. Be specific.

CASE #2: On the Rebound—Shooting for Success

Through finely tuned and deliberate strategies, the National Basketball Association (NBA) emerged as the first truly global sports league. The transformation of a faltering domestic sport into a global commercial success reflected a keen understanding of strategic management. Professional basketball sparked the interest of fans and players around the globe in the mid-1990s, and the NBA cashed in on the game's universal appeal. At one time, if you asked someone in China what the most popular basketball team was, the answer would have been the "Red Oxen" from Chicago. The league wanted to be a global entertainment leader and had the resources and capabilities to make it happen. However, that all changed during the 1998–1999 season. A brutal contract negotiation with players forced the cancellation of more than one-third of the league's games. The lockout frustrated and angered fans. David Stern, NBA commissioner (the top manager), found the league's many business development initiatives grinding to a halt. Then, there was the issue of the NBA's most celebrated icon, Michael Jordan. His retirement in 1999 took away one of the key draws, both as a player and as a celebrity. From its winning streak, the NBA was definitely struggling. However, Stern wasn't throwing in the towel.

To address the challenges facing the NBA, Commissioner Stern looked at what the league had to offer. What it had was consumer familiarity with basketball both domestically and globally, some talented young players (even if they weren't well known yet), and a recognized image and track record. If those resources and capabilities could be exploited, the NBA might get back in the game.

One of the actions that Stern took was to expand its network of offices globally. Why? The league hoped to reignite the NBA's popularity with global consumers by being visible. However, Stern wasn't ready to commit to franchising teams outside the United States. He explained that "The model is the rock concert. Sell lots of records. Tour occasionally."

Another strategic action was the enhancement of the league's Internet presence through its Web site (**www.nba.com**). The NBA's Web site is a constantly changing cornucopia of everything basketball. The NBA is pushing its games and its available products to fans around the world via their computers. In conjunction with the Internet site, the NBA signed a deal with USA Networks to sell league merchandise on its Home Shopping Network. However, some experts question whether fashion trends have moved away from sports merchandise altogether and whether global customers will want NBA merchandise when there are no teams nearby to support. Without the benefit of a globally appealing star like Michael Jordan, the sales of team merchandise may not rebound.

Another action that Stern took was the creation and debut of NBA.com TV in November 1999. Created at a cost of $10 million, NBA.com TV is the first television network ever created by a U.S. sports league. As an extension of the league's Web site, NBA.com TV is a big step forward in the NBA's evolution as a multimedia producer. However, the NBA had to walk a fine line between offering game broadcasts without competing with game telecasts of NBA licensees NBC and Turner Sports. Although an immediate impact on the financials of the NBA is unlikely, the long-term potential is great. With this new venture, the league hopes to be positioned for future growth of sports programming.

Stern and the NBA are definitely taking actions to enhance their resources and capabilities. Whether these are just hoop dreams or can be a reality remains to be seen.

Discussion Questions

1. From this abbreviated description, what resources and capabilities do you think the NBA has?

2. Take each of the four approaches to internal analysis and describe how it could be used in analyzing the strengths and weaknesses of the NBA. Which one do you think is most appropriate for an organization such as the NBA? Support your choice.

3. Look at each of the new strategic initiatives of Stern. Are they exploiting the NBA's strengths and minimizing its weaknesses? Explain.

(**Sources:** Information from NBA's Web site (**www.nba.com**), March 31, 2000; J. Tagliabue, "Hoop Dreams, Fiscal Realities," *New York Times*, March 4, 2000, p. B1; D. Roth, "The NBA's Next Shot," *Fortune*, February 21, 2000, pp. 207–16; A. Bianco, "Now It's NBA All-the-Time TV," *Business Week*, November 15, 1999, pp. 241–42; and D. McGraw and M. Tharp, "Going Out on Top," *U.S. News and World Report*, January 25, 1999, p. 55.)

CASE #3: Revving Up

Porsche. A name that brings to mind the image of the world's best sports cars. The company's Web site (**www.porsche.com**) describes Porsche as pure innovation, emotion, and fascination. Yet, the German company has had its fair share of problems. Wendelin Wiedeking, the current Porsche chairman, is said to have the "automotive world's toughest managerial job." He says, "A company's goal is to make money. If it doesn't make money, it has no reason to exist." However, during the mid-1990s, Porsche wasn't meeting that goal. The daunting task of turning the company around and bringing it back to profitability was given to Wiedeking.

When Wiedeking first took over the production and materials management division in

1991, he found a company saddled with traditional management, a bloated production process, and an ill-conceived plan to add a sedan to its line of high-performance sports cars. His reaction—benchmark every aspect of production to find out how much time, effort, and money was being spent on producing a Porsche. What his team discovered was that Porsche's production process was bloated and wasteful. This evaluation was just a first step, though. Wiedeking's strategic capabilities and sense soon led to his being named chairman of the company. Then he went to work reshaping all aspects of the business from the factory floor to the executive offices to the marketing department.

Concepts such as lean production, just-in-time manufacturing, and one-piece flow were implemented. These changes led to the layoff of nearly one-third of its workforce and a reduction in management layers from six to four. The result? Manufacturing productivity rose sharply. Where it used to take 120 man-hours to produce a Porsche, it now takes 80. In the marketing area, new advertising campaigns were designed to transform Porsche's image of cold, arrogant speed and power into something more friendly, approachable, and fun. One of the company's ads for its Porsche Boxster carried the tag line "Kills bugs fast." This amusing advertising reflects the amazing transformation of an old-line company into something better. Another component of Wiedeking's management philosophy is keeping everyone busy. Since he took over, the company has completely overhauled its processes, simultaneously designed and built the Boxster and retooled the 911, and produced a new 911 Turbo. Now, the company is focusing on developing an SUV. Once that's done, Wiedeking promises there will be another project. He says, "I just started to talk about visions for 2005 and 2010. Where will the company be in 2005 and 2010? This is again, my job, because a company must grow. If a company is not able to grow, it is not able to survive. If you stagnate, I think, that's the beginning of the end."

Discussion Questions

1. How is it possible for a company with significant strengths that have been sources of competitive advantage suddenly to encounter problems?

2. If an organization's distinctive capability is lost or weakened, do you think it can ever be recovered or restored to a competitive advantage? Why or why not?

3. Check out the company's Web site (**www.porsche.com**). Look closely at the information about the company (philosophy, history, etc.) and using a bulleted list format, identify resources and capabilities. Do you feel that Porsche has any distinctive capabilities? Why or why not?

4. Would a company that has a reputation for having the "best" product in its industry ever have a need for competitive intelligence information? Why or why not?

5. How could Wiedeking have used value chain analysis in assessing Porsche's strengths and weaknesses? How about an internal audit? How about the internal environmental analysis process?

(*Sources:* Company's Web site (**www.porsche.com**), March 31, 2000; and T. Mudd, "Back in High Gear," *Industry Week*, February 21, 2000, pp. 38–46.)

ENDNOTES

1. Information on IDG Books Worldwide, Inc. from Hoover's Online (**www.hoovers.com**), March 26, 2000; Company's Web site (**www.idgbooks.com**), January 17, 2000; and S. Sansoni, "It's the Stupid *Name*, Stupid!" *Forbes*, August 10, 1998, pp. 60–61.

2. D. J. Collis, "Research Note: How Valuable Are Organizational Capabilities?" *Strategic Management Journal*, winter 1994, pp. 143–52.

3. R. M. Grant, "The Resource-Based Theory of Competitive Advantage: Implications for Strategy Formulation," *California Management Review*, spring 1991, pp. 114–35.

4. Collis, "Research Note."

5. G. S. Day, "The Capabilities of Market-Driven Organizations," *Journal of Marketing*, October 1994, pp. 37–52; and C. K. Prahalad and G. Hamel, "The Core Competence of the Corporation," *Harvard Business Review*, May–June 1990, pp. 79–91.

6. Day, "The Capabilities of Market-Driven Organizations," p. 39.

7. Prahalad and Hamel, "The Core Competence of the Corporation."

8. L. Kaufman, "Fingerhut Gives Federated Edge in E-Commerce," *New York Times*, July 6, 1999, p. C11; and S. Chandler, "Data Is Power. Just Ask Fingerhut," *Business Week*, June 3, 1996, p. 69.

9. D. J. Teece, G. Pisano, and A. Shuen, "Dynamic Capabilities and Strategic Management," *Strategic Management Journal*, August 1997, pp. 509–33.

10. See M. E. Porter, *Competitive Advantage: Creating and Sustaining Superior Performance*, Chap. 2 (New York: Free Press, 1985).

11. W. J. Duncan, P. M. Ginter, and L. E. Swayne, "Competitive Advantage and Internal Organizational Assessment," *Academy of Management Executive*, August 1998, pp. 6–16.

12. K. E. Marino, "Developing Consensus on Firm Competencies and Capabilities," *Academy of Management Executive*, August 1996, pp. 40–51.

13. This discussion of the capabilities assessment profile is based on Marino, *Academy of Management Executive*.

14. P. Kotler, *Marketing Management*, 8th ed. (Upper Saddle River, NJ: Prentice Hall, 1996), p. 195.

15. H. H. Stevenson, "Defining Corporate Strengths and Weaknesses," *Sloan Management Review*, spring 1967, pp. 51–68.

16. K. Western, "Ethical Spying," *Business Ethics*, September–October 1995, pp. 22–23.

5

FUNCTIONAL STRATEGIES

LEARNING OBJECTIVES

After studying this chapter, you should be able to:

1. Describe what happens after the SWOT analysis is completed.
2. Define functional strategies.
3. Discuss the various production–operations management strategies.
4. Describe the various marketing strategies.
5. Explain high-performance work activities and why they're important.
6. Discuss the various human resource management strategies.
7. Describe the various research and development strategies.
8. Describe a cross-functional team.
9. Describe the types of information systems and their characteristics.
10. Describe the various financial–accounting strategies.
11. Explain how the functional strategies are implemented, evaluated, and changed.
12. Discuss the importance of coordinating the functional strategies with the other organizational strategies.

STRATEGIC MANAGEMENT IN ACTION CASE #1

The Keys to Driving for Success

Making a custom car in five days. Sound like an impossible dream? Not to Toyota Motor Corporation. It says it has developed a way to produce a car within five days of receiving a custom order.[1] Toyota is renowned worldwide for its effectiveness and efficiency in production and manufacturing processes. Its recent manufacturing achievement is likely to give Toyota a significant competitive advantage in an environment where speed to customer is proving to be vital. (Remember how we discussed speed in Chapter 2 as one of the realities of the new situational context.) How has Toyota been able to accomplish such monumental achievements? To understand its successes, we have to look closely at its unique mix of functional strategies.

Many experts have tried to decipher the keys to Toyota's successes. These assessments of Toyota's business reveal that its successes can be attributed to a finely tuned and coordinated mix of strategies. The company leaves nothing to chance. For instance, in Toyota's venerable manufacturing processes, work activities, connections, and production flows are rigidly scripted, yet exceedingly flexible and adaptable. How, you might ask, can this be? How can a rigid system also be flexible? As Toyota has discovered over five decades of operations, those very rigid specifications nourish and preserve the flexibility and creativity. Four rules guide Toyota's Production System. Before we look at these, it's important to recognize and understand the role that the scientific process plays in Toyota's culture. Any change requires a rigorous problem-solving process with a detailed assessment of the current state of affairs and a plan for improvement. This scientific method is so ingrained at Toyota that the system actually inspires workers and managers to engage in the kinds of experimentation that are the hallmarks of a learning organization.

Let's look at the four basic rules that guide the Toyota Production System. They include the following. *Rule 1—All work shall be highly specified as to content, sequence, timing, and outcome.* Toyota recognizes and emphasizes the details. Because employees follow a well-defined sequence of steps for a particular job, deviations are instantly obvious. *Rule 2—Every customer–supplier connection must be direct, and there must be an unambiguous yes-or-no way to send requests and receive responses.* An inherent part of this rule is the recognition that customers aren't only external. Every employee is "serving" some "customer," who may simply be the next person in the assembly process. *Rule 3— The pathway for every product and service must be simple and direct.* Every production line at Toyota is set up so every product and service flows along a simple, specified path. This doesn't mean that each path is dedicated to only one product. In fact, it's quite the opposite. Each production line at a Toyota plant typically accommodates many products. *Rule 4—Any improvement must be made in accordance with the scientific method, under the guidance of a teacher, at the lowest possible level in the organization.* Toyota explicitly teaches people how to improve and expects them to follow the scientific approach when doing so.

These four rules guide Toyota's employees from top to bottom. However, as we said earlier, the production strategies are not the only keys to Toyota's success. All its functional strategies contribute. From Toyota's marketing strategies (see Building Your Skills question 3 at the end of this chapter, which describes Toyota's attempts to attract younger buyers) to its human resource management strategies that emphasize education and training (Toyota's T-Ten—Toyota Technical Education Network—is a partnership with over 50 select vocational and community colleges in the United States that train highly skilled technicians to work on Toyota products) to its research and development strategies (remember the 5-day custom car), Toyota has a firm grasp on its functional strategies.

As our chapter-opening case illustrates, when an organization's functional strategies are managed strategically, it's able to exploit the resources, capabilities, and core competencies found in its various functions. In this chapter, we'll be discussing the role of the various functional level strategies in managing strategically. First, we're going to explain what happens after the SWOT analysis and why we think it's important to look at functional strategies before the competitive or corporate strategies. Next, we'll describe the various types of functional strategies—what they are and how they're implemented. Finally, we'll discuss strategy evaluation, making strategic changes, and coordinating functional strategies with the other organizational strategies.

WHY ARE WE LOOKING AT FUNCTIONAL STRATEGIES FIRST?

In this part of the book, we actually begin to look at *how* strategic decision makers formulate and implement organizational strategies. We're approaching this step in the strategic management process a little differently than do most other strategic management textbooks. That is, we're looking at functional strategies first. However, as you'll see, it seems to make sense to approach strategy formulation and implementation this way.

Strategic Management in Action Process

Although you've already been studying several aspects of strategic management, the whole process of strategic management in action still may appear utterly and totally confusing! (See Figure 5-1.) Just exactly *how* does it work? Although every organizational situation will be different, it's almost like being faced with one of those 500-piece three-dimensional puzzles and you're not quite sure where or how to start. You finally decide that the best way to approach the task is by starting with pieces from the bottom while keeping in mind what the overall goal is (i.e., what the completed puzzle looks like). That's really also the best way for us to look at organizational strategies. The organization's top-level decision makers will develop the overall goal of what the organization hopes to achieve (its vision, mission, and strategic objectives) and establish the overall corporate strategies—think of that picture of the completed puzzle shown on the puzzle box lid. (We'll cover the various corporate strategies in Chapter 7.) Then, all work assembling the puzzle proceeds in light of that completed picture. Yet, that completed picture serves to provide us with only an overall perspective; it doesn't tell us anything about what it takes to get to that completed picture. By looking at the organization's functional strategies first, we're able to see how we get to that completed picture. However, keep in mind that the functional strategies *are* developed in light of the organization's vision, mission(s), overall corporate strategies, and competitive strategies.

There does seem to be one time when discussing corporate strategies first, followed by competitive and then functional strategies, might be logical: when an organization is brand new. At that time, top-level strategists (usually the CEO and his or her top management team) formulate the overall strategic goal(s) and strategies as the organization begins to carry out its vision and organizational members begin performing their work activities. Over time as the organization

Figure 5-1

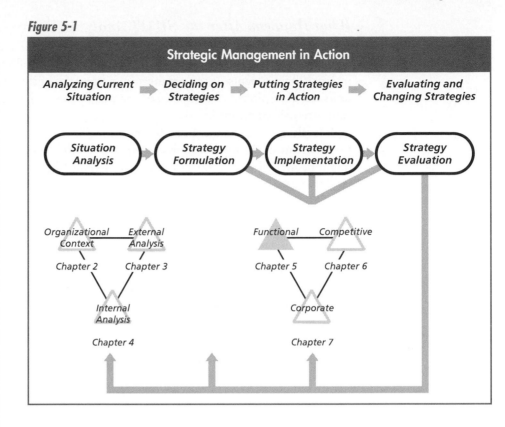

competes in its industry and as organizational members throughout the organization's various units carry out the organization's work—whether it's providing current weather information, writing lines of software code, building a new greenways bike path, or selling telecommunications equipment—organizational resources are used, capabilities are developed, and hopefully distinctive capabilities begin to emerge in the various functional units. The organizational work being done in the various functional units becomes the basic building blocks to achieving competitive advantage. By managing strategically, organizational members in these various functional units work to create a sustainable competitive advantage. The specific strategies being used in the various functional units also serve as the basic building blocks for supporting the business-level (competitive) and corporate-level strategies. Because the vast majority of strategic situations you'll likely be facing will be ones where the organization or organizational unit is *not* new, it makes sense for us to look at the organization's functional strategies first as we look at the process of deciding an organization's most appropriate strategies—that is, the ones that will lead to a sustainable competitive advantage.

What happens if the corporate or competitive strategies aren't working and need to be changed to accommodate changes in either the external or internal environments? What if a sustainable competitive advantage isn't there? Again, strategic decision makers will look to the organization's various functional units and assess what changes need to be made. What *is* and *isn't* working? This is where the information from the SWOT analysis is used.

What Happens After the SWOT Analysis?

After completing the SWOT analysis, an organization's decision makers are armed with information about the positive and negative aspects of both the external and internal environments. If the organization's strengths in the various functional units can be exploited as competitive advantages, particularly in light of any relevant external opportunities, the organization may well be on its way to achieving high levels of performance. In addition, if the SWOT analysis points to negative trends in any of the organization's external areas, changes in functional strategies might be needed to counteract these. Also, serious functional weaknesses that might be preventing a competitive advantage from being developed may need to be corrected or minimized.

The SWOT analysis points to the strategic issues organizational decision makers need to address in their pursuit of sustainable competitive advantage and high performance levels. The vast majority of these strategic issues encompass what performance levels already have been reached (high or low) in the various functional strategies an organization is currently pursuing. Even if it's evident from the SWOT analysis that the organization's corporate or competitive strategies need to be changed, strategists will base their decisions on the resources, capabilities, and core competencies that can be found in the functional areas. These important and fundamental contributions to the organization's performance levels by the various organizational functions and the strategies being employed are another reason why we're looking at functional strategies first.

Now that we've explained why we're looking at the various functional strategies first, what are these strategies and how are they implemented in organizations? That's what we'll be discussing next.

Strategic Management in Action

MTV, a business unit of Viacom, Inc., understands how fragile organizational strengths can be. It's following what seems to be a two-faced marketing strategy as it promotes the latest hot music types while simultaneously being that type of music's loudest ridiculer. For example, the widespread popularity of boy bands such as The Backstreet Boys and 'N Sync didn't stop MTV from airing a made-for-TV movie lampooning boy bands. The company's ability to promote pop culture while at the same time sarcastically ridiculing it is indeed a fine line to walk. So far, MTV has been able to pull it off! What do you think of MTV's approach? What are the dangers inherent in its approach? Could SWOT analysis be useful to an organization such as MTV? How?

Source: E. White, "MTV's Secret: Cheers and Sneers," *Wall Street Journal,* February 18, 2000, p. B1.

WHAT ARE THE VARIOUS FUNCTIONAL STRATEGIES AND HOW ARE THEY IMPLEMENTED?

Each functional unit or department of the organization has a strategy for achieving its own mission and for helping the organization reach its overall vision. We defined an organization's **functional strategies** earlier in Chapter 1 as the short-term goal-directed decisions and actions of the organization's various functional units. All organizations—profit and not-for-profit, large and small—perform three basic functions as they create and deliver goods and services: (1) marketing (first assesses and establishes the demand for the product and then markets and delivers the product after it's produced); (2) production and operations (creates the product or service); and (3) financial and accounting (makes sure payment is received for product and provides information on performance results). These three basic functions, especially for business, are typically expanded into the following classifications: production–operations–manufacturing, marketing, human resource management, research and development, information systems–technology, and financial–accounting. Although each organization will have its own uniquely named functional areas, the basic work activities that comprise these functions remain the same—acquiring, coordinating, processing, and transforming the organization's resources (inputs) into the organization's outputs (goods–services), which are delivered to the organization's customers. Because they're convenient and familiar, we'll use the six typical functional designations as our framework for describing the various functional strategies. Under each functional area, we'll look at some of the most common strategies used in that particular functional area and how these strategies are implemented. In addition, we'll also look at some of the current types of strategies being used by organizations in each of the functional areas. One thing we need to state up front is that our description of the various functional strategies is intended as an *overview* only. We're not attempting to cover the detailed specifics of these strategies. If you want to review this information, you'll need to look at a textbook or other specialized books from that particular functional area.

Production–Operations–Manufacturing Strategies

By this point in your life, you've obviously purchased or used an incredible number and variety of products and services. You may have produced some of these yourself—for example, if you've ever grown produce in a garden, built bookshelves out of scrap wood and bricks, or baked a loaf of bread—but most of the products we consume and use are produced by someone else. The process of creating goods and services in which organizational inputs (resources) are transformed into outputs is called **production**.[2] The production process used to create physical (tangible) products is fairly obvious. However, even the creation and delivery of services requires some type of transformation activities. As our chapter-opening case illustrates, when these various operations strategies are well integrated with the other functional areas of the organization and support the overall company objectives, it's possible to create a sustainable competitive advantage. What we'll look at in this section are some of the common strategic choices in the organization's production function. Table 5-1 provides a concise summary of possible production–operations management strategies.

TABLE 5-1   Possible Production–Operations Management Strategies

Production Process Strategies

Process focused
Product focused
Repetitive focused

Capacity Strategies

Size of facility
Efficient use

Location Strategies

Location selection

Work Design Strategies

Job specialization
Job enlargement
Job enrichment
Ergonomics
Work methods
Motivation–incentive systems
Standards–output levels

Layout Strategies

Fixed position
Process oriented
Office
Retail–service
Warehouse
Product oriented

Production–Operations Management Strategies

Aggregate planning techniques
Just-in-time systems
Purchasing management procedures
Inventory management systems
Materials requirement planning techniques
Short-term scheduling techniques
Project management procedures
Maintenance management

Current Production–Operations Strategies

Integrated manufacturing
    Advanced manufacturing technology
    Total quality management
    Just-in-time inventory control

Production Process Strategies. Different organizations use different approaches to transforming their resources into goods and services. The objective behind an organization's process strategies is to find a way to produce products or services that meet (or exceed) customer requirements in light of certain cost and other managerial constraints. There are three possible process strategies: (1) process focused, which is organized around processes and appropriate for producing high-variety, low-volume products, including things such as gourmet meals, heart transplants, specialized print jobs, or cruise ship vacations; (2) product focused, which is organized around products and appropriate for producing high-volume, low-variety products, including things such as steel, paper, lightbulbs, or bread; (3) repetitive focused, which falls somewhere between process focused and product focused and uses standardized component parts in assembling products like those produced on a typical assembly line, such as motorcycles, televisions, or fast food. Which strategy is most appropriate and will be important to developing a competitive advantage depends on the volume and variety of products being produced. Organizations might also be able to develop a competitive advantage from the specific machinery, equipment, and technology being used if these things result in a production process with lower costs, higher quality, or ability to meet customer needs better.

Capacity Strategies. The size of a facility and how efficiently facilities are used can be important contributors to the development of competitive advantage. Some strategies associated with production capacity include demand management and capacity management. How do organizational members "manage" demand? They'll employ strategies such as making staffing changes (adding or laying off employees), adjusting equipment and processes (purchase, sell, or lease), improving work methods to be more efficient, or redesigning the product. On the other hand, capacity management involves strategies to effectively and efficiently use current facilities, part of which includes determining break-even point. Also, as part of this function, strategic decision makers may have to forecast future capacity requirements in order to assure that facilities are up and running when needed.

Location Strategies. One of the most important competitive decisions a company makes is where to locate its operations. Because location significantly influences an organization's costs and revenues, the objective of the location strategy should be to maximize the benefits and minimize the costs of locating in a particular area. What factors affect location selection? In choosing appropriate location strategies, decision makers will explore factors such as labor costs and availability, proximity to raw materials and suppliers, proximity to markets, state and local government policies and regulations, environmental regulations, utilities, site costs, transportation availability, and quality-of-life issues.

Work Design Strategies. The production–operations function plays a significant role in work design strategies. These strategies determine who can do what, when they can do it, and under what conditions. What are some of these work design strategies? Some of the more common ones encompass job specialization, job enlargement, job enrichment, ergonomics, work methods, and motivation–incentive systems. Work design also involves establishing standards for different jobs and different levels of output for those jobs.

Layout Strategies. How a facility is arranged or laid out to do the organization's work has a significant impact on operational efficiency. The objective of an

Strategic Management in Action

Fruit of the Loom faced very serious production problems in the latter half of 1999. Delays in shipping products and difficulties in customer service were the result of poor strategic decisions. Much of the company's production had been sent overseas, which did reduce costs, but the offshore strategy also led to problems in quality control, production processes, and inventory control. To compensate for these problems, the company cut back on its mostly Caribbean workforce. Then, a surge in customer demand left the company with no way to produce at needed levels. It struggled to find workers and to restart its facilities. For a company that controls over one-third of the U.S. men's and boys' market for underwear, these production problems are particularly disturbing. After all, producing undergarments isn't as complex as producing computer chips. However, its production troubles eventually led to the company's filing for Chapter 11 bankruptcy reorganization in December of 1999. With a new top-level strategic team in place, Fruit of the Loom is hoping that it can correct its many problems. Check out the company's Web site (**www.fruit.com**) and come up with a bulleted list of functional strategies the company has implemented. Note that in addition to production strategies, you'll probably find examples of marketing, research and development, and other functional strategies.

Sources: Company's Web site (**www.fruit.com**), April 12, 2000; and J. P. Miller, "Fruit of the Loom Bottoms Out on Production Troubles," *Wall Street Journal,* September 20, 1999, p. B4.

organization's layout strategy is to develop an economical layout that meets the requirements of product design and volume, process equipment and capacity, quality of work life, and building and site constraints. There are six potential layouts:

1. The *fixed-position layout* is one in which the product remains stationary and requires workers and equipment to come to the work area. Examples include constructing a bridge, building an apartment building or cruise ship, or containing a burning oil well.

2. The *process-oriented layout* is appropriate for low-volume, high-variety (job shop) products where the focus is on the processes being used to create the product or service. Examples include a medical clinic, cafeteria kitchen, or job shop that produces temperature control panels.

3. The *office layout* positions workers, equipment and office spaces to provide for movement of information. Examples include an insurance company, an advertising agency, or a software design firm.

4. The *retail–service layout* arranges people and equipment according to customer needs and behavior. Obviously, the objective behind retail layout is to

maximize profitability per square foot of shelf space or floor space. Examples include grocery store, department store, or office products store.

5. In the *warehouse layout*, the objective is to find the optimum trade-off between product handling cost and warehouse space. Examples include any type of warehouse or distribution facility.

6. The *product-oriented layout* is organized around a product or group of similar high-volume, low-variety products. In this type of repetitive, continuous production, it's important to have layout arrangements that maximize people and machine utilization. Examples include a meatpacking facility, a TV assembly line, or a furniture manufacturer.

Production–Operations Management Strategies. Other production function strategies that an organization might use include those associated with actually managing the production or manufacturing function. These include strategic decisions about areas such as aggregate planning techniques, just-in-time systems, purchasing management procedures, inventory management systems, materials requirement planning techniques, short-term scheduling techniques, project man-

Designing Desirable Work Spaces

Do you study better in some places than in others? What would your ideal study space look like? It used to be that organizational architects were directed to squeeze the largest number of workers into the smallest space possible to balance the cost of expensive real estate. However, today many organizations are discovering that the design of work spaces can have a significant impact on what employees do and how they accomplish their work. For example, the headquarters of Nortel Networks, a global telecommunications company based in Toronto, is a vast indoor cityscape. The former manufacturing plant was transformed into a unique workplace where departmental "neighborhoods" have their own distinctive décor. Employees can go to the plaza outside the Java.cup café at the corner of 20th and Main streets (yes, there are streets and street signs in the facility) or work out in the fitness facility. Why would an organization go to this type of effort—and expense—to create such a work environment? There are several reasons why. First of all, office and work space design has become an important recruiting tool. With an almost full-employment economy, potential employees judge the look and feel of their work spaces and consider it third most important after salary and benefits. Another reason for designing desirable work spaces is the belief that it will lead to more communal bonds among employees. Fostering this community feeling is conducive to employee interaction, trust, and openness. Finally, work space design can be used to foster creativity and innovation. When work spaces are open, flexible, and designed for social interaction, employees mingle and move about. The impromptu conversations and "chance encounters" can lead to sharing of information and new insights—all hallmarks of an innovative organization. Can work space design give an organization a competitive edge? The answer would have to be "not by itself," but having well-designed work spaces can be an important component of an organization's functional strategies.

Sources: M. McDonald, "The Latte Connections," *U.S. News and World Report*, March 29, 1999, pp. 63–66; B. Nussbaum, "Blueprints for Business: Business Week Architectural Record Awards," *Business Week*, November 3, 1997, pp. 112–16; and "Northern Exposure," *Business Week*, November 3, 1997, pp. 124–25.

agement procedures, and maintenance management. Each of these strategies is aimed at making the organization's production as effective and efficient as possible. What we want to look at next are some of the production–operations strategies currently being used by organizations.

Current Production–Operations Strategies. Research studies are beginning to show that an organization's production and manufacturing strategies can (and do) make important strategic contributions to organizational performance.[3] How are today's world-class organizations coping with the demands of designing effective and efficient manufacturing and production strategies that will contribute to high levels of performance and the development of a sustainable competitive advantage? The adoption of integrated manufacturing strategies appears to be central to this challenge. **Integrated manufacturing** is a production–operations philosophy that emphasizes the use of advanced manufacturing technology, total quality management, and just-in-time inventory control in order to create a streamlined flow of materials, people, and work activities for transforming inputs into outputs. What does each of these involve? Advanced manufacturing technology strategies involve the use of flexible manufacturing systems and computer-integrated manufacturing. Total quality management involves production principles such as continuous improvement and teaming up with suppliers to improve quality. Just-in-time inventory control entails work practices that reduce lead time and inventory. Regardless the type, size, or location of the organization, integrated manufacturing strategies are becoming the blue ribbon standard for the design of the production–operations function. Our chapter-opening case on Toyota Motor Corporation provides an excellent example of how an organization can achieve a competitive advantage through integrated manufacturing strategies.

Consider This ◀◀|

✓ How do the functional strategies fit into the strategic management in action process?

✓ Describe how the organizational work being done in the various functional units is the basic building block to achieving competitive advantage.

✓ What information does the SWOT analysis provide strategic decision makers, and why is it important?

✓ Define functional strategies.

✓ Describe the three basic functions that all organizations perform as they create and deliver goods and services.

✓ What is production, and why is it important for both physical products *and* intangible services?

✓ Describe the six basic types of production–operations strategies.

✓ What is integrated manufacturing, and what is its importance to strategic management in action?

Marketing Strategies

An organization's marketing function plays a critical role in the pursuit of sustainable competitive advantage. **Marketing** is a process of assessing and meeting individual's or group's wants and needs by creating, offering, and exchanging products of value.[4] The two biggest factors in marketing—the two Cs—are customers and competitors. An organization's marketing strategies are directed at effectively and efficiently managing these two groups. The main marketing strategies involve segmentation or target market, differentiation, positioning, and marketing mix strategic decisions (the 4 Ps: product, pricing, promotion, and place). Let's look at some of the most common strategic choices for each of these areas. (See Table 5-2 for a concise summary of these.)

Segmentation or Target Market Strategies. Every market consists of potential or actual customers. These customers may differ in one or more ways. These differ-

TABLE 5-2 Possible Marketing Strategies

Segmentation Strategies

Geographic
Demographic
Psychographic
Behavioral

Target Market Selection Strategies

Single-segment concentration
Selective specialization
Product specialization
Market specialization
Full market coverage

Differentiation Strategies

Product itself
Services
Personnel
Image

Positioning Strategies

Attribute positioning
Benefit positioning
Use–application positioning
User positioning
Competitor positioning
Product category positioning
Quality–price positioning

Marketing Mix Strategies

Product
   New-product development
   Product line
   Brand
   Packaging–labeling
   Product life cycle decisions
Pricing
   Markup pricing
   Target-return pricing
   Perceived-value pricing
   Value pricing
   Going-rate pricing
   Sealed-bid pricing

(continues)

TABLE 5-2 Possible Marketing Strategies *(continued)*

Marketing Mix Strategies *(continued)*

Geographical pricing
Price discounts—allowances
Promotional pricing
Discriminatory pricing
Product mix pricing
Promoting
    Advertising
        Billboards
        Point-of-purchase displays
        Symbols and logos
        Packaging inserts
    Sales promotion
    Public relations
    Personal selling
    Direct marketing
Place
    Channel choice
    Market logistics
    Inventory
    Transportation modes—carriers

Current Marketing Strategies

Relationship marketing
Mass customization
Database marketing

ences can be used to segment a market. Market segments are large identifiable groups within a market. At the most basic level, an organization can choose a marketing strategy either to segment the market or to treat it as one homogeneous market. If the organization chooses to segment its market, it can select from several different variables. The major segmentation variables for consumer markets are geographic (region, city or metropolitan area, population density, and climate), demographic (age, gender, family size, family life cycle, income, occupation, education, religion, race, and nationality), psychographic (social class, lifestyle, and personality), and behavioral (occasions of product use, benefits, user status, usage rate, loyalty status, readiness-to-buy stage, and attitude toward product). The major segmentation variables for business markets include demographic (industry type, company size, and location), operating variables (technology, user—nonuser status, and customer capabilities), purchasing approaches (purchasing function organization, power structure, nature of existing relationships, general purchase policies, and purchasing criteria), situational factors (urgency, specific application, and size of order), and personal characteristics (buyer–seller similarity, attitudes toward risk, and loyalty).[5] Once the possible customer segments have been identified, the next step is to determine which ones are the most attractive targets.

Target market selection can take one of five possible strategic approaches. Single-segment concentration means that the organization selects a single segment to target. In selective specialization, the organization chooses to serve a number of equally attractive and appropriate segments that have little or no common characteristics. In product specialization strategy, the organization concentrates on making a certain product that's sold to several segments. In the market specialization strategy, the organization serves many needs of a particular customer group. Finally, the full market coverage strategy means that the organization is attempting to serve all customer groups with all the products they might need or desire.

Differentiation Strategies. Because the vast majority of product and services marketing takes place in competitive markets, organizations look for ways to differentiate their products from those of their competitors. How? Four basic differentiation dimensions have been identified and include the product itself (features, performance, conformance, durability, reliability, repairability, style, and design); services (delivery, installation, customer training, consulting service, repair, and miscellaneous factors); personnel (competence, courtesy, credibility, reliability, responsiveness, and communication abilities); and image (symbols such as a logo, color identifier, or famous person; written and audiovisual media; atmosphere features such as building design, interior design, layout, colors, or furnishings; and sponsored events or causes). Out of all these possibilities, research shows that the main product differentiators organizations use as the basis for developing an effective differentiation strategy are features, performance, conformance, durability, reliability, repairability, style, and design.[6]

Positioning Strategies. Once an organization has identified potential differentiators, it needs to decide which and how many differences to highlight. In other words, it wants to establish a specific and distinct position in the marketplace. At least seven different positioning strategies exist: attribute positioning (on

---

STRATEGIC MANAGEMENT IN AN E-BUSINESS WORLD

If an organization doesn't get its marketing strategies in order, a jump into the online retailing world can lead to a disastrous fall. For instance, when Williams-Sonoma Inc., the esteemed purveyor of upscale kitchenware and home furnishings, launched its sharp, glossy and well-designed Web site on November 1, 1999, it hoped that online holiday orders would pump up its regular catalog and retail unit sales. To be ready for the onslaught of orders, the company stocked up on inventory. However, sales were disappointing and the company ended up with unsold inventory, which lowered its fourth-quarter profits. Williams-Sonoma's story is a reminder that a jazzy Web site isn't enough to guarantee e-commerce success. Do you think marketing strategies for a "bricks-and-mortar" company might have to be changed when it decides to start selling online? Explain.

Sources: Company's Web site (**www.williams-sonoma.com**), April 12, 2000; and L. Lee, "An E-Commerce Cautionary Tale," *Business Week*, March 20, 2000, pp. 46–48.

the basis of certain product attributes), benefit positioning (on the basis of providing certain benefits), use–application positioning (on the basis of a limited use or application), user positioning (on the basis of some customer characteristic), competitor positioning (against one or more competitors), product category positioning (on the basis of some product category), and quality–price positioning (on the basis of quality–price strategies). Each of these possible strategies builds upon what the organization views as its most important differentiators in establishing a competitive advantage. The positioning strategies are also important in influencing the development of appropriate marketing mix strategies.

Marketing Mix Strategies. The marketing mix strategies get into the specific details of what product is going to be offered to customers, how it will be priced, how it will be promoted, and where it will be placed so customers can get it. These are the 4 Ps often referred to in marketing—that is, product, price, promotion, and place. We'll look at each of these separately.

An organization's *product* strategies involve several aspects. One important aspect is how the organization approaches new-product development. (New products can include original products, improved products, modified products, or new brands.) Once new-product ideas have been developed, the organization will have different strategies for developing and testing the actual product itself. If the proposed product passes these stages, then the organization must decide how much and what type of market testing to use, requiring the use of different strategies. Strategic product decisions at this point also involve the width, depth, length, and consistency of the product line(s). There may also be product strategy choices that involve brand decisions such as whether to use a brand name, a brand sponsor, and what type of brand strategy to pursue. Other product strategies involve packaging and labeling decisions. Once the product is out in the market, then product strategies concern managing the various stages in the product life cycle (PLC). The PLC concept is a recognition that a product's sales rise and decline, bringing about the need for different strategies for coping with these ups and downs. (See Figure 5-2 for an example of what a typical PLC looks like.) As you probably know, the various stages of the PLC might require changes not only in the product strategies but also in the other Ps.

The choice of *pricing* strategies depends upon the organization's pricing objectives (survival, maximum current profit, maximum current revenue, maximum sales growth, maximum market skimming, product–quality leadership, or other). It also is influenced by the customers' demand for the product, costs of producing and marketing the product, and competitors' prices. Based on these factors, the company will choose one of the following pricing strategies: markup pricing (by adding a standard markup), target-return pricing (to achieve a targeted or desired return), perceived-value pricing (based on the customers' perception of value), value pricing (based on charging low price for high-quality products), going-rate pricing (based largely on what competitors are charging), or sealed-bid pricing (based on expectations of how competitors will bid). Other decisions to be made in the pricing strategy include decisions about geographical pricing, price discounts and allowances, promotional pricing, discriminatory pricing, or product mix pricing. Also, even though an organization establishes what it feels is an effective and efficient pricing strategy, competitive and marketplace dynamics may require increasing or lowering prices thus creating a need to change the current pricing strategy.

Figure 5-2

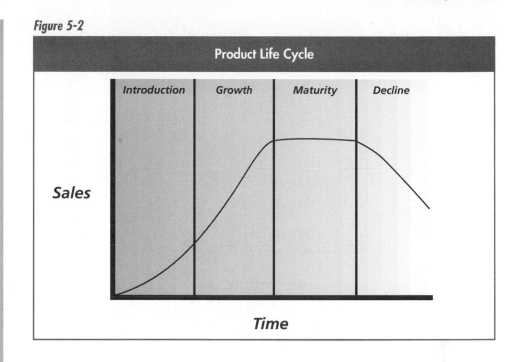

A good overall marketing strategy requires strategies for *promoting* the product. Common strategies for promotion involve the use of the various marketing communication and promotion tools. These include advertising (print and broadcast media ads, brochures and booklets, posters and leaflets, billboards, point-of-purchase displays, symbols and logos, packaging inserts, and many others); sales promotion (contests, games, sweepstakes and lotteries; premiums and gifts; sampling; fairs and trade shows; exhibits; demonstrations; coupons; rebates; trading stamps; product tie-ins; and others); public relations (press kits; speeches; annual reports; charitable contributions, sponsorships; community relations; lobbying; events; company magazine; and others); personal selling (sales presentations, sales meetings, incentive programs, samples, and others); and direct marketing (catalogs, mailings, telemarketing, electronic shopping, and TV shopping). What are appropriate promotional strategic choices? It depends on the target audience and the marketing communication objectives. Once these are determined, then appropriate message, communication channels, promotion budget, and promotion mix strategies can be designed.

The final aspect of the marketing mix strategies involves specific *place* or distribution strategies. What's involved with the place strategy? One important aspect is the choice of channels for distributing the product or service. Alternatives include the type of intermediary to use (e.g., wholesaler, dealer, direct sales, value-added reseller, mail-order marketer, etc.) and the number of intermediaries to use (exclusive distribution, selective distribution, or intensive distribution). Another important aspect of the place strategy involves the actual physical distribution of the product—also referred to as market logistics. Normally, there are four logistics strategies to decide. The first is determining what strategic approaches we'll use in processing customer orders. Next, strategic decision makers must determine what type of warehousing arrangements are most appropriate. Then, decisions about inventory (when to order and how much to order) must be

Strategic Management in Action

A hot and gooey delectable Southern confection. That's the mouth-watering description of Krispy Kreme's original glazed doughnuts. Krispy Kreme, based in Winston-Salem, North Carolina, used to be available mainly in the Southeast. People who grew up with Krispy Kreme and moved away longed to be able to sink their teeth into a Krispy Kreme doughnut. Throughout the years, the company has expanded gradually but still had fewer than 150 stores in only 27 states. However, Krispy Kreme is stepping up its geographic expansion. At what point do a company's products, like Krispy Kreme doughnuts, lose their allure because they become more widely available? That's a problem that Coors beer had. During the 1970s, Coors products were available only in parts of the West. The product developed a cult following among college students in the rest of the country. When it went national in the 1980s, Coors became just another beer. Now, strategic decision makers at Krispy Kreme have to find a way to keep its products' allure alive while continuing to pursue new market opportunities. What are the implications for marketing strategies?

Source: J. R. Hagerty, "Krispy Kreme at a Krossroads," *Wall Street Journal,* February 24, 2000, p. B1.

addressed. Obviously, decisions about inventory strategy should be coordinated with the production–operations function so that finished products are available when needed, in the style and design needed, and at an appropriate cost. Finally, place strategy involves decisions about transportation modes and carriers.

Current Marketing Strategies. Developing effective marketing strategies is getting harder and harder. Why? Customers are becoming more sophisticated and knowledgeable, maybe even cynical, about marketing activities. The number of strategic options in the various aspects of marketing are multiplying, making the choice of appropriate strategies ever more difficult. Also, the increasing extent of global markets and global competitors challenges organizational decision makers who want to strategically manage the marketing function. How are world-class organizations addressing these marketing strategy challenges? One philosophy that they're following is **relationship marketing**, which is a process of building long-term, trusting, "win–win" relationships with valued customers.[7] This strategy emphasizes the importance of building solid and valuable partnerships with customers. How can organizations do this? Three approaches to customer value-building relationships have been identified.

1. Adding *financial* benefits to the customer relationship through programs such as frequent buyers, collectors' societies, kids clubs, and so forth. For instance, Harley-Davidson sponsors the Harley Owners Group (HOG), whose members pay an annual fee to receive a magazine (*Hog Tales*), an

emergency pickup service, touring guides, theft reward service, discount hotel rates, and so forth.

2. Adding *social* benefits to the financial benefits by bonding with customers and building personalized relationships with them through events such as customer appreciation days or hosting a party just for customers. In addition, in today's wired world, these customer connections don't even have to be real, they can be virtual. Many organizations have created **online communities**—constantly changing groups of people who collaborate, share ideas, and build relationships online.

3. Adding *structural* ties as well as financial and social benefits through such activities as, for example, supplying customers with special equipment or computer linkages.[8]

A strategic variation of relationship marketing is approaching customers with "one-to-one marketing" or "mass customization."[9] In mass customization, organizations provide customers with products or services based on what they tell you and what else you may know about them. For instance, customers can get personalized vitamins, custom-fit golf clubs, customized textbooks, or any other number of custom products. Also, the Internet is proving to be a useful ally in the push toward mass customization. Through well-designed Web sites, companies can communicate with customers and tailor product offerings to their unique needs. Amazon.com understands this process well. Let's say, for example, that you've purchased books from Amazon on mountain climbing. As Amazon gets new books on that subject or related subjects, it will contact you to see if you'd like to order. To make this marketing strategy work, all the organization's other business functions must support and facilitate this close connection with customers.

Another current marketing strategy being implemented is **database marketing**, which uses "database technology and sophisticated analytical techniques combined with direct-marketing methods to elicit a desired, measurable response in target groups and individuals."[10] A database marketing system can help in learning customers' buying habits—which products and colors sell best, which time of year is best for selling particular items, and so forth. Having a lot of information about customers can provide an organization a distinct competitive advantage. Many software programs make it possible for organizations to amass detailed profiles of customers and then offer them the things they're likely to buy.[11] For example, American Express amasses large quantities of customer data and then massages them to pinpoint its best customers, who are then targeted in a more personal way. It "mines" the data (data mining) for critical strategic marketing information.

Human Resource Management Strategies

"Our people are our *most* important asset." How often have you seen or heard this assertion? More importantly, can human resource (HR) strategies be used to establish a sustainable competitive advantage? The answer seems to be "yes, they can." Various studies have concluded that an organization's human resources can be a significant source of competitive advantage.[12] Yet, although an organization's HR strategies may lead to competitive advantage, do they also have an impact on performance? Other studies have looked at the link between HR policies–practices and performance. Most have shown that HR policies and practices—ones

FYI

Data Mining

Just like a miner digging for gold, an organization's marketers need to mine their customer data in order to learn more about them and their buying habits. The challenge of data mining is being able to spot the unexpected in the reams of customer information that's collected. There are six basic techniques for data mining. The first is *neural networks*, which attempt to simulate the way the human brain discovers patterns. It involves looking at data and trying to discern possible patterns by thinking the way the customer thinks. The next type of data mining technique is *induction techniques.* In this approach, data miners use a process of reasoning from specific facts to reach a hypothesis. Another technique is using *statistics* by building models that describe the behavior of the data. Then, there's the *visualization technique* that displays analytical data in ways that most nonexperts can understand. Another technique is *online analytical processing,* which is a more sophisticated and complex display of data often across several time periods.

Finally, *query languages* can be used to provide even more explicit descriptions of data. Many of these techniques can be done through software that makes the data miner's job much easier. What happens to data that are "mined"? They can be used to pinpoint which customers are more profitable. They can also help recognize subtle changes in customers' buying habits and patterns. Ultimately, this type of information is needed when designing effective marketing strategies. For example, at Sunglass Hut, strategic managers mine sales data for trends. They pinpoint the 50 top-selling sunglass styles and figure out a way to promote those products. Does data mining work for them? When they noticed that aviator frames were selling well, the merchandising team pulled together an in-store display grouping several designers' versions of the aviator style and sales increased 41 percent!

Sources: L. Bransten, "Looking for Patterns," *Wall Street Journal,* June 21, 1999, p. R16; L. Kroll, "Fashion Statement," *Forbes,* April 19, 1999, p. 168; "Six Data Mining Techniques," *Executive Edge,* April–May 1999, p. 10; J. Teresko, "Information Rich, Knowledge Poor," *Industry Week,* February 1, 1999, pp. 19–24; and P. C. Judge, "What've You Done for Us Lately?" *Business Week,* September 14, 1998, pp. 140–42.

referred to as "high-performance work practices"—*can* have a positive impact on firm performance.[13] What are **high-performance work practices**? They're human resource policies and practices that can lead to both high individual and high organizational performance. They include strategies such as comprehensive employee recruitment and selection procedures, incentive compensation and performance management systems, and extensive employee involvement and training. Table 5-3 lists some of these high-performance work practices that have been identified. These types of HR strategies can improve the knowledge, skills, and abilities of an organization's current and potential employees; increase their motivation; reduce loafing on the job; and enhance retention of quality employees while encouraging nonperformers to leave the organization.[14]

Regardless of the HR strategies used, all should be closely aligned with other functional strategies in order to assure that the right numbers of the appropriately skilled people are in the right place at the right time and that the workforce is being used appropriately. Let's look at some of the strategic HR decisions and options covering such areas as work flows, staffing, employee separations, performance appraisal, training and development, compensation, employee and labor

TABLE 5-3 Examples of High-Performance Work Practices

- Self-directed work team
- Job rotation
- Problem-solving groups
- Total quality management
- Employee suggestions actually implemented
- Contingent pay
- Information sharing
- Attitude surveys

Source: Based on Brian Becker and Barry Gerhart, "The Impact of Human Resource Management on Organizational Performance: Progress and Prospects," *Academy of Management Journal,* August 1996, pp. 779–801.

relations, and employee rights.[15] Table 5-4 lists some common human resource management strategies used in each of these areas.

Work Flows. **Work flow** is the way an organization's work activities are organized so that the vision, mission(s), and objectives are effectively and efficiently accomplished. What do HR strategic choices in work flow involve? Primarily, they're choices about ways to organize work activities—things such as organizing

TABLE 5-4 Possible Human Resource Management Strategies

Work Flows

Organize for efficiency or innovation
Organize for control or flexibility
Use specialized or broad job categories
Use detailed or loose work planning

Staffing

Use internal or external recruitment
Who makes hiring decisions
What's important in hiring
Formal or informal approach

Employee Separations

How to downsize
Hiring freeze
Support for terminated employees
Preferential or nonpreferential rehiring process

(continues)

TABLE 5-4   Possible Human Resource Management Strategies *(continued)*

Performance Appraisal

Customized or uniform appraisals

Appraisal for developmental or control purposes

Multipurpose or focused appraisals

Use multiple inputs or one input

Training and Development

Buy or develop skills

Individual or team-based training

On-the-job or external training

Job-specific or generic training

Compensation

Fixed-pay or variable pay system

Job-based or individual pay

Seniority-based or performance-based system

Centralize or decentralize pay decisions

Employee and Labor Relations

Top-down or bottom-up communications

Interactions with labor unions

Adversarial or cooperative relationship

Employee Rights

Use discipline as control or learning

Protect organization's or employees' rights

Formal or informal ethics program

Current HRM Strategies

Employees as significant resource

High-tech human resources approach

---

for efficiency or innovation; organizing for control or flexibility; using specialized and narrow job descriptions or broad job categories; and using detailed work planning or loose work planning. Inherent in these different approaches are strategic decisions about the use of typical HR tools such as job analysis, job design, job descriptions, and job specifications. However, work-flow strategies also encompass contemporary human resource practices such as boundaryless organizations, business process reengineering, self-managed work teams, contingent workers, and flexible work schedules. Of course, these decisions should be coordinated with the work activities required by the organization's other functions.

What role do an organization's human resource management strategies play in product safety? After a tragic outbreak of E. coli poisonings and the deaths of four children from eating contaminated food at Jack in the Box restaurants in the Pacific Northwest, the parent company, Foodmaker, radically redesigned its food distribution and preparation system. Adapted from a food-safety system developed in the 1960s by NASA and Pillsbury to prepare food for space flights, the system had never been used commercially in fast food. The system involves monitoring food as it travels from supplier (where it's tested extensively for harmful bacteria) through distribution channels, to restaurants, and ultimately to the serving counter. How do HRM strategies come into play? The food-safety consultant hired to design the new system for Foodmaker said, "Although it has technical components, 90% of it is about managing behaviors, people, and culture." What do you think this statement means? What other functional strategies might be impacted by product safety issues? What are the ethical implications for other organizations who must deal with product safety issues as they design their functional strategies?

Source: R. Goff, "Coming Clean," *Forbes*, May 17, 1999, pp. 156–60.

Staffing. Once strategic decisions about work flow have been made, it's time to look at making sure there are appropriately skilled people to perform the work. These staffing decisions involve strategic choices in the following areas: whether to use internal or external recruitment; who will make hiring decisions—HR department or supervisor; what's important in hiring—the "fit" of the applicant with the organizational culture or the applicant's technical qualifications and skills; and whether a formal or informal hiring and socialization approach is taken.

Employee Separations. You've experienced employee separation if you've ever had a summer job and left it at the end of summer to return to school. Whereas staffing strategies deal with getting people *into* the organization, employee separation strategies involve people *leaving* the organization, whether voluntarily or involuntarily. Some strategic choices in terms of employee separation include downsizing by using voluntary inducements to encourage early retirement or using layoffs; implementing a hiring freeze to avoid layoffs or recruiting employees as needed even if this means other employees may be laid off; whether to provide support for terminated employees or let them fend for themselves; and whether to use a preferential or nonpreferential rehiring process.

Performance Appraisal. Tests, in-class assignments, case analysis, group projects—all of these are ways that your professor appraises your "work" performance. The work performed by an organization's employees also needs to be assessed and graded in order to determine whether assigned duties are being completed efficiently and effectively. This is done through a process known as performance appraisal. An appropriately designed performance appraisal system should help the organization achieve two things: employee performance improvement and employee development. Some strategic choices in terms of performance appraisal include whether to use customized or uniform appraisals; whether employee appraisal data will be used for developmental or control purposes; whether appraisals will be multipurpose (i.e., used for training, selection, pay decisions, or promotion) or more narrowly focused (such as for pay decisions only); and whether to have an appraisal system that uses multiple inputs or supervisory input only.

Training and Development. Employee training and development plays a critical role in meeting the challenges of the continuously changing marketplace. We want to make sure that our people have the skills they need to perform their jobs

Skills Gaps

The ever-changing external market-place context creates opportunities that organizations can exploit *if* organizational employees have the skills to harness the changes. Strategic decision makers should be on the lookout for skills gaps—deficiencies in specific skills needed by employees to take advantage of changing situations. For example, if the organization is moving toward an increased e-business presence, are there employees who have the necessary skills in e-commerce or are we going to have to look outside the organization? Once organizations have identified the skills they need for the changing context, there are three ways to get those skills: train current employees, hire new employees, or outsource. Strategically managing skills gaps is critical as an organization's HRM strategies are formulated and implemented.

Source: E. Krell, "Shifting Out of the Skills Gap," *Business Finance*, October 1999, pp. 26–32.

today *and* in the future. That's the role of HRM training and development strategies. What strategic alternatives are there? One important one that influences the organization's entire training approach is whether we intend to "buy" skills by hiring experienced employees (usually at a higher wage) or "develop" skills by training employees (who lack skills but who can usually be hired at a lower wage). Also, will we use individual or team-based training? Will we use on-the-job training or external training? Will training be job specific or generic (such as leadership development, problem-solving skills, listening skills, and so forth)? These are some of the training and development choices.

Compensation. Because all employees do expect to be compensated for their work, it's important to have appropriate compensation strategies. Our compensation system will have a direct impact on attracting, retaining, and motivating organizational members. If we want good people, we've got to have a good compensation system in place. In addition, though, the organization's choice of compensation strategies will impact overall labor costs, which in turn impacts financial performance. So, decision makers have to weigh these two variables—attracting and keeping good people versus what it costs to do so. What strategic choices do we have in strategically managing the compensation system? One decision involves whether to have a system of fixed salaries and benefits or one that uses variable pay components. Another strategic decision revolves around whether to use job-based pay (paying on the basis of the job an individual has) or individual-based pay (paying on the basis of an individual's contributions to the organization). We also must decide whether to use a seniority-based system (compensating on the basis of years with the organization) or a performance-based system (compensating on the basis of performance). Finally, we must decide whether to centralize or decentralize pay decisions.

Employee and Labor Relations. Although it might seem odd to be talking about employee relations *strategies,* the interactions an organization has with its employees can impact how committed they are to the organization and its goals. "Good employee relations involves providing fair and consistent treatment to all employees so that they will be committed to the organization's goals."[16] What

> ## Strategic Management in Action
>
> Ford Motor Company was the first company to offer its 350,000 employees free computers and printers and Internet access for a minimal monthly fee of $5. The computer offer wasn't based on altruism and wasn't meant to be just another employee benefit. Instead, as Ford's CEO Jacques A. Nasser explains, "This program keeps Ford . . . and our worldwide team at the leading edge of e-business technology and skills." Other companies, including Delta Air Lines, Chrysler, and a national health care company, have since put together a similar deal for their employees. What do you think about free PCs as an employee benefit? Could this strategy have a downside? Explain. For Ford, equipping employees with PCs meant an investment of around $300 million. Was this HR strategy a good investment? Explain.
>
> *Sources:* "A PC with Your Paycheck," *Newsweek*, February 14, 2000, p. 65; W. J. Holstein, "Let Them Have PCs," *U.S. News and World Report*, February 14, 2000, p. 43; and K. Kerwin, P. Burrows, and D. Foust, "Workers of the World, Log On," *Business Week*, February 21, 2000, p. 52.

strategic alternatives are part of employee and labor relations? One decision concerns how the organization chooses to communicate with its employees. Is it a strictly top-down system or a bottom-up system of communication and feedback? Another strategic choice—usually described as labor relations—has to do with the organization's interactions with employee unions. Are we actively going to avoid or suppress employee union organization efforts or work closely with employee unions as the employees' representatives? In addition, labor negotiations are likely to be affected by the labor relations strategic approach the organization adopts. The final decision in terms of employee relations strategies addresses how the organization will approach its overall relationship with its employees. Will we take an adversarial approach to employee interactions or will we attempt to address employees' needs? The strategic choices we make here will influence our willingness to implement HRM programs, policies, and systems (including such contemporary workplace practices as family-friendly programs, employee assistance programs, employee recognition programs, etc.) that have the potential to support and strengthen all employee–organization interactions. In other words, it establishes the whole basis for how we're going to treat our employees.

Employee Rights. The final area of HRM strategies that we're going to cover is that of employee rights. This area involves the relationship an organization has with its employees. It's part of the whole approach the organization takes to employee relations but is specifically concerned with employee–management rights and disciplinary strategies. What are the strategic options? One is the approach the organization uses to encourage appropriate work behavior. Do we use discipline as a way to control employee behavior and reduce mistakes, or do we emphasize encouraging appropriate behavior in the first place in order to reduce mistakes? After all, disciplinary measures aren't the only way to encourage appropriate work behavior. Another strategic decision involves whose rights will be protected—the organization's or the employees'. And, not surprisingly, in many instances the rights of the employer and the rights of the employee are in conflict. How will we strategically manage these situations? That depends upon the employee rights strategies we're following. Finally, in the area of employee rights strategies we need to decide how our organization is going to address ethics. Will we rely on informal ethical standards or have explicit ethical codes, standards, and enforcement procedures?

Current HRM Strategies. The HR strategies an organization uses are a pretty good reflection of how it views its *human* resources and the role they're perceived to play in organizational performance. The traditional, often adversarial approach to employees and treating them as any other resource isn't likely to lead to a sustainable competitive advantage. Many examples exist of organizations that view their employees as partners, working together to accomplish the organization's vision, missions, and goals. For instance, at Southwest Airlines (SWA), employees are encouraged to have fun and be playful on the job. Flight attendants often dress up in outrageous outfits on Halloween and other holidays. Stories abound of how flight attendants hide in the plane's overhead storage bins, only to yell "surprise" at the first passenger to open it up. Even Southwest's CEO, Herb Kelleher, has been known to don a costume and show up to entertain the crowd on certain flights. Or, a passenger who is being particularly difficult might find a plastic cockroach in his or her drink. Of course, the added "garnish" will be pointed out to the individual before he or she has had an opportunity to drink out of the cup. All these zany antics are in fun, but SWA is serious about fostering a friendly work environment so that customer service can flourish. In fact, Kelleher himself says, "What we are looking for (in potential hires), first and foremost, is a sense of humor. We look for attitudes. We'll train you on whatever you need to do, but the one thing we can't do is change inherent attitudes in people."[17] Has the company's people focus paid off? Well, it's the only major airline to remain consistently profitable throughout its history. And, it continues to receive awards for outstanding customer service.

Bentonville, Arkansas, doesn't exactly come to mind when you think of meccas for high-tech business. Yet, at the headquarters of Wal-Mart stores, advanced technology is very much in evidence in the company's People Division.[18] With over 3,000 locations worldwide, there's no way that employee training could be totally centralized. Instead, a program called Computer Based Learning was installed in all Wal-Mart stores. Through this program, a series of employee training modules use multimedia devices (audio, video, text, and graphics) to show employees their specific job responsibilities as well as to showcase Wal-Mart's corporate values. This way, the same content and message is delivered to every one of the company's approximately 1,100,000 employees worldwide. Also, because it's computer based, employees can pace themselves on the training, making it more individualized. Another aspect of Wal-Mart's high-tech approach to training can be seen in its own internal satellite network, Wal-Mart Network Television (WMTV). This daily show airs in every store with topics ranging from a company buyer talking about the process behind this season's shoe selections to corporate executives complimenting and motivating employees. Wal-Mart's HRM strategies reflect the latest in high-tech enhancements, and the company feels it's an investment that makes its human resources more efficient and effective.

Consider This ◀◀|

✓ What is marketing, and what are the biggest factors in marketing?

✓ Describe the possible segmentation or target market strategies.

✓ What are the four possible differentiation dimensions? Give some examples of each.

✓ What is positioning, and why is it important to the marketing strategies?

✓ Describe the marketing mix strategies.

✓ How does the product life cycle affect the choice of marketing strategies?

✓ Describe relationship marketing. Why is it becoming so important?

✓ What is database marketing? How might an organization use database marketing as a strategic choice?

✓ Describe high-performance work practices. Why do you think these practices lead to high performance?

✓ What is work flow, and what strategic choices are there in work flow?

✓ Describe possible strategic choices in the following HR areas: staffing, employee separations, performance appraisal, training and development, compensation, employee and labor relations, and employee rights.

✓ What types of current HR strategies are organizations pursuing?

Many other examples exist of organizations that are committed to developing and implementing strong HR management strategies. Reinforcing what was stated earlier, researchers studying the link between an organization's HRM systems and strategies and its performance are finding that, indeed, certain HRM strategies can positively impact a firm's performance.[19] That's a pretty good reason to look at developing appropriate HRM strategies.

Research and Development Strategies

It used to be that when someone talked about a "mouse," he or she was referring to the little gray, furry rodent with a supposedly fond appetite for cheese. Now, however, when a mouse comes up in conversation, it's usually in reference to the hand device used in point-and-click computer technology. How did this man-made mouse come into existence and become a standard feature on most desktops in homes and offices? It's a safe bet that some organization's research and development (R&D) strategies played a significant role. Without R&D, we wouldn't have the scientific breakthroughs, product innovations, or process improvements used in today's world. An organization's R&D strategies should reflect its philosophy about innovation, which we defined earlier in Chapter 2 as the process of taking a creative idea and turning it into a product or process to be used or sold. R&D is how innovation is realized in organizations. In today's fast-changing markets, rapid innovation can lead to a sustainable competitive advantage. What R&D strategies might an organization implement? We're going to look at three strategic areas of R&D: (1) R&D emphasis, (2) R&D timing, and (3) specific product and process development strategies. A summary of possible research and development strategies is provided in Table 5-5.

R&D Emphasis. One strategic decision that has to be made is *what* an organization is going to emphasize in its research and development activities. There are three possible alternatives. (See Figure 5-3.) The first is an emphasis on basic scientific research. This R&D strategy requires the heaviest commitment in terms of resources because it involves the nuts-and-bolts activities and work of scientific research. In numerous industries (e.g., plant and human genetics engineering, computer hardware, or pharmaceuticals), an organization's expertise in basic research can be the key to a sustainable competitive advantage. However, not every industry requires this level of basic scientific research for organizations to achieve high performance levels. That leads us to the second strategic alternative, which is an emphasis on product development. Many organizations depend upon their product development strategies for continued growth in sales and profits.

TABLE 5-5   Possible Research and Development Strategies

R&D Emphasis

Basic scientific research
Product development
Process development

R&D Timing

First mover
Follower

Product and Process Development

Who?
   Separate R&D department
   Cross-functional team
   Some variation
How?
   Formal or informal process
   Use prototypes
   Use product tests
   Use design reviews
   Use test markets
   How to implement new design
   How to evaluate success of new design

Current R&D Strategies

Employee suggestion systems
Risk taking and innovative culture

This strategy requires a significant resource commitment also but not in those work activities associated with basic scientific research. We'll address some specific product development strategies later in this section. The third strategic alternative that an organization might pursue is an emphasis on process development. Using this strategy, an organization looks for ways to improve and enhance any or all of its work processes. We'll also describe some specific process development strategies later in this section.

R&D Timing. The R&D timing an organization uses is another strategic choice. Some organizations want to be the first to bring out or use innovations, whereas other organizations are content to follow or mimic the innovations. An organization that's first to bring a new product innovation to the marketplace or to use a new process innovation is called a **first mover**. Being a first mover has certain strategic advantages and disadvantages as shown in Table 5-6. Some organizations pursue these pioneering approaches or strategies. By doing so, they hope to develop a sustainable competitive advantage. Other organizations have been

Figure 5-3

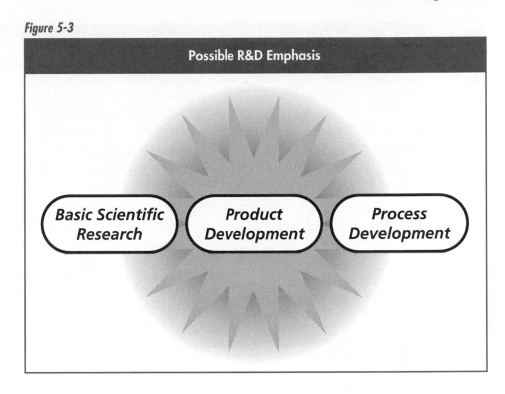

able to develop a sustainable competitive advantage by being the followers in the industry. They let the first movers pioneer the innovations and then mimic their offerings or processes. Which R&D timing strategy an organization chooses to pursue depends upon its overall philosophy and approach to innovation as well as its specific resources and capabilities.

The R&D emphasis and R&D timing strategies an organization chooses will influence its product and process development strategies. We need to look at some specific approaches to these two R&D activities.

Product and Process Development Strategies. Given the dynamics of today's marketplace, organizations need to develop new products. The approaches used to do this are its product development strategies. However, innovation isn't

TABLE 5-6   First Mover Advantages–Disadvantages

Advantages	Disadvantages
• Reputation for being innovative and industry leader	• Uncertainty over exact direction technology and market will go
• Cost and learning benefits resulting from moving along experience curve first	• Risk of competitors imitating innovations (free-rider effect)
• Control over scarce assets preventing competitors from having access to them	• Financial and strategic risks
• Opportunity to begin building customer relationships and customer loyalty	• High development costs

FYI

To Be More Innovative, Get Rid of R&D

You know how important innovation is to an organization's development of a competitive advantage. We've discussed it at various points so far in the text. However, what if to win with innovation, you had to eliminate your organization's R&D efforts? What would you think of that? Some companies in the most innovation-intensive industries (where product life cycles are short and the need for breakthrough products is critical) have pioneered a radically different approach to innovation. How? By engaging the innovation talents of individuals who are not employees. These innovation "superstars" are brought on board to champion the innovation process. Often, they're hired on a project-by-project basis. What this innovative approach to innovation does is nurture outside-the-box, breakout thinking. In industries from entertainment to toys to pharmaceuticals, innovation superstar free agents are changing the face of product development. What do you think about this strategic approach to innovation? Do you think it would work in all types of organizations? Explain. Do you think an organization could ever totally eliminate its R&D function? Why or why not?

Sources: G. Donnelly, "A P&L for R&D," *CFO*, February 2000, pp. 44–50; and C. E. Lucier and J. D. Torsilieri, "To Win with Innovation—Kill R&D," *Strategy & Business* (third quarter 1999), pp. 8–12.

important just for product development; it's also vital for the ways these products are manufactured or marketed—that is, the organization's processes. The strategic alternatives in implementing product and process development revolve around *who* and *how*.

The "who" choices address who's going to be responsible for developing new ideas. Will it be a separate R&D department of scientists–engineers who have total responsibility for creating and implementing new products and processes? Will it be a **cross-functional team**, which is a group of individuals from various functional departments who work together on product or process development, or will it be something in between these two options? More and more organizations are using some type of development team for product and process innovations. And, it appears that these teams are better at developing new and feasible ideas when they include individuals from all the work areas involved with R&D efforts. But, exactly *how* does the R&D effort get done?

The "how" of R&D involves the actual sequence of activities from idea generation to implementation and evaluation. An organization must make several strategic choices as it "does" R&D. Some of these choices include

1. Will we use a formal or informal process for generating ideas for product and process design?
2. Will we use prototypes, and how extensively will we use them?
3. Will we use product tests, and what type will we use?
4. Will we use design reviews in determining manufacturing cost and quality aspects?
5. Will we use test markets, and how extensively will we use them?
6. How will we implement the new product design or process design?
7. How will we evaluate the success of the R&D process?

> ## *Strategic Management in Action*
>
> The CEO of online brokerage E*Trade Group, Christos M. Cotsakos, has built an organization with a culture that's edgy, somewhat bizarre, and usually brilliant. For example, to make his executives move faster on making decisions, he arranged a day of racing Formula One race cars at speeds up to 150 miles an hour. To get employees to loosen up, he has them carry around rubber chickens or wear propeller beanie hats. And, to get his management team to bond together, they attended cooking school where they had to depend on each other to put together a gourmet dinner. Says Cotsakos, "It's all about getting people excited about how they can make a difference as a person and as a team." In the intensely competitive online brokerage industry, a company has to be inventive *and* disciplined. Cotsakos has tried to create a culture in which people are willing to be wildly creative, very competitive, and yet so closely knit that they're like a family. As E*Trade positions itself to become a giant in the online brokerage business, there's no doubt that its R&D strategies are playing a significant role.
>
> *Source:* L. Lee, "Tricks of E*Trade," *Business Week E.Biz,* February 7, 2000, pp. EB18–EB31.

The strategic decisions made depend upon the organization's overall innovation philosophy and whether innovation is a significant source of competitive advantage for the organization. Of course, these decisions must be coordinated with the marketing and production–operations strategies.

Current R&D Strategies. What types of R&D strategies are today's organizations using in their attempts to develop a sustainable competitive advantage? Let's look at a couple of organizations who appear to be strategically managing their R&D strategies.

Where do good ideas come from? Employee suggestion systems can be a good source of process design improvements. For example, at the Johnson Controls Inc. auto-parts factory in Georgetown, Kentucky, employee suggestions have improved efficiency and overall productivity.[20] These suggestions translated into cost savings for the company and bonuses for the employees. Although not every employee suggestion was feasible, this organization has found that employee suggestions could be good sources of ideas for process R&D innovations.

What about product design? Hewlett-Packard (H-P) is widely regarded as an organization that's strong in the area of product design and development. The company has become the dominant player in the laser printer market by consistently developing higher quality and more reliable products at affordable prices. How does it do it? One important aspect is H-P's culture. Its culture encourages risk taking and innovation by product design teams. If product designers come up with something new or different, they're supported even if the product idea never makes it out of design. Also, the company supports its product development people by giving them whatever resources they need to do their jobs.

Information Systems Strategies

How would you like to do your job as a student (study, write papers, take tests, etc.) without information? It would be pretty tough, wouldn't it? You'd probably agree that information affects how effectively and efficiently organizational members do their work. Without information, the payroll clerk doesn't know what deductions to make from paychecks; the sales representative doesn't know what prices to quote a potential customer; or the plant manager doesn't know how this month's product quality levels compared to last month's. It's essential to have information to make decisions and to carry out work duties. How do organizational members get information? That's what an information system does. An **information system** is a set of interrelated components used to collect, process, store, and disseminate information to support decision making, analysis, and management control in organizations.[21] Let's look at two of the strategic decisions associated with the organization's information system. These are the choice of system technology and the choice of what types of information systems to have. Table 5-7 summarizes possible information systems strategies.

System Technology. The choice of system technology is actually pretty simple—the information system can be either manual or computer based. A manual system uses pencil-and-paper technology to collect, store, process, and disseminate information. A computer-based system relies on computer hardware and software technology to do the same. As prices have fallen and computing power has risen, many organizations have moved to more computer-based information systems. However, certain organizations still collect all or some information manually. Which approach an organization uses depends on how important informa-

TABLE 5-7   Possible Information Systems Strategies
System Technology
Manual or computer based
Types of Information Systems
Transaction processing system
Office automation system
Knowledge work system
Management information system
Decision support system
Executive support system
Current Information Systems Strategies
Electronic data sharing
Customer call centers
Internet and World Wide Web

tion is to developing a sustainable competitive advantage. For instance, is it critical that strategic decision makers have rapid access to information from all operational areas of the organization? Is it vital that organizational members have rapid access to information to help them do their jobs effectively and efficiently? Is it critical that organizational units share information? Is information a significant resource in our industry? All these factors will influence the extent to which an organization uses a computer-based or manual system.

Types of Information Systems. An organization's information system isn't just one single system because no single system can provide all the information needed. Instead, an organization will have many different types of information systems serving different organizational levels and functions. We need to look briefly at these six different types of information systems as possible strategic choices. Table 5-8 lists the characteristics of each of these systems.

The first type found at the organization's operational level is typically called a transaction processing system (TPS). These information systems are the basic business systems used in tracking work being done in the various organizational functional areas. Examples include payroll, reservation systems, sales order tracking and processing, and plant scheduling.

The next type of information system is referred to as an office automation system (OAS) and includes all the documents, schedules, and mail generated by an organization's clerical workers. Examples include letters, invoices, press releases, newsletters, or contracts. More and more, this type of information gathering and exchange is being done using word processing, electronic mail, and desktop publishing software.

Another type of information system is called the knowledge work system (KWS). This information system is used primarily by an organization's knowledge workers such as engineers, analysts, designers, attorneys, scientists, or doctors.

Strategic Management—The Global Perspective

The Toronto-based Canadian Imperial Bank of Commerce (CIBC), like other traditional banks, is facing severe competition from Internet banks and brokerage houses that have very low cost structures and can thus offer similar services at cheaper prices. To fight back, CIBC invested in an Internet-based electronic purchasing system. The purchasing function in organizations has been one of the last to convert to automated technology. However, it's an area ripe for information system technology. Some experts say the average cost of processing a paper-based purchase order ranges from $50 to $200. Why? Because purchase orders are typically funneled through layers of costly labor. Therefore, CIBC's strategic decision to move to online procurement was based on the objectives of streamlining administrative routines, discouraging off-contract buying, and consolidating purchasing practices to take advantage of discounts and better service from suppliers. The company's cost-saving goal was 10 percent to 15 percent. You see what advantages CIBC hopes to gain from its strategic move. What challenges do you think it might have to deal with as it implements this system? If you were a strategic manager at CIBC, how would you handle these challenges?

Source: C. Fredman, "The Devil in the Details," *Executive Edge,* April–May 1999, pp. 35–39.

TABLE 5-8   Types of Information Systems and Their Characteristics

Type of System	Information Inputs	Processing	Information Outputs	Users
ESS	Aggregate data; external, internal	Graphics; simulations; interactive	Projections; responses to queries	Senior managers
DSS	Low-volume data; analytic models	Interactive; simulations; analysis	Special reports; decision analyses; responses to queries	Professionals; staff managers
MIS	Summary transaction data; high-volume data; simple models	Routine reports; simple models; low-level analysis	Summary and exception reports	Middle managers
KWS	Design specifications; knowledge base	Modeling; simulations	Models; graphics	Professionals; technical staff
OAS	Documents; schedules	Document management; scheduling; communication	Documents; schedules; mail	Clerical workers
TPS	Transactions; events	Sorting; listing; merging; updating	Detailed reports; lists; summaries	Operations personnel; supervisors

Source: Management Information Systems, 4th ed. by Laudon/Laudon © 1986. Reprinted by permission of Prentice-Hall, Inc., Upper Saddle River, NJ.

What a KWS should do is provide ways to promote and use new knowledge and innovation. Examples include product design graphics (such as computer-aided design, or CAD), legal database search, virtual reality simulations, or financial data analysis.

The next type of information system is the management information system (MIS), which is used by an organization's managers for planning, controlling, and decision making. The MIS typically summarizes and reports on the organization's basic functional activities. It's different from the TPS because it's not designed to report day-to-day activities, but rather to summarize a series of time periods (week, month, quarter, or year). Examples include summary sales reports, cost comparisons from different products, or employee training expenditures for the quarter.

Another type of information system that's also used by managers and other professionals for decision making is called a decision support system (DSS). However, the DSS is different from both the KWS and the MIS because it allows for more powerful data analysis and also allows decision makers to change the assumptions and information to see what impact those changes have on the outcomes. In addition, a DSS is typically designed so that users can work with it directly—that is, the user initiates and controls the information inputs and outputs. These types of information systems are unique to different situations, but some examples might include a financial portfolio analysis with "what-if" scenarios, production facility optimization analysis, evaluation of potential well drilling sites, or defense contract analysis.

The final type of information system an organization might have is an executive support system (ESS). This type of system would be used by an organization's

Strategic Management in Action

Even behind a scary mask, there's a smile on a kid's face who gets any Hershey's candy in a trick-or-treat bag. Yet, at the biggest candy binge of 1999 (Halloween), Hershey Foods Corporation was trying to correct delivery foul-ups caused by a newly installed information system. New technology brought online in July 1999 caused significant problems in the company's ordering and distribution system. The computer system was supposed to automate and modernize all activities from taking candy orders to loading pallets on trucks, but it didn't work as planned. The impact was felt all the way from corporate headquarters to food distributors and retailers. Hershey's third-quarter earnings per share (EPS) dropped 16 percent, and industry experts said that Hershey's may have missed as much as $100 million in sales in the fourth quarter of 1999. You may be saying about now that technology is supposed to help, not hurt! Yet, as this example illustrates, having a successful information systems strategy isn't as easy as it may seem.

Sources: "Cyberwoes Gum Up Hershey Sales," *Springfield News-Leader*, October 30, 1999, p. 9A; and E. Nelson and E. Ramstad, "Hershey's Biggest Dud Has Turned Out to Be New Computer System," *Wall Street Journal*, October 29, 1999, p. A1.

upper-level managers to aid in making unstructured, comprehensive, broad, and complex decisions. An ESS wouldn't be used to help solve specific problems, but rather to provide a generalized approach for looking at a broad array of organizational issues. For instance, an ESS might be designed to help track competitors' actions or to assess the impact of proposed investment tax changes on company earnings.

What role do information and information systems play in managing strategically? It depends on how important it is to have the right types of information when, where, and how organizational members need it. Choosing an appropriate information systems strategy—that is, the system technology to use and the types of information systems to have—involves some important decisions. Let's look at some current information systems strategies being used by organizations.

Current Information Systems Strategies. At the Consumer Brands Division of Sherwin-Williams Company—some of its products include Dutch Boy Paint, Martin-Senour Paint, and Cuprinol Stains—information is an important strategic element.[22] How? Electronic data are shared by marketing and transportation to make sure that retailers' shelves are stocked with the right paint for the right customer at the right time. It has applied information technologies in the following ways: bar coding of paint cans in the manufacturing plants; bar coding of shipping containers and pallet loads for distribution; electronic data interchange (EDI) partnerships with retailers such as Kmart; and an automated warehouse control system including radio frequency data communications. All of these information strategies have allowed the company to enhance its competitiveness in a tough market. And, it has done it by using what it feels are effective and efficient information systems.

At other organizations, the information strategy revolves around customer call centers or customer contact centers.[23] You might not think that the lowly call center would be a strategic part of a business, but many organizations know that it is. For example, at DaimlerChryslerAG, information gleaned from 37,000 calls from car mechanics each month is transferred electronically to engineering, where designers review this information with an eye toward improving the company's cars. Using its information system resources and capabilities, DaimlerChrysler hopes to become the dominant competitor in the intensely competitive automobile market. This company is using its information systems strategies to exploit external marketplace opportunities as well.

Finally, we can't leave the topic of information system strategies without mentioning the pervasiveness of the Internet and World Wide Web. There's hardly an industry that hasn't experienced the power (either positively *or* negatively) of the Internet. The instantaneous availability and interactivity of Web sites gives organizations a powerful tool for collecting, processing, storing, and disseminating information. An organization's decision makers must determine the role of the Internet in its information systems strategies.

Financial–Accounting Strategies

The last functional area we're going to look at involves the organization's financial–accounting strategies. These strategies concern choices about how financial and accounting data are collected and used. We'll be looking at four broad areas: evaluating financial performance; financial forecasting, planning, and budgeting; financing mix; and other financial management decisions.[24] Possible financial–accounting strategies are summarized in Table 5-9.

Evaluating Financial Performance. How do we usually evaluate an organization's financial performance? We do it by looking at the financial statements and evaluating the information they contain. These financial statements include specific pieces of information about the organization's operations. The typical financial statements are the income statement, the balance sheet, and a cash flow statement. By themselves, the financial statements show only results. To evaluate financial performance, we have to look closer at what the statements are telling us. Financial ratios are the principal tool for financial analysis. The financial ratios standardize financial information so that comparisons can be made from time period to time period or of the organization to its industry. The strategic choices in terms of evaluating financial performance revolve around how often to do it and how much analysis to do. Quite often, this is dictated by law or regulation and not entirely open to individual choice. However, even if financial analysis isn't mandated, the fact remains that an organization needs to have in place some mechanism and procedure for evaluating financial performance. Without this information, strategic decision makers would have little knowledge of how the organization is performing, at least from a quantitative and financial standpoint.

Financial Forecasting, Planning, and Budgeting. Financial forecasting is used to estimate an organization's future financial needs. Once forecasts are developed, then decision makers can plan and budget according to the forecasts. The most popular type of financial forecast is the percent of sales method, which involves estimating the potential level of an expense, asset, or liability as a per-

TABLE 5-9   Possible Financial–Accounting Strategies

Evaluating Financial Performance

How often
How much analysis

Financial Forecasting, Planning, and Budgeting

Percentage of sales forecast
Discretionary financial needed model
Sustainable rate of growth model

Financing Mix

Financial structure–capital structure
　　Short-term versus long-term fund sources
　　Permanent or long-term sources

Other Financial Management Decisions

Capital budgeting choices
Stock dividend policy
Capital budgeting
Cash flow management
Working capital management and short-term financing
Cash and marketable securities management
Accounts receivable and inventory management
Use term loans or leases

Current Financial–Accounting Strategies

Controlling costs
Cash flow management by all employees
Valuing intangible assets

centage of the sales forecast. The resulting numbers, then, provide the basis for operational planning and budgeting. Other forecasting models that decision makers might use are the discretionary financial needed (DFN) model (which predicts changes in assets, liabilities, and owners' equity based on predicted changes in sales) or the sustainable rate of growth calculation (which represents the rate at which an organization's sales can maintain its current financial ratios without having to sell new common stock). Again, the strategic choices in terms of financial forecasting, planning, and budgeting would be what financial tools or models are used and how often they're used.

Financing Mix. The financing mix strategies concern decisions about the organization's financial structure and capital structure. **Financial structure** refers to the mix of all items found on the right-hand side of the organization's balance sheet. **Capital structure** refers to the mix of the long-term sources of funds used

The Hitchhiker's Guide to Budgeting

Budgeting is often viewed as the most despised task in organizations. Employees say that it's a meaningless exercise that's only slightly related to the organization's overall objectives, is extremely time-consuming, and that when it's completed has little to do with the realities of conducting business. However, budgeting is an important financial and accounting strategy. How can an organization's budgeting system be improved? Here are some suggestions for effective budgeting:

- Establish a link between what the organization does and what it spends money on.
- Think about what the organization measures. Are the important things being funded?

- Get agreement outside the financial department about what the organization's measures should be.
- Link compensation to budget goals.
- Don't forecast in a vacuum; encourage discussion among all functional areas.
- Reduce the number of budget line items.
- Reduce the time the process takes.
- Give employees the flexibility to meet their budget targets.
- Don't be bound by calendar-based or fiscal year–based forecasts.
- Understand that technology can't solve all the budget-planning challenges. It's only a tool!

Sources: T. Leahy, "Necessary Evil," *Business Finance*, November 1999, pp. 41–45; and R. N. Anthony, J. Dearden, and N. M. Bedford, *Management Control Systems*, 5th ed. (Homewood, IL: Irwin, 1984), Chap. 5–7.

by the organization. How do decision makers determine the optimum financial structure? It primarily depends on two things: (1) how the organization wants to divide its total fund sources between short- and long-term components (maturity composition), and (2) what proportion of total financing the organization wants to be from permanent sources. Answers to these two questions will affect what financing mix strategies the organization chooses. Other factors that influence an organization's strategic choice of financial structure are how much debt capacity it has, whether it has reached its optimum or target amount of debt, the stage in the business cycle, and the amount of risk the organization faces. All of these factors will affect the types and maturities of the financing options an organization has to select from.

Other Financial Management Decisions. Other financial management strategic decisions involve choices about capital budgeting; stock dividend policy; capital budgeting and cash flow management; working capital management and short-term financing; cash and marketable securities management; accounts receivable and inventory management; and the use of term loans and leases. In each of these financial areas, decision makers must choose what to use and how to implement it. For example, are we going to pay shareholder dividends? If so, are we going to try to maintain some standardized payout amount or let it vary? Or, for instance, what's the organization's strategy for maintaining sufficient cash flow? In each of these financial management areas, there are choices to make in strategically managing this particular organization function.

Current Financial–Accounting Strategies. Controlling an organization's costs, especially selling, general, and administrative (SG&A), continues to be an important strategy. For some industries with very narrow profit margins, pennies count. For example, J. B. Hunt, the large trucking company based in Lowell, Arkansas, carefully monitors expenses. Managers and all employees are encouraged to control costs carefully. As an added incentive, every member of management, all operating employees, and most salaried employees are paid a bonus on the company's operating ratio that is based on revenues and expenses. If expenses are not controlled, all bonuses are affected. This is a pretty powerful incentive for all employees to work as a team to control organizational costs.[25] Part of controlling costs has to do with cash flow. At Zytec Corporation, a Minneapolis-based manufacturer of custom-designed computer power sources, cash flow is king.[26] As competition increased, the company, which used to be part of Control Data Corporation, saw its sales volume drop from $80 million to $25 million. In order to survive *and* to keep its commitment to practicing the quality management philosophy espoused by W. Edwards Deming of autonomous decision making by employees, Zytec had to take drastic action. The company's chief financial officer (CFO) stated, "If you have a lot of people making autonomous decisions who don't have any cash sensitivity, all of a sudden you find yourself in a hole at the bank, which is a practical reality that nobody likes." So, the company's strategic decision makers chose to attack the problem head-on through training. The CFO spent an entire year explaining the rudiments of cash flow to all employees at company operations-review meetings. Now, Zytec employees know what cash flow is and why it's so important. Sales revenues have rebounded as well. Now, if there's a cash crunch, all that the financial managers have to do is alert employees to the crisis and remind them to minimize cash outflows and maximize cash inflows.

Finally, we want to look at a current challenge in the area of financial–accounting strategies—valuing intangible assets. The current system of financial

Real Options Theory

A revolutionary concept in corporate finance called "real options theory" states that when the future is highly uncertain, it pays to have a broad range of options open. The real options approach rewards flexibility, which given the realities of today's situational context may make the most strategic sense. Strategic decision makers are encouraged to create lots of possibilities. Then, as different scenarios unfold, certain options may not be worth pursuing, but a few could pay off highly. For instance, Enron Corporation built three gas-fired power plants in northern Mississippi and western Tennessee that were deliberately inefficient. Why? Enron's financial strategists felt that they could generate profits by calculating just the right time to run the plants, taking into consideration prevailing power prices and the costs of powering up and shutting down. According to one consultant, under the options approach, "uncertainty has the potential to be your friend, not your enemy." Other organizations that have used the real options analysis technique in their financial strategies include Hewlett-Packard, Anadarko Petroleum, and Airbus Industries.

Sources: P. Coy, "Exploiting Uncertainty," *Business Week*, June 7, 1999, pp. 118–24; and P. Coy, "Options, Options Everywhere," *Business Week*, June 7, 1999, p. 124.

measurement appears to be inadequate when assessing intellectual capital and other intangible assets. These intangible resources are subjective, nebulous, and hard to define. Even an intangible asset, such as an organization's computer system, that seems relatively straightforward is complicated by issues such as compatibility, software, usage, and bandwidth. To address this glaring weakness in financial-accounting measures, three organizations (*Forbes* magazine, Ernst & Young Center for Business Innovation, and the Wharton Research Program on Value Creation in Organizations) teamed together to research and develop jointly the first practical audit of intangible assets.[27] What the team discovered became the Value Creation Index (VCI), a measurement tool that incorporates the relative importance of each key organizational value driver. What are these value drivers? Through their thorough research, the team uncovered eight organizational functions, which included in order from most important to least important: innovation; ability to attract talented employees; strategic alliances; quality of major processes, products, or services; environmental performance; brand investment; technology; and customer satisfaction. You may be asking yourself, "Why is this such a big deal?" VCI is important because if these truly are the keys behind increasing organizational value, we've identified strategic initiatives that can improve both corporate performance and market value. It represents an important step in unlocking the challenge of measuring intangible assets.

NOW WHAT?

Even though it may seem you've been introduced to all aspects of an organization's functional strategies, we still need to look at a couple of issues. First, what's involved with implementing these strategies? Next, how do we evaluate the functional strategies, and what do we do if they aren't working as well as we'd planned? Finally, how do we coordinate these strategies with the other organizational strategies?

Implementing the Various Functional Strategies

Implementing strategies very simply means *doing* them. What comes to mind is the marketing slogan from the well-known athletic shoe marketer, "Just Do It." Strategy implementation—that is, putting the strategies into action—involves five aspects: processes, activities, budgets, structure, and culture. What this boils down to is simply: What are we going to do? How are we going to do it? Who's going to do it? When are we going to do it? Where are we going to do it? At the functional level, these five aspects are relatively narrow in scope and definition because each functional area has its own specific work to do in contributing to the overall organizational goals. However, this doesn't mean that there's no coordination among the various functional units. Quite the contrary! Coordinating the various functional units is one of the keys to managing strategically at this level. This coordination is important because of the inherent interdependence and interactions of the organization's various functions and their contribution to the organization "doing" what it's in business to do—whether that's manufacturing baseball gloves, designing Web page authoring programs, selling insurance, or building houses. What does this mean for implementation? Managing the organization's various functional areas as separate "chimneys" or "silos" might keep an organization from exploiting its key resources and capabilities and being able to develop them into a sustainable competitive advantage. And, as the functional strategies are implemented through the assorted work processes and activities that are unique to each of these areas, it's important to foster an organizational environment in which all units are working toward fulfilling the organization's vision, missions, and goals. Implementation at the functional level includes both the specific use of certain processes, activities, structure, budget, and culture *and* the coordination of the various functional units.

Evaluating Strategies and Making Changes

How do we know whether the organization's functional strategies are working and what do we do if they're not? Again, if you look at Figure 5-1, you'll see that the processes of evaluating and changing strategies is part of strategic management in action. Strategy evaluation at the functional level involves using specific performance measures—quantitative *and* qualitative—for each of the functional areas. For example, how many product coupons were redeemed from the seasonal sales promotion program; how many and what types of problems have been encountered since the new management information system was put in place; or what's the manufacturing product reject rate? Like any evaluation process, the actual performance measures must be compared against some standard. These standards are the goals established for the strategies in each of the functional areas. For example, if the goal of a new employee safety awareness program were to decrease employee disability claims, did this happen? Was the HRM strategy successful? If the rate of employee disability claims didn't go down, then we'd need to try to determine what happened and why. Maybe the safety information wasn't communicated clearly or maybe the manufacturing unit was behind in its work and employees were being rushed to complete the work and ended up being careless. Strategy evaluation involves looking at what *was* done, what was *supposed* to be done, assessing any variances, and trying to determine what happened. If actual performance wasn't up to standards and if we think a change in a functional strategy is needed, then what? At this point, it depends on how critical the strategy is to the accomplishment of other organizational goals and whether it's something we can control and change. If we determine that the functional strategy is important and controllable, we'd look once again to the first steps in strategic management in action—that is, analyzing the current situation and then formulating appropriate strategies. Any changes in functional strategies would then be implemented and after a certain period of time, evaluated, and changed, if necessary.

Coordinating with Other Organizational Strategies

Not only is it important for the functional strategies to be coordinated with each other, they need to be coordinated with the other organizational strategies. Each organizational level—functional, business, corporate—needs to coordinate with and support the others in order to develop sustainable competitive advantages.[28] Strategic choices made at the business (competitive) and corporate levels do affect and are influenced by the functional strategies being implemented. Depending on what corporate and competitive strategies are being pursued, certain functional areas might be more important in carrying out those strategies. Then, it would be important for the resources, capabilities, and competences in those areas to be

Consider This ◀◀|

✓ What role does research and development play in an organization?

✓ Describe the three R&D activities that could be emphasized.

✓ What is a first mover? What are the advantages and disadvantages of being the first mover?

✓ Why are product and process development strategies important?

✓ What is a cross-functional team, and how might it be used in an organization?

✓ What is an information system?

✓ What are the two strategic decisions associated with an organization's information system?

✓ Differentiate between the six different types of information systems.

✓ Why is financial performance evaluation an important functional strategy?

✓ Describe what other choices must be made in terms of financial strategy.

✓ What is the Value Creation Index? What does it show, and why is it important?

✓ How are the functional strategies implemented?

✓ Why do the functional strategies need to be evaluated?

✓ Why is it important for the functional strategies to be (1) coordinated with each other and (2) coordinated with the other organizational strategies?

more fully developed and exploited. This strategic coordination and interdependency reflects the fact that an organization is a *system* with interrelated and interdependent units.

In addition, if changes are made at the other strategy levels, changes in functional strategies might be warranted. For example, a major strategic change such as reengineering requires examining, evaluating, and redesigning the organization's work processes found at the functional level. Thus, this strategic change might require changes in the functional strategies. Or, say that the organization decides to start selling its products in a foreign market. What is it going to take to implement this major strategy? What it's going to take is the design and implementation of numerous functional strategies—that is, marketing strategies, human resource management strategies, production–operations strategies, and so forth—to implement this change. As you can see, the functional strategies play an important role in executing the vision, missions, and goals of the organization. That's why they need to be coordinated with the other levels of strategies and changed to accommodate changes in those strategies. As we stated at the beginning of this chapter, it's important for an organization's functional strategies to be managed strategically so that its resources, capabilities, and core competencies can be developed into sustainable competitive advantage. Think back to the chapter-opening case. The strategic decision makers at Toyota Motor Corporation have created a system in which the functional level strategies are finely tuned and critical to the company's success. The effectiveness and efficiency of the strategies implemented at the functional levels have had a significant impact on the success of the corporate and business strategies as well as the current and future revenues.

THE BOTTOM LINE

⫸ By looking at the organization's functional strategies first, we're able to see how strategic management really works.

⫸ The functional strategies, however, are developed in light of the organization's vision, missions, overall corporate strategies, and competitive strategies.

⫸ When an organization is brand new, it makes sense to discuss corporate strategies first because no resources, capabilities, or competencies have been developed in the functional areas.

⫸ After completing the SWOT analysis, strategic decision makers can identify positive and negative aspects.

➤ The SWOT analysis points to strategic issues that decision makers need to address in their pursuit of sustainable competitive advantage and high performance levels.

➤ Even if it's evident from the SWOT analysis that the organization's corporate or competitive strategies need to be changed, strategists will base their decisions on the resources, capabilities, and competencies found in the functional areas.

➤ The organization's **functional strategies** are the short-term goal-directed decisions and actions of the organization's various functional units.

➤ The three basic functions (marketing, production and operations, and financial and accounting) are typically expanded to six (production–operation–manufacturing, marketing, human resource management, research and development, information systems–technology, and financial–accounting).

➤ Each organization will have its own uniquely named functional areas, but the basic work activities that comprise these functions remain the same.

➤ Each functional unit of the organization has a strategy for achieving its own mission and for helping the organization reach its overall vision.

➤ The process of creating goods and services in which organizational inputs (resources) are transformed into outputs is called **production**.

➤ Some of the strategic choices in the production function include production process strategies, capacity, location, work design, layout, and production and operations management.

➤ Current production–operations strategies include the use of **integrated manufacturing**, which is a production–operations philosophy that emphasizes the use of advanced manufacturing technology, total quality management, and just-in-time inventory control in order to create a streamlined flow of materials, people, and work activities for transforming inputs into outputs.

➤ **Marketing** is a process of assessing and meeting individual's or group's wants and needs by creating, offering, and exchanging products of value.

➤ In the marketing area, strategic choices include segmentation or target market strategies, differentiation strategies, positioning strategies, and marketing mix strategies.

➤ One current marketing strategy is **relationship marketing**, which is a process of building long-term, trusting, "win–win" relationships with valued customers.

➤ Many organizations have created **online communities**—constantly changing groups of people who collaborate, share ideas, and build relationships online—to build customer connections.

➤ Another current marketing strategy is **database marketing**, which uses database technology and sophisticated analytical techniques combined with direct-marketing methods to elicit desired measurable responses in target groups and individuals.

➤ In the area of human resource management, **high-performance work practices**, which are human resource policies and practices that can lead to both high individual and high organizational performance, have been identified.

➤ These HR strategies can improve the knowledge, skills, and abilities of an organization's current and potential employees; increase their motivation; reduce loafing on the job; and enhance retention of quality employees.

➠ Strategic choices in the HRM area revolve around **work flow** (the way an organization's work activities are organized so that the vision, mission(s), and objectives are effectively and efficiently accomplished), staffing, employee separations, performance appraisal, training and development, compensation, employee and labor relations, and employee rights.

➠ In the research and development area, there are three areas of strategic choices: R&D emphasis, R&D timing, and specific product and process development strategies (which revolve around *who* and *how* decisions).

➠ One particular strategic choice in terms of R&D timing is whether to be a first mover. A **first mover** is an organization that's first to bring a new product innovation to the marketplace or to use a new process innovation.

➠ One R&D "who" strategy involves whether to use a **cross-functional team**, which is a group of individuals from various functional departments who work together on product or process development.

➠ An **information system** is a set of interrelated components used to collect, process, store, and disseminate information to support decision making, analysis, and management control in organizations.

➠ Some of the strategic choices in the information systems function include the choice of system technology and the choice of what types of information systems to use.

➠ Four broad strategic choices exist in the financial–accounting area. These include evaluating financial performance; financial forecasting, planning, and budgeting; financing mix; and other financial management decisions.

➠ The financing mix strategies concern decisions about the organization's **financial structure** (the mix of all items found on the right-hand side of the organization's balance sheet) and **capital structure** (the mix of long-term sources of funds used by the organization).

➠ Once the strategic choices are made in each functional area, the strategies must be implemented.

➠ Functional strategy implementation involves five aspects: processes, activities, budgets, structure, and culture.

➠ At the functional level, these five aspects are relatively narrow in scope and definition because each functional area has its own specific work to do in contributing to the overall organizational goals.

➠ Although implementation involves the specific use of these aspects, it also involves the coordination of the various functional units.

➠ Strategy evaluation at the functional level involves using specific performance measures for each of the functional areas.

➠ The actual performance measures must be compared against some standard (the goals established for the strategies in each functional area).

➠ If actual performance isn't up to standards, what happens next depends on how critical the strategy is to the accomplishment of other organizational goals and whether it's something we can control and change.

➠ The functional strategies need to be coordinated with the other organizational strategies. Strategic choices made at the business (competitive) and corporate levels do affect and are influenced by the functional strategies being implemented.

➠ Depending on what corporate and competitive strategies are being pursued, certain functional areas might be more important in carrying out those strategies.

BUILDING YOUR SKILLS

1. The skirts, shirts, and jackets we wear today aren't a whole lot different than what was worn a decade ago. However, the ways they're produced have been transformed by a forced infusion of information technology. When American apparel makers learned to view their product as a process of harnessing information along a chain that runs from the factory floor to the retail counter, instead of as pieces of fabric sewn together, they improved their performance. Strategic factors such as bar coding, computer systems and software, high-tech distribution centers, and uniform standards have played a role in this reinvention of the clothing industry. How would each of these factors affect a clothing manufacturer's functional strategies in production–operations, marketing, human resource management, research and development, and information systems?

2. Jack Welch, CEO of General Electric, is renowned for his managerial skills and abilities. What's the secret of his success? "Not a series of brilliant insights or bold gambles, but a fanatical attention to detail." What do you think this statement means? What are the implications for strategically managing an organization's functional strategies?

   (*Source:* M. Conlin, "Revealed at Last: The Secret of Jack Welch's Success," *Forbes*, January 26, 1998, p. 44.)

3. Toyota Motor Corporation has a problem. It needs to attract younger buyers. According to Autopacific Inc., the median buyer's age for the 1999 model year were as follows: Volkswagen (36), Honda (37), Nissan (43), Saturn (43), Toyota (46), Chevrolet (47), and Ford (47).

   Toyota had successfully designed a marketing strategy for the baby-boom generation that pulled first-time car buyers in with a low-priced model (the Corolla) and then moved them into bigger, more expensive models as they aged. However, they now need to do the same thing with the younger generation, Generation Y. Which of Toyota's marketing strategies will need to change? How will these marketing strategies need to change? (*Hint:* Look at all the marketing strategies, not just at marketing *mix* strategies.)

   (*Source:* L. Armstrong, "Toyota: Chasing Boomers' Babies," *Business Week*, December 6, 1999, pp. 67–70.)

4. A federal law called the Economic Espionage Act of 1996 protects businesses from having their highly confidential product information stolen. Theft of intellectual property by trusted insiders (employees or contractors) happens a lot. One study estimated that intellectual property loss by U.S. companies amounted to over $250 billion annually. Many types of organizations in many types of industries are vulnerable. What are the implications for the

way an organization's functional strategies are formulated and implemented? Think about each functional area that might be affected.

5. Many organizations are putting customer service activities online (on the Internet) and making them available 24/7 (24 hours a day–7 days a week). What would be the advantages of this strategic approach? The disadvantages? How could strategic decision makers address the disadvantages?

6. During the 1990s, many companies downsized people and production capacity in attempts to run a leaner, more efficient organization. During the period of economic expansion enjoyed at the end of the 1990s through the first part of the twenty-first century, many of these lean companies were stretched thin by surging demand. One manufacturing executive described how his company laid off so many people that capacity was decreased. Another executive described how his company delayed preventive maintenance on machinery in order to meet demand. Could this problem of coping with strong customer demand have been prevented? Explain. Which functional strategies might have to change, and how might they have to change when a company must cope with unexpectedly strong customer demand?

7. Corporate sponsorships of special events and programs (sports programs, entertainment attractions, festivals and fairs, medical–education–social causes, and the arts) are a unique type of marketing strategy. The number of such sponsorships is slowing down. Do some research on corporate sponsorships. Find seven examples of companies using corporate sponsorships. Describe these examples in a brief paper. What types of corporate sponsorships are these companies doing? Given the nature of the company's industry, why do you think they chose the sponsorship they did? Do you think these corporate sponsorships are an effective and efficient marketing strategy? Why or why not?

8. Four emerging departments have been described as essential to running a successful e-business. These departments are Web surfing, information production, content engineering, and measurement and analysis. Describe what you think each of these departments would be responsible for doing. (You might try an Internet search for Internet job descriptions.) In addition, describe what types of strategies might be pertinent to each of these "new" functional areas.

9. How important is a fun workplace to employees? Many experts say that being recognized as a fun place to work can be an important competitive edge when recruiting in a tight labor market. Fun-loving firms indicate that incorporating humor and fun in the workplace reduces stress, increases job satisfaction, stimulates creativity, and increases productivity. Research the topic of fun and humor in the workplace. What are the pros and cons of this strategic choice? Make a bulleted list of your findings. Be prepared to debate the topic (from either side) in class.

10. "Why do companies spend billions of dollars on information technology systems that fail to respond to the needs of those who run them?" This complaint isn't unique. What are the implications for designing effective information systems strategies? Be specific.

11. Revenue management (also called yield management) is a strategic tool that can help strategists make better decisions. Drawing from the fields of operations research, economics, finance, and marketing, revenue management uses

a disciplined approach to forecasting demand for products or services, figuring out how to provide them most efficiently, and using price as a lever to influence demand and generate as much revenue as possible. Research the topic of revenue management. Make a bulleted list of its key points.

12. Customer service would appear to be an important strategic goal of any organization. Yet, surveys of customer satisfaction by the University of Michigan conclude that customer service is bad and has dropped to its lowest level in 30 years. Research the topic of customer service. Then in a short paper, describe which functional strategies might have to change and how they need to change to improve customer service.

(*Sources:* D. Brady, "Why Service Stinks," *Business Week,* October 23, 2000, pp. 118–28; K. Naughton, "Tired of Smile-Free Service," *Newsweek*, March 6, 2000, pp. 44–45; and C. Leaf, "The Death of Customer Service," *SmartMoney,* October 1998, pp. 130–37.)

STRATEGIC MANAGEMENT IN ACTION CASES

CASE #1: The Keys to Driving for Success

Strategic Management in Action case #1 can be found at the beginning of Chapter 5.

Discussion Questions

1. What do you think are the keys to Toyota's success?

2. Do you think production or marketing would be most important to Toyota? Support your choice.

3. Is strategy coordination important to Toyota? Explain.

4. Go to the company's Web site (**www.toyota.com**). Describe what examples of functional strategies you find there.

CASE #2: Cleaning Up at SOL

As one of northern Europe's most admired companies, SOL Cleaning Service, located in Helsinki, Finland, isn't what you might expect. The company's headquarters is located in a renovated film studio and positively "explodes" with color, creativity, and chaos. Walls are painted bright red, white, and yellow, and employees wander the halls talking on bright yellow high-tech portable phones. When necessary, the employees meet in work area "neighborhoods," each with a distinct personality. For instance, one neigh-borhood resembles a tree house. Another has oddly shaped tables that can be fitted together like a jigsaw puzzle. The employee training room looks like a multimedia par-adise—complete with overhead projectors, VCRs, computers, and chalkboards—and the window shades are decorated with bright circus scenes. These bright and energetic surroundings might seem tailor-made for creative, artistic businesses (such as software designers, screenwriters, or advertising executives), but SOL competes in a basic, dirty, and unglamorous business—industrial cleaning. It's a high-energy, fast-paced, knowledge-driven organization whose business is scrubbing hospital floors, making hotel beds, and sweeping grocery store aisles.

The philosophy of Liisa Joronen, SOL's owner, is "In a service business, if you're not happy with yourself, how can you make the customer happy?" Answering that question has made Joronen's company wildly successful. How? The company's unique culture has played an important role.

SOL's culture is characterized by five values. The first value is that hard work has to be fun. Joronen believes that because few people dream of becoming a cleaner, the keys to keeping her employees satisfied on the job are fun and individual freedom. SOL's culture is built around optimism and good cheer. Cleaners wear bright red and yellow jumpsuits that reinforce the company's enthusiastic and fun image. SOL's company logo—a yellow happy face—is plastered on everything from the letterhead to the most important financial statements. Employees also enjoy the freedom of minimal rules and regulations. There are no position titles, individual offices, or set working hours. The company has eliminated all status symbols and benefits that only a select few might get.

The second cultural value that characterizes SOL is that there are no low-skill jobs. The company invests significant amounts of time and money in training employees. There are just so many ways to polish a table or to shampoo a carpet, so SOL employees also study topics such as time management, people skills, and budgeting. Training is focused on turning cleaners into customer service specialists. Joronen says, "Our main goal is to change how cleaners work. To let them use their brains as well as their hands." By

upgrading employees' skills, SOL is upgrading its business. In fact, some of the hospitals that use SOL's cleaners have begun using them for night nurse duties. They do things such as help patients to the bathroom and notify the doctor on call about emergencies. At many of the large grocery stores it services, SOL cleaners stock the shelves as well as sweep the aisles.

Another unique value of SOL is that people who set their own targets shoot for the stars. SOL employees have significant amounts of responsibility. Company supervisors, each of whom heads up a team of up to 50 cleaners, work with the teams to create their own budgets, do their own hiring, and negotiate their own deals with customers. Joronen's philosophy is that people will set targets higher for themselves than what anyone would set for them. These self-managed teams can even build their own offices. SOL has 23 "satellite studios" around Finland. However, a satellite studio opens only when there is enough business to cover the costs of rent, equipment, and employee training. To stay in business, the studio must be profitable.

The fourth value that SOL stresses is that loose organizations need tight measures. Although Joronen believes in employee autonomy, she is a fanatic about performance measurement and accountability. The company measures performance frequently and most of these measures focus on customer satisfaction. Says Joronen, "The more we free our people from rules, the more we need good measurement."

Finally, SOL believes that great customer service demands cutting-edge technology. SOL may be in a "low-end" business, but that doesn't mean it has to be low tech. In fact, laptops and cellular phones are standard equipment for all supervisors at SOL. Why?

This investment in technology frees them to work where they want and how they want. The company also stores all of its critical budget documents and performance reports on its internal information system (its intranet) and uses it for scheduling training, relaying company news, and informing employees about upcoming company events.

Discussion Questions

1. What do you think of this company? Would the five values that characterize SOL's culture be as effective in other types of organizations? Why or why not?

2. Describe what examples of functional strategies you see in this case story. Label your examples and be specific in describing them.

3. How do you think an organization's culture affects its choices of functional strategies? Explain.

(*Source:* G. Imperato, "Dirty Business, Bright Ideas," *Fast Company* Web site (**www.fastcompany.com**), April 16, 1997.

CASE #3: Stringing Together Success

For over a century and a half, the Martin Guitar Company (**www.cfmartin.com**) of Nazareth, Pennsylvania, has been producing acoustic instruments considered to be among the finest in the world. Like a Steinway grand piano, a Buffet clarinet, or a Baccarat crystal vase, a Martin guitar—which can cost more than $10,000—is among the best that money can buy. Annual company revenues for 1999 were close to $58 million. This family business has managed to defy the odds and survive six generations of family members even through to the current CEO, Chris Martin, who continues to be committed to the guitar maker's craft. Few companies, much less a family business, have had the staying power of Martin Guitars.

What's the key to the company's success? It boils down to one word—quality. Even through changes in product design, distribution systems, and manufacturing methods, Martin Guitars has remained committed to making quality products. The company's steadfast adherence to high standards of musical excellence has led to a loyal customer base who demands, and expects, quality. Part of that quality approach encompasses a long-standing ecological policy. The company has embraced the judicious and responsible use of traditional natural materials and encouraged the introduction of sustainable-yield, alternative wood species for manufacturing its guitars. Through customer research, Martin introduced guitars that utilized structurally sound woods with natural cosmetic defects that were once considered unacceptable. In addition, Martin follows the directives of CITES (**www.cites.org**), the Convention on International Trade in Endangered Species of Wild Fauna and Flora. The company has also begun exploring the viability of using Forest Stewardship Council certifiable wood sources and supports the introduction of FSC guitar models as soon as it's commercially feasible. Although it has a long and colorful history, the company also is firmly committed to the future. It's an interesting combination of old and new.

Speaking of new, Christian Martin IV, the current CEO and the great-great-great grandson of the company's founder, is taking Martin Guitars in a new direction. He made a difficult decision to start selling guitars in the under-$800 market segment. This segment accounts for 65 percent of the acoustic guitar industry's sales. Martin's DXM model was introduced in 1998. Although it doesn't look, smell, or feel like the company's pricier models, customers claim it has a better sound than most other instruments in that price range. But, what kind of risk is it to take a company that's dependent on a revered luxury item and to start selling a low-end product? Will those long-time customers be alienated? Martin justifies his decision by saying that, "If Martin just worships its past without trying anything new, there won't be a Martin left to worship." Chris knows that he's going to have to fight to keep his loyal customers playing the expensive models. He's doing this by introducing a series of replicas of the company's flagship product, the Dreadnought guitar, produced before World War II. He's also collaborating on a series of special-edition guitars with Roger McGuinn of the Byrds and Dave Matthews. Chris has also started a custom shop for the guitarist who wants custom features such as his or her name inlaid in mother-of-pearl onto the fingerboard.

Although the company is spreading its wings in new directions, there's still the commitment to making the finest products. There's no doubt that Martin's functional strategies will continue to play a role in its success.

Discussion Questions

1. What functional strategies is Martin Guitars using? Be specific.

2. How has an emphasis on quality led to the company's success? What are the implications for functional strategies?

3. Check out the CITES Web site (**www.cites.org**). What information could a strategic decision maker find there? How might an organization's commitment to social responsibility affect its choice of functional strategies?

4. CEO Chris Martin stated, "If Martin just worships its past without trying anything new, there won't be a Martin left to worship." What do you think his quote means? What are the implications for decisions about functional strategies?

5. What do you think of CEO Chris Martin's new direction for the company? What are the advantages? The drawbacks?

(*Sources:* Company's Web site (**www.cfmartin.com**), January 16, 2000; and S. Fitch, "Stringing Them Along," *Forbes*, July 26, 1999, pp. 90–91.)

ENDNOTES

1. Information from company's Web site (**www.toyota.com**), April 3, 2000; S. Spear and H. K. Bowen, "Decoding the DNA of the Toyota Production System," *Harvard Business Review*, September–October 1999, pp. 96–106; R. L. Simison, "Toyota Finds Way to Make a Custom Car in 5 Days," *Wall Street Journal*, August 6, 1999, p. A4; and D. Bartholomew, "Lean vs. ERP," *Industry Week*, July 19, 1999, pp. 24–30.

2. Information for this section on production–operations–manufacturing is based on J. Heizer and B. Render, *Operations Management*, 5th ed. (Upper Saddle River, NJ: Prentice Hall, 1999).

3. J. W. Dean Jr. and S. A. Snell, "The Strategic Use of Integrated Manufacturing: An Empirical Examination," *Strategic Management Journal*, June 1996, pp. 459–80.

4. Information for this section on marketing is primarily based on P. Kotler, *Marketing Management*, 5th ed. (Upper Saddle River, NJ: Prentice Hall, 2000); and P. Kotler and G. Armstrong, *Principles of Marketing*, 8th ed. (Upper Saddle River, NJ: Prentice Hall, 1999).

5. A thorough description of these major segmentation variables can be found in Kotler, *Marketing Management*, pp. 263–73.

6. See D. A. Garvin, "Competing on the Eight Dimensions of Quality," *Harvard Business Review*, November–December 1987, pp. 101–9.

7. N. Paley, "Romancing Your Customers," *Sales and Marketing Management*, March 1996, pp. 30–32.

8. L. L. Berry and A. Parasuraman, *Marketing Services: Competing Through Quality* (New York: Free Press, 1991), pp. 136–42.

9. J. Lardner, "Your Every Command," *U.S. News and World Report*, July 5, 1999, pp. 44–46; "Mass Customization Becomes the New Marketing Mantra," *Wall Street Journal*, April 29, 1999, p. A1; D. Peppers, M. Rogers, and B. Dorf, "Is Your Company Ready for One-to-One Marketing?" *Harvard Business Review*, January–February 1999, pp. 151–60; and J. H. Gilmore and B. J. Pine II, "The Four Faces of Mass Customization," *Harvard Business Review*, January–February 1997, pp. 91–101.

10. Kotler, *Marketing Management*, pp. 652–56.

11. S. Hamm and R. D. Hof, "An Eagle Eye for Customers," *Business Week*, February 21, 2000, pp. 66–76.

12. J. Pfeffer, *The Human Equation: Building Profits by Putting People First* (Boston: Harvard Business School Press, 1998); A. A. Lado and M. C. Wilson, "Human Resource Systems and Sustained Competitive Advantage: A Competency-Based Perspective," *Academy of Management Review*, October 1994, pp. 699–727; J. Pfeffer, *Competitive Advantage Through People* (Boston: Harvard Business School Press, 1994); and P. M. Wright and G. C. McMahan, "Theoretical Perspectives for Strategic Human Resource Management," *Journal of Management*, Vol. 17 (1991), pp. 295–320.

13. "Human Capital: A Key to Higher Market Value," *Business Finance*, December 1999, p. 15; M. A. Huselid, "The Impact of Human Resource Management Practices on Turnover, Productivity, and Corporate Financial Performance," *Academy of Management Journal*, June 1995, pp. 635–72.

14. U.S. Department of Labor, *High Performance Work Practices and Firm Performance* (Washington, DC: U.S. Government Printing Office, 1993); and G. R. Jones and P. M. Wright, "An Economic Approach to Conceptualizing the Utility of Human Resource Management Practices," in *Research in Personnel and Human Resources Management*, Vol. 10, ed. K. Rowland and G. Ferris (Greenwich, CT: JAI Press, 1992), pp. 271–99.

15. Information for this section was based primarily on L. R. Gomez-Mejia, D. B. Balkin, and R. L. Cardy, *Managing Human Resources* (Upper Saddle River, NJ: Prentice Hall, 1995).

16. Ibid., p. 464.

17. B. P. Sunoo, "How Fun Flies at Southwest Airlines," *Personnel Journal*, June 1995, p. 62.

18. T. L. Shakespeare, "High-tech Training, Wal-Mart Style," *Black Enterprise*, July 1996, p. 54.

19. B. Becker and B. Gerhart, "The Impact of Human Resource Management on Organizational Performance: Progress and Prospects," *Academy of Management Journal*, August 1996, pp. 670–87; J. T. Delaney and M. A. Huselid, "The Impact of Human Resource Management Practices on Perceptions of Organizational Performance," *Academy of Management Journal*, August 1996, pp. 949–69; J. E. Delery and D. H. Doty, "Modes of Theorizing in Strategic Human Resource Management: Tests of Universalistic, Contingency, and Configurational Performance Predictions," *Academy of Management Journal*, August 1996, pp. 802–35; M. A. Youndt, S. A. Snell, J. W. Dean Jr., and D. P. LePak, "Human Resource Management, Manufacturing Strategy, and Firm Performance," *Academy of Management Journal*, August 1996, pp. 836–66; M. J. Koch and R. G. McGrath, "Improving Labor Productivity: Human Resource Management Policies Do Matter," *Strategic Management Journal*, May 1996, pp. 335–54; Huselid, "The Impact of Human Resource Management Practices"; and J. B. Arthur, "Effects of Human Resource Systems on Manufacturing Performance and Turnover," *Academy of Management Journal*, June 1994, pp. 670–87.

20. R. Rose, "Kentucky Plant Workers Are Cranking Out Good Ideas," *Wall Street Journal*, August 13, 1996, p. B1.

21. The information in this section is based on K. C. Laudon and J. P. Laudon, *Essentials of Management Information Systems* (Upper Saddle River, NJ: Prentice Hall, 1995).

22. "Driving Paint to the Marketplace," *Industry Week*, special section on Automatic Data Collection, September 1995, pp. ADCM3–ADCM6.

23. K. M. Kroll, "Bigger Role for Call Centers," *Industry Week*, February 21, 2000, pp. 58–62.

24. Information for this section is based on A. J. Keown, D. F. Scott Jr., J. D. Martin, and J. W. Petty, *Basic Financial Management*, 7th ed. (Upper Saddle River, NJ: Prentice Hall, 1996).

25. S. L. Mintz, "Penny Pinchers: Annual SG&A Survey," *CFO*, December 1999, pp. 44–56.

26. K. M. Kroll, "Cash Wears the Crown," *Industry Week*, May 6, 1996, pp. 16–18.

27. G. Baum, C. Ittner, D. Larcker, J. Low, T. Siesfeld, and M. S. Malone, "Introducing the New Value Creation Index," *Forbes ASAP*, April 3, 2000, pp. 140–43.

28. D. Nath and D. Sudharshan, "Measuring Strategy Coherence Through Patterns of Strategic Choice," *Strategic Management Journal*, January 1994, pp. 43–61.

6

COMPETITIVE STRATEGIES

LEARNING OBJECTIVES

After studying this chapter, you should be able to:

1. Explain the importance of competitive advantage.
2. Define competition.
3. Describe how an organization's competitors can be determined.
4. Explain what a strategic group is.
5. Discuss how resources, capabilities, and core competencies lead to competitive advantage.
6. Explain the relationship between competitive advantage and competitive strategies.
7. Describe Miles and Snow's adaptive strategies.
8. Describe Abell's business definition framework.
9. Discuss Porter's generic competitive strategies.
10. Explain what it means to be "stuck in the middle."
11. Describe an integrated low-cost differentiation strategy.
12. Explain Mintzberg's generic competitive strategies.
13. Describe how an organization's competitive strategies are implemented, evaluated, and changed.
14. Explain what role functional strategies play in an organization's competitive strategies.
15. Discuss the various competitive postures and actions an organization can take.

STRATEGIC MANAGEMENT IN ACTION CASE #1

Pretty in Brown

The package delivery industry has become an all-out war between the two main competitors, UPS and FedEx. Right now, the battle appears to be going in UPS's favor. Smaller, flashier FedEx has been described as a "collection of marketers with trucks and planes" whereas UPS has been described as "industrial engineers with a collection of trucks and planes."[1] In 1999, UPS earned about $2.3 billion on revenues of $27.2 billion. FedEx, on the other hand, earned $631 million on $17.5 billion in revenues. Founded in 1907, UPS is a mainstay of the U.S. economy, delivering more than 6 percent of the nation's gross domestic product. It practically owns the business of economically moving packages by ground and delivering them to any address in the United States and is striving to do the same around the world.

UPS once considered itself a trucking company with technology. Now it considers itself more a technology company with trucks. UPS's daily delivery volume (in early 2000) was a whopping 13 million packages and documents. Its 1999 total delivery volume was over 3.25 billion packages and documents. How did the once unglamorous brown giant (also known as Big Brown and The Brown Blizzard) transform itself into such a global powerhouse?

The transformation was jump-started with a traumatic 15-day UPS drivers' strike in 1997, which allowed competitors such as FedEx and the U.S. Postal Service to capture a combined $350 million in revenue. Although UPS was able to repair its bruised relationships with its popular drivers and angry customers, the company's strategic decision makers also came to another conclusion: a realization that its maturing "brown operations," as marvelous as they were, were not enough to

compete in an industry that was transitioning into a global, knowledge-based logistics business.

Over the years, UPS had developed a successful business model. Uniformity and efficiency were the strategic factors behind the 340 precise methods of how to deliver a package correctly. For instance, its legendary operations training encompassed everything from training drivers to hold their keys on a pinky finger so they don't waste time fumbling in their pockets for the keys to asking employees to clean off their desks at the end of the day so they can have an efficient start the next morning. These strategic factors weren't going to change. Instead, the company began looking at how to build on its key resources, capabilities, and competencies. The new tool—technology. The company has a vast electronic tracking system, but then so does FedEx. FedEx is well wired to the Internet. What UPS did was look for ways to exploit its technology. Technology at UPS spans an incredible range, from specially designed package delivery vehicles to global computer and communications systems. For example, UPS Inventory Express is a contract logistics management service for customers in which UPS stores the customer's merchandise, then ships it as needed . . . just in time. Then, there's its Worldwide Logistics, a comprehensive consulting service

in which UPS assembles services based on the customer's individual needs, which might include freight payment, customs clearance, warehousing, carrier selection, rate negotiation, tracking, fleet management, order processing, electronic data interchange (EDI), and inventory control. UPS's commitment to technology garnered it a "Clicks and Mortar" award at the second Annual eBusiness Awards program at the MIT Sloan School of Management in April 2000. This award recognizes UPS's accomplishments in e-business. As the UPS executive who accepted the award said, "It speaks volumes to our success in applying innovative technology to help our customers transform their businesses for the new digital economy."

As UPS declares on its Web site (**www.ups.com**), it's not just in the delivery business, it's in the customer satisfaction business. Meeting and exceeding customer needs will continue to be the company's driving force. Its highest priorities over the next five years will be to deploy technology that will allow it to continue introducing new services, to provide customers with comprehensive information about their shipments, and to provide training so all employees will clearly understand UPS services, the technologies that make them possible, and be able to communicate that information to the customer.

Competition. It's a given for all organizations, regardless of size, type, or geographic location. Even not-for-profit organizations compete for resources and customers. A small, local community theater faces competition from other entertainment options—both local and global—just as America Online (AOL) faces competition from Microsoft and other Internet service providers. How can organizations cope with competition and still achieve strategic goals? They need to formulate and implement appropriate competitive strategies. For instance, that's exactly what UPS did when it decided to focus on exploiting technology. In this case, it was a savvy and brilliant competitive move that led to increased sales and profits and an enviable competitive position in the marketplace. In this chapter, we're going to look at the various competitive strategies—what they are and how they're implemented, evaluated, and modified. (Figure 6-1 illustrates how an organization's competitive strategies fit into the overall framework of strategic management in action.) First, we're going to review competitive advantage and then discuss the competitive environment.

WHAT IS COMPETITIVE ADVANTAGE AND HOW DO WE GET IT?

As we've said in earlier chapters, competitive advantage is a key concept of strategic management—getting it and keeping it is what managing strategically is all about. Remember that we defined **competitive advantage** as what sets an organization apart—its competitive edge. In other words, the organization does something that others can't or does it better than others do. Or, competitive advantage

Figure 6-1

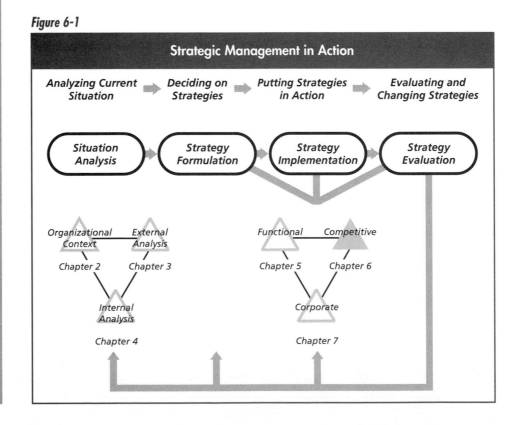

might arise from having something that other competitors don't. Competitive advantage is what an organization's competitive strategies are designed to exploit. Other organizations are also attempting to develop competitive advantage and, in so doing, to attract customers. An organization's competitive advantage can be eroded easily (and often quickly) by competitors' actions. Because competitive advantage implies that there are other competitors, we first need to look at the competitive environment to get a feel for the arena in which competitive advantage is pursued.

Understanding the Competitive Environment

Competition is everywhere. Very few industries or organizations haven't experienced some form and degree of competitiveness. In fact, some strategic management researchers have gone so far as to describe the current business competitive environment as one of **hypercompetition**, which very simply is a situation with very intense and continually increasing levels of competition.[2] Is hypercompetition the only way to describe the competitive environment? Fortunately, no, although it's obvious that the current competitive environment *is* changing and will continue to change. To understand the competitive environment, we first have to understand *what* competition is and then look at *who* our competitors are.

What Is Competition? Competition is when organizations battle or vie for some desired object or outcome—typically customers, market share, survey ranking, or needed resources. Although individuals also often compete for desired objects or outcomes, our primary interest is competition as it relates to organizations. The level of intensity of competition (i.e., how seriously organizations battle for customers or resources) is going to vary depending on several factors, which we describe in Chapter 3 in our discussion of the level of current rivalry in Porter's five forces model. What types of competition might an organization face? This can be answered by looking at who our competitors are.

Who Are Our Competitors? One approach to defining an organization's competitors says that competitors can be described according to an industry perspective or a marketing perspective.[3] Figure 6-2 shows the highlights of each of these.

The industry perspective identifies competitors as organizations that are making the same product or providing the same service; for example, there's the oil industry, the supermarket industry, the automobile industry, the credit card industry, or the dental health care industry. The competitors in each of these industries are producing the same or very similar types of products or services. (To make this concept as clear as possible, take a minute and try to name some of the competitors in these industries.) In addition, these and all other industries can be described according to the number of sellers and whether the products or services are similar or different. The number of sellers and the level of product–service differentiation will affect how intensely competitive the industry is. As Figure 6-2 illustrates, the most intense level of competition will be under situations of pure competition in which there are many sellers and the degree of differentiation among the sellers doesn't exist.

According to the marketing perspective, competitors are organizations that satisfy the same customer need. So, for example, if the customer need is entertainment, competitors might range all the way from video game manufacturers to theme parks to movie theaters to the local community symphony orchestra. If the

Figure 6-2

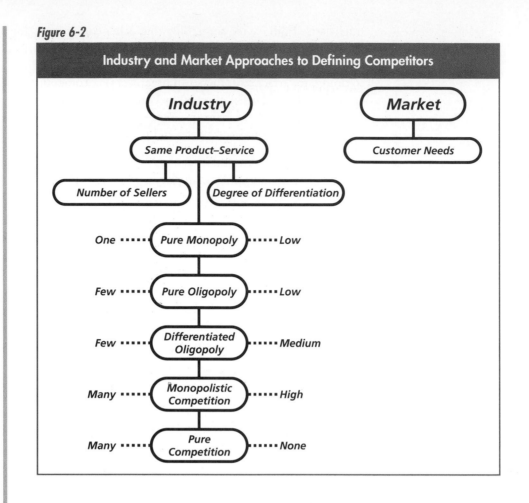

Industry and Market Approaches to Defining Competitors

customer need happens to be package and document delivery, then UPS's competitors would include the likes of FedEx, Airborne Express, and other delivery companies. However, if UPS views its customers' need as logistics support, then its competitors could range from FedEx to software companies to other logistics experts. From the marketing perspective, the intensity of competition depends on how well the customer's need is understood or defined and how well different organizations are able to meet that need.

Another approach to defining *who* competitors are is to use the strategic groups perspective. The concept of strategic groups was developed following an early 1970s study that pinpointed different groups of competitors following similar strategies in the U.S. home appliance industry.[4] We talked about strategic groups earlier in Chapter 3 when we were discussing Porter's five forces model and the level of current rivalry. To refresh your memory, a **strategic group** is a set of firms competing within an industry that have similar strategies and resources.[5] Within a single industry, you might find few or several strategic groups, depending on what strategic factors are important to different groups of customers. For example, two strategic factors found to be valued by customers are price (low to high) and quality (low to high). Competitors would then be grouped according to their price–quality strategies with those following the same or similar approaches in the same strategic group. Keep in mind that the important strategic factors, or strategic dimensions, used to determine an organization's competitors are different

Competitive Strategies **213**

The Grey Zone

The dry cleaning industry is debating the high cost of green management—that is, a recognition of the connection between an organization's decisions and activities and its impact on the natural environment. A vast majority of the over 33,000 dry cleaners in the United States still use toxic chemicals in the dry cleaning process that are linked to cancer, nervous system disorders, and other health hazards. In the early 1990s, green cleaners that used water and biodegradable detergents sprung onto the scene. However, few of the existing businesses were willing to switch to this new process because this form of "wet" cleaning takes longer, increases labor costs, and can easily lead to clothes shrinkage or other quality problems. What if you were a strategic decision maker in this industry? Do you think a competitor who chose to go green could survive? How might you deal with this ethical and social responsibility dilemma of wanting to "do the right thing" yet wanting and needing to stay in business?

Source: B. J. Feder, "Cleaning Up the Dry Cleaners," *New York Times*, February 15, 2000, p. C1.

for every industry and can be different even for different industry segments. Table 6-1 lists some other strategic factors that might be used to distinguish strategic groups. Also, note that an industry strategic grouping is always plotted on a chart with an *X* and *Y* axis and a range of values for the *X-Y* variables. Figure 6-3 is an example of what an industry strategic grouping might look like. It illustrates the relevant strategic groups in the cosmetics industry. Notice in this example that the important strategic factors for grouping the competitors aren't price and quality, but are defined as price and distribution strategies.

According to this approach, the concept of strategic groups is important to understanding who competitors are because your most relevant competitors are those in your strategic group. Although competition might, and often does, come from organizations in other strategic groups, your main competitive concern is those organizations in your own strategic group. The level of intensity of competition from this perspective depends on how effectively each competitor has been able to develop a sustainable competitive advantage and on the competitive strategies and competitive actions that each of the competitors in the strategic group uses.

Although the strategic groups approach is frequently used to define an industry's competitors, you should also be aware that there has been some controversy by strategy researchers over whether specific, identifiable strategic groups even exist.[6] These questions generally concern what factors are used to define a strategic group and how these factors are chosen and used to separate specific and identifiable groups. Despite these concerns over strategic group definition, the strategic groups concept remains a useful approach to determining who an organization's competitors are.

Regardless of how we define our competitors, the fact remains that there *are* other organizations working hard to secure customers, resources, and other desired outcomes. Each of those organizations has resources and capabilities it's attempting to exploit. That's what we're going to look at next—the role resources and capabilities play in competitive advantage.

The Role of Resources, Distinctive Capabilities, and Core Competencies in Gaining Competitive Advantage

What makes some organizations more successful—however you choose to measure success—than others? Why do some professional basketball teams consistently win championships or draw large crowds? Why do some organizations have

TABLE 6-1	**Possible Strategic Dimensions for Identifying Strategic Groups**

- Price
- Quality
- Level of vertical integration
- Geographic scope
- Product line breadth–depth
- Level of diversification
- R&D expenditures
- Market share
- Profits
- Product characteristics
- Any other relevant strategic factor

Figure 6-3

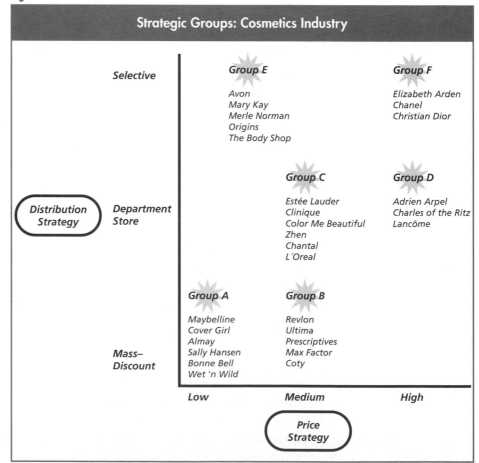

Strategic Groups: Cosmetics Industry

Selective

Group E
Avon
Mary Kay
Merle Norman
Origins
The Body Shop

Group F
Elizabeth Arden
Chanel
Christian Dior

Group C
Estée Lauder
Clinique
Color Me Beautiful
Zhen
Chantal
L'Oreal

Group D
Adrien Arpel
Charles of the Ritz
Lancôme

Distribution Strategy

Department Store

Group A
Maybelline
Cover Girl
Almay
Sally Hansen
Bonne Bell
Wet 'n Wild

Group B
Revlon
Ultima
Prescriptives
Max Factor
Coty

Mass– Discount

Low   Medium   High

Price Strategy

consistent and continuous growth in revenues and profits? Why do some colleges, universities, or departmental majors experience continually increasing enrollments? Why do some organizations appear consistently on lists ranking "the best" or "the most admired" or "the most profitable"? Every organization has resources and work processes–systems to do whatever it's in business to do. However, not every organization is able to exploit effectively the resources or capabilities it has or to obtain the resources or capabilities it needs but doesn't have. It's a classic case of "the haves" and "the have-nots" and "the can dos" and "the can't dos." Some organizations are able to "put it all together" and develop those distinctive organizational capabilities that can provide them with a sustainable competitive advantage. Other organizations never quite get to that point. Organizations will develop strategies to exploit their current resources and capabilities or to vie for needed-but-not-owned resources and capabilities in order to pursue and attain desired outcomes such as customers, market share, resources, or even perhaps, in the case of a college football team, a national championship. They do this while other organizations (few to many) are doing exactly the same thing. Competitive advantage, by its very nature, implies that we're trying to gain the edge on others. As organizations strive for a sustainable competitive advantage, the stage for competition—intense, moderate, or mild—is set.

From Competitive Advantage to Competitive Strategy

In attempting to create a sustainable competitive advantage, organizations are looking for ways to set themselves apart. How an organization chooses to do this is what **competitive strategy** is all about. The choice of competitive strategy is a choice of how an organization or business unit is going to compete in its particular industry or market. The choice of competitive strategy is based on the competitive advantage(s) that the organization has been able to develop. For example, UPS's competitive strategy was based on what it saw as its competitive advantage—the ability to use technology to solve a variety of logistics problems. As an organization refines and sharpens its sustainable competitive advantage (whether found in resources, distinctive capabilities, or core competencies), the basis for the competitive strategy it's going to use is established. After all, that's what the design of competitive strategy is all about—exploiting the organization's competitive advantage by finding ways to use its resources, distinctive capabilities, and core

Strategic Management—The Global Perspective

Butterfly farming is big business in Costa Rica; it's the largest butterfly supplier in the world, exporting more than 300,000 pupae a year. Who buys butterflies? The main customers include zoos, natural history museums, and other tourist attractions. Even some innovative hotels and restaurants have opened butterfly exhibits. Releasing butterflies at weddings has replaced the traditional throwing of rice or bird seed. At one business, Butterfly Paradise, increasing competition has forced owner Mario Polsa to branch out into handicrafts such as mounted, encased butterflies that can be displayed on desks or walls. As in any intensely competitive situation, successful organizations look for some competitive edge.

Source: J. Dulude, "Butterflies Aren't Free," *Latin Trade*, March 2000, pp. 32–34.

Consider This ◀◀|

✓ Is competition an issue for all organizations? Discuss.

✓ What is competitive advantage?

✓ Define competition. Define hyper-competition. What influences the level of competition among organizations?

✓ Compare and contrast the industry and marketing perspectives of defining competitors.

✓ What is a strategic group? Why is the concept of strategic groups important to identifying an organization's competitors?

✓ Describe factors that can be used for grouping competitors.

✓ What role do resources, distinctive capabilities, and core competencies play in gaining competitive advantage?

✓ Define competitive strategy. What's the connection between competitive advantage and competitive strategy?

competencies to set itself apart from competitors. What we need to look at next, then, are the various types of competitive strategies.

WHAT ARE THE COMPETITIVE STRATEGIES?

Although it may seem there are an endless number of possible types of competitive strategies, there are actually a limited number of ways to describe how an organization competes. In this section, we want to look at some of these specific competitive strategy alternatives. We'll look first at some traditional approaches to defining competitive strategies and then discuss some newer perspectives.

Traditional Approaches to Defining Competitive Strategy

Attempts to describe, explain, and categorize specific competitive strategies that organizations use has been a favorite challenge of strategy researchers for a number of years. Three of the most popular approaches that have been the focus of much of this research include Miles and Snow's adaptive strategies (1978), Abell's business definition framework (1980), and Porter's generic competitive strategies (1980).[7] We're going to look at what each approach says about the strategies organizations use to compete.

Miles and Snow's Adaptive Strategies. Miles and Snow's approach is based on the strategies organizations successfully use to adapt to their uncertain competitive environments. According to their approach, four strategic postures are possible: prospector, defender, analyzer, and reactor. What competitive actions are involved with each of these?

The **prospector strategy** is one in which an organization continually innovates by finding and exploiting new product and market opportunities. A prospector's competitive strength is its ability to survey a wide range of rapidly changing environmental conditions, trends, and situations and to create new products and services to fit this dynamic environment. The prospector's competitive strategy is continually to innovate, develop, and test new products and services. It's constantly prospecting—on the lookout—for new directions to pursue. This continual search for innovation creates uncertainties for the prospector's competitors; they never know what's going to happen next or what to expect from the prospector. If the prospector can develop new products or services that the market desires and is willing to pay for, it will have a sustainable competitive advantage. In the broadcast television industry, the Nickelodeon channel and the Fox Broadcasting Network could be considered good examples of organizations using the prospector strategy. Both are noted for their innovative television network programming and willingness to pursue new directions. They've been able to tap into changing societal attitudes and interests and develop television pro-

Strategic Management—The Global Perspective

It's hot! Cholula hot sauce, originally made in Chapala, Guadalajara, in western Mexico, is making its way north of the border, threatening the dominance of Tabasco sauce. When executives at Jose Cuervo, the Mexico City–based tequila company, heard about the hot sauce more than 10 years ago, they bought the license and began marketing it in Mexico. Then, the company decided to take the product north. Throughout the 1990s, specialty food shops and restaurants in the United States tried Cholula and liked customers' responses. Based on its initial successes, Cuervo chose to make an all-out assault on the United States. It hired a spokesman, a well-known Houston chef, and sent him on a 12-city tour to create Cholula-enhanced dishes. The company began running advertisements in trade magazines and putting coupons in newspaper inserts. Sales of Cholula have taken off. It's now the eighth-ranked hot sauce in the United States in terms of retail sales. Although it's got a ways to go to catch up to Tabasco, which controls 23.2 percent of the market, Cholula's sales growth is stronger (27.6 percent versus Tabasco's 8 percent). If you were a strategic decision maker at Cuervo, what would you do at this point? What if you were a strategic decision maker at Tabasco?

Source: C. Poole, "Watch Out, Tabasco," *Latin Trade*, February 2000, pp. 29–30.

grams that appeal to these changes. Their competitive advantage stems from their ability to assess the environmental trends and continually create new and innovative programs.

The **defender strategy** is characterized by the search for market stability and producing only a limited product line directed at a narrow segment of the total potential market. Defenders have well-established businesses that they're seeking to protect (i.e., to "defend"). They'll do whatever it takes to aggressively prevent competitors from coming into their turf. A defender will be successful with this strategy as long as its primary technology and narrow product line remain competitive. Over time, defenders are able to carve out and maintain niches within their industries that competitors find difficult to penetrate. For instance, Union Carbide Company's competitive strategy has been a deliberately defensive one— to remain a chemical company and to be the market leader in each of its market segments. Although it operates in many and varied segments of the chemical industry such as heavy industrial chemicals, specialty chemicals, agricultural chemicals, and plastics, its strategy has been to remain only in those areas where it has expertise, a good chance of attaining a sustainable competitive advantage, and a strong prospect for keeping competitors out. Because Union Carbide vigorously protects its businesses and market share, it is a good example of the defender strategy.

The **analyzer strategy** is one of analysis and imitation. Organizations using this strategy thoroughly analyze new business ideas before jumping in. Analyzers also watch for and copy the successful ideas of prospectors. They compete by following the direction that prospectors pioneer. Even before blindly jumping in, though, analyzers will systematically assess and evaluate whether this move is appropriate for them. For example, in the discount airline industry, many airlines have attempted to imitate Southwest Airlines' enormously successful strategy of short-haul, low-fare flights. Airlines such as United, Delta, and U.S. Air started their low-fare, low-cost operations in an attempt to compete with Southwest and to capture some of the market. These imitative business actions are ideal examples of the analyzer strategy.

Finally, the **reactor strategy** is characterized by the lack of a coherent strategic plan or apparent means of competing. Reactors simply react to environmental changes and make adjustments only when finally forced to do so by environmental pressures. Often, reactors are unable to respond quickly to perceived environmental changes because either they lack the needed resources or capabilities or they're not able to exploit their current resources and capabilities. Obviously, this is *not* a preferred or recommended competitive strategy for developing a sustainable competitive advantage. In fact, the reactor strategy can be thought of as a "default" strategy, almost a nonstrategy position. Some examples of organizations that have used the reactor strategy—willingly or unwillingly—include Sears, Sizzler International Inc. (the steakhouse chain), and Digital Equipment Corporation. In each of these instances, the organization lagged significantly behind its competitors in products or services offered and had no consistent strategic direction. Without significant strategic changes, a reactor will always be in a weak competitive position.

Table 6-2 summarizes the characteristics of each of Miles and Snow's competitive strategies. Strategy research using the Miles and Snow typology continues to verify that these four competitive strategy types are theoretically sound and can be used to describe what competitive strategies organizations are using.[8]

Abell's Business Definition Framework. Another approach suggested for describing the competitive strategies used by organizations is the business definition framework developed by Derek Abell. According to Abell, a business can be defined using three dimensions: (1) customer groups—*who* we're going to serve; (2) customer needs—*what* customer need we're attempting to meet; and (3) technology or distinctive competencies—*how* we're going to meet that need. As you can see, this approach strongly stresses understanding *customers*, not an *industry and its products–services*, when developing an appropriate and effective competitive strategy.

Strategic Management in Action

It's still the largest check printer in the United States (with over 50 percent of the check printing market), but strategic blunders at Deluxe Corporation have weakened the company. Deluxe's strategic decision makers failed to move beyond just printing checks. Growth in the check printing market slowed and Deluxe had nothing to fall back on. Is this an example of the reactor strategy? Explain. How could an industry leader make such a strategic mistake? What could have been done to prevent such a situation?

Source: S. D. Horsburgh, "Deluxe Corporation," *Better Investing,* April 1998, p. 31.

TABLE 6-2   Characteristics of Miles and Snow's Adaptive (Competitive) Strategies

Strategy	Characteristics
Prospector	• Organization seeks innovation • Demonstrated ability to survey dynamic environment and develop new products–services to fit the changing environment • Frequently and continually innovating, developing, and testing new products–services • Competitors are uncertain about prospector's future strategic decisions and actions
Defender	• Searches for market stability • Produces only a limited product line for a narrow segment of total potential market • Seeks to protect (defend) its well-established business • Does whatever is necessary to aggressively prevent competitors from entering their turf • Can carve out and maintain niches within its industry that competitors find difficult to penetrate
Analyzer	• Strategy of analysis and imitation • Thoroughly analyzes new business ideas (products, services, markets) before deciding to jump in • Watches for and copies the promising and successful ideas of prospectors
Reactor	• Lacks coherent strategic plan • Simply reacts to environmental changes • Makes strategic adjustments only when finally forced to do so • Unable to respond quickly to environmental changes because resources–capabilities are lacking or are not developed or exploited properly

Source: Based on R. E. Miles and C. C. Snow, *Organizational Strategy, Structure, and Process* (New York: McGraw-Hill, 1978).

Based on these three dimensions, Abell's competitive strategy classification scheme proposed that a business could be defined by its competitive scope (i.e., broad or narrow markets) and by the extent of competitive differentiation of its product or service offerings (i.e., how differentiated products and services are). The various combinations of these dimensions formed the basis for Abell's three possible competitive strategies: differentiated, undifferentiated, and focus. Figure 6-4 illustrates these three strategies.

Abell's differentiated strategy describes businesses that compete in broad markets and use different competitive weapons to serve the various market segments in which they compete. The undifferentiated strategy also describes businesses with broad competitive scopes, but these businesses use only one common competitive weapon for serving each segment; that is, there's no differentiation in products or services. The focus strategy is used by businesses that compete in a narrow market and also use only one common competitive weapon.

Abell's strict marketing emphasis limits his business definition framework as a widely used and general approach to describing an organization's competitive strategies. However, it does provide clues to two important aspects of competitive strategy—competitive scope and level of product differentiation.

Figure 6-4

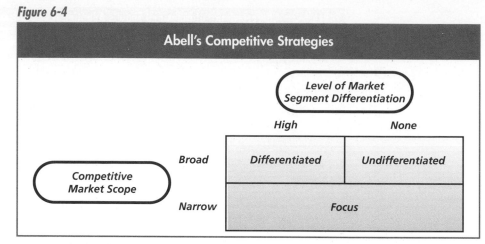

Abell's Competitive Strategies

Level of Market Segment Differentiation

High | None

Competitive Market Scope

Broad | Differentiated | Undifferentiated

Narrow | Focus

Source: Based on J. J. Chrisman, C. W. Hofer, and W. R. Boulton, "Toward a System for Classifying Business Strategies," *Academy of Management Review,* 13, no. 3 (1988), pp. 413–28.

Consider This ◀◀❘

✓ What does Miles and Snow's adaptive strategies approach propose as the basis for developing appropriate competitive strategies? In other words, to what is the organization adapting?

✓ Describe each of Miles and Snow's four adaptive strategies.

✓ In what types of environments do you think each of the adaptive strategies might be most appropriate? Explain.

✓ What are the three dimensions Abell proposed for defining a business?

✓ How does Abell's approach differ from Miles and Snow's approach?

✓ Describe Abell's three competitive strategies.

Porter's Generic Competitive Strategies. Yes, we're once again discussing the same Porter who developed the five forces model (external analysis) and the value chain (internal analysis). We discussed these concepts in earlier chapters as possible approaches for assessing an organization's strengths, weaknesses, opportunities, threats, and competitive advantage(s). These analytical tools are part of the whole strategic package Porter developed for explaining how organizations can create and exploit a sustainable competitive advantage. Why are they important to our discussion of competitive strategies? According to Porter, strategic decision makers would need this information before choosing an appropriate competitive strategy.

What is an "appropriate" competitive strategy? In Porter's approach, it's one based on an organization's competitive advantage.[9] According to Porter, competitive advantage can come from only one of two sources: either from having the lowest costs in the industry or from possessing significant and desirable differences from competitors. Another factor that's important to competitive advantage in Porter's approach is the scope of the product–market in which the organization wishes to compete—that is, broad (all or most market segments) or narrow (only one segment or few segments). The mix of these factors provides the basis for Porter's generic competitive strategies. These include cost leadership, differentiation, and focus (cost and differentiation). Figure 6-5 shows the configurations of these four possible strategies. At this point, you may be wondering why Porter called these strategies *generic*. That term simply refers to the fact that they can be pursued by any type or size organization in any type or size industry. We're going to provide more detail on Porter's strategies

Figure 6-5

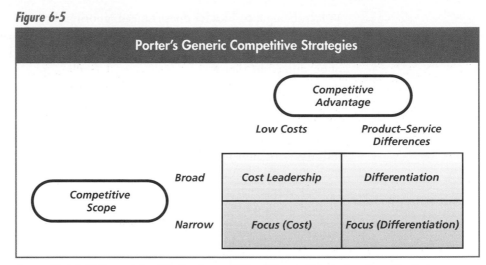

Source: Adapted with the permission of The Free Press, a Division of Simon and Schuster from *Competitive Strategy: Techniques for Analyzing Industries and Competitors* by M. E. Porter. Copyright ©1980 by The Free Press.

because they're well known and have been used numerous times in research on organizations' competitive strategies.

The **cost leadership strategy** is one in which an organization strives to have the lowest costs in its industry and produces products or services for a broad customer base. This strategy is also sometimes called the low-cost strategy. The main goal of the cost leader is to have *the* lowest costs in the industry. Notice that the emphasis here is on *costs*, not on *prices*. In other words, the cost leader is striving to have the lowest total unit costs in the industry. Because the cost leader does have the lowest costs in the industry, it can potentially charge the lowest prices and still earn profits. Although every organization should attempt to keep costs low—that's just smart strategic management—the cost leader is choosing to *compete* on the basis of having the lowest costs. Having the lowest costs means that the cost leader can charge a lower price than its competitors can and still earn significant profits. It also means that when competitive rivalry heats up and competitors begin to compete ferociously on price (i.e., a price war breaks out), the cost leader is in a better position to withstand it and continue earning profits.

What does it take to successfully pursue the cost leadership strategy? Everything the cost leader does—every strategic decision made, every strategic action taken—is aimed at keeping costs as low as possible. Efficiency in all areas of operations is the main objective, and all functional strategies and distinctive capabilities are directed at that. The cost leader isn't going to have deep and wide product lines. Providing these product or service variations is expensive, and the cost leader has chosen to compete on the basis of low costs, not on being different than competitors. The cost leader will market products aimed at the "average" customer. Little or no product frills or differences will be available. The cost leader organization isn't going to have fancy artwork on the walls at corporate headquarters. There won't be any corporate jets or plush office furniture and carpeting. It's unlikely that you'd see a cost leader with an elaborate high-tech, multimedia interactive Web site *unless* it was determined that this would be an extremely cost-effective and efficient way to reach masses of potential customers.

In fact, being a cost leader doesn't mean ignoring the latest advances in technology. Quite the opposite. If new and improved technology can pave the way to further lowering costs, the cost leader will jump on it. For instance, Payless ShoeSource, the shoe retailer with over $2.7 billion in annual sales, has a thoroughly modern automated warehouse in Topeka, Kansas, where corporate headquarters are located. Out of this warehouse, which spans 17 acres under one roof, Payless's approximately 4,400 stores can be restocked with styles and sizes on as little as a day's notice.[10] Because Payless competes in an intensely competitive industry (discount-priced shoes), the cost savings associated with such speed to market is critical. Another example of an organization's pursuing a cost leadership strategy is International Paper, a diversified $24.5 billion corporation.[11] You'd think the world's largest forest-products company that's also one of the largest private landowners in the United States (it owns more than 7 million acres of timberland) would be housed in its own headquarters building. Yet, the company shares a nondescript building in Purchase, New York, with several other companies. If you wanted to visit the executive office suite, you'd have to consult the lobby directory in order to find it. By focusing on efficient, cost-effective performance rather than image, International Paper has been able to survive and succeed in a cutthroat, competitive industry. Other characteristics of cost leaders include strict attention to production controls; rigorous use of budgets; little product differentiation—just enough to satisfy what the mass market might demand; limited market segmentation—products or services aimed at the mass market; emphasis on productivity improvements; and distinctive capabilities (resources and competencies) are found in manufacturing and materials management.

What are the drawbacks of the cost leadership strategy? The main danger is that competitors might find ways of lowering costs even further, taking away the

Strategic Management in Action

Sears considers it to be one of its most fearsome competitors. Is it Wal-Mart? Is it JCPenney? No, it's Kohl's (**www.kohls.com**). The Milwaukee-based chain is moving ahead in its aggressive push out of the Midwest into other U.S. regions. Why has Kohl's been so successful? It maintains a low-cost structure with lean staffs, sophisticated information systems, and centralized buying and distribution. But that's not all. The company combines the cost structure of a discounter with the brand variety of a department store. Kohl's is uniquely positioned to satisfy the vast masses that make up Middle America with its not-too-upscale and not-too-low-scale approach. Check out the company's Web site. Make a bulleted list of the unique strategies that Kohl's is using. How would you classify its competitive strategy? Explain.

Sources: C. Y. Coleman, "Kohl's Officers Plan to Sell Stock in Clothing Seller," *Wall Street Journal,* March 4, 1999, p. B14; and A. Faircloth, "The Best Retailer You've Never Heard Of," *Fortune,* March 16, 1998, pp. 110–11.

cost leader's cost advantage. The cost leader's competitive strategy is successful as long as it can maintain its cost advantage. Another drawback of this strategy is that competitors might easily be able to imitate what the cost leader is doing and erode the cost advantage. Finally, a drawback of the cost leadership strategy is that the cost leader, in its all-out pursuit of lowering costs, might lose sight of changing customer tastes, desires, wants, and needs. In other words, it doesn't matter how cost efficiently you can produce or market a product or service if there's no customer demand and no one willing to purchase it even at rock-bottom prices.

The **differentiation strategy** is a strategy in which the organization competes on the basis of providing unique (different) products or services with features that customers value, perceive as different, and are willing to pay a premium price for. The main goal of the differentiator is to provide products or services that are truly unique and different in the eyes of the customers. The differentiator is competing on the basis of being different and unique. If the differentiator is able to do this, it can charge a premium price because customers perceive that the product or ser-

FYI

Customers as Collaborators

As organizations look for ways to differentiate themselves, they must recognize that the new economy is radically changing the way they must deal with customers. C. K. Prahalad (who, in 1990, along with Gary Hamel proposed that businesses need to identify their core competencies) is now saying that businesses are going to have to recognize that "consumers are going to drive the firm." What does he mean by this? His premise is that a product is no more than an "artifact around which customers have experiences." Because the company can only make the product and can't dictate the customer's experience, that gives customers power. However, this switch isn't as threatening as it may first seem because of the Internet. The Internet makes it possible to reach customers in new ways, and strategic decision makers can use this tool to offer customers an engaging experience. Ideally, that experience would offer enough choices to allow customers to shape their own path. The goal would be to tap into customers' talents, shape their expectations, and encourage communities to form around the product. A company that can do this

can absorb customers' knowledge of the product and their suggestions for making it better. In this approach, customers are no longer simply purchasers of the product, but become collaborators on product design and development. Prahalad and his coresearcher Venkatram Ramaswamy suggest four ways to harness customers' competencies. These include (1) encourage active dialogue (a good example is Amazon.com and its book recommendations and reviews); (2) mobilize customer communities (eBay, Yahoo!, E*Trade are good examples); (3) manage customer diversity (gear products–services to customers' varying skill levels such as Microsoft's Hotmail service); and (4) cocreate personalized experiences (e.g., online florists who let customers customize floral arrangements, vases, and colors). Smart companies must draw customers in and keep them coming back. What's your interpretation of this idea of customers as collaborators? What are the implications for competitive strategy choices?

Sources: F. Andrews, "Regarding Customers as Business Collaborators," *New York Times*, February 9, 2000, p. C10; and C. K. Prahalad and V. Ramaswamy, "Co-opting Customer Competence," *Harvard Business Review*, January–February 2000, pp. 79–87.

vice is different and that it uniquely meets their needs. This premium in price provides the profit incentive to compete on the basis of differentiation.

What does it take to be a successful differentiator? Every strategic decision and strategic action is directed at setting the organization apart from its competitors. All the differentiator's functional strategies and distinctive capabilities are aimed at isolating and understanding specific market segments and developing product features that are valued by customers in these various segments. The differentiator is going to have broad and wide product lines—that is, many different models, features, price ranges, and so forth. In fact, *how* the differentiator chooses to differentiate is practically endless. A differentiator might use countless variations of market segments and product features. What's important to the differentiator is that the customer *perceives* the product or service as different and unique and worth the extra price. Because the differentiation strategy can be expensive, the differentiator also needs to control costs to protect profits, but not to the extent that it loses its source of differentiation. Remember that the differentiator is competing on the basis of being unique, not on having the lowest costs. For example, Gap Inc. has developed a strong—and practically impenetrable—competitive advantage by marketing a wide variety of fashions in different formats.[12] It sells casual clothes in a multitude of styles, colors, and features at its flagship Gap stores. In addition, at its Old Navy stores, The Gap showcases hip-looking up-to-the-minute clothes that appeal to the masses amid 1950s Chevies and merchandise piled in old freezers. However, The Gap isn't selling just a physical product. It's marketing attitude and status. Its ability to differentiate its products has given this clothing company one of the world's greatest brand names. The Gap's differentiation strategy obviously has been implemented with great precision. Another example of a successful differentiation strategy is Kinko's Corporation.[13] Although you may think of Kinko's as simply a place to make copies, it's actually much more than that. This chain of over 900 stores is one of the biggest service providers of office support facilities. At a Kinko's store you can, of course, make copies, but you can also get business cards made, arrange for professional color printing, get a passport photo, pay by the hour for computer use, or even purchase Internet access time. Although competitors such as OfficeMax, Staples, and Office Depot have opened office service centers, none offers Kinko's range of services. Kinko's has attempted to set itself apart by offering a broad spectrum of services.

Other characteristics of differentiators often include differentiating themselves along as many dimensions as possible and segmenting the market into many niches. In addition, the differentiator works hard to establish **brand loyalty**, which describes a situation in which customers consistently and repeatedly seek out, purchase, and use a particular brand. Brand loyalty can be a very powerful competitive weapon for the differentiator. Not surprisingly, the differentiator's distinctive capabilities tend to be in marketing and research and development.

What are the drawbacks of the differentiation strategy? One is that the organization must be able to remain unique in customers' eyes. This may be difficult depending on competitors' abilities to imitate and copy successful differentiation features. If the product loses its uniqueness in customers' eyes, they won't be willing to pay the premium price just to have the differentiated product. Another drawback is that customers might become more price sensitive and the product differences might become less important. In this instance, also, the organization might find that its competitive advantage based on being different and unique no longer works.

The **focus strategy** is when an organization pursues either a cost or a differentiation advantage but in a limited (narrow) customer group or segment. A focuser concentrates on serving a specific market niche. What is a market niche based on?[14] Figure 6-6 shows three possible ways to segment specialized market niches: (1) geographical, (2) type of customer, and (3) product line segment. A geographical niche can be defined in terms of region or locality. For example, Midwest Express Airlines serves 25 midwestern cities from hubs in Omaha,

Figure 6-6

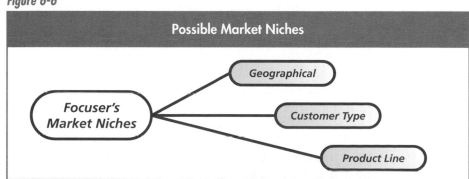

Possible Market Niches

Focuser's Market Niches — Geographical, Customer Type, Product Line

Nebraska, and Milwaukee, Wisconsin.[15] By focusing on this particular geographic area, the company has been able to build a significant customer base. The customer-type niche focuses on a specific group of customers. For instance, Christine Columbus is a mail-order catalog that offers items specifically for women travelers.[16] In this specialized niche, customers can find products tailored to their unique needs. Finally, a product line market niche would focus on a specific and specialized product line. Rhino Entertainment, for example, has built a business producing CDs, videos, books, and even films based on past pop music hit records. The company's collections of pop music and culture created a massive new market niche and revolutionized the record business.[17] All of these organizations have chosen to compete on the basis of some specific and narrow niche.

What is involved with the focus strategy? As stated earlier, the focuser can pursue either a cost or a differentiation advantage. A cost focuser competes by having lower costs than the overall industry cost leader in specific and narrow niches. For instance, MiniMoves Inc. found a lucrative niche by handling small shipments that fell below big moving company minimums and that were too costly and inconvenient for homeowners to box and ship themselves. The company has successfully been able to pursue a cost focus advantage because the big moving companies can't use their low-cost advantages with these small-size shipments.[18] The cost focus strategy also can be successful if an organization can produce complex or custom-built products that don't lend themselves easily to cost efficiencies by the industry's overall cost leaders. The differentiation focuser can use whatever forms of differentiation the broad differentiator might use—product features, product innovations, product quality, customer responsiveness, or whatever. The only difference, however, is that the focuser is specializing in one or a few segments instead of all market segments. A good example of a differentiation focuser is Oink Oink, Inc. of Detroit, Michigan, a specialized pet-food company with over $10 million in annual sales. The company's "Oinkers" roasted pig ears doggie treats are sold—at the rate of more than one million each month—in colorful packaging decorated with playful pigs and poodles.[19] Another company that's successfully pursued a differentiation focus strategy is Yellow Book USA (**www.yellowbook.com**). This company has created its own fantastic niche as an independent publisher of phone directories in 14 states and the District of Columbia.[20]

What are the advantages of the focus strategy? One distinct advantage is that the focuser knows its market niche and knows it well. The focuser can stay close to customers and respond quickly to their changing needs—often much quicker than organizations pursuing a broad market. By effectively and efficiently responding to customers' needs, the focuser can, in turn, develop strong brand loyalty. This brand loyalty can be hard for other competitors to overcome. Also, if the focuser can provide products or services that the broad competitors can't or won't, then it will have the niche all to itself.

What are the drawbacks of the focus strategy? One drawback is that the focuser often operates at a small scale making it difficult to lower costs significantly. However, with technological advancements such as flexible manufacturing systems, this drawback isn't as critical as it once was. In other words, as information and computer technology have become more affordable, focusers have discovered that economies (cost efficiencies) don't necessarily have to come from large-scale production runs. Many times, the focuser can be just as efficient run-

STRATEGIC MANAGEMENT IN AN E-BUSINESS WORLD

The idea seems clever enough—selling pet supplies and treats on the Web. Customers could be serviced anywhere, anytime. And, the market is huge. Sixty percent of all homes in the United States have pets, and Americans spend over $23 billion annually on pet food and supplies. However, "for online pet stores, it's a dog-eat-dog world." Selling pet food and supplies the old-fashioned way in an actual store has never been lucrative, and profit margins are slim (think an average 3 percent, which means for every $1 of sales, the business is making $.03). Therefore, the appeal of selling online has enticed many major pet suppliers to make the jump. However, with so many pet stores now inhabiting the Web, a brutal industry shakeout is looming. Becoming a standout in the crowded market and creating a unique identity costs dearly. Search the Web for sites selling pet supplies and food. How many did you find? Compare and evaluate the players. Describe the three sites you think have the strongest competitive strategies. What are these companies doing? Are they using the same types of competitive actions?

Source: A. Weintraub and R. D. Hof, "For Online Pet Stores, It's Dog-Eat-Dog," *Business Week*, March 6, 2000, pp. 78–80.

ning small batches as the large-scale competitor can running large batches. Another drawback is that the niche customers might change their tastes or needs. Because it's often difficult for a focuser to change niches easily and quickly, this could be a serious problem. In addition, any technological changes that might impact the niche can have a similar effect. Finally, there's always the threat of the broad differentiator taking notice of the focuser's market niche, especially if the focuser is enjoying a significant level of success, and moving in to offer products or services to those customers. In other words, the focuser is subject to being "outfocused" by its competitors—large and small.

The final aspect of Porter's generic competitive strategies is the concept of being **stuck in the middle**, which happens when an organization isn't successfully pursuing either a low-cost or a differentiation competitive advantage. An organization becomes stuck in the middle when its costs are too high to compete with the low-cost leader or when its products and services aren't differentiated enough to compete with the differentiator. As you can well imagine, being stuck in the middle isn't a preferred or profitable strategic direction. Becoming "unstuck" means making consistent strategic decisions about what competitive advantage to pursue and then doing so by aligning resources, distinctive capabilities, and core competencies.

New Perspectives on Competitive Strategy

Although the traditional approaches to describing an organization's competitive strategies are widely used, particularly Porter's generic competitive strategies framework, some of the newer perspectives on competitive strategies provide an expanded, and perhaps more realistic, description of *what* competitive strategies organizations are using. That's what we want to look at in this section. We'll be examining two new perspectives: (1) a refinement of Porter's competitive strategies with the addition of an integrated low-cost differentiation strategy, and (2) a generic strategies framework

> ### Strategic Management in Action ▶
>
> This middle would be a good place to be stuck! For most consumers, the delicious frosting middle is the appeal of chocolate sandwich cookies. What company do you think founded this market? If you said Oreos, you'd be wrong. Hydrox (a product of Sunshine Biscuits) debuted in 1908 and Oreos (a product of National Biscuit, now Nabisco) in 1912. Yet, over the years, Oreos' popularity and market power became so overwhelming that Hydrox languished in obscurity—never able to be a low-cost leader or a differentiator. However, Keebler (now the bakers of Hydrox) is hoping to change all that. The name was changed to Keebler Droxies, the cookie's flavor has been reformulated, and the package redesigned to be more kid oriented. Will these strategic changes be enough to pull the cookie with the tastefully delicious middle out of being stuck in the middle? What do you think?
>
> *Source:* P. Lukas, "Oreos to Hydrox: Resistance Is Futile," *Fortune*, March 15, 1999, pp. 52–54.

Consider This ◀◀|

✓ Why are Porter's competitive strategies called "generic"?

✓ According to Porter, what are the two types of competitive advantage?

✓ What role does competitive scope play in Porter's approach to competitive strategies?

✓ Describe the cost leadership (low-cost leader) strategy. Be sure to note the characteristics of a cost leader and the advantages and disadvantages of this strategy.

✓ Describe the differentiation strategy. Be sure to note the characteristics of a differentiator and the advantages and disadvantages of this strategy.

✓ How is a focus strategy different from the other two generic competitive strategies?

✓ Describe the low-cost focus strategy. Describe the differentiation focus strategy.

✓ What are the advantages of a focus strategy? What are the drawbacks?

✓ What does it mean to be stuck in the middle? How would an organization get unstuck?

proposed by Henry Mintzberg as a better way to take into account the increasing complexity of the competitive environment.

Integrated Low-Cost Differentiation Strategy. Porter's original work on competitive advantage and competitive strategies maintained that an organization couldn't simultaneously pursue a low-cost and a differentiation advantage. To do so meant the risk of being stuck in the middle and not successfully developing or exploiting either competitive advantage. You had to do one or the other.[21] Despite strong empirical support for Porter's strategy framework,[22] several strategy researchers began to question this "mutual exclusivity" of the low-cost and differentiation strategies.[23] Instead of having to pursue *either* low cost *or* differentiation, was it possible that organizations could pursue both strategies simultaneously and successfully? Strategy research evidence is starting to show that organizations *can* successfully pursue an integrated low-cost differentiation strategy.[24]

What is an **integrated low-cost differentiation strategy**? It's one in which an organization develops a competitive advantage by simultaneously achieving low costs and high levels of differentiation. What are some examples of organizations that have implemented such a strategy successfully? One is

Dell Computers, which has succeeded in an intensely competitive market by providing high-quality products and services while undercutting Compaq, IBM, and other PC makers in price.[25] What's Dell's secret? It's been able to keep its costs low and its level of differentiation high by developing and exploiting a competitive advantage that's based on a disciplined, extremely low-cost corporate culture, while still being able to provide high-quality products and services. Other organizations such as Southwest Airlines, Anheuser-Busch, and McDonald's have successfully been able to pursue this hybrid competitive strategy. What makes an integrated low-cost differentiation strategy possible?

The answer is that technological advancements have made it possible for firms to pursue a differentiation strategy at a low cost. Successfully establishing sources of differentiation can be expensive. When creating, manufacturing, and marketing a wide range of quality products or services, it's often difficult to keep costs as low as possible. Yet, the widespread availability and increasing affordability of computer technology has made it easier for organizations to pursue product and service differentiation and yet keep their costs low. Technological advancements such as flexible manufacturing systems, just-in-time inventory systems, and computer-integrated manufacturing systems have opened the door for competing on the basis of having low costs *and* being unique. However, keep in mind that just because these technological advancements are available and accessible doesn't mean that every organization that uses them will successfully be able to implement an integrated low-cost differentiation strategy. It still takes strict attention to keeping costs as low as possible and providing products and services with enough features that the marketplace desires.

Mintzberg's Generic Competitive Strategies. Henry Mintzberg has developed an alternative typology of competitive strategies that he felt better reflected the increasing complexity of the competitive environment.[26] He proposed six possible competitive strategies. Figure 6-7 shows these strategies.

Differentiation by price is a modification of Porter's cost leadership strategy. Mintzberg argued that having the lowest costs didn't provide a competitive advan-

Figure 6-7

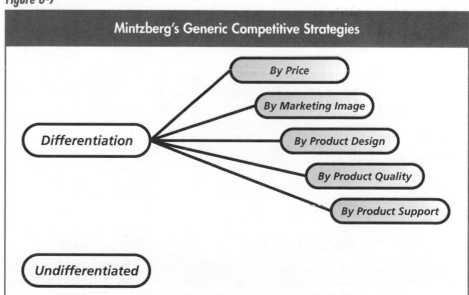

tage by itself, but that the advantage came from the fact it allowed the organization to charge below average market prices. Therefore, the organization pursuing this strategy was instead differentiating on the basis of price. Differentiation by marketing image described a competitive strategy in which an organization attempted to create a certain image in customers' minds. Organizations following this competitive strategy used their marketing image as a potent competitive weapon. The competitive strategy of differentiation by product design can be used to describe organizations that competed on the basis of providing desirable product features and design configurations. An organization that followed this competitive strategy would attempt to give customers a wide selection of product

FYI

New Points of Differentiation

Successful companies realize that points of differentiation between themselves and competitors aren't limited to only products or services. Indeed, a company has the opportunity to differentiate itself at any point where it comes in contact with customers. How? By examining the *consumption chain*, or a customer's entire experience with a product or service. Here are some questions that can help guide this mapping process:

- How do people become aware of their need for your product or service?
- How do consumers find your products being offered?
- How do consumers make their final selections?
- How do customers order and purchase your product or service?
- How is your product or service delivered?
- What happens when your product or service is delivered?
- How is your product installed?
- How is your product or service paid for?
- How is your product stored?
- How is your product moved around?
- What is the customer really using your product for?
- What type of help do customers need as they use your product?
- What about returns or exchanges?

- How is your product repaired or serviced?
- What happens when your product is disposed of or no longer used?

Once you've mapped these issues, you can begin to analyze your customer's experience. The goal is to gain insights into your customers as you look at the context surrounding their consumption chains. Do this by asking what, where, who, when, and how questions. For instance, ask questions such as: What are customers doing at each point in the consumption chain? What problems might they be experiencing? Where are your customers at each point in the consumption chain? Where else would they like to be? Who is with the customer at any point in the consumption chain? Do these other people have influence over the customer? When are customers at any point in the consumption chain? How are customers' needs being addressed? How else might you take care of their needs and concerns? By mapping the consumption chain and analyzing customers' experiences, organizations can uncover many different points of differentiation.

Sources: W. Chan Kim and Renee Mauborgne, "Creating New Market Space," *Harvard Business Review*, January–February 1999, pp. 83–93; and I. C. MacMillan and R. G. McGrath, "Discovering New Points of Differentiation," *Harvard Business Review*, July–August 1997, pp. 133–45.

features and different designs. Differentiation by quality described a strategy in which organizations competed by delivering higher reliability and performance at a comparable price. In this strategy, superior product quality was pursued as the organization's competitive advantage. The competitive strategy of differentiation by product support emphasized the customer support services provided by the organization. In this strategy, competitive advantage would be sought through providing an all-encompassing bundle of desired customer support services. Finally, the undifferentiated strategy described situations in which an organization had no basis for differentiation or when it deliberately followed a copycat strategy.

What's the verdict on Mintzberg's alternative generic competitive strategies typology? It appears that Mintzberg's approach has merit.[27] Research on his strategy typology shows it has strong conceptual clarity and descriptive power. Although it will probably never totally replace the significant popularity of Porter's competitive strategies, Mintzberg's typology does seem to capture the essence of competitive strategies being used by organizations in today's complex and dynamic competitive climate. As such, it provides an alternative way to describe organizations' competitive strategies.

A Brief Recap of the Various Approaches to Describing Competitive Strategies

What is our conclusion about what competitive strategies an organization might use? Undoubtedly, Porter's generic competitive strategy framework remains the most popular approach to describing how organizations compete. Even current business books and periodicals describe how organizations use cost leadership and differentiation strategies to compete. However, if these two competitive strategies are approached as mutually exclusive, Porter's generic strategy typology probably isn't highly relevant or realistic in light of today's competitive environment. On the other hand, if the integrated low-cost differentiation strategy is seen as a legitimate extension of Porter's basic generic strategies, then his framework would appear to be appropriate and suitable for describing an organization's competitive strategies.

This doesn't mean, however, that the other competitive strategy perspectives discussed earlier aren't conceptually sound or appropriate for describing competitive strategies. Mintzberg's typology, with its emphasis on mirroring the realities of today's dynamic competitive environment, seems to have appealing promise as an approach to describing what competitive strategies an organization might pursue. Even Miles and Snow's adaptive strategies can be appropriate and practical choices for describing different organizational competitive approaches.

No matter how you describe them, the main thing to remember about which competitive strategies an organization has at its disposal is that its competitive strategy should exploit the competitive advantage(s) the organization has developed. Without a competitive advantage that's been developed from its resources, distinctive capabilities, or core competencies, it will be extremely difficult for the organization to compete successfully in any given situation.

IMPLEMENTING, EVALUATING, AND CHANGING COMPETITIVE STRATEGY

Look back at the chapter-opening case. What type of competitive strategy did UPS appear to be pursuing? How can you tell? You'll probably notice such things

Consider This ◀◀◀

✓ What is the integrated low-cost differentiation strategy?

✓ How does the integrated low-cost differentiation strategy contradict the concept behind Porter's generic competitive strategies?

✓ What makes the integrated low-cost differentiation strategy possible? Explain.

✓ Describe each of the competitive strategies in Mintzberg's generic strategy typology.

✓ What do you think is the best approach for describing an organization's possible competitive strategies? Support your choice.

✓ What is the main point to remember about what competitive strategy an organization might choose to implement?

as its uniformity and efficiency of operations and its commitment to technology and customer service. The obvious signs of the type of competitive strategy an organization is pursuing can be seen by what's actually being done or implemented. Strategy implementation is critical. If a strategy is not implemented, then it's nothing more than a strategic idea or plan. And, if you remember the entire strategic management process model, once a strategy is implemented, it must be assessed or evaluated, and modified if needed. In this section we want to look at how organizations' competitive strategies are implemented, evaluated, and changed.

Implementing Competitive Strategy

How does The Gap keep current styles in its stores? How does Payless ShoeSource restock its stores within a day's notice? Obviously, workers, facilities and equipment, work activities, and work systems have to be in place to facilitate such accomplishments. (Think in terms of resources, distinctive capabilities, and core competencies.) This is what implementation is all about. Because an organization's resources and capabilities are used and developed within its various functional areas, it shouldn't come as a surprise that the organization's functional strategies play a significant role in implementing competitive strategy. That's what we're going to look at first. Then we'll discuss the various competitive postures or actions an organization might take as it implements its overall competitive strategy.

The Role of Functional Strategies. The challenge in implementing the organization's competitive strategy is to create and exploit a sustainable competitive advantage. As we've discussed many times, competitive advantage comes from the organization's ability to use its resources to develop capabilities that may, in turn, become distinctive. All of these details happen through the actual strategies being used in the organization's various functional work units.

The functional strategies play a dual role in the implementation of competitive strategy. First of all, whatever resources are currently available or being procured, and whatever distinctive capabilities or core competencies are currently in place or being developed, will influence what competitive strategy is most feasible and likely to lead to a sustainable competitive advantage. For instance, each of Porter's generic competitive strategies requires certain skills, resources, and organizational requirements in order to successfully attain a sustainable competitive advantage. Table 6-3 lists these suggested requirements for the generic competitive strategies. However, functional strategies also play another role. Once the organization's competitive strategy is determined, the resources, capabilities, and competencies found in the various functional areas are *how* the competitive strategy is implemented.

We will not repeat all the possible variations of the various functional strategies here (see Chapter 5), but keep in mind that the strategies being used in each functional area should be aligned with whatever competitive advantage—and, of

TABLE 6-3	Requirements for Porter's Generic Competitive Strategies	

Generic Strategy	Commonly Required Skills and Resources	Common Organizational Requirements
Overall cost leadership	Sustained capital investment and access Process engineering skills Intense supervision of labor Products designed for ease of manufacture Low-cost distribution system	Tight cost control Frequent, detailed control reports Structured organization and responsibilities Incentives based on meeting strict quantitative targets
Differentiation	Strong marketing abilities Product engineering Creative flair Strong capability in basic research Corporate reputation for quality or technological leadership Long tradition in the industry or unique combination of skills drawn from other businesses Strong cooperation from channels	Strong coordination among functions in R&D, product development, and marketing Subjective measurement and incentives instead of quantitative measures Amenities to attract highly skilled labor, scientists, or creative people
Focus	Combination of the above policies directed at the particular strategic target	Combination of the above policies directed at the particular strategic target

Source: Adapted with permission of The Free Press, a Division of Simon & Schuster Inc. From *Competitive Strategy: Techniques for Analyzing Industries and Competitors* by Michael E. Porter. Copyright © 1980, 1988 by The Free Press.

course, competitive strategy—is being pursued. This means that, for instance, if we've chosen to compete on the basis of having the lowest costs, then the functional strategies being used should support and reinforce that strategy. Cost efficiencies would be pursued in all operational areas, but particularly in the functional areas of manufacturing and materials management. Financial strategies would support the quest for operational efficiency including such things as capital investment in technology if it's needed and could contribute to lowering costs. All organizational resources, distinctive capabilities, and core competencies would be directed at attaining the goal of having the industry's lowest costs. Likewise, if the organization chose to compete on the basis of both low costs and differentiation, then its functional strategies better reflect that choice or it will never be able to develop a sustainable competitive advantage. To summarize, the functional strategies—that is, how the organization develops and exploits its resources, distinctive capabilities, and core competencies—influence both what competitive strategy is most appropriate and how that strategy is implemented.

It should be fairly obvious by now that an organization's functional strategies play a critical role in the implementation of its competitive strategy. Without the development and exploitation of the organizational resources, capabilities, and competencies—which happens through the functional strategies being used—there will be no hope of developing a sustainable competitive advantage. As we've said from the beginning, developing a sustainable competitive advantage is the whole intent of managing strategically. If the organization doesn't have or can't develop a sustainable competitive advantage—to set it apart from its competi-

> ### Strategic Management in Action
>
> U-Haul International, based in Phoenix, needs to reexamine its functional strategies. The company's financials look great, but customers have had nightmarish experiences. Part of the problem is inconsistent customer service or accountability throughout the organization. More than 93 percent of U-Haul's rental locations are independent dealers whose primary business is something else, such as running a gas station, towing service, or hardware store. U-Haul doesn't insist on high levels of service from these dealers. There are no uniformity requirements as far as cleanliness, dress, or hours of operation. Also, U-Haul keeps no customer information on file. Complaints (common ones include endless waits on the phone, unsafe trucks, rude or untrained staff) are forwarded to a corporate 800 number, which passes along customer data to the dealer in question or to a regional marketing director. However, resolving a problem can take months. With this lack of attention to functional strategies, how has the company stayed competitive? Chairman and President Joe Shoen says his approach is to offer simple pricing and easy-to-use vehicles. What do you think of U-Haul's competitive approach? Do you think strategic changes are necessary? Explain.
>
> *Source:* J. Gordon, "U-Hell," *Forbes*, March 20, 2000, pp. 70–74.

tors—it's going to have a tough time competing and continuing in business. What we're going to discuss next is the types of competitive postures and actions an organization might use as it implements its competitive strategy.

Competitive Postures and Actions. Once an organization's competitive strategy is selected and implemented through specific functional decisions and actions, the real fun begins! The very notion of "competitive" strategy means that the organization is going to be competing "against" other organizations, vying for customers, market share, or other desired objects or outcomes. What happens in this dynamic competitive "dance" is that organizations use certain competitive postures, actions, and tactics in the ongoing battle to keep or acquire whatever object or outcome they're after. What are these competitive postures and actions? Let's look at some.

The competitive postures and actions organizations use are typically described using an old military and sports analogy, offensive and defensive moves. Why? Because that's what organizations are doing when they compete: They're going after competitors' positions or they're defending their position. **Offensive moves** are when an organization attempts to exploit and strengthen its competitive position through attacks on a competitor's position. What offensive moves might an organization use?[28] A frontal assault is when the attacking firm goes head-to-head with its competitor and matches the competitor in every possible category such as price, promotion, product features, and distribution channel. This com-

Aggressive Strategies

Small companies in a variety of industries complain that larger rivals are increasingly using aggressive strategies to eliminate competition. What are some of these aggressive strategies? *Tying* is when a manufacturer makes the sale of a high-demand product conditional to the purchase of a second product. *Market share discounts* are discounts that increase when the purchaser gives the manufacturer a greater share of its business. *Slotting fees* are common in the food-and-

beverage industry and are paid to purchase exclusive shelf space. *Bundled rebates* are given when a buyer purchases more than one product. *Exclusivity incentives* include any form of payment (such as an advertising subsidy) in exchange for a promise not to carry a competitor's products. Find some examples of these types of aggressive competitive strategies. What do you think of these strategies?

Source: M. France, "Are Corporate Predators on the Loose?" *Business Week*, February 23, 1998, pp. 124–26.

petitive move can be an effective way to gain market share from weaker competitors. It's also a good way to slice away rivals' competitive advantages. Another offensive tactic is to attack competitors' weaknesses. How? An organization might concentrate on geographic areas where its competitor is weak. Or it might begin serving customer segments that a competitor is ignoring or where the competitors' offerings are weak. The organization might introduce new product models or product features to fill gaps its competitors aren't serving. This offensive tactic entails attacking wherever the competitor has specific weaknesses. Another offensive tactic is to use an all-out attack on competitors by hitting them from both the product *and* the market segment side. Needless to say, this all-out competitive attack requires significant resources and capabilities. Another type of offensive move is to avoid direct, head-on competitive challenges by maneuvering around competitors and subtly changing the rules of the game. How? Most typically the organization attempts to create new market segments that competitors aren't serving by introducing products with different features. This competitive action cuts the market out from under the competitor and forces the competitor to play catch-up. Finally, another possible offensive tactic is to use "guerilla" attacks. This

Strategic Management—The Global Perspective

Japanese convenience stores are on the offensive! With no further room to physically expand in this country where space is at a premium and in an industry that's intensely competitive, neighborhood convenience stores are moving to embrace new technology. Using interactive computer kiosks, Japanese customers can now order books and concert tickets, make train and plane reservations, and pay on the way out the door. The challenge for the convenience stores is going to be providing online services that customers will be willing to use.

Source: S. Strom, "E-Commerce the Japanese Way," *New York Times*, March 18, 2000, p. B1.

is just what it sounds like—small, intermittent, seemingly random assaults on competitors' markets. For instance, an organization might use special promotions, price incentives, or advertising campaigns to lure away competitors' customers.

Offensive moves are good ways to keep up attacks on competitors and strengthen your own competitive position. What happens when your organization is the one being attacked or threatened with attack? That's when the defensive competitive moves come in.

Defensive moves describe when an organization is attempting to protect its competitive advantage and turf. The use of defensive moves doesn't increase an organization's competitive advantage, but can make that competitive advantage more sustainable.[29] Let's look at some of the defensive moves an organization might use. One is to prevent challengers from attacking by not giving them any areas to attack. For example, an organization could offer a full line of products in every profitable market segment, keep prices low on products that most closely match competitors' offerings, use exclusive agreements with dealers to block competitors from using them, protect technologies through patents or licenses, or use any other number of possible preventive strategic actions. Again, the intent of this particular defensive move is to make sure competitors don't have any holes or weaknesses to attack. Another possible defensive move is to increase competitors' beliefs that significant retaliation can be expected if competitive attacks are initiated. How could an organization signal the market that it's serious about retaliating if attacked? Public announcements by managers to "protect" market share are important as are strong responses to competitors' moves. Doing things such as matching price cuts or matching promotion incentives signals competitors that you aren't going to sit back and let them steal away your customers. Competitive counterattacks are particularly critical if the markets or segments being attacked are crucial to the organization. However, these types of retaliatory actions should be approached cautiously, particularly in instances where the attacker is a new entrant to the market. Why? Research has shown that the typical new entrant doesn't pose a serious threat and aggressive retaliation can be expensive.[30] The final type of defensive move involves lowering the incentive for a competitor to

STRATEGIC MANAGEMENT IN AN E-BUSINESS WORLD

The Book-of-the-Month Club and the Literary Guild have joined forces to combat online competition. The companies have formed an alliance that will transform both into digital hybrids. Although each will retain some features of its traditional customer services, the new alliance will help the companies evolve into interactive digital clubs whereby customers can chat live with authors, express opinions on electronic polls, post notices on member bulletin boards, and read book reviews and book excerpts. One of the principals in the arrangement said, "Without the competitive pressure, we might not have made the deal." What challenges do you think these companies will face as they move into an e-business world? What are the implications for each company's competitive strategy and for the alliance's competitive strategy?

Source: D. Carvajal, "Well-Known Book Clubs Agree to Form Partnership," *New York Times*, March 2, 2000, p. C2.

attack. If a potential attacker is led to believe that the expectations of future profits are minimal, chances are it won't want to challenge the current leader. For instance, an organization might use media announcements to highlight problems in the industry, or it might deliberately keep prices low and continually invest in cost-lowering actions. All of these competitive moves would make it less attractive for a competitor to launch an attack.

Evaluating and Changing Competitive Strategy

As with any other strategic action, the responsibility of managing strategically doesn't stop once the competitive strategy is implemented. The organization's competitive moves, actions, and responses being carried out through the various functional strategies need to be monitored, assessed, and evaluated for performance effectiveness and efficiency. What are the results of the various strategies? Are they having the intended effect? Are we successfully exploiting our competitive advantage? Why or why not? These types of questions need to be asked when evaluating the competitive strategy. Because most organizations' competitive strategies are targeted at increasing sales revenues, market share, or profitability, data on these particular performance areas would be required in order to determine what impact the competitive strategies are having. Likewise, not-for-profit organizations should assess the results of their competitive strategies even though they're not focused on revenues, market share, or profitability. For instance, strategy evaluation might address such areas as did the number of plasma and blood donors increase; did the number of contributors to the church building fund go up or did the average donation amount increase; or did governmental funding of the community drug outreach program increase? No matter what type of organization or what type of competitive strategy is being used, it's important to measure its impact.

However, it's not enough just to measure the results of the competitive strategy. What if results aren't as high as expected, or what if they're better than expected? Then what? Part of the evaluation of the competitive strategy is also to determine what happened and why. We do this by trying to pinpoint areas of competitive weakness. Has the market changed and we haven't? Are the organization's numerous resources and capabilities being used effectively and efficiently so that the needed and crucial competitive advantage is being developed and exploited? Which ones are and which ones aren't? As you can see, the evaluation of the competitive strategy turns out to be an assessment of the organization's various functional areas and the activities being performed there. If this evaluation shows that the strategy isn't having the intended impact or hasn't resulted in desired levels of performance, it may need to be changed. However, a change in the organization's fundamental competitive strategy isn't something that organizations want to do frequently or continually. Why? Remember that each competi-

Consider This ◀◀|

✓ Why is strategy implementation critical?

✓ Describe the role(s) that functional strategies play in implementing the organization's competitive strategy.

✓ What are offensive moves? Describe the offensive competitive actions an organization might use.

✓ What are defensive moves? Describe the defensive competitive actions an organization might use.

✓ Why should the competitive strategy be evaluated? How is it evaluated?

✓ Why is it unlikely that an organization's fundamental competitive strategy will be changed frequently and continually?

✓ What types of competitive changes are likely to be made?

tive strategy entails the development of specific resources, capabilities, and distinctive competences. To change the competitive strategy would mean modifying or redeveloping the organization's resources and capabilities. This is difficult and expensive. However, this doesn't, and shouldn't, mean that an organization would *never* change its basic competitive approach. What it does mean, though, is that this type of major strategic change should be approached realistically and intelligently.

Although changing the organization's basic competitive strategy isn't highly likely, modifying the organization's competitive actions is. Many of the stories in the popular business press are about changes organizations are making in their competitive actions. As competitors battle for desired outcomes or objects, they'll try one thing. If that doesn't work, they'll try something else. That's the reality of the current competitive struggle. As we stated at the beginning of the chapter, competition is a given for all sizes and types of organizations. It's a game that the players are trying to win or to come out on top of. Organizations improve their chances of doing so if they choose a competitive strategy that exploits their competitive advantage. After all, think back to our chapter-opening case. That's what UPS did, and now its sales and earnings are sizzling!

THE BOTTOM LINE

➠ **Competitive advantage**, what sets an organization apart, is a key concept in strategic management.

➠ An organization's competitive advantage can be eroded easily (and often quickly) by competitors' actions.

➠ Because competitive advantage implies that there are other competitors, we need to look at the competitive environment.

➠ Some describe the current business environment as **hypercompetition**, a situation with very intense and continually increasing levels of competition.

➠ Competition is everywhere. **Competition** is organizations battling or vying for some desired object or outcome—typically customers, market share, survey ranking, or needed resources.

➠ The level of intensity of competition depends on factors such as numerous or equally balanced competitors, industry growth rate, presence of high fixed or storage costs, and other factors described in the current rivalry section of Porter's five forces model.

➠ An organization's competitors can be described from the industry perspective, marketing perspective, or strategic groups perspective.

➠ The industry perspective states that competitors are organizations that are making the same product or providing the same service.

➠ The marketing perspective states that competitors are organizations that satisfy the same customer need.

➠ The strategic groups perspective states that competitors are those organizations in your **strategic group**—a group of firms following essentially the same strategy in a particular market or industry.

➠ Some possible dimensions to identify strategic groups include price, quality, product line breadth–depth, market share, geographic scope, and so forth.

➤ Every organization has resources and capabilities to do whatever it's in business to do although not every organization can effectively exploit those resources or capabilities.

➤ **Competitive strategy** is a choice of how an organization or business unit is going to compete in its particular industry or market.

➤ The traditional approaches to defining competitive strategy are Miles and Snow's adaptive strategies, Abell's business definition, and Porter's generic strategies.

➤ Miles and Snow's approach is based on the strategies organizations use to successfully adapt to their uncertain competitive environments.

➤ Their **prospector strategy** is one in which an organization continually innovates by finding and exploiting new product and market opportunities.

➤ Their **defender strategy** is characterized by the search for market stability and producing only a limited product line directed at a narrow segment of the total potential market.

➤ The **analyzer strategy** is one of analysis and imitation.

➤ The **reactor strategy** is characterized by the lack of a coherent strategic plan or apparent means of competing.

➤ Research has shown Miles and Snow's typology to be theoretically sound and an appropriate way to describe the competitive strategies an organization might use.

➤ Abell's business definition framework is heavily marketing focused and proposes defining a business using three dimensions: customer groups (who), customer needs (what), and technology or distinctive competencies (how).

➤ The various combinations of competitive scope and extent of competitive differentiation of products and services provide the basis for Abell's three possible competitive strategies: differentiated, undifferentiated, and focus.

➤ Abell's strict marketing emphasis limits his business definition framework as a widely used and general approach to describing competitive strategies.

➤ Porter's generic competitive strategies are based on the assumption that competitive advantage comes from only one of two possible sources: having the lowest costs in the industry or possessing significant and desirable differences from competitors.

➤ Porter called his competitive strategies generic because they can be pursued by any type or size organization in any type or size industry.

➤ The mix of type of competitive advantage and competitive scope provides the basis for Porter's competitive strategies.

➤ The **cost leadership strategy** is one in which an organization strives to have the lowest costs in its industry and produces products or services for a broad customer base. There are advantages and disadvantages to this approach.

➤ The **differentiation strategy** is one in which the organization competes on the basis of providing unique (different) products or services with features that customers value, perceive as different, and are willing to pay a premium price for. There are advantages and drawbacks to this approach.

➤ A differentiator works hard to establish **brand loyalty**, a situation in which customers consistently and repeatedly seek out, purchase, and use a particular brand.

➠ The **focus strategy** is when an organization pursues either a cost or a differentiation advantage in a limited (narrow) customer group or segment. A focuser concentrates on serving a specific market niche. There are advantages and drawbacks to this approach.

➠ Porter also identified the concept of **stuck in the middle**, which describes an organization that isn't successfully pursuing either a low-cost or a differentiation competitive advantage.

➠ Two newer perspectives on competitive strategy are the integrated low-cost differentiation strategy and Mintzberg's competitive strategy typology.

➠ The **integrated low-cost differentiation strategy** is a strategy whereby an organization develops a competitive advantage by simultaneously achieving low costs and high levels of differentiation.

➠ This hybrid competitive strategy is possible because of technological advancements such as flexible manufacturing systems, just-in-time inventory systems, and computer-integrated manufacturing systems.

➠ Henry Mintzberg's alternative competitive strategy typology was developed to better reflect the increasing complexity of the competitive environment.

➠ His six possible competitive strategies include differentiation by price, marketing image, product design, product quality, product support, and undifferentiation.

➠ The challenge in implementing the organization's competitive strategy is to create and exploit a sustainable competitive advantage.

➠ Competitive strategy implementation is done through the functional strategies. Whatever competitive strategy is selected, certain resources and capabilities will be required to implement it.

➠ In addition, competitive strategy implementation involves various competitive actions. **Offensive moves** are competitive actions taken when an organization attempts to exploit and strengthen its competitive position through attacks on a competitor's position. **Defensive moves** are competitive actions taken when an organization is attempting to protect its competitive advantage and turf.

➠ The organization's competitive strategy must be evaluated to make sure it's doing what it's intended to do.

➠ It's highly unlikely that an organization would continually change its fundamental competitive strategy because each competitive strategy requires certain resources, capabilities, and competencies.

➠ Instead, the organization may change the functional strategies that are being used to implement the competitive strategy, and it may change the competitive actions (both offensive and defensive) it's also using to implement the competitive strategy.

BUILDING YOUR SKILLS

1. A patent is a legal property that allows its holder to prevent others from employing this property for their own use for a specified period of time. A patent protects an invention and is valid for up to 20 years from the date of filing a patent application. Research patents and the patent application

process. (You might want to access the U.S. Patent & Trademark Office Web site at **www.uspto.gov**.) How many types of patents are there? What other interesting information about patents did you find? Would patents play any role in an organization's choice of competitive strategy? Explain.

2. Scented candles are a $2.5-billion-a-year industry, and that sales figure continues to increase. Three leading industry players are Yankee Candle Company (**www.yankeecandle.com**), Illuminations (**www.illuminations. com**), and Wicks and Sticks (**www.wicksandsticks.com**). How are these competitors similar? How are they different? Suppose that an industry newcomer bursts onto the scene. What do you think a newcomer will need to do—that is, what competitive strategy approach—to establish itself as a viable competitor? What will the established competitors need to do?

3. Product comebacks. Long-established brand names are finding it necessary to update their competitive strategies in order to keep up with a continually and rapidly changing economy. For instance, Volvo has moved away from emphasizing safety to advertisements that appeal to younger customers. Find five examples of brands or products that have been "shocked" back to life. Describe what each company has done (is doing) to implement the product comeback. What are the implications for competitive strategy?

(*Sources:* D. Eisenberg, "Trouble in Brand City," *Time*, March 20, 2000, pp. 47–48; and P. Winters Lauro, "Shocking Old Brands Back to Life," *New York Times*, February 10, 2000, p. C10.)

4. Competition is a whole lot like war. What can strategic decision makers learn from military strategists? Sun-Tzu, the great Chinese military strategist, wrote *The Art of War* sometime between 480 and 221 B.C. Could his warfare strategies be used in battling competitors? Here's one person's interpretation of some of these strategies:

- Don't start what you shouldn't begin.
- The impossible is impossible.
- Don't attack a tank with a peashooter.
- Attack what isn't defended.
- If you can't attack, defend.
- Illusion creates confusion.
- Do what they don't expect.
- Rather than assuming they won't attack, position yourself so they can't attack.
- The unprepared can be defeated.
- The unknowing can be outsmarted.
- Do not challenge unless you have the means to win.
- Do not fight unless you're determined to win.

Do you agree with these comments? What implications do you see for competitive strategy in these comments?

(*Source:* S. Marino, "What Wins Wars . . . and Markets," *Industry Week*, December 21, 1998, p. 14.)

5. They were incredibly popular and hunted by consumers of all ages. The cute and cuddly Beanie Babies. Then, Beanie Babies' manufacturer, Ty Inc., announced at the end of 1999 that it was going to "retire" all of the pint-size

stuffed animals by the end of the year. Initially, consumers were upset that the toys might actually be discontinued. Then, customer dismay turned to anger at the possibility that the announcement was nothing more than a publicity stunt. Analyze and evaluate this situation from a competitive strategy point of view.

(*Sources:* D. Canedy, "Requiem for Beanie Babies. Or Maybe Not," *New York Times,* September 4, 1999, p. BU2; and D. Canedy, "Beanie Move Giving Rise to Skepticism," *New York Times,* September 2, 1999, p. C1.)

6. The Maytag repairman won't be lonely for a while because there's plenty to fix at the company. In the intensely competitive appliance industry, Maytag's CEO Lloyd D. Ward (the third-largest appliance manufacturer behind Whirlpool and industry leader GE) has been trying to fashion a competitive strategy that will work. Maytag has long been viewed as the pricier competitor, but both Whirlpool and GE are stepping up their introduction of more competitive products at the high end of the market. Research Maytag. Describe what competitive actions it appears to be using. Do you think these are sufficient? Why or why not? What strategic changes might you propose?

(*Sources:* M. Borden, "Wall Street Puts New Maytag CEO Through Spin Cycle," *Fortune,* May 1, 2000, pp. 54–58; company's Web site (**www.maytag.com**), April 27, 2000; and A. Osterland, "Maytag Through the Wringer," *Business Week,* September 27, 1999, p. 54.)

7. Henry Ford said, "Competition whose motive is merely to compete, to drive some other fellow out, never carries very far. The competitor to be feared is one who never bothers about you at all, but goes on making his own business better all the time. Businesses that grow by development and improvement do not die. But when a business ceases to be creative, when it believes it has reached perfection and needs to do nothing but produce—no improvement, no development—it is done." Are his thoughts still valid in today's environment? Explain.

(*Source:* "Noteworthy Quotes," *Strategy & Business,* 1st quarter 1999, p. 155.)

8. Most organizations face an intensely competitive environment. With this type of competitive pressure, strategic managers might be tempted to engage in unethical competitive actions and activities in order to keep ahead of competitors. Research to find four or five examples of what you think are unfair competitive moves. Write a short paper explaining the examples you've found, why you think they're unfair, and what you'd do about it.

9. Is competition dead? According to James Moore, author of *The Death of Competition* (HarperCollins, 1996), it should be. He says, "There's a growing awareness that competition as we have known it, the head-to-head conflicts of the past, is no longer the way to build a business." Instead, he proposes that organizations should nurture their "ecosystems" of suppliers, customers, and others. "By building links with others, all will evolve and get stronger" (pp. 150–51). What do you think of Moore's belief that competition should be dead? Explain your ideas. Think in terms of the impact on organizational resources, capabilities, and competitive advantage.

10. Select an industry that you know about or are interested in. (You might want to select an industry in which you're concentrating your postgraduation job search.) Do a strategic groups analysis, covering as many of the potential

competitors as you can. Determine what strategic dimensions would be most appropriate for grouping competitors. Then, group competitors according to your strategic dimensions. Be sure to put your analysis on a chart showing the strategic dimensions and the various strategic groups. Write up a brief explanation of one to two pages of what you did, how you did it, and why you did what you did.

STRATEGIC MANAGEMENT IN ACTION CASES

CASE #1: Pretty in Brown

Strategic Management in Action case #1 can be found at the beginning of Chapter 6.

Discussion Questions

1. Describe UPS's competitive strategy using Miles and Snow's framework, Abell's framework, and Porter's framework. Explain each of your choices.
2. What competitive advantage(s) do you think UPS has? Have its resources, capa-

bilities, and core competencies contributed to its competitive advantage(s)? Explain.
3. Do UPS's functional strategies support its competitive strategy? Explain.
4. What do you think UPS is going to have to do to maintain its strong competitive position?

CASE #2: The King of Underwear

Nicholas Graham is the king of underwear and the self-proclaimed "Chief Underpants Officer." His Joe Boxer brand of underwear has grown into a global brand on the strength of its exceptionally wacky and fun boxers and briefs. Underwear, sleepwear, and loungewear for men, women, and kids represent the company's core business. However, other products such as bedding, sportswear, and accessories (watches and mouse pads are two such products that come to mind) are produced under license to other companies.

The San Francisco–based Joe Boxer Company (**www.joeboxer.com**) was founded in 1985 on the premise that the most

basic and utilitarian element of men's clothing should be remade to reflect humor, fashion, and the shifting trends in American culture. Over the years, Graham has guided his company with a bold plan and specific goals. He understood that the clothing industry (even the "under" clothing industry) was intensely competitive and being successful in such an environment would require bold strategic choices.

The company believes strongly in innovation and creativity and emphasizes these core values in product design, merchandising, marketing, customer service, and all business functions. However, in this business, marketing and publicity strategies are the bread-and-butter of Joe Boxer's operation. For example, in 1994, Graham launched the world's largest e-mail message center on a billboard in Times Square. People around the world would send electronic messages and these messages would show up on the billboard. This type of marketing approach is critical to Joe Boxer's identity as a fun, wacky, and exciting business. In addition, many of the company's marketing strategies are tied into socially responsible activities. For example, its Joe Boxer Cab, which cruises the streets of New York and San Francisco, isn't just any cab. It's especially outfitted and decorated with "Licky" face seats (a "Licky" face is the smiley face you'll see on Joe Boxer merchandise), an entertainment center, and handy compartments for a week's supply of Joe Boxer underwear. Cab riders also get a special commemorative treat—a scratch-n'-sniff map of the city on which key destinations can be scratched away to reveal the unique smells of the city. The best part is that 100 percent of the cab fares collected by the Joe Boxer Cab go to support breast cancer research through General Motors' charity venture, Concept: Cure. Another example of the company's unique marketing strategies was its tour sponsorship of British comedian Eddie Izzard. It promoted the tour with displays at bus shelters with real underwear, using the tag line "A show so funny, you'll need new underwear." Then, on opening night of the tour, anyone who showed up in his or her underwear got a new pair of Joe Boxers. Graham states that, "I guess the more people talk about you, the better. Joe Boxer is very eccentric."

Discussion Questions

1. What competitive strategy do you think Joe Boxer Company is following? Explain your choice. Do you think it's the most appropriate competitive choice? Why or why not?

2. What functional strategies would Joe Boxer need to be exceptionally skilled at? Explain.

3. Could there be any drawbacks to the competitive actions that Joe Boxer is using? Explain.

4. What other competitors do you think might be in Joe Boxer's strategic group? (You might have to do some shopping to answer this question.) Compare and evaluate the competitive approaches of these competitors.

(*Sources:* Company's Web site (**www.joeboxer.com**), April 27, 2000; and "Photo Opportunities," *Inc.*, May 1999, pp. 104–5.)

CASE #3: Attack of the Big Orange Box

Its stores have been described as big orange boxes. But behind that colorful and cheerful façade is one of the most terrifying competitors in any industry. Home Depot, founded in Atlanta, Georgia, in 1978, is the world's largest home improvement retailer. At last count, it had over 1,200 stores in the United States, Canada, Puerto Rico, and Chile. By 2003, it intends to be operating over 1,900 stores. In 1999, it earned $2.2 billion (up 37 percent over 1998) on total sales revenues of $38 billion (up 26 percent over 1998). According to an industry analyst, Home Depot grosses $130 per square foot (as compared to a typical home center's $50 per square foot) with $50 of operating profit (as compared to $10 for a typical home center). What does it do with this additional profit? That extra money goes right back into its operations—allowing for such things as smarter and well-trained salespeople, better product selection, and lower prices. There's no doubt that Home Depot knows what it wants to do, and it executes its strategies with exacting precision.

Home Depot's approach has been straightforward. Open massive stores (average 110,000 square feet) at swift speeds (average of three a week) and stock them with every possible item a home improvement do-it-yourselfer might need (about 45,000 items per store). Oh, and one final thing: Keep prices as low as possible. It's a strategic combination that has proven disastrous to competitors.

Some of Home Depot's largest "victims" in the 1990s included Ernst Home Centers (Seattle—liquidated in 1996); Handy Andy (Schaumberg, Illinois—liquidated in 1996); Grossman's (Stoughton, Massachusetts—filed for bankruptcy in 1997); Rickel Home Centers (South Plainfield, New Jersey—liquidated in 1998); and Hechinger (Largo, Maryland—liquidated in 2000). There are several other home improvement chains that Home Depot is attacking and likely to shove under. These now-defunct competitors don't include the numerous small mom-and-pop stores that have been crushed by the big orange stores. Those family-owned stores that have been able to withstand Home Depot's intense market push offered two things that the big orange box couldn't match—friendly, personal service and convenient locations. However, Home Depot is pursuing these rivals by challenging them on the only advantages they have left: service and convenience. How? By opening smaller stores that are "locationally convenient."

These stores, called Villager's Hardware, are designed to compete directly with small rivals. Although this new retail concept of Home Depot's is still in the test stage, the strategic implications are enormous.

Home Depot's one potent competitor is Lowe's, another home improvement chain, that is much smaller than Home Depot. However, Lowe's is an agile and smart competitor that will keep the leader on its toes. The big orange competitor isn't going to rest on its laurels. It intends to maintain its position as America's most admired specialty retailer, as voted by *Fortune* magazine for six straight years.

Discussion Questions

1. Describe the competitors in this industry using the industry perspective. Describe them using the marketing perspective. Finally, describe the competitors using the strategic groups approach.

2. What competitive advantage do you think would be most important to a competitor in this industry? Explain your choice.

3. What competitive advantage does Home Depot have and what competitive strategy do you think Home Depot is using? Explain your choices.

4. Would offensive or defensive moves be more important in this industry? Why?

5. Evaluate Home Depot's strategy. Are there any ethical implications to its approach? Why or why not?

(**Sources:** Company's Web site (**www.homedepot.com**), April 27, 2000; C. Daniels, "To Hire a Lumber Expert, Click Here," *Fortune*, April 3, 2000, pp. 267–70; B. Upbin, "Profit in a Big Orange Box," *Forbes*, January 24, 2000, pp. 122–27; J. Frederick, "Home Depot vs. Lowes," *Money*, March 1999, pp. 60–62; and J. R. Hagerty, "Home Depot Raises the Ante, Targeting Mom-and-Pop Rivals," *Wall Street Journal*, January 25, 1999, p. A1.)

ENDNOTES

1. Information from UPS's Web site (**www.ups.com**), April 17, 2000; B. O'Reilly, "They've Got Mail," *Fortune*, February 7, 2000, pp. 100–12; and K. Barron, "Logistics in Brown," *Forbes*, January 10, 2000, pp. 78–83.

2. R. A. D'Aveni, "Coping with Hypercompetition: Utilizing the New 7S's Framework," *Academy of Management Executive*, August 1995, pp. 45–60.

3. P. Kotler, *Marketing Management*, 5th ed. (Upper Saddle River, NJ: Prentice Hall, 2000), pp. 220–23.

4. M. S. Hunt, "Competition in the Major Home Appliance Industry: 1960–1970," unpublished doctoral dissertation, Harvard University, 1972.

5. See Michael E. Porter, *Competitive Strategy: Techniques for Analyzing Industries and Competitors* (New York: Free Press, 1980), Chap 7.

6. D. Dranove, M. Peteraf, and M. Shanley, "Do Strategic Groups Exist? An Economic Framework for Analysis," *Strategic Management Journal*, November 1998, pp. 1029–44; and J. B. Barney and R. E. Hoskisson, "Strategic Groups: Untested Assertions and Research Proposals," *Managerial and Decision Economics*, 11 (1990), pp. 187–98.

7. R. E. Miles and C. C. Snow, *Organizational Strategy, Structure, and Process* (New York: McGraw-Hill, 1978); D. E. Abell, *Defining the Business: The Starting Point of Strategic Planning* (Upper Saddle River, NJ: Prentice Hall, 1980); and M. E. Porter, *Competitive Strategy*.

8. D. F. Jennings and S. L. Seaman, "High and Low Levels of Organizational Adaptation: An Empirical Analysis of Strategy, Structure, and Performance," *Strategic Management Journal*, July 1995, pp. 459–75; J. Tan and R. J. Litschert, "Environment–Strategy Relationship and Its Performance Implications: An Empirical Study of the Chinese Electronics Industry," *Strategic Management Journal*, January 1994, pp. 1–20; D. H. Doty, W. H. Glick, and G. P. Huber, "Fit, Equifinality, and Organizational Effectiveness: A Test of Two Configurational Theories," *Academy of Management Journal*, December 1993, pp. 1196–250; D. Dvir, E. Segev, and A. Shenhar, "Technology's Varying Impact on the Success of Strategic Business Units Within the Miles and Snow Typology," *Strategic Management Journal*, February 1993, pp. 155–62; S. M. Shortell and E. J. Zajac, "Perceptual and Archival Measures of Miles and Snow's Strategic Types: A Comprehensive Assessment of Reliability and Validity," *Academy of Management Journal*, December 1990, pp. 817–32; S. A. Zahra and J. A. Pearce II, "Research Evidence on the Miles-Snow Typology," *Journal of Management*, December 1990, pp. 751–68; and D. C. Hambrick, "Some Tests of the Effectiveness and Functional Attributes of Miles and Snow's Strategic Types," *Academy of Management Journal*, March 1983, pp. 5–26.

9. M. E. Porter, *Competitive Advantage* (New York: Free Press, 1985); and Porter, *Competitive Strategy*.

10. Information on company from Hoover's Online Web site (**www.hoovers.com**), April 21, 2000; and M. B. Grover, "The Odd Couple," *Forbes*, November 18, 1996, pp. 178–81.

11. Information on company from Hoover's Online Web site (**www.hoovers.com**), April 21, 2000; and R. Osborne, "An Unpretentious Giant," *IW*, June 19, 1995, pp. 73–76.

12. C. Y. Coleman, "Gap Profit Rose 32%," *Wall Street Journal*, February 25, 2000, p. B4; S. Perman, "Mend That Gap," *Time*, February 14, 2000, pp. 60–62; L. Lee, "A Savvy Captain for Old Navy," *Business Week*, November 8, 1999, pp. 133–34; and L. Lee, "Clicks and Mortar at Gap.Com," *Business Week*, October 18, 1999, pp. 150–52.

13. D. Eisenberg, "Offices by the Hours," *Time*, February 1, 1999, pp. 40–41; and L. Flynn, "Kinko's Adds Internet Services to Its Copying Business," *New York Times*, March 18, 1996, p. C6.

14. Porter, *Competitive Strategy*, p. 46.

15. S. Oliver, "Niche Airline," *Forbes*, October 23, 1995, p. 122.

16. H. Page, "For Women Only," *Entrepreneur*, May 1996, p. 42; and M. O. Ray, "Catalog Focuses on Women Travelers," *Marketing News*, February 26, 1996, p. 12.

17. M. Warshaw, "Master the Future," *Success*, October 1996, pp. 28–29.

18. "Think Small," *Wall Street Journal*, April 25, 1996, p. A1.

19. T. Stein, "Build a Brand Name," *Success*, July–August 1996, p. 28.

20. Information from company's Web site (**www.yellowbook.com**), January 17, 2000; and J. Gorham, "Page Turner," *Forbes*, May 3, 1999, pp. 90–91.

21. Porter, *Competitive Advantage*, p. 17.

22. C. Campbell-Hunt, "What Have We Learned About Generic Competitive Strategy? A Meta-Analysis," *Strategic Management Journal*, March 2000, pp. 127–54; R. B. Robinson and J. B. Pearce, "Planned Patterns of Strategic Behavior and Their Relationship to Business Unit Performance," *Strategic Management Journal*, 9, no. 1 (1988), pp. 43–60; D. Miller and P. H. Friesen, "Porter's Generic Strategies and Performance: An Empirical Examination with American Data," *Organization Studies*, 7 (1986), pp. 37–55; G. G. Dess and P. S. Davis, "Porter's Generic Strategies as Determinants of Strategic Group Membership and Organizational Performance," *Academy of Management Review*, 21 (1984), pp. 467–88; and D. Hambrick, "An Empirical Typology of Mature Industrial Product Environments," *Academy of Management Journal*, 26 (1983), pp. 213–30.

23. S. Kotha and B. L. Vadlamani, "Assessing Generic Strategies: An Empirical Investigation of Two Competing Typologies in Discrete Manufacturing Industries," *Strategic Management Journal*, January 1995, pp. 75–83; H. Mintzberg, "Generic Strategies: Toward a Comprehensive Framework," *Advances in Strategic Management*, Vol. 5 (Greenwich, CT: JAI Press, 1988), pp. 1–67; C.W.L. Hill, "Differentiation versus Low Cost or Differentiation and Low Cost," *Academy of Management Review*, July 1988, pp. 401–12; J. J. Chrisman, C. W. Hofer, and W. R. Boulton, "Toward a System for Classifying Business Strategies," *Academy of Management Review*, July 1988, pp. 413–28; and P. Wright, "A Refinement of Porter's Generic Strategies," *Strategic Management Journal*, 8, no. 1 (1987), pp. 93–101.

24. C.W.L. Hill and G. R. Jones, *Strategic Management Theory*, 3rd ed. (Boston: Houghton Mifflin, 1995), pp. 178–79; S. Cappel, P. Wright, M. Kroll, and D. Wyld, "Competitive Strategies and Business Performance: An Empirical Study of Select Service Businesses," *International Journal of Management*, March 1992, pp. 1–11; D. Miller, "The Generic Strategy Trap," *Journal of*

Business Strategy, January–February 1991, pp. 37–41; and R. E. White, "Organizing to Make Business Unit Strategies Work," in *Handbook of Business Strategy*, 2nd ed., ed. H. E. Glass (Boston: Warren, Gorham, and Lamont, 1991), pp. 24.1–24.14.

25. F. Andrews, "Dell, It Turns Out, Has a Better Idea Than Ford," *New York Times*, January 26, 2000, p. C12; D. P. Hamilton, "Dell Surpasses Compaq in U.S. Sales," *Wall Street Journal*, October 25, 1999, p. A3; W. J. Holstein, "No Place Like Home," *U.S. News and World Report*, September 27, 1999, pp. 44–45; and M. Treacy and F. Wiersma, "How Market Leaders Keep Their Edge," *Fortune*, February 6, 1995, p. 90.

26. Mintzberg, "Generic Strategies."

27. Kotha and Vadlamani, "Assessing Generic Strategies."

28. The information in this section is based on various articles in L. Fahey, ed., *The Strategic Management Reader* (Upper Saddle River, NJ: Prentice Hall, 1989), pp. 178–205.

29. The information on this section is based on Porter, *Competitive Advantage*, pp. 482–512.

30. W. T. Robinson, "Marketing Mix Reactions to New Business Ventures," The PIMSletter on Business Strategy, no. 42 (Cambridge, MA: Strategic Planning Institute, 1988), p. 9.

7
CORPORATE STRATEGIES

STRATEGIC MANAGEMENT IN ACTION CASE #1

Pipeline Possibilities

At first, the similarities between oil and fiber optics might be hard to grasp or imagine.[1] After all, we're talking about two vastly different industries. One deals with a natural product extracted from massive wells dug into the earth's crust wherever vast natural resource reserves are found and piped to large refineries where the petroleum and natural gas are processed into various forms. This industry has been a fundamental and integral part of the U.S. business landscape from the earliest days of industrialization. The other industry is a high-tech creation that brings to mind crisp digital images, crystal-clear phone conversations, and instantaneous computer-to-computer response times. It invokes visions of the technologically advanced future of telecommunications. How could one possibly be related to the other? Yet, that odd relationship is exactly what strategic managers at the Williams Companies of Tulsa, Oklahoma, saw. As CEO Keith Bailey said, "There are a lot of analogies between steel pipes and fiber pipes." Williams's strategic decision makers envisioned the inherent interrelatedness and growth potential offered by the two seemingly dissimilar products.

Since its founding in 1908, Williams's strategic decision makers have taken the company in many different directions from making agricultural chemicals, building sidewalks, and producing ethanol, to owning and operating natural gas and petroleum pipeline systems. Today, its main divisions include Williams Gas Pipeline, Williams Communications, Williams Energy Services, and Williams International. The company's 1999 revenues were almost $8.6 billion and net income was $221 million. Although its pipeline systems provide the bulk of the company's revenues, continued steady growth from this core area was uncertain as the U.S. economy continued its shift away from heavy industrialization to information. Was a change in Williams' strategic direction necessary or even possible?

A turning point for the company came in the mid-1980s when Williams was looking for unused assets to put into service or to sell off. One of these unused assets was a decommissioned (unused) petroleum and natural gas pipeline located in the Midwest. During this same time, the phone industry was deregulated. AT&T had spun off the "baby Bells" into separate companies. Competition was now allowed and even encouraged in long-distance phone services. Williams's strategic decision makers believed that there were major opportunities offered by this new competitive telecommunications environment—opportunities they might be able to take advantage of. They decided to put that unused pipeline to a new and vastly different use by pulling fiber optic cable through it and starting a wholesale long-distance company. Such an endeavor had never been attempted before, either by the company or by anyone else in the industry, but the company's managers were willing to take a risk. Williams's engineers invented a process whereby a device called a "pig" was launched through the miles of company pipeline in order to thread the fiber optic cable inside. Getting the cable into the pipeline was just the first step, however. Company engineers also had to write the software to manage the fiber optic network. Did the Williams Companies have any experience running a telecommunications business? No! Neither did it have a customer base nor the traditional assets of a telecommunications company, but in four short years its fiber optics network was one of the country's largest. The experience showed Williams that its skills in managing an oil and natural gas pipeline could be successfully transferred to the high-tech world of fiber optics.

Today, Williams is a global leader in energy and communications. It's the largest-volume transporter of natural gas in the United States. It provides a full range of energy services. And, it offers cutting-edge communications services and products to businesses and individuals throughout the world. Although Williams has transformed itself, its roots remain the same: "We're driven by a belief in honest business dealings and an entrepreneurial spirit that relentlessly pursues innovation."

Deciding the optimal mix of businesses and the overall direction of the organization are key parts of corporate strategy. It involves looking at all aspects of the organization—including resources, distinctive capabilities, core competencies, and competitive advantage(s)—and choosing how best to capitalize on what the organization has or how to compensate for what it doesn't have, in light of critical environmental trends and changes. An example of corporate strategy is shown by the calculated risk that strategic managers at the Williams Companies took when they looked at the possibilities beyond the traditional petroleum-based materials distributed through the company's pipelines. They didn't, and couldn't, know how that strategic change would turn out, but they did know that the convergence of certain environmental opportunities and threats coupled with their organization's distinctive strengths and weaknesses had to be addressed. Although not every organizational risk will turn out as financially successful as the Williams Companies's foray into fiber optics communications, the fact remains that strategic decision makers must look at the broad and long-term strategic issues facing their organizations; that is, they must address the organization's corporate strategies.

In this chapter, we're going to examine all the various aspects of corporate strategy. First, we'll look at how it differs for single- and multiple-business unit organizations. In addition, we explore the role of corporate strategy and how it's related to the other types of organizational strategies we've discussed in previous chapters. Then, we'll get into a comprehensive discussion of the various types of corporate strategies that organizations might choose to implement. Finally, we'll talk about what's involved with evaluating and changing corporate strategies.

A BRIEF OVERVIEW OF CORPORATE STRATEGY

Before we get into the actual nuts-and-bolts of corporate strategy, it would be helpful first to look at some basic information about it. What is it, and how is it related to the other types of organizational strategies?

What Is Corporate Strategy?

We first discussed **corporate strategy** back in Chapter 1. We defined it as those strategies concerned with the broad and long-term questions of what business(es) the organization is in or wants to be in, and what it wants to do with those businesses. Because an organization exists for some purpose (remember the organization's vision and mission), carrying out that purpose means strategic managers must make decisions about the best courses of action or best direction for the organization to take. This is the essence of the corporate strategy—determining the overall direction that will enable the organization to best fulfill its purpose and achieve its strategic goals through the business(es) it chooses to be in. One aspect of corporate strategy that affects how an organization can best fulfill its purpose and achieve its strategic goals is whether the organization is in a single business or in multiple businesses.

Single- and Multiple-Business Organizations. A **single-business organization** operates primarily in one industry. A **multiple-business organization** operates in more than one industry. For instance, Coca-Cola can be considered a single-business organization because it competes primarily in the beverage industry. Even though it has multiple products, multiple markets, and multiple outlets, it still is primarily a beverage company. On the other hand, Coke's biggest competitor, PepsiCo, is an example of a multiple-business organization. Its business units include its snack food business (Frito-Lay) and its beverage business (Pepsi, Diet Pepsi, and its other beverages). (PepsiCo also used to have a restaurant operations unit that included Taco Bell, Pizza Hut, and KFC. It chose to spin off this business unit—now known as Tricon—in early 1997.) Although these industries are similar in many ways, they are different industries. PepsiCo has chosen to follow a corporate strategy in which it operates in more than one industry. That is, it operates as a multiple-business organization. Also, look back at the chapter-opening case. The Williams Companies would be another example of a multiple-business organization because it was operating in at least two different industries—oil and natural gas transmission and fiber optic communications. If it hadn't branched into fiber optics, then it still could be considered a single-business organization. Why is this distinction between single- and multiple-business organizations important? It's important because it influences the organization's overall strategic direction, what corporate strategy is followed, and how that strategy is implemented and managed.

Another general aspect of corporate strategy that should be considered before we discuss the specific types of corporate strategy is its relationship to the other types of organizational strategies. What role does corporate strategy play in the organization and how is it related to the functional and competitive strategies?

Relating Corporate Strategy to Other Organizational Strategies

Whereas the corporate strategy establishes the overall direction that the organization hopes to go in, the other organizational strategies—functional and competitive—provide the means or mechanisms for making sure the organization gets there. A good analogy might be a cargo ship headed across the Pacific Ocean with its payload of containers and crates filled with athletic shoes. The ship's captain sets off in a general direction toward the chosen destination, Seattle. However, the ship doesn't sail by itself. It needs the support provided by the crew, the equipment, the fuel, the navigation tools, and so on. If a significant development arises—perhaps a fierce ocean storm—the ship's crew knows what to do and how to respond. They can take actions to keep the ship headed in the chosen direction. An organization's corporate strategy is much the same. It's used to steer the organization in a certain direction, but the other strategies provide the means for making sure that direction is followed and ensuring that significant changes can be understood and managed. What are these "means"? As we've discussed in earlier chapters, the resources, distinctive capabilities, core competencies, and competitive advantage(s) being developed and used in the organization's functional and competitive strategies are the organization's means and mechanisms for moving in the strategic direction it wants to go. For example, if the organization has an overall objective of increasing its market share, appropriate functional and competitive strategies must be in place that support and enhance the competitive advantage it's using to compete and attract customers. If not, the organization is likely to find that it can't attract customers and thus achieve its goal of increasing its market share. Figure 7-1 shows how corporate strategy fits into the overall strategic management in action process.

Each of the various types of organizational strategies plays a significant role in whether the organization does what it's in business to do and whether it

Figure 7-1

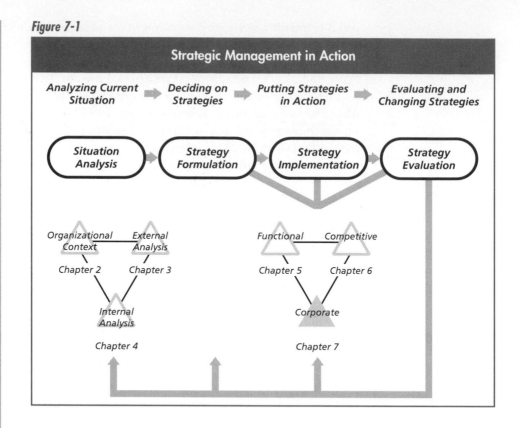

achieves its strategic goals. Coordinating these organizational strategies is critical to managing strategically. The corporate strategy can't be implemented effectively or efficiently without the support provided by the organizational resources, capabilities, and competencies that are developed and used as the competitive and functional strategies are implemented and executed. And, the competitive and functional strategies that are implemented should support the organization's overall strategic direction as reflected by its choice of corporate strategy. In what overall directions can an organization head? That's what we're going to look at next.

What Are the Possible Corporate Strategic Directions?

The number of overall directions strategic managers can choose for the organization is limited. Each of these directions entails the development of certain types of corporate strategies. What are these possible corporate strategic directions? They include (1) moving the organization ahead, (2) keeping the organization where it is, and (3) reversing the organization's decline. What do each of these mean?

Moving ahead means the organization's strategic managers hope to increase its level of operations—that is, to grow. How? By looking at the various corporate growth strategies and choosing one or more that are appropriate given the characteristics and objectives of the particular situation. Choosing to keep the organization where it is means not moving ahead but also not falling behind. This, very simply, is an organizational stability strategy. Finally, reversing the organization's decline describes situations where the organization has minor or major problems and may be seeing a weakening in one or more performance areas. These situations are typically addressed by using organizational renewal strategies.

Now you know the three broad types of corporate strategic direction: organizational growth, organizational stability, and organizational decline–renewal. In the rest of this chapter, we're going to discuss specific corporate strategies that can be used to move the organization in these broad directions and how these corporate strategies are implemented, evaluated, and changed.

ORGANIZATIONAL GROWTH

Organizational growth is viewed as a desirable direction for an organization to go. The pursuit of growth appeals to business and not-for-profit organizations alike. For instance, universities will develop new degree programs or change old ones in order to attract more customers (students) and more resources (funds, books, buildings, equipment, etc.). Or, for example, McDonald's Corporation announces that it's opening additional outlets in various countries throughout Southeast Asia. Also, look at what the Williams Companies did as it added new communications services made possible by the fiber optic cable in its pipelines. All of these strategic decisions and actions involve ways for an organization to grow.

What exactly do we mean by organizational growth? A **growth strategy** involves the attainment of specific growth objectives by increasing the level of an organization's operations. What growth objectives might organizations want to achieve? The typical ones, at least for business organizations, include increases in sales revenues, profits, or other performance measures. However, even not-for-profit organizations have growth objectives; for instance, increasing the number of clients served or patrons attracted, broadening the geographic area of coverage, or even perhaps increasing the number of programs offered. To reach these growth objectives, organizations can use specific growth strategies, which we will look at next.

Types of Growth Strategies

If an organization's strategic managers have decided that growth—in whatever performance area—is the direction they want the organization to go, they can select from some specific corporate growth strategies. Figure 7-2 shows these possibilities. Let's look at each one in more depth.

Concentration. The **concentration strategy** is a growth strategy whereby the organization concentrates on its primary line of business and looks for ways to meet its growth objectives through increasing its level of operations in this primary business. Using the concentration strategy, the organization sticks with its core industry. Thus, when a single-business organization pursues growth, it's using the concentration strategy. As long as desired growth objectives—increases in sales, profits, or whatever—are achieved with this strategy, most organizations will choose to continue with it.

Exactly *how* might an organization use the concentration strategy, particularly when attempting to increase sales and profits? Four concentration options to

Figure 7-2

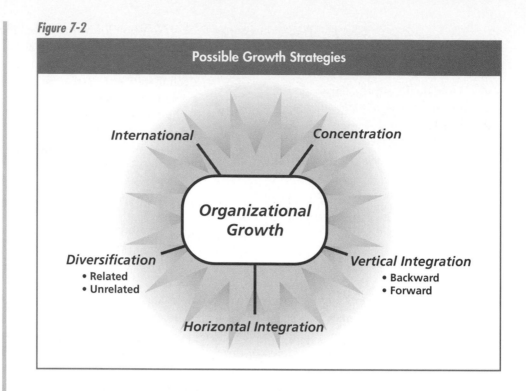

Possible Growth Strategies

International

Concentration

Organizational Growth

Diversification
• **Related**
• **Unrelated**

Vertical Integration
• **Backward**
• **Forward**

Horizontal Integration

use in these circumstances are shown in Figure 7-3.[2] These options, very simply, reflect the various combinations of current product(s) and market(s), and new product(s) and market(s).

The product–market exploitation option describes attempts by the organization to increase sales of its current product(s) in its current market(s). How? The organization will depend on its functional (particularly, marketing and advertising) and its competitive strategies. It might use incentives to get current customers to buy more. Or, it might advertise other uses for the product. For instance, that's what the Church and Dwight Company, Inc. did to increase sales of its Arm & Hammer baking soda. Just think of the numerous ways, beyond using it for baking, consumers are encouraged to use baking soda—as an air freshener, a cleaner, a deodorant, and so forth. L.L. Bean, the catalog company, is using product–market exploitation as it expands its clothing lines, updates its Web site,

Figure 7-3

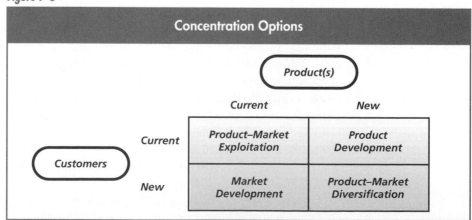

Concentration Options

Product(s)

		Current	*New*
Customers	*Current*	**Product–Market Exploitation**	**Product Development**
	New	**Market Development**	**Product–Market Diversification**

and adds more retail stores—all in an attempt to sell more products to current customers. Of course, organizations try numerous other ways to get current customers to use more of the current product.

Using the product development option, organizations create new products for use by its current market (customers). What is a "new" product? New products may include improved or modified versions of existing products. In addition, new features, options, sizes, and ingredients are often used in developing new products for current customers. For example, Kodak markets film for every conceivable type of camera, light, or situation. Each of these new-product developments is designed to increase sales to its current customers. Another example of product development was when Hershey Food Corporation added new types of candies including Jolly Rancher and Good and Plenty—obviously not chocolates, as are the rest of Hershey's familiar brands—to sell to its current customers.

The market development option, on the other hand, describes when an organization sells its current products in new markets. What are new markets? They might be additional geographic areas, or they might be other market segments not currently served by the organization. For instance, Day Runner, the retail leader in the personal organizer market, developed a line of organizers aimed at 6- to 12-year olds, a segment that it had not sold to previously. This is an example of market development—current product aimed at a new market.

Finally, under the product–market diversification option, the organization seeks to expand into both new products and new markets. At this point, the single-business organization becomes a multiple-business organization because it's now operating in a different industry. An example of product–market diversification can be seen in our chapter-opening case as the Williams Companies moved into both new products (fiber optics products and services) and new markets. We'll discuss the concept of diversification more thoroughly in a later chapter sec-

STRATEGIC MANAGEMENT IN AN E-BUSINESS WORLD

It's a strategic decision that many manufacturers are facing in the ever-changing e-business world. The attractive appeal of selling directly to the final consumer, getting direct customer feedback, and lowering distribution costs by eliminating the middleman is crashing head-on with the reality of the fear of making current distributors and retailers angry. For instance, Rubbermaid Corporation's Web site (**www.rubbermaid. com**) is well designed, but doesn't do the one thing it should: sell merchandise. Rather than risk offending retailers, Rubbermaid's parent company Newell Rubbermaid pulled the plug on Web selling. You can buy Rubbermaid on the Web, but you have to visit the Wal-Mart site to do it (**www.walmart.com**). And, Rubbermaid isn't alone. The Gartner Group estimates that more than 90 percent of manufacturers don't sell online. The main reason: "channel conflict." Manufacturers want to avoid the wrath of retailers that don't want the manufacturers going into business against them. What's your opinion? Should manufacturers sit back and cave in to retailers' demands? Could there be other solutions to this dilemma?

Sources: N. Weinberg, "Not.coms," *Forbes*, April 17, 2000, pp. 424–26; and K. Morris, "Throwing Bricks at the Clicks," *Business Week*, November 15, 1999, p. 39.

tion. To summarize these concentration options, remember that the organization looks for ways to grow in its core business(es) by different combinations of product(s) and market(s). The focus of the concentration strategy is finding ways to meet organizational growth objectives by concentrating on its core business(es).

The advantage of the concentration strategy is that the organization becomes very good at what it does. The strategic managers know the industry and their competitors well. The organization's functional and competitive strategies can be fine-tuned to ensure the development of a sustainable competitive advantage because the strategic managers know what the customers want and they can go about providing it. Everyone in the organization can concentrate on the primary business and on developing and exploiting the key resources, distinctive capabilities, and core competencies that are critical to success in this market.

The main drawback of the concentration strategy is that the organization is vulnerable to industry and other external environmental shifts. This risk can be minimized by remaining alert to significant trends and changes, but strategic managers need to be willing to adjust the organization's direction, should that become necessary. After all, you could be the best buggy whip manufacturer in the world and still not have customers beating down the door for your product. Perhaps an even more relevant example of the risks of the concentration strategy might be the fate suffered by the Royal Typewriter Company when personal computers became the standard equipment for offices and demand for typewriters plummeted. Royal unwisely chose to continue concentrating on typewriter production and as a result doesn't exist anymore. If an organization implements its concentration strategy blindly without understanding the opportunities and threats facing the industry, *not* achieving its growth objectives may be the least of its problems!

It may seem that the concentration strategy is ideal for small organizations, but its use isn't limited to small-size organizations. In fact, large organizations often start off using the concentration strategy and continue to use it to pursue growth. For example, Beckman Coulter, Inc., a Fullerton, California–based organization with annual revenues of over $1.8 billion, has successfully used the concentration strategy to become one of the world's largest medical diagnostics companies.[3] The company has grown by continually innovating new products and processes in this industry. Another example of a large organization that has suc-

Strategic Management in Action

Polaroid, long known for instant photography, is attempting to strategically position itself in its core business even as this core business undergoes radical changes. What does the increasing conversion to a digital world mean for Polaroid? The company's strategic decision makers emphasize the opportunities in such a world. Industry analysts, however, say that the company is in a special position either to exploit its capabilities and competencies in a digital world or to be rendered obsolete by it.

Source: C. H. Deutsch, "Through a Lens, Digitally," *New York Times*, March 27, 2000, p. C1.

cessfully used the concentration strategy is Bose Corporation of Framingham, Massachusetts. The company's innovative audio products have helped make it the world's number-one stereo speaker manufacturer with annual sales of more than $950 million.[4] Again, this organization has grown because of its product development and innovations concentrated in its primary industry.

If the organization isn't able to meet its growth objectives through concentrating on its primary industry, it will begin to look at other corporate growth strategies to meet those goals. Organizations might use the corporate growth strategy of vertical integration.

Vertical Integration (Backward and Forward). The **vertical integration strategy** is an organization's attempt to gain control of its inputs (backward), its outputs (forward), or both. In backward vertical integration, the organization gains controls of its inputs or resources by becoming its own supplier. In forward vertical integration, the organization gains control of its outputs (products or services) by becoming its own distributor, such as through an outlet store or maybe through franchising.

The vertical integration strategy is considered a growth strategy because it expands the organization's operations. However, a single-business organization that implements a vertical integration strategy would still be considered a single-business organization because the organization is not expanding into different industries. It, very simply, is taking another path to meet its organizational growth objectives.

Studies of organizations' vertical integration strategies have shown mixed results in terms of whether the strategy helped or hurt performance. Some of the problems associated with vertical integration include poor performance, higher costs, and a higher risk of bankruptcy.[5] However, studies have also confirmed some of the advantages associated with vertical integration such as better control of costs, more efficient use of inputs, protection of proprietary technology, and creation of barriers to entry to keep out competitors, to name a few.[6] What should we believe? Is the vertical integration strategy an appropriate one to help an organization achieve its growth objectives? In general, we can say that the benefits of vertical integration have been shown to slightly outweigh the costs associated with it.[7] Table 7-1 provides a summary of the benefits and costs associated with vertical integration.

What are some examples of organizations using the vertical integration strategy to meet growth objectives? Oil companies, such as Exxon–Mobil and Amoco–British Petroleum, have long used vertical integration strategies. All have varying levels and types of business operations in the oil exploration, refining, distributing, and selling functions—all the way from oil well to gas pump. Other

TABLE 7-1 Major Benefits and Costs of Vertical Integration	
Benefits	**Costs**
• Reduced purchasing and selling costs	• Reduced flexibility as organization is locked into product(s) and technology
• Improved coordination among functions and capabilities	• Difficulties in integrating various operations
• Protect proprietary technology	• Financial costs of acquiring or starting up

examples of vertical integration from a completely different industry are Walt Disney Company and Time Warner, Inc. and their valued collections of animated cartoon and other fictional characters. Disney, Warner, and other large cartoon producers have taken control over both the programming content *and* the distribution systems to get their programs to the public. Disney has had its Disney Channel for a number of years, and Warner launched its own WB (Warner Brothers) Network showcasing kid favorites such as *Animaniacs, Pinky and the Brain,* and *Sylvester and Tweety.* That's not all that they do, however! These companies also have outlets for distributing (selling) all the consumer products associated with these characters—that is, the Disney and Warner Brothers retail stores where consumers can purchase stuffed animals, clothing, trinkets, jewelry, videos, and any number of their other branded products.

Horizontal Integration. Whereas vertical integration involves an organization remaining in the same industry but supplying its own inputs (resources) or distributing its own outputs (products or services), the **horizontal integration strategy** is expanding the organization's operations through combining with other organizations in the same industry doing the same things it is—that is, it involves combining operations with competitors. This type of growth strategy keeps the organization in the same industry, but provides it with a means of expanding its market share and strengthening its position. Is this legal? Obviously, in the United States, the Federal Trade Commission and the Department of Justice will be assessing the impact of such proposed combinations on the level of competition. They'll be looking to see if it violates antitrust laws. If regulators perceive that competition is likely to be decreased or if the ultimate consumer will be unfairly

e·biz STRATEGIC MANAGEMENT IN AN E-BUSINESS WORLD

The Internet *is* rewriting the old rules about competition and strategy. Some experts believe that the new rules of the e-business world can be exploited through the concept of syndication. Syndication involves the sale of the same product to many customers, who then integrate it with other offerings and redistribute it. It's been a standard practice in the entertainment industry for years. For example, production studios syndicate TV programs to broadcast networks and local stations. Cartoonists syndicate comic strips to newspapers and magazines. How does the concept work in an e-business world? There are three main roles in a syndication strategy. *Originators* create original content. *Syndicators* package content and manage relationships between originators and distributors. *Distributors* deliver content to customers.

Companies can play one role in a syndication network or they may play two or three roles simultaneously. For instance, E*Trade offers its customers a rich assortment of information including financial news, stock quotes, charts, and research. Although it could develop this content on its own, E*Trade chose to purchase its content from outside providers who also sell or syndicate the same information to other broker sites. E*Trade differentiates itself by the way it packages and prices that information. What kind of corporate strategy do you think syndication represents? Explain. Find other examples of the syndication strategy at work. What syndication role(s) is your example playing? Be prepared to share your examples in class.

Source: K. Werbach, "Syndication: The Emerging Model for Business in the Internet Era," *Harvard Business Review,* May–June 2000, pp. 84–93.

impacted, the combined operations of competitors might not be allowed. In industries as diverse as pharmaceuticals, oil, software, and car manufacturing, companies using the horizontal integration strategy have come under FTC scrutiny. However, even with this potential roadblock, many organizations still use the horizontal integration strategy to grow.

For instance, H. J. Heinz Inc., the Pittsburgh-based food-processing company, combined operations with an organic baby food company, Earth's Best, to help its own Heinz baby foods division become more competitive. Another example of the use of the horizontal integration strategy can be seen around the snow-covered mountains of Colorado. Vail Resorts Inc., the nation's largest ski area, wanted to get a lot bigger by combining with other ski areas including Breckenridge, Keystone, and Arapahoe Basin. The Justice Department expressed concern about the proposed combination, however, and studied the potential competitive impact before making a decision about whether to allow the expanded operations. Another example of this particular growth strategy can be seen in the actions of Premier Parks, an amusement-park operator. Its strategy has been to purchase other small amusement-park operators. Horizontal integration is an appropriate corporate growth strategy as long as (1) it enables the company to meet its growth objectives, (2) it can be strategically managed to attain a sustainable competitive advantage, *and* (3) it satisfies legal and regulatory guidelines.

Diversification. We introduced the concept of diversification earlier in our discussion of concentration options. When an organization chooses to go into

Coevolving: Making Synergies Work

"Capturing cross-business synergies is at the heart of corporate strategy—indeed, the promise of synergy is a prime rationale for the existence of the multibusiness corporation." This statement says it all. Organizations diversify in order to exploit anticipated synergies. However, these desired synergies are increasingly difficult to capture. Studies of companies that have successfully achieved synergies show that they've done it, not through the traditional process of collaborating, but through a strategic process called *coevolving.* The concept of coevolution originated in the biology discipline. It refers to the successive changes among two or more ecologically interdependent but separate and unique species such that their evolutionary paths become intertwined over time. As these species adapt to their environment, they also adapt to each other. The result is an ecosystem of partially interdependent species that adapt together. If we take this concept and apply it to business organizations, strategic managers would have to approach diversification efforts differently. First of all, strategies would be determined by business-unit managers rather than by corporate decision makers. And, rather than pursuing collaboration, these managers would pursue coevolution by emphasizing collaboration *and* competition. They would also monitor the number of collaborative links by recognizing that too many links restrict adaptation and too few miss important opportunities for synergies. Coevolving turns the organization into an ecosystem in which the rules are altered, yet it's precisely this unusual twist that gives coevolving companies a competitive edge. What do you think of this concept? Do you agree with its premises? Why or why not?

Source: K. M. Eisenhardt and D. C. Galunic, "Coevolving: At Last, a Way to Make Synergies Work," *Harvard Business Review,* January–February 2000, pp. 91–101.

different products *and* different markets, it *is* diversifying. The **diversification strategy** is a corporate growth strategy in which an organization expands its operations by moving into a different industry. There are two major types of diversification—related and unrelated. **Related (concentric) diversification** is diversifying into a different industry but one that's related in some way to the organization's current operations. **Unrelated (conglomerate) diversification** is diversifying into a completely different industry from the organization's current operations. Any move into a different industry—related or unrelated—automatically makes an organization a multiple-business organization because it's no longer operating in just one industry. Let's look more closely at each of the two different types of diversification.

How can diversification—a term which by itself means "different"—ever be related? In other words, how is a different industry "related" to the one an organization is currently in? An organization using related diversification to achieve its growth objectives is looking for some type of strategic "fit" into which it can transfer its resources, capabilities, and distinctive competencies to the new industry and apply those in such a way that a sustainable competitive advantage results. This is often called the search for strategic "synergy," which very simply is the idea that the performance of the combined operations will be much greater than the performance of each unit separately (the old idea that suggests 2 + 2 can equal 5). How does synergy happen? It comes about because of the interactions and interrelatedness of the combined operations and the sharing of resources, capabilities, and distinctive competencies. A good illustration of what synergy is all about can be seen in a statement made by Steve Perry, the lead singer of Journey (the successful rock music group), when the band got back together in 1996: "Individually, none of us made the music as magically as we collectively make it together."[8] That's what synergy is all about—the combined operations are more "magical" than what each unit could do separately. Figure 7-4 illustrates the various ways that an organization might transfer resources, capabilities, and competencies in order to achieve synergy as it moves into a related industry.

What organizations have used a related diversification strategy? One example is American Standard Companies, based in Piscataway, New Jersey. It is in a variety of businesses including its name-brand bathroom fixtures. It also has diversified into manufacturing air-conditioning and heating units, plumbing parts, and pneumatic truck brakes. What's the strategic fit in these diverse industries? In this case, it happens to be the company's exploitation of its efficiency-oriented manufacturing techniques developed in its bathroom fixtures business and the transferal of these skills to all its other various business units.[9] Another example is DaimlerChrysler AG, the company whose main business is manufacturing Mercedes-Benz and Chrysler automobiles. However, DaimlerChrysler also manufactures heavy-duty trucks—a different type of industry—through its Freightliner unit. Freightliner has diversified into manufacturing school buses and fire vehicles. All of these industries are different but obviously share many common characteristics, which allows DaimlerChrysler to exchange resources, capabilities, and competencies. As with any strategic action, there's no guarantee that related diversification will always succeed at helping the organization reach its strategic goals. Here's an example of a related diversification that didn't work. Anheuser-Busch had entered the snack food industry with its Eagle Snacks business unit because it felt that it could exploit certain marketing synergies (distribution channels, cus-

Figure 7-4

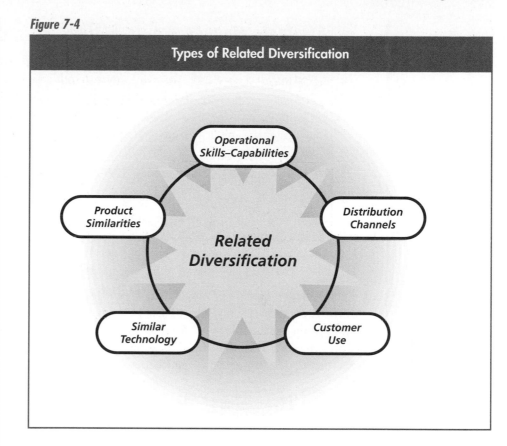

Types of Related Diversification

tomer use, product similarities) developed as the market leader in the beer business and transfer those resources and capabilities to the snack food industry. However, it was never able to develop a sustainable competitive advantage against snack food industry leader, Frito-Lay (a business unit of PepsiCo) in this intensely competitive market. As a result, Anheuser-Busch shut down Eagle Snacks in 1996. Anheuser-Busch had already sold its baseball team, the St. Louis Cardinals, in 1995. However, it can still be considered a related diversified company because, although it's still primarily a beer company, it has also retained its Sea World and Busch Gardens theme parks.

What about unrelated diversification? This growth strategy involves the organization moving into industries in which there is absolutely no strategic fit to be exploited. Why in the world would an organization choose to be in industries where there were no possible connections, relationships, or potential synergies? Most often, an organization will use this approach when its core industry and any related industries don't offer enough growth potential. For the organization to pursue and achieve its growth objectives, it has to look elsewhere. Also, some organizations might choose unrelated diversification if their specialized resources, capabilities, and competencies can't be easily applied to other industries outside its core business. This would obviously limit the options for growth. That's why an organization in this situation might look at the unrelated diversification strategy.

Because of the challenges of strategically managing such entirely different businesses, not many companies use this growth strategy. However, some organizations do use it. For instance, Fortune Brands is a crazy quilt of businesses pro-

Strategic Management in Action

Dennis Kozlowski, CEO of Tyco Inc., has pursued an unrelated diversification strategy. The company is divided into four basic product areas: electronics and telecommunications, health care, fire and security devices, and industrial valves. Go to Tyco's Web site (**www.tyco.com**) and research the company. Does it still appear to be following an unrelated diversification strategy? Explain. Does this strategy appear to have been successful? Explain.

Sources: Company's Web site (**www.tyco.com**), May 8, 2000; and "Deal-a-Day Dennis," *Business Week*, November 1, 1999, p. 164.

ducing market leading products such as Jim Beam bourbon, Moen faucets, DeKuyper cordials, Titleist golf balls, Foot Joy retail outlets, Swingline staplers, and Master Lock padlocks.[10] Another example is Lancaster Colony Corporation, which makes and markets salad dressing, car mats, and fragrant candles.[11] Finally, another example from the global arena is the Charoen Pokphand Group, headquartered in Bangkok, Thailand. Its widely diverse businesses include agricultural business operations (feed production, animal breeding, meat processing, shrimp farming, etc.), industrial operations (production of petrochemicals, leather goods, toys, telecommunications equipment, motorcycles, beer, etc.), and investment properties and investment holdings (real estate and other types of financial investments).[12]

What is our conclusion about the usefulness of the diversification strategy? Is it an effective growth strategy for organizations? Research studies of organizations using the diversification strategy have shown that, for the most part, related diversification is superior to unrelated diversification.[13] If an organization can develop and exploit the potential synergies in the resources, capabilities, and competencies of its diversified operations, then it's likely to create a sustainable competitive advantage. However, the strategic vision of being able to achieve these desired synergies doesn't, by any means, happen easily or automatically. The ability to strategically manage these diverse businesses and develop a sustainable competitive advantage—no matter how related the different industries might be—is crucial. Also, even though organizations' unrelated diversification efforts haven't fared as well in performance measures according to certain

Consider This ◀◀▌

✓ Define growth strategy.

✓ What types of growth objectives might business (for-profit) organizations have? How about not-for-profit organizations?

✓ What are the various corporate growth strategies?

✓ Describe the concentration strategy. (Look at the ways organizations can use it, the advantages and drawbacks, and what types of organizations might use it.)

✓ What is the vertical integration strategy? How is it a growth strategy?

✓ What are some of the benefits and costs associated with the vertical integration strategy?

✓ Describe the horizontal integration strategy. When is it an appropriate growth strategy?

✓ What is the diversification strategy? Describe the two major types of diversification.

✓ Explain the concept of synergy and how it relates to the diversification strategy.

✓ Is diversification an effective growth strategy for organizations? Explain.

research studies, the unrelated diversification strategy probably can be just as valuable a growth strategy as the related one. Once again, it depends on how effectively the diverse operations are strategically managed as a sustainable competitive advantage is sought.[14]

International. Strategic decision makers will undoubtedly have to deal with international issues as they manage strategically. An organization's corporate strategies are likely to involve looking for ways to grow by taking advantage of the potential revenues–profits offered by global markets or to stabilize or revitalize the organization's core operations because of global competitors.[15] One thing we need to clarify up front about international growth is that it's possible for an organization to "go international" as it pursues growth using any of the other corporate growth strategies. This means that if an organization chooses to vertically integrate, then this particular growth strategy could be implemented globally as well as domestically. If a related diversification strategy is being implemented, it could involve combining the operations of organizations in different countries as well as those in just the home market. You need to know about some specific international growth issues, however, and that's why we've also included it as a specific type of growth strategy.

The first issues we need to examine in relation to the international growth strategy are the advantages and drawbacks of international expansion. These are summarized in Table 7-2. Essentially, the advantages and drawbacks of international growth boil down to the fact that it provides significant opportunities for organizations to create and exploit sustainable competitive advantages, but their ability to do so is not easily or automatically achieved. Although international expansion—of markets or operational resources and capabilities—is a common strategic approach, it, like everything else we've discussed, must be managed strategically in order to contribute to the development of a sustainable competitive advantage.

Another international growth issue that must be resolved is what general approach the organization is going to take as it goes international. There are basically three choices: (1) multidomestic, (2) global, and (3) transnational.[16] Each approach entails a unique configuration of two factors: the need for the organization to be responsive to local needs and differences (i.e., the organization's competitive strategy is to pursue a differentiation advantage), and the need for it to

TABLE 7-2 Advantages and Drawbacks of International Expansion	
Advantages	**Drawbacks**
• Could lower operational costs	• Poses greater economic, strategic, and financial risks
• Provides a way to supplement or strengthen domestic growth	• Process of managing strategically becomes more complex and challenging
• Contributes to achieving benefits of economies of scale	• Finding similarities in markets or operational capabilities is more difficult
• Becomes a stronger competitor both domestically and internationally	• Capturing and exploiting advantages is not easy or automatic

globally integrate and standardize operations (i.e., the organization's competitive strategy is to pursue a low-cost advantage). These combinations are shown in Figure 7-5. In the **multidomestic approach** (high local market responsiveness–low global integration of operations), the organization implements its global expansion strategy by decentralizing operational decisions and activities to each country in which it's operating and by tailoring its products and services to each market. This approach is designed with the organization's differentiation advantage in mind. The **global approach** (low local market responsiveness–high global integration of operations) involves the organization providing more standardized products—not tailored to each specific country—and using significantly integrated operations. This approach is designed to enhance the development of a low-cost advantage. Finally, in the **transnational approach** (high local market responsiveness–high global integration of operations), the organization wants to achieve both global efficiency through globally integrating operations *and* product differentiation through tailoring products and services to the local market. You can see that the choice of approach to international strategy hinges on the organization's desired competitive advantage.

The final issue that we need to look at in relation to the organization's international expansion strategy is the various ways an organization enters a foreign

Figure 7-5

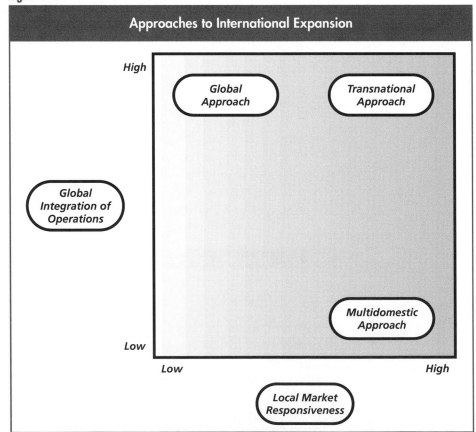

Source: From *Strategic Management: Competitiveness and Globalization* by Hitt, Ireland, Hoskisson. Copyright ©1997 by permission of South-Western College Publishing, a division of International Thomson Publishing Inc., Cincinnati, Ohio, 45227.

> ### Strategic Management in Action
>
> The world's major automobile manufacturers have followed different roads in going global. General Motors prefers minority stakes or alliances even though it took full ownership of Saab. It holds 49 percent of Isuzu Motors, 10 percent of Suzuki Motor, 20 percent of Fuji Heavy Industries (maker of Subaru cars), and 20 percent of Fiat. Ford believes in acquisitions and acquired Jaguar in 1989, Volvo in 1999, and Land Rover in 2000. It owns 33 percent and controls Mazda Motor and is currently pursuing Daewoo and Mitsubishi. DaimlerChrysler prefers outright ownership. Daimler-Benz merged with Chrysler in 1998. It's also currently pursuing a controlling stake in Mitsubishi. Finally, Toyota prefers alliances, just like GM does. It owns 51 percent of Daihatsu and 33.8 percent of Hino Motors, Japan's biggest truck maker. It also builds cars in California with GM. What does this description tell you about strategies for global growth? Update the information on the car makers' alliances and acquisitions.
>
> **Sources:** K. Kerwin, "At Ford, the More Brands, the Merrier," *Business Week*, April 3, 2000, p. 58; K. Kerwin et al., "For GM, Once Again, Little Ventured, Little Gained," *Business Week*, March 27, 2000, pp. 42–43; and K. Bradsher, "Gentlemen, Merge Your Manufacturers," *New York Times*, March 23, 2000, p. C1.

market. The four main ways to do this are exporting, licensing, franchising, and direct investment. In *exporting*, the organization manufactures its products in its home country and then transports those products to other countries to be sold there through an existing distribution channel. *Licensing* is an arrangement in which a foreign licensee buys the rights to manufacture and market a company's product in that country for a negotiated fee. In *franchising*—which is mainly used by service providers—the company sells franchisees in the foreign country limited rights to use its brand name in return for a lump-sum payment and a share of the franchisee's profits. In *direct investment*, the organization actually owns assets in the foreign country.

What are some examples of the international growth strategy? London publisher Dorling Kindersley Holdings PLC has used different ways to grow.[17] It uses direct selling of its products through in-home parties in the various countries it's in, including Australia, Russia, the United States, and of course, Britain. It also has chosen to publish its own titles in foreign markets rather than licensing the titles to some other organization. Why? The company wanted to retain strong control over its marketing. MTV is another company still growing in the global marketplace. MTV is in over 70 million homes in the United States, but over 100 million homes in Asia. It also has expanded into Russia. MTV tailors its programming to specific markets. Another example of a different international experience altogether is the challenge that Newell Rubbermaid Inc., the U.S.-based manufacturer of plastic household and other consumer products, faced as it attempted to enter foreign markets.[18] The company's strategic decision makers soon discovered that its products would have to be tailored to each foreign market—something it hadn't wanted or planned to do. Whereas most Americans preferred Rubbermaid's storage containers in neutral blues and almond colors, consumers in southern Europe preferred red containers, and customers in Holland wanted white. Also, in markets outside the United States, Rubbermaid faced consumer resistance to plastic furniture and cleaning tools. Even though Rubbermaid has a strong brand name and a reputation for quality in the United States, customers in other parts of the world tended to perceive that plastic products were cheap and cheaply made. The H. J. Heinz Company also faced problems with 14 different recipes for its ketchup around the world. That tailor-made ketchup meant higher costs and lower profits. Therefore, Heinz found a way to make the most widely accepted versions at the lowest cost. As Rubbermaid's and Heinz's experiences in international expansion illustrate, even given the vast growth opportunities presented by foreign markets, there are still significant strategic challenges associated with the international growth strategy.

You've now been introduced to all the types of corporate growth strategies that an organization can use to pursue its growth objectives: concentration, vertical integration, horizontal integration, diversification, and international. Next we look at the mechanisms that organizations use to implement these growth strategies.

Implementing Growth Strategies

As we've just discussed, organizations can use specific corporate strategy alternatives to pursue growth objectives, if growth is the overall direction strategic managers have decided to go. However, as we've discussed in previous chapters, just choosing an appropriate strategic alternative is only part of the picture. That strategy must be implemented. For corporate growth strategies, the mechanisms for implementing are fairly straightforward. The three broad options are (1) mergers–acquisitions, (2) internal development, and (3) strategic partnering.

Mergers–Acquisitions. One way that an organization can implement the growth strategies is by "purchasing" what it needs to expand its operations. These purchases are called mergers and acquisitions. You might think "mergers" and "acquisitions" are synonymous, but they're not. Both describe situations when an organization combines its operations with another's, but each involves a different approach. A **merger** is a legal transaction in which two or more organizations combine operations through an exchange of stock, but only one organization entity will actually remain. Mergers usually take place between organizations that are similar in size. And, mergers are usually friendly—that is, a merger is usually acceptable to all the concerned parties. On the other hand, an **acquisition** is an outright purchase of an organization by another. The purchased organization is completely absorbed by the purchasing organization. Acquisitions usually are between organizations of unequal sizes and can be friendly or hostile. Friendly acquisitions are ones in which the combination is desired by the respective organizations. In a hostile acquisition, called a **takeover**, the organization being acquired doesn't want to be acquired. In fact, the target of a takeover often will take steps to prevent the acquisition. Table 7-3 lists some possible defensive manuevers a takeover target might use to scare off the acquiring organization.

How common are mergers and acquisitions for implementing organizations' growth strategies? Research has shown that the popularity of mergers and acquisitions as a strategic growth mechanism seems to go in cycles.[19]

TABLE 7-3 Possible Defensive Mechanisms Used by Takeover Targets
• Buys up (repurchases) its stock
• Looks for a "friendly" merger partner, often referred to as a *white knight*
• Takes on significant amounts of long-term debt that become due and payable if it's acquired, often referred to as a *cyanide pill*
• Calls in government regulators to initiate an antitrust suit
• Staggers the terms (time frames) its board members serve
• Gives current shareholders the right to purchase additional stock at a substantial discount, often called a *poison pill*

Keep in mind that a merger or acquisition could be used by an organization when implementing *any* of the growth strategies—concentration, vertical integration, horizontal integration, diversification, or global. The main distinguishing feature of mergers–acquisitions as a mechanism for implementing growth strategies is that the organization is "buying" its way into expanded operations. We want to look next at another alternative mechanism for implementing the growth strategies.

Internal Development. In **internal development**, the organization chooses to expand its operations by starting a new business from the ground up. In this approach, the organization believes that it has the necessary resources, capabilities, and competencies to "start from scratch." Using internal development, strategic managers choose to provide the resources and develop the capabilities needed to meet the desired growth objectives internally rather than dealing with the risks, aggravations, and challenges of combining two or more different organizations. This doesn't mean, though, that there aren't risks, aggravations, and challenges associated with starting a new business. But, again, with internal development, strategic managers believe that the best way for the organization to expand its operations in order to achieve growth objectives is to do it themselves.

When would purchasing (mergers or acquisitions) be preferable, and when would doing it yourself (internal development) be preferable? Research has shown that the choice between the two approaches depends on these factors: (1) the new industry's barriers to entry, (2) the relatedness of the new business to the existing

Strategic Management—The Global Perspective

PriceSmart is rolling out membership shopping across Central America. The membership concept, where store customers pay an annual fee to join a "club" so they can access the store's low prices and bulk purchases, is being brought to shoppers in Panama, Costa Rica, Honduras, Guatemala, and El Salvador. Internal expansion plans call for further stores in Nicaragua, the Dominican Republic, and Trinidad and Tobago. Rather than acquiring regional retailers, PriceSmart chose to develop stores on its own. Do you think this is the best approach? Why or why not?

Source: "Attention, Central American Shoppers," *Latin Trade*, February 2000, pp. 25–26.

one, (3) the speed and development costs associated with each approach, (4) the risks associated with each approach, and (5) the stage of the industry life cycle.[20] These factors are summarized in Table 7-4.

Although both mergers–acquisitions and internal development continue to be popular ways to implement the growth strategy, organizations are using some newer approaches. These tactics fall under the category of "strategic partnering," which we'll look at next.

Strategic Partnering. Is it possible for an organization to exploit the benefits of combining operations with other organization(s) in order to pursue growth objectives while also minimizing the challenges and risks of buying a business or developing one from scratch? Welcome to the world of strategic partnering! Exactly what is **strategic partnering**? It's a situation when two or more organizations establish a legitimate relationship (partnership) by combining their resources, distinctive capabilities, and core competencies for some business purpose. This umbrella term covers a variety of situations from loose relationships among partnering organizations to formal legal arrangements among the strategic partners. These cooperative arrangements can be used to implement any of the growth strategies. For instance, an organization may decide to strategically partner with one of its suppliers or distributors (vertical integration), or it may develop a strategic relationship with one of its competitors (horizontal integration) or with an organization in a related industry (related diversification). Rather than buying or internally developing what's needed to expand its operations, an organization's strategic decision makers instead might choose to develop a strategic partnership. The three main types of strategic partnerships are: (1) joint ventures, (2) long-term contracts, and (3) strategic alliances.

In a **joint venture**, two or more separate organizations form a separate independent organization for strategic purposes. In this cooperative arrangement, the strategic partners will typically own equal shares of the new joint venture. A joint venture is often used when the partners do not want to or cannot legally join together permanently. Instead, the partners create this separate entity to perform whatever business activity they're joining together to do. These business activities range from manufacturing to marketing a product or service. Also, a joint venture is a popular partnering method in global growth strategies because it can minimize the financial and political–legal constraints that plague mergers–acquisitions and internal development. For example, a long-running joint venture is the New

TABLE 7-4 Mergers–Acquisitions or Internal Development	
Use Merger–Acquisition When:	**Use Internal Development When:**
• Maturity stage	• Embryonic or growth stage
• High barriers to entry	• Low barriers to entry
• New industry not closely related to existing one	• New industry closely related to existing one
• Unwilling to accept time frame and development costs of starting new business	• Willing to accept time frame and development costs of starting new business
• Unwilling to accept risks of starting new business	• Willing to accept risks of starting new business

United Motor Manufacturing Company (NUMMI) formed by General Motors and Toyota in 1984. This joint venture was created to help introduce a new automobile production system into the United States. Another example of a joint venture between global companies is the strategic partnership between Siemens (a German company) and Corning (a U.S. company). This joint venture, Siecor, was entered into to create a fiber optic cable business. Finally, Hewlett-Packard Company, the computer equipment manufacturer, has had numerous joint ventures with various suppliers around the globe.

Another type of strategic partnership arrangement is the **long-term contract**. This is a long-term legal contract between organizations covering a specific business purpose. Long-term contracts have been used typically between an organization and its suppliers. They're often viewed as a new variation of vertical integration without the organization's having to buy the supplier or internally develop its own supply source. Instead, in this way, the organization locks a supplier into a long-term relationship wherein both partners understand the importance of developing resources, capabilities, and core competencies for a sustainable competitive advantage. The organization benefits by having an assured source of supplies that meets its cost and quality expectations. The supplier benefits by having an assured outlet for its supplies. The partners in a long-term contract often find it in their best interest to share resources, capabilities, and core competencies in order for both to capture the potential benefits. Again, that's the beauty of the long-term contract as a strategic partnership. The partners recognize and accept that they must work together in order for both to profit.

The last type of strategic partnership we're going to discuss is the **strategic alliance** in which two or more organizations share resources, capabilities, or competencies to pursue some business purpose. You might be saying to yourself about now that this sounds very similar to a joint venture. In the case of a strategic alliance, however, there's no formation of a separate entity. Instead, the partnering organizations simply share whatever they need to in order to do whatever they want to do. Most often, strategic alliances are pursued in order to encourage

Why Alliances Make Sense

Companies worldwide are finding ways to build bridges to each other. Although these resulting alliances may not always work, they often make more sense than acquisitions do. Here are some reasons why alliances make sense: flexibility and informality of arrangements promote efficiencies; provide access to new markets and technologies; entail less paperwork when creating and disbanding projects; risks and expenses are shared by multiple parties; independent brand identification is kept and can be exploited; working with partners possessing multiple skills can create major synergies; rivals can often work together harmoniously; alliances can take on varied forms from simple to complex; dozens of participants can be accommodated in alliance arrangements; and antitrust laws can protect R&D activities. Do alliances make strategic sense? One expert says that "The future of business is that fewer companies will succeed by going it alone."

Sources: D. Sparks, "Partners," *Business Week*, October 25, 1999, pp. 106–12, and D. Brady, "When Is Cozy Too Cozy?" *Business Week*, October 25, 1999, pp. 127–30.

product innovation, bring stability to cyclical businesses, expand product line offerings, or to cement relationships with suppliers, distributors, or competitors. For example, PepsiCo and Lipton joined together to sell canned iced tea beverages jointly. PepsiCo brought to the alliance its marketing strengths in canned beverages, and Lipton brought its recognized tea brand and customer base. Although each organization could have attempted this on its own, the hurdles to developing a sustainable competitive advantage would have been much higher. By combining their strengths, the two partners hoped to dominate this product line. Another example of a strategic alliance would be the partnership arrangement between Tyson Foods (U.S.), C-Itoh (Japan), and Provemex (Mexico). This alliance was established to process Japanese-style *yakatori* chicken products for export to Japan. Under this arrangement, Tyson Foods found a new market for its dark chicken meat; Provemex, the second-largest chicken producer in Mexico, provided the know-how and inexpensive labor to debone the dark meat for use in the *yakatori* products; and C-Itoh provided the marketing outlet for the chicken products in Japan. As you can see, each partner in the strategic alliance can reap the benefits of expanded operations by contributing to the alliance its unique resources, capabilities, or competencies.

Strategic partnering arrangements are growing in popularity among organizations.[21] Keep in mind that the intent of all of these types of strategic partnerships—joint venture, long-term contract, and strategic alliance—is to gain the benefits of expanding business operations (growth) while minimizing some of the drawbacks of buying or internally developing the means to expand. Strategic partnerships should be approached with the same careful preparation and diligence as an acquisition–merger or an internally developed business. There's no guarantee that the hoped-for strategic benefits will be realized using these arrangements, and there's no doubt that trust among all strategic partners is a critical component to making these arrangements successful.[22]

We have now discussed all the ways that an organization can implement its growth strategies. We will look next at when the organization's strategic managers decide that the best organizational direction is for it to stay where it is.

> ## Consider This ◀◀|
>
> ✓ How can international growth be used in all the other growth strategies?
> ✓ Describe the advantages and drawbacks of international expansion.
> ✓ Compare and contrast the three approaches an organization can take as it goes international.
> ✓ What are the four main ways an organization can enter a foreign market?
> ✓ What is a merger? An acquisition? A takeover? When are mergers and acquisitions preferable for implementing an organization's growth strategies?
> ✓ What is internal development? When is it preferable for implementing an organization's growth strategies?
> ✓ What is strategic partnering?
> ✓ Compare and contrast the three main types of strategic partnerships.

ORGANIZATIONAL STABILITY

Although it may seem inconceivable that an organization would want to stand still, there are times when its resources, distinctive capabilities, and core competencies are stretched to their limits and expanding operations any further might risk the organization's competitive advantage. At times like these, the organization's strategic managers may decide that it's best for the organization to stay where it is. The **stability strategy** is one in which the organization maintains its current size and current level of business operations.

When Is Stability an Appropriate Strategic Choice?

When might strategic managers decide that the stability strategy is the most appropriate direction for the organization? One situation might be that the industry is in a period of rapid upheaval with several key industry and general external forces drastically changing, making the future highly uncertain. At times like this, the strategic managers might decide that the prudent course of action is to sit tight and wait to see what happens. This doesn't mean that organizational resources and capabilities would be allowed to deteriorate. Quite the contrary! In order to stabilize and maintain the organization's current position, it's important to keep up levels of investment and commitment in the various business functions or units. The stability strategy shouldn't mean slipping backward, but it also doesn't mean moving ahead. It's simply stabilizing at the current level of operations.

Another situation in which strategic managers might pursue the stability strategy is if the industry is facing slow- or no-growth opportunities. In this instance, the strategic managers might decide to keep the organization operating at its current levels before making any strategic moves into new industries. This period of stability would allow them time to analyze their strategic options, such as diversification, vertical integration, or even perhaps horizontal integration, to address the disadvantages of being in a low- or no-growth industry.

An organization's strategic managers might also choose a stability strategy if it has just completed a frenzied period of growth and needs to have some "down" time in order for its resources and capabilities to build up strength again. For example, in its early days of rapid growth, Apple Computer Inc. would stabilize for a short period of time because it didn't have the managerial resources it needed to effectively manage the company's operations at that level. Once its essential managerial resources (and probably other resources, as well) were in place, Apple would once again pursue rapid growth.

> ### *Strategic Management in Action* ▶
>
> The sporting goods industry is a mature one. Although Rawlings Sporting Goods, based in St. Louis, dominates the market for baseball equipment, it lags far behind other sporting goods manufacturers (Nike, Spalding, and Wilson). Interest in baseball has been stagnant for years in the face of newer, hipper sports such as in-line skating and lacrosse. Where does this leave the over 100-year-old Rawlings? With revenues that have been stagnating for years. Check out the company's Web site (**www.rawlings.com**). Is it still following a stability strategy? Explain.
>
> *Sources:* Company's Web site (**www.rawlings.com**), May 8, 2000; and M. M. Stichnoth, "Baseball and Beyond," *New York Times*, March 15, 1998, p. BU4.

Stability might also be an appropriate strategy for large firms in a large industry that's in the maturity stage of the industry life cycle. In this situation, if profits and other performance results are satisfactory *and* if strategic decision makers are relatively risk averse, they may choose to "stay as they are" rather than pursue growth.

Finally, whereas most strategic managers in large organizations prefer pursuing growth (and often are rewarded for pursuing growth), many small business owners may follow a stability strategy indefinitely. Why? These small business owners may feel that their business is successful enough just as it is and that it adequately meets their personal objectives.

Although there may be other times when a stability strategy is the most appropriate organizational direction, these are the most common situations. One thing we need to emphasize about the stability strategy is that it typically should be a short-run strategy. Because industry and competitive conditions don't stop changing while an organization stabilizes, it's important for an organization's strategic managers to get its resources, capabilities, and core competencies aligned and strengthened once again, so it doesn't lose its competitive position or competitive advantage.

Implementing the Stability Strategy

There's not much to implementing the stability strategy. Primarily it involves *not* expanding the level of the organization's operations. In other words, during stability, the organization won't be doing such things as putting new products out on the market, developing new programs, or adding production capacity. This doesn't mean that organizational resources, capabilities, and core competencies don't change during periods of stability—they just don't expand. In fact, organizations often use the period of stability to assess operations and activities, and strengthen and reinforce those that need bolstering or revitalizing. The stability period essentially gives the organization an opportunity to "take a breath" and prepare itself for the return to pursuing growth and the strategic challenges associated with that particular corporate strategy. For example, at Geon Company, one of the largest global producers of polyvinyl chloride resins, the stability strategy implemented by CEO William Patient was designed to "put it into a position to succeed" in a fiercely competitive market.[23] Once Geon had strengthened its resources, capabilities, and core competencies, it was ready to grow once again.

As a possible direction for the organization to go, stability can be an appropriate choice. Again, it's important to remember that stability probably should be a short-run strategy. If the organization becomes too complacent, it's susceptible to losing its competitive position. And, if the organization finds during its period of stability that significant organizational weaknesses exist or that its performance, using whatever measures are appropriate, is declining, then it may be necessary for the organization to look at a different strategic direction altogether—organizational renewal. That's the next topic we will discuss.

ORGANIZATIONAL RENEWAL

The popular business periodicals frequently report stories of organizations that aren't meeting their strategic objectives or whose performance is declining. It's obvious that strategic managers in these organizations have *not* done an effective job of managing strategically and have been unable to develop or exploit a sustainable competitive advantage. The organization is in trouble and something needs to be done or it can't achieve high levels of success; maybe even in the worst-case scenario, it won't survive. Given these circumstances, the organization's situation can be described as "falling back," and the strategic managers need to implement strategies that reverse the organizational decline and put it back on a more appropriate path to successfully achieving its strategic goals. The strategies used to accomplish this are called the **renewal strategies**. In this section, we will discuss the two main types of organizational renewal strategies—retrenchment and turnaround—and the mechanisms used to implement them. However, first we need to look at some of the possible causes of corporate decline and also at some indicators of possible decline.

We can say that, generally speaking, an organization's strategic managers don't deliberately make ineffective or inappropriate strategic decisions that are going to cause the organization to decline. However, strategic decisions they do make or strategies that they do implement may create conditions that keep the organization from developing or exploiting a sustainable competitive advantage. Without this competitive advantage, it's going to be difficult for an organization to meet its strategic goals and have desirable performance results. What leads to this situation? What have researchers identified as some of the causes of corporate decline? Figure 7-6 shows the main ones.[24] As you can see, the main reason behind corporate decline is poor management. In fact, all of the other causes of

Figure 7-6

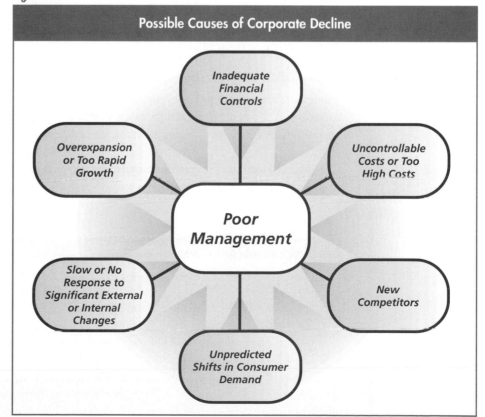

decline can be traced back to poor management, as well. If strategic managers are inept or incompetent or they don't strategically manage all aspects of the organization, then organizational performance is likely to suffer. And, strategic decisions to overexpand or expand too rapidly indicate poor management judgment. In addition, if the organization has inadequate financial controls or if costs are out of control or too high to be competitive, then strategic managers aren't being effective. Likewise, there's no excuse for not anticipating new competitors or shifts in consumer demand. Strategic managers don't have crystal balls that give them all the answers, but they should—as we discussed in Chapter 3—systematically scan and evaluate the external environment for significant changes and trends. There's no excuse for strategic managers not to be aware of what's happening in their external environment. That's simply poor management! Finally, managers who are slow to respond or who never respond to significant changes in their external and internal situations are doing a poor job of managing strategically. Inertia can be a kiss of death in the dynamic and complex competitive environment that most organizations face!

Can strategic managers estimate when performance declines might be imminent? Are there certain signals to look for? Yes, some signs indicate that the organization might have some strategic problems that would require the eventual implementation of renewal strategies.[25] These are listed in Table 7-5. Again, if everyone in the organization is managing strategically and focused on developing and exploiting the organization's competitive advantage, then performance declines shouldn't happen. However, we know that this scenario of perfection isn't likely or probably even realistic. Even the best-managed organizations sometimes find that performance isn't what was expected and performance results aren't meeting strategic goals. If the organization's overall performance—in whatever ways it's measured—is falling back, then organizational renewal strategies may need to be implemented.

Types of Renewal Strategies

There are two main types of organizational renewal strategies: retrenchment and turnaround. Both are designed to halt the organization's declining performance and to return it to more desirable performance levels. Let's look at each one more closely.

Retrenchment. The **retrenchment strategy** is a common short-run strategy designed to address organizational weaknesses that are leading to performance

TABLE 7-5   Signs of Potential Performance Decline
• Excess numbers of personnel • Unnecessary and cumbersome administrative procedures • Fear of conflict or taking risk • Tolerating work incompetence at any level or in any area • Lack of clear vision, mission, or goals • Ineffective or poor communication within various units and between various units

declines. In a retrenchment situation, an organization doesn't necessarily have negative financial returns. Although it may have had some time periods when revenues didn't cover expenses, this isn't the typical sign that an organization needs to retrench. Instead, the usual situation in retrenchment is that the organization hasn't been able to meet its strategic objectives, in whatever areas. Revenues and profits may be declining, but aren't negative, and it needs to do something to reverse the slide or it soon may face significant performance declines leading to severe financial problems.

The word *retrenchment* is a military term that describes situations when a military unit "goes back to the trenches" in order to stabilize, revitalize, and prepare for entering battle again. That's pretty descriptive of what organizations must do, as well, in retrenching. The organization's strategic managers must stabilize operations, replenish or revitalize organizational resources and capabilities, and prepare to compete once again. At a later point, we'll look at how retrenchment strategies are implemented.

What happens if the organization's circumstances are more serious? What if the organization's profits aren't just declining, but instead there *aren't* any profits, just losses? And, what if other performance results are also significantly low or maybe negative? This type of situation calls for a more dramatic strategic response.

Turnaround. The **turnaround strategy** is an organizational renewal strategy that's designed for situations in which the organization's performance problems are more serious. This organization has to be "turned around" or its very survival is in jeopardy. Some well-known companies that have had to use a turnaround strategy include Sears, Kmart, Chrysler, Motorola, Mitsubishi, and Apple. In each of these instances, the organization faced severe external and internal pressures and had to make strategic changes in order to remain a viable entity. There's no guarantee that a turnaround strategy will accomplish the desired results and make the organization a strong competitor once again, but without it the organization is doomed to fail.

How are both retrenchment and turnaround strategies implemented? What are the strategic tools and mechanisms that strategic managers can draw on to renew the organization's performance? That's what we want to look at next.

Implementing Renewal Strategies

The implementation of both organizational renewal strategies is primarily dependent on two strategic actions: cutting costs and restructuring. A retrenchment strategy typically will not involve as extensive a use of these measures as a turnaround strategy will. The retrenchment strategy may, in fact, require only selected cost cutting to get organizational performance back on track. We need to look more closely at each of these implementation tools.

Cost Cutting. In Chapter 6 we discussed the concept of having low costs or even having the *lowest* costs in the industry as a source of competitive

Consider This ◀◀|

✓ What is a stability strategy?

✓ Why might an organization choose a stability strategy?

✓ Describe the implementation of a stability strategy.

✓ Why is it important that a stability strategy be a short-run strategy?

✓ What are renewal strategies?

✓ Describe some of the causes of corporate decline.

✓ Why is poor management the root problem of almost all organizational decline?

✓ What are some signs that declining performance might be imminent?

✓ Describe the two types of organizational renewal strategies.

advantage. However, cost cutting as a response to declining performance has little to do with developing a sustainable competitive advantage. Instead, the necessity to cut costs is approached as a tactic to bring the organization's performance results back in line with expectations. The organization's strategic managers want to avoid severely cutting costs in those critical areas the organization feels it needs in order to retain or exploit a competitive advantage, however weak that advantage may be. As they cut costs, the organization's strategic managers are trying to revitalize the organization's performance (retrenchment) or save the organization (turnaround).

Cost cutting can be approached from the angle of across-the-board cuts (implemented in all areas of the organization) or selective cuts (implemented in selected areas of the organization). Obviously, in a turnaround strategy, the cuts may need to be more extensive and comprehensive—that is, wide and deep.

How will organizations try to cut costs? Strategic decision makers will evaluate to see if there are any waste, redundancies, or inefficiencies in work tasks and activities (i.e., in the organization's capabilities) that could be eliminated. They'll also look to see if certain resources could be eliminated or used more efficiently. For example, UPS found that it could cut costs by over $200,000 annually by changing the lightbulbs in the "Exit" signs in its buildings to a lower wattage. That might not seem like a significant amount to an organization whose revenues are in the multibillions, but keep in mind that this is just one small cost cut with savings that could be redirected to resources or capabilities that UPS needs for a sustainable competitive advantage, or the cost cut savings can be applied directly to the bottom line. Either way, the company comes out ahead!

Generally, if additional cuts are needed to keep performance from declining further, the strategic managers may have to look at reducing and eliminating certain work tasks and activities or even entire departments, units, or divisions. We'll discuss this type of more serious cost cutting when we get into the restructuring section and look at reengineering and downsizing as strategic implementation options.

Restructuring. Another strategic action that an organization might take as it implements a retrenchment or turnaround strategy is restructuring its operations. An organization can restructure its operations in a number of ways. In many instances, the restructuring involves the organization's strategic managers deciding to refocus on their primary business(es) as it sells off, spins off, liquidates, reengineers, or downsizes. In fact, organizational refocusing has been found to be the most beneficial form of restructuring an organization can do.[26] Let's look closer at the various ways that an organization can restructure and refocus itself.

One possible strategic action that the organization might take is to sell off one or more of its business units. Frequently, when an organization finds that a business unit isn't performing up to expectations or that the business unit doesn't fit in with the organization's long-run direction or plans, strategic managers will choose to sell it. The process of selling off a business to someone else where it will continue as an ongoing business is called **divestment**. To whom might an organization sell the business unit? Three possible types of buyers include independent investors, other companies, and the management of the business unit being divested. For example, at Figgie International—a conglomerate of businesses with products ranging from protective breathing equipment for firefighting and industrial use to thermometers, barometers, hygrometers, and other precision measur-

Strategic Management—The Global Perspective

BMW, the German luxury car manufacturer, needs to chart a new strategic course. Chairman Joachim Milberg is taking the first step by selling off the Land Rover unit to Ford Motor Company. That action would free BMW to concentrate its resources and capabilities where it traditionally has seen its biggest payoff—in luxury cars. However, even that strategic action has its risks. To be a strong competitor in the global market, BMW has to look for ways to expand its model range.

Sources: C. Tierney, "BMW: Unloading Rover May Not Win the Race," *Business Week*, April 3, 2000, p. 59; and M. Karnitschnig, "BMW Could Use a Little Skid Control," *Business Week*, January 24, 2000, p. 134.

ing devices—a critically needed turnaround strategy included selling off a dozen of these widely diverse businesses to other companies. Keep in mind from our earlier discussion of ways to implement corporate growth strategies that one avenue for organizations to grow is through acquisition. Those acquisitions have to come from somewhere. So, when one company is acquiring, that means another company has to be selling.

Another possibility for restructuring the organization is to remove a business unit by spinning it off. A **spin-off** typically involves setting up the business unit as a separate business through a distribution of shares of stock. For example, in the late 1990s, 3M Company spun off its data storage and imaging business into a separate company called Imation. Why did 3M choose to spin off this business unit? Corporate managers at 3M had to make some hard choices about resource allocation and, because this unit had mediocre earnings compared to other units, they chose to spin it off as a separate business.[27]

What happens if there's no buyer for a business unit or if there's no possibility of spinning off the business unit separately? The only strategic option at that point might be **liquidation**, which is shutting down the business completely. A business unit that's liquidated will not continue as an ongoing, viable business. There may be ways to sell off the business's assets, but that's the only revenue an organization could see from liquidating a business unit. As you can well imagine, liquidation is often a strategic action of last resort. It may be the only option if a turnaround strategy hasn't had the intended effects.

If an organization finds that performance in any of its various business units or areas isn't up to par and isn't meeting strategic goals, another implementation option that an organization might use in restructuring is to rethink completely the way it works. This fundamental rethinking and radical redesign of the organization's business processes is called **reengineering**.[28] Reengineering is a procedure in which traditional assumptions and approaches are questioned and the organization's work activities are radically redesigned and changed. When an organization's strategic managers choose to reengineer, they're asking, "How would we do this if we started from scratch and we didn't have to do it the way we've always done it?" During reengineering, the organization's current resources, capabilities, and core competencies are irrelevant because strategic managers are looking to see if work processes can be designed better. As you can well imagine, reengineering involves radical and often drastic change. Yet, in a retrenchment or turnaround situation, these types of extreme changes may be necessary to get the organization and its various units back on track. For example, at Cigna Corporation, reengineering of its property and casualty claims unit and its system unit resulted in a 1,200 percent improvement in transaction processing time and a 42 percent reduction in costs.[29] Although many reengineering efforts show significant performance improvements, not all have.[30] There's no guarantee that a reengineering effort is going to work. Why? Reengineering involves radical changes, and not every organization that's attempted it has been able to do the type of extensive analysis required, or the organization may have been unwilling to make the drastic changes involved. Again, if the organization is faced with a situation in which it has to make some changes or find its performance results continuing to decline, then reengineering may be an action chosen by strategic managers.

Part of an organization's cost cutting or restructuring efforts might involve **downsizing**, which is an organizational restructuring in which individuals are laid off from their jobs. Although downsizing can be a quick way to pare costs, simply cutting the number of employees without some type of strategic analysis of where employee cuts might be most beneficial is dangerous.[31] In order to maintain strategic competitiveness for the eventual emergence of the organization from retrenchment or turnaround—if and when that happens—it's important that downsizing be done for the right reasons. In fact, research has shown that downsizing efforts actually improve stockholder wealth when they're done for strategic purposes.[32] How can strategic managers ensure that their downsizing actions are appropriate and effective? Table 7-6 lists some recommendations.[33]

The final option we want to look at for restructuring the organization is one of last resort: bankruptcy. **Bankruptcy** is the failure of a business and involves dissolving or reorganizing the business under the protection of bankruptcy legislation. It's typically the result of years of significant performance declines during which other restructuring or cost cutting actions have had little effect or have not been implemented effectively. What happens when an organization "goes bank-

Strategic Management—The Global Perspective

Deutsche Bank is struggling to be one of the top five banking companies in the world. It has 1,500 local offices and 7 million retail banking customers, and the largest branch banking network in Germany. Yet, that network barely makes a profit and drags down the bank's overall performance. To address that weakness, Chairman Rolf-Ernst Breuer is looking at a radical strategic change. He is contemplating letting someone else have a controlling stake in his bank's branches. Breuer contends that the Internet will cannibalize conventional banking channels and lead to a continued reduction of profit margins. However, he also believes that the Internet opens up new opportunities for geographic expansion across Europe without having physical locations. It's a strategic gamble, but one that leaves little choice to an organization that's struggling to correct its performance declines.

Sources: C. Rhoads and E. Portanger, "Dresdner Scraps Deutsche Bank Merger," *Wall Street Journal*, April 6, 2000, p. A3; and E. L. Andrews, "Streamlining a German Blimp," *New York Times*, February 29, 2000, p. C1.

TABLE 7-6	Recommendations for Making Downsizing Appropriate and Effective

- Communicate openly and honestly about needed actions
- Clarify goals and expectations before, during, and after downsizing
- Eliminate unnecessary work *activities* rather than making across-the-board cuts in *people*
- Outsource work if it can be done more inexpensively and more effectively elsewhere
- Provide whatever assistance is appropriate to downsized individuals
- Counsel, communicate with, and seek input from those employees not downsized
- Ensure that those individuals remaining after downsizing know they are a valuable and much-needed organizational resource

rupt"? The act of going bankrupt was dramatically changed on October 1, 1979, with the passage of the Bankruptcy Reform Act.[34] This legislative change encouraged firms to reorganize (Chapter 11 bankruptcy) rather than liquidate their assets (Chapter 7 bankruptcy). Therefore, the aftermath of bankruptcy depends on which type of bankruptcy filing is used. An organization in Chapter 7 bankruptcy will have its assets liquidated by the court with the proceeds used to pay off all outstanding obligations (debts). An organization in Chapter 11 bankruptcy reorganizes its debts and is protected from creditors collecting on their debts until such time it can emerge from bankruptcy. Although bankruptcy may not be a preferred strategic action, if an organization's turnaround strategy hasn't been effective, it may be the *only* option open to the organization.

We need to clarify a couple of issues regarding the alternatives for implementing the organizational renewal strategies. One issue is that these strategic actions typically aren't used one at a time and by themselves. Instead, it's often necessary for the organization to use some combination of these alternatives as it struggles to regain or develop a sustainable competitive advantage. In fact, most organizations faced with the need to retrench or to do some serious restructuring (needed for a turnaround) will look at a coordinated long-run program of strategic actions. Another issue we need to discuss is that although we chose to discuss restructuring and cost cutting actions in relation to retrenchment and turnaround strategies, the fact is that organizations *don't* have to be pursuing just these strategies to implement some of these actions. Strategic managers may choose to use selected cost cutting or restructuring actions (such as divesting selected business units or reengineering work processes in certain areas) even during periods of organizational growth if these strategic actions are viewed as contributing to the organization's development or exploitation of a competitive advantage. That's the important key—is the organization's competitive advantage(s) enhanced and strengthened with these actions?

You have now been introduced to all the possible corporate strategic directions: organizational growth, organizational stability, and organizational renewal. You should also be familiar with the various options for implementing these strategies. What we need to look at next is how strategic managers evaluate the corporate strategies and make any needed changes.

Consider This ◀◀|

✓ What are the two strategic actions used in implementing the organization's renewal strategies?

✓ How could the organization use cost cutting in retrenching? In turnaround?

✓ Describe organizational restructuring.

✓ What is divestment?

✓ What are the three possible types of buyers for a business unit?

✓ How is a spin-off different from divestment?

✓ Describe liquidation.

✓ What is reengineering, and how might it be used in organizational renewal?

✓ What is downsizing, and how can strategic managers ensure that their downsizing efforts are effective?

✓ Describe bankruptcy.

✓ What's the difference between Chapter 7 and Chapter 11 bankruptcy?

✓ Why are most organizational renewal strategies used in combination?

EVALUATING AND CHANGING CORPORATE STRATEGY

The organization's corporate strategy has been implemented. The competitive strategy and various functional strategies are aligned with the overall direction that strategic managers have chosen for the organization and are being implemented, as well. How do you know it's all working as it should? How do you know whether the corporate strategy has been successful? How could the corporate strategy be evaluated? That's what we will discuss in this section.

Evaluating Corporate Strategies

Evaluation is an important part of the entire strategic management process. Without evaluation, strategic managers wouldn't have a clue about whether the implemented strategies—at any level of the organization—were working. We've discussed the specifics of evaluating the functional and competitive strategies in earlier chapters. Now we need to look at how the corporate strategy is assessed and evaluated. It shouldn't come as a surprise that the tools used in evaluating corporate strategy tend to be broader and encompass the overall performance of the organization rather than just focusing on narrow functional areas. We will look at four main evaluation techniques: (1) corporate objectives; (2) efficiency, effectiveness, and productivity measures; (3) benchmarking; and (4) portfolio analysis.

Corporate Objectives or Goals. The corporate objectives or goals indicate the desired results or targets that strategic managers have established. Whereas each functional area and each business unit also should have goals that are being pursued, the corporate objectives tend to be broader, more comprehensive, and more long run than these other levels. However, remember that success in meeting the goals at the functional and competitive (business) levels determines whether the corporate goals are met. In other words, the attainment of functional and competitive targets (goals) is how the organization achieves its corporate goals. If the functional and competitive targets aren't being reached, it's impossible for the organization to reach its corporate goals. Again, this simply reflects the inherent interaction and interdependence among the various strategy levels in the organization.

What types of corporate goals or objectives might an organization have? Figure 7-7 lists some of the more common organization-wide goals. For a publicly held corporation, maximizing stockholder wealth ranks right at the top of its goals. Why? As the company's legal owners and in exchange for providing capital, the stockholders expect an appropriate return on their investment. However, even not-for-profit, government, and privately held organizations need corporate goals to guide decision making. Don't forget that the goals should reflect the organization's vision and various missions and the overall direction it intends to go.

Figure 7-7

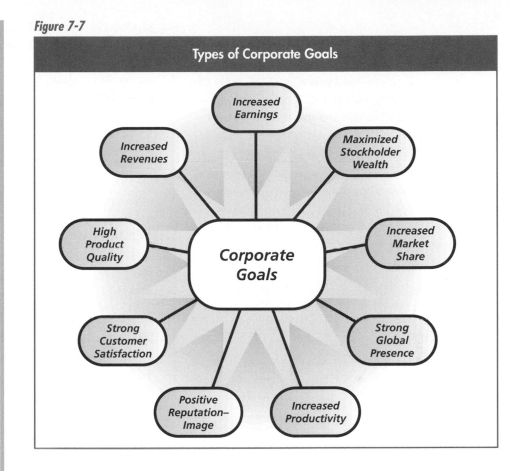

How are corporate objectives or goals used in evaluating corporate strategy? These become the standards against which performance is measured. Say, for instance, that one of the corporate goals is to increase the organization's market share by 1 percent. The evaluation would be did this happen or didn't it? It's helpful for corporate goals to be quantified whenever possible, but that may not always be possible in certain situations. This doesn't mean that the nonquantifiable areas shouldn't be evaluated. Sometimes a qualitative (subjective) assessment can be just as useful in evaluating performance as can a quantitative one. Also, we need to remember that not every organization is going in the direction of expanding operations—that is, not every organization is pursuing growth. Organizations that are using the stability strategy or renewal strategies will have goals that reflect those organizational directions. In these situations, the attainment of those objectives should be evaluated as well.

Efficiency, Effectiveness, and Productivity Measures. Three specific organizational measures that deserve special attention are efficiency, effectiveness, and productivity. Why? They represent the organization's ability to use its limited resources strategically and wisely in achieving high levels of corporate performance.

Efficiency is the ability of the organization to minimize the use of resources in achieving organizational objectives. **Effectiveness** is the organization's ability to complete or reach goals. **Productivity** is a specific measure typically used in the

An organization's objectives often include being a good corporate citizen by emphasizing ethical and socially responsible decisions and actions. What happens when an organization's values are continually on public display? Executives at Wal-Mart, the world's largest retailer, face this situation. Wal-Mart, by virtue of its enormous size and reach, has played an unwanted role of national conscience enforcer. Don Soderquist, senior vice chairman, says it best, "The watchword for all of our people is 'Do what is right.' That's what we really preach and teach and we want, but there's so much gray." For instance, handguns were booted off the shelves in 1994, but the company sells hunting rifles as part of its strategy to create a dominant sporting goods department for males. Alcohol isn't sold in traditional Wal-Mart stores, but is sold in its superstores in locations where it's legal. Wal-Mart clearly articulates its role as an "agent" for the consumer. The company views its job as finding out what customers want and getting those products into stores at the lowest possible cost. What are the ethical implications of this "public display" phenomenon for an organization measuring its performance to see if corporate strategies are effective? *Can* corporate morality be "practical"? *Should* it be practical? Explain your position.

Source: B. Saporito, "Wrestling with Your Conscience," *Time,* November 15, 1999, pp. 72–73.

production–operations–manufacturing area of how many inputs it took to produce outputs and is measured by taking the overall output of goods and services produced, divided by the inputs needed to generate that output.

Although these organizational measures aren't easy to calculate or evaluate, strategic decision makers should attempt to gauge how efficient, effective, and productive the organization is. They should be concerned not only with getting activities completed (effectiveness) but also with doing so efficiently and productively. Because total organizational performance is a result of the interaction of a vast variety of work activities at many different levels and in different areas of the organization, these three measures can serve as appropriate assessments of how well or how successfully the organization works *and* how well it's doing at going in the desired corporate direction (growth, stability, or renewal).

Benchmarking. **Benchmarking** is the search for the best practices from other leading organizations (competitors or noncompetitors) that are believed to have contributed to their superior performance. Whereas the actual process of benchmarking may be useful for implementing strategy, the specific benchmarks or best practices can be a standard against which to measure corporate strategy performance. In Chapter 2 we discussed that a world-class organization strives to be the best in the world at what it does. With the benchmarks, an organization's strategic managers can evaluate whether the organization is being strategically managed as a world-class organization and where improvements are needed. Is the overall organizational performance up to the standards of the best in the world? For example, Southwest Airlines studied Indy 500 pit crews, who can change a race car tire in under 15 seconds, to see how their gate crews could make their gate turnaround times even faster. Why benchmark against Indy pit crews? Southwest felt they were the best in the world at incredibly fast turnaround, and as Southwest's strategic managers reasoned, you don't make money sitting on the ground. You've got to have quick ground turnaround time and get the planes back in the air flying passengers to the next location. The benchmark or best practice was a standard against which to measure one aspect of performance.

Portfolio Analysis. The last approach to evaluating corporate performance that we're going to look at is the use of portfolio analysis. What is in an organization's "portfolio"? The answer would be the organization's various business units. If the organization has only one business unit, then portfolio analysis would be useless because there's no evaluation or comparison of specific businesses. (We should mention that some single businesses that have multiple brands use portfolio analysis to evaluate those brands. But that's not our focus here.) However, if the organization has multiple business units—in the same or different industries—then portfolio analysis can be used to evaluate strategic performance.

Portfolio analysis is done with two-dimensional matrices that summarize internal and external factors. There are three main ones you should know about: (1) the BCG matrix, (2) the McKinsey–GE stoplight matrix, and (3) the product–market evolution matrix.

The BCG matrix (also known as the growth–share matrix) was created by the Boston Consulting Group as a way to determine whether a business unit is a cash producer or a cash user. It's a simple, four-cell matrix. (See Figure 7-8.) The *Y* axis is a measure of the business unit's relative market share. In a very general sense, market share is a proxy for the business unit's internal strengths and weaknesses. Relative market share is defined as the ratio of a business unit's market share compared to the market share held by the largest rival in the industry. If the ratio is greater than 1.0, then the business unit is said to have high relative market share. If it's less than 1.0, then the business unit has low relative market share. (Note that only if a business unit is the market leader in its industry will it have a

Figure 7-8

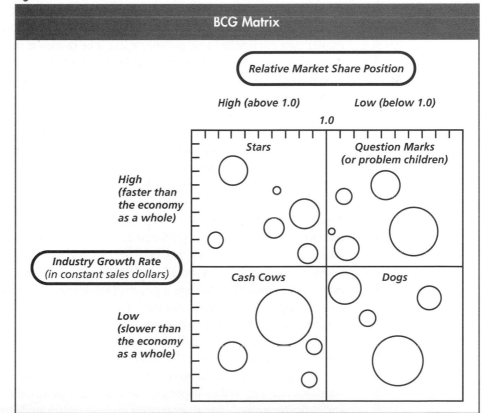

Source: The original growth–share matrix was developed by the Boston Consulting Group.

relative market share greater than 1.0.) Some analysts have concluded that this 1.0 figure is too restrictive and have recommended using lower figures such as .75 or even .50.

The *X* axis is a measure of the industry growth rate. Likewise, in a very general sense, the industry growth rate is a proxy for the external opportunities and threats facing the business unit. We want to know whether this industry is growing faster than the overall economy as a whole. If it is, then industry growth rate is evaluated as high. If it's not growing faster, the industry growth rate is low.

Each of the organization's business units would be assessed according to these guidelines and placed in the appropriate cell on the matrix. On the sample BCG matrix shown in Figure 7-8, the circles represent an organization's various business units. The size of the circle corresponds to the size of the business unit, using some measure such as business unit proportion of total corporate revenues. You can tell from the matrix the relative size of the organization's various business units—some are bigger and some are smaller. The business units are plotted on the matrix according to their scores on relative market share and industry growth rate.

A business unit with low relative market share and low industry growth rate is classified as a *dog*. According to the BCG analysis, a dog offers few growth prospects and, in fact, may require significant investments of cash just to maintain its position. The strategic recommendation for a business unit evaluated as a dog often is to exit that industry by either divesting or liquidating. However, a strategy of harvesting—that is, gradually letting the business unit decline in a controlled and calculated fashion and using any excess cash flows to support other, more desirable business units—may be an option *if* the business unit is profitable. A business unit with low relative market share and high industry growth rate is classified as a *question mark*. The question marks are low in competitive strengths, but they're in an industry where there's a lot of potential. The recommendation for a business unit evaluated as a question mark is that those with the weakest or most uncertain long-term potential should be divested. Why? Meeting the cash needs of too many business units may spread organizational resources too thinly and result in none being able to achieve star status. However, question marks are easy to sell because of the attractiveness of the industries. Those question marks with more potential should be infused with cash to attempt to turn them into market leaders. A business unit with high relative market share and high industry growth rate is classified as a *star*. Stars are the leading business units in an organization's portfolio. Depending on how competitive the industry is, stars may take significant cash resources to maintain their market leadership position, or they may take little cash if they're in an industry where competitive rivalry isn't high. The recommendation for a business unit evaluated as a star is to maintain its strong position while taking advantage of the significant growth opportunities in the industry. Finally, a business unit with high relative market share but low industry growth rate is a *cash cow*. Cash cows are strong cash providers. The positive cash flows from cash cows should be used to support those question marks with potential and to support the stars.

Although the BCG matrix is relatively simple to use, its simplicity is both its biggest advantage and its biggest drawback. The reliance on relative market share and industry growth rate to evaluate a business unit's performance and future potential is an extremely limited view. The fact that the BCG matrix is easy to use and understand is the main reason for its continued popularity as a portfolio assessment tool.

The McKinsey–GE stoplight matrix was developed by McKinsey and Company for General Electric. This nine-cell matrix (shown in Figure 7-9) provides a more comprehensive analysis of a business unit's internal and external factors. In this matrix, the *Y* axis is defined as business strength–competitive position. What's included in this analysis? It's more than just relative market share! It includes an analysis of the internal resources and capabilities that are believed by strategic managers to be important for success in this business. For instance, it might include an analysis of economies of scale, manufacturing flexibility, workforce morale, product quality, company image, and so forth—whatever strategic managers think the business needs to be good at in order to be competitive. The evaluation scale used in this analysis typically ranges from 1 (very weak) to 5 (very strong). The *X* axis is defined as industry attractiveness, which again provides a much broader analysis than the BCG's industry growth rate. Industry attractiveness might include such factors as average industry profitability, number of competitors, ethical standards, technological stability of the market, market growth

Figure 7-9

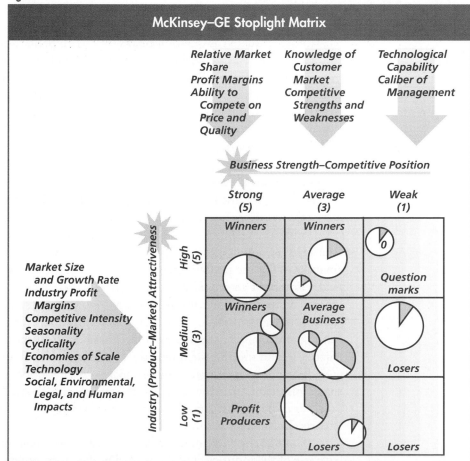

Source: Adapted from *Strategic Management in GE*, Corporate Planning and Development, General Electric Corporation. Used by permission of General Electric Company.

rate, and so forth. Again, strategic managers would use a measurement scale from 1 (very unattractive) to 5 (very attractive) to evaluate the industry a business unit is in. An organization's business units would be plotted on the matrix using these two measures.

As with the BCG matrix, the number of circles on the McKinsey matrix corresponds to the number of business units. In this instance, however, the size of the circle corresponds to the relative size of the industry and the shaded wedge corresponds to the market share held by the organization's business unit. With this matrix, we have a little more information to judge a business unit's position. How should strategic managers evaluate the placement of the business units on the matrix?

The three cells in the lower right-hand corner of the matrix are evaluated as *losers*. These business units have weak competitive position–low industry attractiveness; weak competitive position–medium industry attractiveness; and average competitive position–low industry attractiveness. In the original GE stoplight matrix, these cells were colored "red" indicating to stop investing in these business units. The three cells in the upper left-hand corner of the matrix are described as *winners*. These business units are evaluated as strong competitive position–high industry atttractiveness; strong competitive position–medium industry attractiveness; and average competitive position–high industry attractiveness. As you can probably guess, these cells were colored "green" indicating to go ahead, invest in, and grow these business units. Finally, the three cells along the diagonal in the matrix are evaluated as question marks (weak competitive position–high industry attractiveness), average businesses (average competitive position–medium industry attractiveness), and profit producers (strong competitive position–low industry attractiveness). These cells were colored "yellow" indicating caution in strategic decisions about these business units. Obviously, the profit producers would be milked for their cash flows with the cash going to support the winners and those question marks with potential to turn into winners.

The McKinsey matrix overcame the problem of simplistic analysis that plagued the BCG matrix tool. However, its main drawback is the subjectivity of the analysis. Because the factors to measure competitive position and industry attractiveness were created by an organization's decision makers and also because these individuals then rated business units on these factors, there was a risk that the analysis might be too subjective. Another drawback (also shared by the BCG matrix) is that the performance analysis is static. It's similar to what accountants often say about an organization's balance sheet—that it's a snapshot of the performance of business units at one point in time. Unless a series of "snapshots" are taken, strategic managers would have no way to interpret whether a business unit's performance is improving or declining. So even though the McKinsey matrix was an improvement over the BCG matrix, it still had its shortcomings.

The product–market evolution matrix was developed by C. W. Hofer and is based on the product life cycle, which serves as the *X* axis. The *Y* axis (internal analysis of the business unit) is the competitive position as used in the McKinsey matrix. This matrix is shown in Figure 7-10.

Also like the McKinsey matrix, the size of the circles corresponds to the relative size of the industry, and the shaded wedge corresponds to the market share of that business unit. Business units are placed on the matrix according to their individual evaluation on competitive position and stage in the product life cycle.

Figure 7-10

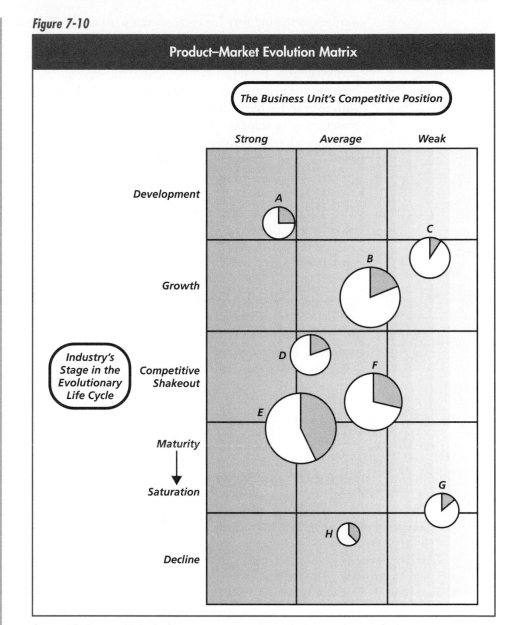

Product–Market Evolution Matrix

The Business Unit's Competitive Position

| | Strong | Average | Weak |

Industry's Stage in the Evolutionary Life Cycle

Development

Growth

Competitive Shakeout

Maturity

Saturation

Decline

Source: John Pearce and Richard Robinson, *Strategic Management,* 5th ed. (Burr Ridge: IL, Richard D. Irwin, 1994), p. 278.

Once all business units are plotted on the matrix, strategic managers have an indicator of the range of business units in various stages of the product life cycle. Say, for instance, that most of the organization's business units were positioned in the maturity or even decline stages. Then the strategic managers should be looking at ways to balance the organization's portfolio with some business units in earlier stages of the life cycle in order to provide long-run potential.

Although Hofer's product–market evolution matrix attempts to provide some semblance of the dynamic nature of an organization's business units through its use of the product life cycle, it still suffers from the same subjectivity biases that the McKinsey matrix does. In addition, many products don't fit nicely and neatly into the industry life cycle, so this particular evaluation tool also has drawbacks that limit its usefulness.

As an evaluation tool, the portfolio matrices do provide a way to assess the performance of the organization's various business units. With this evaluation, an organization's strategic decision makers have information for deciding what to do with the various business units. Should they be supported and strengthened? Should they be sold? Do we need to start looking for businesses to acquire? Because each of the various portfolio analysis techniques suffers from serious drawbacks, they should be used with caution or at least in conjunction with other strategy evaluation measures.

What happens after evaluating the corporate strategy? If the evaluation indicates that performance results aren't as strategic managers had hoped, then strategic changes are in order.

Changing Corporate Strategies

If the evaluation shows that the corporate strategies aren't having the intended results—growth objectives aren't being attained, organizational stability is instead causing the organization to fall behind, or if organizational renewal efforts aren't working—then some changes are obviously needed. Once strategic managers have evaluated the outcomes of the corporate strategy, through whatever measures are being used, then they have to decide whether to act and what actions to take.

If it's determined that changes are needed, they might look at changing the functional and competitive strategies that have been implemented. Perhaps some modifications to those will be enough to bring about the desired results. On the other hand, strategic managers might decide that more drastic action is needed and the corporate direction should be changed. If so, changes might also be necessary in the way the corporate strategy is being implemented. For example, when Microsoft's strategic managers realized that the Internet and World Wide Web were continuing to alter the future of computing, they did a complete about-face and changed the corporate direction with an all-out focus on this area. What did this corporate strategic change involve? Several actions! Microsoft began acquiring various Internet and Web start-up companies, reshuffled administrative duties, redesigned software already under development, and basically did what it had to in order to build up its commitment to this new corporate direction.[35] Notice how, in this example, the corporate strategy change affected the organization's functional and competitive strategies, as well.

An organization's corporate strategy is important to establishing the overall direction the organization wants to go. As the chapter-opening case illustrated, strategic managers have to understand

Consider This ◀◀|

✓ Why is an evaluation of corporate strategies important?

✓ What are the four ways to evaluate corporate strategies?

✓ How would objectives and goals be used in evaluating corporate strategy?

✓ Differentiate between efficiency, effectiveness, and productivity. How would each of these be used to evaluate corporate strategy?

✓ What is benchmarking, and how could it be used to evaluate corporate strategy?

✓ What is an organization's portfolio?

✓ How is portfolio analysis important as an evaluation tool?

✓ Describe each of the portfolio analysis matrices including how it's used, the cells in the matrix, and its advantages and drawbacks.

✓ Why might an organization's corporate strategy need to be changed?

✓ How might an organization's corporate strategy be changed?

both the opportunities–threats and the strengths–weaknesses facing the organization in order to design appropriate strategies—ones that will develop or exploit the resources, distinctive capabilities, and core competencies the organization has in its various business units in order to realize a sustainable competitive advantage. Each level of the organization's strategies is linked through this all-encompassing effort to develop a sustainable competitive strategy. Each strategy level plays a different role in this process, but each role is important.

THE BOTTOM LINE

▶ An organization's **corporate strategy** describes those strategies concerned with the broad and long-term questions of what business(es) the organization is in or wants to be in, and what it wants to do with those businesses.

▶ It involves looking at all aspects of the organization, including the other types of strategies and choosing how best to capitalize on what the organization has or how to compensate for what it doesn't have, in light of critical environmental trends and changes.

▶ One aspect of corporate strategy that's important to understand is whether the organization is a **single-business organization** (operates primarily in one industry) or a **multiple-business organization** (operates in more than one industry).

▶ Each of the various types of organizational strategies plays a significant role in whether the organization does what it's in business to do and whether it achieves its strategic goals.

▶ Coordinating these organizational strategies is critical to managing strategically.

▶ The corporate strategy can't be implemented effectively or efficiently without the support provided by the organizational resources, capabilities, and core competencies that are developed and used as the competitive and functional strategies are implemented and executed.

▶ In addition, the competitive and functional strategies that are implemented should support the organization's overall strategic direction as reflected by its choice of corporate strategy.

▶ The possible corporate strategic directions include moving the organization ahead, keeping the organization where it is, and reversing the organization's decline.

▶ The corporate strategies associated with these directions are growth, stability, and renewal.

▶ A **growth strategy** involves the attainment of specific growth objectives by increasing the level of an organization's operations. There are five main growth strategies.

▶ In the **concentration strategy**, the organization concentrates on its primary line of business.

▶ Possible ways for an organization to concentrate include product–market exploitation (current products–current customers), product development (new products–current customers), market development (current products–new customers), and product–market diversification (new products–new customers).

➠ In the **vertical integration strategy**, the organization attempts to gain control of its inputs (backward vertical integration) or its outputs (forward vertical integration) or both.

➠ In **horizontal integration**, the organization expands by combining with other organizations in the same industry (i.e., competitors).

➠ The **diversification strategy** is a growth strategy in which the organization expands by moving into a different industry.

➠ Diversification can be either **related (concentric) diversification** (diversifying into a different industry but one that's related in some way to the organization's current operations) or **unrelated (conglomerate) diversification** (diversifying into a completely different industry that has no relationship to the current industry).

➠ International growth is the last strategic growth option an organization might use.

➠ It is possible for an organization to "go international" as it concentrates, vertically integrates, horizontally integrates, or diversifies.

➠ There are three general approaches to international growth.

➠ The **multidomestic approach** is one in which the organization decentralizes operational decisions and activities to each country in which it is operating and tailors its products and services to each market in order to be highly differentiated.

➠ The **global approach** is one in which the organization provides more standardized products and uses significantly integrated operations in order to be highly efficient.

➠ The **transnational approach** is one in which the organization hopes to be both efficient and differentiated by globally integrating operations and tailoring products and services to local markets.

➠ An organization might choose to enter a foreign market by exporting, licensing, franchising, or direct investment.

➠ There are three main options for implementing corporate growth strategy: mergers and acquisitions, internal development, and strategic partnering.

➠ A **merger** is a legal transaction in which two or more organizations combine operations through an exchange of stock, but only one organization entity will remain.

➠ An **acquisition** is a purchase of an organization by another. If the acquisition is hostile (the organization being acquired doesn't want to be acquired), then it is known as a **takeover**.

➠ In **internal development**, the organization chooses to expand its operations by starting a new business from the ground up.

➠ The choice of internal development or mergers–acquisitions would depend on the new industry's barriers to entry, the relatedness of the new business to the existing one, the speed and development costs associated with each approach, the risks associated with each approach, and the stage of the industry life cycle.

➠ The **strategic partnering** approach describes a situation in which two or more organizations establish a legitimate relationship (partnership) by combining their resources, capabilities, and core competencies for some business purpose. There are three types of strategic partnerships.

➤ One type of strategic partnership is a **joint venture** in which two or more separate organizations form a separate, independent organization for strategic purposes.

➤ Another type of strategic partnership is a **long-term contract** in which two or more organizations establish a long-term legal contract covering a specific business purpose.

➤ The final type of strategic partnership is the **strategic alliance** in which two or more organizations share resources, capabilities, or core competencies to pursue some business purpose.

➤ The **stability strategy** is a corporate strategy in which an organization maintains its current size and current level of business operations. The stability strategy is typically a short-run strategy, although small businesses may pursue it long term.

➤ The stability strategy might be an appropriate choice if the organization's industry is in a period of rapid upheaval, if the industry is facing slow- or no-growth opportunities, and if the organization has just completed a frenzied period of growth.

➤ The stability strategy doesn't mean that organizational resources, capabilities, and core competencies don't change; they just don't expand.

➤ When organizations aren't meeting their strategic objectives or when performance results are declining, organizational renewal strategies are needed.

➤ A **renewal strategy** is designed to stop an organization's decline and put it back on a more appropriate path to achieving its strategic goals. There are two main types of renewal strategies.

➤ The **retrenchment strategy** is a short-run strategy designed to address organizational weaknesses that are leading to performance declines.

➤ The **turnaround strategy** is designed for situations in which the organization's problems are more serious as reflected by its performance measures.

➤ Both organizational renewal strategies are implemented through cost cutting and restructuring.

➤ Cost cutting might be across the board or selective.

➤ Restructuring involves various actions to refocus the organization.

➤ **Divestment** is a restructuring action that involves selling off a business unit to someone else where it will continue as an ongoing business.

➤ A **spin-off** is a restructuring action in which a business unit is set up as a separate business through a distribution of shares of stock.

➤ **Liquidation** is a restructuring action in which a business unit is shut down completely.

➤ In **reengineering** as a restructuring action, the organization's business processes are fundamentally rethought and radically redesigned.

➤ **Downsizing** is a restructuring action in which individuals are laid off from their jobs.

➤ The restructuring option of last resort is **bankruptcy** in which a business has failed and is either dissolved or reorganized under the protection of bankruptcy legislation.

⇒ These organizational renewal strategies aren't typically used one at a time and by themselves. It's often necessary for the organization to use some combination of these alternatives as it struggles to regain or develop a competitive advantage.

⇒ In addition, organizations don't necessarily have to be pursuing renewal in order to implement some of these actions. Strategic decision makers may choose to use cost cutting or restructuring at other times especially if these strategic actions are viewed as contributing to the organization's development or exploitation of a competitive advantage.

⇒ Once the corporate strategy has been implemented, it should be evaluated and changed if necessary. There are four main evaluation techniques.

⇒ One evaluation technique is comparing results against corporate objectives or goals (such as increased market share, increased earnings, strong customer satisfaction, etc.).

⇒ Another evaluation technique involves measuring **efficiency** (the ability of an organization to minimize the use of resources in achieving organizational objectives), **effectiveness** (the ability to complete or reach goals), and **productivity** (a specific performance measure typically used in the production and operations area that looks at how many inputs it took to produce outputs).

⇒ **Benchmarking** is another evaluation technique that involves searching for the best practices from other leading organizations (competitors or noncompetitors) that are believed to have contributed to their superior performance.

⇒ Finally, the organization could use portfolio analysis in which it evaluates the performance of the businesses in its portfolio.

⇒ The three main portfolio analysis tools are the BCG matrix, the McKinsey–GE stoplight matrix, and the product–market evolution matrix.

⇒ If the evaluation of corporate strategies shows that the strategy isn't having the intended results—growth objectives aren't being met, organizational stability is causing the organization to fall behind, or organizational renewal efforts aren't working—it may be time to make some changes.

BUILDING YOUR SKILLS

1. Banking with State Farm Insurance? You can now bank with the "Good Neighbor" people. State Farm Bank® offers a variety of deposit and lending products such as checking accounts, savings accounts, money market accounts, certificates of deposit, car loans, mortgages, home equity loans, and lines of credit. What type of growth strategy would you call this? Explain your choice.

2. Coca-Cola Company and America Online have formed a strategic alliance to develop programs to market their brands online and off-line. What benefits do you see accruing to each strategic partner? What challenges do you think this strategic alliance faces?

3. Gillette Company has faced some critical strategic decisions. For years, its portfolio of related diversified companies (Gillette razors, blades, and other shaving products; Oral B toothbrushes; Braun household appliances; and Parker, PaperMate, and Waterman pens) seemed to work well. Now, CEO

Michael C. Hawley is pruning back to the core businesses (blades, batteries, and oral care). He vows that "We're going to be the fiercest competitors in the world" in these areas. Research Gillette's financial performance from 1995 to the present. What story do the performance measures tell? Would you say its corporate strategy was working during this time? Explain.

4. What were the five largest mergers–acquisitions last year? Make a list of the merger–acquisition partners. What reasons were given for the merger–acquisition? What do you think of each of these strategic actions? Do you think they made strategic sense? Explain.

5. Using the Internet (company's Web site, **www.hoovers.com**, or other Web sites), research each of the companies in the following list and answer these questions:

   a. What corporate strategy(ies) does the company appear to be following? Explain your choice.

   b. Evaluate the company's performance using financial and any other measures you choose.

   c. What changes might you recommend to the company's strategic direction? Explain why you did or did not recommend changes.

COMPANIES

Cemex (**www.cemex.com**)
United Technologies (**www.utc.com**)
AmeriServe (**www.ameriserve.com**)
Unilever (**www.unilever.com**)
Toshiba (**www.toshiba.com**)
Smith Corona (**www.smithcorona.com**)

6. A company growing at an annual rate of 35 percent will double in size in just two years. A company growing at an 18 percent rate will double in size in four years. A company growing by 12 percent will double in size in six years. Persistent long-term growth is most achievable in moderate rates. Do you agree? Why or why not?

7. Globalization is here to stay. Has it been beneficial for the United States? Here are some of its pluses and minuses:

PLUSES OF GLOBALIZATION

Productivity grows more quickly.
Global competition and cheap imports keep a lid on prices, holding down inflation.
An open economy spurs innovation.
Export jobs often pay more.
Unfettered capital flows give U.S. access to foreign investment and keep interest rates low.

MINUSES OF GLOBALIZATION

Millions of people have lost jobs due to production shifts abroad.
Millions fear losing their jobs.
Workers face pay-cut demands from employers.
Service and white-collar jobs are increasingly vulnerable to moving offshore.
U.S. employees can lose their comparative advantage.

What do you think of these statements of globalization pluses and minuses? Is globalization good for a country? Explain.

8. Find examples of each of the types of corporate strategy (each of the types of growth strategies, stability strategy, and each of the types of renewal strategies). Describe your example. Be sure to provide your citation information.

9. "The acid test for any corporate strategy is that the company's businesses must not be worth more to another owner." Do you agree with this statement? Explain your choice.

10. Can corporate growth have a downside? Explain. How might these drawbacks be addressed?

STRATEGIC MANAGEMENT IN ACTION CASES

CASE #1: Pipeline Possibilities

Strategic Management in Action case #1 can be found at the beginning of Chapter 7.

Discussion Questions

1. What examples of corporate strategies do you see in this situation? Explain.

2. What corporate strategy evaluation measures might you suggest that the company use? Explain your choices.

3. What is Williams's mission? How is its mission related to its corporate strategy?

4. The last statement in the case is "We're driven by a belief in honest business dealings and an entrepreneurial spirit that relentlessly pursues innovation." How do you see this exhibited in the company's corporate strategy?

CASE #2: A Little Slice of Nice

Lawyers running a specialty restaurant. Now that seems to be as unlikely a combination as tandoori chicken or barbecued chicken on pizza. Yet, Rick Rosenfield and Larry Flax have built a successful company called California Pizza Kitchen (CPK) (**www.cpk.com**). The two former federal prosecutors decided to trade in the courtroom for the dining room and opened a unique restaurant that offers creative hearth-baked pizzas and other tasty dishes.

The pair opened their first CPK in Beverly Hills in 1985. Since that time, the company has grown to over 100 units in 20 states and 2 other countries outside the United States. Sales for 1999 were estimated at $200 million. As the leading premium pizza chain,

Rosenfield and Flax have built a successful business by carefully managing their organizational strategies. However, things weren't always that way.

In 1992, PepsiCo Inc. bought 67 percent of the CPK chain for $100 million. Rosenfield and Flax pocketed $34 million in cash and kept a minimal stake in the company. Both stayed on as co-CEOs and had the go-ahead from Pepsi to grow the company using corporate money for expansion. Pepsi's mandate: Open as many restaurants as possible. The only problem was that no one had a real plan about how to do that. At most the pair had opened seven locations in one year. Pepsi sent in some corporate accountants to keep an eye on CPK's fairly loose organization. During the first 18 months under Pepsi's ownership, the company opened nearly 40 new restaurants. Although sales revenues doubled, occupancy costs were skyrocketing. Pepsi's accountants responded by cutting corners. Instead of grilled fresh vegetables on the pizzas, frozen vegetables were used. Instead of fresh mozzarella cheese, frozen was used. Customers noticed! Sales revenue growth crashed. Pepsi's strategic decision makers were alarmed, needless to say. They tried several things, but to no avail. For the five years Pepsi owned CPK, the company lost money. Fortunately, at the time of the sale, Rosenfield and Flax had negotiated a buyout strategy. Pepsi sold the unit to an investment banking firm and the cofounders got 24 percent of the company back through a unique buyback arrangement. They immediately took steps to improve operations.

First they hired an experienced chief executive, Frederick Hipp, who had run Houlihans, a successful chain of contemporary restaurants. Hipp brought logical planning to the operation. He shut down the worst performing locations and revised the growth plans. He's not in any rush to open new stores and says, "I'll wait up to two years for the right site." His goal is to fill in existing markets by opening sites in malls with strong anchors. In addition, Hipp brought back CPK's once notable quality. CPK made the switch back to fresh ingredients. In addition, CPK decided to increase the size of the pizzas with no price increase. Once again, customers noticed.

Same-store sales shot up 8 percent. In an attempt to grow sales, Hipp has entered CPK into a strategic alliance with Kraft Foods to market a frozen version of CPK's pizza in grocery stores. Also, CPK has started some CPK-ASAP faster-service stores to capture customers who want the product, but don't have the time for a sit-down, dine-in experience.

Great food and service are crucial for any restaurant wanting to succeed. CPK has that, and more. By continuing to strategically manage the business, Rosenfield and Flax hope to maintain CPK's position as the leading premium pizza chain.

Discussion Questions

1. What types of corporate strategy do you see in this example? Be specific and explain your choices.
2. What lessons about growth can be learned from the CPK story?
3. What relationships between functional, competitive, and corporate strategies do you see here? Explain.
4. What might have been some signs of problems or opportunities in CPK's strategies?
5. What corporate strategy evaluation tools would you recommend for CPK? Explain your choices.

(Sources: Company's Web site (**www.cpk.com**), May 10, 2000, and from Hoover's Online Web site (**www.hoovers.com**), May 10, 2000; K. Hubbard and J. Hannah, "Dough Boys," *People*, March 13, 2000, pp. 143–45; A. Linsmayer, "Smothered by Money," *Forbes*, November 30, 1998, pp. 138–40; and K. Morris, "How to Have Your Pie and Eat It Too," *Business Week*, November 16, 1998, pp. 100–2.)

CASE #3: Clearing the Paper Jam

Xerox, a name synonymous with copying machines, was facing serious challenges. CEO Rick Thoman had tried different strategic initiatives to secure the company's future. However, his efforts were falling short.

Xerox had seen much of its traditional market slipping away. Sales of the classic Xerox copier—an analog stand-alone machine—fell 21 percent in 1999. Now, customers wanted their printed documents to come out of digital machines. Although Xerox is a major force in the digital document-handling business, it doesn't "own" that field as it did the analog copier business. It must compete for every digital sale, not only with other copier companies but also with computer companies that sell digital printing equipment. In fact, Xerox's biggest worry is that customers prefer document output on their own desktop printer, not on a copier down the hall. In the desktop printer business, Xerox hadn't been able to make any serious inroads against the market leader, Hewlett-Packard.

Overcoming obstacles wasn't anything new to Xerox. In the early 1980s, Japanese rivals Canon and Ricoh appeared on the copier scene with cheap, quality machines. Xerox's strategic decision makers were caught off guard, and the company almost went under. However, it refocused the business on costs and quality and recovered quite nicely. Then in the early 1990s, Xerox diversified into the insurance business, but soon discovered that that strategy hadn't been a good one and sold that business.

When Thoman took over the CEO reins in April 1999 (he already was Xerox's chief operating officer), the company's board of directors charged him with transforming the company into a high-tech powerhouse. Two things Xerox had going for it were its size and its reputation. Xerox's product line was revamped to be better and broader than ever. In addition, its huge direct sales and service force was well positioned to serve large institutions around the world in solving their corporate document management problems. What does Xerox do for these customers? It analyzes all aspects of document handling and creates a more efficient and effective document system by integrating fax machines, printers, scanners, and copiers, as well as PC

and workstation software. Xerox also sells supplies (ink, paper, and toner) and provides document outsourcing services. All these actions seem to make perfect strategic sense, right? Things haven't quite worked out that way, however, because moving in this direction required some corporate restructuring and refocusing, which haven't been executed well.

One of the bungled restructuring efforts was a revamping of the company's customer administration centers. In Europe, the majority of the tasks handled by Xerox's 53 administration centers were consolidated in a single center in Ireland. In the United States, most of the work of 36 centers was consolidated into 3 locations. The result was chaos. Invoices and shipping orders weren't handled in a timely manner. Sales representatives ended up spending their time getting orders right and answering billing questions. Instead of cutting expenses, the transition cost Xerox money and customer goodwill. After the fact, Thoman said, "We screwed up. We acted too quickly." As if that strategic action weren't bad enough, another restructuring effort focused on the sales force. The decision was made in early 1999 to reorganize the sales force from a geographic focus to an industry focus. This sounded like a good idea on paper because half of the company's revenues come from large corporate and public sector customers. However, this new industry focus created chaos. Almost two-thirds of Xerox's sales force had to change the customers they contacted. In addition, the sales force was asked to sell solutions and networked systems, not just pieces of equipment. This new focus meant a total retraining of the sales force. The company's decision makers chose to do this using virtual classrooms. However, the software used in the training wasn't ready initially, and sales representatives were baffled by the amount of information they were being forced to absorb. As CEO Thoman was finding out, changing a company with a proud heritage and over 95,000 employees wasn't an easy task! Meanwhile, Xerox's stock price was being badly beaten up (the company lost $20 billion in stock market value in just over a year's time) as analysts and investors worried about the direction Xerox was headed.

Meanwhile, Thoman was trying to fulfill the mandate he had been given—to transform Xerox into a high-tech powerhouse. New emphasis was placed on capitalizing on the technological innovations coming out of the company's Palo Alto Research Center (PARC). Although long recognized for its innovative efforts, Xerox had never really fully taken advantage of PARC's output. Now, the ideas coming out of the research and development operation became core components in the company's main products and others became the basis for start-up companies partly owned by Xerox. In addition, a couple of key strategic alliances were pursued. One of these strategic alliances was with Imation, a leader in color management technologies and the graphic arts market. This strategic alliance was formed to introduce printing, proofing, and imaging products to the graphics arts industry. Another strategic alliance

was with Microsoft in a spin-off of Xerox's ContentGuard technology. ContentGuard creates a hard-to-crack electronic envelope for moving advertisements, videos, books, music, and other content over the Internet and protects copyrights by giving the sender control over how the material is used. Will these strategic actions work?

Discussion Questions

1. What examples of corporate strategy do you see in this case? Explain.

2. What lessons about corporate strategy can be learned from Xerox's experiences?

3. What relationships between functional, competitive, and corporate strategies do you see here? Explain.

4. Update what is happening with Xerox. What strategies is it using? How is its performance?

Epilogue: On May 11, 2000, Xerox CEO Rick Thoman resigned under pressure. His struggles to turn Xerox around led to his departure. The company's chairman (and former CEO before Thoman), Paul A. Allaire, assumed the CEO position.

(Sources: Information on company from Xerox Web site (**www.xerox.com**), *USA Today* Web site (**www.usatoday.com**), *Wall Street Journal Interaction Edition* Web site (**www.wsj.com**), and Hoover's Online Web site (**www.hoovers.com**), May 12, 2000; P. L. Moore, "Still Looking for Wall Street's Respect," *Business Week*, May 8, 2000, pp. 136–37; and P. Klebnikov, "Paper Jam," *Forbes*, March 20, 2000, pp. 146–54.)

ENDNOTES

1. Information from company's Web Site (**www.williams.com**), May 1, 2000; C. Poole, "From Pipe to Fiber," *Latin Trade*, March 2000, pp. 28–29; B. Wysocki Jr., "Corporate America Confronts the Meaning of a 'Core' Business," *Wall Street Journal*, November 9, 1999, p. A1; A. M. Borrego, "Williams Cos. to Sell Stake in Unit to Public," *Wall Street Journal*, November 20, 1998, p. B6; and S. Schiesel, "From a Supplier of Gas Comes a Digital Pipeline," *New York Times*, January 12, 1998, p. C8.

2. The discussion of these concentration strategy options has been slightly modified from information found in P. Kotler, *Marketing Management,* 10th ed. (Upper Saddle River, NJ: Prentice Hall, 2000), pp. 74–75.

3. Information from company's Web site (**www.coulter.com**), May 1, 2000; and B. Upbin, "What Have You Invented for Me Lately?" *Forbes*, December 16, 1996, pp. 330–34.

4. Information from company's Web site (**www.bose.com**), May 1, 2000; and W. M. Bulkeley, "How an MIT Professor Came to Dominate Stereo Speaker Sales," *Wall Street Journal*, December 31, 1996, p. A1.

5. R. A. D'Aveni and A. V. Illinitch, "Complex Patterns of Vertical Integration in the Forest Products Industry: Systematic and Bankruptcy Risk," *Academy of Management Journal*, 35 (1992), pp. 596–625; J. B. Quinn, T. L. Doorley, and P. C. Paquette, "Technology in Services: Rethinking Strategic Focus," *Sloan Management Review*, 31, no. 2 (1990), pp. 79–87; R. E. Miles and C. C. Snow, "Organizations: New Concepts for New Forms," *California Management Review*, 28, no. 3 (1986), pp. 62–73; K. R. Harrigan, "Strategies for Intrafirm Transfers and Outside Sourcing," *Academy of Management Journal*, 28 (1985), pp. 914–25; K. R. Harrigan, *Strategies for Joint Ventures* (Lexington, MA: Heath & Lexington Books, 1985); R. P. Rumelt, "Diversification Strategy and Profitability," *Strategic Management Journal*, 3 (1982), pp. 359–70; and R. P. Rumelt, *Strategy, Structure and Economic Performance* (Cambridge, MA: Harvard University Press, 1974).

6. J. T. Mahoney, "The Choice of Organizational Form: Vertical Ownership versus Other Methods of Vertical Integration," *Strategic Management Journal*, 13 (1992), pp. 559–84; M. K. Perry, "Vertical Integration: Determinants and Effects," in *Handbook of Industrial Organization*, Vol. 1, ed. R. Schmalansee and R. D. Willig (New York: Elsevier Science, 1989), pp. 185–255; G. R. Jones and C.W.L. Hill, "Transaction Cost Analysis of Strategy-Structure Choice," *Strategic Management Journal*, 9 (1988), pp. 159–72; M. H. Riordan and D.E.M. Sappington, "Information, Incentives, and Organizational Mode," *Quarterly Journal of Economics*, 102 (1987), pp. 243–63; M. K. Perry and R. H. Groff, "Resale Price Maintenance and Forward Integration into a Monopolistically Competitive Industry," *Quarterly Journal of Economics*, 100 (1985), pp. 1293–311; S. C. Salop and D. T. Scheffman, "Raising Rivals' Costs," *American Economic Review*, 73 (1983), pp. 267–71; K. R. Harrigan, *Strategies for Vertical Integration* (Lexington, MA: Heath & Lexington Books, 1983); F. M. Westfield, "Vertical Integration: Does Product Price Rise or Fall?" *American Economic Review*, 71 (1981), pp. 334–46; M. A. Porter, *Competitive Strategy: Techniques for Analyzing Industries and Competitors* (New York: Free Press, 1980); M. K. Perry, "Forward Integration by Alcoa: 1888–1930," *Journal of Industrial Economics*, 29 (1980), pp. 159–70; O. E. Williamson, "The Vertical Integration of Production: Market Failure Considerations," *American Economic Review*, 61 (1971), pp. 112–23; J. M. Vernon and D. A. Graham, "Profitability of Monopolization by Vertical Integration," *Journal of Political Economy*, 79 (1971), pp. 924–25; J. S. Bain, *Barriers to New Competition* (Cambridge, MA: Harvard University Press, 1956); and G. J. Stigler, "The Division of Labor Is Limited by the Extent of the Market," *Journal of Political Economy*, 59 (1951), pp. 185–93.

7. R. D'Aveni and D. J. Ravenscraft, "Economies of Integration versus Bureaucracy Costs: Does Vertical Integration Improve Performance," *Academy of Management Journal*, October 1994, pp. 1167–206.

8. The Associated Press, "Journey Back with New Album, Tour Plans," *Springfield News-Leader*, January 21, 1997, p. 5B.

9. J. Weber, "American Standard Wises Up," *Business Week*, November 18, 1996, pp. 70–74.

10. S. Oliver, "I Love These Brands," *Forbes*, September 25, 1995, pp. 94–96.

11. *Better Investing*, June 1996, p. 6.

12. E. A. Gargan, "From Chickens to Chemicals," *New York Times*, November 14, 1995, p. D1.

13. L. E. Palich, G. R. Carini, and S. L. Seaman, "Internationalization as a Moderator in the Diversification-Performance Relationship: An Empirical Assessment," *Academy of Management Proceedings on CD-ROM*, August 1996; I. Goll and R. B. Sambharya, "Corporate Ideology, Diversification and Firm Performance," *Organization Studies*, 16, no. 5 (1995), pp. 823–46; C. C. Markides and P. J. Williamson, "Related Diversification, Core Competencies, and Corporate Performance," *Strategic Management Journal*, 15 (1994), pp. 149–65; H. Singh and C. A. Montgomery, "Corporate Acquisition Strategies and Economic Performance," *Strategic Management Journal*, 8, no. 4 (1987), pp. 377–86; K. Palepu, "Diversification Strategy, Profit Performance, and the Entropy Measure," *Strategic Management Journal*, 6, no. 3 (1985), pp. 239–55; D. J. Lecraw, "Diversification Strategy and Performance," *Journal of Industrial Economics*, 33, no. 2 (1984), pp. 179–98; R. A. Bettis, "Performance Differences in Related and Unrelated Diversified Firms," *Strategic Management Journal*, 2, no. 4 (1981), pp. 379–93; R. Rumelt, *Strategy, Structure and Economic Performance;* and H. I. Ansoff, *Corporate Strategy* (New York: McGraw-Hill, 1965).

14. Palich, Carini, and Seaman, "Internationalization as a Moderator"; R. B. Sambharya, "The Combined Effect of International Diversification and Product Diversification Strategies on the Performance of U.S.-Based Multinational Corporations," *Management International Review*, 35, no. 3 (1995), pp. 197–218; V. L. Blackburn, J. R. Lang, and K. H. Johnson, "Mergers and Shareholder Returns: The Roles of Acquiring Firms' Ownership and Diversification Strategy," *Journal of Management*, December 1990, pp. 769–82; B. W. Keats, "Diversification and Business Economic Performance Revisited: Issues of Measurement and Causality," *Journal of Management*, March 1990, pp. 61–72; and A. Seth, "Value Creation in Acquisitions: A Re-examination of Performance Issues," *Strategic Management Journal*, February 1990, pp. 99–115.

15. J. Birkinshaw, A. Morrison, and J. Hulland, "Structural and Competitive Determinants of a Global Integration Strategy," *Strategic Management Journal*, 15 (1995), pp. 637–55; "Competitors: Some Criteria for Success," *Business Horizons*, January–February 1988, pp. 34–41; and B. S. Chakravarthy and H. V. Perlmutter, "Strategic Planning for a Global Business," *Columbia Journal of World Business*, spring 1985, pp. 3–10.

16. C. A. Bartlett and S. Ghosal, *Managing Across Borders: The Transnational Solution* (Boston: Harvard Business School Press, 1989); and S. Ghoshal, "Global Strategy: An Organizing Framework," *Strategic Management Journal*, 8 (1987), pp. 425–40.

17. H. Dawley, "A British Publisher's Dreams of Empire," *Business Week*, November 18, 1996, p. 66.

18. R. Narisetti, "Can Rubbermaid Crack Foreign Markets?" *Wall Street Journal*, June 20, 1996, p. B1.

19. L. Capron, "Historical Analyses of Three Waves of Mergers and Acquisitions in the United States: Triggering Factors, Motivations, and Performance," *Academy of Management Proceedings on CD-ROM*, August 1996; and M. H. Lubatkin and

P. J. Lane, "Psst . . . the Merger Mavens Still Have It Wrong," *Academy of Management Executive*, February 1996, pp. 21–39.

20. P. Haspeslagh and D. Jemison, *Managing Acquisitions* (New York: Free Press, 1991); E. R. Biggadike, *Corporate Diversification: Entry, Strategy, and Performance* (Cambridge, MA: Division of Research, Harvard Business School, 1983); G. S. Yip, "Diversification Entry: Internal Development versus Acquisition," *Strategic Management Journal*, 3 (1982), pp. 331–45; M. S. Salter and W. A. Weinhold, *Diversification Through Acquisition: Strategies for Creating Economic Value* (New York: Free Press, 1979); and H. L. Ansoff, *Corporate Strategy* (New York: McGraw-Hill, 1965).

21. C. Ellis, "Making Strategic Alliances Succeed," *Harvard Business Review*, July–August 1996, pp. 8–9; C. M. Brown, "Partnering for Profit," *Black Enterprise*, June 1995, p. 43; R. Maynard, "Striking the Right Match," *Nation's Business*, May 1995, pp. 18–28; Roundtable Discussion, "Strategic Partnering," *Chief Executive*, November 1995, pp. 52–62; D. E. Gumpert, "Business 2000: Partnerships for Success," *Inc.*, December 1995, pp. 133–46; N. Templin, "More and More Firms Enter Joint Ventures with Big Competitors," *Wall Street Journal*, November 1, 1995, p. A1; N. S. Levinson and M. Asahi, "Cross-National Alliances and Interorganizational Learning," *Organizational Dynamics*, Autumn 1995, pp. 50–63; and J. Bleeke and D. Ernst, "Is Your Strategic Alliance Really a Sale?" *Harvard Business Review*, January–February 1995, pp. 97–105.

22. M. Kotabe and K. S. Swan, "The Role of Strategic Alliances in High Technology New Product Development," *Strategic Management Journal*, 16 (1995), pp. 621–36; J. B. Barney and M. H. Hansen, "Trustworthiness: Can It Be a Source of Competitive Advantage?" *Strategic Management Journal*, 15 (Special Issue 1994), pp. 175–203; and C.W.L. Hill, "Cooperation, Opportunism, and the Invisible Hand: Implications for Transaction Cost Theory," *Academy of Management Review*, 15 (1990), pp. 500–13.

23. M. A. Verespej, "Stability Before Growth," *Industry Week*, April 15, 1996, pp. 12–16.

24. See C. Siafter, *Corporate Recovery: Successful Turnaround Strategies and Their Implementation* (Hammondsworth, England: Penguin Books), 1984; R. C. Hoffman, "Strategies for Corporate Turnarounds: What Do We Know About Them?" *Journal of General Management*, 14 (1984), pp. 46–66; D. Schendel, G. R. Patton, and J. Riggs, "Corporate Turnaround Strategies: A Study of Profit Decline and Recovery," *Journal of General Management*, 2 (1976), pp. 1–22; and J. Argenti, *Corporate Collapse: Causes and Symptoms* (New York: McGraw-Hill, 1976).

25. P. Lorange and R. T. Nelson, "How to Recognize—and Avoid—Organizational Decline," *Sloan Management Review*, spring 1987, pp. 41–48.

26. C. C. Markides, "Diversification, Restructuring, and Economic Performance," *Strategic Management Journal*, February 1995, pp. 101–18; W. W. Lewis, "Strategic Restructuring: A Critical Requirement in the Search for Corporate Potential," in *Corporate Restructuring*, ed. M. L. Rock and R. H. Rock (New York: McGraw-Hill, 1990), pp. 43–55; and "Shifting Strategies: Surge in Restructuring is Profoundly Altering Much of U.S. Industry," *Wall Street Journal*, August 12, 1985, p. 1.

27. J. Greenwald, "Spinning Away," *Time*, August 26, 1996, pp. 30–31.

28. M. Hammer and J. Champy, *Reengineering the Corporation* (New York: HarperCollins, 1995).

29. S. Helldorfer and M. Daly, "Reengineering Brings Together Units," *Best's Review*, October 1993, pp. 82–84.

30. B. S. Moskal, "Reengineering Without Downsizing," *Industry Week*, February 19, 1996, pp. 23–28; R. D. Boyle, "Avoiding Common Pitfalls of Reengineering," *Management Accounting*, October 1995, pp. 24–33; M. A. Verespej, "New Rules for a New Century," *Industry Week*, September 18, 1995, pp. 19–20; and N. Fitzgerald, "A Process of Change," *CA Magazine*, July 1994, pp. 38–42.

31. G. D. Bruton, J. K. Keels, and C. L. Shook, "Downsizing the Firm: Answering the Strategic Questions," *Academy of Management Executive*, May 1996, pp. 38–45; and W. McKinley, C. M. Sanchez, and A. G. Schick, "Organizational Downsizing: Constraining, Cloning, and Learning," *Academy of Management Executive*, August 1995, pp. 32–44.

32. D. L. Worrell, W. M. Davidson, and V. M. Sharma, "Layoff Announcements and Stockholder Wealth," *Academy of Management Journal*, 34 (1991), pp. 662–78.

33. There are numerous articles written about organizational downsizing. Here are some of the most informative: a series of articles on "The Downsizing of America" can be found in the *New York Times*, March 1996; S. Greengard, "Don't Rush Downsizing: Plan, Plan, Plan," *Personnel Journal*, November 1993, pp. 64–72; W. F. Cascio, "Downsizing: What Do We Know? What Have We Learned?" *Academy of Management Executive*, February 1993, p. 96; K. S. Cameron, S. J. Freeman, and A. K. Miskra, "Best Practices in White-Collar Downsizing: Managing Contradictions," *Academy of Management Executive*, August 1991, pp. 57–73; R. Henkoff, "Cost Cutting: How to Do It Right," *Fortune*, April 9, 1990, pp. 40–49; and D. A. Heenan, "The Downside of Downsizing," *Journal of Business Strategy*, November–December 1989, pp. 18–23.

34. Y. Chen, J. F. Weston, and E. I. Altman, "Financial Distress and Restructuring Models," *Financial Management*, summer 1995, pp. 57–75; J. P. Sheppard, "Strategy and Bankruptcy: An Exploration into Organizational Death," *Journal of Management*, 20, no. 4 (1994), pp. 795–833; and C. M. Daily, "Bankruptcy in Strategic Studies: Past and Promise," *Journal of Management*, 20, no. 2 (1994), pp. 263–95.

35. J. Markoff, "Tomorrow, the World Wide Web," *New York Times*, January 16, 1996, p. C1; and K. Rebello, "Inside Microsoft," *Business Week*, July 15, 1996, pp. 56–67.

8

STRATEGIC MANAGEMENT IN OTHER ORGANIZATION TYPES

LEARNING OBJECTIVES

After studying this chapter, you should be able to:

1. Differentiate between a small business and an entrepreneurial venture.
2. Explain why small businesses and entrepreneurial ventures are important.
3. Describe how the strategic management process is used in small businesses and entrepreneurial ventures.
4. Discuss the special strategic issues facing small businesses and entrepreneurial ventures.
5. Define not-for-profit organization and public sector organization.
6. Describe the various types of not-for-profit organizations.
7. Describe how the strategic management process is used in not-for-profit and public sector organizations.
8. Discuss the special strategic issues facing not-for-profit and public sector organizations.
9. Describe the unique strategies developed by not-for-profit organizations.

STRATEGIC MANAGEMENT IN ACTION CASE #1

Shooting the Moon

Brenda Laurel had some great ideas for computer video games.[1] Because most video games were designed for and marketed at adolescent boys, she felt that a vast potential audience—preteen and young adolescent girls—was being missed. Also, she felt that the computer games for girls that were on the market focused on trivial matters such as eye shadow selection, nail-polish tricks, hairdo changes, and other fashion and makeup issues. Laurel believed that girls could use video games to solve challenges and to get immersed in complex situations in which they had to use their knowledge and skills to resolve pressing issues. Her creation was a character, Rockett Movado, who became the star computer game character of Laurel's company, Purple Moon.

Rockett is a lot like her creator, a spunky heroine. Brenda Laurel worked for Atari as a game designer in the early 1980s. Purple Moon evolved out of her belief that girls "played" differently than boys. She interviewed 1,000 girls to find out how to apply their principles of play to computer games. It soon became clear to her that girls were not turned off by the violence in boys' games as much as they found the dying and starting over again—a significant feature of most video action games— tedious and meaningless. Whereas boys liked superheroes and fantasy adventures, girls liked challenges they could recognize from their own lives. The company's initial exhaustive market research continued with 25 additional studies. For instance, an ethnographic study of girls' interest in sports led to the creation of a video game line, Starfire Soccer, featuring, as is probably obvious, girls and soccer.

The first Rockett game, "Rockett's New School," was introduced in 1997. Purple Moon used radically different game features such as emotional navigation and relationship hierarchies to position a product for girls in a market that had long been targeted at boys. Eventually, Purple Moon was able to capture 5.7 percent of the girls' software market. However, this was a far cry from the market shares of the industry leaders—Mattel with 64.5 percent and the Learning Company with 21.6 percent. Unfortunately, even with the best ideas, thorough market research, and entrepreneurial intentions behind it, Purple Moon's story doesn't have a storybook ending. The company's attempt to "shoot the moon" turned out to be unsuccessful in the long run.

Purple Moon was acquired by Mattel, the toy company, in the spring of 1999. Mattel expanded the Rockett brand by introducing new CD-ROMs, including Rockett's Camp Adventures®. Another strategic direction for the Purple Moon division was the development of the *Rockett's World* book series in conjunction with Scholastic Inc. In addition, Mattel enhanced the popular Purple Moon Web site (**www.purple-moon.com**) to make it even more appealing to its targeted market of 8- to 12-year-old girls.

Brenda Laurel attributes Purple Moon's failure to make it as an independent entrepreneurial venture on tough competition, bad timing, and perhaps even unrealistic expectations about what the company could accomplish. Despite the unfortunate ending, Laurel suggested that Purple Moon did help broaden girls' attitudes toward technology and the software industry's attitude about girls and technology. That, in itself, may have been its most significant accomplishment!

The story of Purple Moon's rise and fall as an independent business illustrates how strategic management and managing strategically can be applied and are important in unique types of organizations. Brenda Laurel's recognition of environmental opportunities, her strategic plan for targeting girls with appropriately designed software, and the venture's acquisition by toy industry giant Mattel are all examples of strategic management in action in an entrepreneurial venture. Although we may have a tendency to think of competitive advantage, internal and external analysis, strategy formulation, and strategy implementation as important concepts for corporate America, the fact is that strategic management is important for all types and sizes of organizations. Although we've used examples of not-for-profit organizations and other types of organizations in previous chapters as we discussed various strategy topics, in this chapter we want to focus exclusively on what it means to manage strategically in some of these other unique types of organizations—that is, organizations that aren't your standard business corporations. Why do we need to look at these types of organizations separately? The best answer is that these organizations may face unique types of challenges and issues when managing strategically. Yet, it's still important for them to think and manage strategically.

There are three "other" types of organizations that we will examine. First, we'll take a look at small businesses and entrepreneurial ventures. What role does strategic management play in these organizations, how is it used, and what types of unique strategic issues do these types of organizations specifically have to deal with both in the initial start-up phase and as they grow? Then, we'll look at the broad category of not-for-profit organizations, including public sector organizations. Again, we'll examine the role strategic management plays, how it's used, and the unique strategic issues that strategic managers in these types of organizations might have to deal with.

SMALL BUSINESSES AND ENTREPRENEURIAL VENTURES

In this section, we want to look at the process of managing strategically in small businesses and entrepreneurial ventures. Before we can do that, however, we need to know what these organization types are, how they're the same, and how they're different.

What Is a Small Business and What Is an Entrepreneurial Venture?

Although you may lump these two organizational types together and think they're one and the same, there are some important differences that might influence the process of managing strategically and strategic decisions and actions. Let's look first at what a small business is.

What constitutes a "small" business? There is no universally accepted definition of a small business, but most definitions use some measure of number of employees or annual revenues. Also, the Small Business Administration (SBA), the U.S. federal agency that provides assistance and loans to small businesses, has different definitions for a small business depending on what industry it's in. For instance, the cutoff point for a "small" business in the metal can fabrication industry is 1,000 employees, whereas in the wholesale hardware industry, it's 100 employees.[2]

We're going to define a **small business** as one that is independently owned, operated, and financed; has fewer than 100 employees; doesn't engage in any new marketing or innovative practices; and has relatively little impact on its industry.[3]

The whole idea of entrepreneurship involves the discovery of opportunities and the resources to exploit them.[4] We're going to define an **entrepreneurial venture** as a business that is characterized by innovative strategic practices and that has profitability and growth as its main goals.[5] Obviously some definitional and actual overlap exists between small businesses and entrepreneurial ventures, but we're going to look at them as two different organizational types. A small business isn't necessarily entrepreneurial in nature just because it's small. To be entrepreneurial means being innovative and seeking out new opportunities—being willing to take risks. Although entrepreneurial ventures may start small, they do pursue growth. Some new small firms may grow, but many will remain small businesses.

Yes, there are some distinct differences between small businesses and entrepreneurial ventures. The primary one is their perspective on growth and innovation. These differences are summarized in Table 8-1.

At this point, you may be asking yourself why we're emphasizing small businesses and entrepreneurial ventures as "special" types of organizations. The fact is that both small businesses and entrepreneurial ventures play an important role in the global economy.

Why Are These Types of Organizations Important?

Using any number of information or media sources, you can read statistics about how many small businesses there are, how many workers they employ, and how much of the gross national economic output they're responsible for. The headlines "scream" the facts: Small businesses represent over 99 percent of all employers, employ 53 percent of the private nonfarm workforce, contribute 47 percent of all sales in the United States, and are responsible for 51 percent of the private gross domestic product. In addition, during the 1990–1995 time period, small firms with fewer than 500 employees created 76 percent of net new jobs.[6]

Small businesses and entrepreneurial ventures are important to every industry sector in the U.S. and global economies. For instance, over 60 percent of all retail businesses in the United States can be classified as small businesses, and almost 90 percent of construction companies fall into this category. Small busi-

TABLE 8-1 Characteristics of Small Business versus Entrepreneurial Venture	
Small Business	**Entrepreneurial Venture**
• Independently owned, operated, and financed	• Innovative strategic practices
• Fewer than 100 employees	• Strategic goals are profitability and growth
• Doesn't emphasize new or innovative practices	• Seeks out new opportunities
• Little impact on industry	• Willingness to take risks

nesses also dominate what is broadly known as the "service" industry, which covers a wide variety of organizations from restaurants to dry cleaners to lawn care. In all types of industries, small businesses and entrepreneurial ventures play a significant role. Many of the cost advantages that large organizations traditionally realized because of their size are being eroded and diminished by advances in technology. Continual changes in the external environment—competition, technology, customer desires, and so forth—provide a fertile climate for small businesses and entrepreneurial ventures because these organizations are often better able to respond quickly to changing conditions than are larger, more bureaucratic, and less flexible organizations. Indeed, that may be one reason why we're continuing to see an increase in the number of new businesses started.

In 1970, some 264,000 new businesses were launched.[7] By 1980, that figure had more than doubled to 532,000. The number of new businesses started in 1990 was 647,000 and in 1995, 819,000 were started. The latest figures show that in 1998, new business formation reached another record level at 898,000 new firms.[8] Add these new start-ups to the large number of small businesses already operating and you can begin to understand the economic importance of small business and entrepreneurial ventures. However, this still doesn't answer the question of how many total small businesses and entrepreneurial ventures there are.

Right off, we need to say that there's no one single answer to that question. Why? It goes back to the definitional problem—the number of small businesses depends on how you define a small business. For instance, the SBA reports that the number of business tax returns filed in the United States was 24.8 million in 1998, with more than 99 percent of those filed by firms defined as small businesses.[9] However, Dun and Bradstreet (**www.dnb.com**), the organization that collects and disseminates all kinds of business information and reports, pegs the number at around 10 million small businesses. Dun and Bradstreet's number is significantly lower because it includes only what it calls "economically active" businesses.[10] Regardless of what figure we use, it's clear that there are large numbers of small businesses and entrepreneurial ventures.

Finally, you can understand why small businesses and entrepreneurial ventures are important when you look at the number of jobs created by those types of organizations. Figure 8-1 illustrates that a significant number of jobs were created between 1992 and 1996 (the latest figures available) in organizations with fewer than 100 employees. Small businesses and entrepreneurial ventures create jobs both when they're started and when they expand. Many analysts concur that these types of organizations are, indeed, creating the most new jobs in today's economy.

There's no doubt that small businesses and entrepreneurial ventures play a significant role in the U.S. economy and the global economy. Their economic importance will undoubtedly continue. That's why we need to look at what it means to manage strategically in these types of organizations. Both of these types of business organizations face unique strategic challenges. Before we look at these unique issues, though, we need to discuss how the strategic management process might be used in small businesses and entrepreneurial ventures. One thing that can help strategic managers in small businesses and entrepreneurial ventures is information and assistance in strategically managing their organizations. The FYI box points out that there's plenty of information on the Web to help in this area.

Figure 8-1

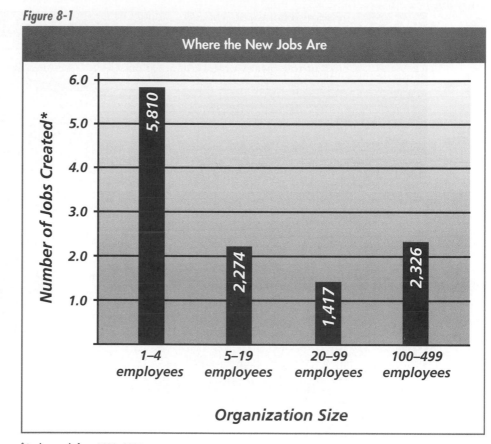

Where the New Jobs Are

In thousands from 1992–1996
Source: Small Business Administration, Office of Advocacy, "Small Business Answer Card 1998."

The Strategic Management Process in Small Businesses and Entrepreneurial Ventures

Developing and exploiting a sustainable competitive advantage is an important task for strategic managers in small businesses and entrepreneurial ventures, just as it is for large, single-business or multiple-business organizations. As we've discussed numerous times in previous chapters, securing a sustainable competitive advantage means developing those organizational resources and capabilities that result in distinctive capabilities and core competencies that competitors can't duplicate and that provide customers with products or services they desire. Getting to that point isn't easy no matter what size or type organization. Again, that's the intent behind managing strategically—using the strategic management process to identify and assess the important internal and external factors that influence appropriate strategic choices and decisions. What are "appropriate" strategic choices and decisions? Of course, they're those that lead to the development or exploitation of a sustainable competitive advantage. What's different or unique about the way that strategic managers in small businesses and entrepreneurial ventures do this? Let's look more closely at the strategic management process in small businesses and entrepreneurial ventures.

Value of Strategic Planning. The first thing we need to address is whether strategic managers in small businesses and entrepreneurial ventures should actu-

FYI

Web Sites for Entrepreneurs

The Web is a wonderful source of information for strategic decision makers in small businesses and entrepreneurial ventures. Here are just a few of the best sites:

The Business Planning Resource Center (**www.bplans.com**)

The Business Forum Online® (**www. businessforum.com**)

The Business Resource Center (**www.morebusiness.com**)

Business Week Online: The Small Business Resource (**www.businessweek. com/smallbiz**)

CEO Express Executive Gateway (**www.ceoexpress.com**)

Entrepreneur Magazine Online Small Business Authority (**www.entrepreneur mag.com**)

Entrepreneurial Edge (**www.edgeonline.com**)

EntreWorld Resources for Entrepreneurs (**www.entreworld.org**)

Garage.com (**www.garage.com**)

Idea Café (**www.ideacafe.com**)

Inc. Online: The Web Site for Growing Companies (**www.inc.com**)

New Venture Café (**www.mgt.smsu.edu/nvcafe**)

Small Business Administration (**www.sbaonline.sba.gov**)

SBFocus.com (**www.smallbizplanet.com**)

Smart Business Supersite (**www.smart biz.com**)

U.S. Business Advisor (**www.business.gov**)

Look up five of these sites. In a paper, describe and evaluate what's on each site. Then discuss what strategic decision makers in small businesses and entrepreneurial ventures could learn from each site to help them be better strategists.

---

ally do any strategic planning. What's the value of strategic planning for these types of organizations? Strategy research on the value of general planning in these types of organizations and on the value of pre–start-up planning in particular has shown mixed results. Several studies have shown positive linkages between planning and business performance.[11] Others have not uncovered any such relationship between planning and performance or have shown that the relationship depends on the industry.[12] What's our conclusion? Despite the contradictory findings in the research studies, we believe that the benefits to be gained from strategic planning by strategic managers in small businesses and entrepreneurial ventures *do* outweigh the drawbacks of doing so. Table 8-2 summarizes both the benefits and drawbacks of strategic planning for these organizations. If we conclude that strategic planning is important, how should it be done?

The Overall Approach to the Strategic Planning Process. Most researchers generally agree that the strategic planning process in small organizations should be far less formal than that in large organizations.[13] If the process becomes too formal, rigid, and cumbersome for the strategic managers, a small business or entrepreneurial venture can lose much of the flexibility that's often crucial to its

TABLE 8-2 Benefits and Drawbacks of Strategic Planning for Small Businesses and Entrepreneurial Ventures

Benefits	Drawbacks
• Positive impact on organizational performance	• Takes time and resources to complete
• Positive impact on long-run success and survival	• Strategic manager may not know how to do it or may lack skills to do it
• More complete knowledge of strategic issues facing the organization	• Plans are just that—plans. Implementation is the important thing
• Forces strategic managers to identify and assess external and internal factors	• Too much planning can be harmful if by the time an opportunity is investigated fully, it no longer exists
• Positive influence on product–service innovation	

Consider This ◀◀|

✓ What is a "small" business?

✓ How is an entrepreneurial venture defined?

✓ How are small businesses and entrepreneurial ventures different?

✓ Why are small businesses and entrepreneurial ventures important to the U.S. and global economies?

✓ Is strategic planning valuable to small businesses and entrepreneurial ventures? Explain.

✓ Why should the strategic planning process be more informal in small businesses and entrepreneurial ventures?

competitive success. In fact, the value of strategic planning for small businesses and entrepreneurial ventures lies more in the "doing"—that is, in the process itself—not in the outcome of the process, a formal strategic "plan." Most of the value of the strategic planning process comes from its emphasis on analyzing and evaluating the external and internal environments of the organization. Obviously, both external and internal analyses are important to effective strategic planning.

External and Internal Environmental Analysis. Strategic managers in small businesses and entrepreneurial ventures need to expend the time and resources to know what's happening both externally and internally. There are a couple of reasons why. One reason is that many aspects of an organization's external environment have been shown to influence performance, particularly in new entrepreneurial ventures.[14] Even for established small businesses, however, external analysis could provide crucial information for developing or exploiting a sustainable competitive advantage. Another reason why it's important for strategic managers in both small businesses and entrepreneurial ventures to do an external analysis is to have information about changes and trends in customer expectations, competitors and their actions, economic factors, technological advances, and other marketplace features.[15] As we discussed in Chapter 3, the information from this external analysis provides an indication of the various opportunities and threats in the external environment. If an external analysis isn't done, then it's impossible to know what positive or negative changes and trends are occurring. The same thing holds true for an internal analysis. If strategic managers don't assess the organization's strengths and weaknesses, then it's going to be difficult to know what strategic decisions and actions are needed to help develop or exploit the organization's sustainable competitive advantage. In other words, what resources, capabilities, and core competencies does the organization have and not have? Remember from our discussion in Chapter 4 that identifying these things is the whole purpose behind doing an internal analysis. Although it may be difficult for a small business owner to be totally objective in analyzing strengths and weaknesses, such an analysis *is* necessary.

There is one final reason why the process of environmental analysis is so important to small businesses and entrepreneurial ventures. This reason has to do with a concept called the "boiled frog phenomenon," which is a classic psychological experiment.[16] In the experiment, when a live frog is dropped into a boiling pan of water, it reacts instantaneously and jumps out. However, if a live frog is dropped into mild water that's gradually heated to the boiling point, the frog fails to react and dies. The same concept can be applied to small businesses and entrepreneurial ventures. Research has shown that in small businesses, when negative changes in organizational performance are gradual, a serious response to do something about it is never triggered or at least isn't triggered until it's too late.[17] Therefore, strategic managers need to analyze both the external and internal environments in order to detect subtle, but potentially damaging, changes in their

FYI

Trend Spotting for Opportunities and Threats

The skill of observing. Do you have it? Can you pick up on what people think is "hot" or popular? Faith Popcorn, an author and well-known trend spotter, actually says that you don't have to be a pro to be good at it. In fact, professionals may be constrained by rigid organizational structures and their past successes. So, how can *you* become more in tune with what's happening and hone your skills at trend spotting? Here are some suggestions:

1. Remember that valuable information is everywhere around you. Look for it everywhere and anywhere. Read magazines you don't normally read. Watch television shows or movies that you personally might not be interested in. Go to places. Do things. Talk to people. Information is the bread and butter of a good trend spotter.

2. File that information away. If your memory isn't as good as it should be, use note cards. What you write down doesn't have to be long and complex. It could be something as simple as "avocado seems to be a hot color," "teens seem to be flocking to organized fitness programs," or whatever.

3. Determine whether the fads seem to be part of deeper, wider trends that can be good sources of entrepreneurial opportunity. You can do this by assessing whether the fad seems to have staying power, whether the fad is a reflection of a change in people's attitudes or behaviors, and whether you see the fad in more than a few places.

4. Test your ideas about trends on intelligent friends of various ages and incomes. Bounce your ideas off of them. What do they say? Make sure, however, that these people will be honest with you.

5. Don't expect trends to jump out at you. After all, if they were easy to spot, everyone would be doing it. You have to be alert, be open to new and unusual possibilities, and be willing to work at it. Don't worry if you miss a trend. After all, there will be more.

Sources: K. G. Salwen, "Thinking About Tomorrow: An Interview with David Birch," *Wall Street Journal*, May 24, 1999, p. R30; and R. Furchgott, "Trend-Spotting: Anyone Can Play," *Business Week Enterprise*, March 2, 1998, pp. ENT12–ENT16.

organization's competitive advantage. They don't want to be like the frog that waits too long to jump out of the boiling water.

Strategy Choices. Small businesses and entrepreneurial ventures are going to have most of the same types of strategic choices as large firms do, but there are some differences. Let's look at the three different strategy levels to see what these differences are.

At the functional levels, strategies for the various functional areas have to be decided. For instance, what production and operations strategies will the organization use? What human resource management strategies will be used? What financing strategies will be adopted? Look back at the chapter-opening case. What types of research and development strategies did Purple Moon use? The main difference in the functional strategies of small businesses and entrepreneurial ventures and large businesses is the extent or range of the possible strategies. Small size doesn't mean that the functional strategies aren't used. It just means that small businesses and entrepreneurial ventures are limited in terms of the resources and capabilities that are available to implement those strategies.

The competitive strategy choices for small businesses and entrepreneurial ventures often are limited to focus (either low-cost focus or differentiation focus) strategies because of their small size and narrow competitive scope. It would be extremely difficult, even with technological advances, for a small-size organization to compete in a broad market, head-to-head with a large organization on the basis of low costs, and probably even on differentiation. However, small businesses and entrepreneurial ventures can compete successfully in narrow market niches by developing a low-cost, differentiation, or integrated competitive advantage. Which one the strategic managers decide to develop or exploit depends on the resources, capabilities, and core competencies present in the functional areas of the organization.

Finally, it probably seems strange to talk about "corporate" strategies for a small business or entrepreneurial venture, especially if you think of corporate strategy as encompassing several of an organization's businesses. However, strate-

Strategic Management—The Global Perspective

Although market success is something that most entrepreneurs work hard to achieve, success can bring about production and other strategic challenges. Carla Haeussler Baudillo of Puerto Rico had this problem, albeit a good one! Carla's Sweets Corporation produces bite-size miniatures of merengue, a favorite Caribbean dessert. When she first created her concoctions, the desserts sold like hotcakes at her parents' gourmet café. With this initial positive reaction from customers, Baudillo went from store to store and landed accounts with the island's top grocery stores and movie theater chains. However, all this market success meant larger and larger production facilities to make the desserts. During its first five years, the company moved four different times because it outgrew its current facilities. For Carla's Sweets, growth has been the result of good strategic choices in all areas and levels of the organization.

Source: J. P. Marino, "Success Is Sweets," *Business Week Enterprise,* March 1, 1999, p. ENT22.

How far should a business go in exploiting its competitive advantage? Chipotle Mexican Grill, a Denver-based chain of 50 restaurants, is pushing the limits with its advertising. The ads show a foil-wrapped package of Mexican food that looks very much like a package of marijuana wrapped for shipment. The ad's copy reads "Usually when you roll something this good, it's illegal." The only other words in small print in a bottom corner of the ad are "Gourmet burritos. Addictive flavor." There's also a Chipotle logo in the bottom corner. The ads have run in Chicago and Denver editions of *The Onion*, a newspaper known for its satirical views and commentaries. One other twist to this story is that the controlling stockholder of the Chipotle chain is McDonald's Corporation. Do these ads sound like an appropriate strategic choice? When does a business cross the line between humor and bad taste? Should the fact that Chipotle's majority stockholder is a successful family-oriented company play any role in the choice of and evaluation of strategies? Explain. Are there ethical guidelines that you might propose?

Source: "Fast Food for the Munchies," *Business Week*, February 21, 2000, p. 10.

gic managers in these types of businesses do need to decide on a broad and comprehensive strategy for the organization. In what broad, overall direction is the organization going to go? The possible strategic directions are the same as for a large organization: Is the organization going to grow, stabilize, or reverse a decline by renewing? Again, however, there are limits to the range of strategic options available to small businesses and entrepreneurial ventures in each of these directions. For example, most entrepreneurial ventures will choose to grow using the concentration strategy, because vertical and horizontal integration or diversification are not financially or operationally feasible. Organization renewal actions may be limited to cost cutting and simple restructuring activities. Although the strategic options at the broad, corporate level may be limited, strategic managers in these types of organizations still need to determine what strategic direction they'd like to take the organization.

One final point we need to stress about the strategy choices for small businesses and entrepreneurial ventures is that the whole process boils down to the strategic manager(s) deciding what business to be in, what competitive advantages are needed to be successful in that business, and what strategies are necessary to get there. This encompasses the whole range of strategic activities from developing or exploiting organizational resources, capabilities, and core competencies to building or exploiting a sustainable competitive advantage from these in order to move the firm in the desired direction.

Strategy Evaluation and Control. The evaluation and control phase of the strategic management process for small businesses and entrepreneurial ventures is similar to what would be used in large organizations. The organization's strategies might be evaluated in terms of performance as measured by attainment of goals or objectives at the various levels. Strategy evaluation might also include an assessment of certain performance trends and a comparison of the organization to its competitors. The organization's strategic managers want to know (and *need* to know) whether the implemented strategies are having the intended effect. If not, why not, and what changes might be necessary? The main difference between large and small organizations' strategy evaluation efforts will be in terms of the magnitude or extent of evaluation that is done.

All in all, the strategic management process in small businesses and entrepreneurial ventures is very similar to that used in larger organizations. Figure 8-2 illustrates this process. As we stated earlier, the main differences will be in terms

Figure 8-2

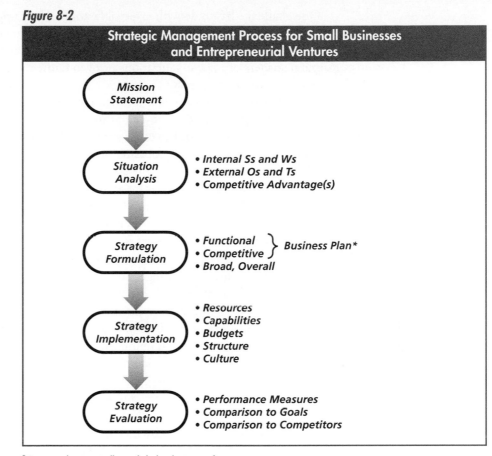

Strategic Management Process for Small Businesses and Entrepreneurial Ventures

- Mission Statement
- Situation Analysis
  - • *Internal Ss and Ws*
  - • *External Os and Ts*
  - • *Competitive Advantage(s)*
- Strategy Formulation
  - • *Functional* ⎫
  - • *Competitive* ⎬ *Business Plan**
  - • *Broad, Overall* ⎭
- Strategy Implementation
  - • *Resources*
  - • *Capabilities*
  - • *Budgets*
  - • *Structure*
  - • *Culture*
- Strategy Evaluation
  - • *Performance Measures*
  - • *Comparison to Goals*
  - • *Comparison to Competitors*

* Business plan is typically needed when business is first starting up.

of "how much" the small business or entrepreneurial venture can do these things. Because of their limited resources and capabilities, strategic managers in the small business or entrepreneurial venture often find their strategic options and actions limited. As we've already stated, however, this doesn't mean that strategic managers in these organizations don't—or shouldn't—do these things; it just means they don't have the range or extent of alternatives to choose from.

Specific Strategic Issues Facing Small Businesses and Entrepreneurial Ventures

The strategic management process for small business and entrepreneurial ventures is virtually identical to that for larger organizations, but these smaller organizations do face some unique strategic issues. These issues include global–international opportunities and challenges, human resource management issues, and innovation and flexibility considerations. Let's take a closer look at each of these.

Global–International Opportunities and Challenges. International markets offer small companies many opportunities for long-term growth and profitability.[18] Just because an organization is small doesn't mean it cannot pursue global growth. In fact, small organizations are capable of entering the same markets as larger firms.[19] Size limits only the number of markets a small organization can serve. However, certain challenges exist for small businesses and entrepreneurial ventures associated with pursuing international operations. What kinds of challenges?

One challenge has to do with external factors such as understanding the cultural, economic, and legal–political factors of the country(ies) in which the small organization wishes to do business. It's not easy to get this information, but strategic managers of small organizations need to know the ins and outs of doing business in a particular country.

The other challenges associated with going international have to do with internal factors—that is, with the organization's resources and capabilities. Strategic managers would want to make sure that the organization's resources and capabilities are adequate and appropriate for doing business on an international scale. You don't want to jeopardize any competitive advantages you may have developed domestically. However, if these competitive advantages can be appropriately transferred to other countries, there are prime opportunities for enhancing the organization's growth and profitability.

Human Resource Management Issues. One of the most valuable resources and competitive advantages a small organization has is its employees. Yet, research indicates that recruiting, motivating, and retaining employees is one of the biggest problems for small organizations.[20] Human resource management (HRM) issues are among the most significant ones for small businesses and entrepreneurial ventures. A large organization typically enjoys a wider range of HR strategy options in terms of recruiting, selecting, training, appraising, and compensating employees; a smaller organization usually doesn't have as many options. However, just because small businesses and entrepreneurial ventures don't have the wide range of HR strategies doesn't mean that they should just forget about strategies for managing their human resources. Quite the opposite, in fact! Strategic managers in these organizations should recognize how important human resources are and commit whatever time and other resources are necessary to develop appropriate strategies for attracting and keeping good people. It's an investment that small businesses and entrepreneurial ventures can't ignore.

Innovation and Flexibility Considerations. One of the primary advantages that small businesses and entrepreneurial ventures can develop is a commitment to being flexible and innovative.[21] Because large organizations are usually concerned with producing large quantities of products in order to take advantage of economies of scale, they often can't be as flexible as small organizations. Their

---

e·biz

STRATEGIC MANAGEMENT IN AN E-BUSINESS WORLD

How about those stock options? You've all read the stories about the dot.com millionaires—individuals who went to work for a small Internet company, took most of their compensation in the form of stock options, and then when the company went public, the person became an instant millionaire or multimillionaire. Are stock options good strategic choices for entrepreneur-ial ventures and small businesses? Research the topic of stock options. Come up with a bulleted list of pros and cons regarding stock options as a human resource management strategy. (Be sure to think about the pros and cons from the perspectives of both the company *and* the employees.) Be prepared to debate either side in class.

Consider This ◀◀|

✓ Why is environmental analysis (both external and internal) important to small businesses and entrepreneurial ventures?

✓ How do strategic choices for small businesses and entrepreneurial ventures differ from those of larger organizations?

✓ Describe the strategic management process for small businesses and entrepreneurial ventures.

✓ What is the boiled frog phenomenon, and how does it apply to small businesses and entrepreneurial ventures?

✓ Describe the specific strategic issues that face small businesses and entrepreneurial ventures.

✓ What is creative destruction, and why is it important to small businesses and entrepreneurial ventures?

resource commitments often prevent them from responding to new and quickly changing markets as effectively as small, nimble businesses can. Therefore, strategic managers at small businesses and entrepreneurial ventures need to capitalize on this flexibility advantage and be aware of and open to environmental changes (another good reason for doing an external analysis while managing strategically).

Also, small businesses and entrepreneurial ventures have the potential, more so than large organizations, to come up with real innovations. Why? Larger organizations tend to concentrate on improving products they already have in order to justify large expenditures on facilities and equipment. Small businesses and entrepreneurial ventures are in a better position to develop innovations in technology, markets, products, and ideas. Economist Joseph Schumpeter referred to this process in which existing products, processes, ideas, and businesses are replaced with better ones as **creative destruction**. Small businesses and entrepreneurial ventures are the driving force of change in the process of creative destruction. Developing and exploiting a sustainable competitive advantage may mean that strategic managers at small businesses and entrepreneurial ventures need to be on the lookout for ways to "creatively destruct"!

NOT-FOR-PROFIT AND PUBLIC SECTOR ORGANIZATIONS

In this section we're going to look at managing strategically in public sector (governmental) organizations and in other types of not-for-profit organizations. We'll start off by defining these organizational types and looking at how they're different from for-profit organizations. Then, we'll discuss the details of the strategic management process for these types of organizations and finish up with a discussion of some special strategic issues with which these organizations might have to contend.

What Are Not-for-Profit Organizations and What Are Public Sector Organizations?

One thing we need to clarify up front is that public sector organizations *are* not-for-profit organizations, also. However, we have chosen to define them separately because of their unique importance to our economic system. Before we define public sector organizations, let's look first at what a not-for-profit organization is.

A **not-for-profit organization** is one whose purpose is to provide some service or good with no intention or goal of earning a profit and, as such, has met the requirements of Section 501(c)(3) of the U.S. Internal Revenue Service tax code as a tax-exempt organization. Note that "not-for-profit" doesn't mean "no revenue." Just because a not-for-profit (NFP) organization has no intention of earning a profit doesn't mean that it doesn't need some source of income. An organization can't exist without some means of covering the expenses associated with providing a good or service. Where can an NFP's revenues come from? Figure 8-3 lists the typical sources of revenue: taxes; dues; donations; product sales; permits, fees, and charges; and grants. In many instances, an NFP gets its revenues from a combination of these sources. What happens if an NFP's revenues actually *exceed* its expenses? Because an NFP can't earn a profit and retain its not-for-profit status, usually it will use any excess of revenues over expenses to improve those goods or services it's providing or to reduce the price of those goods or services. It's not uncommon for an NFP to set aside a specified amount of funds in some type of reserve accounts to be used when revenues *don't* meet expenses.

Just as business (for-profit) organizations aren't all alike, neither are NFPs! There are a number of different types of not-for-profit organizations. We've already mentioned one of those types, the public sector organization, which we'll discuss more fully later. What are some other types of NFPs? The main ones include educational (public schools, colleges, and universities); charitable (United Way, American Cancer Society, Children's Miracle Network, etc.); religious (churches, synagogues, and other religious associations); social service (Junior League, American Red Cross, Camp Fire, Habitat for Humanity, Big Brothers–Big Sisters, Mothers Against Drunk Drivers, etc.); professional membership associations (American Bar Association, Academy of Management, etc.); health service (hospitals, medical clinics, and other health care–related organizations); cultural and recreational (theaters, museums, dance troupes, symphonies,

Figure 8-3

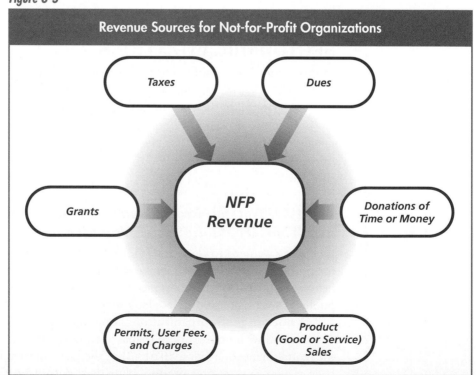

Revenue Sources for Not-for-Profit Organizations

Taxes

Dues

Grants

NFP Revenue

Donations of Time or Money

Permits, User Fees, and Charges

Product (Good or Service) Sales

parks, zoos, and other arts or recreation-oriented organizations); cause related (Save the Whales, Republican or Democratic National Party, Nature Conservancy, American Association of Retired Persons, etc.); and foundations (Rockefeller Foundation, Bill and Melinda Gates Foundation, college or university alumni foundations, Foundation for the Health and Safety of American Firefighters, etc.). Figure 8-4 summarizes the various types of not-for-profit organizations.

The other main type of NFP is the public sector organization. A **public sector organization** is a not-for-profit organization created, funded, and regulated by the public sector or government. Public sector organizations include governmental units, offices, departments, agencies, and divisions at all levels—federal, state, and local. Public sector organizations provide those public services that a society needs to be able to exist and operate, such as police protection, paved roads and other transportation needs, recreation facilities, care and help for needy and disabled citizens, laws and regulations to protect and enhance life, and so forth.

Both public sector organizations and other types of NFPs are important to society. These organizations provide for many of society's essential needs that either can't be or shouldn't be provided by for-profit businesses. After all, for example, most individual citizens couldn't afford to pay for private police protection, but instead rely on the government to provide this protection; the American

Figure 8-4

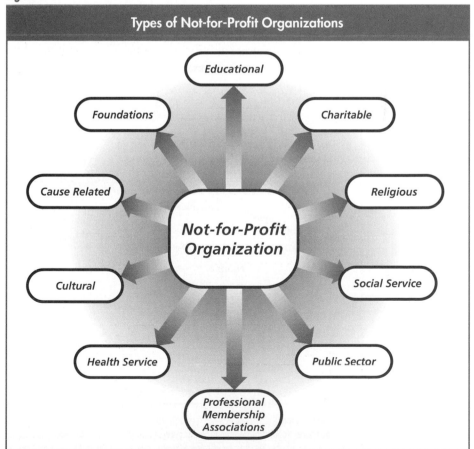

Cancer Society provides funds for cancer research and to help educate people about cancer and its causes; and any child born with birth defects is eligible for help from the March of Dimes. Many of the services and goods that NFPs provide are important to the quality of life in society. NFPs also play a significant role in maintaining an economic, social, and political system that encourages, facilitates, and protects the development and continued existence of for-profit organizations. Although the vast array of laws and regulations may seem overly cumbersome and meaningless at times, most have been enacted with society's best interests in mind. Finally, NFPs are an important economic activity. Figure 8-5 shows that these organizations (both public and other types of NFPs) provide a significant portion of the gross national product. In addition, NFPs employ a large number of individuals who, in turn, have income to pay taxes and to spend on goods and services.

You may not have realized that there was such a wide variety of not-for-profit organizations, understood the extent of what NFPs did, or recognized the economic significance of these types of organizations. Not-for-profit and public sector organizations are important to our society as well as to other societies around the world. Strategically managing these types of organizations would also appear to be a necessity. That's what we want to look at next—how the strategic management process is used in NFPs.

The Strategic Management Process in Not-for-Profit and Public Sector Organizations

Because these types of organizations aren't struggling to "make a profit," you may think that managing strategically isn't necessary or maybe even possible. However, developing and exploiting a sustainable competitive advantage is an important task for strategic managers in NFPs and public sector organizations. Why?

Figure 8-5

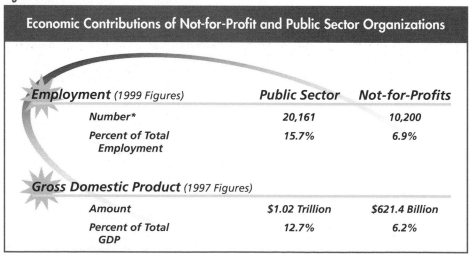

Economic Contributions of Not-for-Profit and Public Sector Organizations		
Employment (*1999 Figures*)	**Public Sector**	**Not-for-Profits**
Number*	20,161	10,200
Percent of Total Employment	15.7%	6.9%
Gross Domestic Product (*1997 Figures*)		
Amount	$1.02 Trillion	$621.4 Billion
Percent of Total GDP	12.7%	6.2%

* In thousands

Sources: Nonprofit Information Center (**www.independentsector.org**), May 17, 2000; "Employment Report," U.S. Department of Labor, Bureau of Labor Statistics, February 2000, p. 45; *Statistical Abstract of the United States*, 1999, p. 460.

Because, believe it or not, NFPs are also competing for resources and customers! For example, the American Heart Association competes with other social services, health services, and charitable and religious organizations for volunteers. A local community theater or symphony competes with other community arts organizations and with "entertainment" businesses for customers, volunteers, and corporate and private donations. A state university is competing with countless other organizations for state budget funds, employees, and "customers" (that's you, and the rest of your fellow students!). That means the NFP also needs to develop and exploit a competitive advantage—something that sets it apart and gives it a competitive edge. So, the strategic management process is clearly needed by these types of organizations.

Unfortunately, most of the research on the strategic management process and organizational strategy actions and decisions has taken place in for-profit organizations. Yet, strategy researchers have recognized the need to look at strategic management concepts and techniques in not-for-profit organizations.[22] As in for-profit organizations, there does appear to be a positive link between strategic planning efforts in NFPs and organizational performance measures.[23] So, what does the strategic management process involve for not-for-profit and public sector organizations?

External and Internal Environmental Analysis. Both external and internal analyses can reveal important information for strategically managing NFPs. Not-for-profit organizations are facing increasingly dynamic environments just as business organizations are. The external analysis provides an assessment of the positive and negative environmental trends and changes that might impact the NFP's

Strategic Management in Action

Even the U.S. military is acutely aware of the demographic and sociocultural trends: Employment is high, college financial aid is there for the taking, and dot.com success stories are big news. With all these attractive choices, getting kids to sign up for military service is, to put it mildly, a huge struggle. To deal with the threats, the U.S. military has chosen to redo its image. It's launched an all-out assault on Generation Y with money (the Marine Corps is a sponsor of *The X Games*, a televised extreme sports competition popular with teens), technology (the Air Force sends out a technology-intense road show with flight simulators and an F-16 fighter jet to shopping mall parking lots and high schools), and celebrity marketing (the Navy's commercials are directed by Spike Lee and the Pentagon is going after Tom Cruise and Harrison Ford to appear in ads). Will these new strategies work? Military recruiters are hoping so. What other external trends can you think of that might impact military organizations' strategies?

Source: D. Brady, "Uncle Sam Wants You . . . To Have Fun!" *Business Week,* February 21, 2000, pp. 98–101.

strategic decisions and actions, just as it does for the for-profit organizations. For example, economic trends might positively or negatively influence the amount of tax revenues or the level of private and corporate donations an NFP or public sector organization might expect. Changing societal attitudes toward respect for others and individual responsibility can influence the willingness of individuals to volunteer time and work or to make contributions to a particular cause. A new community arts organization (a new "competitor") can affect the program offerings and revenues of other community arts organizations. Even a long-running governmental monopoly such as the U.S. Postal Service faces competition from such technological advances as e-mail, fax machines, and overnight package delivery services. It should be quite evident to you that strategic managers at NFPs and public sector organizations need to analyze the external factors in order to assess the positive and negative impacts of changes and trends on the organization's strategic decisions and actions. The NFPs face opportunities and threats just as for-profit organizations do.

The internal analysis provides an assessment of the not-for-profit organizations' resources and capabilities and its strengths and weaknesses in specific areas. What resources and capabilities does it have? Which ones are inadequate or absent? With this information, strategic managers can look to see what distinctive capabilities, core competencies, and competitive advantage(s) the NFP might have or might need to develop. The different functional areas of an NFP are probably not called the same as those of a for-profit organization, but the process of analyzing the functional areas *is* similar. Even in an NFP, the product or service must be produced and delivered to the "customer," and revenues must be accounted for in some way. What the internal analysis shows, as we well know, is how efficient and effective the organization is at doing these things. An internal audit would be an appropriate tool for assessing an NFP's resources and capabilities and where the organization's strengths and weaknesses are.

What happens after we have the information from the SWOT analysis? If you remember, strategic managers use this information to assess their various strategy options and choices for creating or exploiting a competitive advantage.

Strategy Choices. The idea that NFPs and public sector organizations have strategic options and choices still may seem rather odd to you. After all, NFPs aren't "selling" anything and aren't competing with other organizations, and they certainly aren't motivated to be efficient and effective in developing a competitive advantage because they don't have to make a profit to stay in business. These statements are definitely *not* true! Strategic managers at NFPs face similar constraints of limited resources, competition for customers and resources, performance measurement, and long-run survival, just as strategic managers at for-profit organizations do. Thus, at some point, an NFP's strategic managers must make some decisions about strategies the organization is going to use to fulfill its vision and mission(s). The strategic options that an NFP or a public sector orga-

Consider This ◀◀|

- ✓ What is a not-for-profit organization?
- ✓ Do not-for-profit organizations need revenue? How about profits? Explain.
- ✓ Describe the typical sources of revenues for not-for-profit organizations.
- ✓ What are the main types of not-for-profit organizations? Give some examples of each type.
- ✓ What is a public sector organization, and what does it provide?
- ✓ Why are public sector organizations and other types of NFPs important to society?
- ✓ Explain how not-for-profits "compete."
- ✓ How would strategic managers in an NFP do an external analysis? An internal analysis?

nization has are similar in many respects to those available to businesses. Let's look first at the functional types of strategies.

At the functional level, the NFP or public sector organization must have strategies that allow it to do what it's set up to do—whether that's collecting taxes; imprisoning or rehabilitating convicted felons; developing and showcasing community art, dance, and music; or providing regional home health care assistance to elderly individuals. Every NFP or public sector organization must have resources and capabilities to perform whatever service or to provide whatever good(s) it's set up to do. As we know from earlier discussions, the functional strategies are the various ways an organization might choose to do these things. The main difference between the functional strategies of business organizations and NFPs is that not-for-profits can't choose from a wide variety of strategic alternatives because of scarce and limited resources or because there are external constraints. Whereas scarce and limited resources affect both public sector organizations and other types of not-for-profits, external constraints are most common in public sector organizations, particularly in functional areas such as purchasing or employee hiring–firing. These types of constraints limit strategic managers' discretion in choosing appropriate and feasible functional strategies.

Competition doesn't cease to exist just because an organization isn't profit oriented. As we stated earlier, not-for-profits and public sector organizations *do*

STRATEGIC MANAGEMENT IN AN E-BUSINESS WORLD

Have you ever waited in line—it seems like forever—at the local office of your state's motor vehicle department to register your car or to renew your car tags? Or have you ever applied for a visa and had to go from office to office to fill out all that paperwork? All that governmental hassle is about to change. Welcome to the world of e-government! Public agencies at all levels of government are putting an increasing variety of services online. As local, state, and federal agencies go online, millions of dollars could be saved on staffing and mailing expenses. However, declining costs of delivering services is only one benefit of online government services. There's also the convenience factor. For instance, motorists in Alabama, Alaska, Arizona, Michigan, and other states can register a car and get new license plates via their home computer any time of the day or night. Residents of Georgia can purchase hunting, fishing, and boating licenses on the Internet. Parking tickets can be paid online in Boston, Indianapolis, and Seattle. Even college students can apply for financial aid on an Education Department Web site. Yet, with all the progress in online governmental services, there's still a long way to go. Every year, businesses and individuals conduct about $600 billion worth of government transactions and less than 1 percent of that takes place online. However, despite all the advantages associated with going online, the biggest drawback is the widespread lack of access to the Internet for many citizens. Often, those individuals lacking access are society's poorest and most disadvantaged. This is an aspect of this strategy that governmental decision makers will have to address as they look at future strategic actions.

Source: A. Borrus, "Click Here to Pay Your Parking Ticket," *Business Week,* January 17, 2000, pp. 76–78.

compete for resources (financial and human) and customers (clients, users, members, etc.) just like business organizations do. These NFPs are competing with each other and, in many instances, with business organizations for these resources and customers. Very little research has been done on specific competitive strategies that NFPs and public sector organizations use. One study of community arts organizations did show that these organizations competed on the basis of keeping costs low, being different, or focusing on a specific niche—Porter's cost leadership, differentiation, and focus strategies.[24] However, even without a significant amount of research on specific competitive strategies in NFPs and public sector organizations, we do know that these organizations must develop and exploit a sustainable competitive advantage to ensure their continued existence. How the strategic managers choose to do that is the essence of their organization's competitive strategy.

Finally, not-for-profits and public sector organizations face the same types of corporate strategy choices as do businesses: Should the organization grow, and what are its options for growth? Does the organization need to stabilize its operations, or does it need to correct declining performance and renew itself? The main difference between corporate strategies for business organizations and for NFPs and public sector organizations is the limited range of strategic options. For instance, concentration is a frequently used growth strategy for NFPs, but diversification would be rare, if not nonexistent. For example, strategic managers at the headquarters of the United Way had to use a turnaround strategy to correct its rapidly declining performance. Their strategic actions involved cost cutting, restructuring, and reestablishing good relationships with member chapters throughout the United States. However, even if possible corporate strategy actions are somewhat limited, NFPs and public sector organizations *do* look at ways to grow, stabilize, or renew—they're faced with the same kinds of broad, comprehensive, and long-run strategic decisions that for-profit organizations face.

Strategy Evaluation and Control. As we've said many times before, formulating and implementing a strategy is only part of the job of managing strategically. Once the strategy has been implemented, strategic managers must evaluate whether the strategy had the intended effect and, if it didn't, do some type of corrective action. Even though we know that strategy evaluation and control are important, this is the part of the strategic management process that's probably the most difficult for not-for-profit and public sector organizations. Why? Primarily because clearly stated performance standards (typically, goals and objectives) are not easy to develop for these types of organizations. Without clearly stated goals, strategy evaluation and control become more difficult. In these types of organizations there's not one simple measure of performance like the profit standard used for business organizations. Instead, strategic managers may have to look at several measures of strategic performance. For example, what are some ways that a church's strategic performance could be measured? One measure might be whether member contributions increased. Another might be the increase (or decrease) in the number of members. The fact that strategic managers at these types of organizations may have to look at several different performance measures makes the process of strategy evaluation and control a little more cumbersome and difficult. Also, because it's often easier for strategic managers of not-for-profit organizations to measure the resources coming into the organization (inputs) than the services or goods being provided (outputs), they often tend to focus more on

New IRS Rule Affects Not-for-Profit Organizations

A new regulation from the Internal Revenue Service requires many not-for-profit groups to provide detailed financial information. Colleges, universities, hospitals, publicly supported charities, and other tax-exempt organizations now must provide, on request, copies of their financial filings. These forms, filed annually with the IRS, include information about executive salaries and other sensitive facts. Before the IRS rule went into effect on June 8, 1999, tax-exempt organizations had to make their financial forms available only for public "inspection" at their offices. A former IRS official said, "The new rules, backed by significantly increased penalties, will lead to sharply increased scrutiny and a higher level of accountability for the nation's nonprofit organizations." Organizations that post their documents on the Internet in a prescribed format will be exempt from the new rules. How might these rules benefit not-for-profits? Other stakeholders? What drawbacks might there be to the new rules? How might these rules affect strategy formulation, implementation, and evaluation in not-for-profits?

Source: T. Herman, "Nonprofit Groups Ordered to Open Their Books," *Wall Street Journal*, April 9, 1999, p. A2.

the resources coming into the organization than on how the resources are being used—that is, how the organization is performing.[25] Again, this reflects the difficulties strategic managers in these types of organizations face as they attempt to develop appropriate ways to evaluate and control the strategies.

However, even given the difficulties associated with strategy evaluation and control in not-for-profit and public sector organizations, strategic managers need to assess the strategies being used to see if they're doing what was intended. Without some performance or other types of evaluation measures, it would be difficult to assess the appropriateness of functional, competitive, and corporate strategies.

Specific Strategic Issues Facing Not-for-Profit and Public Sector Organizations

Because of their unique purposes and designs, not-for-profit and public sector organizations often must deal with some specific strategic issues that other types of organizations do not. The issues we'll discuss include the misperception that strategic management isn't needed in or can't be applied to these types of organizations, the challenges of managing multiple stakeholders, and some specific strategies that not-for-profits have developed in response to environmental pressures.

Misperception About the Usefulness of Strategic Management. You'd probably agree that strategic management is useful and necessary in for-profit organizations. Somehow, when "profit" is involved, the utility of the process makes sense. However, many people question the usefulness of the strategic management process for not-for-profits. Many not-for-profit managers themselves also aren't aware of what managing strategically is and why it's important. They don't understand why and how strategic management should be used. Some of these managers even go so far as to say that management, in general, isn't needed. Their rationale: We're not a business, so why should we be worried about managing the organization like a business?

Of course, we're well aware that these types of attitudes are simply misperceptions about what strategic management is and its purposes. As we've stated numerous times, managing strategically in order to develop a sustainable competitive advantage is a task that *all* strategic decision makers face. The caseload manager at a local Social Security Administration office and even the executive director of a community ballet school should be concerned with managing strategically. Tasks such as developing an organizational vision and mission(s), analyzing positive and negative external trends, assessing internal resources and capabilities, and designing appropriate programs and services are all key aspects of managing strategically.

Fortunately, these misperceptions about the usefulness of strategic management for not-for-profit organizations are changing, although they are changing slowly. As academic research studies and even media reports on successful strategic management outcomes in these types of organizations continue to appear, these misperceptions will continue to change. However, not-for-profit and public sector organizations still face this issue.

Multiple Stakeholders. We know that strategic managers in business organizations must cope with multiple stakeholders. However, this issue is magnified in not-for-profit organizations and particularly in public sector organizations. Public sector organizations are best described as the government—at all levels—doing its work. This fact means that public sector organizations are closely intertwined with politics and the political process. Strategic managers in public sector organizations may find their plans and strategies ignored by political leaders who may be interested only in getting reelected. In addition, in the United States, our fundamental assumption about government is that individual citizens *are* the government—government of the people, by the people, and for the people, as our Constitution so eloquently states. Public sector organizations, then, are "owned" by all citizens, and strategic managers may find that their decisions and actions

---

Strategic Management in Action

Even paradise has problems. For the state of Hawaii, a vacation paradise, a prolonged slump in tourism has brought a host of problems. Throughout much of the early and mid-1990s, Hawaiian officials saw visitor counts increasing. However, in 1997, the number of visitors began to drop and has remained down. As the numbers of tourists fell, retail sales plunged and bankruptcies reached a record number. As Hawaiian officials attempt to regain the state's competitive advantage, what stakeholders might be affected? Check out the state's Web site (**www.state.hi.us**). Make a list of possible stakeholders and the concerns each might have.

Sources: Information from the State of Hawaii Web site (**www.state.hi.us**), May 21, 2000; and J. Carlton, "Reeling Hawaii Tries to Get Tourists Back," *Wall Street Journal*, March 1, 1999, p. A2.

are more closely monitored. Public sector managers also may find their actions scrutinized by oversight agencies such as courts, legislative bodies, and political commissions. They may find their strategic decisions second-guessed by individuals who feel they have the right to voice their opinion.

Just as strategic managers in public sector organizations face multiple and often conflicting stakeholder demands, strategic managers in other types of not-for-profit organizations may find themselves dealing with multiple stakeholders who have different agendas to push. For instance, think of the public school superintendent and the various stakeholder groups he or she must consider when making decisions and taking actions, or think of the executive director of a local Red Cross organization and the many stakeholders that might influence strategic decisions and actions. The challenge of coping with these multiple stakeholders is compounded if the not-for-profit organization relies on these different stakeholders for revenues. You can begin to imagine how difficult that situation might be! Multiple stakeholders do represent a unique strategic issue with which NFP and public sector decisions makers have to deal.

Unique Strategies Developed by Not-for-Profit Organizations. Because not-for-profit organizations often rely on variable and unpredictable revenue sources, many have developed some unique strategies to cope with the changing environmental conditions—both external and internal. We need to look at three of these unique strategies: (1) cause-related marketing, (2) marketing alliances, and (3) strategic piggybacking.

Many not-for-profit organizations are participating in cause-related marketing activities. **Cause-related marketing** is a strategic practice in which for-profit businesses link up with a social cause that fits in well with the company's product or service. For instance, Avon Products, Inc. (the makeup company) developed the Avon Breast Cancer Crusade (**www.avoncrusade.com**). Its mission has been to provide women, particularly those who are medically underserved, with direct access to breast cancer education and early detection screening services. The Avon Breast Cancer Crusade in the United States is one of 30 Avon-sponsored programs in countries around the world that support women's health. These programs are known as the Avon Worldwide Fund for Women's Health and have raised over $75 million since 1992. The company saw this as a way to fund a good cause that was meaningful to its target customers. Cause-related marketing can, and does, benefit the not-for-profit organizations through public exposure and corporate donations, but the primary intent of the strategy is to enhance the image of the supporting company.[26] Although cause-related marketing may be designed for the strategic advantage of the sponsoring corporation, the NFPs can also benefit from the marketing link, and many NFPs have chosen to participate in these types of activities.

Some not-for-profits have taken cause-related marketing a step further and have actively pursued and initiated alliances between themselves and corporate partners. These **not-for-profit marketing alliances** are strategic partnerships between a not-for-profit organization and one or more corporate partners in which the corporate partner(s) agrees to undertake a series of marketing actions that will benefit both the NFP and the corporate partner(s).[27] These marketing alliances are an extension of cause-related marketing, with the main difference being that the not-for-profit organization is the one that proposes and initiates the alliance. Figure 8-6 illustrates the three different types of these marketing alliances.

Figure 8-6

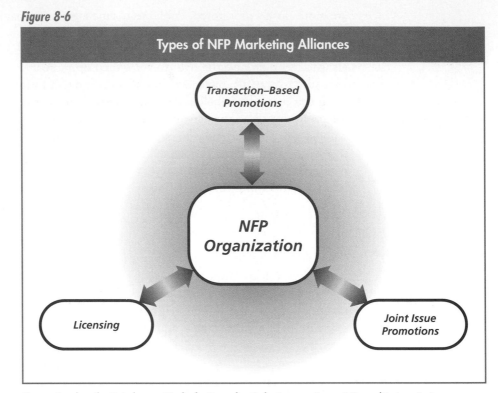

Types of NFP Marketing Alliances

Transaction–Based Promotions

NFP Organization

Licensing

Joint Issue Promotions

Source: Based on Alan R. Andreason, "Profits for Nonprofits: Find a Corporate Partner," *Harvard Business Review,* November–December 1996, p. 49.

The transaction-based promotion is an alliance in which the corporate partner donates a specific amount of cash, food, or equipment in direct proportion to sales revenues, typically up to a certain limit. American Express's Charge Against Hunger is an example of this type of not-for-profit marketing alliance. In this program, American Express donates three cents (up to a total of $5 million annually) to Share Our Strength, a hunger-relief program, every time someone uses an American Express card between November 1 and December 31 of any year.

The joint issue promotion is an alliance in which the partners agree to tackle a social problem through actions such as advertising and distributing products and promotional materials. For instance, *Glamour* magazine and Hanes Hosiery teamed up with the National Cancer Institute, the American College of Obstetricians and Gynecologists, and the American Health Foundation to distribute health materials and magazine articles about breast cancer to young women between the ages of 18 and 39.

The last type of not-for-profit marketing alliance involves licensing names and logos of not-for-profits in return for a fee or percentage of revenues. For example, the Arthritis Foundation allowed McNeil Consumer Products, a division of Johnson & Johnson, to market a line of pain relievers called "Arthritis Foundation Pain Relievers." In return, the foundation receives a minimum of $1 million annually to fund research. Another good example of licensing you might be more familiar with is the licensing of a university's name and logo for use on clothing and other types of merchandise. In return for allowing its name and logo

STRATEGIC MANAGEMENT IN AN E-BUSINESS WORLD

Not-for-profit organizations are finding ways to get e-commerce to work for them. For instance, Save the Children, an international children's relief charity, sells ties, jewelry, and other goods online at its Web site (**www.savethechildren. org**). This merchandise is still available in its catalog, but because the organization couldn't afford to send out more than one catalog annually to its 100,000 patrons, the Web site seemed a perfect solution. Through its Web site (**www.secondharvest.org**), individuals who wish to donate to Second Harvest, a food bank

clearinghouse, can choose a location where they want their dollars to go. There's no doubt that the Web will play an increasing role in strategies developed by decision makers at not-for-profit organizations. Find some other examples of how not-for-profits are using the Web to advance their cause. Write up a description of these examples.

Sources: B. Tedeschi, "Charitable Groups Find New Revenue in Retailing Goods via Their Own Web Sites," *New York Times*, March 27, 2000, p. C11; and M. M. Buechner, "Giving It Up Online," *Timedigital.com*, March 8, 1999, pp. 62–63.

Consider This ◀◀|

✓ What kinds of strategic choices do strategic managers at not-for-profit and public sector organizations face?

✓ Describe how functional, competitive, and corporate strategies might be used in NFPs and public sector organizations.

✓ What types of strategy evaluation and control issues do strategic managers of NFPs face?

✓ How would you address the misperceptions that strategic management isn't useful for or isn't needed in not-for-profit and public organizations?

✓ What types of challenges do NFPs face in dealing with multiple stakeholders, and how can strategic managers address these challenges?

✓ Describe cause-related marketing.

✓ How are marketing alliances different from cause-related marketing efforts?

✓ What are the three different types of not-for-profit marketing alliances?

✓ What is strategic piggybacking, and what are its benefits and drawbacks?

to be used, the university or college receives licensing fees. In fact, some universities generate significant funds through these licensing arrangements.

These not-for-profit marketing alliances can be an excellent way for not-for-profits to cope with the uncertainties of revenue sources. However, NFP strategic managers *do* need to ensure that the marketing alliance doesn't waste scarce organizational resources, reduce other types of donations, bring about restricted flexibility in decision making, or establish partnerships with unethical or questionable corporate partners.

The last unique NFP strategy we want to look at is **strategic piggybacking**. This term describes the development of a new activity that would generate revenue for the not-for-profit organization.[28] For example, when the Special Olympics organization sells clothing and other related merchandise, it's generating revenue through strategic piggybacking. A community symphony may decide to sell cookbooks or other types of merchandise to supplement revenue from symphony memberships. One cautionary note regarding strategy piggybacking is that the Internal Revenue Service watches these activities very closely. If an NFP engages in a business "not substantially related" to its exempt purposes, it may jeopardize its tax-exempt status. Obviously, the strategic managers would want to monitor these activities closely.

THE BOTTOM LINE

➠ Strategic management is important for all types and sizes of organizations.

➠ Strategic managers of small businesses and entrepreneurial ventures and of not-for-profit organizations face some unique challenges in managing strategically.

➠ A small business and an entrepreneurial venture are different types of organizations.

➠ A **small business** is independently owned, operated, and financed; has fewer than 100 employees; doesn't engage in any new marketing or innovative practices; and has relatively little impact on its industry.

➠ An **entrepreneurial venture** is a business that is characterized by innovative strategic practices and that has profitability and growth as its main goals.

➠ The primary difference between these two types of organizations is their differing perspective on growth and innovation.

➠ Small businesses and entrepreneurial ventures are important to every industry sector and play a significant role in the global economy.

➠ Continual changes in the external environment provide a fertile climate for small businesses and entrepreneurial ventures to flourish because these organizations are often better able to respond quickly to changing conditions than are larger organizations.

➠ The number of new start-up businesses continues to increase.

➠ The total number of small businesses and entrepreneurial ventures is also a reflection of their economic importance.

➠ The last factor that establishes the economic importance of small businesses and entrepreneurial ventures is the number of new jobs created by these types of organizations, which most analysts concur are creating the most new jobs in today's economy.

➠ It's important that the strategic management process be used in small businesses and entrepreneurial ventures.

➠ Generally speaking, the benefits to be gained from strategic planning in these organizations outweigh the drawbacks of doing so.

➠ Most researchers generally agree that the strategic planning process in small organizations and entrepreneurial ventures should be far less formal than that found in large organizations.

➠ The process shouldn't become too formal, rigid, or cumbersome or you risk the flexibility that's often crucial to a small business's competitive success.

➠ The value of strategic planning for small businesses and entrepreneurial ventures lies more in the "doing" than in the "outcome."

➠ The strategic management process in small businesses and entrepreneurial ventures involves external and internal environmental analysis, strategy choices, and strategy evaluation and control.

➠ External and internal environmental analyses play an important part in assessing the opportunities, threats, strengths, and weaknesses of the organization.

➠ Also, the boiled frog phenomenon has been shown to be relevant to small organizations.

⏩ Strategic managers at small businesses and entrepreneurial ventures have similar strategy choices as far as functional, competitive, and corporate strategies as larger organizations do. The main difference is the range or extent of possible strategies.

⏩ A small organization often will not have as many strategic options as the larger organization.

⏩ Strategy evaluation and control is similar to that used in large organizations. Again, the main difference will be in terms of the magnitude or extent of evaluation that can be done.

⏩ Some of the special strategic issues facing small businesses and entrepreneurial ventures include global–international opportunities and challenges, human resource management issues, and innovation and flexibility considerations.

⏩ Small businesses and entrepreneurial ventures are positioned to engage in **creative destruction**, the process in which existing products, processes, ideas, and businesses are replaced with better ones.

⏩ The other types of special organizations include not-for-profit and public sector organizations.

⏩ A **not-for-profit organization** is one that has met the requirements of Section 501(c)(3) of the U.S. Internal Revenue Service tax code because its purpose is to provide some good or service with no intention or goal of earning a profit.

⏩ The wide variety of NFPs include educational, charitable, religious, social service, professional membership associations, health service, cultural and recreational, cause related, and foundations.

⏩ **Public sector organizations** are also not-for-profit and are defined as organizations that are created, funded, and regulated by the public sector or government.

⏩ Both not-for-profit and public sector organizations are important to society.

⏩ The strategic management process in NFPs has not been well researched, but we know that managing strategically is important for these organizations.

⏩ The strategic management process for these types of organizations involves external and internal environmental analysis, strategy choices (functional, competitive, and corporate), and strategy evaluation and control.

⏩ Some specific strategic issues facing not-for-profit organizations include the misperception about the usefulness of strategic management, multiple stakeholders, and some unique strategies used by NFPs in response to the variable and unpredictable revenue sources.

⏩ The unique strategies used by NFPs include **cause-related marketing** (a strategic practice in which for-profit businesses link up with a social cause that fits in well with the company's product or service), **not-for-profit marketing alliances** (strategic partnerships between a not-for-profit organization and one or more corporate partners in which the corporate partner agrees to undertake a series of marketing actions that will benefit both the NFP and the corporate partner), and **strategic piggybacking** (the development of a new activity that would generate revenue for the not-for-profit organization).

BUILDING YOUR SKILLS

1. The American Lung Association (**www.lungusa.org**) is facing some serious strategic challenges. First established to combat the lung disease tuberculosis (TB), the organization has done such an effective job helping to educate individuals about TB and to eradicate the disease that the ALA no longer has an identity or a cause to rally people around. Its well-known annual Christmas Seal campaign, the organization's revenue generator, is losing its pull because a new generation of donors has more "attractive" causes to support. Log on to the organization's Web site and familiarize yourself with its mission and activities. You might even want to contact the local chapter for more information. With the information you get, do a brief SWOT analysis. Then, come up with some strategies that the ALA could use to make itself more appealing to potential donors.

   (*Sources:* Information from ALA Web site (**www.lungusa.org**), May 21, 2000; and M. Langley, "Waiting to Exhale," *Wall Street Journal,* April 14, 1999, p. A1.)

2. The Gooseberry Patch Company catalog is one of thousands of catalogs mailed annually in the United States. The direct-mail catalog industry is a cutthroat one, and the cofounders behind Gooseberry Patch, Jo Ann Martin and Vickie L. Hutchins, are trying to make good strategic decisions to keep their company growing. Check out their Web site at (**www.gooseberry patch.com**). Do some research on the direct-marketing industry by going to the Direct Marketing Association Web site (**www.the-dma.org**). Come up with a bulleted list of recommendations you'd make to Martin and Hutchins to continue growing their company.

3. Association Central is a Web site (**www.associationcentral.com**) that provides access to information, products, and services of trade associations, professional societies, and other not-for-profit organizations in the United States. Research 10 different associations (see if you can find some unusual ones!), and write up a short description of the association's mission, activities, and other information. Be sure to include the association's Web site address.

4. Judo strategy just might be an appropriate description of what successfully competing in today's dynamic context requires. A successful judo practitioner needs three things: rapid movement, flexibility, and leverage. Write a paper that addresses the following issues:

   a. What do you think each of these characteristics refers to in relation to competing in today's dynamic context?

   b. What impact might these three characteristics have as strategic decision makers in entrepreneurial ventures and small businesses strategically manage their businesses?

   c. Find two examples of entrepreneurial ventures or small businesses (check out *Business 2.0, Fast Company, Inc.,* or other sources) that you feel fit the characteristics of a judo strategy. Describe what they're doing and why you think they're good examples of a judo strategy.

   (*Source:* D. B. Yoffie and M. A. Cusumano, "Judo Strategy: The Competitive Dynamics of Internet Time," *Harvard Business Review,* January–February 1999, pp. 71–81.)

5. In order to cope with dwindling budgets and growing maintenance backlogs, many state parks are becoming entrepreneurs. How? In Ohio, for example,

campers who don't own their own gear or who don't want to haul their gear around can rent cots, coolers, cook stoves, and even teepees at many of the state parks. In New York, the state park system now serves Coke products as its "official" soft drink thanks to a $2 million alliance with the Coca-Cola Company. Many park administrators around the United States believe that they don't have any choice but to pursue revenues on their own. Park attendance is up, but overall state park budgets have decreased by an estimated 22 percent since 1980, and funds for capital improvements and maintenance have declined 68 percent. One analyst says, "Entrepreneurial fund raising is the wave of the future for state parks and someday, national parks." What type of not-for-profit strategy would you call these activities by parks? What conflicts might these types of "entrepreneurial" activities raise for strategic decision makers at state parks? What recommendations would you make for strategically managing in the changing type of environment that state parks face?

(*Source:* T. Ewing, "Meet the New Entrepreneurs," *Wall Street Journal,* February 11, 1997, p. B1.)

6. Trends can be a powerful source for entrepreneurial ideas. However, how do you know when something is really a trend and not simply a fad? For instance, think of the "clear" colas. Why did these turn out to be a fad? Do some research on trends and fads. Write up a report that includes suggestions for strategic decision makers about understanding trends and fads.

7. The Sierra Club (**www.sierraclub.org**) is a well-known environmental organization. In fact, it's the world's largest grassroots environmental organization, with over 600,000 members and a $45 million budget. What is the Sierra Club's mission? What stakeholders do you think the Sierra Club might have to contend with? What are its strategic goals and policies? If you were the club's president, how would you use the strategic management process to help you strategically manage this not-for-profit organization? Be specific.

8. An article on small business growth strategies in *Entrepreneur* magazine stated, "A good growth strategy is in focus with what the business owner has in mind for the company. In other words, the best growth strategy is a well-planned one." What's your interpretation of this statement? On a piece of paper, make two columns with one listing reasons why this statement is a good description of growth strategy for small businesses and entrepreneurial ventures and the other listing some reasons why it isn't a good description. Be prepared to debate both sides in a class discussion.

(*Source:* L. Beresford, "Growing Up," *Entrepreneur,* July 1996, pp. 124–28.)

9. You've probably watched its shows on public television. WGBH of Boston (**www.wgbh.org**) is a highly successful not-for-profit organization. For more than 40 years, it has produced hits such as *NOVA, This Old House, Evening at Pops,* and many others. How has it been so successful? There's no doubt that strategic management has contributed to its success. Using the organization's Web site, make a bulleted list of what you see as examples of good strategic choices. Be specific in describing both the *what* and *why* of your examples. That includes identifying whether the strategic choices are functional, competitive, or corporate.

STRATEGIC MANAGEMENT IN ACTION CASES

CASE #1: Shooting the Moon

Strategic Management in Action case #1 can be found at the beginning of Chapter 8.

Discussion Questions

1. Would you call Purple Moon a small business or an entrepreneurial venture? Explain your choice.

2. What examples of managing strategically can you identify in this case? Be specific.

3. Purple Moon did exhaustive market research (over 25 studies), but still failed as an independent business. What's your explanation? What are some possible reasons why this happened? Does this mean that competitor intelligence and market intelligence is useless? Explain.

4. Which part of the strategic management process is most important to strategic decision makers in small businesses and entrepreneurial ventures? Explain your answer.

CASE #2: Delivering Success

The U.S. Postal Service is a large organization. You may not realize just how large it is. Its fiscal 1996 revenues were $56.4 billion, and it ranked as the United States' ninth largest enterprise. With its career workforce of more than 760,000 employees, it's the nation's largest employer next to the Department of Defense. The U.S. Postmaster General and CEO of this not-for-profit organization, William J. Henderson, faced strategic issues that would challenge even the most effective private sector manager.

One thing that makes Henderson's job challenging is the severe constraints on operating freedom with which he has to deal. Although the U.S. Postal Service is no longer a Cabinet-level department, it is still subject to oversight control by the Congress, which has never been shy about expressing or exercising its will. The quasi-governmental organization also reports to a nine-member board of governors appointed by the President of the United States. In addition, several federal departments can control its actions. For instance, if it wants to enter new businesses, the Treasury Department must give its approval; the Department of Transportation sets rates for overseas air mail; and the Office of Personnel Management works with the agency on appeals to the Merit Systems Protection Board.

The Postal Service can't even establish its own postal rates. It can only make recommendations to the Postal Rate Commission, which either approves, disapproves, or changes them. This decision process can drag on for several months, leaving the Postal Service vulnerable to changing markets or competitors who *can* compete ferociously on price of services.

Even given all the constraints posed by these various factors, the biggest lack of self-determination that the Postal Service must contend with is that it can't pick and choose its markets and services. Its mandate is to provide universal service at a uniform price—delivering mail to *any* address in the United States regardless of how remote or dangerous an area may be, six days a week, and at a standard rate. Whereas competitors can select target markets and customers who represent the best potential profits, the Postal Service doesn't have this luxury. Some of the other strategic challenges facing Henderson included (1) quick, flexible competitors who continued to peck away at the Postal Service's markets; (2) an organizational structure that was overly bureaucratic and weak on technology; (3) no profits (i.e., no excess revenues); and (4) strained relations with the postal unions. Nonetheless, Henderson (and the previous Postmaster General, William T. Runyon) has fashioned an effective and successful slate of strategies.

Marketing innovations have been instrumental in the agency's operations. Part of this approach has been making post offices look user friendly with bright, colorful postal stores with automatic teller machines and clerks who smile. Customers can use credit cards, an innovation that took two years to get approved by Congress. The agency's Priority Mail also has been aggressively marketed. Other product innovations have included self-stick (no lick) stamps, Global Priority Mail, and Global Package Link. To counteract some of the electronic competition, the Postal Service has developed Smart-Stamp electronic stamps by which postage prints directly off a personal computer and printer; Electronic Postmark, which builds on the Postal Service's unique capability of being a "trusted third party" by certifying e-mail messages; and kiosks that offer consumers one-stop shopping

for federal services. In addition, the Postal Service is going after the Web delivery market. As more and more individuals shop online, the Postal Service wants to be the deliverer of choice.

The Postal Service hasn't ignored other strategic areas, either. On the operations side of the business, the Postal Service has installed sophisticated automated equipment to improve efficiency and on-time delivery. In the human resources area, the Postal Service was reorganized by eliminating four layers of management. The leaner organization has made it possible for communications from top to bottom to become much more effective.

All of these strategic actions have had a profound impact on the Postal Service's performance. It posted a profit in 1997 and in 1998. Although profit isn't the agency's goal, the excess revenues allowed the organization to continue its efficiency and effectiveness pursuits.

Discussion Questions

1. Although the U.S. Postal Service is a public sector organization, how does it exhibit some of the characteristics of a small business or entrepreneurial venture?
2. What types of constraints do strategic decision makers at the USPS face?
3. What should an external analysis for the Postal Service include? Be specific.
4. What types of strategic evaluation and control would you recommend that the Postal Service might use? Be sure and explain not only *what* you would recommend, but *how* it would work.
5. Log on to the U.S. Postal Service Web site (**www.usps.com**) and find the cur-

rent Annual Performance Plan. What strategic goals and initiatives is the organization pursuing? How will these strategies be measured?

(*Sources:* Information from U.S. Postal Service Web site (**www.usps.com**), including the 2000 U.S.P.S. Annual Performance Plan, May 21, 2000; K. Kranhold, "Postal Service Seeks More Web Deliveries," *Wall Street Journal*, August 27, 1999, p. B2; D. Kushner, "Post Office Spurring the Pony Express into the Next Century," *New York Times*, December 24, 1998, p. D5; G. Anders, "It's Digital, It's Encrypted — It's Postage," *Wall Street Journal*, September 21, 1998, p. B1; The Associated Press, "E-stamps Replacing Sticking with Clicking," *Springfield News Leader*, April 1, 1998, p. 12A; M. B. Regan, "The Post Office Delivers a Banner Year," *Business Week*, January 19, 1998, p. 38; W. Dowell et al., "Zapping the Post Office," *Time*, January 19, 1998, pp. 46–47; and W. H. Miller, "Runyon Delivers a Turnaround," *Industry Week*, November 18, 1996, pp. 44–49.)

CASE #3: Recipe for Success

William Williams, cofounder of Glory Foods (**www.gloryfoods.com**) has followed his own recipe for success. Glory Foods, Inc., based in Columbus, Ohio, has annual revenues approaching $15 million. It sells "down-home tasting" southern cuisine specialties that are quick and easy to prepare, a delicious alternative to the traditional southern cooking that takes hours. The company has successfully cornered a market niche by following a conservative path to growth.

Williams formed the company after he saw all the ethnic foods being sold — Hispanic, Asian, Jewish, everything but African American food — while walking down a grocery store aisle. As the owner of a soul food restaurant in Columbus, Williams "smelled" opportunity. The traditional southern cuisine — foods such as black-eyed peas, collard greens, grits, peppered vinegar, and hot sauce — are all very labor intensive to prepare. People were busy; they probably didn't have the time or energy to spend hours cooking and baking even though they loved these kinds of food. Williams felt there had to be a market for ready-prepared African American food. The big food manufacturers such as Swanson and Green Giant weren't targeting any specific niches, and the companies that were had overlooked this particular food market. Williams decided to pursue his entrepreneurial idea.

Williams brought together three partners, all with food industry experience. They pooled their money and launched Glory Foods. From the beginning the founders followed a conservative path. Each kept their day jobs until the business was financially stable. That way no one would be taking a salary out of the business because capital was scarce in the early days. The foursome worked two years to develop their recipes. They took their time because their goal was making food that tasted delicious and authentic, yet would be healthier, lower in fat, cholesterol, and salt. Throughout that time, Williams tested recipes at his restaurant to see how people responded. The partners deliberately chose not to go to market with their products until they had all 17 specialties ready.

Once the products were of the desired quality, Glory Foods test-marketed its products in Kroger grocery stores for 90 days. Although Kroger wanted to place the food products in all 90 of its stores in central Ohio, Williams decided to take only part of the order — enough for 40 stores. His rationale was that he felt that Glory Foods was underfinanced for such a large order. Although it was a difficult decision to make, it turned out to be a smart one. With the Kroger order, Williams was able to get a bank line of credit. He then went to South Carolina and contracted with farmers to grow fresh vegetables and with a factory to process the food. At that time there was no money left for advertising, so Williams resorted to down-home marketing. He recruited women's auxiliary groups from local black churches to give out food samples in the Kroger stores. For their services, Glory made donations to the churches and paid the women $10 an hour. For the first six months of their debut, Glory Foods' products sold slowly. However, another large grocery chain, Food Lion, heard of Glory Foods and placed an order for its 1,400 stores. Cash flow constraints kept Glory Foods from taking on the full order, but it did stock 600 Food Lion stores with its products.

Even with its calculated, careful growth, the time was fast approaching when the company would need more capital to continue in business. The four partners each agreed to invest additional money and to sell 17 percent of the company to 40 investors. These investors were mainly friends and a few relatives.

Williams's decision to move slowly was based mostly on the fact that he didn't want to dilute the founders' equity portions down to minority levels. Several venture capitalists expressed strong interest in the company, but the partners turned them down. Although the slow growth approach may have taken more time, Glory Foods' partners felt it was worth it because each owns nearly 21 percent of the business and among them, they have total control over what happens to the company. The company continues its slow growth approach, even today. Its product line has expanded to include additional grocery products, frozen entrees, and side dishes, but only after carefully considering and testing each new item. It seems that Williams's recipe for success has turned out to be sweet, indeed.

Discussion Questions

1. If you were William Williams and his co-owners, how would you measure growth in your business? Why would these measures be important?

2. Is slow, cautious growth a good strategy in the food industry? Explain.

3. How have Glory Foods' strategic decision makers used strategic management in their business? Be specific.

(*Sources:* Company's Web site (**www.gloryfoods.com**), May 21, 2000; and C. Shook, "Making Haste Slowly," *Forbes*, September 22, 1997, pp. 220–22.)

ENDNOTES

1. Information from Purple Moon Web site (**www.purple-moon.com**), May 15, 2000; K. T. Greenfeld, "Mattel: Some (Re)Assembly Required," *Time*, October 25, 1999, pp. 58–59; A. Harmon, "With the Best Research and Intentions, a Game Maker Fails," *New York Times*, March 22, 1999, p. C1; and L. Bannon, "Mattel's Barbie Gains New Friend, Rockett, Who's Really Serious," *Wall Street Journal*, March 19, 1999, p. A3.

2. Code of Federal Regulations 13:121 (Washington, DC: U.S. Government Printing Office, January 1, 1994), pp. 354–67.

3. T. L. Hatten, *Small Business: Entrepreneurship and Beyond* (Upper Saddle River, NJ: Prentice Hall, 1997), p. 5; and J. W. Carland, F. Hoy, W. R. Boulton, and J. C. Carland, "Differentiating Entrepreneurs from Small Business Owners: A Conceptualization," *Academy of Management Review*, 9, no. 2 (1984), pp. 354–59.

4. L. W. Busenitz, "Research on Entrepreneurial Alertness," *Journal of Small Business Management*, October 1996, pp. 35–44.

5. Carland, Hoy, Boulton, and Carland, "Differentiating Entrepreneurs."

6. "The Facts About Small Business 1999" (Washington, DC: U.S. Small Business Administration, Office of Advocacy), available from SBA Online Web site (**www.sba.gov/advo**), May 19, 2000, p. 1.

7. *Statistical Abstract of the United States*, 1993.

8. "The Facts About Small Business 1999," p. 1; J. Chun and C. E. Griffin, "The Mouse That Roared: The True State of Small Business," *Entrepreneur*, September 1996, pp. 118–22; and L. M. Litvan, "The Hot Zones for Entrepreneurs," *Nation's Business*, June 1996, pp. 42–43.

9. "The Facts About Small Business 1999," p. 1.

10. Chun and Griffin, "The Mouse That Roared," p. 120.

11. C. Schwenk and C. B. Shrader, "Effects of Formal Strategic Planning on Financial Performance in Small Firms: A Meta-Analysis," *Entrepreneurship Theory and Practice*, 17, no. 3 (1993), pp. 53–64; J. Bracker, B. Keats, and J. Pearson, "Planning and Financial Performance Among Small Firms in a Growth Industry," *Strategic Management Journal*, 9 (1988), pp. 591–603; J. Bracker and J. Pearson, "Planning and Financial Performance of Small, Mature Firms," *Strategic Management Journal*, 7 (1986), pp. 503–22; R. Ackelsberg and P. Arlow, "Small Businesses Do Plan and It Pays Off," *Long Range Planning*, 18, no. 3 (1985), pp. 61–67; C. Orpen, "The Effects of Long-Range Planning on Small Business Performance," *Journal of Small Business Management*, January 1985, pp. 16–23; R. Robinson and J. Pearce, "Research Thrusts in Small Firm Strategic Planning," *Academy of Management Review*, 9 (1984), pp. 128–37; P. Wood and R. LaForge, "The Impact of Comprehensive Planning on Financial Performance," *Academy of Management Journal*, 22 (1979), pp. 516–26; R. Robinson, "Forecasting and Small Business: A Study of the Strategic Planning Process," *Journal of Small Business Management*, 17, no. 3 (1979), pp. 19–27; P. Karger and R. Mali, "Long Range Planning and Organizational Performance," *Long Range Planning*, 8, no. 6 (1975), pp. 61–64; D. Herold, "Long Range Planning and Organizational Performance: A Cross-Validation Study," *Academy of Management Journal*, 15 (1972), pp. 91–102; and H. I. Ansoff et al., "Does Planning Pay? The Effect of Planning on Success of Acquisition in American Firms," *Long Range Planning*, 3, no. 2 (1970), pp. 2–7.

12. C. B. Shrader, C. Mulford, and V. Blackbrun, "Strategic and Operational Planning, Uncertainty, and Performance in Small Firms," *Journal of Small Business Management*, October 1989, pp. 45–60; R. Robinson and J. Pearce, "The Impact of Formalized Strategic Planning on Financial Performance in Small Organizations," *Strategic Management Journal*, 4 (1983), pp. 197–207; W. Lindsay et al., "Strategic Planning: Determining the Impact of Environmental Characteristics and Uncertainty," *Academy of Management Journal*, 25 (1982), pp. 500–9; R. Hogarth and S. Makridakis, "Forecasting and Planning: An Evaluation," *Management Science*, 27, no. 2 (1981), pp. 115–38; M. Leontiades and A. Tezel, "Planning Perceptions and Planning Results," *Strategic Management Journal*, 1 (1980), pp. 65–76; R. Kudla, "The Effects of Strategic Planning on Common Stock Returns," *Academy of Management Journal*, 23 (1980), pp. 5–20; R. Fulmer and L. Rue, "The Practice and Profitability of Long-Range Planning," *Managerial Planning*, May–June 1974, pp. 1–7; and S. Thune and R. House, "Where Long Range Planning Pays Off," *Business Horizons*, 13, no. 4 (1970), pp. 81–87.

13. T. J. Callahan and M. D. Cassar, "Small Business Owners' Assessment of Their Abilities to Perform and Interpret Formal Market Studies," *Journal of Small Business Management*, October 1995, pp. 1–9; Shrader et al., "Strategic and Operational Planning"; L. R. Smeltzer, G. L. Fann, and V. N. Nikolaisen, "Environmental Scanning Practices in Small Businesses," *Journal of Small Business Management*, July 1988, pp. 56–62; S. W. McDaniel and A. Parasuraman, "Practical Guidelines for Small Business Marketing Research," *Journal of Small Business Management*, January 1986, pp. 1–9; and S. W. McDaniel and A. Parasuraman, "Small Business Experience with and Attitudes Toward Formal Marketing Research," *American Journal of Small Business*, spring 1985, pp. 1–6.

14. S. Shane and L. Kolvereid, "National Environment, Strategy, and New Venture Performance: A Three Country Study," *Journal of Small Business Management*, April 1995, pp. 37–50.

15. A. Bhide, "The Questions Every Entrepreneur Must Answer," *Harvard Business Review*, November–December 1996, pp. 120–30; S. I. Mohan-Neill, "The Influence of Firm's Age and Size on Its Environmental Scanning Activities," *Journal of Small Business Management*, October 1995, pp. 10–21; T. J. Callahan and M. D. Cassar, *Journal of Small Business Management*, October 1995; J. Masten, G. B. Hartmann, and A. Safari, "Small Business Strategic Planning and Technology Transfer: The Use of Publicly Supported Technology Assistance Agencies," *Journal of Small Business Management*, July 1995, pp. 26–37; and A. Shama, "Marketing Strategies During Recession: A Comparison of Small and Large Firms," *Journal of Small Business Management*, July 1993, pp. 62–72.

16. N. M. Tichy and M. A. Devenna, *The Transformational Leader* (New York: John Wiley, 1986).

17. S. D. Chowdhury and J. R. Lang, "Crisis, Decline, and Turnaround: A Test of Competing Hypotheses for Short-Term Performance Improvement in Small Firms," *Journal of Small Business Management*, October 1993, pp. 8–17.

18. J. L. Calof, "The Impact of Size on Internationalization," *Journal of Small Business Management*, October 1993, pp. 60–69; and P. C. Wright, "The Personal and the Personnel Adjustments and Costs for Small Businesses Entering the International Market Place," *Journal of Small Business Management*, January 1993, pp. 83–93.

19. Calof, "The Impact of Size on Internationalization."

20. S. P. Deshpande and D. Y. Golhar, "HRM Practices in Large and Small Manufacturing Firms: A Comparative Study," *Journal of Small Business Management*, April 1994, pp. 49–56.

21. See Hatten, *Small Business: Entrepreneurship and Beyond*, pp. 17–18.

22. K. Ascher and B. Nare, "Strategic Planning in the Public Sector," in *International Review of Strategic Management*, Vol. 1, ed. D. E. Hussey (New York: John Wiley, 1988), pp. 297–315; M. S. Wortman Jr., "Strategic Management in Nonprofit Organizations: A Research Typology and Research Prospectus," in *Strategic Management Frontiers*, ed. J. H. Grant (Greenwich, CT: JAI Press, 1988), pp. 425–42; J. W. Harvey and K. F. McCrohan, "Strategic Issues for Charities and Philanthropies," *Long Range Planning*, December 1988, pp. 44–55; D. Harvey and J. D. Snyder, "Charities Need a Bottom Line, Too," *Harvard Business Review*, January–February 1987, pp. 14–22; I. Unterman and R. H. Davis, *Strategic Management of Not-for-Profit Organizations* (New York: Praeger, 1984); J. M. Stevens and R. P. McGowan, "Managerial Strategies in Municipal Government Organizations," *Academy of Management Journal*, 26, no. 3 (1983), pp. 527–34.

23. A. Howard and J. Magretta, "Surviving Success: An Interview with the Nature Conservancy's John Sawhill," *Harvard Business Review*, September–October 1995, pp. 108–18; P. V. Jenster and G. A. Overstreet, "Planning for a Non-Profit Service: A Study of U.S. Credit Unions," *Long Range Planning*, April 1990, pp. 103–11; and G. J. Medley, "Strategic Planning for the World Wildlife Fund," *Long Range Planning*, February 1988, pp. 46–54.

24. M. Coulter, "Competitive Strategies of Community Arts Organizations," working paper from a research study of community arts organizations in the Midwest, 1996.

25. R. M. Kanter and D. V. Summers, "Doing Well While Doing Good: Dilemmas of Performance Measurement in Nonprofit Organizations and the Need for a Multiple-constituency Approach," in *The Nonprofit Sector: A Research Handbook*, ed. W. W. Powell (New Haven, CT: Yale University Press, 1987).

26. See, for example, G. Smith and R. Stodghill II, "Are Good Causes Good Marketing?" *Business Week*, March 21, 1994, pp. 64–65; G. Levin, "Green Marketing Gets Cautious," *Advertising Age*, July 5, 1993, p. 4; "Cause-Related Marketing," *Inc.*, July 1991, p. 72; and "Marketing: Cause-Related Marketing," *Wall Street Journal*, February 19, 1987, p. B1.

27. A. R. Andreason, "Profits for Nonprofits: Find a Corporate Partner," *Harvard Business Review*, November–December 1996, pp. 47–59.

28. R. P. Nielsen, "Piggybacking Strategies for Nonprofits: A Shared Costs Approach," *Strategic Management Journal*, May–June 1986, pp. 209–11; R. P. Nielsen, "Piggybacking for Business and Nonprofits: A Strategy for Hard Times," *Long Range Planning*, April 1984, pp. 96–102; and R. P. Nielsen, "SMR Forum: Strategic Piggybacking—A Self-Subsidizing Strategy for Nonprofit Institutions," *Sloan Management Review*, summer 1982, pp. 65–69.

COMPREHENSIVE CASES FOR ANALYSIS

Amazon.com

Amazon.com (**www.amazon.com**) is one of the interesting stories of the e-commerce revolution. Its numbers are eye-opening: $16 billion in market value (it's been as high as $23 billion), $1 billion in cash and marketable securities, $1.5 billion in long-term debt, $1.6 billion in revenues (at the end of 1999), 135.2 percent revenue growth rate (12 months ended 1999), 229.9 percent revenue growth rate (36 months ended 1999), and zero profits ($720 million loss in 1999). And that's only from having been in business a short period of time (since 1994). However, as the e-world continues to grow, evolve, and shift, will there be a place for Amazon.com? How long can the company continue to operate without profits? Will Jeff Bezos, founder–CEO and an innovative retail visionary, be able to strategically manage Amazon's future?

BACKGROUND

By now, most of us have heard the captivating story behind Amazon.com. The company is the realization of Jeff Bezos's dream of retailing on the Internet. In 1994, Bezos was a successful programmer on Wall Street, but statistics on the explosive use of the Internet and World Wide Web (at that time, it was growing at the rate of about 2,300 percent a month) kept nagging at him. After presenting his idea for selling on the Internet to his employer, hedge fund company D. E. Shaw, and being turned down, he decided to quit his job and pursue his vision. Bezos drew up a list of 20 products that he figured could be sold online (including books, music, magazines, and PC hardware and software) and finally narrowed the list down to books or music. He settled on books for two simple reasons: There were more products to sell (more than 2 million titles in print versus 300,000 music titles), and the giant publishing companies were not as ferociously competitive as the six (at that time) record companies. After pinpointing the product he would retail, Bezos piled his family's belongings into a moving van and ordered the drivers to head west. He told them he would contact them when he'd decided whether the destination would be Colorado, Oregon, or Washington. Bezos, his wife, and their Labrador retriever headed off in the same direction.

They eventually landed in Seattle. Why Seattle? Because it had a pool of talented computer professionals (Microsoft and numerous computer software start-ups are located there), and it was near two major book wholesalers. Bezos sold his first book from his Web site in July of 1995. Bezos and his team innovated features that now seem commonplace and ordinary to online shoppers: one-click shopping, customer reviews, and e-mail order verification. Now, just like its namesake river, Amazon.com keeps branching out into new territories.

CURRENT OPERATIONS

Amazon.com, billed as the Internet's largest retailer, serves over 20 million accounts in all 50 states and over 160 countries. Although it still competes directly with Barnes & Noble and others in the book business, Amazon.com has branched out into a vast and varied network of Internet sites. Its online partners offer a host of other consumer goods, including jewelry, prescription goods, electronics, music, DVDs, videos, software, and home improvement products. Amazon also has created Web-based marketplaces (Amazon.com Auctions, zShops, and sothebys.amazon.com) where buyers and sellers can enter into transactions on a wide range and variety of products. These online auction services were formed to compete directly with eBay, the largest online auction company.

Amazon has continued to expand through new divisions and alliances online. For instance, in June 1999, Amazon started offering digital downloads of complete musical works. It bought stakes in other dot.com retailers such as drugstore.com, living.com, HomeGrocer.com, and Pets.com. Here is a complete listing of Amazon's products and affiliated operations (as of June 2000):

Affiliates
Accept.com (online transaction technology)
Alexa Internet (Web tracking and recommendation site)
Ashford.com (luxury and premium goods)
Audible (downloadable audio content)
Back to Basics (toy catalog)
Basis Technology (develops international Web sites of U.S. online companies)
Della.com (online wedding registry)
drugstore.com (health and beauty products and prescription drugs)
Exchange.com (rare products)
eZiba.com (world crafts)
Gear.com (brand-name sporting goods at discount prices)
Greenlight.com (online car sales)
Greg Manning Auctions (online auctioneer doing business in the United States, China, and Europe)
HomeGrocer.com (home delivery service for groceries and other products)
Kozmo.com (one-hour delivery service for entertainment and convenience products)

living.com (furniture store)

NextCard (co-branded consumer credit card)

Pets.com (pet supply store)

sothebys.amazon.com (auctions of collectibles and other valuables)

Tool Crib of the North (tools and equipment catalog)

Wineshopper.com (wine)

Selected Products Sold on Amazon.com

Books

Cameras

Cars

CDs

Computer games

DVDs

Furniture

Home electronics

Home improvement items

Jewelry

Kitchen gear

Lawn mowers

Outdoor grills

Patio furniture

Software

Tools

Toys

Videos

Wine

Other Businesses

Amazon.com Anywhere (Web site for wireless phones, handheld units, and other noncomputer devices)

Amazon.co.uk (Amazon's U.K. business)

Amazon.de (Amazon's German business)

Internet Movie Database (comprehensive and authoritative source of information on movies, entertainment programs, and cast–crew members)

Junglee (online comparison shopping services)

LiveBid Auctions (sole provider of live-event auctions)

PlanetAll (online address book, calendar, and reminder service)

An important component of Amazon's operations are its distribution facilities. The geographic coverage of the distribution centers and their capacity has dramatically improved Amazon's order fulfillment capabilities. Having its own distribution network also allows Amazon to better control the distribution process and facilitate its ability to deliver merchandise to customers on a timely and reliable basis. The company has ten distribution warehouses including one in England and one in Germany. The U.S. locations include Seattle, Washington (also company headquarters); New Castle, Delaware; McDonough, Georgia; Coffeyville, Kansas; Campbellsville and Lexington, Kentucky;

Fernley, Nevada; and Grand Forks, North Dakota. These distribution facilities play an important role in warehousing and shipping the products ordered by Amazon's customers.

Amazon purchases products from a network of manufacturers, distributors, publishers, and labels. When it doesn't have the needed inventory on hand to fill customers' orders, the company's proprietary software selects orders that can be filled by electronic interfaces with vendors and forwards the others to the special orders group. The special orders group has developed customized information systems that trained ordering personnel use to locate hard-to-find merchandise.

Amazon is affected to some extent by seasonal fluctuations in Internet usage and in retail ordering. Internet usage usually declines during the summer months because users engage in outdoors and other recreational activities. Retail seasonality revolves around the enormous jump in demand in the last three months of a year.

TECHNOLOGY

Maintaining a viable and reliable technology base is obviously critical to Amazon's operations. Because its operations are dependent on the continuous use of computer software and hardware, Amazon has invested significant resources (people and equipment) in the development and maintenance of its technology base.

The company has implemented numerous Web site management, search, customer interaction, recommendation, transaction-processing, and fulfillment services and systems. Although it uses some commercially available licensed technologies, many of its technologies are proprietary. Amazon's current strategy is to focus development efforts on creating and enhancing the specialized, proprietary software that's unique to its business. However, Amazon is willing to license or acquire commercially developed technology if it's available and appropriate.

Amazon's Web sites, network operations, and transaction-processing systems are monitored continuously. The continued, uninterrupted operation of its Web sites and transaction-processing systems is critical to Amazon's business. Currently, the company uses the services of three Internet service providers so it can maintain constant connectivity, both domestically and internationally.

MARKETING AND CUSTOMER SERVICE

Amazon's marketing strategy is designed to strengthen the Amazon.com brand name; increase customer traffic to the Web site; build customer loyalty; encourage repeat purchases; and develop complementary, incremental product and service revenue opportunities. The company's marketing strategy is implemented through creative applications of technology to customers' experiences. Innovations such as personalized programs and services, as well as flexible merchandising, are all part of Amazon's approach to marketing. The company uses a variety of media, promotional methods, and public relations activities to achieve its marketing goals. Amazon, and particularly Jeff Bezos, is featured in news publications and in other news sources quite frequently.

With all the marketing exchanges taking place in Amazon's online world, it should come as no surprise that customer service is a high priority, particularly because the interactions take place in a virtual world and the only connection is by computers and phone lines. From the beginning, Amazon's focus has been on offering customers compelling value. It set out to offer customers something they couldn't get in any other way: more selection than in a physical store presented in a useful, easy-to-search, and easy-to-browse format in a store open 365 days a year, 24 hours a day. It has maintained a dogged focus on improving customers' online shopping experiences.

Delivering outstanding customer service isn't easy in this online environment. The reality of online shopping is that it increases the odds of communications mix-ups and angry accusations. However, Amazon has taken steps to keep its customers satisfied.

Every day, Amazon hears from more than 20,000 customers who have a problem. Maybe the merchandise they ordered hasn't showed up or wasn't what they expected. Even first-time visitors to Amazon's Web site may want help placing an order. The company's more than 200 customer service representatives, working in five customer service centers (Seattle and Tacoma, Washington; Slough, England; Regensburg, Germany; and Grand Forks, North Dakota), are trained to work with customers and attempt to resolve their problems. New customer service centers opened in Huntington, West Virginia, and The Hague, Netherlands, in 2000. These reps deal with a constant stream of e-mails, phone calls, and even letters, although most of the complaints come in electronically. Phrases such as "thank you" and "we're sorry" are used over and over again. If the situation turns hostile, these reps are authorized to waive shipping charges and placate customers with gift certificates.

Amazon must be doing something right in this area. Its prices for books are only the sixth-lowest among 14 major online merchants. However, a publisher of Internet shopping guides rates Amazon as the best overall online bookstore, mostly because of its strong showing in customer service–oriented categories such as customer confidence and ease of use. How does the company do it?

The customer service department at Amazon is a curious mix of old-fashioned hand-holding, traditional factory procedures, and modern technology. Bill Price, Amazon's head of customer service, has tried to turn the customer service function into a series of simple routines. Yet he readily acknowledges that the most important parts of the job can't be automated. He says, "To do this job right, you need a real passion for the consumer" (Anders, p. R12). The best customer service reps are individuals who have a lot of empathy for frustrated customers.

The reps work in long rows of gray cubicles. As customers' complaints come up on their computer screens, the reps choose from a library of 1,400 prescripted remarks that are then customized with the customer's name and a few other details. There are remarks to address almost every conceivable issue. In fact, many customer complaints have more than one prescripted remark, and the reps can use their own good judgment to decide which to respond with. These responses are sent out electronically. If a service rep resolves an especially difficult situation, he or she gets a "CPR" from the quality assurance department recognizing a "customer permanently retained." Another form of recognition by Amazon's management was the handing out of hundreds of tiny green ceramic turtles to top service representatives. The story behind this was that an unhappy customer is like a turtle on its back. The turtle wants to get back on its feet but doesn't know how. That's where the customer service rep comes in—the rep helps the turtle (the customer) get back on its feet.

HUMAN RESOURCE MANAGEMENT

Amazon.com started with a mission "to use the Internet to transform book buying into the fastest, easiest, and most enjoyable shopping experience possible." Amazon is committed to customer satisfaction and the delivery of an educational and inspiring shopping experience.

The company's philosophy is to work hard, have fun, and make history. Employees are passionate about what they do and many have a financial stake in the company's future through stock options. There is no "Amazon.com" type. Certain Amazon employees have three masters' degrees and some speak five languages. Among other employees are a professional figure skater, race car drivers, and a husband–wife–dog team. There are people who have worked at Procter & Gamble and Microsoft, and people who have worked at *Rolling Stone* and *The Village Voice*. The company experienced its first layoff of 150 employees in January 2000.

The employees (as of the end of 1999, there were 7,600) are not unionized. They wear jeans to work, and although casualness is encouraged, that casual attitude does not spill over to work ethic expectations. Amazon's employees work hard at being innovative and original. The software engineers work to develop programs that are the first of their kind; the editors work to create original content; and the site team works to design site features that can't be found anywhere else. Their philosophy is that innovation *and* execution go hand-in-hand. It doesn't do any good to innovate if the innovations aren't implemented.

The company's executive officers are as follows:

Jeff Bezos   Founder and Chief Executive Officer
Bezos founded Amazon in 1994. Prior to that he was employed by D. E. Shaw & Company, a Wall Street investment firm. He has a B.S. degree in Electrical Engineering and Computer Science from Princeton University.

Joe Galli   President and Chief Operating Officer
Galli joined Amazon in June 1999. Prior to that he held a variety of positions with The Black and Decker Corporation, including president of Black and Decker's Worldwide Power Tools and Accessories. He has a B.S. in Business Administration degree from the University of North Carolina and an M.B.A. from Loyola College.

Warren Jenson   Chief Financial Officer and Senior Vice President
Jenson joined Amazon in September 1999. Prior to that, he was CFO and EVP of Delta Air Lines, CFO and SVP for the National Broadcasting Company (NBC), and participated in efforts to develop MSNBC. He has a B.S. in Accounting degree and a Masters of Accountancy from Brigham Young University.

Diego Piacentini   General Manager, International and Senior Vice President
Piacentini joined Amazon in February 2000. He was VP and GM of Europe of Apple Computer, Inc. prior to coming to Amazon. He has a degree in Economics from Bocconi University in Milan, Italy.

Rick Dalzell   Chief Information Officer
Dalzell joined Amazon in August 1997. Prior to his arrival at Amazon, he held several management positions with the IS Division at Wal-Mart Stores, Inc. He has a B.S. in Engineering degree from the United States Military Academy, West Point.

David Risher   General Manager, U.S. Retail Group and Senior Vice President
Risher joined Amazon in February 1997 as Vice President of Product Development. He held a variety of marketing and management positions at Microsoft prior to joining Amazon. He has a B.A. degree in Comparative Literature from Princeton University and an M.B.A. from Harvard Business School.

Jeff Wilke   Vice President and General Manager, Operations

Wilke joined Amazon in September 1999. Prior to that he was employed in various executive positions at AlliedSignal and was a technology consultant at Andersen Consulting. He has a B.S.E. degree in chemical engineering from Princeton University and an M.B.A. and Master of Science in chemical engineering from MIT.

Mark Britto   Vice President, Strategic Alliances

Britto joined Amazon in June 1999 as part of the acquisition of Accept.com. Prior to his cofounding of Accept.com, he held executive positions at FirstUSA Bank and NationsBank. He holds a B.S. in Industrial Engineering and Operations Research degree and an M.S. in Operations Research from the University of California at Berkeley.

Mark S. Peek   Chief Accounting Officer

Peek joined Amazon in March 2000. Prior to joining Amazon, he was a partner at Deloitte & Touche LLP where he was lead partner for a number of multinational technology clients. He has a B.S. degree in Accounting, Economics, and International Business from Minnesota State University.

FINANCIAL

Financially, Amazon has continued to be an enigma. It has produced only losses since its beginning. However, its market valuation continues to be in the stratosphere. Amazon's 1999 revenues of $1.6 billion took only four years to achieve. In contrast, when Wal-Mart went public in 1970, it had only $31 million in annual revenues eight years later. Amazon epitomizes the potential of Internet-based companies. As one expert explained, Internet retailers are unconstrained by the realities of the physical world and are rewarded with continuously increasing returns as they grow. "When a customer in Beijing buys a book or a toy at Amazon, Amazon has just opened up a store in that neighborhood. And it cost the company nothing to do so" (Rothfeder, p. 20). But, how long do investors wait for the company to prove its worth? Financial highlights for 1996, 1997, 1998, and 1999 follow.

Income Statement (all dollar amounts in millions)	Dec. 99	Dec. 98	Dec. 97	Dec. 96
Revenue	$1,639.8	$ 609.8	$147.8	$15.7
Cost of goods sold	1,349.1	476.1	118.9	12.3
Gross profit	290.6	133.7	28.8	3.5
Operating expenses	896.4	242.7	61.4	9.9
Loss from operations	(605.8)	(109)	(32.6)	(6.4)
Net interest income	(37.4)	(12.6)	1.6	.2
Loss before equity in losses of equity-method investees	(643.2)	(121.6)	(31.0)	(6.2)
Equity in losses of equity-method investees	(76.8)	(2.9)	—	—
Net loss	$ (720)	$(124.5)	$(31.0)	$ (6.2)

Balance Sheet (in millions)	Dec. 99	Dec. 98	Dec. 97	Dec. 96
Cash	$ 117.0	$ 25.6	$ 1.8	$ .864
Marketable securities	589.2	347.9	123.5	5.4
Working capital	273.2	262.7	93.2	1.7
Total assets	2,472.6	648.5	149.8	8.4
Long-term debt	1,466.3	348.1	76.7	—
Stockholder's equity	$ 266.3	$ 138.7	$ 28.6	$ 2.9

(Financial information from Amazon.com's *1999 Annual Report*, p. 22.)

Fiscal results for the first quarter of 2000 showed slight improvement. The company lost $308 million in the first quarter on revenues of $574 million. Revenues rose 95 percent over the same period the previous year. Of those sales, the U.S. book, music, and video business represented $401 million, up 50 percent from figures in the same period a year earlier. Sales in its British and German subsidiaries increased by 300 percent to $75 million. Sales in its other units (including toys, tools, and auctions) were $97 million.

Stock analysts praised the company for its increased focus on efficiency and financial prudence. Amazon's chief financial officer stressed that the company was moving toward profitability. Financial improvements were to come mainly from increased efficiency in the company's distribution warehouses. During this quarter, Amazon said it spent $41 million in marketing. That represented $13 for each of its three million new customers, a far lower cost than that of any other major online retailer. In addition, those customers that were active spent an average of $121 during the first quarter of 2000, compared to $107 for the first quarter of 1999.

The company's cash position at the end of the first quarter was strong. It had $1 billion in cash, and the company's chief financial officer said Amazon was not at risk of running out of cash. He stressed that the company would generate enough cash from its operations over the remainder of 2000 to cover its planned capital expenses.

INDUSTRY AND COMPETITOR INFORMATION

The online retailing industry is a chaotic one, at best. The 1999 holiday selling season, while setting record sales, also precipitated a shakeout in the industry as weaker competitors struggled to stay in business. The online book segment of retailing, Amazon's major market, has experienced several changes. The advent of electronic books, competitor mergers and acquisitions, and legal wranglings over content and process patents are just a few of the major challenges facing the online retailing industry.

Some of Amazon's major competitors include Barnes & Noble, CDNow, and eBay. Here's some brief information on each of these companies.

Barnes & Noble, Inc. (**www.barnesandnoble.com**)

Barnes & Noble is the number-one bookseller in the United States with a market share of 15 percent. It operates about 1,000 stores, including about 520 superstores and a decreasing number of mall stores. The company's principal business is the bricks-and-mortar retail sale of trade books (generally hardcover and paperback consumer titles), mass-market paperbacks, children's books, bargain books, and magazines. Barnes & Noble also owns video game retailer Babbage's Etc. and 49 percent of publishing portal iUniverse.com. It maintains a mail-order catalog and a book publishing business. Its e-commerce site allows access to more than 750,000 titles ready for immediate delivery, and the Web site database features more than 6.5 million out-of-print and rare books as well as the largest online selection of bargain books discounted up to 90 percent.

CDNow, Inc.

CDNow is an online retailer that sells CDs, DVDs, videos, and T-shirts. It also offers music downloads and related content. CDNow offers about 500,000 titles to around 3.5

million customers. In 1999, the company purchased rival N2K (Music Boulevard). However, an agreement to be purchased by Columbia House (the music joint venture between Sony and Time Warner) fell through in early March 2000. The company is desperate for cash and in serious trouble.

eBay, Inc.

eBay is an online auction service with over 4,500 categories being used by over 12 million registered users. The company profits by taking a percentage of each sale. The eBay business model is one of community. eBay users use the site as a place to socialize, discuss topics of common interest, and ultimately to conduct business in an online trading environment. Through eBay, individuals can buy and sell items ranging from sports memorabilia, computers, Beanie Babies, magazines, electronics, and gemstones. eBay is proving to be a formidable competitor, and unlike most other online retailers, it's profitable. The company's 1999 revenues were $224.7 million with profits after tax of $10.8 million.

FUTURE CHALLENGES

Jeff Bezos has attempted to position Amazon to be the dominant winner in the online retail market. His five-year plan is for Amazon to be a place where you can buy anything and everything. To accomplish that, the company needs a partnership strategy—partners of all sizes and business models. He also aims to continue Amazon's claim to being the world's most customer-centric company.

However, serious challenges face Amazon as well. These include losing substantial market share if it can't keep up with the intense competition in the online retail market; experiencing system interruptions that can affect the volume of orders and, ultimately, Amazon's brand name; significant strains on management, operational, and financial resources caused by rapid growth; inventory risk because of changes in customer demand and product cycles; expense and strain of continuing to enter new business areas; necessity for continually effective and efficient expansion and operation of distribution centers; seasonality of sales, particularly in the fourth quarter, can create significant strains; being able to adapt quickly to changing customer requirements and industry standards; continuing to find and integrate strategic alliance partners successfully; loss of senior managers; long-term viability of Internet as a medium for commerce; product liability claims if customers are injured by products sold; uncertainty of government regulation of Internet including sales tax issue; liabilities arising from fraudulent activities or security breaches on the Web site; maintaining protection of intellectual property rights; and necessity of continuing successful international expansion. Even with this long list of challenges, Amazon's strategic managers remain convinced that they can strategically manage the company's future.

Sources: Wired Editors, "A Conversation with Jeff Bezos and *Wired* Editors," *Wired*, July 2000, pp. 252–55; company information from Hoover's Online (**www.hoovers.com**), and Amazon.com Web sites, June 20, 2000; C. J. Loomis, "Amazon So Far Has Produced Nothing but Losses. . . ," *Fortune*, May 1, 2000, pp. 128–32; S. Hansell, "Amazon.com Reports a Loss of $308 Million," *Wall Street Journal*, April 27, 2000, p. C2; K. Swisher, "Why Is Jeff Bezos Still Smiling?" *Wall Street Journal*, April 24, 2000, p. B1; G. Anders, "At Your Service," *Wall Street Journal*, April 17, 2000, p. R12; M. Peers, "Ex-Web Darling CDNow Hunts for a New Deal," *Wall Street Journal*, April 3, 2000, p. B1; R. Spector, "Going for Broke," *Business 2.0*, April 2000, pp. 256–72; M. Richtel, "CDNow Deal with Sony and Time Warner Is Called Off," *Wall Street Journal*, March 14, 2000, p. C1; J. Rothfeder, "Perpetual Motion," *Executive Edge*, October–November 1999, pp. 18–22; K. Brooker, "Amazon vs. Everybody," *Fortune*, November 8, 1999, pp. 120–28; J. McHugh, "The $29 Billion Flea Market," *Forbes*, November 1, 1999, pp. 66–68; and R. D. Hof and S. Hamm, "Amazon.com Throws Open Its Doors," *Business Week*, October 11, 1999, p. 44.

Eatertainment Industry

During the 1990s, it was the fastest-growing segment of the restaurant industry. The major competitors in the *eatertainment* industry—a term that's not a fluke and not even misspelled, because it describes a restaurant designed to combine the act of eating with the art of entertaining—are facing serious challenges. Strategic managers at Hard Rock Café, Darden Restaurants, Inc., Brinker International, Rainforest Café, and especially Planet Hollywood are looking for the answers that will allow them to prosper in this intensely competitive environment.

BACKGROUND

These eatertainment theme restaurants are a combination amusement park, diner, souvenir stand, and museum. One of the first of these themed dining chains was the rock music–oriented Hard Rock Café (**www.hardrock.com**), with its vast array of fascinating music memorabilia and collectible merchandise. It used to be the essence of "cool" to have a T-shirt or some other article of clothing from a Hard Rock Café. The success of these restaurants tempted others to enter the game. Other popular themed dining chains soon included Planet Hollywood, Motown Café, the Official All-Star Café, Harley-Davidson Café, Rainforest Café, Fashion Café, and Dive! Even large media companies such as United Artists and Viacom jumped in. Many of these chains didn't make it, and the remaining ones are struggling to keep the diners coming.

Each of these restaurants used a theme—such as Planet Hollywood and its Hollywood movie themes and product tie-ins; Rainforest Café's incredibly lush tropical settings including live birds and fake snakes; Fashion Café and its fashion industry theme; and the submarine-oriented Dive!—to entice customers. Each was aiming for that "WOW!" factor that would dazzle, astound, and ultimately attract a hungry and cash-flush audience. As Tim Zagat, publisher of the Zagat restaurant guides stated, "The food doesn't have to be all that good, as long as it doesn't poison you. You go because you're interested" (Morris, p. 60). Attracting and maintaining customer interest was critical.

For these theme restaurants, the food, drink, and entertainment were just the beginning stages of what the owners hoped became a sought-after brand name. That's where the big bucks were—selling merchandise with the themed logo. The logo gear was always far more profitable than was the food. However, competition in the merchandising area was just as fierce as in the restaurants themselves.

WHAT'S HAPPENING IN THE INDUSTRY?

Over $1 billion a day. That's what Americans are spending on dining out in restaurants. The restaurant industry's sales for 2000 were predicted to jump 5 percent over 1999's sales. The fastest-growing part of the restaurant business, according to the National Restaurant Association (**www.restaurant.org**) was dining at "white tablecloth" restaurants where the average bill runs $25 a person. However, casual dining was on the rise, also, as were takeout orders and purchases of prepared meals from supermarkets. Steven Anderson, president and CEO of the National Restaurant Association, said, "We used to be perceived as the leisure part of the economy. But now, with people having less time, people are ordering carryout as well as dining out. People used to say at the end of the day, 'What do you want to eat?' Now they say, 'Where do you want to meet?' " (*Wall Street Journal*, May 24, 2000). Also, consumers have more disposable income and are willing to spend it on more expensive foods.

Although Americans are dining out more than ever, one survey by a restaurant-marketing consulting firm suggested that a significant number of them are enjoying it less and less. Poor service, mediocre meals, bad atmosphere, and poor value are some of the things that diners hate. An average of 7 percent of patrons polled in this survey said they would never return to the same restaurant because of lousy service or other complaints. That number rose to 12 percent for customers of upscale steakhouses or gourmet restaurants. Another study of restaurant employees found that almost half of them would not recommend their own place as somewhere good to eat. Obviously there are some problems that the restaurant industry, as a whole, needs to address. Attracting, keeping, and training staff is a major challenge for restaurants in all categories. Finding experienced staff and retaining them is made more difficult by a tight labor market where employees can readily find other jobs.

One significant trend that's affecting many different industries, including the restaurant one, is that customers are placing more and more importance on the "experiences" they receive from their goods and services. Successful businesses realize that it's no longer enough to sell a quality product at a fair price. They have to provide distinct and memorable experiences to be competitive. What is an experience? It's "a memorable event that engages the customer in a personal way" (Caudron, p. 39). This trend has affected organizations in various industries from "shoppertainment" to "edutainment" to "eatertainment."

WHAT'S HAPPENING WITH THE EATERTAINMENT COMPETITORS?

The five major competitors in this industry are Hard Rock Café International, Inc.; Planet Hollywood International, Inc.; Rainforest Café, Inc.; Darden Restaurants, Inc.; and Brinker International, Inc. Let's take a closer look at each.

Hard Rock Café International, Inc.

Hard Rock Café International (**www.hardrock.com**) operates the Hard Rock Café chain of theme restaurants in 36 countries. Currently, the 100 locations in major cities around the world combine classic American food, rock music memorabilia, and branded merchandise. Hard Rock has expanded to support music-related products and programs such as television shows, live music venues, a record label, hotels, and an alliance with the National Basketball Association to create NBA City restaurant units. The company also produces television shows and operates two hotels.

The first Hard Rock Café (HRC) opened in 1971 in London, England. Founded by Isaac Tigrett and Peter Morton, two enterprising and music-loving Americans, HRC was an instant hit, attracting droves of customers with its first-rate, but moderately priced, casual American fare, friendly service, and ubiquitous rock 'n' roll music. Hard Rock's memorabilia collection, which consists of more than 60,000 pieces that are rotated from restaurant to restaurant, provides a marvelous comprehensive "visual history" of rock 'n' roll. Some of these treasures include an incredible collection of classic guitars and other instruments, posters, costumes, music and lyric sheets, album art, platinum and gold LPs, photos, and much more. Like the "living" museum it is, Hard Rock Café's memorabilia collection continues to be a work in progress.

Even after more than a quarter-century in operation, HRC remains true to its original intentions. Its rock 'n' roll image remains at the very center of all Hard Rock restaurants. The company attempts to maintain a capable, caring, and attentive wait staff, and it has a strong commitment to wide-ranging altruistic causes under its banner "Save the Planet." The company is committed to being important, contributing members of the communities in which they do business. It strives to offer the Hard Rock "family" a fun, healthy, and nurturing work environment. Throughout its history, Hard Rock Café has been guided by a service philosophy of "Love All—Serve All." Its mission is "to spread the spirit of rock 'n' roll by delivering an exceptional entertainment and dining experience."

In 1996, Hard Rock became a subsidiary of The Rank Group PLC, a U.K. company with businesses in the leisure and entertainment industries. Some of its other divisions include a gambling company, a film processing company, and vacation resorts. Fiscal results for 1998 for Hard Rock (the most current information available) were as follows:

Sales:	$396.7 million
Sales growth:	2.6 percent
Net income:	$79.7 million
Net income growth:	3 percent
Employees:	5,900
Employee growth:	15.7 percent

Planet Hollywood International, Inc.

Planet Hollywood (**www.planethollywood.com**) was started in 1991 by a veteran executive from the Hard Rock Café chain, Robert Earl, and by Keith Barish, a producer. The chain started from one location that was heavily promoted by stars such as Arnold Schwarzenegger, Bruce Willis, Demi Moore, and Sylvester Stallone in return for stock. Over the decade, Planet Hollywood expanded into prime tourist locations in the United States and abroad.

Planet Hollywood International, Inc. was launched to capitalize on the universal appeal of movies, sports, and other entertainment-based themes. It utilized a marketing strategy based on its widely recognized trademark and distinctive logo to promote its theme restaurants, Planet Hollywood and the Official All-Star Café. In 1996, Planet Hollywood began opening stand-alone retail stores. Then over the next two years, it opened two Manhattan hotels, Cool Planet Ice Cream dessert cafés, and entered into a joint venture with AMC to develop a giant movie theater complex and eatery. This was in addition to launching the All-Star Cafés. It was a lot to swallow.

Planet Hollywood soon found itself spread too thin, suffering from weak repeat business and intense competition from other theme restaurants. The company was forced to scale back its expansion plans. It tried bringing on board a turnaround specialist in

1998, but he lasted less than a year. Fiscal results for 1998 were dismal. Revenues were $387 million (down from $475 million in 1997) and the company had a net loss of $244 million (versus a profit of $8.3 million in 1997). In October of 1999, Planet Hollywood filed for Chapter 11 bankruptcy protection. The company emerged from bankruptcy in early 2000.

Planet Hollywood International currently operates about 60 Planet Hollywood restaurants in 27 countries around the world and 8 sports-themed Official All-Star Cafés (although the All-Star Cafés are up for sale). As part of its bankruptcy reorganization plan, an investment group led by Saudi Prince al-Waleed bin Talal, Ong Beng Seng, and CEO Robert Earl invested $30 million in return for 70 percent of the new stock. Planet Hollywood is facing an uphill battle to survive.

Rainforest Café, Inc.

Rainforest Café, Inc. (**www.rainforestcafe.com**) owns, operates, and licenses themed restaurant–retail facilities under the name Rainforest Café—A Wild Place to Shop and Eat. As of February 2000, the company owned and operated 28 units in the United States and licensed 10 units globally (England, Mexico, Canada, Hong Kong, and France). Most are located in upscale shopping malls, but two (at Disney's Florida theme parks) are free-standing.

The Rainforest Cafés are designed to provide a visually and audibly stimulating and entertaining rainforest environment that appeals to a broad range of customers of all ages. Each café consists of a Restaurant and a Retail Village. The Restaurants provide customers a full menu of high-quality food and beverage items, generous portions, and excellent service in a unique and exciting environment. The Retail Villages feature apparel, toys, and gifts with the Rainforest Café logo and other items reflecting the rainforest theme, such as Iggy (an iguana) and Cha! Cha! (a tree frog). Because of its theme, The Rainforest Café strongly encourages education and emphasizes learning about endangered rain forests through free presentations. Company programs include a resident parrot program, on-site educational tours, educational outreach programs, support for Earth month, and rainforest preservation kits. The company also supports educational and environmental programs through The Rainforest Café Friends of the Future Foundation.

Rainforest Café, Inc. suffered the same fate as some of the other theme restaurants. Repeat business was lacking and same-store sales began to slide. In 1999, the company introduced membership programs, targeting both children and adults, in hopes of increasing repeat business. Lakes Gaming agreed to purchase the company in late 1999, but the deal was terminated. Then, another purchase offer from Landry's Seafood Restaurants was presented, but it, too, did not work out. Here are selected financial results:

Income Statement (all dollar amounts in millions)	Dec. 99	Dec. 98	Dec. 97
Revenues	$259.5	$211.7	$108.1
Net income	$ 5.7	$ 10.8	$ 12.3
Balance Sheet (in millions)			
Cash	$ 11.5	$ 16.9	$ 53.6
Total assets	261.7	255.5	246.1
Total liabilities	$ 59.4	$ 42.5	$ 23.0

Darden Restaurants, Inc.

Darden Restaurants (**www.darden.com**) isn't a direct competitor in the eatertainment industry, but it is the number-one casual-dining restaurant operator in the United States. The Orlando, Florida–based chain consists of 650 Red Lobster restaurants, 465 Olive Garden Italian restaurants, and 6 Bahama Breeze Caribbean restaurants. The restaurant empire has been built (with the exception of 38 licensed units in Japan) without the benefit of franchises.

The Red Lobster and Olive Garden restaurants were once part of the General Mills Corporation. However, in 1995, General Mills decided to spin off its restaurant business as a public company. The General Mills Restaurants (which also included China Coast restaurants) were renamed Darden Restaurants in honor of the original founder of the Red Lobster restaurant chain. Current CEO Joe Lee was hired to run the company. He immediately shut down the China Coast restaurants and closed underperforming Red Lobster and Olive Garden units. Then, in 1997, Lee oversaw the opening of the Bahama Breeze restaurants. These casual-dining restaurants seem to be popular with customers and expansion is in the works. As it did with all its innovative restaurant concepts, the company opened its first test prototype of Smokey Bones BBQ in Orlando. If this new casual-dining option succeeds, Darden will move to expand its locations. Selected financial results follow:

Income Statement (all dollar amounts in millions)	May 99	May 98	May 97
Revenue	$3,458.1	$3,287	$3,171.8
Net income	$ 140.5	$ 101.7	$ (91)
Balance Sheet (in millions)			
Cash	$ 41	$ 33.5	$ 25.5
Total assets	1,905.7	1,984.7	1,963.7
Long-term debt	314.1	310.6	313.2
Total liabilities	$ 941.7	$ 964.9	$ 882.5

Brinker International, Inc.

Based out of Dallas, Brinker International (**www.brinker.com**) operates several chains of concept eateries including Chili's Grill & Bar (southwestern theme), Romano's Macaroni Grill (family-style Italian dining), On the Border Café (casual-style Mexican), Corner Bakery (retail Old World bakery and quick foods), Cozymel's Coastal Mexican Grill (upscale Mexican dining), and Maggiano's Little Italy (1940s-style Italian diner). There are over 1,000 of these restaurants in 47 U.S. states, Canada, as well as Asia, Australia, Europe, and the Middle East. In addition, Brinker has jointly developed with other partners restaurant concepts including Big Bowl (Asian cuisine), EatZi's Market and Bakery (home meal replacement), and Wildfire (1940s-style steak house).

Norman Brinker, founder of Brinker International, pioneered the casual-dining segment in 1966 when he opened his first Steak & Ale in Dallas. In 1976, Pillsbury bought the chain. Brinker left Pillsbury in 1983 to take over Chili's. He expanded Chili's and soon added other casual-dining chains to his business. Today, CEO Ronald McDougall is leading the company into different themed segments.

Brinker is one of the strongest competitors financially in the casual-dining segment. Some selected financial information follows:

Income Statement (all dollar amounts in millions)	June 99	June 98	June 97
Revenues	$1,870.6	$1,574.4	$1,335.3
Net income	$ 78.8	$ 69.1	$ 60.5
Balance Sheet (in millions)			
Cash	$ 12.6	$ 31.1	$ 23.2
Total assets	1,085.6	989.4	996.9
Long-term debt	183.2	147.3	287.5
Total liabilities	$ 424.2	$ 395.7	$ 473.1

WHAT DOES THE FUTURE HOLD FOR THE INDUSTRY?

The restaurant industry in general appears strong with lots of opportunities because more and more people eat out more often. However, the eatertainment industry faces the huge challenge of creating demand for its theme restaurants. As these restaurants serve high-priced food and lose entertainment hype, companies such as Hard Rock Café, Planet Hollywood, and Rainforest Café need to take a long, hard look at their strategies.

Sources: Company information from respective Web sites and Hoover's Online (**www.hoovers.com**), June 21, 2000; "Restaurant Industry Sees Sales Reaching $376 Billion This Year," *Wall Street Journal*, May 24, 2000, p. B10; S. Caudron, "The Experience Factor," *Business Finance*, May 2000, pp. 39–44; M. Lord, "There's a Fly in My Soup," *U.S. News and World Report*, November 22, 1999, p. 53; L. Kroll, "Clawing Back," *Forbes*, July 26, 1999, p. 80; and K. Morris, "Oh Yeah, They Also Serve Food," *Business Week*, February 24, 1997, p. 60.

Greeting-Card Industry

INTRODUCTION

Following the sentiments of one of its many products, strategic managers in the greeting-card industry are looking at ways to help their companies get well. Sales revenues in the traditional greeting-card market have been growing slowly, about 4 percent annually, because customers have been finding easier and more convenient ways to keep in touch. Technology advances in areas such as e-mail and increasingly inexpensive long-distance phone service have sent industry competitors scrambling to find ways to keep those greeting cards flowing out the doors. Even the U.S. Postmaster General conceded that as much as 25 percent of future mail volume and revenue were "at risk" because of electronic alternatives.

Advances in computer technology have provided both opportunities and threats to companies in the greeting-card industry. The choices are to embrace the changes and develop strategies that take advantage of them or to develop alternative products for specific and narrow customer segments that aren't looking for technological sophistication in their greeting cards.

However, the opportunities and threats for greeting-card companies aren't just from changes in technology. Changes in customers' tastes and shopping habits are forcing companies to change the variety of products offered and where customers can buy them. Industry competitors are making sure that their products are in the places where customers want them. Because more than 66 percent of greeting cards sold are purchased in drugstores, supermarkets, and other mass-retail outlets, industry competitors have beefed up their product offerings in these places.

There are two major players in the traditional greeting-card industry. Number one in the industry, Hallmark, Inc., has 47 percent of the greeting card market. Then, in 1999, there was a merger of number three in the industry (Gibson Greetings) with number two in the industry (American Greetings Corporation). Other competitors include CSS Industries, Inc., a maker of seasonal consumer products such as gift wrapping, bows, and Christmas cards; Blue Mountain Arts, the Web-based greeting card company; and Amazon.com, the online retailer. Each of these competitors is looking for the "perfect package" of strategies to get that competitive edge.

COMPETITORS

Hallmark, Inc. (www.hallmark.com)

Hallmark is the number-one greeting-card company in the world. The company's cards are sold under brand names such as Hallmark, Shoebox, and Ambassador. Although the company is best known for its personal expression products and collectible ornaments, it has diversified into a variety of other areas. For example, it owns Binney & Smith, the maker of Crayola brand crayons and markers. It also owns The Picture People, a mall-based chain of portrait studios. For a number of years, Hallmark has produced television movies through its Hallmark Entertainment unit. Not to be left behind, Hallmark also has a Web site that offers electronic greeting cards, gift items, and flowers. An analysis of Hallmark's Web site described it as very "practical." It was the one site (other sites evaluated were Amazon and Blue Mountain Arts) that provided card content and related merchandise in one place. In other words, if a customer wanted flowers to go with a condolence card or with a Valentine's Day card, he or she could purchase both very conveniently right there. However, the Web site was also described as "dull."

In the fall of 1999, Hallmark announced its newest venture—next-day delivery of fresh flower bouquets. This new business is part of the company's ambitious strategy to triple annual sales over the next 10 years (the goal is $12 billion by 2010). One industry analyst said that "They're [Hallmark] not going to make $12 billion selling just greeting cards, I can tell you that. So I guess this is one way they plan on finding new revenue sources." Other avenues being explored by Hallmark include markets such as personal development and family entertainment.

Hallmark's culture can be described as "social responsibility plus!" Company programs promoting social responsibility include environmental conservation efforts, energy efficiency, recycled paper, ink changes, and waste recovery and reduction. It's also a member of Business for Social Responsibility (**www.bsr.org**), Environmental Excellence Business Network, Earth Day (**www.earthday.net**) activities, Sustainable Forestry Initiative, Greening the Supply Chain Initiative, and Missouri Choose Environmental Excellence Campaign.

The Kansas City–based company is privately held so little financial information is available. Revenues for a five-year period from 1995 to 1999 were $3.4 billion, $3.6 billion, $3.7 billion, $3.9 billion, and $4.2 billion. It has operations in Australia, Belgium, Canada, France, Japan, Mexico, the Netherlands, New Zealand, Puerto Rico, Spain, the United Kingdom, and the United States. Its products are marketed in more than 100 countries.

American Greetings Corporation (**www.americangreetings.com**)

As the number-two maker of greeting cards in the United States, American Greetings creates, manufactures, and distributes greeting cards and special occasion products. Its products can be found in over 110,000 retail outlets worldwide (over 80 countries) including grocery stores, specialty card and gift shops, department stores, bookstores, and airports. The company's products include greeting cards, gift wrap, paper party goods, candles, balloons, stationery, giftware, and supplemental educational products. These products are manufactured and sold in the United States by American Greetings Corporation; Plus Mark, Inc.; Carlton Cards Retail, Inc.; Learning Horizons; and other subsidiaries in Canada, the United Kingdom, France, Mexico, Australia, New Zealand, and South Africa. Personalized greeting cards are sold through CreataCard machines, which are located in retail outlets where the company's products are marketed. CreataCard Interactive, Inc. markets e-mail greetings, personalized greeting cards, and other products through the company's Web site. In addition, American Greetings' subsidiary Magnivision is one of the largest makers of nonprescription reading glasses.

American Greetings is headquartered in Cleveland, Ohio, and has over 21,000 associates worldwide. The company's mission statement says that the American Greetings mission is to "help people everywhere express their innermost thoughts and feelings, enhance meaningful relationships and celebrate life's milestones and special occasions." The company strongly emphasizes creativity and innovation, customer service, technology, shareholder value, high standards, superior performance, and community involvement.

Most of American Greetings revenues are from sales in the United States. Of the $2.1 billion in sales for 2000, 81 percent were from the United States. Also, a breakdown of product contributions to revenues shows that 45 percent came from everyday greeting cards, 20 percent came from seasonal greetings cards, 14 percent came from gift wrap and wrap accessories, and 21 percent came from other products. Other key financial statistics are shown here:

	Feb. 00	Feb. 99	Feb. 98
	(all dollar amounts in millions)		
Revenues	$2,175.2	$2,205.7	$2,198.8
Profits	90.0	180.2	190.1
Cash	61.0	144.6	47.6
Total assets	2,518	2,419.3	2,145.9
Current liabilities	582.5	417.7	517.2
Total liabilities	$1,265.6	$1,072.7	$ 800.6

Blue Mountain Arts (**www.bluemountain.com**)

Blue Mountain Arts, based in Boulder, Colorado, started as a family business in 1971 by an idealistic young couple, Stephen and Susan Polis Schutz. They started producing inspirational posters and greeting cards with a "hippie" feel—pastel, mellow birds-and-trees, and landscapes. Stephen and Susan soon found that their all-occasion cards had a devoted audience and branched out into books, calendars, and other products. By 1986, the market for the company's feel-good cards had grown so large that Hallmark began copying what Blue Mountain was doing. After two years of legal wrangling, Hallmark agreed to stop selling its copycat cards. Over the next several years, Blue Mountain prospered but remained a strictly niche-market business.

In the early 1990s, the couple's son Jared, became acquainted with the Internet and the World Wide Web while a student at Princeton University. He called his father and told him that they needed to jump on this new medium. Stephen said about this new venture, "I just wanted to do it for fun, basically." From this subtle beginning, Blue Mountain was one of the top 10 Internet sites in 1998 and 1999. After an inability to turn a profit, the company sold its bluemountain.com operations to popular search engine Excite in 1999. Blue Mountain's self-described hippie founders, Stephen (a physicist, by training) and Susan (a poet) said they sold the Web site so they could devote time and money to charitable pursuits. Jared has taken the reins of Blue Mountain Arts and planned to improve its remaining operations, which include traditional greeting cards, poetry and gift book publishing, and stationery.

Blue Mountain's Web site generates a lot of visits—over 12 million monthly. For a company with so much eyeball traffic, it's kept a remarkably low profile. How did the company get so big? By offering users free electronic greeting cards. However, like many Web "successes," it's trying to figure out how to make money (a viable revenue stream) from all these visitors. Since creating the Web site, Blue Mountain has seen a 20 percent annual increase in sales of its paper cards although it doesn't offer them for sale on the site.

Blue Mountain is privately owned but sales at the end of 1998 were estimated at $60 million.

THE FUTURE

Competitors in the greeting card industry have several opportunities and threats facing them. There are many questions to be answered in terms of the role of the Web and traditional outlets for the industry's products.

Sources: Company information from respective Web sites and Hoover's Online (**www.hoovers.com**), June 21, 2000; Associated Press, "New Venture Is Blooming for Hallmark," *Springfield News Leader*, February 13, 2000, p. 9B; T. J. Mullaney, "You'll Laugh, You'll Cry, You'll Send a Card," *Business Week E.Biz*, November 1, 1999, pp. EB80–EB82; and G. Beato, "Fire on the Mountain," *Business 2.0*, September, 1999, pp. 128–38.

Kellogg Company

The snap, crackle, and pop is pretty muffled around Kellogg Company, the Battle Creek, Michigan–based breakfast giant. The company is facing serious strategic challenges as it looks for ways to regain its dominant position in the industry. The stock market hasn't been forgiving of Kellogg's problems as its share price fell 45 percent during 1999. CEO Carlos M. Gutierrez is looking for some answers.

BACKGROUND

Kellogg Company was founded in 1894 and pioneered the ready-to-eat cereal industry. Some of its classic products with the all-familiar names include Frosted Flakes, Corn Flakes, Rice Krispies, Special K, and Froot Loops. Another of Kellogg's early innovations was the waxed inner lining in cereal boxes to keep cereal fresh. Another of Kellogg's products, the Pop Tart, was introduced in 1964. Then in the 1970s, Kellogg added to its breakfast-food menu by acquiring Eggo Waffles. The decade of the 1980s was one of intense competition from General Mills and other rivals. To offset some of the intense competition domestically, Kellogg began marketing its products to adults and aggressively went after the fast-growing European market. However, no new major brands were introduced between 1983 and 1991. The 1990s were a time of reengineering and restructuring. Kellogg created its USA Convenience Foods Division and sold off noncore assets such as a container manufacturer and an Argentine snack-food maker. In 1994, Kellogg teamed with ConAgra to create a health-oriented cereal line sold under the popular Healthy Choice label. Then in 1996, Kellogg's market position was eroded further by stiff store-brand competition and price wars. It was forced to drop its prices an average of 19 percent on 16 popular brands after Kraft Foods lowered its Post-brand cereal prices. This same year, it purchased Lender's Bagels from Kraft. In 1997 and 1998, Kellogg expanded its international operations in Australia, the United Kingdom, Asia, and Latin America. It downsized, laying off about 25 percent of its North American employees. The company also decided to raise prices on most of its cereal products. Because of continuing problems, several top officers left the company in 1998 and 1999. The current CEO was brought on board in April 1999. He decided to sell the Lender's Bagels division because its sales were never what the company hoped for or needed. The company did purchase Worthington Foods, a non–breakfast-food manufacturer whose main products included Morningstar Farms meat alternatives and Harvest Burgers. By November of 1999, Kellogg's main competitor, General Mills, had closed the market share gap and taken over the market leader position for the first time ever. Kellogg has found itself needing fresh strategies.

CURRENT BUSINESS

Currently, the company sells its products in over 160 countries and manufactures in 20 countries on 6 continents. These products are ready-to-eat cereals and grain-based convenience foods. Cereals include Apple Jacks, Froot Loops, Frosted Flakes, Rice Krispies, and Special K. Grain-based convenience foods include Eggo Waffles, Pop Tarts, Rice Krispies

Treats, Snack'Ums, and Nutri-Grain Bars. New products include Racing Apple Jacks cereal with red, blue, and yellow colors; Rice Krispies Treats Squares featuring double chocolate chunk flavor; and Froot Loops cereal with CherryBerry swirls. These new products are a reflection of the commitment made by CEO Gutierrez to reenergizing Kellogg's new-product development strategies.

Kellogg's mission states, "Kellogg is a global company committed to building long-term growth in volume and profit and to enhancing its worldwide leadership position by providing nutritious food products of superior value." It lives this mission with a dedicated management philosophy that holds people above profits. Kellogg's strategic leaders are also committed to an advertising and marketing philosophy that seeks to associate the Kellogg name with wholesome, truthful advertising. And, Kellogg icons such as Tony the Tiger and Snap, Crackle, and Pop are among the most recognized characters in advertising.

Kellogg prides itself on environmental responsibility in action. The company initiates partnerships with like-minded community organizations to raise local environmental awareness. For example, Kellogg Company headquarters in Battle Creek regularly sponsors community environmental programs, including Adopt-A-Highway and Hazardous Waste Day (for safe disposal of hazardous household waste). Kellogg is committed to promoting and maintaining environmentally responsible practices for the communities in which it is located. This includes an environmental audit program that evaluates all Kellogg's manufacturing practices. The audit includes air and water quality, waste management practices, spill prevention and control, hazardous materials management, and employee awareness. Kellogg has historically used recycled material in packaging, but also uses recycled materials in corporate communications such as annual reports and company newsletters. It also uses recycled materials in items such as office supplies, park benches, T-shirts, and air filters.

CEO Gutierrez has been taking steps to bring the snap, crackle, and pop back to Kellogg. He outlined his vision for the company's future, in which noncereal products account for 40 percent of revenues, compared to 24 percent today. He's also spending more money on marketing and advertising. In early spring 2000, the company unveiled its first new characters in 30 years—EET, a horse, and ERN, a pig. These characters are part of a new Web-based program that allows consumers to earn points from selected products and redeem them online at Web sites such as fogdog.com and toysmart.com. Gutierrez is more optimistic about Kellogg's future. His optimism comes after a year (1999) of radical and difficult changes at the company. Among his strategic actions was the replacement or reshuffling of eight of the company's top ten executives. He also closed Kellogg's oldest Corn Flakes plant, a facility that dated back to 1900. Although it was a smart strategic move because of cost inefficiencies at the plant, it still was a difficult decision given the culture and history of the company. Gutierrez expanded the company's emphasis on its convenience foods such as Rice Krispies Treats Squares, Nutri-Grain Twist Bars, and Snack'Ums. He also made the decision to move more fully into nutritionally enhanced foods, including a new soy breakfast cereal introduced in early 2000.

FINANCIAL HIGHLIGHTS

Kellogg's financial performance reflects the problems it's facing internally and externally. Selected financial measures are as follows:

Income Statement (all dollar amounts in millions)	1999	1998
Net sales		
North America	$4,358.3	$4,175.9
Europe	1,614.4	1,698.5
Asia–Pacific	442.0	377.0
Latin America	567.0	510.7
Corporate and other	2.5	—
Consolidated	$6,984.2	$6,762.1

Operating profit	1999	1998
North America	$ 866.7	$ 831.6
Europe	224.1	211.4
Asia–Pacific	53.2	48.3
Latin America	141.3	107.2
Corporate and other	(211.9)	(232.9)
Consolidated	$1,073.4	$ 965.6

Balance Sheet (in millions)	1999	1998
Current assets		
Cash and cash equivalents	$ 150.6	$ 136.4
Accounts receivable, net	678.5	693.0
Inventories:		
Raw materials and supplies	141.2	133.3
Finished goods and materials in process	362.6	318.1
Other current assets	236.3	215.7
Total current assets	1,569.2	1,469.5
Property, net of accumulated depreciation of $2,515.8 and $ 2,358.0	2,640.9	2,888.8
Other assets	598.6	666.2
Total assets	4,808.7	$5,051.5
Current liabilities		
Current maturities of long-term debt	$ 2.9	$ 1.1
Notes payable	518.6	620.4
Accounts payable	305.3	386.9
Income taxes	83.5	69.4
Other current liabilities	677.5	640.7
Total current liabilities	1,587.8	1,718.5
Long-term debt	1,612.8	1,614.5
Nonpension postretirement benefits	424.9	435.2
Deferred income taxes and other liabilities	370.0	393.5
Shareholders' equity		
Common stock, $.25 par value	103.8	103.8
Capital in excess of par value	104.5	105.0
Retained earnings	1,317.2	1,367.7
Treasury stock, at cost	(380.9)	(394.3)

Accumulated other comprehensive income	(331.4)	(292.4)
Total shareholders' equity	813.2	889.8
Total liabilities and shareholders' equity	$4,808.7	$5,051.5

(Financial information from Kellogg Company's Web site (**www.kellogg.com**) Investor Relations, June 22, 2000.)

THE CEREAL INDUSTRY

The cereal industry is changing because of shifts in consumer tastes and preferences. Interest in breakfast is waning, so companies in the industry are striving to boost bottom lines with breakfast alternatives, such as cereal bars and snack foods. Kellogg's major competitors include General Mills, Kraft Foods, and the Quaker Oats Company.

General Mills (**www.generalmills.com**)

General Mills, Inc. is engaged in the manufacture and marketing of consumer foods products. It produces and sells a number of ready-to-eat cereals as well as a line of dessert mixes under the Betty Crocker trademark. This line includes such familiar products as SuperMoist layer cakes, Rich & Creamy and Soft Whipped ready-to-spread frostings, Supreme brownie and dessert bar mixes, muffin mixes, Stir'n'Bake mixes, and Sweet Rewards fat-free and reduced-fat mixes.

General Mills is Kellogg's strongest competitor and is making great strides in market share and sales. The company passed Kellogg's in market share of cereal sales as measured by dollars in early 1999. It also surpassed Kellogg's as the biggest U.S. cereal company in December of 1999.

Kraft Foods (**www.kraft.com**)

Kraft Foods is the North American food business of the Philip Morris Companies. Kraft is the largest packaged food company in the United States and Canada. Its 10 business divisions include beverages and desserts, Boca foods, e-commerce, Maxwell House and Post Cereals, Kraft Canada, Kraft Cheese, Kraft Food Services, the New Meals division, Oscar Mayer Foods, and pizza.

Quaker Oats Company (**www.quakeroats.com**)

Quaker operates in the packaged food industry and manufactures hot cereals, pancake mixes, grain-based snacks, value-added rice products, sports beverages, syrups, and pasta products.

FUTURE CHALLENGES

Considering the intense competitiveness of the ready-to-eat cereal business, both Kellogg and General Mills are furiously developing their convenience-food businesses. General Mills has had great success with its yogurt products as well as its Betty Crocker snack foods. As far as Kellogg, is it headed in the right direction? What strategic actions does the company need to make?

Sources: Company information from respective company Web sites and Hoover's Online (**www.hoovers.com**), June 22, 2000; A. Carter, "General Mills vs. Kellogg," *Money*, June 2000, p. 52C; Associated Press, "Kellogg Confident Changes Will Pay Off," *Springfield News Leader*, May 7, 2000, p. 13B; A. Kover, "Why the Cereal Business Is Soggy," *Fortune*, March 6, 2000, p. 74; and A. Taylor III, "Kellogg Cranks Up Its Idea Machine," *Fortune*, July 5, 1999, pp. 181–82.

Levi-Strauss & Company

Levi-Strauss & Company is the world's number-one maker of brand-name clothing. It manufactures and sells branded jeans and casual sportswear clothing under the Levi's®, Dockers®, and Slates® brand names in more than 60 countries. The company employs a staff of approximately 1,300 people at its San Francisco headquarters and approximately 17,000 people worldwide. Levi's has been in business for almost 150 years, but is currently facing its most serious strategic problems. The company's CEO, Philip Marineau, brought on board in 1999 to restore Levi's image and performance, is searching for the correct combination of strategies.

INDUSTRY AND COMPETITORS

The clothing apparel industry, particularly for companies with brand-name fashions, is a volatile and fickle one. Consumer tastes, whims, and wants can change as quickly as teenagers in a department store dressing room full of clothes. However, clothing manufacturers aren't just at the mercy of consumers—they're at the mercy of retailers that also face serious competitive challenges and profit pressures. Although both manufacturers and retailers want the same thing—products that consumers demand and purchase—they don't always hold the same views about the most effective strategic decisions for achieving this goal.

Some of the major competitors in the jeans–casual sportswear clothing apparel industry include Gap, Tommy Hilfiger, and VF Corporation. Here is some additional information on each of these competitors.

Gap, Inc. (www.gap.com)

Gap, Inc. has over 3,100 stores in the United States, Canada, France, Germany, Japan, and the United Kingdom. Gap offers men's and women's casual clothing. Its other chains include Banana Republic, GapKids, babyGap, and Old Navy. Gap is having its share of problems as its same-store sales growth has plummeted. However, Gap CEO Mickey Drexler is a retailing–fashion brain and is repositioning the company.

Tommy Hilfiger Corporation (www.tommy.com)

Tommy Hilfiger Corporation sells men's and women's casual wear, denim wear, athletic wear, children's wear, and accessories. The company also offers fragrances, belts, bedding, home furnishings, and cosmetics. Tommy Hilfiger, the actual designer namesake of the company, has found his reputation boosted by his fashions' popularity with hip-hop stars and fashion-conscious youth. However, Hilfiger also finds itself struggling with disappointing sales and a gloomy outlook.

VF Corporation (www.vfc.com)

VF Corporation has over 25 percent of the U.S. market for jeans. Its brands include Lee, Rustler, Brittania, and Wrangler. The company's other brand names include Vanity Fair, Jantzen, Jansport, Red Kap, and Healthtex. VF licenses sports apparel, Nike apparel, and NASCAR apparel, which, because of its increasing popularity, has proved to be a strategically sound arrangement. Wal-Mart, the world's largest retailer, accounts for around 12 percent of VF's sales.

COMPANY HISTORY

The company was founded in 1853 by Levi Strauss, who arrived in San Francisco from New York to start a wholesale dry goods business. A gold prospector told Strauss of miners' problems in finding sturdy pants that held up under the pressures of panning for gold. In response, Strauss made a pair of pants out of canvas for the prospector. Word of the durable pants spread quickly. During the 1860s, Strauss switched the fabric to a durable French cloth (serge de Nimes), which soon became known as denim. He colored the fabric with an indigo dye and, together with a Nevada tailor, patented the process of putting rivets in pants for strength. Thus was created Levi's jeans. The pants quickly became the clothing choice for cowboys, oil drillers, lumberjacks, farmers, and railroad workers. From this beginning of being a company whose clothes were favored by blue-collar, physical laborers, Levi's jeans became the preferred clothing choice of teens around the world. No longer were jeans viewed as something worn only by hardworking laborers. The strong popularity and appeal of the Levi's brands would last well into the 1990s before problems hit. Sales in 1998 plummeted 13 percent from the previous year.

CURRENT OPERATIONS

Levi-Strauss is a global corporation composed of three business units including the Levi-Strauss Americas Division; the Levi-Strauss Europe, Middle East, and Africa Division; and the Asia–Pacific Division. The company has wholly owned and operated businesses, joint ventures, and licensing agreements that cover the right to make and market apparel and accessories in countries outside of the United States under the Levi's, Dockers, and Slates brand names.

The significant sales decrease in 1998 triggered some serious changes in Levi's operations strategies. It closed 30 of its 51 factories and laid off about 15,000 (about 40 percent) of its employees. This shift of manufacturing from company-owned plants to contractors created some problems, as well. Production and logistics systems didn't work as smoothly as they should have. Retailers frequently received the wrong merchandise or got it late. However, a computerized "automatic replenishment" system to keep retailers' shelves stocked with key products was being installed gradually and carefully.

Although some of its products are still company produced, Levi's gradual change to outsourcing is reflected by the fact that much of its clothing is now produced by approximately 600 cutting, sewing, and finishing contractors in more than 60 countries. This strategic move presented its own challenges because of Levi-Strauss's strong commitment to socially responsible business practices. To ensure that contractors' practices were ethical and responsible, the company developed Global Sourcing and Operating Guidelines to help it select business partners who followed stringent workplace standards and business practices consistent with Levi's ethical and socially responsible values. These requirements were applied to every contractor that manufactured or finished products for Levi-Strauss & Company. Trained inspectors closely audit and monitor compliance among these contractors.

MARKETING

One of the company's most valuable assets is its Levi's trademark. Yet, that venerable Levi's brand has lost much of its popularity, particularly with younger consumers. Industry analysts estimate that Levi's share of the jeans market fell from 31 percent to about 17 percent over the latter half of the 1990s. The marketing challenge for Levi's is making its products appealing to a new generation of kids while continuing to attract its core customers—the aging baby boomers. How can a company be "young and hip" without alienating the "no-longer young and hip"?

Levi-Strauss's advertising has had some classics. From the colorful, dream-like ads with a "hippie, flower-power" feel to the "nice pants" theme, Levi's has always been able to tap into the prevailing social consciousness. However, even the company's advertising lost its focus in the late 1990s as the company struggled to define (redefine) who it was and what it was. The company's new advertising emphasis was on showcasing the products themselves rather than trying to convey "attitude."

PRODUCT DEVELOPMENT AND INNOVATION

Levi's was (the question is—is it still?) a fashion innovator. After all, it created the jeans market. The company has consistently been a fashion innovator because of its unique ability to "read" the market and respond with variations of its core products. However, that same success with its core products led to its failure to see the shift away from the traditional jeans styling. As one retailer said, "When fashion shifted, Levi's never caught on to what youth wanted" (Lee, 8/13/00, p. 148). CEO Marineau admits that the company missed fashion trends from flared jeans legs to stretchy fabrics. However, Marineau implemented some strategic changes to address these shortcomings.

One of Levi's newest innovations was a line called "Engineered Jeans." This line was being promoted as a "reinvention" of the classic five-pocket style. It featured side seams that followed the line of the leg and a bottom hem that was slightly shorter in the back so it didn't drag on the ground. The pants also had a larger pocket to accommodate essential gear such as pagers or cell phones. Then, in the youth-oriented Silver Tab line, Levi's introduced the Mobile Zip-Off Pant with legs that zip off and the loose Ripcord Pant with legs that roll up easily. The other Levi's clothing lines (Dockers khakis and Slates dressy casual) have also been updated as the company continued to add new styles, colors, and features.

FINANCIAL

For its first 100 years, Levi-Strauss & Company was a private company. Relatives of Levi Strauss owned nearly all the stock, and company employees owned most of the remaining shares. In 1971, the company traded shares publicly to finance further growth and diversification. However, in August 1981, the publicly held shares were repurchased in a leveraged buyout transaction—one of the largest ever in U.S. corporate history. Today, Levi-Strauss & Company is a privately held corporation controlled by chairman Robert Haas, a great-great-grandnephew of Levi Strauss, and three other relatives. Even though the company is privately held, selected financial data is available. Revenues for 1999 fell to $5.1

billion from revenues in 1998 of $6 billion. Profits fell to $5.4 million in 1999 from $102.5 million in 1998. Other financial information is shown here.

Consolidated Statements of Income (loss)
(all dollar amounts in thousands, unaudited)

	Three Months Ended		Six Months Ended	
	May 28, 2000	May 30, 1999	May 28, 2000	May 30, 1999
Net sales	$1,149,044	$1,227,910	$2,231,481	$2,506,232
Cost of goods sold	661,469	737,303	1,293,911	1,551,976
Gross profit	487,575	490,607	937,570	954,256
Marketing, general and administrative expenses	367,417	407,677	689,528	826,762
Excess capacity/restructuring charge	—	11,780	—	405,885
Operating income (loss)	120,158	71,150	248,042	(278,391)
Interest expense	60,989	43,819	117,771	86,976
Other income, net	(10,100)	(20,931)	(39,241)	(37,058)
Income (loss) before taxes	69,269	48,262	169,512	(328,309)
Income tax expense (benefit)	24,245	17,857	59,329	(121,474)
Net income (loss)	$ 45,024	$ 30,405	$ 110,183	$ (206,835)

Net Sales by Region
(all dollar amounts in millions, unaudited)

	Three Months Ended			Six Months Ended		
Net Sales	May 28, 2000	May 30, 1999	Percent Change	May 28, 2000	May 30, 1999	Percent Change
Americas	$ 762.1	$ 801.8	(4.9%)	$1,452.6	$1,621.6	(10.4%)
Europe	278.7	337.3	(17.4%)	581.7	714.3	(18.6%)
Asia	108.3	88.8	21.9%	197.2	170.4	15.7%
Total company	$1,149.0	$1,227.9	(6.4%)	$2,231.5	$2,506.2	(11.0%)

Net Sales at Prior-Year Currency Exchange Rates	Three Months Ended			Six Months Ended		
	May 28, 2000 (Restated)	May 30, 1999	Percent Change	May 28, 2000 (Restated)	May 30, 1999	Percent Change
Americas	$ 761.5	$ 801.8	(5.0%)	$1,450.1	$1,621.6	(10.6%)
Europe	299.1	337.3	(11.3%)	640.9	714.3	(10.3%)
Asia	102.6	88.9	15.5%	187.0	170.4	9.8%
Total company	$1,163.2	$1,227.9	(5.3%)	$2,277.9	$2,506.2	(9.1%)

Condensed Consolidated Balance Sheets
(all dollar amounts in thousands)

Assets	May 28, 2000 (Unaudited)	November 28, 1999
Cash and cash equivalents	$ 128,363	$ 192,816
Trade receivables, net	625,912	759,273
Total inventories	588,131	671,487
Property, plant and equipment, net	579,324	685,026
Other assets	1,234,976	1,356,915
Total assets	$3,156,706	$3,665,517

Liabilities and Stockholders' Deficit		
Current maturities of long-term debt and short-term borrowings	$ 232,165	$ 233,992
Accounts payable	201,891	262,389
Restructuring reserves	107,546	258,784
Long-term debt, less current maturities	2,070,556	2,430,617
Long-term employee related benefits	330,334	325,518
Postretirement medical benefits	549,380	541,815
Other liabilities	858,864	900,964
Total liabilities	4,350,736	4,954,079
Total stockholders' deficit	(1,194,030)	(1,288,562)
Total liabilities and stockholders' deficit	$3,156,706	$3,665,517

(Financial information from company Web site (**www.levistrauss.com**) press release, June 23, 2000.)

COMPANY CULTURE

Levi-Strauss's mission is to achieve and sustain commercial success as a global marketer of branded apparel. Its vision is to be the world's foremost authority in casual apparel through a relentless focus on consumers, innovation, and people. The company supports this mission and vision with its values, including integrity in business dealings and ethical behavior, commitment to people, and diversity. Levi's also encourages innovation, informed risk taking, decisiveness and results orientation, leveraging, accountability, and recognition of results.

Levi-Strauss & Company has a long history of commitment to its employees and to the communities in which it does business. This heritage goes back to Levi Strauss himself, who devoted substantial time and resources to charitable and philanthropic activities.

The company encourages its employees to take an active part in their communities. It pioneered an employee volunteer effort called "Community Involvement Teams" (CITs) in 1984. There are now more than 100 CITs worldwide.

Levi-Strauss & Company and the Levi-Strauss Foundation operate a global giving program through which they give gifts to community organizations in more than 40 countries. In 2000, the budgeted amount for giving was $16 million. These funds support programs that help people achieve economic self-sufficiency, fight the spread of AIDS, confront discrimination and racism, and give young people a voice in their communities.

The company's long-standing commitment to social responsibility and ethics is reflected in all of its business operations. In 1998, Levi-Strauss & Company received the Ron Brown Award for Corporate Leadership, the first Presidential Award to honor companies for outstanding achievements in community and employee relations. The company was honored for its Project Change, an antiracism initiative of the Levi-Strauss Foundation.

Another area where Levi-Strauss & Company has played a leadership role is in educational programs and policies on AIDS in the workplace. The company has received numerous awards and recognition for its efforts to combat HIV. It received the first National Business and Labor Award for Leadership on HIV–AIDS in 1997 from the United States Center for Disease Control.

The company's commitment to workplace standards continued throughout 1999 with outreach and collaboration with stakeholder groups to promote respect for workers' rights. Consistent with the company's philosophy of continuous improvement, it adopted NGO recommendations for production partnership facilities in Dominican Republic and the Philippines. (NGOs are nongovernmental organizations associated with the United Nations whose goals are to promote collaborations among NGOs around the globe; to effectively partner with the United Nations and each other; and to create a more peaceful, just, equitable, and sustainable world for generations to come.)

LEVI-STRAUSS'S CLUMSY MOVE INTO E-BUSINESS

Believe it or not, Levi-Strauss was an Internet pioneer, launching its first Web site in 1994. However, in late 1999, the company decided to pull the plug on its e-commerce capabilities. A Levi spokesperson said, "We determined that running a world-class e-commerce site was unaffordable" (Kroll, p. 181). Levi's encountered some significant problems in its e-business push.

One problem was its indecision about what the Web site should offer. It took Levi's management four years to decide whether to sell merchandise from the site. The company didn't want to alienate its all-important retailers by competing with them. Another problem was that when it did decide to sell online, it didn't stock the popular Levi's 501 blues initially because it didn't want to upset European and Asian customers who couldn't buy online. In addition, many people wanted to avoid shipping charges and wanted the ability to return products to bricks-and-mortar stores, something Levi's didn't want to do and didn't have the ability to do. Other internal problems arose. Across-the-board corporate budget cuts because of the sharp decline in sales and profits meant that all Web advertising was canceled, including a planned television ad campaign. Without marketing support, the Web site never got the needed point-and-click traffic. The budget cuts also led to the departure of talented employees who immediately headed for Internet start-ups. Another problem was that retailers that initially went along with Levi's decision not to let them sell its products online soon tried to get the company to change its mind.

Companies such as JCPenney and Macy's repeatedly begged Levi's to let them sell Levi's products on their Web sites. Levi's finally decided it wasn't worth fending off the retailers because they might choose to retaliate by cutting back orders to their physical stores and relented. However, a consumer can't purchase Levi's products on Levi's own Web site.

FUTURE CHALLENGES

Levi-Strauss & Company has to make some serious strategic decisions. The challenge for the company is going to be retaining and increasing its brands' appeal and image. Keeping the blues just in its famous jeans is going to be a tough strategic challenge, indeed.

Sources: Company information from respective Web sites and Hoover's Online (**www.hoovers.com**), June 21, 2000; C. Y. Coleman, "Gap Inc. Battles Decrease in Same-Store Sales," *Wall Street Journal*, May 9, 2000, p. B11; "Levi's Profit Fell Sharply in '99," *Wall Street Journal*, May 8, 2000, p. C17; L. Lee, "Gaping Holes at the Gap," *Business Week*, April 24, 2000, pp. 54–55; T. Agins, "Not So Haute: Hilfiger Shares Plunge on Lackluster Forecast for Fiscal Year," *Wall Street Journal*, April 10, 2000, p. B21; L. Lee, "Can Levi's Be Cool Again?" *Business Week*, March 13, 2000, pp. 144–48; and L. Kroll, "Denim Disaster," *Forbes*, November 29, 1999, p. 181.

Southwest Airlines

Simple and *fun.* These two words sum up Southwest Airlines. Yet, behind these two very plain words lies the heart and soul of a company's strategies that have helped it achieve an enviable record in the intensely competitive airline industry—27 consecutive years of profitability (through 1999). As Southwest continues to grow, can it maintain that commitment to simplicity and fun?

BACKGROUND

Southwest Airlines began service in June of 1971, with three planes flying between three Texas cities: Houston, Dallas, and San Antonio. Herb Kelleher, the colorful character who is Southwest's current CEO, recalls, "A lot of people figured us for road kill at that time." And the company's strategic approach was unlike anything that the other major airlines were doing at that time. The state of air service in the early 1970s could best be described as airfares being too high, flight schedules being too inconvenient, ticketing being too complicated, and the whole flying experience (driving to the airport, parking at the airport, and finally getting underway) being too long and inconvenient. Southwest began with a simple notion—get your passengers to their destinations when they want to get there, on time, at the lowest possible fares, and make sure they have a good time doing it. To deliver this type of service, Southwest's strategy was to fly short-haul routes where the fares were competitive with driving. In these short-haul markets, speed and convenience would be essential to marketplace success. Therefore, Southwest's overall strategy was to minimize total travel time for customers, including ticketing and boarding and providing service out of airports convenient to doing business or vacationing in a city. Simple, yet effective. A timeline of Southwest's growth is shown in Exhibit 1.

Southwest has had a busy and impressive 29 years. The company has earned a title that no other airline can claim: the only short-haul, low-fare, high-frequency, point-to-point service in the United States.

CURRENT OPERATIONS

The mission of Southwest Airlines (as stated on the company's Web site found at [**www.iflyswa.com**]) is as follows:

> The mission of Southwest Airlines is dedication to the highest quality of Customer Service delivered with a sense of warmth, friendliness, individual pride, and Company Spirit.

This mission statement affects the way Southwest employees do their work. It emphasizes the company's strong desire to serve its customers and provides guidance when employees have to make service-related decisions. In fact, employees are continually reminded that Southwest is in the customer service business—and its business just happens to be airline transportation that is provided to customers. The goal is not only getting customers from point A to point B but also doing it in a way that is right for the customer.

Southwest Airlines is the only U.S. domestic airline that provides short-haul, low-fare, high-frequency, point-to-point service. As of June 2000, this included 56 cities (57

EXHIBIT 1   Timeline of Southwest Airlines

1971   Southwest begins passenger service between Dallas, Houston, and San Antonio with President Lamar Muse at the helm.

1972   Houston service is transferred to Hobby Airport from Houston Intercontinental to save customers time and hassle.

1973   Southwest files with the Texas Aeronautics Commission to provide service to the Rio Grande Valley. Cargo service is introduced, and the company has its first profitable year.

1974   The year of the one millionth passenger!

1975   Permission was finally granted to fly to the Rio Grande Valley.

1976   Southwest begins service to other Texas cities: Austin, Corpus Christi, El Paso, Lubbock, and Midland–Odessa.

1977   The year of the five millionth passenger! The company's stock is listed on the NYSE as LUV (for Dallas's Love Field, its base of operations).

1978   Lamar Muse steps down and Herb Kelleher, cofounder, is named interim president, CEO, and chairman of the board.

1979   Self-ticketing machines are introduced in 10 cities. Service begins between New Orleans and Dallas—the first city outside of Texas to be added.

1980   The twenty-second Boeing 737 (the only plane style that Southwest uses) is added to the fleet.

1981   Southwest celebrates a decade of "Love Southwest Style."

1982   Kelleher is named permanent president, CEO, and chairman of the board. Service is expanded to San Francisco, Los Angeles, San Diego, Las Vegas, and Phoenix.

1983   Major schedule increases are adopted. Southwest has flown over 9.5 million customers.

1984   The fourth consecutive year that Southwest is ranked number one in customer satisfaction ranking.

1985   New service to St. Louis and Chicago is introduced. The Ronald McDonald House is named as the company's primary charity.

1986   The company celebrates 15 years of low fares, good times, and high spirits.

1987   The sixth consecutive year that Southwest is awarded the Best Consumer Satisfaction record of any continental U.S. airline.

1988   Southwest and Sea World of Texas join together to promote Texas as a major tourist attraction. One of the company's 737s is painted to look like Shamu, the killer whale. The company wins the Triple Crown of airlines: Best On-Time Record, Best Baggage Handling, and Fewest Customer Complaints.

1989   The company wins its second Triple Crown. Shamu Two is put into service, and Oakland is added to the system.

1990   Southwest reaches the $1 billion revenue mark. Lone Star One becomes the company's twentieth anniversary flagship Boeing 737.

1991   Twenty years of serving and loving customers!

1992   Southwest wins the first *annual* Triple Crown—something no other airline has been able to do even in monthly rankings.

1993   Service begins to the East Coast. The company wins the second annual Triple Crown.

1994   Southwest introduces Ticketless Travel in four cities. The company merges with Morris Air in the Southwest. New destinations include Seattle, Spokane, Portland, and Boise. And, Southwest wins the third consecutive Triple Crown.

1995   Ticketless Travel becomes available throughout Southwest's system. Service to Omaha is added, and it wins its fourth consecutive Triple Crown.

1996   Service to Florida and Rhode Island is added. The company's impressive record for the Triple Crown continues—it wins its fifth one.

(continues)

EXHIBIT 1   Timeline of Southwest Airlines *(continued)*

1997	The fiftieth city—Jacksonville, Florida—is added to Southwest's service. Triple Crown One, a 737 dedicated as a tribute to Southwest's employees, joins the fleet.
1998	Southwest begins service to Manchester, New Hampshire.
1999	Southwest begins service to Islip, New York, and Raleigh–Durham, North Carolina.
2000	The company adds service to Albany and Buffalo, New York.

airports) in 29 states. Southwest focuses primarily on point-to-point rather than hub-and-spoke service, which is where an airline will bring flights into a hub (such as the St. Louis hub for TWA or Newark Airport hub for Continental) and then reconnect passengers on to their next location. The point-to-point service strategy allows Southwest to provide more direct, nonstop routes for customers. The company emphasizes that its approach minimizes connections, delays, and total trip time for customers.

Quick turnaround of its planes is an essential component of this strategy. To facilitate quick turnaround, Southwest flies only one type of jet: the 737 model. As of April 25, 2000, it operated 318 of these planes as follows:

Type	Number	Available Seats
737-200	35	122
737-300	194	137
737-500	25	122
737-700	64	137

The use of one type of aircraft also minimizes employee training and maintenance costs. The average age of Southwest's fleet is only 8.4 years, making it one of the newest fleets in the industry. During 2000, an additional twenty-six 737-700s will be delivered, and two of the older 737-200s will be retired. Each of Southwest's aircraft flies an average of almost 9 flights per day (about 12 hours). The average trip length is about 462 miles with an average duration of about 1 hour and 24 minutes. More than 2,550 flights are offered daily throughout all of Southwest's route system. The company's top eight airports are (in descending order): Phoenix (178 daily departures); Las Vegas (153 daily departures); Houston Hobby (149 daily departures); Dallas Love Field (139 daily departures); Los Angeles (122 daily departures); Chicago Midway (121 daily departures); Oakland, California (112 daily departures); and Baltimore (95 daily departures).

Other strategies that facilitate the quick turnaround necessary to successfully implement Southwest's short-haul approach are that there are no reserved seats and no checked baggage. Only one class of service is offered, and no meals are served. To make itself even better at gate turnaround, Southwest benchmarked its performance against Indy race car crews that are renowned for getting a car back into the race within seconds—just the perfect example of quick turnaround!

Southwest offers a ticketless travel system, which trims the need for travel agents and thus travel agents' fees. It operates nine reservations centers located in Dallas, San

Antonio, Houston, Phoenix, Albuquerque, Chicago, Salt Lake City, Little Rock, and Oklahoma City. In addition to these phone reservations centers, Southwest offers online travel purchases. The company's SWABIZ Web site allows business travelers to plan, book, and purchase ticketless travel. Corporate travel departments can use SWABIZ to plan and purchase travel on Southwest Airlines. Each company is provided a company ID number, which is then used on all business travel reservations. When a reservation is made, the traveler receives a detailed itinerary via fax from Southwest. In addition, corporate travel managers can log on to the Web site at any time and view all bookings made by their employees for the previous day or the last 12 months—a useful tool for tracking and reporting of business travel. Online reservations aren't just for business travelers, however. Personal or leisure travelers can log on to the Web site (**www.southwest.com**) to purchase their tickets. Southwest's Web sites have been extremely successful—so successful in fact, that Southwest announced in March 2000 that more than one quarter of its passenger revenue in February came from bookings on its Web sites. That achievement caught other competitors in the airline industry by surprise and raised the bar for the future.

SOUTHWEST'S CULTURE AND PEOPLE

Southwest has one of the most unique cultures among those of all major U.S. corporations. It's a high-spirited, often irreverent culture, much like its CEO, Herb Kelleher. Flight attendants have been known to dress up as the Easter Bunny or with Halloween masks on those respective holidays. They've hidden in the overhead baggage compartments and jumped out at passengers who first opened them on a flight. No matter how fun and goofy it may get, however, no one at Southwest loses sight of the fact that the focus is on customers. The company is extremely concerned about its people and seeks to provide fun and challenging jobs. Southwest was ranked second in the January 2000 issue of *Fortune* magazine's 100 Best Companies to Work for in America. It topped the list in 1998 and was number four in 1999. All of these high rankings reflect Southwest's commitment to its more than 29,000 total active employees. What makes Southwest's people emphasis even more impressive is that approximately 85 percent of its workforce is unionized, a reality, that has often proved to be very divisive and confrontational for the industry, but not at Southwest.

The company invests heavily in building its human capital. For instance, to fill 4,200 job openings in 1999, it interviewed almost 80,000 people (chosen out of over 144,442 résumés received). Candidates endure a rigorous interview process that can take as long as six weeks. Southwest wants the best of the best. Once on board, about 20 percent of new hires fail to make it through the training period. However, according to the company's vice president of people, Libby Sartain, the payback for this intense people commitment is low turnover, high customer satisfaction, and a self-monitoring culture of self-motivated employees. She explains, "We don't keep them if they don't fit into our culture. A lot of people think we're just relaxed, loosey-goosey, but we have a lot of discipline" (Donnelly, p. 68). Southwest's employee turnover rate is about 9 percent, considerably lower than the industry average.

FINANCIAL HIGHLIGHTS

For 1999, Southwest Airlines posted record operating revenues, record operating income, the highest operating profit margin since 1981 (16.5 percent), and a record load factor of 69.0 percent (Load factor is a measure or production or utilization of capacity used to analyze a transportation company. It's calculated by dividing revenue passenger miles by available seat miles.) The company's string of years of posting a profit reached 27. Balance sheet information for 1998 and 1999 and income statement information for 1997, 1998, and 1999 are provided in Exhibits 2, 3, and 4 (see pages 372–375).

COMPANY AWARDS AND RECOGNITIONS

When you do outstanding work, you get recognized, and Southwest Airlines is no exception. Here are just a few of the company's many distinctions:

- Southwest has ranked number one in fewest customer complaints for the last nine consecutive years as published in the Department of Transportation's *Air Travel Consumer Report.*
- Southwest has ranked number one in on-time performance for the last seven out of eight years according to the same report.
- Southwest began the first profit-sharing plan in the U.S. airline industry in 1974. Employees now own about 13 percent of the company's stock.
- Herb Kelleher, CEO, was named CEO of the Year in 1999 by *Chief Executive Magazine.*
- Southwest was the first airline to set up a home page on the Web.
- Southwest has appeared frequently on the list of 100 Best Companies to Work for in America as published by *Fortune* magazine.
- Southwest also has been the most admired airline in *Fortune* magazine's annual survey of corporate reputations in 1996, 1997, and 1998. Among all industries, the company has been listed year after year on the most admired list. In 2000, it was the number-six most admired corporation.
- Southwest was cited in 1999 for having one of the best national reputations as shown by the results of a consumer survey conducted for the *Wall Street Journal.* It was the only airline to make the list.
- The company has been recognized as one of the world's safest airlines by *Conde Nast Traveler* magazine and has been named a charter member of the International Airline Passengers Association's Honor Roll of Airlines among the World's Safest Airlines.

THE AIRLINE INDUSTRY AND MAJOR COMPETITORS

The airline industry is one of the most intensely competitive industries. Many external factors influence the potential profitability of each competitor, both positively and negatively. Several competitors have tried to duplicate Southwest's formula, but with little success. However, as Southwest branches into more and more markets, particularly on the East Coast, and as it begins to offer more long-haul flights, the company may find that competitors have become more adept and are more savvy about those markets. Consolidations (mergers and alliances) among industry players are a real possibility, although the Federal Trade Commission will examine any proposed mergers very carefully. However, as the industry continues to change, competitors need to make sure that their strategies are aligned with the needs of the marketplace so that they can achieve successful levels of performance, financial and otherwise.

THE FUTURE

Southwest Airlines has been an anomaly among airlines. Its performance has consistently been among the industry's best. However, Southwest will face challenges as it seeks to become a true national carrier. In addition, the announcement in August of 1999 that Southwest's CEO, Herb Kelleher, had prostate cancer presents additional strategic challenges for the company.

Sources: Company information from Southwest Airlines Web site (**www.iflyswa.com**), and Hoover's Online (**www.hoovers.com**), June 21, 2000; J. Sharkey, "Southwest Airlines' Success with Online Bookings Has Caught the Travel Industry by Surprise," *Wall Street Journal*, March 1, 2000, p. C10; G. Donnelly, "Recruiting Retention," *CFO*, March 2000, pp. 68–76; "Southwest Airlines: A Stock to Study," *Better Investing*, February 2000, p. 14; H. Lancaster, "Herb Kelleher Has One Main Strategy: Treat Employees Well," *Wall Street Journal*, August 31, 1999, p. B1; W. Zellner, "Earth to Herb: Pick a Co-Pilot," *Business Week*, August 16, 1999, p. 70; R. Abelson, "Southwest's Chairman Has Cancer; Succession Issue Is Raised," *New York Times*, August 12, 1999, p. C1; S. McCartney, "Southwest Airlines Chief to Be Treated for Prostate Cancer, but Stay on Job," *Wall Street Journal*, August 12, 1999, p. B11; "How Herb Keeps Southwest Hopping: Investing Stocks Q & A," *Money*, June 1999, pp. 61–62; D. Pederson, "Wal-Mart of the Sky," *Newsweek*, March 1, 1999, p. 47; and W. Zellner, "Southwest's New Direction," *Business Week*, February 8, 1999, pp. 58–59.

EXHIBIT 2   Consolidated Balance Sheet

	Years Ended December 31	
(in thousands except per share amounts)	1999	1998
ASSETS		
Current assets:		
Cash and cash equivalents	$ 418,819	$ 378,511
Accounts receivable	73,448	88,799
Inventories of parts and supplies, at cost	65,152	50,035
Deferred income taxes (Note 11)	20,929	20,734
Prepaid expenses and other current assets	52,657	36,076
Total current assets	631,005	574,155
Property and equipment, at cost (Notes 3, 5, and 6):		
Flight equipment	5,768,506	4,709,059
Ground property and equipment	742,230	720,604
Deposits on flight equipment purchase contracts	338,229	309,356
	6,848,965	5,739,019
Less allowance for depreciation	1,840,799	1,601,409
	5,008,166	4,137,610
Other assets	12,942	4,231
	$5,652,113	$4,715,996
LIABILITIES AND STOCKHOLDERS' EQUITY		
Current liabilities:		
Accounts payable	$ 156,755	$ 157,415
Accrued liabilities (Note 4)	535,024	477,448
Air traffic liability	256,942	200,078
Current maturities of long-term debt (Note 5)	7,873	11,996
Other current liabilities	3,872	3,716
Total current liabilities	960,466	850,653
Long-term debt less current maturities (Note 5)	871,717	623,309
Deferred income taxes (Note 11)	692,342	549,207
Deferred gains from sale and leaseback of aircraft	222,700	238,412
Other deferred liabilities	69,100	56,497
Commitments and contingencies (Notes 3, 6, and 11)		
Stockholders' equity (Notes 8 and 9):		
Common stock, $1.00 par value: 1,300,000 shares authorized; 505,005 and 335,904 shares issued in 1999 and 1998, respectively	505,005	335,904
Capital in excess of par value	35,436	89,820
Retained earnings	2,385,854	2,044,975
Treasury stock, at cost: 5,579 and 5,402 shares in 1999 and 1998, respectively	(90,507)	(72,781)
Total stockholders' equity	2,835,788	2,397,918
	$5,652,113	$4,715,996

(*Source:* Southwest Airlines, *1999 Annual Report.*)

EXHIBIT 3 Consolidated Statement of Income

(in thousands except per share amounts)	Years Ended December 31		
	1999	1998	1997
OPERATING REVENUES:			
Passenger	$4,499,360	$3,963,781	$3,639,193
Freight	102,990	98,500	94,758
Other	133,237	101,699	82,870
Total operating revenues	4,735,587	4,163,980	3,816,821
OPERATING EXPENSES:			
Salaries, wages, and benefits (Note 10)	1,455,237	1,285,942	1,136,542
Fuel and oil	492,415	388,348	494,952
Maintenance materials and repairs	367,606	302,431	256,501
Agency commissions	156,419	157,766	157,211
Aircraft rentals	199,740	202,160	201,954
Landing fees and other rentals	242,002	214,907	203,845
Depreciation (Note 2)	248,660	225,212	195,568
Other operating expenses	791,932	703,603	646,012
Total operating expenses	3,954,011	3,480,369	3,292,585
OPERATING INCOME	781,576	683,611	524,236
OTHER EXPENSES (INCOME):			
Interest expense	54,145	56,276	63,454
Capitalized interest	(31,262)	(25,588)	(19,779)
Interest income	(25,200)	(31,083)	(36,616)
Other (gains) losses, net	10,282	(21,106)	221
Total other expenses (income)	7,965	(21,501)	7,280
INCOME BEFORE INCOME TAXES	773,611	705,112	516,956
PROVISION FOR INCOME TAXES (Note 11)	299,233	271,681	199,184
NET INCOME	$ 474,378	$ 433,431	$ 317,772
NET INCOME PER SHARE, BASIC (Notes 8, 9, and 12)	$.94	$.87	$.64
NET INCOME PER SHARE, DILUTED (Notes 8, 9, and 12)	$.89	$.82	$.62

(*Source:* Southwest Airlines, *1999 Annual Report.*)

EXHIBIT 4   Ten-Year Summary

Selected Consolidated Financial Data[1]

(in thousands except per share amounts)	1999	1998	1997	1996
Operating revenues:				
Passenger	$4,499,360	$3,963,781	$3,639,193	$3,269,238
Freight	102,990	98,500	94,758	80,005
Other	133,237	101,699	82,870	56,927
Total operating revenues	4,735,587	4,163,980	3,816,821	3,406,170
Operating expenses	3,954,011	3,480,369	3,292,585	3,055,335
Operating income	781,576	683,611	524,236	350,835
Other expenses (income), net	7,965	(21,501)	7,280	9,473
Income before income taxes	773,611	705,112	516,956	341,362
Provision for income taxes[3]	299,233	271,681	199,184	134,025
Net income[3]	$474,378	$433,431	$317,772	$207,337
Net income per share, basic[3]	$.94	$.87	$.64	$.42
Net income per share, diluted[3]	$.89	$.82	$.62	$.41
Cash dividends per common share	$.02150	$.01889	$.01471	$.01303
Total assets	$5,652,113	$4,715,996	$4,246,160	$3,723,479
Long-term debt	$871,717	$623,309	$628,106	$650,226
Stockholders' equity	$2,835,788	$2,397,918	$2,009,018	$1,648,312

Consolidated Financial Ratios[1]

	1999	1998	1997	1996
Return on average total assets	9.2%	9.7%	8.0%	5.9%
Return on average stockholders' equity	18.1%	19.7%	17.4%	13.5%

Consolidated Operating Statistics[2]

	1999	1998	1997	1996
Revenue passengers carried	57,500,213	52,586,400	50,399,960	49,621,504
RPMs (000s)	36,479,322	31,419,110	28,355,169	27,083,483
ASMs (000s)	52,855,467	47,543,515	44,487,496	40,727,495
Passenger load factor	69.0%	66.1%	63.7%	66.5%
Average length of passenger haul	634	597	563	546
Trips flown	846,823	806,822	786,288	748,634
Average passenger fare	$78.25	$75.38	$72.21	$65.88
Passenger revenue yield per RPM	12.33¢	12.62¢	12.84¢	12.07¢
Operating revenue yield per ASM	8.96¢	8.76¢	8.58¢	8.36¢
Operating expenses per ASM	7.48¢	7.32¢	7.40¢	7.50¢
Fuel cost per gallon (average)	52.71¢	45.67¢	62.46¢	65.47¢
Number of employees at year-end	27,653	25,844	23,974	22,944
Size of fleet at year-end[9]	312	280	261	243

[1] The Selected Consolidated Financial Data and Consolidated Financial Ratios for 1992 through 1990 have been restated to include the financial results of Morris Air Corporation (Morris).

[2] Prior to 1993, Morris operated as a charter carrier; therefore, no Morris statistics are included for these years.

	1995	1994	1993	1992	1991	1990
	$2,760,756	$2,497,765	$2,216,342	$1,623,828	$1,267,897	$1,144,421
	65,825	54,419	42,897	33,088	26,428	22,196
	46,170	39,749	37,434	146,063	84,961	70,659
	2,872,751	2,591,933	2,296,673	1,802,979	1,379,286	1,237,276
	2,559,220	2,275,224	2,004,700	1,609,175	1,306,675	1,150,015
	313,531	316,709	291,973	193,804	72,611	87,261
	8,391	17,186	32,336	36,361	18,725	6,827[6]
	305,140	299,523	259,637	157,443	53,886	80,434
	122,514	120,192	105,353	60,058	20,738	29,829
	$182,626	$179,331	$154,284[4]	$97,385[5]	$33,148	$50,605
	$.38	$.37	$.32[4]	$.21[5]	$.08	$.11
	$.37	$.36	$.31[4]	$.20[5]	$.07	$.11
	$.01185	$.01185	$.01146	$.01047	$.00987	$.00955
	$3,256,122	$2,823,071	$2,576,037	$2,368,856	$1,854,331	$1,480,813
	$661,010	$583,071	$639,136	$735,754	$617,434	$327,553
	$1,427,318	$1,238,706	$1,054,019	$879,536	$635,793	$607,294
	6.0%	6.6%	6.2%[4]	4.6%[5]	2.0%	3.5%
	13.7%	15.6%	16.0%[4]	12.9%	5.3%	8.4%
	44,785,573	42,742,602[7]	36,955,221[7]	27,839,284	22,669,942	19,830,941
	23,327,804	21,611,266	18,827,288	13,787,005	11,296,183	9,958,940
	36,180,001	32,123,974	27,511,000	21,366,642	18,491,003	16,411,115
	64.5%	67.3%	68.4%	64.5%	61.1%	60.7%
	521	506	509	495	498	502
	685,524	624,476	546,297	438,184	382,752	338,108
	$61.64	$58.44	$59.97	$58.33	$55.93	$57.71
	11.83¢	11.56¢	11.77¢	11.78¢	11.22¢	11.49¢
	7.94¢	8.07¢	8.35¢	7.89¢	7.10¢	7.23¢
	7.07¢	7.08¢	7.25¢[8]	7.03¢	6.76¢	6.73¢
	55.22¢	53.92¢	59.15¢	60.82¢	65.69¢	77.89¢
	19,933	16,818	15,175	11,397	9,778	8,620
	224	199	178	141	124	106

[3] Pro forma for 1992 through 1990 assuming Morris, an S-Corporation prior to 1993, was taxed at statutory rates.
[4] Excludes cumulative effect of accounting changes of $15.3 million ($.03 per share).
(**Source:** Southwest Airlines, *1999 Annual Report.*)

Starbucks Corporation

If a steaming cup of aromatic specialty coffee is your thing, you've undoubtedly heard of Starbucks Corporation. Starbucks is the number-one specialty coffee retailer with over 2,500 locations in the United States and 15 other countries. Its coffee shops and kiosks are located in shopping centers, airports, office buildings, bookstores, and as stand-alone stores. Can Starbucks' managers keep the company's growth percolating along?

INDUSTRY AND COMPETITORS

The coffee industry is an interesting one indeed. Staying competitive presents challenges for strategic managers. Fewer people are drinking coffee now, and those who do consume it are indulging in fewer cups. Consumption of fruit-based drinks and bottled water are growing. Despite decreasing demand for coffee, the success of Starbucks has been beneficial for all coffee distributors in the United States and has encouraged innovation in the industry.

Among coffee makers, illycaffè (**www.illy.com**) may be one of Starbucks's strongest competitors because it is well placed to occupy the premium sector. illycaffè is an Italian premium coffee manufacturer that offers only one kind of coffee—espresso. Being a single product company, illycaffè differentiates its packages of espresso coffee only based on weight (from 3 kilograms for professional consumption and from 125 to 150 grams for individual consumption), on form (ground coffee, beans, or other), and on type (regular or decaffeinated). illycaffè serves over 3 million espresso coffees daily—2 million in Italy alone. Using a unique preservation of the product—through the use of pressurization—illycaffè has expanded into strategic locations in the United States, Europe, and Japan.

Bab Holdings, Inc. (**www.babholdings.com**), based in Chicago, franchises or licenses almost 300 bagel, muffin, and coffee shops across 28 states and Canada, as well as in Egypt, Peru, South Korea, and the United Arab Emirates. BAB is struggling under a debt load brought on by rapid expansion. Therefore, it's selling company-owned stores to concentrate on franchising. BAB plans to spin off its bagel business to a subsidiary and change strategic direction by acquiring an Internet investment company.

Another competitor in the industry is Einstein–Noah Bagel Corporation (**www.ein steinbros.com**), based in Golden, Colorado. Einstein–Noah Bagel is the number-one operator of bagel shops in the United States. It operates almost 460 Einstein Brothers Bagels and Noah's New York Bagels restaurants in 29 states and the District of Columbia.

The Swiss Company, Nestlé SA (**www.nestle.com**)—the world's number-one food company—is also the world leader in coffee with its Nescafe brand and also in bottled water with its Perrier and Poland Spring brands. Nestlé is a formidable player that other competitors must keep an eye on. Any strategic moves that it makes may necessitate strategic changes on the part of industry competitors.

Other potential competitors include:

ABP (**www.aubonpain.com**)

AFC Enterprises (**www.afc-online.com**)

Allied Domecq, PLC (**www.allieddomecqplc.com**)

Churchill Coffee Company (**www.churchillcoffee.com**)

Diedrich Coffee (**www.diedrich.com**)

Farmer Brothers

Green Mountain Coffee (**www.greenmountaincoffee.com**)

Kraft Foods (**www.kraftfoods.com**)

New World Coffee (**www.nwcb.com**)

Panera Bread–St. Louis Bread Company (**www.panerabread.com**)

Peet's (**www.peets.com**)

Procter & Gamble (**www.pg.com**)

Sara Lee (**www.saralee.com**)

Tully's Coffee Corporation (**www.tullys.com**)

STARBUCKS—THE COMPANY

Starbucks purchases and roasts high-quality whole bean coffees and sells them, along with rich fresh-brewed coffees, Italian-style espresso beverages, a variety of pastries and confections, and coffee-related accessories and equipment—mostly through its company-owned and -operated retail stores. In addition, Starbucks also sells primarily whole-bean coffees through a specialty sales group, a direct response business, supermarkets, and online at (**www.starbucks.com**). The company's office coffee programs are aimed at large offices, small offices, and everything in between. It even has a special program for companies that want Starbucks coffee bundled with their office supplies. Starbucks also offers food services for hotels, colleges and universities, businesses, and health care facilities. Additionally, Starbucks produces and sells bottled Frappuccino® bottled coffee drinks through an alliance with PepsiCo and a coffee ice cream through an alliance with Dreyer's. The company has joined with Kraft Foods to sell its coffee in U.S. grocery stores and has signed an agreement with Albertson's supermarket chain to open more than 100 coffee bars in some of its stores. In 1999, Starbucks acquired Tazo, a Portland, Oregon–based tea company. Tazo is known for producing authentic, premium tea products.

Starbucks's objective is to establish itself as the most recognized and respected brand in the world. Thus, it's using its name to sell more than coffee. For instance, in its retail coffee stores, customers can purchase Starbucks board games, Starbucks CDs, and other products with the Starbucks name and logo. The company has started test marketing upscale breakfast, lunch, and dinner items in a few U.S. cities. Other strategies Starbucks is using to achieve its goal include continuing the rapid expansion of retail operations, increasing specialty sales and other operations, and selectively pursuing opportunities to leverage the Starbucks brand through the introduction of new products and the pursuit of new distribution channels.

How rapidly has Starbucks grown? The following chart provides some clues.

1971	First Starbucks opens in Seattle's famous Pike Place Market. Founded by Gordon Bowker, Jerry Baldwin, and Ziv Siegl, who named the company for the coffee-loving first mate in the book *Moby Dick* and created its recognizable two-tailed siren logo.

1982	Starbucks begins providing coffee to fine restaurants and espresso bars in Seattle.
	Starbucks company-owned locations: 5
	Howard Schultz joins the company.
1984	Starbucks tests the first coffee bar concept in downtown Seattle.
1987	Starbucks company-owned locations: 17
1988	Starbucks company-owned locations: 33
1989	Starbucks company-owned locations: 55
1990	Starbucks company-owned locations: 84
1991	Starbucks company-owned locations: 116
1992	Starbucks company-owned locations: 165
1993	Starbucks company-owned locations: 272
1994	Starbucks company-owned locations: 425
1995	Starbucks company-owned locations: 676
1996	Starbucks company-owned locations: 1,015
1997	Starbucks company-owned locations: 1,412
1998	Starbucks company-owned locations: 1,886
1999	Starbucks company-owned locations: 2,135
2000	Starbucks company-owned locations: Goal is 2,500

Starbucks mission statement (found at **www.starbucks.com**) is as follows:

To establish Starbucks as the premier purveyor of the finest coffee in the world while maintaining our uncompromising principles as we grow.

In conjunction with the mission statement, company employees use six guiding principles (found on the company Web site) to measure the appropriateness of their decisions:

- Provide a great work environment and treat each other with respect and dignity.
- Embrace diversity as an essential component in the way we do business.
- Apply the highest standards of excellence to the purchasing, roasting, and fresh delivery of our coffee.
- Develop enthusiastically satisfied customers all of the time.
- Contribute positively to our communities and our environment.
- Recognize that profitability is essential to our future success.

In addition to its corporate statement of mission, Starbucks has developed an environmental mission as a framework for employee decision making. This mission is as follows:

Starbucks is committed to a role of environmental leadership in all facets of our business.

The company intends to fulfill this mission through its commitment to the following:

- Understanding of environmental issues and sharing information with all our partners
- Developing innovative and flexible solutions to bring about change
- Striving to buy, sell, and use environmentally friendly products
- Recognizing that fiscal responsibility is essential to our environmental future

- Instilling environmental responsibility as a corporate value
- Measuring and monitoring our progress for each project

Starbucks's CEO Howard Schultz, the visionary behind Starbucks, announced in April 2000 that he was taking on a new role in the company. Starbucks chief operating officer (COO) Orin Smith took over his duties. Schulz described his new role as "working with strategic partners and alliances around the world to speed up Starbucks' entry into supermarkets, as well as opening new stores" (*Wall Street Journal*, April 8, 2000). His feeling was that Starbucks had accomplished only one-third of its potential. Starbucks Corporation's other executive officers and board of directors is shown in Exhibit 1.

STARBUCKS—THE PEOPLE

In its 1999 Annual Report, CEO Schultz states that "We know that our people are the heart and soul of our success." The more than 37,000 partners (employees) of Starbucks serve over 10 million customers each week. That's a lot of opportunities to either please or displease the customer. The experiences customers enjoy in the stores ultimately affect the company's all-important brand image. Starbucks has made a commitment to both its full-

---

EXHIBIT 1   Starbucks Corporation Executive Officers and Board of Directors

Executive Officers

Howard Schultz, Chairman of the Board and Chief Executive Officer
Orin C. Smith, President and Chief Operating Officer
John B. Richards, President, North American Operations
Paul D. Davis, President Retail North America
Peter Maslen, President, Starbucks Coffee International, Inc.
Deidra Wager, Executive Vice President, Retail
Eduardo R. Garcia, Executive Vice President, Supply Chain and Coffee Operations
Michael Casey, Executive Vice President, Chief Financial Officer, and Chief Administrative Officer

Board of Directors

Howard Schultz
Orin C. Smith
Arlen I. Prentice, Co-Chairman and Chief Executive Officer of Kibble & Prentice
Barbara Bass, President, Gerson Bakar Foundation
Craig J. Foley, President, Wickham Capital Corporation
Craig E. Weatherup, Chairman and Chief Executive Officer, The Pepsi Bottling Group
Gregory B. Maffei, Senior Vice President and Chief Financial Officer, Microsoft Corporation
Howard P. Behar, Director
James G. Shennan Jr., General Partner, Trinity Ventures

time and part-time partners (who make up 83 percent of the company's workforce). Employees who work 20 hours per week receive full benefits plus a pound of free coffee each week. They also receive stock options in Starbucks through its Bean Stock program.

STARBUCKS—THE FINANCIALS

The year 1999 was a record one for Starbucks in many ways. It opened 625 new stores system wide, the most new stores in Starbucks history. Part of this expansion was the addition of 157 international locations and expansion into New Zealand, Beijing, Malaysia, South Korea, and Kuwait. Revenues for 1999 were $1.7 billion and profits were over $100 million. However, an announcement in the third quarter of 1999 that earnings would fall short of estimates caused a 28 percent decline in the company's stock price, the first downfall in the seven years that Starbucks had been a publicly held corporation. Analysts believed that the earnings shortfall could be attributed to Schulz's preoccupation with Starbucks's Internet strategy to become a lifestyle site by partnering with gourmet food sellers and home-furnishings stores. Delayed new store openings and lower-than-expected sales at existing stores put a damper on earnings. After the stock price plummet, Schultz said, "Our management team is 100% focused on growing our core business without distraction or dilution from any other initiative" (Lee, p. 92). Additional company financial information is provided in Exhibits 2 and 3.

Starbucks's philosophy is that it should share its good fortune with others. The company has provided millions of dollars in support to communities around the world. It is the largest North American contributor to CARE, the international aid and development organization. The work done by CARE helps Starbucks give back to the coffee-origin countries where it does business. In addition, the Starbucks Foundation reaches thousands of families and children in North America through literacy grant programs. Starbucks also has partnered with Earvin "Magic" Johnson through his Johnson Development Corporation to hasten Starbucks's presence in underserved neighborhoods in key metropolitan areas.

THE FUTURE

What does the future hold for Starbucks Corporation? Does the company need to bring its focus back to its core business of coffee shops, or should it continue its current path? What are the implications of declining consumer demand for coffee? How can the company remain "relevant" to its customers? How can Starbucks best achieve its goal of establishing itself as the most recognized and respected brand in the world? These are just a few of the strategic issues that Starbucks's managers have to address.

Sources: Company information from Starbucks Corporation and Hoover's Online Web sites, June 21, 2000; "Behind Starbucks' New Venture: Beans, Beatniks, and Booze," *Fortune*, May 15, 2000, p. 80; "Starbucks Founder Taking on New Role," *Wall Street Journal*, April 8, 2000, p. B14; V. Vishwanath and D. Harding, "The Starbucks Effect," *Harvard Business Review*, March–April 2000, pp. 17–18; B. Tedeschi, "E-Commerce Report," *New York Times*, February 28, 2000, p. C10; L. Lee, "Now, Starbucks Uses Its Bean," *Business Week*, February 14, 2000, pp. 92–93; A. Barrett, "Illycaffe Moves Full Steam into Starbucks Turf," *Wall Street Journal*, November 8, 1999, p. 47A; R. McNatt, "A Coffee Break at Starbucks," *Business Week*, August 2, 1999, p. 4; D. A. Kaplan, "Trouble Brewing," *Newsweek*, July 19, 1999, pp. 40–41; R. Gibson, "Starbucks Holders Wake UP, Smell the Coffee and Sell," *Wall Street Journal*, July 2, 1999, p. B3; N. Deogun, "Joe Wakes Up, Smells the Soda," *Wall Street Journal*, June 8, 1999, p. B1; K. Barron, "The Cappuccino Conundrum," *Forbes*, February 22, 1999, pp. 54–55.

EXHIBIT 2   **Financial Highlights**

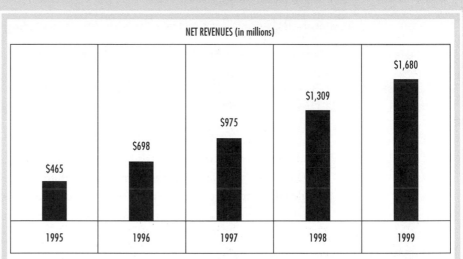

NET REVENUES (in millions)

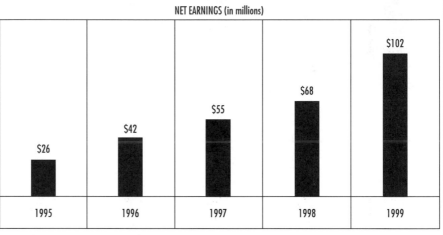

NET EARNINGS (in millions)

RETAIL STORE COUNT (at fiscal year-end)

LICENSED STORES   COMPANY-OWNED STORES

Source: *Starbucks Annual Report, 1999, p. 17.*

EXHIBIT 3   Selected Financial Data

(in thousands, except earnings per share and store operating data)

The following selected financial data have been derived from the consolidated financial statements of the Company.

As of and for the fiscal year ended[1]	Oct. 3, 1999 (53 Wks)	Sept. 27, 1998 (52 Wks)	Sept. 28, 1997 (52 Wks)	Sept. 29, 1996 (52 Wks)	Oct. 1, 1995 (52 Wks)
Results of Operations Data					
Net revenues					
Retail	$1,423,389	$1,102,574	$836,291	$601,458	$402,655
Specialty[2]	256,756	206,128	139,098	96,414	62,558
Total net revenues	1,680,145	1,308,702	975,389	697,872	465,213
Merger expenses[3]	—	8,930	—	—	—
Operating income	156,711	109,216	86,199	56,575	40,116
Gain on sale of investment[4]	—	—	—	9,218	—
Net earnings	$ 101,693	$ 68,372	$ 55,211	$ 41,710	$ 26,102
Net earnings per common share—diluted[5]	$ 0.54	$ 0.37	$ 0.33	$ 0.27	$ 0.18
Cash dividends per share	—	—	—	—	—
Balance Sheet Data					
Working capital	$ 134,903	$ 157,805	$172,079	$239,365	$134,304
Total assets	1,252,514	992,755	857,152	729,227	468,178
Long-term debt (including current portion)	9,057	1,803	168,832	167,980	81,773
Shareholders' equity	961,013	794,297	533,710	454,050	312,231

EXHIBIT 3   Selected Financial Data

The following selected financial data have been derived from the consolidated financial statements of the Company.

As of and for the fiscal year ended[1]	Oct. 3, 1999 (53 Wks)	Sept. 27, 1998 (52 Wks)	Sept. 28, 1997 (52 Wks)	Sept. 29, 1996 (52 Wks)	Oct. 1, 1995 (52 Wks)
Store Operating Data					
Percentage change in comparable store sales[6]	6%	5%	5%	7%	9%
Stores open at year-end					
Continental North America					
Company-operated stores	2,038	1,622	1,270	929	627
Licensed stores	179	133	94	75	49
International					
Company-operated stores—					
United Kingdom	97	66	31	9	1
Licensed stores	184	65	17	2	—
Total stores	2,498	1,886	1,412	1,015	677

[1] The Company's fiscal year ends on the Sunday closest to September 30. Fiscal year 1999 includes 53 weeks, and fiscal years 1995 to 1998 each included 52 weeks.

[2] Specialty revenues includes product sales to and royalties and fees from the Company's licensees.

[3] Merger expenses relate to the business combination with Seattle Coffee Holdings Limited in fiscal 1998.

[4] Gain on sale of investment relates to the sale of Noah's New York Bagels, Inc. stock in fiscal 1996.

[5] Earnings per share is based on the weighted average number of shares outstanding during the period plus common stock equivalents consisting of certain shares subject to stock options. In addition, the presentation of diluted earnings per share assumes conversion of the Company's formerly outstanding convertible subordinated debentures using the "if converted" method when such securities were dilutive, with net income adjusted for the after-tax interest expense and amortization applicable to these debentures. Earnings per share data for fiscal years 1995 through 1998 have been restated to reflect the two-for-one stock splits in fiscal 1999 and 1996.

[6] Includes only Company-operated stores open 13 months or longer.

Source: *Starbucks Annual Report, 1999,* pp. 19, 27, 28.

EXHIBIT 3   Selected Financial Data (continued)

Consolidated Balance Sheets

(in thousands, except share data)

Assets	Oct. 3, 1999 (53 weeks)	Sept. 27, 1998 (52 weeks)
Current assets		
Cash and cash equivalents	$ 66,419	$101,663
Short-term investments	51,367	21,874
Accounts receivable	47,646	50,972
Inventories	180,886	143,118
Prepaid expenses and other current assets	19,049	11,205
Deferred income taxes, net	21,133	8,448
Total current assets	386,500	337,280
Joint ventures and other investments	68,060	38,917
Property, plant and equipment, net	760,289	600,794
Deposits and other assets	23,474	15,685
Goodwill, net	14,191	79
Total	$1,252,514	$992,755

Liabilities and Shareholders' Equity

	Oct. 3, 1999	Sept. 27, 1998
Current liabilities		
Accounts payable	$ 56,108	$ 49,861
Checks drawn in excess of bank balances	64,211	33,634
Accrued compensation and related costs	43,872	35,941
Accrued occupancy costs	23,017	17,526
Accrued taxes	30,752	18,323
Other accrued expenses	33,637	24,190
Total current liabilities	251,597	179,475
Deferred income taxes, net	32,886	18,983
Long-term debt	7,018	—
Commitments and contingencies (Notes 5, 9, and 13)		

Shareholders' Equity

	Oct. 3, 1999	Sept. 27, 1998
Common stock—Authorized, 300,000,000 shares; issued and outstanding, 183,282,095 and 179,266,956 shares, respectively (includes 848,550 common stock units in both years)	651,020	589,214
Retained earnings	313,939	212,246
Accumulated other comprehensive loss	(3,946)	(7,163)
Total shareholders' equity	961,013	794,297
Total	$1,252,514	$992,755

See Notes to Consolidated Financial Statements.

EXHIBIT 3 Selected Financial Data

Consolidated Statements of Earnings

(in thousands, except earnings per share)

Fiscal year ended	Oct 3, 1999	Sept. 27, 1998	Sept. 28, 1997
Net revenues	$1,680,145	$1,308,702	$975,389
Cost of sales and related occupancy costs	741,010	578,483	436,942
Gross margin	939,135	730,219	538,447
Store operating expenses	543,572	418,476	314,064
Other operating expenses	51,374	43,479	28,239
Depreciation and amortization	97,797	72,543	52,801
General and administrative expenses	89,681	77,575	557,144
Merger expenses	—	8,930	—
Operating income	156,711	109,216	86,199
Interest and other income	8,678	8,515	12,393
Interest and other expense	(1,363)	(1,381)	(7,282)
Earnings before income taxes	164,026	116,350	91,310
Income taxes	62,333	47,978	36,099
Net earnings	$ 101,693	$ 68,372	$ 55,211
Net earnings per common share—basic	$ 0.56	$ 0.39	$ 0.35
Net earnings per common share—diluted	$ 0.54	$ 0.37	$ 0.33
Weighted average shares outstanding			
Basic	181,842	176,110	159,289
Diluted	188,531	183,771	180,317

See Notes to Consolidated Financial Statements.

Index